THE OPEN SOCIETY
AND ITS ENEMIES

KARL POPPER

Volume II

THE HIGH TIDE OF PROPHECY:
HEGEL, MARX,
AND THE AFTERMATH

London

First published 1945
by Routledge & Kegan Paul Ltd

Reprinted 1947
Reprinted 1949
Second edition (revised) 1952
Third edition (revised) 1957
Fourth edition (revised) 1962

Published as a Routledge paperback 1962
Reprinted 1963
Fifth edition (revised) 1966
Reprinted six times

Reprinted 1990, 1992, 1993, 1996, 1999 by Routledge
11 New Fetter Lane, London EC4P 4EE

Printed in Great Britain by
T.J. International Ltd,
Padstow, Cornwall

British Library Cataloguing in Publication Data
A catalogue record for this book is available from the British Library

ISBN 0–415–05134–7

CONTENTS

VOLUME II : THE HIGH TIDE OF PROPHECY

To the débâcle of liberal science can be
traced the moral schism of the modern world
which so tragically divides enlightened men.

WALTER LIPPMANN.

THE OPEN SOCIETY AND ITS ENEMIES

VOL. II

THE HIGH TIDE OF PROPHECY

THE RISE OF ORACULAR PHILOSOPHY

CHAPTER 11: THE ARISTOTELIAN ROOTS OF HEGELIANISM

The task of writing a history of the ideas in which we are interested—of historicism and its connection with totalitarianism --will not be attempted here. The reader will remember, I hope, that I do not even try to give more than a few scattered remarks which may throw light on the background of the modern version of these ideas. The story of their development, more particularly during the period from Plato to Hegel and Marx, could not possibly be told while keeping the size of the book within reasonable limits. I shall therefore not attempt a serious treatment of Aristotle, except in so far as his version of Plato's essentialism has influenced the historicism of Hegel, and thereby that of Marx. The restriction to those ideas of Aristotle with which we have become acquainted in our criticism of Plato, Aristotle's great master, does not, however, create as serious a loss as one might fear at first sight. For Aristotle, in spite of his stupendous learning and his astonishing scope, was not a man of striking originality of thought. What he added to the Platonic store of ideas was, in the main, systematization and a burning interest in empirical and especially in biological problems. To be sure, he is the inventor of logic, and for this and his other achievements, he amply deserves what he himself claimed (at the end of his *Sophistic Refutations*)—our warm thanks, and our pardon for his shortcomings. Yet for readers and admirers of Plato these shortcomings are formidable.

1

I

In some of Plato's latest writings, we can find an echo of the contemporary political developments in Athens—of the consolidation of democracy. It seems that even Plato began to doubt whether some form of democracy had not come to stay. In Aristotle, we find indications that he did not doubt any longer. Although he is no friend of democracy, he accepts it as unavoidable, and is ready to compromise with the enemy.

An inclination to compromise, strangely mixed with an inclination to find fault with his predecessors and contemporaries (and with Plato in particular), is one of the outstanding characteristics of Aristotle's encyclopædic writings. They show no trace of the tragic and stirring conflict that is the motive of Plato's work. Instead of Plato's flashes of penetrating insight, we find dry systematization and the love, shared by so many mediocre writers of later times, for settling any question whatever by issuing a ' sound and balanced judgement ' that does justice to everybody ; which means, at times, by elaborately and solemnly missing the point. This exasperating tendency which is systematized in Aristotle's famous ' doctrine of the mean ' is one of the sources of his so often forced and even fatuous criticism of Plato [1]. An example of Aristotle's lack of insight, in this case of historical insight (he also was a historian), is the fact that he acquiesced in the apparent democratic consolidation just when it had been superseded by the imperial monarchy of Macedon ; a historical event which happened to escape his notice. Aristotle, who was, as his father had been, a courtier at the Macedonian court, chosen by Philip to be the teacher of Alexander the Great, seems to have underrated these men and their plans ; perhaps he thought he knew them too well. ' Aristotle sat down to dinner with Monarchy without becoming aware of it ', is Gomperz's appropriate comment. [2]

Aristotle's thought is entirely dominated by Plato's. Somewhat grudgingly, he followed his great teacher as closely as his temperament permitted, not only in his general political outlook but practically everywhere. So he endorsed, and systematized, Plato's naturalistic theory of slavery [3] : ' Some men are by nature free, and others slaves ; and for the latter, slavery is fitting as well as just. . . A man who is by nature not his own, but another's, is by nature a slave. . . Hellenes do not like to call themselves slaves, but confine this term to barbarians. . . The slave is totally devoid of any faculty of reasoning ', while free women have just a very little of it. (We owe to Aristotle's criticisms and denunciations most of our knowledge of the Athenian movement against slavery. By arguing against the fighters for freedom, he preserved some of their utterances.) In some minor points Aristotle slightly mitigates Plato's theory of slavery, and duly censures his teacher for being too harsh. He could neither resist an opportunity for criticizing Plato, nor one for a compromise, not even if it was a compromise with the liberal tendencies of his time.

But the theory of slavery is only one of Plato's many political ideas to be adopted by Aristotle. Especially his theory of the Best State, as far as we know it, is modelled upon the theories of the *Republic* and the *Laws* ; and his version throws considerable light on Plato's. Aristotle's Best State is a compromise between three things, a romantic Platonic aristocracy, a ' sound and balanced ' feudalism, and some democratic ideas ; but feudalism has the best of it. With the democrats, Aristotle holds that all citizens should have the right to participate in the government. But this, of course, is not meant to be as radical as it sounds, for Aristotle explains at once that not only slaves but all members of the producing classes are excluded from citizenship. Thus he teaches with Plato that the working classes must not rule and the ruling classes must not work, nor earn any money. (But they are supposed to have plenty.) They own the land, but must not work it themselves. Only hunting, war, and similar hobbies are considered worthy of the feudal rulers. Aristotle's fear of any form of money earning, i.e. of all professional activities, goes perhaps even further than Plato's. Plato had used the term ' banausic ' [4] to describe a plebeian, abject, or depraved state of mind. Aristotle extends the disparaging use of the term so as to cover all interests which are not pure hobbies. In fact, his use of the term is very near to our use of the term ' professional ', more especially in the sense in which it disqualifies in an amateur competition, but also in the sense in which it applies to any specialized expert, such as a physician. For Aristotle, every form of professionalism means a loss of caste. A feudal gentleman, he insists [5], must never take too much interest in ' any occupation, art or science. . . There are also some *liberal arts*, that is to say, arts which a gentleman may acquire, but always only to a certain degree. For if he takes too much interest in them, then these evil effects will follow ', namely, he will become proficient, like a professional, and lose caste. This is Aristotle's idea of a *liberal education*, the idea, unfortunately not yet obsolete [6], of a gentleman's education, as opposed to the education of a slave, serf, servant, or professional man. It is in the same vein that he repeatedly insists that ' the first principle of all action is leisure ' [7]. Aristotle's admiration and deference for the leisured classes seems to be the expression of a curious feeling of uneasiness. It looks as if the son of the Macedonian court physician was troubled by the question of his own social position, and especially by the possibility that he might lose caste because of his own scholarly interests which might be considered professional. ' One is tempted to believe ', says Gomperz [8], ' that he feared to hear such denunciations from his aristocratic friends . . It is indeed strange to see that one of the greatest scholars of all time, if not the greatest, does not wish to be a professional scholar. He would rather be a dilettante, and a man of the world . .' Aristotle's feelings of inferiority have, perhaps, still another basis, apart from his wish to prove his independence of Plato, apart from his own ' professional ' origin, and apart from the fact that he was, undoubtedly, a professional ' sophist ' (he even taught rhetoric). For with Aristotle, Platonic philosophy gives up her great aspirations, her claims to power. From this moment, it could continue only as a teaching profession. And since hardly anybody but a feudal lord had the money and the leisure for studying philosophy, all that philosophy could aspire to was to become an annex to the traditional education of a gentleman. With this more modest aspiration in view, Aristotle finds it very necessary to persuade the feudal gentleman that philosophical speculation and contemplation may become a most important part of his ' good life ' ; for it is the happiest and noblest and the most refined method of whiling away one's time, if one is not occupied with political intrigues or by war. It is the best way of spending one's leisure since, as Aristotle himself puts it, ' nobody . . would arrange a war for that purpose ' [9].

It is plausible to assume that such a courtier's philosophy will tend to be optimistic, since it will hardly be a pleasant pastime otherwise. And indeed, in its optimism lies the one important adjustment made by Aristotle in his systematization [10] of Platonism. Plato's sense of drift had expressed itself in his theory that all change, at least in certain cosmic periods, must be for the worse ; all change is degeneration. Aristotle's theory admits of changes which are improvements ; thus change may be progress. Plato had taught that all development starts from the original, the perfect Form or Idea, so that the developing thing must lose its perfection in the degree in which it changes and in which its similarity to the original decreases. This theory was given up by his nephew and successor, Speusippus, as well as by Aristotle. But Aristotle censured Speusippus' arguments as going too far, since they implied a general biological evolution towards higher forms. Aristotle, it seems, was opposed to the much-discussed evolutionary biological theories of his time [11]. But the peculiar optimistic twist which he gave to Platonism was an outcome of biological speculation also. It was based upon the idea of a *final cause*.

According to Aristotle, one of the four causes of anything— also of any movement or change—is the final cause, or the end towards which the movement aims. In so far as it is an aim or a desired end, the final cause is also *good*. It follows from this that some *good* may not only be the starting point of a movement (as Plato had taught, and as Aristotle admitted [12]) but that some good must also stand at its end. And this is particularly important for anything that has a beginning in time, or, as Aristotle puts it, for anything that comes into being. *The Form or essence of anything developing is identical with the purpose or end or final state towards which it develops.* Thus we obtain after all, in spite of Aristotle's disclaimer, something very closely resembling Speusippus' adjustment of Platonism. The Form or Idea, which is still, with Plato, considered to be good, stands at the end, instead of the beginning. This characterizes Aristotle's substitution of optimism for pessimism.

Aristotle's teleology, i.e. his stress upon the end or aim of change as its final cause, is an expression of his predominantly *biological* interests. It is influenced by Plato's biological theories [13], and also by Plato's extension of his theory of justice to the universe. For Plato did not confine himself to teaching that each of the different classes of citizens has its natural place in society, a place to which it belongs and for which it is naturally fitted ; he also tried to interpret the world of physical bodies and their different classes or kinds on similar principles. He tried to explain the weight of heavy bodies, like stones, or earth, and their tendency to fall, as well as the tendency of air and fire to rise, by the assumption that they strive to retain, or to regain, the place inhabited by their kind. Stones and earth fall because they strive to be where most stones and earth are, and where they belong, in the just order of nature ; air and fire rise because they strive to be where air and fire (the heavenly bodies) are, and where they belong, in the just order of nature [14]. This theory of motion appealed to the zoologist Aristotle ; it combines easily with the theory of final causes, and it allows an explanation of all motion as being analogous with the canter of horses keen to return to their stables. He developed it as his famous theory of *natural places*. Everything if removed from its own natural place has a natural tendency to return to it.

Despite some alterations, Aristotle's version of Plato's essentialism shows only unimportant differences. Aristotle insists, of course, that unlike Plato he does not conceive the Forms or Ideas as existing apart from sensible things. But in so far as this difference is important, it is closely connected with the adjustment in the theory of change. For one of the main points in Plato's theory is that he must consider the Forms or essences or originals (or fathers) as existing prior to, and therefore apart from, sensible things, since these move further and further away from them. Aristotle makes sensible things move towards their final causes or ends, and these he identifies [15] with their Forms or essences. And as a biologist, he assumes that sensible things carry potentially within themselves the seeds, as it were, of their final states, or of their essences. This is one of the reasons why he can say that the Form or essence is *in* the thing, not, as Plato said, prior and external to it. For Aristotle, all movement or change means the realization (or ' actualization ') of some of the potentialities inherent in the essence of a thing [16]. It is, for example, an essential potentiality of a piece of timber, that it can float on water, or that it can burn ; these potentialities remain inherent in its essence even if it should never float or burn. But if it does, then it realizes a potentiality, and thereby changes or moves. Accordingly, the essence, which embraces all the potentialities of a thing, is something like its internal source of change or motion. This Aristotelian essence or Form, this ' formal ' or ' final ' cause, is therefore practically identical with Plato's ' nature ' or ' soul ' ; and this identification is corroborated by Aristotle himself. ' Nature ', he writes [17] in the *Metaphysics*, ' belongs also to the same class as potentiality ; for it is a principle of movement inherent in the thing itself.' On the other hand, he defines the ' soul ' as the ' first entelechy of a living body ', and since ' entelechy ', in turn, is explained as the Form, or the formal cause, considered as a motive force [18], we arrive, with the help of this somewhat complicated terminological apparatus, back at Plato's original point of view : that the soul or nature is something akin to the Form or Idea, but inherent in the thing, and its principle of motion. (When Zeller praised Aristotle for his ' definite use and comprehensive development of a scientific terminology ' [19], I think he must have felt a bit uneasy in using the word ' definite ' ; but the comprehensiveness is to be admitted, as well as the most deplorable fact that Aristotle, by using this complicated and somewhat pretentious jargon, fascinated only too many philosophers ; so that, as Zeller puts it, ' for thousands of years he showed philosophy her way '.)

Aristotle, who was a historian of the more encyclopædic type, made no direct contribution to historicism. He adhered to a more restricted version of Plato's theory that floods and other recurring catastrophes destroy the human race from time to time, leaving only a few survivors. [20] But he does not seem, apart from this, to have interested himself in the problem of historical trends. In spite of this fact, it may be shown here how his theory of change lends itself to historicist interpretations, and that it contains all the elements needed for elaborating a grandiose historicist philosophy. (This opportunity was not fully exploited before Hegel.) Three historicist doctrines which directly follow from Aristotle's essentialism may be distinguished. (1) Only if a person or a state develops, and only by way of its history, can we get to *know* anything about its ' hidden, undeveloped essence ' (to use a phrase of Hegel's [21]). This doctrine leads later, first of all, to the adoption of an historicist method ; that is to say, of the principle that we can obtain any knowledge of social entities or essences only by applying the historical method, by studying social changes. But the doctrine leads further (especially when connected with Hegel's moral positivism which identifies the known as well as the real with the good) to the worship of History and its exaltation as the Grand Theatre of Reality as well as the World's Court of Justice. (2) Change, by revealing what is hidden in the undeveloped essence, can only make apparent the essence, the potentialities, the seeds, which from the beginning have inhered in the changing object. This doctrine leads to the historicist idea of an historical fate or an inescapable essential destiny ; for, as Hegel [22] showed later, ' what we call principle, aim, *destiny* ' is nothing but the

'hidden undeveloped essence'. This means that whatever may
befall a man, a nation, or a state, must be considered to emanate
from, and to be understandable through, the essence, the real
thing, the real 'personality' that manifests itself in this man,
this nation, or this state. 'A man's fate is immediately connected with his own being ; it is something which, indeed, he
may fight against, but which is really a part of his own life.'
This formulation (due to Caird [23]) of Hegel's theory of fate is
clearly the historical and romantic counterpart of Aristotle's
theory that all bodies seek their own 'natural places'. It is,
of course, no more than a bombastic expression of the platitude,
that what befalls a man depends not only on his external
circumstances, but also on himself, on the way he reacts to them.
But the naïve reader is extremely pleased with his ability to
understand, and to feel the truth of this depth of wisdom that
needs to be formulated with the help of such thrilling words as
'fate' and especially 'his own being'. (3) In order to become
real or actual, the essence must unfold itself in change. This
doctrine assumes later, with Hegel, the following form [24] : 'That
which exists for itself only, is . . a mere potentiality : it has
not yet emerged into Existence. . . It is only by activity that
the Idea is actualized.' Thus if I wish to 'emerge into Existence' (surely a very modest wish), then I must 'assert my
personality'. This still rather popular theory leads, as Hegel
sees clearly, to a new justification of the theory of slavery. For
self-assertion means [25], in so far as one's relations to others are
concerned, the attempt to dominate them. Indeed, Hegel
points out that all personal relations can thus be reduced to the
fundamental relation of master and slave, of domination and
submission. Each must strive to assert and prove himself, and
he who has not the nature, the courage, and the general capacity
for preserving his independence, must be reduced to servitude.
This charming theory of personal relations has, of course, its
counterpart in Hegel's theory of international relations. Nations
must assert themselves on the Stage of History ; it is their duty
to attempt the domination of the World.

All these far-reaching historicist consequences, which will be
approached from a different angle in the next chapter, were
slumbering for more than twenty centuries, 'hidden and
undeveloped', in Aristotle's essentialism. Aristotelianism was
more fertile and promising than most of its many admirers
know.

II

> The chief danger to our philosophy, apart from
> laziness and woolliness, is scholasticism, . . which
> is treating what is vague as if it were precise . .
>   F. P. RAMSEY.

We have reached a point from which we could without delay
proceed to an analysis of the historicist philosophy of Hegel,
or, at any rate, to the brief comments upon the developments
between Aristotle and Hegel and upon the rise of Christianity
that conclude, as section III, the present chapter.   As a kind
of digression, however, I shall next discuss a more technical
problem, Aristotle's *essentialist method of Definitions*.

The problem of definitions and of the ' meaning of terms '
does not directly bear upon historicism.   But it has been an
inexhaustible source of confusion and of that particular kind of
verbiage which, when combined with historicism in Hegel's
mind, has bred that poisonous intellectual disease of our own
time which I call *oracular philosophy*.   And it is the most important
source of Aristotle's regrettably still prevailing intellectual influence, of all that verbal and empty scholasticism that haunts not
only the Middle Ages, but our own contemporary philosophy ;
for even a philosophy as recent as that of L. Wittgenstein [26]
suffers, as we shall see, from this influence.   The development
of thought since Aristotle could, I think, be summed up by saying
that every discipline, as long as it used the Aristotelian method of
definition, has remained arrested in a state of empty verbiage
and barren scholasticism, and that the degree to which the various
sciences have been able to make any progress depended on the
degree to which they have been able to get rid of this essentialist
method.   (This is why so much of our ' social science ' still belongs
to the Middle Ages.)   The discussion of this method will have to
be a little abstract, owing to the fact that the problem has been
so thoroughly muddled by Plato and Aristotle, whose influence
has given rise to such deep-rooted prejudices that the prospect
of dispelling them does not seem very bright.   In spite of all
that, it is perhaps not without interest to analyse the source of
so much confusion and verbiage.

Aristotle followed Plato in distinguishing between *knowledge*
and *opinion* [27].   Knowledge, or science, according to Aristotle,
may be of two kinds—either demonstrative or intuitive.   *Demonstrative knowledge* is also **a** knowledge of ' causes '.   It consists of

statements that can be demonstrated—the conclusions—together with their syllogistic demonstrations (which exhibit the ' causes ' in their ' middle terms '). *Intuitive knowledge* consists in grasping the ' indivisible form ' or essence or essential nature of a thing (if it is ' immediate ', i.e. if its ' cause ' is identical with its essential nature) ; it is the originative source of all science since it grasps the original basic premises of all demonstrations.

Undoubtedly, Aristotle was right when he insisted that we must not attempt to prove or demonstrate *all* our knowledge. Every proof must proceed from premises ; the proof as such, that is to say, the derivation from the premises, can therefore never finally settle the truth of any conclusion, but only show that the conclusion must be true *provided* the premises are true. If we were to demand that the premises should be proved in their turn, the question of truth would only be shifted back by another step to a new set of premises, and so on, to infinity. It was in order to avoid such an infinite regress (as the logicians say) that Aristotle taught that we must assume that there are premises which are indubitably true, and which do not need any proof ; and these he called ' basic premises '. If we take for granted the methods by which we derive conclusions from these basic premises, then we could say that, according to Aristotle, the whole of scientific knowledge is contained in the basic premises, and that it would all be ours if only we could obtain an encyclopædic list of the basic premises. But how to obtain these basic premises ? Like Plato, Aristotle believed that we obtain all knowledge ultimately by an intuitive grasp of the essences of things. ' We can know a thing only by knowing its essence ', Aristotle writes [28], and ' to know a thing is to know its essence '. A ' basic premise ' is, according to him, nothing but a statement describing the essence of a thing. But such a statement is just what he calls [29] a definition. Thus *all ' basic premises of proofs ' are definitions.*

What does a definition look like ? An example of a definition would be : ' A puppy is a young dog.' The subject of such a definition-sentence, the term ' puppy ', is called the *term to be defined* (or *defined term*) ; the words ' young dog ' are called the *defining formula*. As a rule, the defining formula is longer and more complicated than the defined term, and sometimes very much so. Aristotle considers [30] the term to be defined as a name of the essence of a thing, and the defining formula as the description of that essence. And he insists that the defining formula must give an exhaustive description of the essence or the essential properties of the thing in question ; thus a statement like ' A puppy has four legs ', although true, is not a satisfactory definition, since it does not exhaust what may be called the essence of puppiness, but holds true of a horse also ; and similarly the statement ' A puppy is brown ', although it may be true of some, is not true of all puppies ; and it describes what is not an essential but merely an accidental property of the defined term.

But the most difficult question is how we can get hold of definitions or basic premises, and make sure that they are correct—that we have not erred, not grasped the wrong essence. Although Aristotle is not very clear on this point [31], there can be little doubt that, in the main, he again follows Plato. Plato taught [32] that we can grasp the Ideas with the help of some kind of unerring *intellectual intuition* ; that is to say, we visualize or look at them with our ' mental eye ', a process which he conceived as analogous to seeing, but dependent purely upon our intellect, and excluding any element that depends upon our senses. Aristotle's view is less radical and less inspired than Plato's, but in the end it amounts to the same [33]. For although he teaches that we arrive at the definition only after we have made many observations, he admits that sense-experience does not in itself grasp the universal essence, and that it cannot, therefore, fully determine a definition. Eventually he simply postulates that we possess an intellectual intuition, a mental or intellectual faculty which enables us unerringly to grasp the essences of things, and to know them. And he further assumes that if we know an essence intuitively, we must be capable of describing it and therefore of defining it. (His arguments in the *Posterior Analytic* in favour of this theory are surprisingly weak. They consist merely in pointing out that our knowledge of the basic premises cannot be demonstrative, since this would lead to an infinite regress, and that the basic premises must be at least as true and as certain as the conclusions based upon them. ' It follows from this ', he writes, ' that there cannot be demonstrative knowledge of the primary premises ; and since nothing but intellectual intuition can be more true than demonstrative knowledge, it follows that it must be intellectual intuition that grasps the basic premises.' In the *De Anima*, and in the theological part of the *Metaphysics*, we find more of an argument ; for here we have a *theory* of intellectual intuition— that it comes into contact with its object, the essence, and that it even becomes one with its object. ' Actual knowledge is identical with its object.')

Summing up this brief analysis, we can give, I believe, a fair description of the Aristotelian ideal of perfect and complete knowledge if we say that he saw the ultimate aim of all inquiry in the compilation of an encyclopædia containing the intuitive definitions of all essences, that is to say, their names together with their defining formulæ ; and that he considered the progress of knowledge as consisting in the gradual accumulation of such an encyclopædia, in expanding it as well as in filling up the gaps in it and, of course, in the syllogistic derivation from it of ' the whole body of facts' which constitute demonstrative knowledge.

Now there can be little doubt that all these essentialist views stand in the strongest possible contrast to the methods of modern science. (I have the empirical sciences in mind, not perhaps pure mathematics.) First, although in science we do our best to find the truth, we are conscious of the fact that we can never be sure whether we have got it. We have learned in the past, from many disappointments, that we must not expect finality. And we have learned not to be disappointed any longer if our scientific theories are overthrown ; for we can, in most cases, determine with great confidence which of any two theories is the better one. We can therefore know that we are making progress ; and it is this knowledge that to most of us atones for the loss of the illusion of finality and certainty. In other words, we know that our scientific theories must always remain hypotheses, but that, in many important cases, we can find out whether or not a new hypothesis is superior to an old one. For if they are different, then they will lead to different predictions, which can often be tested experimentally ; and on the basis of such a crucial experiment, we can sometimes find out that the new theory leads to satisfactory results where the old one breaks down. Thus we can say that in our search for truth, we have replaced scientific certainty by scientific progress. And this view of scientific method is corroborated by the development of science. For science does not develop by a gradual encyclopædic accumulation of essential information, as Aristotle thought, but by a much more revolutionary method ; it progresses by bold ideas, by the advancement of new and very strange theories (such as the theory that the earth is not flat, or that ' metrical space ' is not flat), and by the overthrow of the old ones.

But this view of scientific method means [34] that in science there is no ' *knowledge* ', in the sense in which Plato and Aristotle understood the word, in the sense which implies finality ; in science, we never have sufficient reason for the belief that we have attained the truth. What we usually call ' scientific knowledge ' is, as a rule, not knowledge in this sense, but rather information regarding the various competing hypotheses and the way in which they have stood up to various tests ; it is, using the language of Plato and Aristotle, information concerning the latest, and the best tested, scientific ' *opinion* '. This view means, furthermore, that we have no proofs in science (excepting, of course, pure mathematics and logic). In the empirical sciences, which alone can furnish us with information about the world we live in, proofs do not occur, if we mean by ' proof' an argument which establishes once and for ever the truth of a theory. (What may occur, however, are refutations of scientific theories.) On the other hand, pure mathematics and logic, which permit of proofs, give us no information about the world, but only develop the means of describing it. Thus we could say (as I have pointed out elsewhere [35]) : ' In so far as scientific statements refer to the world of experience, they must be refutable ; and, in so far as they are irrefutable, they do not refer to the world of experience.' But although proof does not play any part in the empirical sciences, argument still does [36] ; indeed, its part is at least as important as that played by observation and experiment.

The rôle of definitions in science, especially, is also very different from what Aristotle had in mind. Aristotle taught that in a definition we have first pointed to the essence—perhaps by naming it—and that we then describe it with the help of the defining formula ; just as in an ordinary sentence like ' This puppy is brown ', we first point to a certain thing by saying ' this puppy ', and then describe it as ' brown '. And he taught that by thus describing the essence to which the term points which is to be defined, we determine or explain the *meaning* [37] of the term also. Accordingly, the definition may at one time answer two very closely related questions. The one is ' What is it ? ', for example, ' What is a puppy ? ' ; it asks what the essence is which is denoted by the defined term. The other is ' What does it mean ? ', for example, ' What does " puppy " mean ? ' ; it asks for the meaning of a term (namely, of the term that denotes the essence). In the present context, it is not necessary to distinguish between these two questions ; rather, it is important to see what they have in common ; and I wish, especially, to draw attention to the fact that both *questions are*

*raised by the term that stands, in the definition, on the left side and
answered by the defining formula which stands on the right side.* This
fact characterizes the essentialist view, from which the scientific
method of definition radically differs.

While we may say that the essentialist interpretation reads
a definition ' normally ', that is to say, from the *left to the right*,
we can say that *a definition, as it is normally used in modern science,
must be read back to front, or from the right to the left* ; for it starts
with the defining formula, and asks for a short label to it. Thus
the scientific view of the definition ' A puppy is a young dog '
would be that it is an answer to the question ' *What shall we call
a young dog ?* ' rather than an answer to the question ' *What is*
a puppy ? '. (Questions like ' *What is* life ? ' or ' *What is* gravity ? '
do not play any rôle in science.) The scientific use of definitions,
characterized by the approach ' from the right to the left ', may
be called its *nominalist* interpretation, as opposed to its Aristotelian or *essentialist* interpretation [38]. In modern science, only [39]
nominalist definitions occur, that is to say, shorthand symbols
or labels are introduced in order to cut a long story short. And
we can at once see from this that definitions do *not* play any
very important part in science. For shorthand symbols can
always, of course, be replaced by the longer expressions, the
defining formula, for which they stand. In some cases this
would make our scientific language very cumbersome ; we should
waste time and paper. But we should never lose the slightest
piece of factual information. Our ' scientific knowledge ', in
the sense in which this term may be properly used, remains
entirely unaffected if we eliminate all definitions ; the only
effect is upon our language, which would lose, not precision [40],
but merely brevity. (This must not be taken to mean that in
science there cannot be an urgent practical need for introducing
definitions, for brevity's sake.) There could hardly be a greater
contrast than that between this view of the part played by
definitions, and Aristotle's view. For Aristotle's essentialist
definitions are the principles from which all our knowledge is
derived ; they thus contain all our knowledge ; and they serve
to substitue a long formula for a short one. As opposed to this,
the scientific or nominalist definitions do not contain any knowledge whatever, not even any ' opinion ' ; they do nothing but
introduce new arbitrary shorthand labels ; they cut a long
story short.

In practice, these labels are of the greatest usefulness. In order to see this, we only need to consider the extreme difficulties that would arise if a bacteriologist, whenever he spoke of a certain strain of bacteria, had to repeat its whole description (including the methods of dyeing, etc., by which it is distinguished from a number of similar species). And we may also understand, by a similar consideration, why it has so often been forgotten, even by scientists, that scientific definitions must be read ' from the right to the left ', as explained above. For most people, when first studying a science, say bacteriology, must try to find out the meanings of all these new technical terms with which they are faced. In this way, they really *learn* the definition ' from the left to the right ', substituting, as if it were an essentialist definition, a very long story for a very short one. But this is merely a psychological accident, and a teacher or writer of a textbook may indeed proceed quite differently ; that is to say, he may introduce a technical term only after the need for it has arisen [41].

So far I have tried to show that the scientific or nominalist use of definitions is entirely different from Aristotle's essentialist method of definitions. But it can also be shown that the essentialist view of definitions is simply untenable in itself. In order not to prolong this digression unduly [42], I shall criticize two only of the essentialist doctrines ; two doctrines which are of significance because some influential modern schools are still based upon them. One is the esoteric doctrine of intellectual intuition, and the other the very popular doctrine that ' we must define our terms ', if we wish to be precise.

Aristotle held with Plato that we possess a faculty, intellectual intuition, by which we can visualize essences and find out which definition is the correct one, and many modern essentialists have repeated this doctrine. Other philosophers, following Kant, maintain that we do not possess anything of the sort. My opinion is that we can readily admit that we possess something which may be described as ' intellectual intuition ' ; or more precisely, that certain of our intellectual experiences may be thus described. Everybody who ' understands ' an idea, or a point of view, or an arithmetical method, for instance, multiplication, in the sense that he has ' got the feel of it ', might be said to understand that thing intuitively ; and there are countless intellectual experiences of that kind. But I would insist, on the other hand, that these experiences, important as they may be for our scientific endeavours, can never serve to establish the truth of any idea

or theory, however strongly somebody may feel, intuitively, that
it must be true, or that it is ' self-evident ' [43]. Such intuitions
cannot even serve as an argument, although they may encourage
us to look for arguments. For somebody else may have just
as strong an intuition that the same theory is false. The way of
science is paved with discarded theories which were once declared
self-evident ; Francis Bacon, for example, sneered at those who
denied the self-evident truth that the sun and the stars rotated
round the earth, which was obviously at rest. Intuition
undoubtedly plays a great part in the life of a scientist, just
as it does in the life of a poet. It leads him to his discoveries.
But it may also lead him to his failures. And it always remains
his private affair, as it were. Science does not ask how he has
got his ideas, it is only interested in arguments that can be
tested by everybody. The great mathematician, Gauss, described this situation very neatly once when he exclaimed : ' I
have got my result ; but I do not know yet how to get it.' All
this applies, of course, to Aristotle's doctrine of intellectual
intuition of so-called essences [44], which was propagated by
Hegel, and in our own time by E. Husserl and his numerous
pupils ; and it indicates that the ' intellectual intuition of
essences ' or ' pure phenomenology ', as Husserl calls it, is a
method of neither science nor philosophy. (The much debated
question whether it is a new invention, as the pure phenomeno-
logists think, or perhaps a version of Cartesianism or Hegelianism,
can be easily decided ; it is a version of Aristotelianism.)

The second doctrine to be criticized has even more important
connections with modern views ; and it bears especially upon
the problem of verbalism. Since Aristotle, it has become
widely known that one cannot prove all statements, and that
an attempt to do so would break down because it would lead
only to an infinite regression of proofs. But neither he [45] nor,
apparently, a great many modern writers seem to realize that
the analogous attempt to define the meaning of all our terms
must, in the same way, lead to an infinite regression of definitions. The following passage from Crossman's *Plato To-Day*
is characteristic of a view which by implication is held by
many contemporary philosophers of repute, for example, by
Wittgenstein [46] : ' . . if we do not know precisely the meanings
of the words we use, we cannot discuss anything profitably.
Most of the futile arguments on which we all waste time are
largely due to the fact that we each have our own vague meanings

for the words we use and assume that our opponents are using them in the same senses. If we defined our terms to start with, we could have far more profitable discussions. Again, we have only to read the daily papers to observe that propaganda (the modern counterpart of rhetoric) depends largely for its success on confusing the meaning of the terms. If politicians were compelled by law to define any term they wished to use, they would lose most of their popular appeal, their speeches would be shorter, and many of their disagreements would be found to be purely verbal.' This passage is very characteristic of one of the prejudices which we owe to Aristotle, of the prejudice that language can be made more precise by the use of definitions. Let us consider whether this can really be done.

First, we can see clearly that if ' politicians ' (or anybody else) ' were compelled by law to define any term they wished to use ', their speeches would not be shorter, but infinitely long. For a definition cannot establish the meaning of a term any more than a logical derivation [47] can establish the truth of a statement ; both can only shift this problem back. The derivation shifts the problem of truth back to the premises, the definition shifts the problem of meaning back to the defining terms (i.e., the terms that make up the defining formula). But these, for many reasons [48], are likely to be just as vague and confusing as the terms we started with ; and in any case, we should have to go on to define them in turn ; which leads to new terms which too must be defined. And so on, to infinity. One sees that the demand that all our terms should be defined is just as untenable as the demand that all our statements should be proved.

At first sight this criticism may seem unfair. It may be said that what people have in mind, if they demand definitions, is the elimination of the ambiguities so often connected with words such as [49] ' democracy ', ' liberty ', ' duty ', ' religion ', etc. ; that it is clearly impossible to define all our terms, but possible to define some of these more dangerous terms and to leave it at that ; and that the defining terms have just to be accepted, i.e., that we must stop after a step or two in order to avoid an infinite regression. This defence, however, is untenable. Admittedly, the terms mentioned are much misused. But I deny that the attempt to define them can improve matters. It can only make matters worse. That by ' defining their terms ' even once, and leaving the defining terms undefined, the politicians would not be able to make their speeches shorter, is

clear ; for any essentialist definition, i.e. one that 'defines our
terms' (as opposed to the nominalist one which introduces new
technical terms), means the substitution of a long story for a
short one, as we have seen. Besides, the attempt to define
terms would only increase the vagueness and confusion. For
since we cannot demand that all the defining terms should be
defined in their turn, a clever politician or philosopher could
easily satisfy the demand for definitions. If asked what he means
by 'democracy', for example, he could say 'the rule of the
general will' or 'the rule of the spirit of the people'; and
since he has now given a definition, and so satisfied the highest
standards of precision, nobody will dare to criticize him any
longer. And, indeed, how could he be criticized, since the
demand that 'rule' or 'people' or 'will' or 'spirit' should
be defined in their turn, puts us well on the way to an infinite
regression so that everybody would hesitate to raise it ? But
should it be raised in spite of all that, then it can be equally
easily satisfied. On the other hand, a quarrel about the question
whether the definition was correct, or true, can only lead to an
empty controversy about words.

Thus the essentialist view of definition breaks down, even if
it does not, with Aristotle, attempt to establish the 'principles'
of our knowledge, but only makes the apparently more modest
demand that we should 'define the meaning of our terms'.

But undoubtedly, the demand that we speak clearly and
without ambiguity is very important, and must be satisfied.
Can the nominalist view satisfy it ? And can nominalism
escape the infinite regression ?

It can. For the nominalist position there is no difficulty
which corresponds to the infinite regression. As we have seen,
science does not use definitions in order to determine the meaning
of its terms, but only in order to introduce handy shorthand
labels. And it does not depend on definitions ; all definitions
can be omitted without loss to the information imparted. It
follows from this that in science, *all the terms that are really needed
must be undefined terms.* How then do the sciences make sure of
the meanings of their terms ? Various replies to this question
have been suggested [50], but I do not think that any of them are
satisfactory. The situation seems to be this. Aristotelianism
and related philosophies have told us for such a long time how
important it is to get a precise knowledge of the meaning of our
terms that we are all inclined to believe it. And we continue

to cling to this creed in spite of the unquestionable fact that philosophy, which for twenty centuries has worried about the meaning of its terms, is not only full of verbalism but also appallingly vague and ambiguous, while a science like physics which worries hardly at all about terms and their meaning, but about facts instead, has achieved great precision. This, surely, should be taken as indicating that, under Aristotelian influence, the importance of the meaning of terms has been grossly exaggerated. But I think that it indicates even more. For not only does this concentration on the problem of meaning fail to establish precision ; it is itself the main source of vagueness, ambiguity, and confusion.

In science, we take care that the statements we make should never *depend* upon the meaning of our terms. Even where the terms are defined, we never try to derive any information from the definition, or to base any argument upon it. This is why our terms make so little trouble. We do not overburden them. We try to attach to them as little weight as possible. We do not take their ' meaning ' too seriously. We are always conscious that our terms are a little vague (since we have learned to use them only in practical applications) and we reach precision not by reducing their penumbra of vagueness, but rather by keeping well within it, by carefully phrasing our sentences in such a way that the possible shades of meaning of our terms do not matter. This is how we avoid quarrelling about words.

The view that the precision of science and of scientific language depends upon the precision of its terms is certainly very plausible, but it is none the less, I believe, a mere prejudice. The precision of a language depends, rather, just upon the fact that it takes care not to burden its terms with the task of being precise. A term like ' sand-dune ' or ' wind ' is certainly very vague. (How many inches high must a little sand-hill be in order to be called ' sand-dune ' ? How quickly must the air move in order to be called ' wind ' ?) However, for many of the geologist's purposes, these terms are quite sufficiently precise ; and for other purposes, when a higher degree of differentiation is needed, he can always say ' dunes between 4 and 30 feet high ' or ' wind of a velocity of between 20 and 40 miles an hour '. And the position in the more exact sciences is analogous. In physical measurements, for instance, we always take care to consider the range within which there may be an error ; and precision does not consist in trying to reduce this range to nothing, or in pretending that there is no such range, but rather in its explicit recognition.

Even where a term has made trouble, as for instance the term ' simultaneity ' in physics, it was not because its meaning was unprecise or ambiguous, but rather because of some intuitive theory which induced us to burden the term with too much meaning, or with too ' precise ' a meaning, rather than with too little. What Einstein found in his analysis of simultaneity was that, when speaking of simultaneous events, physicists made a false assumption which would have been unchallengeable were there signals of infinite velocity. The fault was not that they did not mean anything, or that their meaning was ambiguous, or the term not precise enough ; what Einstein found was, rather, that the elimination of a theoretical assumption, unnoticed so far because of its intuitive self-evidence, was able to remove a difficulty which had arisen in science. Accordingly, he was not really concerned with a question of the meaning of a term, but rather with the truth of a theory. It is very unlikely that it would have led to much if someone had started, apart from a definite physical problem, to improve the concept of simultaneity by analysing its ' essential meaning ', or even by analysing what physicists ' really mean ' when they speak of simultaneity.

I think we can learn from this example that we should not attempt to cross our bridges before we come to them. And I also think that the preoccupation with questions concerning the meaning of terms, such as their vagueness or their ambiguity, can certainly not be justified by an appeal to Einstein's example. Such a preoccupation rests, rather, on the assumption that much depends upon the meaning of our terms, and that we operate with this meaning ; and therefore it must lead to verbalism and scholasticism. From this point of view, we may criticize a doctrine like that of Wittgenstein [51], who holds that while science investigates matters of fact, it is the business of philosophy to clarify the meaning of terms, thereby purging our language, and eliminating linguistic puzzles. It is characteristic of the views of this school that they do not lead to any chain of argument that could be rationally criticized ; the school therefore addresses its subtle analyses [52] exclusively to the small esoteric circle of the initiated. This seems to suggest that any preoccupation with meaning tends to lead to that result which is so typical of Aristotelianism : scholasticism and mysticism.

Let us consider briefly how these two typical results of

Aristotelianism have arisen.   Aristotle insisted that demonstration or proof, and definition, are the two fundamental methods of obtaining knowledge.   Considering the doctrine of proof first, it cannot be denied that it has led to countless attempts to prove more than can be proved ;   medieval philosophy is full of this scholasticism and the same tendency can be observed, on the Continent, down to Kant.   It was Kant's criticism of all attempts to prove the existence of God which led to the romantic reaction of Fichte, Schelling, and Hegel.   The new tendency is to discard proofs, and with them, any kind of rational argument.   With the romantics, a new kind of dogmatism becomes fashionable, in philosophy as well as in the social sciences.   It confronts us with its dictum.   And we can *take it or leave it*.   This romantic period of an oracular philosophy, called by Schopenhauer the ' age of dishonesty ', is described by him as follows [53] : ' The character of honesty, that spirit of undertaking an inquiry together with the reader, which permeates the works of all previous philosophers, disappears here completely.   Every page witnesses that these so-called philosophers do not attempt to teach, but to bewitch the reader.'

A similar result was produced by Aristotle's doctrine of definition.   First it led to a good deal of hairsplitting.   But later, philosophers began to feel that one cannot argue about definitions.   In this way, essentialism not only encouraged verbalism, but it also led to the disillusionment with argument, that is, with reason.   Scholasticism and mysticism and despair in reason, these are the unavoidable results of the essentialism of Plato and Aristotle.   And Plato's open revolt against freedom becomes, with Aristotle, a secret revolt against reason.

As we know from Aristotle himself, essentialism and the theory of definition met with strong opposition when they were first proposed, especially from Socrates' old companion Antisthenes, whose criticism seems to have been most sensible [54].   But this opposition was unfortunately defeated.   The consequences of this defeat for the intellectual development of mankind can hardly be overrated.   Some of them will be discussed in the next chapter.   With this I conclude my digression, the criticism of the Platonic-Aristotelian theory of definition.

III

It will hardly be necessary again to stress the fact that my treatment of Aristotle is most sketchy—much more so than my treatment of Plato. The main purpose of what has been said about both of them is to show the rôle they have played in the rise of historicism and in the fight against the open society, and to show their influence on problems of our own time—on the rise of the oracular philosophy of Hegel, the father of modern historicism and totalitarianism. The developments between Aristotle and Hegel cannot be treated here at all. In order to do anything like justice to them, at least another volume would be needed. In the remaining few pages of this chapter I shall, however, attempt to indicate how this period might be interpreted in terms of the conflict between the open and the closed society.

The conflict between the Platonic-Aristotelian speculation and the spirit of the Great Generation, of Pericles, of Socrates, and of Democritus, can be traced throughout the ages. This spirit was preserved, more or less purely, in the movement of the Cynics who, like the early Christians, preached the brotherhood of man, which they connected with a monotheistic belief in the fatherhood of God. Alexander's empire as well as that of Augustus was influenced by these ideas which had first taken shape in the imperialist Athens of Pericles, and which had always been stimulated by the contact between West and East. It is very likely that these ideas, and perhaps the Cynic movement itself, influenced the rise of Christianity also.

In its beginning, Christianity, like the Cynic movement, was opposed to the highbrow Platonizing Idealism and intellectualism of the ' scribes ', the learned men. (' Thou hast hid these things from the wise and prudent and hast revealed them unto the babes.') I do not doubt that it was, in part, a protest against what may be described as Jewish Platonism in the wider sense [55], the abstract worship of God and His Word. And it was certainly a protest against Jewish tribalism, against its rigid and empty tribal taboos, and against its tribal exclusiveness which expressed itself, for example, in the doctrine of the chosen people, i.e. in an interpretation of the deity as a tribal god. Such an emphasis upon tribal laws and tribal unity appears to be characteristic not so much of a primitive tribal society as of a desperate attempt to restore and arrest the old forms of tribal life ; and in the case of Jewry, it seems to have originated as a reaction to the impact of the Babylonian conquest on Jewish tribal life. But side by side with this movement towards greater rigidity we find another movement which apparently originated at the same time, and which produced humanitarian ideas that resembled the response of the Great Generation to the dissolution of Greek tribalism. This process, it appears, repeated itself when Jewish independence was ultimately destroyed by Rome. It led to a new and deeper schism between these two possible solutions, the return to the tribe, as represented by orthodox Jewry, and the humanitarianism of the new sect of Christians, which embraced barbarians (or gentiles) as well as slaves. We can see from the *Acts* [56] how urgent these problems were, the social problem as well as the national problem. And we can see this from the development of Jewry as well ; for its conservative part reacted to the same challenge by another movement towards arresting and petrifying their tribal form of life, and by clinging to their ' laws ' with a tenacity which would have won the approval of Plato. It can hardly be doubted that this development was, like that of Plato's ideas, inspired by a strong antagonism to the new creed of the open society ; in this case, of Christianity.

But the parallelism between the creed of the Great Generation, especially of Socrates, and that of early Christianity goes deeper. There is little doubt that the strength of the early Christians lay in their moral courage. It lay in the fact that they refused to accept Rome's claim ' that it was entitled to compel its subjects to act against their conscience ' [57]. The Christian martyrs who rejected the claims of might to set the standards of right suffered for the same cause for which Socrates had died.

It is clear that these matters changed very considerably when the Christian faith itself became powerful in the Roman empire. The question arises whether this official recognition of the Christian Church (and its later organization after the model of Julian the Apostate's Neo-Platonic Anti-Church [58]) was not an ingenious political move on the part of the ruling powers, designed to break the tremendous moral influence of an equalitarian religion —a religion which they had in vain attempted to combat by force as well as by accusations of atheism and impiety. In other words, the question arises whether (especially after Julian) Rome did not find it necessary to apply Pareto's advice, ' to take advantage of sentiments, not wasting one's energies in futile efforts to destroy them '. This question is hard to answer ; but it certainly cannot be dismissed by appealing (as Toynbee does [59]) to our ' historical sense that warns us against attributing ', to

the period of Constantine and his followers, ' . . motives that
are anachronistically cynical ', that is to say, motives that are
more in keeping with our own ' modern Western attitude to
life '. For we have seen that such motives are openly and
' cynically ', or more precisely, shamelessly, expressed as early as
in the fifth century B.C., by Critias, the leader of the Thirty
Tyrants ; and similar statements can be found frequently during
the history of Greek philosophy [60]. However this may be, it
can hardly be doubted that with Justinian's persecution of non-
Christians, heretics, and philosophers (A.D. 529), the dark ages
began. The Church followed in the wake of Platonic-Aristotelian
totalitarianism, a development that culminated in the Inquisition.
The theory of the Inquisition, more especially, can be described
as purely Platonic. It is set out in the last three books of the
Laws, where Plato shows that it is the duty of the shepherd rulers
to protect their sheep at all costs by preserving the rigidity of
the laws and especially of religious practice and theory, even if
they have to kill the wolf, who may admittedly be an honest and
honourable man whose diseased conscience unfortunately does
not permit him to bow to the threats of the mighty.

It is one of the characteristic reactions to the strain of civilization in our own time that the allegedly ' Christian ' authoritarianism of the Middle Ages has, in certain intellectualist circles,
become one of the latest fashions of the day [61]. This, no doubt,
is due not only to the idealization of an indeed more ' organic '
and ' integrated ' past, but also to an understandable revulsion
against modern agnosticism which has increased this strain beyond
measure. Men believed God to rule the world. This belief
limited their responsibility. The new belief that they had to rule
it themselves created for many a well nigh intolerable burden of
responsibility. All this has to be admitted. But I do not doubt
that the Middle Ages were, even from the point of view of Christianity, not better ruled than our Western democracies. For we
can read in the Gospels that the founder of Christianity was
questioned by a certain ' doctor of the law ' about a criterion by
which to distinguish between a true and a false interpretation of
His words. To this He replied by telling the parable of the
priest and the Levite who both, seeing a wounded man in great
distress, ' passed by on the other side ', while the Samaritan bound
up his wounds, and looked after his material needs. This parable,
I think, should be remembered by those ' Christians ' who long
not only for a time when the Church suppressed freedom and

conscience, but also for a time in which, under the eye and with
the authority of the Church, untold oppression drove the people
to despair. As a moving comment upon the suffering of the
people in those days and, at the same time, upon the ' Christianity ' of the now so fashionable romantic medievalism which
wants to bring these days back, a passage may be quoted here
from H. Zinsser's book, *Rats, Lice, and History*,[62] in which he
speaks about epidemics of dancing mania in the Middle Ages,
known as ' St. John's dance ', ' St. Vitus' dance ', etc. (I do not
wish to invoke Zinsser as an authority on the Middle Ages—
there is no need to do so since the facts at issue are hardly controversial. But his comments have the rare and peculiar touch
of the practical Samaritan—of a great and humane physician.)
' These strange seizures, though not unheard of in earlier times,
became common during and immediately after the dreadful
miseries of the Black Death. For the most part, the dancing
manias present none of the characteristics which we associate
with epidemic infectious diseases of the nervous system. They
seem, rather, like *mass hysterias, brought on by terror and despair, in
populations oppressed, famished, and wretched to a degree almost un-
imaginable to-day*. To the miseries of constant war, political and
social disintegration, there was added the dreadful affliction of
inescapable, mysterious, and deadly disease. Mankind stood
helpless as though trapped in a world of terror and peril against
which there was no defence. God and the devil were living
conceptions to the men of those days who cowered under the
afflictions which they believed imposed by supernatural forces.
For those who broke down under the strain there was no road
of escape except to the inward refuge of mental derangement
which, under the circumstances of the times, took the direction
of religious fanaticism.' Zinsser then goes on to draw some
parallels between these events and certain reactions of our time
in which, he says, ' economic and political hysterias are substituted for the religious ones of the earlier times ' ; and after this,
he sums up his characterization of the people who lived in those
days of authoritarianism as ' a terror-stricken and wretched
population, which had broken down under the stress of almost
incredible hardship and danger '. Is it necessary to ask which
attitude is more Christian, one that longs to return to the ' un-
broken harmony and unity ' of the Middle Ages, or one that
wishes to use reason in order to free mankind from pestilence
and oppression ?

But some part at least of the authoritarian Church of the Middle Ages succeeded in branding such practical humanitarianism as ' worldly ', as characteristic of ' Epicureanism ', and of men who desire only to ' fill their bellies like the beasts '. The terms ' Epicureanism ', ' materialism ', and ' empiricism ', that is to say, the philosophy of Democritus, one of the greatest of the Great Generation, became in this way the synonyms of wickedness, and the tribal Idealism of Plato and Aristotle was exalted as a kind of Christianity before Christ. Indeed, this is the source of the immense authority of Plato and Aristotle, even in our own day, that their philosophy was adopted by medieval authoritarianism. But it must not be forgotten that, outside the totalitarian camp, their fame has outlived their practical influence upon our lives. And although the name of Democritus is seldom remembered, his science as well as his morals still live with us.

CHAPTER 12 : HEGEL AND THE NEW TRIBALISM

> The philosophy of Hegel, then, was . . a scrutiny
> of thought so profound that it was for the most
> part unintelligible. . .
>
> J. H. STIRLING.

I

Hegel, the source of all contemporary historicism, was a direct
follower of Heraclitus, Plato, and Aristotle. Hegel achieved
the most miraculous things. A master logician, it was child's
play for his powerful dialectical methods to draw real physical
rabbits out of purely metaphysical silk-hats. Thus, starting from
Plato's *Timaeus* and its number-mysticism, Hegel succeeded in
' proving ' by purely philosophical methods (114 years after
Newton's *Principia*) that the planets must move according to
Kepler's laws. He even accomplished [1] the deduction of the
actual position of the planets, thereby proving that no planet
could be situated between Mars and Jupiter (unfortunately, it
had escaped his notice that such a planet had been discovered
a few months earlier). Similarly, he proved that magnetizing
iron means increasing its weight, that Newton's theories of
inertia and of gravity *contradict* each other (of course, he could
not foresee that Einstein would show the *identity* of inert and
gravitating mass), and many other things of this kind. That
such a surprisingly powerful philosophical method was taken
seriously can be only partially explained by the backwardness
of German natural science in those days. For the truth is, I
think, that it was not at first taken really seriously by serious
men (such as Schopenhauer, or J. F. Fries), not at any rate by
those scientists who, like Democritus [2], ' would rather find a
single causal law than be the king of Persia '. Hegel's fame
was made by those who prefer a quick initiation into the deeper
secrets of this world to the laborious technicalities of a science
which, after all, may only disappoint them by its lack of power to
unveil all mysteries. For they soon found out that nothing could
be applied with such ease to any problem whatsoever, and at
the same time with such impressive (though only apparent) difficulty, and with such quick and sure but imposing success,
nothing could be used as cheaply and with so little scientific training and knowledge, and nothing would give such a

spectacular scientific air, as did Hegelian *dialectics*, the mystery method that replaced ' barren formal logic '. Hegel's success was the beginning of the ' age of dishonesty ' (as Schopenhauer [3] described the period of German Idealism) and of the ' age of irresponsibility ' (as K. Heiden characterizes the age of modern totalitarianism) ; first of intellectual, and later, as one of its consequences, of moral irresponsibility ; of a new age controlled by the magic of high-sounding words, and by the power of jargon.

In order to discourage the reader beforehand from taking Hegel's bombastic and mystifying cant too seriously, I shall quote some of the amazing details which he discovered about sound, and especially about the relations between sound and heat. I have tried hard to translate this gibberish from Hegel's *Philosophy of Nature* [4] as faithfully as possible ; he writes : ' § 302. Sound is the change in the specific condition of segregation of the material parts, and in the negation of this condition ;— merely an *abstract* or an ideal *ideality*, as it were, of that specification. But this change, accordingly, is itself immediately the negation of the material specific subsistence ; which is, therefore, *real ideality* of specific gravity and cohesion, i.e.—*heat*. The heating up of sounding bodies, just as of beaten or rubbed ones, is the appearance of heat, originating conceptually together with sound.' There are some who still believe in Hegel's sincerity, or who still doubt whether his secret might not be profundity, fullness of thought, rather than emptiness. I should like them to read carefully the last sentence—the only intelligible one— of this quotation, because in this sentence, Hegel gives himself away. For clearly it means nothing but : ' The heating up of sounding bodies . . is heat . . together with sound.' The question arises whether Hegel deceived himself, hypnotized by his own inspiring jargon, or whether he boldly set out to deceive and bewitch others. I am satisfied that the latter was the case, especially in view of what Hegel wrote in one of his letters. In this letter, dated a few years before the publication of his *Philosophy of Nature*, Hegel referred to another *Philosophy of Nature*, written by his former friend Schelling : ' I have had too much to do . . with mathematics . . differential calculus, chemistry ', Hegel boasts in this letter (but this is just bluff), ' to let myself be taken in by the humbug of the Philosophy of Nature, by this philosophizing without knowledge of fact . . and by the treatment of *mere fancies, even imbecile fancies, as ideas*.' This is a very fair characterization of Schelling's method, that is to say, of that audacious way of bluffing which Hegel himself copied, or rather aggravated, as soon as he realized that, if it reached its proper audience, it meant success.

In spite of all this it seems improbable that Hegel would ever have become the most influential figure in German philosophy without the authority of the Prussian state behind him. As it happened, he became the first official philosopher of Prussianism, appointed in the period of feudal ' restoration ' after the Napoleonic wars. Later, the state also backed his pupils (Germany had, and still has, only state-controlled Universities), and they in their turn backed one another. And although Hegelianism was officially renounced by most of them, Hegelianizing philosophers have dominated philosophical teaching and thereby indirectly even the secondary schools of Germany ever since. (Of German-speaking Universities, those of Roman Catholic Austria remained fairly unmolested, like islands in a flood.) Having thus become a tremendous success on the continent, Hegelianism could hardly fail to obtain support in Britain from those who, feeling that such a powerful movement must after all have something to offer, began to search for what Stirling called *The Secret of Hegel*. They were attracted, of course, by Hegel's ' higher ' idealism and by his claims to ' higher ' morality, and they were also somewhat afraid of being branded as immoral by the chorus of the disciples ; for even the more modest Hegelians claimed [5] of their doctrines that ' they are acquisitions which must . . ever be reconquered in the face of assault from the powers eternally hostile to spiritual and moral values '. Some really brilliant men (I am thinking mainly of McTaggart) made great efforts in constructive idealistic thought, well above the level of Hegel ; but they did not get very far beyond providing targets for equally brilliant critics. And one can say that outside the continent of Europe, especially in the last twenty years, the interest of philosophers in Hegel has slowly been vanishing.

But if that is so, why worry any more about Hegel ? The answer is that Hegel's influence has remained a most powerful force, in spite of the fact that scientists never took him seriously, and that (apart from the ' evolutionists ' [6]) many philosophers are beginning to lose interest in him. Hegel's influence, and especially that of his cant, is still very powerful in moral and social philosophy and in the social and political sciences (with the sole exception of economics). Especially the philosophers of history, of politics, and of education are still to a very large extent under its sway. In politics, this is shown most drastically by the fact that the Marxist extreme left wing, as well as the conservative centre, and the fascist extreme right, all base their political philosophies on Hegel ; the left wing replaces the war of nations which appears in Hegel's historicist scheme by the war of classes, the extreme right replaces it by the war of races ; but both follow him more or less consciously. (The conservative centre is as a rule less conscious of its indebtedness to Hegel.)

How can this immense influence be explained ? My main intention is not so much to explain this phenomenon as to combat it. But I may make a few explanatory suggestions. For some reason, philosophers have kept around themselves, even in our day, something of the atmosphere of the magician. Philosophy is considered as a strange and abstruse kind of thing, dealing with those mysteries with which religion deals, but not in a way which can be ' revealed unto babes ' or to common people ; it is considered to be too profound for that, and to be the religion and theology of the intellectuals, of the learned and wise. Hegelianism fits these views admirably ; it is exactly what this kind of popular superstition supposes philosophy to be. It knows all about everything. It has a ready answer to every question. And indeed, who can be sure that the answer is not true ?

But this is not the main reason for Hegel's success. His influence, and the need to combat it, can perhaps be better understood if we briefly consider the general historical situation.

Medieval authoritarianism began to dissolve with the Renaissance. But on the Continent, its political counterpart, medieval feudalism, was not seriously threatened before the French Revolution. (The Reformation had only strengthened it.) The fight for the open society began again only with the ideas of 1789 ; and the feudal monarchies soon experienced the seriousness of this danger. When in 1815 the reactionary party began to resume its power in Prussia, it found itself in dire need of an ideology. Hegel was appointed to meet this demand, and he did so by reviving the ideas of the first great enemies of the open society, Heraclitus, Plato, and Aristotle. Just as the French Revolution rediscovered the perennial ideas of the Great Generation and of Christianity, freedom, equality, and the brotherhood of all men, so Hegel rediscovered the Platonic ideas which lie behind the perennial revolt against freedom and reason. Hegelianism is the renaissance of tribalism. The historical significance of Hegel may be seen in the fact that he represents the ' missing link ', as it were, between Plato and the modern form of totalitarianism. Most of the modern totalitarians are quite unaware that their ideas can be traced back to Plato. But many know of their indebtedness to Hegel, and all of them have been brought up in the close atmosphere of Hegelianism. They have been taught to worship the state, history, and the nation. (My view of Hegel presupposes, of course, that he interpreted Plato's teaching in the same way as I did here, that is to say, as totalitarian, to use this modern label ; and indeed, it can be shown [7], from his criticism of Plato in the *Philosophy of Law*, that Hegel's interpretation agrees with ours.)

In order to give the reader an immediate glimpse of Hegel's Platonizing worship of the state, I shall quote a few passages, even before I begin the analysis of his historicist philosophy. These passages show that Hegel's radical collectivism depends as much on Plato as it depends on Frederick William III, king of Prussia in the critical period during and after the French Revolution. Their doctrine is that the state is everything, and the individual nothing ; for he owes everything to the state, his physical as well as his spiritual existence. This is the message of Plato, of Frederick William's Prussianism, and of Hegel. ' The Universal is to be found in the State ', Hegel writes [8]. ' The State is the Divine Idea as it exists on earth. . . We must therefore worship the State as the manifestation of the Divine on earth, and consider that, if it is difficult to comprehend Nature, it is infinitely harder to grasp the Essence of the State. . . The State is the march of God through the world. . . The State must be comprehended as an organism. . . To the complete State belongs, essentially, consciousness and thought. The State knows what it wills. . . The State is real ; and . . true reality is necessary. What is real is eternally necessary. . . The State . . exists for its own sake. . . The State is the actually existing, realized moral life.' This selection of utterances may suffice to show Hegel's Platonism and his insistence upon the absolute moral authority of the state, which overrules all personal morality, all conscience. It is, of course, a bombastic and hysterical Platonism, but this only makes more obvious the fact that it links Platonism with modern totalitarianism.

One could ask whether by these services and by his influence upon history, Hegel has not proved his genius. I do not think this question very important, since it is only part of our romanticism that we think so much in terms of ' genius ' ; and apart from that, I do not believe that success proves anything, or that history is our judge [9] ; these tenets are rather part of Hegelianism. But as far as Hegel is concerned, I do not even think that he was talented. He is an indigestible writer. As even his most ardent apologists must admit [10], his style is ' unquestionably scandalous '. And as far as the content of his writing is concerned, he is supreme only in his outstanding lack of originality. There is nothing in Hegel's writing that has not been said better before him. There is nothing in his apologetic method that is not borrowed from his apologetic forerunners [11]. But he devoted these borrowed thoughts and methods with singleness of purpose, though without a trace of brilliancy, to one aim : to fight against the open society, and thus to serve his employer, Frederick William of Prussia. Hegel's confusion and debasement of reason is partly necessary as a means to this end, partly a more accidental but very natural expression of his state of mind. And the whole story of Hegel would indeed not be worth relating, were it not for its more sinister consequences, which show how easily a clown may be a ' maker of history '. The tragicomedy of the rise of ' German Idealism ', in spite of the hideous crimes to which it has led, resembles a comic opera much more than anything else ; and these beginnings may help to explain why it is so hard to decide of its latter-day heroes whether they have escaped from the stage of Wagner's Grand Teutonic Operas or from Offenbach's farces.

My assertion that Hegel's philosophy was inspired by ulterior motives, namely, by his interest in the restoration of the Prussian government of Frederick William III, and that it cannot therefore be taken seriously, is not new. The story was well known to all who knew the political situation, and it was freely told by the few who were independent enough to do so. The best witness is Schopenhauer, himself a Platonic idealist and a conservative if not a reactionary [12], but a man of supreme integrity who cherished truth beyond anything else. There can be no doubt that he was as competent a judge in philosophical matters as could be found at the time. Schopenhauer, who had the pleasure of knowing Hegel personally and who suggested [13] the use of Shakespeare's words, ' such stuff as madmen tongue and brain not ', as the motto of Hegel's philosophy, drew the following excellent picture of the master : ' Hegel, installed from above, by the powers that be, as the certified Great Philosopher, was a

flat-headed, insipid, nauseating, illiterate charlatan, who reached
the pinnacle of audacity in scribbling together and dishing up
the craziest mystifying nonsense. This nonsense has been noisily
proclaimed as immortal wisdom by mercenary followers and
readily accepted as such by all fools, who thus joined into as
perfect a chorus of admiration as had ever been heard before.
The extensive field of spiritual influence with which Hegel was
furnished by those in power has enabled him to achieve the
intellectual corruption of a whole generation.' And in another
place, Schopenhauer describes the political game of Hegelianism
as follows : ' Philosophy, brought afresh to repute by Kant . .
had soon to become a tool of interests ; of state interests from
above, of personal interests from below. . . The driving forces
of this movement are, contrary to all these solemn airs and
assertions, not ideal ; they are very real purposes indeed, namely
personal, official, clerical, political, in short, material interests.
. . Party interests are vehemently agitating the pens of so many
pure lovers of wisdom. . . Truth is certainly the last thing they
have in mind. . . Philosophy is misused, from the side of the
state as a tool, from the other side as a means of gain. . . Who
can really believe that truth also will thereby come to light, just
as a by-product ? . . *Governments make of philosophy a means
of serving their state interests, and scholars make of it a trade. . .*'
Schopenhauer's view of Hegel's status as the paid agent of
the Prussian government is, to mention only one example,
corroborated by Schwegler, an admiring disciple [14] of Hegel.
Schwegler says of Hegel : ' The fullness of his fame and activity,
however, properly dates only from his call to Berlin in 1818.
Here there rose up around him a numerous, widely extended,
and . . exceedingly active school ; here too, he acquired, from
his connections with the Prussian bureaucracy, political influence
for himself as well as the recognition of his system as the official
philosophy ; not always to the advantage of the inner freedom
of his philosophy, or of its moral worth.' Schwegler's editor,
J. H. Stirling [15], the first British apostle of Hegelianism, of course
defends Hegel against Schwegler by warning his readers not to
take too literally ' the little hint of Schwegler's against . . the
philosophy of Hegel as a state-philosophy '. But a few pages
later, Stirling quite unintentionally confirms Schwegler's representation of the facts as well as the view that Hegel himself
was aware of the party-political and apologetic function of his
philosophy. (The evidence quoted [16] by Stirling shows that

Hegel expressed himself rather cynically on this function of his philosophy.)   And a little later, Stirling unwittingly gives away the ' secret of Hegel ' when he proceeds to the following poetic as well as prophetic revelations [17], alluding to the lightning attack made by Prussia on Austria in 1866, the year before he wrote : ' Is it not indeed to Hegel, and especially his philosophy of ethics and politics, that Prussia owes that mighty life and organization she is now rapidly developing ?   Is it not indeed the grim Hegel that is the centre of that organization which, maturing counsel in an invisible brain, strikes, lightning-like, with a hand that is weighted from the mass ?   But as regards the value of this organization, it will be more palpable to many, should I say, that, while in constitutional England, Preference-holders and Debenture-holders are ruined by the prevailing commercial immorality, the ordinary owners of Stock in Prussian Railways can depend on a safe average of 8·33 per cent.   This, surely, is saying something for Hegel at last !

' The fundamental outlines of Hegel must now, I think, be evident to every reader.   I have gained much from Hegel . .' Stirling continues his eulogy.   I too hope that Hegel's outlines are now evident, and I trust that what Stirling had gained was saved from the menace of the commercial immorality prevailing in an un-Hegelian and constitutional England.

(Who could resist mentioning in this context the fact that Marxist philosophers, always ready to point out how an opponent's theory is affected by his class interest, habitually fail to apply this method to Hegel ?   Instead of denouncing him as an apologist for Prussian absolutism, they regret [18] that the works of the originator of dialectics, and especially his works on logic, are not more widely read in Britain—in contrast to Russia, where the merits of Hegel's philosophy in general, and of his logic in particular, are officially recognized.)

Returning to the problem of Hegel's political motives, we have, I think, more than sufficient reason to suspect that his philosophy was influenced by the interests of the Prussian government by which he was employed.   But under the absolutism of Frederick William III, such an influence implied more than Schopenhauer or Schwegler could know ;   for only in the last decades have the documents been published that show the clarity and consistency with which this king insisted upon the complete subordination of all learning to state interest.   ' Abstract sciences ', we read in his educational programme [19], ' that touch only the academic world, and serve only to enlighten this group, are of course without value to the welfare of the State ; it would be foolish to restrict them entirely, but it is healthy to keep them within proper limits.' Hegel's call to Berlin in 1818 came during the high tide of reaction, during the period which began with the king's purging his government of the reformers and national liberals who had contributed so much to his success in the ' War of Liberation '. Considering this fact, we may ask whether Hegel's appointment was not a move to ' keep philosophy within proper limits ', so as to enable her to be healthy and to serve ' the welfare of the State ', that is to say, of Frederick William and his absolute rule. The same question is suggested to us when we read what a great admirer says [20] of Hegel : ' And in Berlin he remained till his death in 1831, the acknowledged dictator of one of the most powerful philosophic schools in the history of thought.' (I think we should substitute ' lack of thought ' for ' thought ', because I cannot see what a dictator could possibly have to do with the history of thought, even if he were a dictator of philosophy. But otherwise, this revealing passage is only too true. For example, the concerted efforts of this powerful school succeeded, by a conspiracy of silence, in concealing from the world for forty years the very fact of Schopenhauer's existence.) We see that Hegel may indeed have had the power to ' keep philosophy within proper limits ', so that our question may be quite to the point.

In what follows, I shall try to show that Hegel's whole philosophy can be interpreted as an emphatic answer to this question ; an answer in the affirmative, of course. And I shall try to show how much light is thrown upon Hegelianism if we interpret it in this way, that is to say, as an apology for Prussianism. My analysis will be divided into three parts, to be treated in sections II, III, and IV of this chapter. Section II deals with Hegel's historicism and moral positivism, together with the rather abstruse theoretical background of these doctrines, his dialectic method and his so-called philosophy of identity. Section III deals with the rise of nationalism. In section IV, a few words will be said on Hegel's relation to Burke. And section V deals with the dependence of modern totalitarianism upon the doctrines of Hegel.

II

I begin my analysis of Hegel's philosophy with a general comparison between Hegel's historicism and that of Plato.

Plato believed that the Ideas or essences exist *prior* to the things in flux, and that the trend of all developments can be explained as a movement away from the perfection of the Ideas, and therefore as a descent, as a movement towards decay. The history of states, especially, ·is one of degeneration ; and ultimately this degeneration is due to the racial degeneration of the ruling class. (We must here remember the close relationship between the Platonic notions of ' race ', ' soul ', ' nature ', and ' essence ' [21].) Hegel believes, with Aristotle, that the Ideas or essences are *in* the things in flux ; or more precisely (as far as we can treat a Hegel with precision), Hegel teaches that they are identical with the things in flux : ' Everything actual is an Idea ', he says [22]. But this does not mean that the gulf opened up by Plato between the essence of a thing and its sensible appearance is closed ; for Hegel writes : ' Any mention of Essence implies that we distinguish it from the Being ' (of the thing) ; ' . . upon the latter, as compared with Essence, we rather look as mere appearance or semblance. . . Everything has an Essence, we have said ; that is, things are not what they immediately show themselves to be.' Also like Plato and Aristotle, Hegel conceives the essences, at least those of organisms (and therefore also those of states), as souls, or ' Spirits '.

But unlike Plato, Hegel does not teach that the trend of the development of the world in flux is a descent, away from the Idea, towards decay. Like Speusippus and Aristotle, Hegel teaches that the general trend is rather towards the Idea ; it is progress. Although he says [23], with Plato, that ' the perishable thing has its basis in Essence, and originates from it ', Hegel insists, in opposition to Plato, that even the essences develop. In Hegel's world, as in Heraclitus', *everything* is in flux ; and the essences, originally introduced by Plato in order to obtain something stable, are not exempted. But this flux is not decay. Hegel's historicism is optimistic. His essences and Spirits are, like Plato's souls, self-moving ; they are self-developing, or, using more fashionable terms, they are ' emerging ' and ' self-creating '. And they propel themselves in the direction of an Aristotelian ' final cause ', or, as Hegel puts it [24], towards a ' self-realizing and self-realized final cause in itself'. This final cause or end of the development of the essences is what Hegel calls ' The absolute Idea ' or ' The Idea '. (This Idea is, Hegel tells us, rather complex : it is, all in one, the Beautiful ; Cognition and Practical Activity ; Comprehension ; the Highest Good ; and the Scientifically Contemplated Universe. But we really need not worry about minor difficulties such as these.) We can say that Hegel's world of flux is in a state of 'emergent' or ' creative evolution ' [25] ; each of its stages contains the preceding ones, from which it originates ; and each stage supersedes all previous stages, approaching nearer and nearer to perfection. The general law of development is thus one of progress ; but, as we shall see, not of a simple and straightforward, but of a ' dialectic ' progress.

As previous quotations have shown, the collectivist Hegel, like Plato, visualizes the state as an organism ; and following Rousseau who had furnished it with a collective ' general will ', Hegel furnishes it with a conscious and thinking essence, its ' reason ' or ' Spirit '. This Spirit, whose ' very essence is activity ' (which shows its dependence on Rousseau), is at the same time the collective *Spirit of the Nation* that forms the state.

To an essentialist, knowledge or understanding of the state must clearly mean knowledge of its essence or Spirit. And as we have seen [26] in the last chapter, we can know the essence and its ' potentialities ' only from its ' actual ' history. Thus we arrive at the fundamental position of historicist method, that the way of obtaining knowledge of social institutions such as the state is to study its history, or the history of its ' Spirit '. And the other two historicist consequences developed in the last chapter follow also. The Spirit of the nation determines its hidden historical destiny ; and every nation that wishes ' to emerge into existence ' must assert its individuality or soul by entering the ' Stage of History ', that is to say, by fighting the other nations ; the object of the fight is world domination. We can see from this that Hegel, like Heraclitus, believes that war is the father and king of all things. And like Heraclitus, he believes that war is just : ' The History of the World is the World's court of justice ', writes Hegel. And like Heraclitus, Hegel generalizes this doctrine by extending it to the world of nature, interpreting the contrasts and oppositions of things, the polarity of opposites, etc., as a kind of war, and as a moving force of natural development. And like Heraclitus, Hegel believes in the unity or identity of opposites ; indeed, the unity of opposites plays such an important part in the evolution, in the ' dialectical ' progress, that we can describe these two Heraclitean ideas, the war of opposites, and their unity or identity, as the main ideas of Hegel's *dialectics*.

So far, this philosophy appears as a tolerably decent and

honest historicism, although one that is perhaps a little unoriginal [27]; and there seems to be no reason to describe it, with Schopenhauer, as charlatanism. But this appearance begins to change if we now turn to an analysis of Hegel's dialectics. For he proffers this method with an eye to Kant, who, in his attack upon metaphysics (the violence of these attacks may be gauged from the motto to my ' Introduction '), had tried to show that all speculations of this kind are untenable. Hegel never attempted to refute Kant. He bowed, and twisted Kant's view into its opposite. This is how Kant's ' dialectics ', the attack upon metaphysics, was converted into Hegelian ' dialectics ', the main tool of metaphysics.

Kant, in his *Critique of Pure Reason*, asserted under the influence of Hume that pure speculation or reason, whenever it ventures into a field in which it cannot possibly be checked by experience, is liable to get involved in contradictions or ' antinomies ' and to produce what he unambiguously described as ' mere fancies '; ' nonsense '; ' illusions '; ' a sterile dogmatism '; and ' a superficial pretension to the knowledge of everything ' [28]. He tried to show that to every metaphysical assertion or *thesis*, concerning for example the beginning of the world in time, or the existence of God, there can be contrasted a counter-assertion or *antithesis* ; and both, he held, may proceed from the same assumptions, and can be proved with an equal degree of ' evidence '. In other words, when leaving the field of experience, our speculation can have no scientific status, since to every argument there must be an equally valid counter-argument. Kant's intention was to stop once and forever the ' accursed fertility ' of the scribblers on metaphysics. But unfortunately, the effect was very different. What Kant stopped was only the attempts of the scribblers to use rational argument ; they only gave up the attempt to teach, but not the attempt to bewitch the public (as Schopenhauer puts it [29]). For this development, Kant himself undoubtedly bears a very considerable share of the blame ; for the obscure style of his work (which he wrote in a great hurry, although only after long years of meditation) contributed considerably to a further lowering of the low standard of clarity in German theoretical writing [30].

None of the metaphysical scribblers who came after Kant made any attempt to refute him [31] ; and Hegel, more particularly, even had the audacity to patronize Kant for ' reviving the name of Dialectics, which he restored to their post of honour '.

He taught that Kant was quite right in pointing out the anti-nomies, but that he was wrong to worry about them. It just lies in the nature of reason that it must contradict itself, Hegel asserted ; and it is not a weakness of our human faculties, but it is the very essence of all rationality that it must work with contradictions and antinomies ; for this is just the way in which *reason develops*. Hegel asserted that Kant had analysed reason as if it were something static ; that he forgot that mankind develops, and with it, our social heritage. But what we are pleased to call our own reason is nothing but the product of this social heritage, of the historical development of the social group in which we live, the nation. This development proceeds *dialectically*, that is to say, in a three-beat rhythm. First a *thesis* is proffered ; but it will produce criticism, it will be contradicted by opponents who assert its opposite, an *antithesis* ; and in the conflict of these views, a *synthesis* is attained, that is to say, a kind of unity of the opposites, a compromise or a reconciliation on a higher level. The synthesis absorbs, as it were, the two original opposite positions, by superseding them ; it reduces them to components of itself, thereby negating, elevating, and preserving them. And once the synthesis has been established, the whole process can repeat itself on the higher level that has now been reached. This is, in brief, the three-beat rhythm of progress which Hegel called the ' dialectic triad '.

I am quite prepared to admit that this is not a bad description of the way in which a critical discussion, and therefore also scientific thought, may sometimes progress. For all criticism consists in pointing out some contradictions or discrepancies, and scientific progress consists largely in the elimination of contradictions wherever we find them. This means, however, that science proceeds on the assumption that *contradictions are impermissible and avoidable*, so that the discovery of a contradiction forces the scientist to make every attempt to eliminate it ; and indeed, once a contradiction is admitted, all science must collapse [32]. But Hegel derives a very different lesson from his dialectic triad. Since contradictions are the means by which science progresses, he concludes that contradictions are not only permissible and unavoidable but also highly desirable. This is a Hegelian doctrine which must destroy all argument and all progress. For if contradictions are unavoidable and desirable, there is no need to eliminate them, and so all progress must come to an end.

But this doctrine is just one of the main tenets of Hegelianism. Hegel's intention is to operate freely with all contradictions. 'All things are contradictory in themselves', he insists [33], in order to defend a position which means the end not only of all science, but of all rational argument. And the reason why he wishes to admit contradictions is that he wants to stop rational argument, and with it scientific and intellectual progress. By making argument and criticism impossible, he intends to make his own philosophy proof against all criticism, so that it may establish itself as a *reinforced dogmatism*, secure from every attack, and the unsurmountable summit of all philosophical development. (We have here a first example of a typical *dialectical twist* ; the idea of progress, popular in a period which leads to Darwin, but not in keeping with conservative interests, is twisted into its opposite, that of a development which has arrived at an end—an arrested development.)

So much for Hegel's dialectic triad, one of the two pillars on which his philosophy rests. The significance of the theory will be seen when I proceed to its application.

The other of the two pillars of Hegelianism is his so-called *philosophy of identity*. It is, in its turn, an application of dialectics. I do not intend to waste the reader's time by attempting to make sense of it, especially since I have tried to do so elsewhere [34] ; for in the main, the philosophy of identity is nothing but shameless equivocation, and, to use Hegel's own words, it consists of nothing but 'fancies, even imbecile fancies'. It is a maze in which are caught the shadows and echoes of past philosophies, of Heraclitus, Plato, and Aristotle, as well as of Rousseau and Kant, and in which they now celebrate a kind of witches' sabbath, madly trying to confuse and beguile the naïve onlooker. The leading idea, and at the same time the link between Hegel's dialectics and his philosophy of identity, is Heraclitus' doctrine of the unity of opposites. 'The path that leads up and the path that leads down are identical', Heraclitus had said, and Hegel repeats this when he says : 'The way west and the way east are the same.' This Heraclitean doctrine of the identity of opposites is applied to a host of reminiscences from the old philosophies which are thereby 'reduced to components' of Hegel's own system. Essence and Idea, the one and the many, substance and accident, form and content, subject and object, being and becoming, everything and nothing, change and rest, actuality and potentiality, reality and appearance, matter and spirit, all these ghosts from the past seem to haunt the brain of the Great Dictator while he performs his dance with his balloon, with his puffed-up and fictitious problems of God and the World. But there is method in this madness, and even Prussian method. For behind the apparent confusion there lurk the interests of the absolute monarchy of Frederick William. The philosophy of identity serves to justify the existing order. Its main upshot is an *ethical and juridical positivism*, the doctrine that what is, is good, since there can be no standards but existing standards ; it is the doctrine that *might is right.*

How is this doctrine derived ? Merely by a series of equi-vocations. Plato, whose Forms or Ideas, as we have seen, are entirely different from ' ideas in the mind ', had said that the Ideas alone are real, and that perishable things are unreal. Hegel adopts from this doctrine the equation *Ideal = Real.* Kant talked, in his dialectics, about the ' Ideas of pure Reason ', using the term ' Idea ' in the sense of ' ideas in the mind '. Hegel adopts from this the doctrine that the Ideas are something mental or spiritual or rational, which can be expressed in the equation *Idea = Reason.* Combined, these two equations, or rather equivocations, yield *Real = Reason* ; and this allows Hegel to maintain that everything that is reasonable must be real, and everything that is real must be reasonable, and that the development of reality is the same as that of reason. And since there can be no higher standard in existence than the latest development of Reason and of the Idea, everything that is now real or actual exists by necessity, and must be reasonable as well as good [35]. (Particularly good, as we shall see, is the actually existing Prussian state.)

This is the philosophy of identity. Apart from ethical positivism a theory of truth also comes to light, just as a by-product (to use Schopenhauer's words). And a very convenient theory it is. All that is reasonable is real, we have seen. This means, of course, that all that is reasonable must conform to reality, and therefore must be true. Truth develops in the same way as reason develops, and everything that appeals to reason in its latest stage of development must also be true for that stage. In other words, everything that seems certain to those whose reason is up to date, must be true. Self-evidence is the same as truth. Provided you are up to date, all you need is to believe in a doctrine ; this makes it, by definition, true. In this way, the opposition between what Hegel calls ' the Subjective ', i.e.

belief, and ' the Objective ', i.e. truth, is turned into an identity ; and this unity of opposites explains scientific knowledge also. ' The Idea is the union of Subjective and Objective . . Science presupposes that the separation between itself and Truth is already cancelled.' [36]

So much on Hegel's philosophy of identity, the second pillar of wisdom on which his historicism is built. With its erection, the somewhat tiresome work of analysing Hegel's more abstract doctrines comes to an end. The rest of this chapter will be confined to the practical political applications made by Hegel of these abstract theories. And these practical applications will show us more clearly the apologetic purpose of all his labours.

Hegel's dialectics, I assert, are very largely designed to pervert the ideas of 1789. Hegel was perfectly conscious of the fact that the dialectic method can be used for twisting an idea into its opposite. 'Dialectics', he writes [37], 'are no novelty in philosophy. Socrates . . used to simulate the wish for some clearer knowledge about the subject under discussion, and after putting all sorts of questions with that intention, he brought those with whom he conversed round to the opposite of what their first impression had pronounced correct.' As a description of Socrates' intentions, this statement of Hegel's is perhaps not very fair (considering that Socrates' main aim was the exposure of cocksureness rather than the conversion of people to the opposite of what they believed before) ; but as a statement of Hegel's own intention, it is excellent, even though in practice Hegel's method turns out to be more clumsy than his programme indicates.

As a first example of this use of dialectics, I shall select the problem of *freedom of thought*, of the independence of science, and of the standards of objective truth, as treated by Hegel in the *Philosophy of Law* (§ 270). He begins with what can only be interpreted as a demand for freedom of thought, and for its protection by the state : ' The state ', he writes, ' has . . thought as its essential principle. Thus freedom of thought, and science, can originate only in the state ; it was the church that burnt Giordano Bruno, and forced Galileo to recant . . . Science, therefore, must seek protection from the state, since . . the aim of science is knowledge of objective truth.' After this promising start which we may take as representing the ' first impressions ' of his opponents, Hegel proceeds to bring them ' to the opposite of what their first impressions pronounced correct ', covering his change of front by another sham attack on the Church : ' But such knowledge does, of course, not always conform with the standards of science, it may degenerate into mere opinion . . ; and for these opinions . . it ' (i.e. science) ' may raise the same pretentious demand as the church—the demand to be free in its opinions and convictions.' Thus the demand for freedom of thought, and of the claim of science to judge for itself, is described as ' pretentious ' ; but this is merely the first step in Hegel's twist. We next hear that, if faced with subversive opinions, ' the state must protect objective truth ' ; which raises the fundamental question : who is to judge what is, and what is not, objective truth ? Hegel replies : ' The state has, in general, . . to make up its own mind concerning what is to be considered as objective truth.' With this reply, freedom of thought, and the claims of science to set its own standards, give way, finally, to their opposites.

As a second example of this use of dialectics, I select Hegel's treatment of the demand for a *political constitution*, which he combines with his treatment of *equality* and *liberty*. In order to appreciate the problem of the constitution, it must be remembered that Prussian absolutism knew no constitutional law (apart from such principles as the full sovereignty of the king) and that the slogan of the campaign for democratic reform in the various German principalities was that the prince should ' grant the country a constitution '. But Frederick William agreed with his councillor Ancillon in the conviction that he must never give way to ' the hotheads, that very active and loud-voiced group of persons who for some years have set themselves up as the nation and have cried for a constitution ' [38]. And although, under great pressure, the king promised a constitution, he never fulfilled his word. (There is a story that an innocent comment on the king's ' constitution ' led to the dismissal of his unfortunate court-physician.) Now how does Hegel treat this ticklish problem ? ' As a living mind ', he writes, ' the state is an organized whole, articulated into various agencies . . . The *constitution* is this articulation or organization of state power . . . The constitution is existent *justice* . . . Liberty and equality are . . the final aims and results of the constitution.' This, of course, is only the introduction. But before proceeding to the dialectical transformation of the demand for a constitution into one for an absolute monarchy, we must first show how Hegel transforms the two ' aims and results ', liberty and equality, into their opposites.

Let us first see how Hegel twists equality into inequality :
' That the citizens are equal before the law ', Hegel admits [39],
'contains a great truth. But expressed in this way, it is only
a tautology ; it only states in general that a legal status exists,
that the laws rule. But to be more concrete, the citizens . . are
equal before the law only in the points in which they are equal
outside the law also. *Only that equality which they possess in property,
age, . . etc., can deserve equal treatment before the law* . . The laws
themselves . . presuppose unequal conditions . . . It should
be said that it is just the great development and maturity of form
in modern states which produces the supreme concrete inequality
of individuals in actuality.'

In this outline of Hegel's twist of the ' great truth ' of equalitarianism into its opposite, I have radically abbreviated his
argument ; and I must warn the reader that I shall have to do
the same throughout the chapter ; for only in this way is it at all
possible to present, in a readable manner, his verbosity and the
flight of his thoughts (which, I do not doubt, is pathological [40]).

We may consider liberty next. ' As regards liberty ', Hegel
writes, ' in former times, the legally defined rights, the private as
well as public rights of a city, etc., were called its " liberties ".
Really, every genuine law is a liberty ; for it contains a reasonable principle . . ; which means, in other words, that it embodies
a liberty . . .' Now this argument which tries to show that
' liberty ' is the same as ' a liberty ' and therefore the same as
' law ', from which it follows that the more laws, the more liberty,
is clearly nothing but a clumsy statement (clumsy because it relies
on a kind of pun) of the paradox of freedom, first discovered by
Plato, and briefly discussed above [41] ; a paradox that can be
expressed by saying that unlimited freedom leads to its opposite,
since without its protection and restriction by law, freedom must
lead to a tyranny of the strong over the weak. This paradox,
vaguely restated by Rousseau, was solved by Kant, who demanded
that the freedom of each man should be restricted, but not beyond
what is necessary to safeguard an equal degree of freedom for all.
Hegel of course knows Kant's solution, but he does not like it,
and he presents it, without mentioning its author, in the following
disparaging way : ' To-day, nothing is more familiar than the
idea that each must restrict his liberty in relation to the liberty of
others ; that the state is a condition of such reciprocal restrictions ; and that the laws are restrictions. But ', he goes on to
criticize Kant's theory, ' this expresses the kind of outlook that

views freedom as casual good-pleasure and self-will.' With this cryptic remark, Kant's equalitarian theory of justice is dismissed.

But Hegel himself feels that the little jest by which he equates liberty and law is not quite sufficient for his purpose ; and somewhat hesitatingly he turns back to his original problem, that of the constitution. ' The term political liberty ', he says [42], ' is often used to mean a formal participation in the public affairs of the state by . . those who otherwise find their chief function in the particular aims and business of civil society ' (in other words, by the ordinary citizen). ' And it has . . become a custom to give the title " constitution " only to that side of the state which establishes such participation . . , and to regard a state in which this is not formally done as a state without a constitution.' Indeed, this has become a custom. But how to get out of it ? By a merely verbal trick—by a definition : ' About this use of the term, the only thing to say is that by a constitution we must understand the determination of laws in general, that is to say, of liberties . .' But again, Hegel himself feels the appalling poverty of the argument, and in despair he dives into a collectivist mysticism (of Rousseau's making) and into historicism [43] : ' The question " To whom . . belongs the power of making a constitution ? " is the same as " Who has to make the Spirit of a Nation ? ". Separate your idea of a constitution ', Hegel exclaims, ' from that of a collective Spirit, as if the latter exists, or has existed, without a constitution, and your fancy proves how superficially you have apprehended the nexus ' (namely, that between the Spirit and the constitution). ' . . It is the indwelling Spirit and the history of the Nation—which only is that Spirit's history—by which constitutions have been and are made.' But this mysticism is still too vague to justify absolutism. One must be more specific ; and Hegel now hastens to be so : ' The really living totality,' he writes, ' that which preserves, and continually produces, the State and its constitution, is the *Government* . . . In the Government, regarded as an organic totality, the Sovereign Power or Principate is . . the all-sustaining, all-decreeing Will of the State, its highest Peak and all-pervasive Unity. In the perfect form of the State in which each and every element . . has reached its free existence, this will is that of *one actual decreeing Individual* (not merely of a majority in which the unity of the decreeing will has no *actual* existence) ; it is *monarchy*. The monarchical constitution is therefore the constitution of developed reason ; and all other constitutions belong to lower grades of the development and the self-realization of reason.' And to be still more specific, Hegel explains in a parallel passage of his *Philosophy of Law*—the foregoing quotations are all taken from his *Encyclopædia*—that 'ultimate decision . . *absolute* self-determination constitutes the power of the prince as such', and that 'the *absolutely decisive* element in the whole . . is a single individual, the monarch.'

Now we have it. How can anybody be so stupid as to demand a 'constitution' for a country that is blessed with an absolute monarchy, the highest possible grade of all constitutions anyway? Those who make such demands obviously know not what they do and what they are talking about, just as those who demand freedom are too blind to see that in the Prussian absolute monarchy, 'each and every element has reached its free existence'. In other words, we have here Hegel's absolute dialectical proof that Prussia is the 'highest peak', and the very stronghold, of freedom ; that its absolutist constitution is the goal (not as some might think, the gaol) towards which humanity moves ; and that its government preserves and keeps, as it were, the purest spirit of freedom—in concentration.

Plato's philosophy, which once had claimed mastership in the state, becomes with Hegel its most servile lackey.

These despicable services [44], it is important to note, were rendered voluntarily. There was no totalitarian intimidation in those happy days of absolute monarchy ; nor was the censorship very effective, as countless liberal publications show. When Hegel published his *Encyclopædia* he was professor in Heidelberg. And immediately after the publication, he was called to Berlin to become, as his admirers say, the 'acknowledged dictator' of philosophy. But, some may contend, all this, even if it is true, does not prove anything against the excellence of Hegel's dialectic philosophy, or against his greatness as a philosopher. To this contention, Schopenhauer's reply has already been given : 'Philosophy is misused, from the side of the state as a tool, from the other side as a means of gain. *Who can really believe that truth also will thereby come to light, just as a by-product?*'

These passages give us a glimpse of the way in which Hegel's dialectic method is applied in practice. I now proceed to the combined application of dialectics and the philosophy of identity.

Hegel, we have seen, teaches that everything is in flux, even essences. Essences and Ideas and Spirits develop ; and their development is, of course, self-moving and dialectical [45]. And the latest stage of every development must be reasonable, and therefore good and true, for it is the apex of all past developments, superseding all previous stages. (Thus things can only get better and better.) Every real development, since it is a real process, must, according to the philosophy of identity, be a rational and reasonable process. It is clear that this must hold for history also.

Heraclitus had maintained that there is a hidden reason in history. For Hegel, history becomes an open book. The book is pure apologetics. By its appeal to the wisdom of Providence it offers an apology for the excellence of Prussian monarchism ; by its appeal to the excellence of Prussian monarchism it offers an apology for the wisdom of Providence.

History is the development of something real. According to the philosophy of identity, it must therefore be something rational. The evolution of the real world, of which history is the most important part, is taken by Hegel to be ' identical ' with a kind of logical operation, or with a process of reasoning. History, as he sees it, is the thought process of the ' Absolute Spirit ' or ' World Spirit '. It is the manifestation of this Spirit. It is a kind of huge dialectical syllogism [46] ; reasoned out, as it were, by Providence. The syllogism is the plan which Providence follows ; and the logical conclusion arrived at is the end which Providence pursues—the perfection of the world. ' The only thought ', Hegel writes in his *Philosophy of History*, ' with which Philosophy approaches History, is the simple conception of Reason; it is the doctrine that Reason is the Sovereign of the World, and that the History of the World, therefore, presents us with a *rational process*. This conviction and intuition is . . no hypothesis in the domain of Philosophy. It is there proven . . that Reason . . is *Substance* ; as well as *Infinite Power* ; . . *Infinite Matter* . . ; *Infinite Form* . . ; *Infinite Energy* . . . That this " Idea " or " Reason " is the *True*, the *Eternal*, the absolutely *Powerful Essence* ; that it reveals itself in the World, and that in that World nothing else is revealed but this and its honour and glory—this is a thesis which, as we have said, has been proved in Philosophy, and is here regarded as demonstrated.' This gush does not carry us far. But if we look up the passage in ' Philosophy ' (i.e., in his *Encyclopædia*) to which Hegel refers, then we see a little more of his apologetic purpose. For here we read : ' That History, and above all Universal History, is founded on an essential and actual aim, which *actually is*, and will be, *realized in it*—the Plan of Providence ; that, in short, there is Reason in History, must be decided

on strictly philosophical grounds, and thus shown to be essential
and in fact necessary.' Now since the aim of Providence ' actually is realized ' in the results of history, it might be suspected
that this realization has taken place in the actual Prussia. And
so it has ; we are even shown how this aim is reached, in three
dialectical steps of the historical development of reason, or, as
Hegel says, of ' Spirit ', whose ' life . . is a cycle of progressive
embodiments ' [47]. The first of these steps is Oriental despotism,
the second is formed by the Greek and Roman democracies and
aristocracies, and the third, and highest, is the Germanic Monarchy, which of course is an absolute monarchy. And Hegel
makes it quite clear that he does not mean a Utopian monarchy
of the future : ' Spirit . . has no past, no future,' he writes, ' but
is essentially *now* ; this necessarily implies that the present form
of the Spirit contains and surpasses all earlier steps.'

But Hegel can be even more outspoken than that. He subdivided the third period of history, Germanic Monarchy, or
' the German World ', into three divisions too, of which he
says [48] : ' First, we have to consider *Reformation* in itself—the all-
enlightening *Sun*, following on that blush of dawn which we
observed at the termination of the medieval period ; next, the
unfolding of that state of things which succeeded the Reformation ; and lastly, Modern Times, dating from the end of the
last century ', i.e. the period from 1800 down to 1830 (the last
year in which these lectures were delivered). And Hegel proves
again that this present Prussia is the pinnacle and the stronghold
and the goal of freedom. ' On the Stage of Universal History ',
Hegel writes ' on which we can observe and grasp it, Spirit displays itself in its most concrete reality.' And the essence of Spirit,
Hegel teaches, is freedom. ' Freedom is the sole truth of Spirit.'
Accordingly, the development of Spirit must be the development
of freedom, and the highest freedom must have been achieved in
those thirty years of the Germanic Monarchy which represent
the last subdivision of historical development. And indeed, we
read [49] : ' The German Spirit is the Spirit of the new World.
Its aim is the realization of absolute Truth as the unlimited self-
determination of Freedom.' And after a eulogy of Prussia, the
government of which, Hegel assures us, ' rests with the official
world, whose apex is the personal decision of the Monarch ; for
a final decision is, as shown above, an absolute necessity ', Hegel
reaches the crowning conclusion of his work : ' This is the
point ', he says, ' which consciousness has attained, and these

are the principal phases of that form in which Freedom has realized itself; for the History of the World is nothing but the development of the Idea of Freedom . . . That the History of the World . . is the realization of Spirit, this is the true Theodicy, the justification of God in History . . . What has happened and is happening . . is essentially His Work . .'

I ask whether I was not justified when I said that Hegel presents us with an apology for God and for Prussia at the same time, and whether it is not clear that the state which Hegel commands us to worship as the Divine Idea on earth is not simply Frederick William's Prussia from 1800 to 1830. And I ask whether it is possible to outdo this despicable perversion of every-thing that is decent ; a perversion not only of reason, freedom, equality, and the other ideas of the open society, but also of a sincere belief in God, and even of a sincere patriotism.

I have described how, starting from a point that appears to be progressive and even revolutionary, and proceeding by that general dialectical method of twisting things which by now will be familiar to the reader, Hegel finally reaches a surprisingly conservative result. At the same time, he connects his philosophy of history with his ethical and juridical positivism, giving the latter a kind of historicist justification. History is our judge. Since History and Providence have brought the existing powers into being, their might must be right, even Divine right.

But this moral positivism does not fully satisfy Hegel. He wants more. Just as he opposes liberty and equality, so he opposes the brotherhood of man, humanitarianism, or, as he says, ' philanthropy '. Conscience must be replaced by blind obedi-ence and by a romantic Heraclitean ethics of fame and fate, and the brotherhood of man by a *totalitarian nationalism*. How this is done will be shown in section III and especially [50] in section IV of this chapter.

III

I now proceed to a very brief sketch of a rather strange story —the story of the *rise of German nationalism*. Undoubtedly the tendencies denoted by this term have a strong affinity with the revolt against reason and the open society. Nationalism appeals to our tribal instincts, to passion and to prejudice, and to our nostalgic desire to be relieved from the strain of individual responsibility which it attempts to replace by a collective or group responsibility. It is in keeping with these tendencies that we find that the oldest works on political theory, even that of the Old Oligarch, but more markedly those of Plato and of Aristotle, express decidedly nationalist views ; for these works were written in an attempt to combat the open society and the new ideas of imperialism, cosmopolitanism, and equalitarianism [51]. But this early development of a nationalist political theory stops short with Aristotle. With Alexander's empire, genuine tribal nationalism disappears for ever from political practice, and for a long time from political theory. From Alexander onward, all the civilized states of Europe and Asia were empires, embracing populations of infinitely mixed origin. European civilization and all the political units belonging to it have remained international or, more precisely, inter-tribal ever since. (It seems that about as long before Alexander as Alexander was before us, the empire of ancient Sumer had created the first international civilization.) And what holds good of political practice holds good of political theory ; until about a hundred years ago, the Platonic-Aristotelian nationalism had practically disappeared from political doctrines. (Of course, tribal and parochial feelings were always strong.) When nationalism was revived a hundred years ago, it was in one of the most mixed of all the thoroughly mixed regions of Europe, in Germany, and especially in Prussia with its largely Slav population. (It is not well known that barely a century ago, Prussia, with its then predominantly Slav population, was not considered a German state at all ; though its kings, who as princes of Brandenburg were ' Electors ' of the German Empire, were considered German princes. At the Congress of Vienna, Prussia was registered as a ' Slav kingdom ' ; and in 1830 Hegel still spoke [52] even of Brandenburg and Mecklenburg as being populated by ' Germanized Slavs '.)

Thus it is only a short time since the *principle of the national state* was reintroduced into political theory. In spite of this fact, it iş so widely accepted in our day that it is usually taken for granted, and very often unconsciously so. It now forms, as it were, an implicit assumption of popular political thought. It is even considered by many to be the basic postulate of political ethics, especially since Wilson's well-meant but less well-considered principle of national self-determination. How anybody who had the slightest knowledge of European history, of the shifting and mixing of all kinds of tribes, of the countless waves of peoples who had come forth from their original Asian habitat and split up and mingled when reaching the maze of peninsulas called the European continent, how anybody who knew this could ever have put forward such an inapplicable principle, is hard to understand. The explanation is that Wilson, who was a sincere democrat (and Masaryk also, one of the greatest of all fighters for the open society [53]), fell a victim to a movement that sprang from the most reactionary and servile political philosophy that had ever been imposed upon meek and long-suffering mankind. He fell a victim to his upbringing in the metaphysical political theories of Plato and of Hegel, and to the nationalist movement based upon them.

The *principle of the national state*, that is to say, the political demand that the territory of every state should coincide with the territory inhabited by one nation, is by no means so self-evident as it seems to appear to many people to-day. Even if anyone knew what he meant when he spoke of nationality, it would be not at all clear why nationality should be accepted as a funda-mental political category, more important for instance than religion, or birth within a certain geographical region, or loyalty to a dynasty, or a political creed like democracy (which forms, one might say, the uniting factor of multi-lingual Switzer-land). But while religion, territory, or a political creed can be more or less clearly determined, nobody has ever been able to explain what he means by a nation, in a way that could be used as a basis for practical politics. (Of course, if we say that a nation is a number of people who live or have been born in a certain state, then everything is clear ; but this would mean giving up the principle of the national state which demands that the state should be determined by the nation, and not the other way round.) None of the theories which maintain that a nation is united by a common origin, or a common language, or a com-mon history, is acceptable, or applicable in practice. The principle of the national state is not only inapplicable but it has never been clearly conceived. It is a myth. It is an irrational, a romantic and Utopian dream, a dream of naturalism and of tribal collectivism.

In spite of its inherent reactionary and irrational tendencies, modern nationalism, strangely enough, was in its short history before Hegel a revolutionary and liberal creed. By something like an historical accident—the invasion of German lands by the first national army, the French army under Napoleon, and the reaction caused by this event—it had made its way into the camp of freedom. It is not without interest to sketch the history of this development, and of the way in which Hegel brought nationalism back into the totalitarian camp where it had belonged from the time when Plato first maintained that Greeks are related to barbarians like masters to slaves.

Plato, it will be remembered [54], unfortunately formulated his fundamental political problem by asking : Who should rule ? Whose will should be law ? Before Rousseau, the usual answer to this question was : The prince. Rousseau gave a new and most revolutionary answer. Not the prince, he maintained, but the people should rule ; not the will of one man but the will of all. In this way, he was led to invent the people's will, the collective will, or the ' general will ', as he called it ; and the people, once endowed with a will, had to be exalted into a super-personality ; ' in relation to what is external to it ' (i.e. in relation to other peoples), Rousseau says, ' it becomes one single being, one individual '. There was a good deal of romantic collectivism in this invention, but no tendency towards nationalism. But Rousseau's theories clearly contained the germ of nationalism, whose most characteristic doctrine is that the various nations must be conceived as personalities. And a great practical step in the nationalist direction was made when the French Revolution inaugurated a people's army, based on national conscription.

One of the next to contribute to the theory of nationalism was J. G. Herder, a former pupil and at the time a personal friend of Kant. Herder maintained that a good state should have natural borders, namely those which coincide with the places inhabited by its ' nation ' ; a theory which he first proffered in his *Ideas towards a Philosophy of the History of Mankind* (1785). ' The most natural state ', he wrote [55], ' is a state composed of a single people with a single national character . . .   A people is a natural growth like a family, only spread more widely . . . As in all human communities, . . so, in the case of the state, the natural order is the best—that is to say, the order in which everyone fulfils that function for which nature intended him.' This theory, which tries to give an answer to the problem of the ' natural ' borders of the state [56], an answer that only raises the new problem of the ' natural ' borders of the nation, did not at first exert much influence. It is interesting to see that Kant at once realized the dangerous irrational romanticism in this work of Herder's, of whom he made a sworn enemy by his outspoken criticism. I shall quote a passage from this criticism, because it excellently sums up, once and for all, not only Herder, but also the later oracular philosophers like Fichte, Schelling, Hegel, together with all their modern followers : ' A sagacity quick in picking up analogies ', Kant wrote, ' and an imagination audacious in the use it makes of them are combined with a capability for enlisting emotions and passions in order to obtain interest for its object— an object that is always veiled in mystery. These emotions are easily mistaken for the efforts of powerful and profound thoughts, or at least of deeply significant allusions ; and they thus arouse higher expectations than cool judgement would find justified . . . Synonyms are passed off as explanations, and allegories are offered as truths.'

It was Fichte who provided German nationalism with its first theory. The borders of a nation, he contended, are determined by language. (This does not improve matters. Where do differences of dialect become differences of language ? How many different languages do the Slavs or the Teutons speak, or are the differences merely dialects ?)

Fichte's opinions had a most curious development, especially if we consider that he was one of the founders of German nationalism. In 1793, he defended Rousseau and the French Revolution, and in 1799 he still declared [57] : ' It is plain that from now on the French Republic alone can be the fatherland of the upright man, that he can devote his powers to this country alone of all, since not only the dearest hopes of humanity but also its very existence are bound up with the victory of France . . . I dedicate myself and all my abilities to the Republic.' It may be noted that when Fichte made these remarks he was negotiating for a university position in Mainz, a place then controlled by the French. ' In 1804 ', E. N. Anderson writes in his interesting study on nationalism, ' Fichte ∴ was eager to leave Prussian service and to accept a call from Russia. The Prussian government had not appreciated him to the desired financial extent and he hoped for more recognition from Russia, writing to the Russian negotiator that if the government would make him a member of the St. Petersburg Academy of Science and pay him a salary of not less than four hundred roubles, " I would be theirs until death " . . Two years later ', Anderson continues, ' the transformation of Fichte the cosmopolitan into Fichte the nationalist was completed.'

When Berlin was occupied by the French, Fichte left, out of patriotism ; an act which, as Anderson says ' he did not allow . . to remain unnoticed by the Prussian king and government '.

When A. Mueller and W. von Humboldt had been received by
Napoleon, Fichte wrote indignantly to his wife : ' I do not envy
Mueller and Humboldt ; I am glad that I did not obtain that
shameful honour . . It makes a difference to one's conscience
and apparently also to one's later success if . . one has openly shown
devotion to the good cause.' On this, Anderson comments :
' As a matter of fact, he did profit ; undoubtedly his call to the
University of Berlin resulted from this episode. This does not
detract from the patriotism of his act, but merely places it in its
proper light.' To all this we must add that Fichte's career as a
philosopher was from the beginning based on a fraud. His first
book was published anonymously, when Kant's philosophy of
religion was expected, under the title *Critique of All Revelation*. It
was an extremely dull book, which did not prevent it from being
a clever copy of Kant's style ; and everything was set in motion,
including rumours, to make people believe that it was Kant's
work. The matter appears in its right light if we realize that
Fichte only obtained a publisher through the kindheartedness of
Kant (who was never able to read more than the first few pages
of the book). When the press extolled Fichte's work as one of
Kant's, Kant was forced to make a public statement that the
work was Fichte's, and Fichte, upon whom fame had suddenly
descended, was made professor in Jena. But Kant was later
forced to make another declaration, in order to dissociate himself
from this man, a declaration in which occur the words [58] :
' May God protect us from our friends. From our enemies, we
can try to protect ourselves.'

These are a few episodes in the career of the man whose
' windbaggery ' has given rise to modern nationalism as well as to
modern Idealist philosophy, erected upon the perversion of Kant's
teaching. (I follow Schopenhauer in distinguishing between
Fichte's ' windbaggery ' and Hegel's ' charlatanry ', although I
must admit that to insist on this distinction is perhaps a little
pedantic.) The whole story is interesting mainly because of the
light it throws upon the ' history of philosophy ' and upon ' history ' in general. I mean not only the perhaps more humorous
than scandalous fact that such clowns are taken seriously, and that
they are made the objects of a kind of worship, of solemn although
often boring studies (and of examination papers to match). I
mean not only the appalling fact that the windbag Fichte and the
charlatan Hegel are treated on a level with men like Democritus,
Pascal, Descartes, Spinoza, Locke, Hume, Kant, J. S. Mill, and

Bertrand Russell, and that their moral teaching is taken seriously and perhaps even considered superior to that of these other men. But I mean that many of these eulogist historians of philosophy, unable to discriminate between thought and fancy, not to mention good and bad, dare to pronounce that their history is our judge, or that their history of philosophy is an implicit criticism of the different ' systems of thought '.   For it is clear, I think, that their adulation can only be an implicit criticism of their histories of philosophy, and of that pomposity and conspiracy of noise by which the business of philosophy is glorified.   It seems to be a law of what these people are pleased to call ' human nature ' that bumptiousness grows in direct proportion to deficiency of thought and inversely to the amount of service rendered to human welfare.

At the time when Fichte became the apostle of nationalism, an instinctive and revolutionary nationalism was rising in Germany as a reaction to the Napoleonic invasion.   (It was one of those typical tribal reactions against the expansion of a super-national empire.)   The people demanded democratic reforms which they understood in the sense of Rousseau and of the French Revolution, but which they wanted without their French conquerors. They turned against their own princes and against the emperor at the same time.   This early nationalism arose with the force of a new religion, as a kind of cloak in which a humanitarian desire for freedom and equality was clad. ' Nationalism ', Anderson writes [59], ' grew as orthodox Christianity declined, replacing the latter with belief in a mystical experience of its own.'   It is the mystical experience of community with the other members of the oppressed tribe, an experience which replaced not only Christianity but especially the feeling of trust and loyalty to the king which the abuses of absolutism had destroyed.   It is clear that such an untamed new and democratic religion was a source of great irritation, and even of danger, to the ruling class, and especially to the king of Prussia.   How was this danger to be met?   After the wars of liberation, Frederick William met it first by dismissing his nationalist advisers, and then by appointing Hegel.   For the French Revolution had proved the influence of philosophy, a point duly emphasized by Hegel (since it is the basis of his own services) : ' The Spiritual ', he says [60], ' is now the essential basis of the potential fabric, and *Philosophy* has thereby become dominant.   It has been said that the French Revolution resulted from Philosophy, and it is not without reason that Philosophy has been described as World Wisdom ; Philosophy is not only Truth in and for itself . . but also Truth as exhibited in worldly matters. We should not, therefore, contradict the assertion that the Revolution received its first impulse from Philosophy.' This is an indication of Hegel's insight into his immediate task, to give a counter impulse ; an impulse, though not the first, by which philosophy might strengthen the forces of reaction. Part of this task was the perversion of the ideas of freedom, equality, etc. But perhaps an even more urgent task was the taming of the revolutionary nationalist religion. Hegel fulfilled this task in the spirit of Pareto's advice ' to take advantage of sentiments, not wasting one's energies in futile efforts to destroy them '. He tamed nationalism not by outspoken opposition but by transforming it into a well-disciplined Prussian authoritarianism. And it so happened that he brought back a powerful weapon into the camp of the closed society, where it fundamentally belonged.

All this was done rather clumsily. Hegel, in his desire to please the government, sometimes attacked the nationalists much too openly. ' Some men ', he wrote [61] in the *Philosophy of Law*, ' have recently begun to talk of the " sovereignty of the people " in opposition to the sovereignty of the monarch. But when it is contrasted with the sovereignty of the monarch, then the phrase " sovereignty of the people " turns out to be merely one of those confused notions which arise from a wild idea of the " people ". Without its monarch . . the people are just a formless multitude.' Earlier, in the *Encyclopædia*, he wrote : ' The aggregate of private persons is often spoken of as the *nation*. But such an aggregate is a rabble, not a people ; and with regard to it, it is the one aim of the state that a nation should *not* come into existence, to power and action, as such an aggregate. Such a condition of a nation is a condition of lawlessness, demoralization, brutishness. In it, the nation would only be a shapeless wild blind force, like that of a stormy elemental sea, which however is not self-destructive, as the nation—a spiritual element—would be. Yet one can often hear such a condition described as pure freedom.' There is here an unmistakable allusion to the liberal nationalists, whom the king hated like the plague. And this is even clearer when we see Hegel's reference to the early nationalists' dreams of rebuilding the German empire : ' The fiction of an Empire ', he says in his eulogy of the latest developments in Prussia, ' has utterly vanished. It is broken into Sovereign States.' His anti-liberal tendencies induced Hegel to refer to England as the most characteristic example of a nation in the bad sense. ' Take the case of England,' he writes, ' which, because private persons have a predominant share in public affairs, has been regarded as having the freest of all constitutions. Experience shows that that country, as compared with the other civilized states of Europe, is the most backward in civil and criminal legislation, in the law and liberty of property, and in arrangements for the *arts and sciences*, and that objective freedom or rational right is *sacrificed* to formal [62] right and particular private interest : and that this happens even in the institutions and possessions dedicated to religion.' An astonishing statement indeed, especially when the ' arts and sciences ' are considered, for nothing could have been more backward than Prussia, where the University of Berlin had been founded only under the influence of the Napoleonic wars, and with the idea, as the king said [68], that ' the state must replace with intellectual prowess what it has lost in physical strength '. A few pages later, Hegel forgets what he has said about the arts and sciences in England; for he speaks there of ' England, where the art of historical writing has undergone a process of purification and arrived at a firmer and more mature character '.

We see that Hegel knew that his task was to combat the liberal and even the imperialist leanings of nationalism. He did it by persuading the nationalists that their collectivist demands are automatically realized by an almighty state, and that all they need do is to help to strengthen the power of the state. ' The Nation State is Spirit in its substantive rationality and immediate actuality ', he writes [64] ; ' it is therefore the absolute power on earth . . . The state is the Spirit of the People itself. The actual State is animated by this spirit, in all its particular affairs, its Wars, and its Institutions . . . The self-consciousness of one particular Nation is the vehicle for the . . development of the collective spirit ; . . in it, the Spirit of the Time invests its Will. Against this Will, the other national minds have no rights : *that* Nation dominates the World.' It is thus the nation and its spirit and its will that act on the stage of history. History is the contest of the various national spirits for world domination. From this it follows that the reforms advocated by the liberal nationalists are unnecessary, since the nation and its spirit are the leading actors anyway ; besides, ' every nation . . has the constitution which is appropriate to it and belongs to it '. (Juri-

dical positivism.)   We see that Hegel replaces the liberal elements
in nationalism not only by a Platonic-Prussianist worship of the
state, but also by a worship of history, of historical success.
(Frederick William had been successful against Napoleon.)   In
this way, Hegel not only began a new chapter in the history of
nationalism, but he also provided nationalism with a new theory.
Fichte, we have seen, had provided it with the theory that it was
based on language.   Hegel introduced the *historical theory of the
nation*.   A nation, according to Hegel, is united by a spirit that
acts in history.   It is united by the common foe, and by the
comradeship of the wars it has fought.   (It has been said that
a race is a collection of men united not by their origin but by
a common error in regard to their origin.   In a similar way, we
could say that a nation in Hegel's sense is a number of men
united by a common error in regard to their history.)   It is clear
how this theory is connected with Hegel's historicist essentialism.
The history of a nation is the history of its essence or ' Spirit ',
asserting itself on the ' Stage of History '.

In concluding this sketch of the rise of nationalism, I may
make a remark on the events down to the foundation of Bismarck's
German empire.   Hegel's policy had been to take advantage of
nationalist sentiments, instead of wasting energy in futile efforts
to destroy them.   But sometimes this celebrated technique
appears to have rather strange consequences.   The medieval
conversion of Christianity into an authoritarian creed could not
fully suppress its humanitarian tendencies ;   again and again,
Christianity breaks through the authoritarian cloak (and is persecuted as heresy).   In this way, Pareto's advice not only serves
to neutralize tendencies that endanger the ruling class, but
can also unintentionally help to preserve these very tendencies.
A similar thing happened to nationalism.   Hegel had tamed it,
and had tried to replace German nationalism by a Prussian
nationalism.   But by thus ' reducing nationalism to a component ' of his Prussianism (to use his own jargon) Hegel ' preserved ' it ;   and Prussia found itself forced to proceed on the
way of taking advantage of the sentiments of German nationalism.
When it fought Austria in 1866 it had to do so in the name of
German nationalism, and under the pretext of securing the
leadership of ' Germany '.   And it had to advertise the vastly
enlarged Prussia of 1871 as the new ' German Empire ', a new
' German Nation '—welded by war into a unit, in accordance
with Hegel's historical theory of the nation.

IV

In our own time, Hegel's hysterical historicism is still the fertilizer to which modern totalitarianism owes its rapid growth. Its use has prepared the ground, and has educated the intelligentsia to intellectual dishonesty, as will be shown in section v of this chapter. We have to learn the lesson that intellectual honesty is fundamental for everything we cherish.

But is this all ? And is it just ? Is there nothing in the claim that Hegel's greatness lies in the fact that he was the creator of a new, of a historical way of thinking—of a new historical sense ?

Many of my friends have criticized me for my attitude towards Hegel, and for my inability to see his greatness. They were, of course, quite right, since I was indeed unable to see it. (I am so still.) In order to remedy this fault, I made a fairly systematic inquiry into the question, Wherein lies Hegel's greatness ?

The result was disappointing. No doubt, Gegel's talk about the vastness and greatness of the historical drama created an atmosphere of interest in history. No doubt, his vast historicist generalizations, periodizations, and interpretations fascinated some historians and challenged them to produce valuable and detailed historical studies (which nearly invariably showed the weakness of Hegel's findings as well as of his method). But was this challenging influence the achievement of either a historian or a philosopher ? Was it not, rather, that of a propagandist ? Historians, I found, tend to value Hegel (if at all) as a philosopher, and philosophers tend to believe that his contributions (if any) were to the understanding of history. But historicism is not history, and to believe in it reveals neither historical understanding nor historical sense. And if we wish to evaluate Hegel's greatness, as a historian or as a philosopher, we should not ask ourselves whether some people found his vision of history inspiring, but whether there was much truth in this vision.

I found only one idea which was important and which might be claimed to be implicit in Hegel's philosophy. It is the idea which leads Hegel to attack abstract rationalism and intellectualism which does not appreciate the indebtedness of reason to tradition. It is a certain awareness of the fact (which, however, Hegel forgets in his Logic) that men cannot start with a blank, creating a world of thought from nothing ; but that their thoughts are, largely, the product of an intellectual inheritance.

I am ready to admit that this is an important point, and one which might be found in Hegel if one is willing to search for it. But I deny that it was Hegel's own contribution. It was the common property of the Romantics. That all social entities are products of history ; not inventions, planned by reason, but formations emerging from the vagaries of historical events, from the interplay of ideas and interests, from sufferings and from passions, all this is older than Hegel. It goes back to Edmund Burke, whose appreciation of the significance of tradition for the functioning of all social institutions had immensely influenced the political thought of the German Romantic Movement. The trace of his influence can be found in Hegel, but only in the exaggerated and untenable form of an historical and evolutionary relativism—in the form of the dangerous doctrine that what is believed to-day is, in fact, true to-day, and in the equally dangerous corollary that what was true yesterday (*true*, and not merely ' believed ') may be false to-morrow—a doctrine which, surely, is not likely to encourage an appreciation of the significance of tradition.

V

I now proceed to the last part of my treatment of Hegelianism, to the analysis of the dependence of the new tribalism or totalitarianism upon the doctrines of Hegel.

If it were my aim to write a history of the rise of totalitarianism, I should have to deal with Marxism first ; for fascism grew partly out of the spiritual and political breakdown of Marxism. (And, as we shall see, a similar statement may be made about the relationship between Leninism and Marxism.) Since my main issue, however, is historicism, I propose to deal with Marxism later, as the purest form of historicism that has so far arisen, and to tackle fascism first.

Modern totalitarianism is only an episode within the perennial revolt against freedom and reason. From older episodes it is distinguished not so much by its ideology, as by the fact that its leaders succeeded in realizing one of the boldest dreams of their predecessors ; they made the revolt against freedom a popular movement. (Its popularity, of course, must not be overrated ; the intelligentsia are only a part of the people.) It was made possible only by the breakdown, in the countries concerned, of another popular movement, Social Democracy or the democratic version of Marxism, which in the minds of the working people stood for the ideas of freedom and equality. When it became obvious that it was not just by chance that this movement had failed in 1914 to make a determined stand against war ; when it became clear that it was helpless to cope with the problems of peace, most of all with unemployment and economic depression ; and when, at last, this movement defended itself only half-heartedly against fascist aggression, then the belief in the value of freedom and in the possibility of equality was seriously threatened, and the perennial revolt against freedom could by hook or by crook acquire a more or less popular backing.

The fact that fascism had to take over part of the heritage of Marxism accounts for the one ' original ' feature of fascist ideology, for the one point in which it deviates from the traditional make-up of the revolt against freedom. The point I have in mind is that fascism has not much use for an open appeal to the supernatural. Not that it is necessarily atheistic or lacking in mystical or religious elements. But the spread of agnosticism through Marxism led to a situation in which no political creed aiming at popularity among the working class could bind itself to any of the traditional religious forms. This is why fascism added to its official ideology, in its early stages at least, some admixture of nineteenth-century evolutionist materialism.

Thus the formula of the fascist brew is in all countries the same : Hegel plus a dash of nineteenth-century materialism (especially Darwinism in the somewhat crude form given to it by Haeckel [65]). The ' scientific ' element in racialism can be traced back to Haeckel, who was responsible, in 1900, for a prize-competition whose subject was : ' What can we learn from the principles of Darwinism in respect of the internal and political development of a state ? ' The first prize was allotted to a voluminous racialist work by W. Schallmeyer, who thus became the grandfather of racial biology. It is interesting to observe how strongly this materialist racialism, despite its very different origin, resembles the naturalism of Plato. In both cases, the basic idea is that degeneration, particularly of the upper classes, is at the root of political decay (read : of the advance of the open society). Moreover, the modern myth of Blood and Soil has its exact counterpart in Plato's Myth of the Earthborn. Nevertheless, not ' Hegel + Plato ', but ' Hegel + Haeckel ' is the formula of modern racialism. As we shall see, Marx replaced Hegel's ' Spirit ' by matter, and by material and economic interests. In the same way, racialism substitutes for Hegel's ' Spirit ' something material, the quasi-biological conception of Blood or

Race.   Instead of ' Spirit ', Blood is the self-developing essence ;
instead of ' Spirit ', Blood is the Sovereign of the world, and
displays itself on the Stage of History ; and instead of its ' Spirit ',
the Blood of a nation determines its essential destiny.

The transubstantiation of Hegelianism into racialism or of
Spirit into Blood does not greatly alter the main tendency of
Hegelianism.   It only gives it a tinge of biology and of modern
evolutionism.   The outcome is a materialistic and at the same
time mystical religion of a self-developing biological essence,
very closely reminiscent of the religion of creative evolution
(whose prophet was the Hegelian [66] Bergson), a religion which
G. B. Shaw, more prophetically than profoundly, once characterized as ' a faith which complied with the first condition of all
religions that have ever taken hold of humanity : namely, that
it must be . . a *meta-biology* '.   And indeed, this new religion
of racialism clearly shows a *meta*-component and a *biology*-
component, as it were, or Hegelian mystical metaphysics and
Haeckelian materialist biology.

So much about the difference between modern totalitarianism
and Hegelianism.   In spite of its significance from the point of
view of popularity, this difference is unimportant so far as their
main political tendencies are concerned.   But if we now turn
to the similarities, then we get another picture.   Nearly all
the more important ideas of modern totalitarianism are directly
inherited from Hegel, who collected and preserved what
A. Zimmern calls [67] the ' armoury of weapons for authoritarian
movements '.   Although most of these weapons were not forged
by Hegel himself, but discovered by him in the various ancient
war treasuries of the perennial revolt against freedom, it is
undoubtedly his effort which rediscovered them and placed them
in the hands of his modern followers.   Here is a brief list of
some of the most precious of these ideas.   (I omit Platonic
totalitarianism and tribalism, which have already been discussed,
as well as the theory of master and slave.)

(*a*) Nationalism, in the form of the historicist idea that the
state is the incarnation of the Spirit (or now, of the Blood) of the
state-creating nation (or race) ; one chosen nation (now, the
chosen race) is destined for world domination.   (*b*) The state as
the natural enemy of all other states must assert its existence in
war.   (*c*) The state is exempt from any kind of moral obligation ;
history, that is, historical success, is the sole judge ; collective
utility is the sole principle of personal conduct ; propagandist

lying and distortion of the truth is permissible.   (*d*) The ' ethical ' idea of war (total and collectivist), particularly of young nations against older ones ; war, fate and fame as most desirable goods. (*e*) The creative rôle of the Great Man, the world-historical personality, the man of deep knowledge and great passion (now, the principle of leadership).   (*f*) The ideal of the heroic life (' live dangerously ') and of the ' heroic man ' as opposed to the petty bourgeois and his life of shallow mediocrity.

This list of spiritual treasures is neither systematic nor complete.   All of them are part and parcel of an old patrimony.   And they were stored up, and made ready for use, not only in the works of Hegel and his followers, but also in the minds of an intelligentsia fed exclusively for three long generations on such debased spiritual food, early recognized by Schopenhauer [68] as an ' intelligence-destroying pseudo-philosophy ' and as a ' mischievous and criminal misuse of language '.   I now proceed to a more detailed examination of the various points in this list.

(*a*) According to modern totalitarian doctrines, the state as such is not the highest end.   This is, rather, the Blood, and the People, the Race.   The higher races possess the power to create states.   The highest aim of a race or nation is to form a mighty state which can serve as a powerful instrument of its self-preservation.   This teaching (but for the substitution of Blood for Spirit) is due to Hegel, who wrote [69] : ' In the existence of a *Nation*, the substantial aim is to be a State and preserve itself as such.   A Nation that has not formed itself into a State—*a mere Nation*—has strictly speaking no history, like the Nations . . which existed in a condition of savagery.   What happens to a Nation . . has its essential significance in relation to the State.'   The state which is thus formed is to be totalitarian, that is to say, its might must permeate and control the whole life of the people in all its functions : ' The State is therefore the basis and centre of all the concrete elements in the life of a people : of Art, Law, Morals, Religion, and Science . . .   The substance that . . exists in that concrete reality which is the state, is the Spirit of the People itself.   The actual State is animated by this Spirit in all its particular affairs, in its Wars, Institutions, etc.'   Since the state must be powerful, it must contest the powers of other states.   It must assert itself on the ' Stage of History ', must prove its peculiar essence or Spirit and its ' strictly defined ' national character by its historical deeds, and must ultimately aim at world domination.   Here is an outline of this historicist essentialism in Hegel's words : ' The very essence of Spirit is activity ; it actualizes its potentiality, and makes itself its own deed, its own work . . Thus it is with the Spirit of a Nation ; it is a Spirit having strictly defined characteristics which exist and persist . . in the events and transitions that make up its history. That is its work—that is what this particular Nation *is*. Nations are what their deeds are . . . A Nation is moral, virtuous, vigorous, as long as it is engaged in realizing its grand objects . . . The constitutions under which World-Historical Peoples have reached their culminations are peculiar to them . . Therefore, from . . the political institutions of the ancient World-Historical Peoples, nothing can be learned . . . Each particular National Genius is to be treated as only One Individual in the process of Universal History.' The Spirit or National Genius must finally prove itself in World-Domination : ' The self-consciousness of a particular Nation . . is the objective actuality in which the Spirit of the Time invests its Will. Against this absolute Will the other particular national minds have no rights : *that* Nation dominates the World . .'

But Hegel not only developed the historical and totalitarian theory of nationalism, he also clearly foresaw the psychological possibilities of nationalism. He saw that nationalism answers a need—the desire of men to find and to know their definite place in the world, and to belong to a powerful collective body. At the same time he exhibits that remarkable characteristic of German nationalism, its strongly developed feelings of inferiority (to use a more recent terminology), especially towards the English. And he consciously appeals, with his nationalism or tribalism, to those feelings which I have described (in chapter 10) as the *strain of civilization* : ' Every Englishman ', Hegel writes [70], ' will say : We are the men who navigate the ocean, and who have the commerce of the world ; to whom the East Indies belong and their riches . . . The relation of the individual man to that Spirit is . . that it . . enables him to have a definite place in the world—to be *something*. For he finds in . . the people to which he belongs an already established, firm world . . with which he has to incorporate himself. In this its work, and therefore its world, the Spirit of the people enjoys its existence and finds satisfaction.'

(*b*) A theory common to both Hegel and his racialist followers is that the state by its very essence can exist only through its contrast to other individual states. H. Freyer, one of the leading sociologists of present-day Germany, writes [71] : ' A being that draws itself round its own core creates, even unintentionally, the boundary-line. And the frontier—even though it be unintentionally—creates the enemy.' Similarly Hegel : ' Just as the individual is not a real person unless related to other persons so the State is no real individuality unless related to other States . . . The relation of one particular State to another presents . . the most shifting play of . . passions, interests, aims, talents, virtues, power, injustice, vice, and mere external chance. It is a play in which even the Ethical Whole, the Independence of the State, is exposed to accident.' Should we not, therefore, attempt to regulate this unfortunate state of affairs by adopting Kant's plans for the establishment of eternal peace by means of a federal union ? Certainly not, says Hegel, commenting on Kant's plan for peace : ' Kant proposed an alliance of princes ', Hegel says rather inexactly (for Kant proposed a federation of what we now call democratic states), ' which should settle the controversies of States ; and the Holy Alliance probably aspired to be an institution of this kind. The State, however, is an individual ; and in individuality, negation is essentially contained. A number of States may constitute themselves into a family, but this confederation, as an individuality, must create opposition and so beget an enemy.' For in Hegel's dialectics, negation equals limitation, and therefore means not only the boundary-line, the frontier, but also the creation of an opposition, of an enemy : ' The fortunes and deeds of States in their relation to one another reveal the dialectic of the finite nature of these Spirits.' These quotations are taken from the *Philosophy of Law* ; yet in his earlier *Encyclopædia*, Hegel's theory anticipates the modern theories, for instance that of Freyer, even more closely : ' The final aspect of the State is to appear in immediate actuality as a single nation . . . As a single individual it is exclusive of other like individuals. In their mutual relations, waywardness and chance have a place . . . This independency . . reduces disputes between them to terms of mutual violence, to a *state of war* . . . It is this state of war in which the omnipotence of the State manifests itself . .' Thus the Prussian historian Treitschke only shows how well he understands Hegelian dialectic essentialism when he repeats : ' War is not only a practical necessity, it is also a theoretical necessity, an exigency of logic. The concept of the State implies the concept of war, for the essence of the State is Power. The State is the People organized in sovereign Power.'

(c) The State *is* the Law, the moral law as well as the juridical law. Thus it cannot be subject to any other standard, and especially not to the yardstick of civil morality. Its historical responsibilities are deeper. Its only judge is the History of the World. The only possible standard of a judgement upon the state is the world historical *success* of its actions. And this success, the power and expansion of the state, must overrule all other considerations in the private life of the citizens ; right is what serves the might of the state. This is the theory of Plato ; it is the theory of modern totalitarianism ; and it is the theory of Hegel : it is the Platonic-Prussian morality. ' The State ', Hegel writes [72], ' is the realization of the ethical Idea. It is the ethical Spirit as revealed, self-conscious, substantial Will.' Consequently, there can be no ethical idea above the state. ' When the particular Wills of the States can come to no agreement, their controversy can be decided only by war. What offence shall be regarded as a breach of treaty, or as a violation of respect and honour, must remain indefinite. . . The State may identify its infinitude and honour with every one of its aspects.' For ' . . the relation among States fluctuates, and no judge exists to adjust their differences.' In other words : ' Against the State there is no power to decide what is . . right. . . States . . may enter into mutual agreements, but they are, at the same time, superior to these agreements ' (i.e. they need not keep them). . . ' Treaties between states . . depend ultimately on the particular sovereign wills, and for that reason, they must remain unreliable.'

Thus only *one* kind of ' judgement ' can be passed on World-Historical deeds and events : their result, their success. Hegel can therefore identify [73] ' the essential *destiny*—the absolute *aim*, or, what amounts to the same—the true *result* of the World's History '. To be successful, that is, to emerge as the strongest from the dialectical struggle of the different National Spirits for power, for world-domination, is thus the only and ultimate aim and the only basis of judgement ; or as Hegel puts it more poetically : ' Out of this dialectic rises the universal Spirit, the unlimited World-Spirit, pronouncing its judgement—and its judgement is the highest—upon the finite Nations of the World's History ; for the History of the World is the World's court of justice.'

Freyer has very similar ideas, but he expresses them more frankly [74] : ' A manly, a bold tone prevails in history. He who has the grip has the booty. He who makes a faulty move is done for . . he who wishes to hit his mark must know how to shoot.' But all these ideas are, in the last instance, only repetitions of Heraclitus : ' War . . proves some to be gods and others to be mere men, by turning the latter into slaves and the former into masters. . . War is just.' According to these theories, there can be no moral difference between a war in which we are attacked, and one in which we attack our neighbours ; the only possible difference is success. F. Haiser, author of the book *Slavery : Its Biological Foundation and Moral Justification* (1923), a prophet of a master race and of a master morality, argues : ' If we are to defend ourselves, then there must also be aggressors . . ; if so, why then should we not be the aggressors ourselves ? ' But even this doctrine (its predecessor is Clausewitz's famous doctrine that an attack is always the most effective defence) is Hegelian ; for Hegel, when speaking about offences that lead to war, not only shows the necessity for a ' war of defence ' to turn into a ' war of conquest ', but he informs us that some states which have a strong individuality ' will naturally be more inclined to irritability ', in order to find an occasion and a field for what he euphemistically calls ' intense activity '.

With the establishment of historical success as the sole judge in matters relating to states or nations, and with the attempt to break down such moral distinctions as those between attack and defence, it becomes necessary to argue against the morality of conscience. Hegel does it by establishing what he calls ' true morality or rather social virtue ' in opposition to ' false morality '. Needless to say, this ' true morality ' is the Platonic totalitarian morality, combined with a dose of historicism, while the ' false morality ' which he also describes as ' mere formal rectitude ' is that of personal conscience. ' We may fairly ', Hegel writes [75], ' establish the true principles of morality, or rather of social virtue, in opposition to false morality ; for the History of the World occupies a higher ground than that morality which is personal in character—the conscience of individuals, their particular will and mode of action. . . What the absolute aim of Spirit requires and accomplishes, what Providence does, transcends . . the imputation of good and bad motives. . . Consequently it is only formal rectitude, deserted by the living Spirit and by God, which those who take their stand upon ancient right and order maintain.' (That is to say, the moralists who refer, for example, to the New Testament.) ' The deeds of Great Men,

of the Personalities of World History, . . must not be brought
into collision with irrelevant moral claims. *The Litany of private
virtues, of modesty, humility, philanthropy, and forbearance*, must not
be raised against them. The History of the World can, in
principle, entirely ignore the circle within which morality . .
lies.' Here, at last, we have the perversion of the third of the
ideas of 1789, that of fraternity, or, as Hegel says, of philanthropy,
together with the ethics of conscience. This Platonic-Hegelian
historicist moral theory has been repeated over and over again.
The famous historian E. Meyer, for example, speaks of the ' flat
and moralizing evaluation, which judges great political undertakings with the yardstick of civil morality, ignoring the
deeper, the truly moral factors of the State and of historical
responsibilities '.

When such views are held, then all hesitation regarding
propagandist lying and distortion of the truth must disappear,
particularly if it is successful in furthering the power of the state.
Hegel's approach to this problem, however, is rather subtle :
' A great mind has publicly raised the question ', he writes [76],
' whether it is permissible to deceive the People. The answer is
that the People will not permit themselves to be deceived concerning their substantial basis ' (F. Haiser, the master moralist,
says : ' no error is possible where the racial soul dictates ') ' but
it deceives *itself*', Hegel continues, ' about the way it knows
this. . . Public opinion deserves therefore to be esteemed as
much as to be despised. . . Thus to be independent of public
opinion is the first condition of achieving anything great. . .
And great achievements are certain to be subsequently recognized
and accepted by public opinion . .' In brief, it is always success
that counts. If the lie was successful, then it was no lie, since
the People were not deceived concerning their substantial basis.

(*d*) We have seen that the State, particularly in its relation
to other states, is exempt from morality—it is a-moral. We
may therefore expect to hear that war is not a moral evil, but
morally neutral. However, Hegel's theory defies this expectation ; it implies that war is good in itself. ' There is an ethical
element in war ', we read [77]. ' It is necessary to recognize that
the Finite, such as property and life, is accidental. This necessity
appears first under the form of a force of nature, for all things
finite are mortal and transient. In the ethical order, in the
State, however, . . this necessity is exalted to a work of freedom,
to an ethical law. . . War . . now becomes an element . .

of . . right. . . War has the deep meaning that by it the ethical health of a nation is preserved and their finite aims uprooted. . . War protects the people from the corruption which an everlasting peace would bring upon it. History shows phases which illustrate how successful wars have checked internal unrest. . . These Nations, torn by internal strife, win peace at home as a result of war abroad.' This passage, taken from the *Philosophy of Law*, shows the influence of Plato's and Aristotle's teaching on the ' dangers of prosperity ' ; at the same time, the passage is a good instance of the identification of the moral with the healthy, of ethics with political hygiene, or of right with might ; this leads directly, as will be seen, to the identification of virtue and vigour, as the following passage from Hegel's *Philosophy of History* shows. (It follows immediately after the passage already mentioned, dealing with nationalism as a means of getting over one's feelings of inferiority, and thereby suggests that even a war can be an appropriate means to that noble end.) At the same time, the modern theory of the virtuous aggressiveness of the young or have-not countries against the wicked old possessor countries is clearly implied. ' A Nation ', Hegel writes, ' is moral, virtuous, vigorous while it is engaged in realizing its grand objects. . . But this having been attained, the activity displayed by the Spirit of the People . . is no longer needed. . . The Nation can still accomplish much in war and peace . . but the living substantial soul itself may be said to have ceased its activity. . . The Nation lives the same kind of life as the individual when passing from maturity to old age. . . This mere *customary life* (the watch wound up and going of itself) is that which brings on natural death. . . Thus perish individuals, thus perish peoples by a natural death. . . A people can only die a violent death when it has become naturally dead in itself.' (The last remarks belong to the decline-and-fall tradition.)

Hegel's ideas on war are surprisingly modern ; he even visualizes the moral consequences of mechanization ; or rather, he sees in mechanical warfare the consequences of the ethical Spirit of totalitarianism or collectivism [78] : ' There are different kinds of bravery. The courage of the animal, or the robber, the bravery that arises from a sense of honour, chivalrous bravery, are not yet the true forms of bravery. In civilized nations true bravery consists in the readiness to give oneself wholly to the service of the State so that the individual counts but as *one among many*.' (An allusion to universal conscription.) ' Not personal valour is significant ; the important aspect lies in *self-subordination to the universal.* This higher form causes . . bravery to appear more mechanical. . . Hostility is directed not against separate individuals, but against a hostile whole ' (here we have an anticipation of the principle of *total war*) ; '. . personal valour appears as impersonal. This principle has caused the invention of the gun ; it is not a chance invention . .' In a similar vein, Hegel says of the invention of gunpowder : ' Humanity needed it, and it made its appearance forthwith.' (How kind of Providence !)

It is thus purest Hegelianism when the philosopher E. Kaufmann, in 1911, argues against the Kantian ideal of a community of free men : ' Not a community of men of free will but a *victorious war* is the social ideal . . it is in war that the State displays its true nature ' [79] ; or when E. Banse, the famous ' military scientist ', writes in 1933 : ' War means the highest intensification . . of all spiritual energies of an age . . it means the utmost effort of the people's Spiritual power . . Spirit and Action linked together. Indeed, war provides the basis on which the human soul may manifest itself at its fullest height . . . Nowhere else can the Will . . of the Race . . rise into being thus integrally as in war.' And General Ludendorff continues in 1935 : ' During the years of the so-called peace, politics . . have only a meaning inasmuch as they prepare for total war.' He thus only formulates more precisely an idea voiced by the famous essentialist philosopher Max Scheler in 1915 : ' War means the State in its most actual growth and rise : it means politics.' The same Hegelian doctrine is reformulated by Freyer in 1935 : ' The State, from the first moment of its existence, takes its stand in the sphere of war. . . War is not only the most perfect form of State activity, it is the very element in which the State is embedded ; war delayed, prevented, disguised, avoided, must of course be included in the term.' But the boldest conclusion is drawn by F. Lenz, who, in his book *The Race as the Principle of Value*, tentatively raises the question : ' But if humanity were to be the goal of morality, then have not *we*, after all, taken the wrong side ? ' and who, of course, immediately dispels this absurd suggestion by replying : ' Far be it from us to think that humanity should condemn war : nay, it is war that condemns humanity.' This idea is linked up with historicism by E. Jung, who remarks : ' Humanitarianism, or the idea of mankind . . is no regulator of history.' But it was Hegel's predecessor, Fichte, called by Schopenhauer the ' wind-bag ', who must be credited with the original anti-humanitarian argument. Speaking of the word 'humanity', Fichte wrote : 'If one had presented, to the German, instead of the Roman word "*humaneness*" its proper translation, the word "*manhood*", then . . he would have said : " It is after all not so very much to be a man instead of a wild beast ! " This is how a German would have spoken—in a manner which would have been impossible for a Roman. For in the German language, 'manhood' has remained a merely phenomenal notion ; it has never become a super-phenomenal idea, as it did among the Romans. Whoever might attempt to smuggle, cunningly, this alien Roman symbol ' (viz., the word ' humaneness ') ' into the language of the Germans, would thereby manifestly debase their ethical standards . .' Fichte's doctrine is repeated by Spengler, who writes : ' Manhood is either a zoological expression or an empty word ' ; and also by Rosenberg, who writes : ' Man's inner life became debased when . . an alien motive was impressed upon his mind : salvation, humanitarianism, and the culture of humanity.'

Kolnai, to whose book I am deeply indebted for a great deal of material to which I would otherwise have had no access, says [80] most strikingly : ' All of us . . who stand for . . rational, civilized methods of government and social organization, agree that war is in itself an evil. . .' Adding that in the opinion of most of us (except the pacifists) it might become, under certain circumstances, a necessary evil, he continues : ' The nationalist attitude is different, though it need not imply a desire for perpetual or frequent warfare. It sees in a war a good rather than an evil, even if it be a dangerous good, like an exceedingly heady wine that is best reserved for rare occasions of high festivity.' War is not a common and abundant evil but a precious though rare good :—this sums up the views of Hegel and of his followers.

One of Hegel's feats was the revival of the Heraclitean idea of fate ; and he insisted [81] that this glorious Greek idea of fate as expressive of the essence of a person, or of a nation, is opposed to the nominalist Jewish idea of universal laws, whether of nature, or of morals. The essentialist doctrine of fate can be derived (as shown in the last chapter) from the view that the essence of a nation can reveal itself only in its history. It is not ' fatalistic ' in the sense that it encourages inactivity ; ' destiny ' is not to be identified with ' predestination '. The opposite is the case. Oneself, one's real essence, one's innermost soul, the stuff one is made of (will and passion rather than reason) are of decisive importance in the formation of one's fate. Since Hegel's amplification of this theory, the idea of fate or destiny has become a favourite obsession, as it were, of the revolt against freedom. Kolnai rightly stresses the connection between racialism (it is fate that makes one a member of one's race) and hostility to freedom : ' The principle of Race ', Kolnai says [82], ' is meant to embody and express the utter negation of human freedom, the denial of equal rights, a challenge in the face of mankind.' And he rightly insists that racialism tends ' to oppose *Liberty* by *Fate*, individual consciousness by the compelling urge of the Blood beyond control and argument '. Even this tendency is expressed by Hegel, although as usual in a somewhat obscure manner : ' What we call *principle*, *aim*, *destiny*, or the nature or idea of Spirit ', Hegel writes, ' is a hidden, undeveloped essence, which *as such*—however true in itself—is not completely real. . . The motive power that . . gives them . . existence is the *need, instinct, inclination and passion* of men.' The modern philosopher of total education, E. Krieck, goes further in the direction of fatalism : ' All rational will and activity of the individual is confined to his everyday life ; beyond this range he can only achieve a higher destiny and fulfilment in so far as he is gripped by superior powers of fate.' It sounds like personal experience when he continues : ' Not through his own rational scheming will he be made a creative and relevant being, only through forces that work above and beneath him, that do not originate in his own self but sweep and work their way through his self . .' (But it is an unwarranted generalization of the most intimate personal experiences when the same philosopher thinks that not only ' the epoch of " objective " or " free " science is ended ', but also that of ' pure reason '.)

Together with the idea of fate, its counterpart, that of fame is also revived by Hegel : ' Individuals . . are *instruments*. . . What they personally gain . . through the individual share they take in the substantial business (prepared and appointed independently of them) is . . *Fame*, which is their reward.' [83] And Stapel, a propagator of the new paganized Christianity, promptly repeats : ' All great deeds were done for the sake of fame or glory.' But this ' Christian ' moralist is even more radical than Hegel : ' Metaphysical glory is the one true morality ', he teaches, and the ' Categorical Imperative ' of this one true morality runs accordingly : ' Do such deeds as spell glory ! '

(e) Yet glory cannot be acquired by everybody ; the religion of glory implies anti-equalitarianism—it implies a religion of 'Great Men'. Modern racialism accordingly 'knows no equality between souls, no equality between men' [84] (Rosenberg). Thus there are no obstacles to adopting the Leader Principle from the arsenal of the perennial revolt against freedom, or as Hegel calls it, the idea of the World Historical Personality. This Idea is one of Hegel's favourite themes. In discussing the blasphemous 'question whether it is permissible to deceive a people' (see above), he says : ' In public opinion all is false and true, but to discover the truth in it is the business of the Great Man. The Great Man of his time is *he who expresses the will of his time* ; *who tells his time what it wills* ; *and who carries it out.* He acts according to the inner Spirit and Essence of his time, which he realizes. And he who does not understand *how to despise public opinion*, as it makes itself heard here and there, will never accomplish anything great.' This excellent description of the Leader— the Great Dictator—as a publicist is combined with an elaborate myth of the Greatness of the Great Man, that consists in his being the foremost instrument of the Spirit in history. In this discussion of ' Historical Men—World Historical Individuals ' Hegel says : ' They were practical, political men. But at the same time they were thinking men, who had an insight into the requirements of the time—into what was ripe for development. . . World Historical Men—the Heroes of an epoch—must therefore be recognized as its clear-sighted ones ; *their* deeds, *their* words are the best of that time. . . It was they who best understood affairs ; from whom others learned, and approved, or at least acquiesced in—their policy. For the Spirit which has taken this fresh step in History is the inmost soul of all individuals ; but in a state of unconsciousness which aroused the Great Men. . . Their fellows, therefore, follow those Soul-Leaders, for they feel the irresistible power of their own inner Spirit thus embodied.' But the Great Man is not only the man of greatest understanding and wisdom but also the Man of Great Passions—foremost, of course, of political passions and ambitions. He is thereby able to arouse passions in others. ' Great Men have formed purposes to satisfy themselves, not others. . . They are Great Men because they willed and accomplished something great. . . Nothing Great in the World has been accomplished without *passion. . . This may be called the cunning of reason—that it sets the passions to work for itself. . .* Passion, it is true, is not quite the suitable word for what I wish to express. I mean here nothing more than human activity as resulting from *private* interests—particular, or if you will, self-seeking designs—with the qualification that the whole energy of will and character is devoted to their attainment. . . Passions, private aims, and the satisfaction of selfish desires are . . most effective springs of action. Their power lies in the fact that they respect none of the limitations which justice and morality would impose on them ; and that these natural impulses have a more direct influence over their fellow-men than the artificial and tedious discipline that tends to order and self-restraint, law and morality.' From Rousseau onwards, the Romantic school of thought realized that man is not mainly rational. But while the humanitarians cling to rationality as an aim, the revolt against reason exploits this psychological insight into the irrationality of man for its political aims. The fascist appeal to ' human nature ' is to our passions, to our collectivist mystical needs, to ' man the unknown '. Adopting Hegel's words just quoted, this appeal may be called the *cunning of the revolt against reason.* But the height of this cunning is reached by Hegel in this boldest dialectical twist of his. While paying lip-service to rationalism, while talking more loudly about ' reason ' than any man before or after him, he ends up in irrationalism ; in an apotheosis not only of passion, but of brutal force : ' It is ', Hegel writes, ' the absolute interest of Reason that this Moral Whole ' (i.e. the State) ' should exist ; and herein lies the justification and merit of heroes, the founders of States—however cruel they may have been. . . Such men may treat other great and even sacred interests inconsiderately. . . But so mighty a form must trample down many an innocent flower ; it must crush to pieces many an object on its path.'

(f) The conception of man as being not so much a rational as an heroic animal was not invented by the revolt against reason ; it is a typical tribalist ideal. We have to distinguish between this ideal of the Heroic Man and a more reasonable respect for heroism. Heroism is, and always will be, admirable ; but our admiration should depend, I think, very largely on our appreciation of the cause to which the hero has devoted himself. The heroic element in gangsterism, I think, deserves little appreciation. But we should admire Captain Scott and his party, and if possible even more, the heroes of X-ray or of Yellow Fever research ; and certainly those who defend freedom.

The tribal ideal of the Heroic Man, especially in its fascist form, is based upon different views. It is a direct attack upon those things which make heroism admirable to most of us—such things as the furthering of civilization. For it is an attack on the idea of civil life itself ; this is denounced as shallow and material-istic, because of the idea of security which it cherishes. *Live dangerously !* is its imperative ; the cause for which you undertake to follow this imperative is of secondary importance ; or as W. Best says [85] : ' Good fighting as such, not a " good cause " . . is the thing that turns the scale. . . It merely matters *how*, not for what object we fight '. Again we find that this argument is an elaboration of Hegelian ideas : ' In peace ', Hegel writes, ' civil life becomes more extended, every sphere is hedged in . . and at last all men stagnate. . . From the pulpits much is preached concerning the insecurity, vanity, and instability of temporal things, and yet everyone . . thinks that he, at least, will manage to hold on to his possessions. . . It is necessary to recognize . . property and life as accidental. . . Let insecurity finally come in the form of Hussars with glistening sabres, and show its earnest activity ! ' In another place, Hegel paints a gloomy picture of what he calls ' mere customary life ' ; he seems to mean by it something like the normal life of a civilized com-munity : ' Custom is activity without opposition . . in which fullness and zest is out of the question—a merely external and sensuous ' (i.e. what some people in our day like to call ' materialist ') ' existence which has ceased to throw itself enthu-siastically into its object . . , an existence without intellect or vitality.' Hegel, always faithful to his historicism, bases his anti-utilitarian attitude (in distinction to Aristotle's utilitarian comments upon the ' dangers of prosperity ') on his interpretation of history : ' The History of the World is no theatre of happiness. Periods of happiness are blank pages in it, for they are periods of harmony.' Thus, liberalism, freedom and reason are, as usual, objects of Hegel's attacks. The hysterical cries : We want our history ! We want our destiny ! We want our fight ! We want our chains ! resound through the edifice of Hegelianism, through this stronghold of the closed society and of the revolt against freedom.

In spite of Hegel's, as it were, official optimism, based on his theory that what is rational is real, there are features in him to which one can trace the *pessimism* which is so characteristic of the more intelligent among the modern racial philosophers ; not so much, perhaps, of the earlier ones (as Lagarde, Treitschke, or Moeller van den Bruck) but of those who came after Spengler, the famous historicist. Neither Spengler's biological holism, intuitive understanding, Group-Spirit and Spirit of the Age, nor even his Romanticism, helps this fortune-teller to escape a very pessimistic outlook. An element of blank despair is unmistakable in the ' grim ' activism that is left to those who foresee the future and feel instrumental in its arrival. It is interesting to observe that this gloomy view of affairs is equally shared by both wings of the racialists, the ' Atheist ' as well as the ' Christian ' wing.

Stapel, who belongs to the latter (but there are others, for example Gogarten), writes [86] : ' Man is under the sway of original sin in his totality . . The Christian knows that it is strictly impossible for him to live except in sin . . Therefore he steers clear of the pettiness of moral hair-splitting. . . An ethicized Christianity is a counter-Christianity through and through. . . God has made this world perishable, it is doomed to destruction. May it, then, go to the dogs according to destiny ! Men who imagine themselves capable of making it better, who want to create a " higher " morality, are starting a ridiculous petty revolt against God. . . The hope of Heaven does not mean the expect- ation of a happiness of the blessed ; it means obedience and War-Comradeship.' (The return to the tribe.) ' If God orders His man to go to hell, then his sworn adherent . . will accord- ingly go to hell. . . If He allots to him eternal pain, this has to be borne too. . . Faith is but another word for victory. It is victory that the Lord demands . .'

A very similar spirit lives in the work of the two leading philosophers of contemporary Germany, the ' existentialists ' Heidegger and Jaspers, both originally followers of the essentialist philosophers Husserl and Scheler. Heidegger has gained fame by reviving the Hegelian *Philosophy of Nothingness* : Hegel had ' established ' the theory [87] that ' Pure Being ' and ' Pure Noth- ingness ' are identical ; he had said that if you try to think out the notion of a *pure* being, you must abstract from it all particular ' determinations of an object ', and therefore, as Hegel puts it— ' nothing remains '. (This Heraclitean method might be used for proving all kinds of pretty identities, such as that of pure wealth and pure poverty, pure mastership and pure servitude, pure Aryanism and pure Judaism.) Heidegger ingeniously applies the Hegelian theory of Nothingness to a practical Philo- sophy of Life, or of ' Existence '. Life, Existence, can be understood only by understanding Nothingness. In his *What is Metaphysics?* Heidegger says : ' The enquiry should be into the Existing or else into—nothing ; . . into the existing alone, and beyond it into—*Nothingness.*' The enquiry into nothingness (' Where do we search for Nothingness? Where can we find Nothingness? ') is made possible by the fact that ' we know Nothingness ' ; we know it through fear : ' Fear reveals Nothingness.'

Fear ; the fear of nothingness ; the anguish of death ; these are the basic categories of Heidegger's Philosophy of Existence ; of a life whose true meaning it is [88] ' to be cast down into existence, directed towards death '. Human existence is to be interpreted as a ' Thunderstorm of Steel ' ; the ' determined existence ' of a man is ' to be a self, passionately free to die . . in full self-consciousness and anguish '. But these gloomy confessions are not entirely without their comforting aspect. The reader need not be quite overwhelmed by Heidegger's passion to die. For the will to power and the will to live appear to be no less developed in him than in his master, Hegel. ' The German University's Will to the Essence ', Heidegger writes in 1933, ' is a Will to Science ; it is a Will to the historico-spiritual mission of the German Nation, as a Nation experiencing itself in its State. Science and German Destiny must attain Power, especially in the essential Will.' This passage, though not a monument of originality or clarity, is certainly one of loyalty to his masters ; and those admirers of Heidegger who in spite of all this continue to believe in the profundity of his ' Philosophy of Existence ' might be reminded of Schopenhauer's words : ' Who can really believe that truth also will come to light, just as a by-product ? ' And in view of the last of Heidegger's quotations, they should ask themselves whether Schopenhauer's advice to a dishonest guardian has not been successfully administered by many educationists to many promising youths, inside and outside of Germany. I have in mind the passage : ' Should you ever intend to dull the wits of a young man and to incapacitate his brains for any kind of thought whatever, then you cannot do better than give him Hegel to read. For these monstrous accumulations of words that annul and contradict one another drive the mind into tormenting itself with vain attempts to think anything whatever in connection with them, until finally it collapses from sheer exhaustion. Thus any ability to think is so thoroughly destroyed that the young man will ultimately mistake empty and hollow verbiage for real thought. A guardian fearing that his ward might become too intelligent for his schemes might prevent this misfortune by innocently suggesting the reading of Hegel.'

Jaspers declares [89] his nihilist tendencies more frankly even, if that is possible, than Heidegger. Only when you are faced with Nothingness, with annihilation, Jaspers teaches, will you be able to experience and appreciate Existence. In order to live in the essential sense, one must live in a crisis. In order to taste life one has not only to risk, but to lose !—Jaspers carries the historicist idea of change and destiny recklessly to its most gloomy extreme. All things must perish ; everything ends in failure : in this way does the historicist law of development present itself to his disillusioned intellect. But face destruction—and you will get the thrill of your life ! Only in the ' marginal situations ', on the edge between existence and nothingness, do we really live. The bliss of life always coincides with the end of its intelligibility, particularly with extreme situations of the body, above all with bodily danger. You cannot taste life without tasting failure. Enjoy yourself perishing !

This is the philosophy of the gambler—of the gangster. Needless to say, this demoniac ' religion of Urge and Fear, of the Triumphant or else the Hunted Beast ' (Kolnai [90]), this absolute nihilism in the fullest sense of the word, is not a popular creed. It is a confession characteristic of an esoteric group of intellectuals who have surrendered their reason, and with it, their humanity.

There is another Germany, that of the ordinary people whose brains have not been poisoned by a devastating system of higher education. But this ' other ' Germany is certainly not that of her thinkers. It is true, Germany had also some ' other ' thinkers (foremost among them, Kant) ; however, the survey just finished is not encouraging, and I fully sympathize with Kolnai's remark [91] : ' Perhaps it is not . . a paradox to solace our despair at German culture with the consideration that, after all, there is another Germany of Prussian Generals besides the Germany of Prussian Thinkers.'

VI

I have tried to show the identity of Hegelian historicism with the philosophy of modern totalitarianism. This identity is seldom clearly enough realized. Hegelian historicism has become the language of wide circles of intellectuals, even of candid ' anti-fascists ' and ' leftists '. It is so much a part of their intellectual atmosphere that, for many, it is no more noticeable, and its appalling dishonesty no more remarkable, than the air they breathe. Yet some racial philosophers are fully conscious of their indebtedness to Hegel. An example is H. O. Ziegler, who in his study, *The Modern Nation*, rightly describes [92] the introduction of Hegel's (and A. Mueller's) idea of ' collective Spirits conceived as Personalities ', as the ' Copernican revolution in the Philosophy of the Nation '. Another illustration of this awareness of the significance of Hegelianism, which might specially interest British readers, can be found in the judgements passed in a recent German history of British philosophy (by R. Metz, 1935). A man of the excellence of T. H. Green is here criticized, not of course because he was influenced by Hegel, but because he ' fell back into the typical individualism of the English. . . He shrank from such radical consequences as Hegel has drawn '. Hobhouse, who fought bravely against Hegelianism, is contemptuously described as representing ' a typical form of bourgeois liberalism, defending itself against the omnipotence of the State because it feels its freedom threatened thereby '—a feeling which to some people might appear well founded. Bosanquet of course is praised for his genuine Hegelianism. But the significant fact is that this is all taken perfectly seriously by most of the British reviewers.

I mention this fact mainly because I wish to show how difficult and, at the same time, how urgent it is to continue Schopenhauer's fight against this shallow cant (which Hegel himself accurately fathomed when describing his own philosophy as of ' the most lofty depth '). At least the new generation should be helped to free themselves from this intellectual fraud, the greatest, perhaps, in the history of our civilization and its quarrels with its enemies. Perhaps they will live up to the expectations of Schopenhauer, who in 1840 prophesied [93] that ' this colossal mystification will furnish posterity with an inexhaustible source of sarcasm '. (So far the great pessimist has proved a wild optimist concerning posterity.) The Hegelian farce has done enough harm. We must stop it. We must speak—even at the price of soiling ourselves by touching this scandalous thing which, unfortunately without success, was so clearly exposed a hundred years ago. Too many philosophers have neglected Schopenhauer's incessantly repeated warnings ; they neglected them not so much at their own peril (they did not fare badly) as at the peril of those whom they taught, and at the peril of mankind.

It seems to me a fitting conclusion to this chapter if I leave the last word to Schopenhauer, the anti-nationalist who said of Hegel a hundred years ago : 'He exerted, not on philosophy alone but on all forms of German literature, a devastating, or more strictly speaking, a stupefying, one could also say, a pestiferous, influence. To combat this influence forcefully and on every occasion is the duty of everybody who is able to judge independently. *For if we are silent, who will speak?*'

> The collectivists . . have the zest for progress, the sympathy for the poor, the burning sense of wrong, the impulse for great deeds, which have been lacking in latter-day liberalism. But their science is founded on a profound misunderstanding . . , and their actions, therefore, are deeply destructive and reactionary. So men's hearts are torn, their minds divided, they are offered impossible choices.
>
> WALTER LIPPMANN.

CHAPTER 13 : MARX'S SOCIOLOGICAL DETERMINISM

It has always been the strategy of the revolt against freedom ' to take advantage of sentiments, not wasting one's energies in futile efforts to destroy them ' [1]. The most cherished ideas of the humanitarians were often loudly acclaimed by their deadliest enemies, who in this way penetrated into the humanitarian camp under the guise of allies, causing disunion and thorough confusion. This strategy has often been highly successful, as is shown by the fact that many genuine humanitarians still revere Plato's idea of ' justice ', the medieval idea of ' Christian ' authoritarianism, Rousseau's idea of the ' general will ', or Fichte's and Hegel's ideas of ' national freedom '.[2] Yet this method of penetrating, dividing and confusing the humanitarian camp and of building up a largely unwitting and therefore doubly effective intellectual fifth column achieved its greatest success only after Hegelianism had established itself as the basis of a truly humanitarian movement : of Marxism, so far the purest, the most developed and the most dangerous form of historicism.

It is tempting to dwell upon the similarities between Marxism, the Hegelian left-wing, and its fascist counterpart. Yet it would be utterly unfair to overlook the difference between them. Although their intellectual origin is nearly identical, there can be no doubt of the humanitarian impulse of Marxism. Moreover, in contrast to the Hegelians of the right-wing, Marx made an honest attempt to apply rational methods to the most urgent problems of social life. The value of this attempt is unimpaired by the fact that it was, as I shall try to show, largely unsuccessful.

81

Science progresses through trial *and* error. Marx tried, and although he erred in his main doctrines, he did not try in vain. He opened and sharpened our eyes in many ways. A return to pre-Marxian social science is inconceivable. All modern writers are indebted to Marx, even if they do not know it. This is especially true of those who disagree with his doctrines, as I do ; and I readily admit that my treatment, for example of Plato [3] and Hegel, bears the stamp of his influence.

One cannot do justice to Marx without recognizing his sincerity. His open-mindedness, his sense of facts, his distrust of verbiage, and especially of moralizing verbiage, made him one of the world's most influential fighters against hypocrisy and pharisaism. He had a burning desire to help the oppressed, and was fully conscious of the need for proving himself in deeds, and not only in words. His main talents being theoretical, he devoted immense labour to forging what he believed to be scientific weapons for the fight to improve the lot of the vast majority of men. His sincerity in his search for truth and his intellectual honesty distinguish him, I believe, from many of his followers (although unfortunately he did not altogether escape the corrupting influence of an upbringing in the atmosphere of Hegelian dialectics, described by Schopenhauer as ' destructive of all intelligence ' [4]). Marx's interest in social science and social philosophy was fundamentally a practical interest. He saw in knowledge a means of promoting the progress of man [5].

Why, then, attack Marx ? In spite of his merits, Marx was, I believe, a false prophet. He was a prophet of the course of history, and his prophecies did not come true ; but this is not my main accusation. It is much more important that he misled scores of intelligent people into believing that historical prophecy is the scientific way of approaching social problems. Marx is responsible for the devastating influence of the historicist method of thought within the ranks of those who wish to advance the cause of the open society.

But is it true that Marxism is a pure brand of historicism ? Are there not some elements of social technology in Marxism ? The fact that Russia is making bold and often successful experiments in social engineering has led many to infer that Marxism, as the science or creed which underlies the Russian experiment, must be a kind of social technology, or at least favourable to it. But nobody who knows anything about the history of Marxism can make this mistake. Marxism is a purely historical theory, a theory which aims at predicting the future course of economic and power-political developments and especially of revolutions. As such, it certainly did not furnish the basis of the policy of the Russian Communist Party after its rise to political power. Since Marx had practically forbidden all social technology, which he denounced as Utopian [6], his Russian disciples found themselves at first entirely unprepared for their great tasks in the field of social engineering. As Lenin was quick to realize, Marxism was unable to help in matters of practical economics. ' I do not know of any socialist who has dealt with these problems ', said Lenin [7], after his rise to power ; ' there was nothing written about such matters in the Bolshevik textbooks, or in those of the Mensheviks.' After a period of unsuccessful experiment, the so-called ' period of war-communism ', Lenin decided to adopt measures which meant in fact a limited and temporary return to private enterprise. This so-called NEP (New Economic Policy) and the later experiments—five-year plans, etc.—have nothing whatever to do with the theories of ' Scientific Socialism ' once propounded by Marx and Engels. Neither the peculiar situation in which Lenin found himself before he introduced the NEP, nor his achievements, can be appreciated without due consideration of this point. The vast economic researches of Marx did not even touch the problems of a constructive economic policy, for example, economic planning. As Lenin admits, *there is hardly a word on the economics of socialism to be found in Marx's work* —apart from such useless [8] slogans as ' from each according to his ability, to each according to his needs '. The reason is that the economic research of Marx is completely subservient to his historical prophecy. But we must say even more. Marx strongly emphasized the opposition between his purely historicist method and any attempt to make an economic analysis with a view to rational planning. Such attempts he denounced as Utopian, and as illegitimate. In consequence, Marxists did not even study what the so-called ' bourgeois economists ' attained in this field. They were by their training even less prepared for constructive work than some of the ' bourgeois economists ' themselves.

Marx saw his specific mission in the freeing of socialism from its sentimental, moralist, and visionary background. Socialism was to be developed from its Utopian stage to its scientific stage [9] ; it was to be based upon the scientific method of analysing cause and effect, and upon scientific prediction. And since he assumed prediction in the field of society to be the same as historical prophecy, scientific socialism was to be based upon a study of historical causes and historical effects, and finally upon the prophecy of its own advent.

Marxists, when they find their theories attacked, often withdraw to the position that Marxism is primarily not so much a doctrine as a method. They say that even if some particular part of the doctrines of Marx, or of some of his followers, were superseded, his method would still remain unassailable. I believe that it is quite correct to insist that Marxism is, fundamentally, a method. But it is wrong to believe that, as a method, it must be secure from attacks. The position is, simply, that whoever wishes to judge Marxism has to probe it and to criticize it as a method, that is to say, he must measure it by methodological standards. He must ask whether it is a fruitful method or a poor one, i.e. whether or not it is capable of furthering the task of science. The standards by which we must judge the Marxist method are thus of a practical nature. By describing Marxism as purest historicism, I have indicated that I hold the Marxist method to be very poor indeed [10].

Marx himself would have agreed with such a practical approach to the criticism of his method, for he was one of the first philosophers to develop the views which later were called ' pragmatism '. He was led to this position, I believe, by his conviction that a scientific background was urgently needed by the practical politician, which of course meant the socialist politician. Science, he taught, should yield practical results. Always look at the fruits, the practical consequences of a theory ! They tell something even of its scientific structure. A philosophy or a science that does not yield practical results merely interprets the world we live in ; but it can and it should do more ; it should change the world. ' The philosophers ', wrote Marx [11] early in his career, ' have only interpreted the world in various ways ; the point however is to change it.' It was perhaps this pragmatic attitude that made him anticipate the important methodological doctrine of the later pragmatists that the most characteristic task of science is not to gain knowledge of past facts, but to predict the future.

This stress on scientific prediction, in itself an important and progressive methodological discovery, unfortunately led Marx astray. For the plausible argument that science can predict the future only if the future is predetermined—if, as it were, the future is present in the past, telescoped in it—led him to adhere to the false belief that a rigidly scientific method must be based on a rigid determinism. Marx's ' inexorable laws ' of nature and of historical development show clearly the influence of the Laplacean atmosphere and that of the French Materialists. But the belief that the terms ' scientific ' and ' determinist ' are, if not synonymous, at least inseparably connected, can now be said to be one of the superstitions of a time that has not yet entirely passed away [12]. Since I am interested mainly in questions of method, I am glad that, when discussing its method-ological aspect, it is quite unnecessary to enter into a dispute concerning the metaphysical problem of determinism. For whatever may be the outcome of such metaphysical controversies as, for example, the bearing of the Quantum theory on ' free-will ', one thing, I should say, is settled. No kind of determinism, whether it be expressed as the principle of the uniformity of nature or as the law of universal causation, can be considered any longer a necessary assumption of scientific method ; for physics, the most advanced of all sciences, has shown not only that it can do without such assumptions, but also that to some extent it contradicts them. Determinism is not a necessary pre-requisite of a science which can make predictions. Scientific method cannot, therefore, be said to favour the adoption of strict determinism. Science can be rigidly scientific without this assumption. Marx, of course, cannot be blamed for having held the opposite view, since the best scientists of his day did the same.

It must be noted that it is not so much the abstract, theoretical doctrine of determinism which led Marx astray, but rather the practical influence of this doctrine upon his view of scientific method, upon his view of the aims and possibilities of a social science. The abstract idea of ' causes ' which ' determine ' social developments is as such quite harmless as long as it does not lead to historicism. And indeed, there is no reason whatever why this idea should lead us to adopt a historicist attitude towards social institutions, *in strange contrast to the obviously technological attitude taken up by everybody, and especially by determinists, towards mechanical or electrical machinery.* There is no reason why we should believe that, of all sciences, social science is capable of realizing the age-old dream of revealing what the future has in store for us. This belief in scientific fortune-telling is not founded on determinism alone ; its other foundation is the confusion between *scientific prediction*, as we know it from physics or astronomy, and *large-scale historical prophecy*, which foretells in broad lines the main tendencies of the future development of society. These two kinds of prediction are very different (as I have tried to show elsewhere [13]), and the scientific character of the first is no argument in favour of the scientific character of the second.

Marx's historicist view of the aims of social science greatly upset the pragmatism which had originally led him to stress the predictive function of science. It forced him to modify his earlier view that science should, and that it could, change the world. For if there was to be a social science, and accordingly, historical prophecy, the main course of history must be predetermined, and neither good-will nor reason had power to alter it. All that was left to us in the way of reasonable interference was to make sure, by historical prophecy, of the impending course of development, and to remove the worst obstacles in its path. ' When a society has discovered ', Marx writes in *Capital* [14], ' the natural law that determines its own movement, . . even then it can neither overleap the natural phases of its evolution, nor shuffle them out of the world by a stroke of the pen. But this much it can do ; it can shorten and lessen its birth-pangs.' These are the views that led Marx to denounce as ' Utopianists ' all who looked upon social institutions with the eyes of the social engineer, holding them to be amenable to human reason and will, and to be a possible field of rational planning. These ' Utopianists ' appeared to him to attempt with fragile human hands to steer the colossal ship of society against the natural currents and storms of history. All a scientist could do, he thought, was to forecast the gusts and vortices ahead. The practical service he could achieve would thus be confined to issuing a warning against the next storm that threatened to take the ship off the right course (the right course was of course the left !) or to advising the passengers as to the side of the boat on which they had better assemble. Marx saw the real task of scientific socialism in the annunciation of the impending socialist millennium. Only by way of this annunciation, he holds, can scientific socialist teaching contribute to bringing about a socialist world, whose coming it can further by making men conscious of the impending change, and of the parts allotted to them in the play of history. Thus scientific socialism is not a social technology ; it does not teach the ways and means of constructing socialist institutions. Marx's views of the relation between socialist theory and practice show the purity of his historicist views.

Marx's thought was in many respects a product of his time, when the remembrance of that great historical earthquake, the French Revolution, was still fresh. (It was revived by the revolution of 1848.) Such a revolution could not, he felt, be planned and staged by human reason. But it could have been foreseen by a historicist social science ; sufficient insight into the social situation would have revealed its causes. That this historicist attitude was rather typical of the period can be seen from the close similarity between the historicism of Marx and that of J. S. Mill. (It is analogous to the similarity between the historicist philosophies of their predecessors, Hegel and Comte.) Marx did not think very highly of ' bourgeois economists such as . . J. S. Mill ' [15] whom he viewed as a typical representative of ' an insipid, brainless syncretism '. Although it is true that in some places Marx shows a certain respect for the ' modern tendencies ' of the ' philanthropic economist ' Mill, it seems to me that there is ample circumstantial evidence against the conjecture that Marx was directly influenced by Mill's (or rather by Comte's) views on the methods of social science. The agreement between the views of Marx and of Mill is therefore the more striking. Thus when Marx says in the preface to *Capital*, ' It is the ultimate aim of this work to lay bare the . . law of motion of modern society ' [16], he might be said to carry out Mill's programme : ' The fundamental problem . . of the social science, is to find the law according to which any state of society produces the state which succeeds it and takes its place.' Mill distinguished fairly clearly the possibility of what he called ' two kinds of sociological inquiry ', the first closely corresponding to what I call social technology, the second corresponding to historicist prophecy, and he took sides with the latter, characterizing it as the ' general Science of Society by which the conclusions of the other and more special kind of inquiry must be limited and controlled '. This general science of society is based upon the principle of causality, in accordance with Mill's view of scientific method ; and he describes this causal analysis of society as the ' Historical Method '. Mill's ' states of society ' [17] with ' properties . . changeable . . from age to age ' correspond exactly to Marxist ' historical periods ', and Mill's optimistic belief in progress resembles Marx's, although it is of course much more naïve than its dialectical counterpart. (Mill thought that the type of movement ' to which human affairs must conform . . must be . . one or the other ' of two possible astronomical movements, viz., ' an orbit ' or ' a trajectory '. Marxist dialectics is less certain of the simplicity of the laws of historical development ; it adopts a combination, as it were, of Mill's two movements—something like a wave or a corkscrew movement.)

There are more similarities between Marx and Mill ; for example, both were dissatisfied with *laissez-faire* liberalism, and both tried to provide better foundations for carrying into practice the fundamental idea of liberty. But in their views on the method of sociology, there is one very important difference. Mill believed that the study of society, in the last analysis, must be reducible to psychology ; that the laws of historical development must be explicable in terms of *human nature*, of the ' laws of the mind ', and in particular, of its progressiveness. ' The progressiveness of the human race ', says Mill, ' is the foundation on which a method of . . social science has been . . erected, far superior to . . the modes . . previously . . prevalent . .' [18] The theory that sociology must in principle be reducible to social psychology, difficult though the reduction may be because of the complications arising from the interaction of countless individuals, has been widely held by many thinkers ; indeed, it is one of the theories which are often simply taken for granted. I shall call this approach to sociology (methodological) *psychologism* [19]. Mill, we can now say, believed in psychologism. But Marx challenged it. ' Legal relationships ', he asserted [20], ' and the various political structures cannot . . be explained by . . what has been called the general " progressiveness of the human mind ".' To have questioned psychologism is perhaps the greatest achievement of Marx as a sociologist. By doing so he opened the way to the more penetrating conception of a specific realm of sociological laws, and of a sociology which was at least partly autonomous.

In the following chapters, I shall explain some points of Marx's method, and I shall try always to emphasize especially such of his views as I believe to be of lasting merit. Thus I shall deal next with Marx's attack on psychologism, i.e. with his arguments in favour of an autonomous social science, irreducible to psychology. And only later shall I attempt to show the fatal weakness and the destructive consequences of his historicism.

Chapter 14 : THE AUTONOMY OF SOCIOLOGY

A concise formulation of Marx's opposition to psychologism [1], i.e. to the plausible doctrine that all laws of social life must be ultimately reducible to the psychological laws of ' human nature ', is his famous epigram : ' It is not the consciousness of man that determines his existence—rather, it is his social existence that determines his consciousness.' [2] The function of the present chapter as well as of the two following ones is mainly to elucidate this epigram. And I may state at once that in developing what I believe to be Marx's anti-psychologism, I am developing a view to which I subscribe myself.

As an elementary illustration, and a first step in our examination, we may refer to the problem of the so-called rules of exogamy, i.e. the problem of explaining the wide distribution, among the most diverse cultures, of marriage laws apparently designed to prevent inbreeding. Mill and his psychologistic school of sociology (it was joined later by many psychoanalysts) would try to explain these rules by an appeal to ' human nature ', for instance to some sort of instinctive aversion against incest (developed perhaps through natural selection, or else through ' repression ') ; and something like this would also be the naïve or popular explanation. Adopting the point of view expressed in Marx's epigram, however, one could ask whether it is not the other way round, that is to say, whether the apparent instinct is not rather a product of education, the effect rather than the cause of the social rules and traditions demanding exogamy and forbidding incest [3]. It is clear that these two approaches correspond exactly to the very ancient problem whether social laws are ' natural ' or ' conventional ' (dealt with at length in chapter 5). In a question such as the one chosen here as an illustration, it would be difficult to determine which of the two theories is the correct one, the explanation of the traditional social rules by instinct or the explanation of an apparent instinct by traditional social rules. The possibility of deciding such questions by experiment has, however, been shown in a similar case, that of the apparently instinctive aversion to snakes. This aversion has a greater semblance of being instinctive or ' natural ' in that it is exhibited not only by men but also by all anthropoid apes and by most monkeys as well. But experiments seem to indicate that this fear is conventional. It appears to be a product of education, not only in the human race but also for instance in chimpanzees, since [4] both young children and young chimpanzees who have not been taught to fear snakes do not exhibit the alleged instinct. This example should be taken as a warning. We are faced here with an aversion which is apparently universal, even beyond the human race. But although from the fact that a habit is not universal we might perhaps argue against its being based on an instinct (but even this argument is dangerous since there are social customs enforcing the suppression of instincts), we see that the converse is certainly not true. The universal occurrence of a certain behaviour is not a decisive argument in favour of its instinctive character, or of its being rooted in ' human nature '.

Such considerations may show how naïve it is to assume that all social laws must be derivable, in principle, from the psychology of ' human nature '. But this analysis is still rather crude. In order to proceed one step further, we may try to analyse more directly the main thesis of psychologism, the doctrine that, society being the product of interacting minds, social laws must ultimately be reducible to psychological laws, since the events of social life, including its conventions, must be the outcome of motives springing from the minds of individual men.

Against this doctrine of psychologism, the defenders of an autonomous sociology can advance *institutionalist* views [5]. They can point out, first of all, that no action can ever be explained by motive alone ; if motives (or any other psychological or behaviourist concepts) are to be used in the explanation, then they must be supplemented by a reference to the general situation, and especially to the environment. In the case of human actions, this environment is very largely of a social nature ; thus our actions cannot be explained without reference to our social environment, to social institutions and to their manner of functioning. It is therefore impossible, the institutionalist may contend, to reduce sociology to a psychological or behaviouristic analysis of our actions ; rather, every such analysis presupposes sociology, which therefore cannot wholly depend on psychological analysis. Sociology, or at least a very important part of it, must be autonomous.

Against this view, the followers of psychologism may retort that they are quite ready to admit the great importance of environmental factors, whether natural or social ; but the

structure (they may prefer the fashionable word ' pattern ') of
the social environment, as opposed to the natural environment,
is man-made ; and therefore it must be explicable in terms of
human nature, in accordance with the doctrine of psychologism.
For instance, the characteristic institution which economists call
' the market ', and whose functioning is the main object of their
studies, can be derived in the last analysis from the psychology
of ' economic man ', or, to use Mill's phraseology, from the
psychological ' phenomena . . of the pursuit of wealth ' [6].
Moreover, the followers of psychologism insist that it is because
of the peculiar psychological structure of human nature that
institutions play such an important rôle in our society, and that,
once established, they show a tendency to become a traditional
and a comparatively fixed part of our environment.   Finally—
and this is their decisive point—the *origin as well as the development*
of traditions must be explicable in terms of human nature.
When tracing back traditions and institutions to their origin,
we must find that their introduction is explicable in psychological
terms, since they have been introduced by man for some purpose
or other, and under the influence of certain motives.   And even
if these motives have been forgotten in the course of time, then
that forgetfulness, as well as our readiness to put up with
institutions whose purpose is obscure, is in its turn based on human
nature.   Thus ' all phenomena of society are phenomena of
human nature ' [7], as Mill said ; and ' the Laws of the phenomena
of society are, and can be, nothing but the laws of the actions
and passions of human beings ', that is to say, ' the laws of
individual human nature.   Men are not, when brought together,
converted into another kind of substance . .' [8]

This last remark of Mill's exhibits one of the most praiseworthy
aspects of psychologism, namely, its sane opposition to collectivism
and holism, its refusal to be impressed by Rousseau's or Hegel's
romanticism—-by a general will or a national spirit, or perhaps, by
a group mind.   Psychologism is, I believe, correct only in so far as
it insists upon what may be called ' methodological individualism '
as opposed to ' methodological collectivism ' ; it rightly insists
that the ' behaviour ' and the ' actions ' of collectives, such as
states or social groups, must be reduced to the behaviour and to
the actions of human individuals.   But the belief that the choice
of such an individualistic method implies the choice of a psychological method is mistaken (as will be shown below in this chapter),
even though it may appear very convincing at first sight.   And

that psychologism as such moves on rather dangerous ground, apart from its commendable individualistic method, can be seen from some further passages of Mill's argument. For they show that *psychologism is forced to adopt historicist methods*. The attempt to reduce the facts of our social environment to psychological facts forces us into speculations about origins and developments. When analysing Plato's sociology, we had an opportunity of gauging the dubious merits of such an approach to social science (compare chapter 5). In criticizing Mill, we shall now try to deal it a decisive blow.

It is undoubtedly Mill's psychologism which forces him to adopt a historicist method ; and he is even vaguely aware of the barrenness or poverty of historicism, since he tries to account for this barrenness by pointing out the difficulties arising from the tremendous complexity of the interaction of so many individual minds. ' While it is . . imperative ', he says, '. . never to introduce any generalization . . into the social sciences until sufficient grounds can be pointed out in human nature, I do not think any one will contend that it would have been possible, setting out from the principle of human nature and from the general circumstances of the position of our species, to determine *a priori* the order in which human development must take place, and to predict, consequently, the general facts of history up to the present time.' [9] The reason he gives is that ' after the first few terms of the series, the influence exercised over each generation by the generations which preceded it becomes . . more and more preponderant over all other influences '. (In other words, the social environment becomes a dominant influence.) ' So long a series of actions and reactions . . could not possibly be computed by human faculties . .'

This argument, and especially Mill's remark on ' the first few terms of the series ', are a striking revelation of the weakness of the psychologistic version of historicism. If all regularities in social life, the laws of our social environment, of all institutions, etc., are ultimately to be explained by, and reduced to, the ' actions and passions of human beings ', then such an approach forces upon us not only the idea of historico-causal development, but also the idea of the *first steps* of such a development. For the stress on the psychological origin of social rules or institutions can only mean that they can be traced back to a state when their introduction was dependent solely upon psychological factors, or more precisely, when it was independent of any established social institutions.   Psychologism is thus forced, whether it likes it or not, to operate with the idea of a *beginning of society*, and with the idea of a human nature and a human psychology as they existed prior to society.   In other words, Mill's remark concerning the 'first few terms of the series' of social development is not an accidental slip, as one might perhaps believe, but the appropriate expression of the desperate position forced upon him.   It is a desperate position because this theory of a pre-social human nature which explains the foundation of society—a psychologistic version of the 'social contract'—is not only an historical myth, but also, as it were, a methodological myth.   It can hardly be seriously discussed, for we have every reason to believe that man or rather his ancestor was social prior to being human (considering, for example, that language presupposes society).   But this implies that social institutions, and with them, typical social regularities or sociological laws [10], must have existed prior to what some people are pleased to call ' human nature ', and to human psychology.   If a reduction is to be attempted at all, it would therefore be more hopeful to attempt a reduction or interpretation of psychology in terms of sociology than the other way round.

This brings us back to Marx's epigram at the beginning of this chapter.   Men—i.e. human minds, the needs, the hopes, fears, and expectations, the motives and aspirations of human individuals—are, if anything, the product of life in society rather than its creators.   It must be admitted that the structure of our social environment is man-made in a certain sense ;   that its institutions and traditions are neither the work of God nor of nature, but the results of human actions and decisions, and alterable by human actions and decisions.   But this does not mean that they are all consciously designed, and explicable in terms of needs, hopes, or motives.   On the contrary, even those which arise as the result of conscious and intentional human actions are, as a rule, *the indirect, the unintended and often the unwanted by-products of such actions*.   ' Only a minority of social institutions are consciously designed, while the vast majority have just " grown ", as the undesigned results of human actions ', as I have said before [11] ;   and we can add that even most of the few institutions which were consciously and successfully designed (say, a newly founded University, or a Trade Union) do not turn out according to plan—again because of the unintended social repercussions resulting from their intentional creation.   For their creation affects not only many other social institutions but also

' human nature '—hopes, fears, and ambitions, first of those more immediately involved, and later often of all members of the society. One of the consequences of this is that the moral values of a society—the demands and proposals recognized by all, or by very nearly all, of its members—are closely bound up with its institutions and traditions, and that they cannot survive the destruction of the institutions and traditions of a society (as indicated in chapter 9 when we discussed the ' canvas-cleaning ' of the radical revolutionary).

All this holds most emphatically for the more ancient periods of social development, i.e. for the closed society, in which the conscious design of institutions is a most exceptional event, if it happens at all. To-day, things may begin to be different, owing to our slowly increasing knowledge of society, i.e. owing to the study of the unintended repercussions of our plans and actions ; and one day, men may even become the conscious creators of an open society, and thereby of a greater part of their own fate. (Marx entertained this hope, as will be shown in the next chapter.) But all this is partly a matter of degree, and although we may learn to foresee many of the unintended consequences of our actions (the main aim of all social technology), there will always be many which we did not foresee.

The fact that psychologism is forced to operate with the idea of a psychological origin of society constitutes in my opinion a decisive argument against it. But it is not the only one. Perhaps the most important criticism of psychologism is that it fails to understand the main task of the explanatory social sciences.

This task is not, as the historicist believes, the prophecy of the future course of history. It is, rather, the discovery and explanation of the less obvious dependences within the social sphere. It is the discovery of the difficulties which stand in the way of social action—the study, as it were, of the unwieldiness, the resilience or the brittleness of the social stuff, of its resistance to our attempts to mould it and to work with it.

In order to make my point clear, I shall briefly describe a theory which is widely held but which assumes what I consider the very opposite of the true aim of the social sciences ; I call it the ' *conspiracy theory of society* '. It is the view that an explanation of a social phenomenon consists in the discovery of the men or groups who are interested in the occurrence of this phenomenon (sometimes it is a hidden interest which has first to be revealed), and who have planned and conspired to bring it about.

This view of the aims of the social sciences arises, of course, from the mistaken theory that, whatever happens in society—especially happenings such as war, unemployment, poverty, shortages, which people as a rule dislike—is the result of direct design by some powerful individuals and groups. This theory is widely held ; it is older even than historicism (which, as shown by its primitive theistic form, is a derivative of the conspiracy theory). In its modern forms it is, like modern historicism, and a certain modern attitude towards ' natural laws ', a typical result of the secularization of a religious superstition. The belief in the Homeric gods whose conspiracies explain the history of the Trojan War is gone. The gods are abandoned. But their place is filled by powerful men or groups—sinister pressure groups whose wickedness is responsible for all the evils we suffer from—such as the Learned Elders of Zion, or the monopolists, or the capitalists, or the imperialists.

I do not wish to imply that conspiracies never happen. On the contrary, they are typical social phenomena. They become important, for example, whenever people who believe in the conspiracy theory get into power. And people who sincerely believe that they know how to make heaven on earth are most likely to adopt the conspiracy theory, and to get involved in a counter-conspiracy against non-existing conspirators. For the only explanation of their failure to produce their heaven is the evil intention of the Devil, who has a vested interest in hell.

Conspiracies occur, it must be admitted. But the striking fact which, in spite of their occurrence, disproves the conspiracy theory is that few of these conspiracies are ultimately successful. *Conspirators rarely consummate their conspiracy.*

Why is this so ? Why do achievements differ so widely from aspirations ? Because this is usually the case in social life, conspiracy or no conspiracy. Social life is not only a trial of strength between opposing groups: it is action within a more or less resilient or brittle framework of institutions and traditions, and it creates—apart from any conscious counter-action—many unforeseen reactions in this framework, some of them perhaps even unforeseeable.

To try to analyse these reactions and to foresee them as far as possible is, I believe, the main task of the social sciences. It is the task of analysing the unintended social repercussions of intentional human actions—those repercussions whose significance is neglected both by the conspiracy theory and by psychologism,

as already indicated.   An action which proceeds precisely according to intention does not create a problem for social science
(except that there may be a need to explain why in this particular case no unintended repercussions occurred).   One of the
most primitive economic actions may serve as an example in
order to make the idea of unintended consequences of our actions
quite clear.   If a man wishes urgently to buy a house, we can
safely assume that he does not wish to raise the market price of
houses.   But the very fact that he appears on the market as a
buyer will tend to raise market prices.   And analogous remarks
hold for the seller.   Or to take an example from a very different
field, if a man decides to insure his life, he is unlikely to have the
intention of encouraging some people to invest their money in
insurance shares.   But he will do so nevertheless.   We see here
clearly that not all consequences of our actions are intended
consequences ; and accordingly, that the conspiracy theory of
society cannot be true because it amounts to the assertion that all
results, even those which at first sight do not seem to be intended
by anybody, are the intended results of the actions of people who
are interested in these results.

The examples given do not refute psychologism as easily as
they refute the conspiracy theory, for one can argue that it is the
sellers' *knowledge* of a buyer's presence in the market, and their
hope of getting a higher price—in other words, psychological
factors—which explain the repercussions described.   This, of
course, is quite true ; but we must not forget that this knowledge
and this hope are not ultimate data of human nature, and that
they are, in their turn, explicable in terms of the *social situation*—
the market situation.

This social situation is hardly reducible to motives and to the
general laws of ' human nature '.   Indeed, the interference of
certain ' traits of human nature ', such as our susceptibility to
propaganda, may sometimes lead to deviations from the economic
behaviour just mentioned.   Furthermore, if the social situation
is different from the one envisaged, then it is possible that the
consumer, by the action of buying, may indirectly contribute to
a cheapening of the article ; for instance, by making its mass-
production more profitable.   And although this effect happens to
further his interest as a consumer, it may have been caused just
as involuntarily as the opposite effect, and altogether under precisely similar psychological conditions.   It seems clear that the
social situations which may lead to such widely different unwanted

or unintended repercussions must be studied by a social science which is not bound to the prejudice that ' it is imperative never to introduce any generalization into the social sciences until sufficient grounds can be pointed out in human nature ', as Mill said [12]. They must be studied by an autonomous social science.

Continuing this argument against psychologism we may say that our actions are to a very large extent explicable in terms of the situation in which they occur. Of course, they are never fully explicable in terms of the situation alone ; an explanation of the way in which a man, when crossing a street, dodges the cars which move on it may go beyond the situation, and may refer his motives, to an ' instinct ' of self-preservation, or to his wish to avoid pain, etc. But this ' psychological ' part of the explanation is very often trivial, as compared with the detailed determination of his action by what we may call the *logic of the situation* ; and besides, it is impossible to include all psychological factors in the description of the situation. The analysis of situations, the situational logic, plays a very important part in social life as well as in the social sciences. It is, in fact, the method of economic analysis. As to an example outside economics, I refer to the ' logic of power ' [13], which we may use in order to explain the moves of power politics as well as the working of certain political institutions. The method of applying a situational logic to the social sciences is not based on any psychological assumption concerning the rationality (or otherwise) of ' human nature '. On the contrary : when we speak of ' rational behaviour ' or of ' irrational behaviour ' then we mean behaviour which is, or which is not, in accordance with the logic of that situation. In fact, the psychological analysis of an action in terms of its (rational or irrational) motives presupposes—as has been pointed out by Max Weber [14]—that we have previously developed some standard of what is to be considered as rational in the situation in question.

My arguments against psychologism should not be misunderstood [15]. They are not, of course, intended to show that psychological studies and discoveries are of little importance for the social scientist. They mean, rather, that psychology—the psychology of the individual—is one of the social sciences, even though it is not the basis of all social science. Nobody would deny the importance for political science of psychological facts such as the craving for power, and the various neurotic phenomena connected with it. But ' craving for power ' is undoubtedly a social notion as well as a psychological one : we must not forget that, if we study, for example, the first appearance in childhood of this craving, then we study it in the setting of a certain social institution, for example, that of our modern family. (The Eskimo family may give rise to rather different phenomena.) Another psychological fact which is significant for sociology, and which raises grave political and institutional problems, is that to live in the haven of a tribe, or of a 'community' approaching a tribe, is for many men an emotional necessity (especially for young people who, perhaps in accordance with a parallelism between ontogenetic and phylogenetic development, seem to have to pass through a tribal or 'American-Indian' stage). That my attack on psychologism is not intended as an attack on all psychological considerations may be seen from the use I have made (in chapter 10) of such a concept as the 'strain of civilization' which is partly the result of this unsatisfied emotional need. This concept refers to certain feelings of uneasiness, and is therefore a psychological concept. But at the same time, it is a sociological concept also ; for it characterizes these feelings not only as unpleasant and unsettling, etc., but relates them to a certain social situation, and to the contrast between an open and a closed society. (Many psychological concepts such as ambition or love have an analogous status.) Also, we must not overlook the great merits which psychologism has acquired by advocating a methodological individualism and by opposing a methodological collectivism ; for it lends support to the important doctrine that all social phenomena, and especially the functioning of all social institutions, should always be understood as resulting from the decisions, actions, attitudes, etc., of human individuals, and that we should never be satisfied by an explanation in terms of so-called 'collectives' (states, nations, races, etc.). The mistake of psychologism is its presumption that this methodological individualism in the field of social science implies the programme of reducing all social phenomena and all social regularities to psychological phenomena and psychological laws. The danger of this presumption is its inclination towards historicism, as we have seen. That it is unwarranted is shown by the need for a theory of the unintended social repercussions of our actions, and by the need for what I have described as the logic of social situations.

In defending and developing Marx's view that the problems of society are irreducible to those of 'human nature', I have permitted myself to go beyond the arguments actually propounded by Marx. Marx did not speak of 'psychologism', nor did he criticize it systematically ; nor was it Mill whom he had in mind in the epigram quoted at the beginning of this chapter. The force of this epigram is directed, rather, against ' idealism ', in its Hegelian form. Yet so far as the problem of the psychological nature of society is concerned, Mill's psychologism can be said to coincide with the idealist theory combated by Marx [16]. As it happened, however, it was just the influence of another element in Hegelianism, namely Hegel's Platonizing collectivism, his theory that the state and the nation is more ' real ' than the individual who owes everything to them, that led Marx to the view expounded in this chapter. (An instance of the fact that one can sometimes extract a valuable suggestion even from an absurd philosophical theory.) Thus, historically, Marx developed certain of Hegel's views concerning the superiority of society over the individual, and used them as arguments against other views of Hegel. Yet since I consider Mill a worthier opponent than Hegel, I have not kept to the history of Marx's ideas, but have tried to develop them in the form of an argument against Mill.

To see Marx presented in this way, that is to say, as an opponent of any psychological theory of society, may possibly surprise some Marxists as well as some Anti-Marxists. For there seem to be many who believe in a very different story. Marx, they think, taught the all-pervading influence of the economic motive in the life of men ; he succeeded in explaining its over-powering strength by showing that ' man's overmastering need was to get the means of living ' [1] ; he thus demonstrated the fundamental importance of such categories as the profit motive or the motive of class interest for the actions not only of individuals but also of social groups ; and he showed how to use these categories for explaining the course of history. Indeed, they think that the very essence of Marxism is the doctrine that *economic motives* and especially *class interest* are the driving forces of history, and that it is precisely this doctrine to which the name *'materialistic interpretation of history'* or *'historical materialism'* alludes, a name by which Marx and Engels tried to characterize the essence of their teaching.

Such opinions are very common ; but I have no doubt that they misinterpret Marx. Those who admire him for having held them, I may call Vulgar Marxists (alluding to the name ' Vulgar Economist ' given by Marx to certain of his opponents [2]). The average Vulgar Marxist believes that Marxism lays bare the sinister secrets of social life by revealing the hidden motives of greed and lust for material gain which actuate the powers behind the scenes of history ; powers that cunningly and consciously create war, depression, unemployment, hunger in the midst of plenty, and all the other forms of social misery, in order to gratify their vile desires for profit. (And the Vulgar Marxist is sometimes seriously concerned with the problem of reconciling the claims of Marx with those of Freud and Adler ; and if he does not choose the one or the other of them, he may perhaps decide that hunger, love and lust for power [3] are the Three Great Hidden Motives of Human Nature brought to light by Marx, Freud, and Adler, the Three Great Makers of the modern man's philosophy. . .)

Whether or not such views are tenable and attractive, they certainly seem to have very little to do with the doctrine which

Marx called ' historical materialism '.   It must be admitted that
he sometimes speaks of such psychological phenomena as greed
and the profit motive, etc., but never in order to explain history.
He interpreted them, rather, as symptoms of the corrupting
influence of the *social system*, i.e. of a system of institutions
developed during the course of history ; as effects rather than
causes of corruption ; as repercussions rather than moving forces
of history.   Rightly or wrongly, he saw in such phenomena as
war, depression, unemployment, and hunger in the midst of
plenty, not the result of a cunning conspiracy on the part of
' big business ' or of ' imperialist war-mongers ', but the unwanted
social consequences of actions, directed towards different results,
by agents who are caught in the network of the social system.   He
looked upon the human actors on the stage of history, including
the ' big ' ones, as mere puppets, irresistibly pulled by economic
wires—by historical forces over which they have no control.   The
stage of history, he taught, is set in a social system which binds
us all ; it is set in the ' kingdom of necessity '.   (But one day
the puppets will destroy this system and attain the ' kingdom of
freedom '.)

This doctrine of Marx's has been abandoned by most of his
followers—perhaps for propagandist reasons, perhaps because
they did not understand him—and a Vulgar Marxist Conspiracy
Theory has very largely replaced the ingenious and highly original
Marxian doctrine.   It is a sad intellectual come-down, this come-
down from the level of *Capital* to that of *The Myth of the 20th
Century*.

Yet such was Marx's own philosophy of history, usually called
' historical materialism '.   It will be the main theme of these
chapters.   In the present chapter, I shall explain in broad outlines its ' materialist ' or economic emphasis ; after that, I shall
discuss in more detail the rôle of class war and class interest and
the Marxist conception of a ' social system '.

I

The exposition of Marx's economic historicism [4] can be
conveniently linked up with our comparison between Marx and
Mill.   Marx agrees with Mill in the belief that social phenomena
must be explained historically, and that we must try to understand any historical period as a historical product of previous
developments.   The point where he departs from Mill is, as
we have seen, Mill's psychologism (corresponding to Hegel's

idealism).   This is replaced in Marx's teaching by what he calls *materialism*.

Much has been said about Marx's materialism that is quite untenable.   The often repeated claim that Marx does not recognize anything beyond the ' lower ' or ' material ' aspects of human life is an especially ridiculous distortion.   (It is another repetition of that most ancient of all reactionary libels against the defenders of freedom, Heraclitus' slogan that ' they fill their bellies like the beasts ' [5].)   But in this sense, Marx cannot be called a materialist at all, even though he was strongly influenced by the eighteenth-century French Materialists, and even though he used to call himself a materialist, which is well in keeping with a good number of his doctrines.   For there are some important passages which can hardly be interpreted as materialistic.   The truth is, I think, that he was not much concerned with purely philosophical issues—less than Engels or Lenin, for instance— and that it was mainly the sociological and methodological side of the problem in which he was interested.

There is a well-known passage in *Capital* [6], where Marx says that ' in Hegel's writing, dialectics stands on its head ; one must turn it the right way up again . .'   Its tendency is clear.   Marx wished to show that the ' head ', i.e. human thought, is not itself the basis of human life but rather a kind of superstructure, on a physical basis.   A similar tendency is expressed in the passage :   ' The ideal is nothing other than the material when it has been transposed and translated inside the human head.' But it has not, perhaps, been sufficiently recognized that these passages do not exhibit a radical form of materialism ; rather, they indicate a certain leaning towards a dualism of body and mind.   It is, so to speak, a practical dualism.   Although, theoretically, mind was to Marx apparently only another *form* (or another aspect, or perhaps an epi-phenomenon) of matter, in practice it is different from matter, since it is *another* form of it. The passages quoted indicate that although our feet have to be kept, as it were, on the firm ground of the material world, our heads—and Marx thought highly of human heads—are concerned with thoughts or ideas.   In my opinion, Marxism and its influence cannot be appreciated unless we recognize this dualism.

Marx loved freedom, real freedom (not Hegel's ' real freedom ').   And as far as I am able to see he followed Hegel's famous equation of freedom with spirit, in so far as he believed that we can be free only as spiritual beings.   At the same time he recognized in practice (as a practical dualist) that we are spirit *and* flesh, and, realistically enough, that the flesh is the fundamental one of these two. This is why he turned against Hegel, and why he said that Hegel puts things upside down. But although he recognized that the material world and its necessities are fundamental, he did not feel any love for the ' kingdom of necessity ', as he called a society which is in bondage to its material needs. He cherished the spiritual world, the ' kingdom of freedom ', and the spiritual side of ' human nature ', as much as any Christian dualist ; and in his writings there are even traces of hatred and contempt for the material. What follows may show that this interpretation of Marx's views can be supported by his own text.

In a passage of the third volume of *Capital* [7], Marx very aptly describes the material side of social life, and especially its economic side, that of production and consumption, as an extension of human metabolism, i.e. of man's exchange of matter with nature. He clearly states that our freedom must always be limited by the necessities of this metabolism. All that can be achieved in the direction of making us more free, he says, is ' to conduct this metabolism rationally, . . with a minimum expenditure of energy and under conditions most dignified and adequate to human nature. Yet it will still remain the kingdom of necessity. Only outside and beyond it can that development of human faculties begin which constitutes an end in itself—the true kingdom of freedom. But this can flourish only on the ground occupied by the kingdom of necessity, which remains its basis . .' Immediately before this, Marx says : ' The kingdom of freedom actually begins only where drudgery, enforced by hardship and by external purposes, ends ; it thus lies, quite naturally, beyond the sphere of proper material production.' And he ends the whole passage by drawing a practical conclusion which clearly shows that it was his sole aim to open the way into that non-materialist kingdom of freedom for all men alike : ' The shortening of the labour day is the fundamental pre-requisite. '

In my opinion this passage leaves no doubt regarding what I have called the dualism of Marx's practical view of life. With Hegel he thinks that freedom is the aim of historical development. With Hegel he identifies the realm of freedom with that of man's mental life. But he recognizes that we are not purely spiritual beings ; that we are not fully free, nor capable of ever achieving full freedom, unable as we shall always be to emancipate ourselves entirely from the necessities of our metabolism, and thus from productive toil. All we can achieve is to improve upon the exhausting and undignified conditions of labour, to make them more worthy of man, to equalize them, and to reduce drudgery to such an extent that *all of us can be free for some part of our lives*. This, I believe, is the central idea of Marx's ' view of life ' ; central also in so far as it seems to me to be the most influential of his doctrines.

With this view, we must now combine the methodological determinism which has been discussed above (in chapter 13). According to this doctrine, the scientific treatment of society, and scientific historical prediction, are possible only in so far as society is determined by its past. But this implies that science can deal only with the kingdom of necessity. If it were possible for men ever to become perfectly free, then historical prophecy, and with it, social science, would come to an end. ' Free ' spiritual activity as such, if it existed, would lie beyond the reach of science, which must always ask for causes, for determinants. It can therefore deal with our mental life only in so far as our thoughts and ideas are caused or determined or necessitated by the ' kingdom of necessity ', by the material, and especially by the economic conditions of our life, by our metabolism. Thoughts and ideas can be treated scientifically only by considering, on the one hand, the material conditions under which they originated, i.e. the economic conditions of the life of the men who originated them, and on the other hand, the material conditions under which they were assimilated, i.e. the economic conditions of the men who adopted them. Hence from the scientific or causal point of view, thoughts and ideas must be treated as ' ideological superstructures on the basis of economic conditions '. Marx, in opposition to Hegel, contended that the clue to history, even to the history of ideas, is to be found in the development of the relations between man and his natural environment, the material world ; that is to say, in his economic life, and not in his spiritual life. This is why we may describe Marx's brand of historicism as *economism*, as opposed to Hegel's idealism or to Mill's psychologism. But it signifies a complete misunderstanding if we identify Marx's economism with that kind of materialism which implies a depreciatory attitude towards man's mental life. Marx's vision of the ' kingdom of freedom ', i.e. of a partial but equitable liberation of men from the bondage of their material nature, might rather be described as idealistic.

Considered in this way, the Marxist view of life appears to be consistent enough ; and I believe that such apparent contradictions and difficulties as have been found in its partly determinist and partly libertarian view of human activities disappear.

II

The bearing of what I have called Marx's dualism and his scientific determinism on his view of history is plain.   Scientific history, which to him is identical with social science as a whole, must explore the laws according to which man's exchange of matter with nature develops.   Its central task must be the explanation of the development of the conditions of production. Social relationships have historical and scientific significance only in proportion to the degree in which they are bound up with the productive process—affecting it, or perhaps affected by it. ' Just as the savage must wrestle with nature in order to satisfy his needs, to keep alive, and to reproduce, so must the civilized man ; and he must continue to do so in all forms of society and under all possible forms of production.   This kingdom of necessity expands with its development, and so does the range of human needs.   Yet at the same time, there is an expansion of the productive forces which satisfy these needs.' [8]   This, in brief, is Marx's view of man's history.

Similar views are expressed by Engels.   The expansion of modern means of production, according to Engels, has created ' for the first time . . the possibility of securing for every member of society . . an existence not only . . sufficient from a material point of view, but also . . warranting the . . development and exercise of his physical and mental faculties ' [9]. With this, freedom becomes possible, i.e. the emancipation from the flesh. ' At this point . . man finally cuts himself off from the animal world, leaves . . animal existence behind him and enters conditions which are really human.'   Man is in fetters exactly in so far as he is dominated by economics ; when ' the domination of the product over producers disappears . . , man . . becomes, for the first time, the conscious and real master of nature, by becoming master of his own social environment . .   Not until then will man himself, in full consciousness, make his own history . .   It is humanity's leap from the realm of necessity into the realm of freedom.'

If now again we compare Marx's version of historicism with

that of Mill, then we find that Marx's economism can easily solve the difficulty which I have shown to be fatal to Mill's psychologism. I have in mind the rather monstrous doctrine of a beginning of society which can be explained in psychological terms—a doctrine which I have described as the psychologistic version of the social contract. This idea has no parallel in Marx's theory. To replace the priority of psychology by the priority of economics creates no analogous difficulty, since ' economics ' covers man's metabolism, the exchange of matter between man and nature. Whether this metabolism has always been socially organized, even in pre-human times, or whether it was once dependent solely on the individual, can be left an open question. No more is assumed than that the science of society must coincide with the history of the development of the economic conditions of society, usually called by Marx ' the conditions of production '.

It may be noted, in parentheses, that the Marxist term ' production ' was certainly intended to be used in a wide sense, covering the whole economic process, including distribution and consumption. But these latter never received much attention from Marx and the Marxists. Their prevailing interest remained production in the narrow sense of the word. This is just another example of the naïve historico-genetic attitude, of the belief that science must only ask for causes, so that, even in the realm of man-made things, it must ask ' Who has made it ? ' and ' What is it made of ? ' rather than ' Who is going to use it ? ' and ' What is it made for ? '

III

If we now proceed to a criticism as well as to an appreciation of Marx's ' historical materialism ', or of so much of it as has been presented so far, then we may distinguish two different aspects. The first is historicism, the claim that the realm of social sciences coincides with that of the historical or evolutionary method, and especially with historical prophecy. This claim, I think, must be dismissed. The second is economism (or ' materialism '), i.e. the claim that the economic organization of society, the organization of our exchange of matter with nature, is fundamental for all social institutions and especially for their historical development. This claim, I believe, is perfectly sound, so long as we take the term ' fundamental ' in an ordinary vague sense, not laying too much stress upon it. In other words, there can be no doubt that practically all social studies, whether institutional or historical, may profit if they are carried out with an eye to the ' economic conditions' of society. Even the history of an abstract science such as mathematics is no exception [10]. In this sense, Marx's economism can be said to represent an extremely valuable advance in the methods of social science.

But, as I said before, we must not take the term ' fundamental' too seriously. Marx himself undoubtedly did so. Owing to his Hegelian upbringing, he was influenced by the ancient distinction between ' reality' and ' appearance', and by the corresponding distinction between what is ' essential' and what is ' accidental'. His own improvement upon Hegel (and Kant) he was inclined to see in the identification of ' reality' with the material world [11] (including man's metabolism), and of ' appearance' with the world of thoughts or ideas. Thus all thoughts and ideas would have to be explained by reducing them to the underlying essential reality, i.e. to economic conditions. This philosophical view is certainly not much better [12] than any other form of essentialism. And its repercussions in the field of method must result in an over-emphasis upon economism. For *although the general importance of Marx's economism can hardly be overrated, it is very easy to overrate the importance of the economic conditions in any particular case.* Some knowledge of economic conditions may contribute considerably, for example, to a history of the problems of mathematics, but a knowledge of the problems of mathematics themselves is much more important for that purpose ; and it is even possible to write a very good history of mathematical problems without referring at all to their ' economic background'. (In my opinion, the ' economic conditions' or the ' social relations' of science are themes which can easily be overdone, and which are liable to degenerate into platitude.)

This, however, is only a minor example of the danger of over-stressing economism. Often it is sweepingly interpreted as the doctrine that all social development depends upon that of economic conditions, and especially upon the development of the physical means of production. But such a doctrine is palpably false. There is an interaction between economic conditions and ideas, and not simply a unilateral dependence of the latter on the former. If anything, we might even assert that certain ' ideas', those which constitute our knowledge, are more fundamental than the more complex material means of production, as may be seen from the following consideration. Imagine that our economic system, including all machinery and all social organizations, was destroyed one day, but that technical and scientific knowledge was preserved. In such a case it might conceivably not take very long before it was reconstructed (on a smaller scale, and after many had starved). But imagine *all knowledge* of these matters to disappear, while the material things were preserved. This would be tantamount to what would happen if a savage tribe occupied a highly industrialized but deserted country. It would soon lead to the complete disappearance of all the material relics of civilization.

It is ironical that the history of Marxism itself furnishes an example that clearly falsifies this exaggerated economism. 'Marx's *idea* 'Workers of all countries, unite!' was of the greatest significance down to the eve of the Russian Revolution, and it had its influence upon economic conditions. But with the revolution, the situation became very difficult, simply because, as Lenin himself admitted, there were no further constructive ideas. (See chapter 13.) Then Lenin had some new ideas which may be briefly summarized in the slogan : ' Socialism is the dictatorship of the proletariat, plus the widest introduction of the most modern electrical machinery.' It was this new idea that became the basis of a development which changed the whole economic and material background of one-sixth of the world. In a fight against tremendous odds, uncounted material difficulties were overcome, uncounted material sacrifices were made, in order to alter, or rather, to build up from nothing, the conditions of production. And the driving power of this development was the enthusiasm for an *idea*. This example shows that in certain circumstances, ideas may revolutionize the economic conditions of a country, instead of being moulded by these conditions. Using Marx's terminology, we could say that he had underrated the power of the kingdom of freedom and its chances of conquering the kingdom of necessity.

The glaring contrast between the development of the Russian Revolution and Marx's metaphysical theory of an economic reality and its ideological appearance can best be seen from the following passages : ' In considering such revolutions ', Marx writes, ' it is necessary always to distinguish between the material revolution in the economic conditions of production, which fall within the scope of exact scientific determination, and the juridical, political, religious, æsthetic, or philosophic—in a word, ideological forms of appearance . .' [13] In Marx's view, it is vain to expect that any important change can be achieved by the use of legal or political means ; a *political revolution* can only lead to one set of rulers giving way to another set—a mere exchange of the persons who act as rulers. Only the evolution of the underlying essence, the economic reality, can produce any essential or real change—a *social revolution*. And only when such a social revolution has become a reality, only then can a political revolution be of any significance. But even in this case, the political revolution is only the outward expression of the essential or real change that has occurred before. In accordance with this theory, Marx asserts that every social revolution develops in the following way. The material conditions of production grow and mature until they begin to conflict with the social and legal relations, outgrowing them like clothes, until they burst. ' Then an epoch of social revolution opens ', Marx writes. ' With the change in the economic foundation, the whole vast superstructure is more or less rapidly transformed . . New, more highly productive relationships ' (within the superstructure) ' never come into being before the material conditions for their existence have been brought to maturity within the womb of the old society itself.' In view of this statement, it is, I believe, impossible to identify the Russian Revolution with the social revolution prophesied by Marx ; it has, in fact, no similarity with it whatever [14].

It may be noted in this connection that Marx's friend, the poet H. Heine, thought very differently about these matters. ' Mark this, ye proud men of action ', he writes ; ' ye are nothing but unconscious instruments of the men of thought who, often in humblest seclusion, have appointed you to your inevitable task. Maximilian Robespierre was merely the hand of Jean-Jacques Rousseau . .' [15] (Something like this might perhaps be said of the relationship between Lenin and Marx.) We see that Heine was, in Marx's terminology, an idealist, and that he applied his idealistic interpretation of history to the French Revolution, which was one of the most important instances used by Marx in favour of his economism, and which indeed seemed to fit this doctrine not so badly—especially if we compare it now with the Russian Revolution. Yet in spite of this heresy, Heine remained Marx's friend [16] ; for in those happy days, excommunication for heresy was still rather uncommon among those who fought for the open society, and tolerance was still tolerated.

My criticism of Marx's ' historical materialism ' must certainly not be interpreted as expressing any preference for Hegelian 'idealism' over Marx's 'materialism'; I hope I have made it clear that in this conflict between idealism and materialism my sympathies are with Marx. What I wish to show is that Marx's 'materialist interpretation of history', valuable as it may be, must not be taken too seriously; that we must regard it as nothing more than a most valuable suggestion to us to consider things in their relation to their economic background.

Chapter 16 : THE CLASSES

An important place among the various formulations of Marx's ' historical materialism ' is occupied by his (and Engels') statement : ' The history of all hitherto existing society is a history of class struggle.' [1] The tendency of this statement is clear. It implies that history is propelled and the fate of man determined by the war of classes and not by the war of nations (as opposed to the views of Hegel and of the majority of historians). In the causal explanation of historical developments, including national wars, class interest must take the place of that allegedly national interest which, in reality, is only the interest of a nation's ruling class. But over and above this, class struggle and class interest are capable of explaining phenomena which traditional history may in general not even attempt to explain. An example of such a phenomenon which is of great significance for Marxist theory is the historical trend towards increasing productivity. Even though it may perhaps record such a trend, traditional history, with its fundamental category of military power, is quite unable to explain this phenomenon. Class interest and class war, however, can explain it fully, according to Marx ; indeed, a considerable part of *Capital* is devoted to the analysis of the mechanism by which, within the period called by Marx ' capitalism ', an increase in productivity is brought about by these forces.

How is the doctrine of class war related to the institutionalist doctrine of the autonomy of sociology discussed above [2] ? At first sight it may seem that these two doctrines are in open conflict, for in the doctrine of class war, a fundamental part is played by class interest, which apparently is a kind of *motive*. But I do not think that there is any serious inconsistency in this part of Marx's theory. And I should even say that nobody has understood Marx, and particularly that major achievement of his, anti-psychologism, who does not see how it can be reconciled with the theory of class struggle. We need not assume, as Vulgar Marxists do, that class interest must be interpreted psychologically. There may be a few passages in Marx's own writings that savour a little of this Vulgar Marxism, but wherever he makes serious use of anything like class interest, he always means a thing within the realm of autonomous sociology, and not a psychological category. He means a thing, a situation, and not a state of mind, a thought, or a feeling of being interested in a thing. It is simply that thing or that social institution or situation which is advantageous to a class. The interest of a class is simply everything that furthers its power or its prosperity.

According to Marx, class interest in this institutional, or, if we may say so, ' objective ', sense exerts a decisive influence on human minds. Using Hegelian jargon, we might say that the objective interest of a class becomes conscious in the subjective minds of its members ; it makes them class-interested and class-conscious, and it makes them act accordingly. Class interest as an institutional or objective social situation, and its influence upon human minds, is described by · Marx in the epigram which I have quoted (at the beginning of chapter 14) : ' It is not the consciousness of man that determines his existence— rather, it is his social existence that determines his consciousness.' To this epigram we need add only the remark that it is, more precisely, the place where man stands in society, his class situation, by which, according to Marxism, his consciousness is determined.

Marx gives some indication of how this process of determination works. As we learned from him in the last chapter, we can be free only in so far as we emancipate ourselves from the productive process. But now we shall learn that, in any hitherto existing society, we were not free even to that extent. For how could we, he asks, emancipate ourselves from the productive process ? Only by making others do the dirty work for us. We are thus forced to use them as means for our ends ; we must degrade them. We can buy a greater degree of freedom only at the cost of enslaving other men, by splitting mankind into *classes* ; the ruling class gains freedom at the cost of the ruled class, the slaves. But this fact has the consequence that the members of the ruling class must pay for their freedom by a new kind of bondage. They are *bound* to oppress and to fight the ruled, if they wish to preserve their own freedom and their own status ; they are compelled to do this, since he who does not do so ceases to belong to the ruling class. Thus the rulers are determined by their class situation ; they cannot escape from their social relation to the ruled ; they are bound to them, since they are bound to the social metabolism. Thus all, rulers as well as ruled, are caught in the net, and forced to fight one another. According to Marx, it is this bondage, this determination, which brings their struggle within the reach of scientific method, and of scientific historical prophecy ; which makes it possible to treat the history of society scientifically, as the history of class struggle.   This social net in which the classes are caught, and forced to struggle against one another, is what Marxism calls the economic structure of society, or the social system.

According to this theory, social systems or class systems change with the conditions of production, since on these condi- tions depends the way in which the rulers can exploit and fight the ruled.   To every particular period of economic development corresponds a particular social system, and a historical period is best characterized by its social system of classes ; this is why we speak of ' feudalism ', ' capitalism ', etc.   ' The hand-mill ', Marx writes [3], ' gives you a society with the feudal lord ; the steam-mill gives you a society with the industrial capitalist.' The class relations that characterize the social system are inde- pendent of the individual man's will.   The social system thus resembles a vast machine in which the individuals are caught and crushed.   ' In the social production of their means of existence ', Marx writes [4], ' men enter into definite and unavoid- able relations which are independent of their will.   These productive relationships correspond to the particular stage in the development of their material productive forces.   The system of all these productive relationships constitutes the economic structure of society ', i.e. the social system.

Although it has a kind of logic of its own, this social system works blindly, not reasonably.   Those who are caught in its machinery are, in general, blind too—or nearly so.   They cannot even foresee some of the most important repercussions of their actions.   One man may make it impossible for many to procure an article which is available in large quantities ; he may buy just a trifle and thereby prevent a slight decrease of price at a critical moment.   Another may in the goodness of his heart distribute his riches, but by thus contributing to a lessening of the class struggle, he may cause a delay in the libera- tion of the oppressed.   Since it is quite impossible to foresee the more remote social repercussions of our actions, since we are one and all caught in the network, we cannot seriously attempt to cope with it.   We obviously cannot influence it from outside ; but blind as we are, we cannot even make any plan for its improvement from within.   Social engineering is impossible, and a social technology therefore useless.   We cannot impose our interests upon the social system ; instead, the system forces upon us what we are led to *believe* to be our interests. It does so by forcing us to act in accordance with our class interest. It is vain to lay on the individual, even on the individual ' capitalist ' or ' bourgeois ', the blame for the injustice, for the immorality of social conditions, since it is this very system of conditions that forces the capitalist to act as he does. And it is also vain to hope that circumstances may be improved by improving men ; rather, men will be better if the system in which they live is better. ' Only in so far ', Marx writes in *Capital* [5], ' as the capitalist is personified capital does he play a historical rôle . . But exactly to that extent, his motive is not to obtain and to enjoy useful commodities, but to increase the production of commodities for exchange ' (his real historical task). ' Fanatically bent upon the expansion of value, he ruthlessly drives human beings to produce for production's sake . . With the miser, he shares the passion for wealth. But what is a kind of mania in the miser is in the capitalist the effect of the social mechanism in which he is only a driving-wheel . . Capitalism subjects any individual capitalist to the immanent laws of capitalist production, laws which are external and coercive. Without respite, competition forces him to extend his capital for the sake of maintaining it.'

This is the way in which, according to Marx, the social system determines the actions of the individual ; the ruler as well as the ruled ; capitalist or bourgeois as well as proletarian. It is an illustration of what has been called above the ' logic of a social situation '. To a considerable degree, all the actions of a capitalist are ' a mere function of the capital which, through his instrumentality, is endowed with will and consciousness ', as Marx puts it [6], in his Hegelian style. But this means that the social system determines their thoughts too ; for thoughts, or ideas, are partly *instruments* of actions, and partly—that is, if they are publicly expressed—an important *kind* of social action ; for in this case, they are immediately aimed at influencing the actions of other members of the society. By thus determining human thoughts, the social system, and especially the ' objective interest ' of a class, becomes conscious in the subjective minds of its members (as we said before in Hegelian jargon [7]). Class struggle, as well as competition between the members of the same class, are the means by which this is achieved.

We have seen why, according to Marx, social engineering,

and consequently, a social technology, are impossible ; it is
because the causal chain of dependence binds us to the social
system, and not *vice versa*. But although we cannot alter the
social system at will [8], capitalists as well as workers are bound
to contribute to its transformation, and to our ultimate liberation
from its fetters. By driving ' human beings to produce for
production's sake ' [9], the capitalist coerces them ' to develop
the forces of social productivity, and to create those material
conditions of production which alone can form the material
bases of a higher type of society whose fundamental principle
is the full and free development of every human individual.'
In this way, even the members of the capitalist class must play
their rôle on the stage of history and further the ultimate coming
of socialism.

In view of subsequent arguments, a linguistic remark may be
added here on the Marxist terms usually translated by the words
' class-conscious ' and ' class consciousness '. These terms indicate, first of all, the result of the process analysed above, by
which the objective class situation (class interest as well as class
struggle) gains consciousness in the minds of its members, or,
to express the same thought in a language less dependent on
Hegel, by which members of a class become conscious of their
class situation. Being class-conscious, they know not only their
place but their true class interest as well. But over and above
this, the original German word used by Marx suggests something
which is usually lost in the translation. The term is derived
from, and alludes to, a common German word which became
part of Hegel's jargon. Though its literal translation would be
' self-conscious ', this word has even in common use rather the
meaning of being *conscious of one's worth and powers*, i.e. of being
proud and fully assured of oneself, and even self-satisfied. Accordingly, the term translated as ' class-conscious ' means in
German not simply this, but rather, ' assured or proud of one's
class ', and bound to it by the consciousness of the need for
solidarity. This is why Marx and the Marxists apply it nearly
exclusively to the workers, and hardly ever to the ' bourgeoisie '.
The class-conscious proletarian—this is the worker who is not
only aware of his class situation, but who is also class-proud,
fully assured of the historical mission of his class, and believing
that its unflinching fight will bring about a better world.

How does he know that this will happen ? Because being
class-conscious, he must be a Marxist. The Marxist theory

itself and its scientific prophecy of the advent of socialism are part and parcel of the historical process by which the class situation ' emerges into consciousness ', establishing itself in the minds of the workers.

II

My criticism of Marx's theory of the classes, as far as its historicist emphasis goes, follows the lines taken up in the last chapter. The formula ' all history is a history of class struggle ' is very valuable as a suggestion that we should look into the important part played by class struggle in power politics as well as in other developments ; this suggestion is the more valuable since Plato's brilliant analysis of the part played by class struggle in the history of Greek city states was only rarely taken up in later times. But again, we must not, of course, take Marx's word ' all ' too seriously. Not even the history of class issues is always a history of class struggle in the Marxian sense, considering the important part played by dissension within the classes themselves. Indeed, the divergence of interests within both the ruling and the ruled classes goes so far that Marx's theory of classes must be considered as a dangerous over-simplification, even if we admit that the issue between the rich and the poor is always of fundamental importance. One of the great themes of medieval history, the fight between popes and emperors, is an example of dissension within the ruling class. It would be palpably false to interpret this quarrel as one between exploiter and exploited. (Of course, one can widen Marx's concept ' class ' so as to cover this and similar cases, and narrow the concept ' history ', until ultimately Marx's doctrine becomes trivially true—a mere tautology ; but this would rob it of any significance.)

One of the dangers of Marx's formula is that if taken too seriously, it misleads Marxists into interpreting all political conflicts as struggles between exploiters and exploited (or else as attempts to cover up the ' real issue ', the underlying class conflict). As a consequence there were Marxists, especially in Germany, who interpreted a war such as the First World War as one between the revolutionary or ' have-not ' Central Powers and an alliance of conservative or ' have ' countries—a kind of interpretation which might be used to excuse any aggression. This is only one example of the danger inherent in Marx's sweeping historicist generalization.

On the other hand, his attempt to use what may be called the ' logic of the class situation ' to explain the working of the institutions of the industrial system seems to me admirable, in spite of certain exaggerations and the neglect of some important aspects of the situation ; admirable, at least, as a sociological analysis of that stage of the industrial system which Marx has mainly in mind : the system of ' unrestrained capitalism ' (as I shall call it [10]) of one hundred years ago.

Chapter 17 : THE LEGAL AND THE SOCIAL SYSTEM

We are now ready to approach what is probably the most crucial point in our analysis as well as in our criticism of Marxism ; it is Marx's theory of the state and—paradoxical as it may sound to some—of the impotence of all politics.

I

Marx's theory of the state can be presented by combining the results of the last two chapters. The legal or juridico-political system—the system of legal institutions enforced by the state—has to be understood, according to Marx, as one of the superstructures erected upon, and giving expression to, the actual productive forces of the economic system ; Marx speaks [1] in this connection of 'juridical and political superstructures'. It is not, of course, the only way in which the economic or material reality and the relations between the classes which correspond to it make their appearance in the world of ideologies and ideas. Another example of such a superstructure would be, according to Marxist views, the prevailing moral system. This, as opposed to the legal system, is not enforced by state power, but sanctioned by an ideology created and controlled by the ruling class. The difference is, roughly, one between persuasion and force (as Plato [2] would have said) ; and it is the state, the legal or political system, which uses force. It is, as Engels [3] puts it, ' a special repressive force ' for the coercion of the ruled by the rulers. ' Political power, properly so called,' says the *Manifesto* [4], ' is merely the organized power of one class for oppressing the other.' A similar description is given by Lenin [5] : ' According to Marx, the state is an organ of class *domination*, an organ for the oppression of one class by another ; its aim is the creation of an ' order ' which legalizes and per-petuates this oppression . .' The state, in brief, is just part of the machinery by which the ruling class carries on its struggle.

Before proceeding to develop the consequences of this view of the state, it may be pointed out that it is partly an institutional and partly an essentialist theory. It is institutional in so far as Marx tries to ascertain what practical functions legal institu-tions have in social life. But it is essentialist in so far as Marx neither inquires into the variety of ends which these institutions may possibly serve (or be made to serve), nor suggests what institutional reforms are necessary in order to make the state serve those ends which he himself might deem desirable.   Instead of making his demands or proposals concerning the functions which he wants the state, the legal institutions or the government to perform, he asks, ' *What is* the state ? ' ; that is to say, he tries to discover the *essential* function of legal institutions.   It has been shown before [6] that such a typically essentialist question cannot be answered in a satisfactory way ; yet this question, undoubtedly, is in keeping with Marx's essentialist and metaphysical approach which interprets the field of ideas and norms as the appearance of an economic reality.

What are the consequences of this theory of the state ?   The most important consequence is that all politics, all legal and political institutions as well as all political struggles, can never be of primary importance.   *Politics are impotent.*   They can never alter decisively the economic reality.   The main if not the only task of any enlightened political activity is to see that the alterations in the juridico-political cloak keep pace with the changes in the social reality, that is to say, in the means of production and in the relations between the classes ; in this way, such difficulties as must arise if politics lag behind these developments can be avoided.   Or in other words, political developments are either superficial, unconditioned by the deeper reality of the social system, in which case they are doomed to be unimportant, and can never be of real help to the suppressed and exploited ; or else they give expression to a change in the economic background and the class situation, in which case they are of the character of volcanic eruptions, of complete revolutions which can perhaps be foreseen, as they arise from the social system, and whose ferocity might then be mitigated by non-resistance to the eruptive forces, but which can be neither caused nor suppressed by political action.

These consequences show again the unity of Marx's historicist system of thought.   Yet considering that few movements have done as much as Marxism to stimulate interest in political action, the theory of the fundamental impotence of politics appears somewhat paradoxical. (Marxists might, of course, meet this remark with either of two arguments.   The one is that in the theory expounded, political action *has* its function ; for even though the workers' party cannot, by its actions, improve the lot of the exploited masses, its fight awakens class consciousness and thereby prepares for the revolution. This would be the argument of the radical wing. The other argument, used by the moderate wing, asserts that there may exist historical periods in which political action can be directly helpful ; the periods, namely, in which the forces of the two opposing classes are approximately in equilibrium. In such periods, political effort and energy may be decisive in achieving very significant improvements for the workers.—It is clear that this second argument sacrifices some of the fundamental positions of the theory, but without realizing this, and consequently without going to the root of the matter.)

It is worth noting that according to Marxist theory, the workers' party can hardly make political mistakes of any import-ance, as long as the party continues to play its assigned rôle, and to press the claims of the workers energetically. For political mistakes cannot materially affect the actual class situation, and even less the economic reality on which everything else ultimately depends.

Another important consequence of the theory is that, in principle, all government, even democratic government, is a dictatorship of the ruling class over the ruled. ' The executive of the modern state ', says the *Manifesto* [7], ' is merely a committee for managing the economic affairs of the whole bourgeoisie . .' What we call a democracy is, according to this theory, nothing but that form of class dictatorship which happens to be most convenient in a certain historical situation. (This doctrine does not agree very well with the class equilibrium theory of the moderate wing mentioned above.) And just as the state, under capitalism, is a dictatorship of the bourgeoisie, so, after the social revolution, it will at first be a dictatorship of the proletariat. But this proletarian state must lose its function as soon as the resistance of the old bourgeoisie has broken down. For the proletarian revolution leads to a one-class society, and therefore to a classless society in which there can be no class-dictatorship. Thus the state, deprived of any function, must disappear. ' *It withers away* ', as Engels said [8].

II

I am very far from defending Marx's theory of the state. His theory of the impotence of all politics, more particularly, and his view of democracy, appear to me to be not only mistakes, but fatal mistakes. But it must be admitted that behind these grim as well as ingenious theories, there stood a grim and depressing experience. And although Marx, in my opinion, failed to understand the future which he so keenly wished to foresee, it seems to me that even his mistaken theories are proof of his keen sociological insight into the conditions of his own time, and of his invincible humanitarianism and sense of justice.

Marx's theory of the state, in spite of its abstract and philosophical character, undoubtedly furnishes an enlightening interpretation of his own historical period. It is at least a tenable view that the so-called 'industrial revolution' developed at first mainly as a revolution of the 'material means of production ', i.e. of machinery ; that this led, next, to a transformation of the class structure of society, and thus to a new social system ; and that political revolutions and other transformations of the legal system came only as a third step. Even though this Marxist interpretation of the 'rise of capitalism ' has been challenged by historians who were able to lay bare some of its deep-lying ideological foundations (which were perhaps not quite unsuspected by Marx [9], although destructive to his theory), there can be little doubt about the value of the Marxist interpretation as a first approximation, and about the service rendered to his successors in this field. And even though some of the developments studied by Marx were deliberately fostered by legislative measures, and indeed made possible only by legislation (as Marx himself says [10]), it was he who first discussed the influence of economic developments and economic interests upon legislation, and the function of legislative measures as weapons in the class struggle, and especially as means for the creation of a 'surplus population ', and with it, of the industrial proletariat.

It is clear from many of Marx's passages that these observations confirmed him in his belief that the juridico-political system is a mere 'superstructure' [11] on the social, i.e. the economic, system; a theory which, although undoubtedly refuted by subsequent experience [12], not only remains interesting, but also, I suggest, contains a grain of truth.

But it.was not only Marx's general views of the relations between the economic and the political system that were in this way influenced by his historical experience ; his views on liberalism and democracy, more particularly, which he considered to be nothing but veils for the dictatorship of the bourgeoisie, furnished an interpretation of the social situation of his time which appeared to fit only too well, corroborated as it was by sad experience. For Marx lived, especially in his younger years, in a period of the most shameless and cruel exploitation. And this shameless exploitation was cynically defended by hypocritical apologists who appealed to the principle of human freedom, to the right of man to determinate his own fate, and to enter freely into any contract he considers favourable to his interests.

Using the slogan ' equal and free competition for all ', the unrestrained capitalism of this period resisted successfully all labour legislation until the year 1833, and its practical execution for many years more [13]. The consequence was a life of desolation and misery which can hardly be imagined in our day. Especially the exploitation of women and children led to incredible suffering. Here are two examples, quoted from Marx's *Capital* : ' William Wood, 9 years old, was 7 years and 10 months when he began to work . . He came to work every day in the week at 6 a.m., and left off about 9 p.m. . .' ' Fifteen hours of labour for a child 7 years old ! ' exclaims an official report [14] of the Children's Employment Commission of 1863. Other children were forced to start work at 4 a.m., or to work throughout the night until 6 a.m., and it was not unusual for children of only six years to be forced to a daily toil of 15 hours.—' Mary Anne Walkley had worked without pause 26½ hours, together with sixty other girls, thirty of them in one room . . A doctor, Mr. Keys, called in too late, testified before the coroner's jury that " Mary Anne Walkley had died from long hours of work in an over-crowded workroom . .". Wishing to give this gentleman a lecture in good manners, the coroner's jury brought in a verdict to the effect that " the deceased had died of apoplexy, but there is reason to fear that her death had been accelerated by overwork in an overcrowded workroom ".' [15] Such were the conditions of the working class even in 1863, when Marx was writing *Capital* ; his burning protest against these crimes, which were then tolerated, and sometimes even defended, not only by professional economists but also by churchmen, will secure him forever a place among the liberators of mankind.

In view of such experiences, we need not wonder that Marx did not think very highly of liberalism, and that he saw in parliamentary democracy nothing but a veiled dictatorship of the bourgeoisie. And it was easy for him to interpret these facts as supporting his analysis of the relationship between the legal and the social system. According to the legal system, equality and freedom were established, at least approximately. But what did this mean in reality ! Indeed, we must not blame Marx for insisting that the economic facts alone are ' real ' and that the legal system may be a mere superstructure, a cloak for this reality, and an instrument of class domination.

The opposition between the legal and the social system is most clearly developed in *Capital*. In one of its theoretical parts (treated more fully in chapter 20), Marx approaches the analysis of the capitalist economic system by using the simplifying and idealizing assumption that the legal system is perfect in every respect. Freedom, equality before the law, justice, are all assumed to be guaranteed to everybody. There are no privileged classes before the law. Over and above that, he assumes that not even in the economic realm is there any kind of ' robbery ' ; he assumes that a ' just price ' is paid for all commodities, including the labour power which the worker sells to the capitalist on the labour market. The price for all these commodities is ' just ', in the sense that all commodities are bought and sold in proportion to the average amount of labour needed for their reproduction (or using Marx's terminology, they are bought and sold according to their true ' value ' [16]). Of course, Marx knows that all this is an over-simplification, for it is his opinion that the workers are hardly ever treated as fairly as that ; in other words, that they are usually cheated. But arguing from these idealized premises, he attempts to show that even under so excellent a legal system, the economic system would function in such a way that the workers would not be able to enjoy their freedom. In spite of all this ' justice ', they would not be very much better off than slaves [17]. For if they are poor, they can only sell themselves, their wives and their children on the labour market, for as much as is necessary for the reproduction of their labour power. That is to say, for the whole of their labour power, they will not get more than the barest means of existence. This shows that exploitation is not merely robbery. It cannot be eliminated by merely legal means.   (And Proudhon's criticism that ' property is theft ' is much too superficial [18].)

In consequence of this, Marx was led to hold that the workers cannot hope much from the improvement of a legal system which as everybody knows grants to rich and poor alike the freedom of sleeping on park benches, and which threatens them alike with punishment for the attempt to live ' without visible means of support '. In this way Marx arrived at what may be termed (in Hegelian language) the distinction between *formal* and *material* freedom.   Formal [19] or legal freedom, although Marx does not rate it low, turns out to be quite insufficient for securing to us that freedom which he considered to be the aim of the historical development of mankind.   What matters is real, i.e. economic or material, freedom.   This can be achieved only by an equal emancipation from drudgery.   For this emancipation, ' the shortening of the labour day is the fundamental pre-requisite '.

III

What have we to say to Marx's analysis ?   Are we to believe that politics, or the framework of legal institutions, are intrinsically impotent to remedy such a situation, and that only a complete social revolution, a complete change of the ' social system ', can help ?   Or are we to believe the defenders of an unrestrained ' capitalist ' system who emphasize (rightly, I think) the tremendous benefit to be derived from the mechanism of free markets, and who conclude from this that a truly free labour market would be of the greatest benefit to all concerned ?

I believe that the injustice and inhumanity of the unrestrained ' capitalist system ' described by Marx cannot be questioned ; but it can be interpreted in terms of what we called, in a previous chapter [20], the *paradox of freedom*.   Freedom, we have seen, defeats itself, if it is unlimited.   Unlimited freedom means that a strong man is free to bully one who is weak and to rob him of his freedom.   This is why we demand that the state should limit freedom to a certain extent, so that everyone's freedom is protected by law.   Nobody should be at the *mercy* of others, but all should have a *right* to be protected by the state.

Now I believe that these considerations, originally meant to apply to the realm of brute-force, of physical intimidation, must be applied to the economic realm also.   Even if the state protects its citizens from being bullied by physical violence (as it does, in principle, under the system of unrestrained capitalism), it may defeat our ends by its failure to protect them from the misuse of economic power.   In such a state, the economically strong is still free to bully one who is economically weak, and to rob him of his freedom.   Under these circumstances, unlimited economic freedom can be just as self-defeating as unlimited physical freedom, and economic power may be nearly as danger-ous as physical violence ;   for those who possess a surplus of food can force those who are starving into a ' freely ' accepted servitude, without using violence. And assuming that the state limits its activities to the suppression of violence (and to the protection of property), a minority which is economically strong may in this way exploit the majority of those who are economically weak.

If this analysis is correct [21], then the nature of the remedy is clear. It must be a *political* remedy—a remedy similar to the one which we use against physical violence. We must construct social institutions, enforced by the power of the state, for the protection of the economically weak from the economically strong. The state must see to it that nobody need enter into an inequitable arrangement out of fear of starvation, or economic ruin.

This, of course, means that the principle of non-intervention, of an unrestrained economic system, has to be given up ; if we wish freedom to be safeguarded, then we must demand that the policy of unlimited economic freedom be replaced by the planned economic intervention of the state. We must demand that unrestrained *capitalism* give way to an *economic interventionism* [22]. And this is precisely what has happened. The economic system described and criticized by Marx has everywhere ceased to exist. It has been replaced, not by a system in which the state begins to lose its functions and consequently ' shows signs of withering away ', but by various interventionist systems, in which the functions of the state in the economic realm are extended far beyond the protection of property and of ' free contracts '. (This development will be discussed in the next chapters.)

IV

I should like to characterize the point here reached as the most central point in our analysis. It is only here that we can begin to realize the significance of the clash between historicism and social engineering, and its effect upon the policy of the friends of the open society.

Marxism claims to be more than a science. It does more than make a historical prophecy. It claims to be the basis for practical political action. It criticizes existing society, and it asserts that it can lead the way to a better world. But according to Marx's own theory, we cannot at will alter the economic reality by, for example, legal reforms. Politics can do no more than ' shorten and lessen the birth-pangs '.[23] This, I think, is an extremely poor political programme, and its poverty is a consequence of the third-rate place which it attributes to political power in the hierarchy of powers. For according to Marx, the real power lies in the evolution of machinery ; next in importance is the system of economic class-relationships ; and the least important influence is that of politics.

A directly opposite view is implied in the position we have reached in our analysis. It considers political power as fundamental. Political power, from this point of view, can control economic power. This means an immense extension of the field of political activities. We can ask what we wish to achieve and how to achieve it. We can, for instance, develop a rational political programme for the protection of the economically weak. We can make laws to limit exploitation. We can limit the working day ; but we can do much more. By law, we can insure the workers (or better still, all citizens) against disability, unemployment, and old age. In this way we can make impossible such forms of exploitation as are based upon the helpless economic position of a worker who must yield to anything in order not to starve. And when we are able by law to guarantee a livelihood to everybody willing to work, and there is no reason why we should not achieve that, then the protection of the freedom of the citizen from economic fear and economic intimidation will approach completeness. From this point of view, political power is the key to economic protection. Political power and its control is everything. Economic power must not be permitted to dominate political power ; if necessary, it must be fought and brought under control by political power.

From the point of view reached, we can say that Marx's disparaging attitude towards political power not only means that he neglects to develop a theory of the most important potential means of bettering the lot of the economically weak, but also that he neglected the greatest potential danger to human freedom. His naïve view that, in a classless society, state power would lose its function and ' wither away' shows very clearly that he never grasped the paradox of freedom, and that he never understood the function which state power could and should perform, in the service of freedom and humanity. (Yet this view of Marx stands witness to the fact that he was, ultimately, an individualist, in spite of his collectivist appeal to class consciousness.) In this way, the Marxian view is analogous to the liberal belief that all we need is ' equality of opportunity '. We certainly need this. But it is not enough. It does not protect those who are less gifted, or less ruthless, or less lucky, from becoming objects of exploitation for those who are more gifted, or ruthless, or lucky.

Moreover, from the point of view we have reached, what Marxists describe disparagingly as ' mere formal freedom ' becomes the basis of everything else. This ' mere formal freedom ', i.e. democracy, the right of the people to judge and to dismiss their government, is the only known device by which we can try to protect ourselves against the misuse of political power [24] ; it is the control of the rulers by the ruled. And since political power can control economic power, political democracy is also the only means for the control of economic power by the ruled. Without democratic control, there can be no earthly reason why any government should not use its political and economic power for purposes very different from the protection of the freedom of its citizens.

V

It is the fundamental rôle of ' formal freedom ' which is overlooked by Marxists who think that formal democracy is not enough and wish to supplement it by what they usually call ' economic democracy ' ; a vague and utterly superficial phrase which obscures the fact that ' merely formal freedom ' is the only guarantee of a democratic economic policy.

Marx discovered the significance of economic power ; and it is understandable that he exaggerated its status. He and the Marxists see economic power everywhere. Their argument runs : he who has the money has the power ; for if necessary, he can buy guns and even gangsters. But this is a roundabout argument. In fact, it contains an admission that the man who has the gun has the power. And if he who has the gun becomes aware of this, then it may not be long until he has both the gun and the money. But under an unrestrained capitalism, Marx's argument applies, to some extent ; for a rule which develops institutions for the control of guns and gangsters but not of the power of money is liable to come under the influence of this power. In such a state, an uncontrolled gangsterism of wealth may rule. But Marx himself, I think, would have been the first to admit that this is not true of all states ; that there have been times in history when, for example, all exploitation was looting, directly based upon the power of the mailed fist. And to-day there

will be few to support the naïve view that the ' progress of
history ' has once and for all put an end to these more direct
ways of exploiting men, and that, once formal freedom has
been achieved, it is impossible for us to fall again under the sway
of such primitive forms of exploitation.

These considerations would be sufficient for refuting the
dogmatic doctrine that economic power is more fundamental
than physical power, or the power of the state. But there are
other considerations as well. As has been rightly emphasized
by various writers (among them Bertrand Russell and Walter
Lippmann [25]), it is only the active intervention of the state—the
protection of property by laws backed by physical sanctions—
which makes of wealth a potential source of power ; for without
this intervention, a man would soon be without his wealth.
Economic power is therefore entirely dependent on political and
physical power. Russell gives historical examples which illustrate
this dependence, and sometimes even helplessness, of wealth :
' Economic power within the state,' he writes [26], ' although
ultimately derived from law and public opinion, easily acquires
a certain independence. It can influence law by corruption
and public opinion by propaganda. It can put politicians under
obligations which interfere with their freedom. It can threaten
to cause a financial crisis. *But there are very definite limits to what
it can achieve.* Cæsar was helped to power by his creditors, who
saw no hope of repayment except through his success ; but
when he had succeeded he was powerful enough to defy them.
Charles V borrowed from the Fuggers the money required to
buy the position of Emperor, but when he had become Emperor
he snapped his fingers at them and they lost what they had lent.'

The dogma that economic power is at the root of all evil
must be discarded. Its place must be taken by an understanding of the dangers of *any* form of uncontrolled power. Money
as such is not particularly dangerous. It becomes dangerous
only if it can buy power, either directly, or by enslaving the
economically weak who must sell themselves in order to live.

We must think in these matters in even more materialist
terms, as it were, than Marx did. We must realize that the
control of physical power and of physical exploitation remains
the central political problem. In order to establish this control,
we must establish ' merely formal freedom '. Once we have
achieved this, and have learned how to use it for the control of
political power, everything rests with us. We must not blame

anybody else any longer, nor cry out against the sinister economic demons behind the scenes. For in a democracy, we hold the keys to the control of the demons. We can tame them. We must realize this and use the keys ; we must construct institutions for the democratic control of economic power, and for our protection from economic exploitation.

Much has been made by Marxists of the possibility of buying votes, either directly or by buying propaganda. But closer consideration shows that we have here a good example of the power-political situation analysed above. Once we have achieved formal freedom, we can control vote-buying in every form. There are laws to limit the expenditure on electioneering, and it rests entirely with us to see that much more stringent laws of this kind are introduced [27]. The legal system can be made a powerful instrument for its own protection. In addition, we can influence public opinion, and insist upon a much more rigid moral code in political matters. All this we can do ; but we must first realize that social engineering of this kind is our task, that it is in our power, and that we must not wait for economic earthquakes miraculously to produce a new economic world for us, so that all we shall have to do will be to unveil it, to remove the old political cloak.

VI

Of course, in practice Marxists never fully relied on the doctrine of the impotence of political power. So far as they had an opportunity to act, or to plan action, they usually assumed, like everybody else, that political power can be used for the control of economic power. But their plans and actions were never based on a clear refutation of their original theory, nor upon any well-considered view of that most fundamental problem of all politics : the control of the controller, of the dangerous accumulation of power represented in the state. They never realized the full significance of democracy as the only known means to achieve this control.

As a consequence they never realized the danger inherent in a policy of increasing the power of the state. Although they abandoned more or less unconsciously the doctrine of the impotence of politics, they retained the view that state power presents no important problem, and that it is bad only if it is in the hands of the bourgeoisie. They did not realize that *all* power, and political power at least as much as economic power, is dangerous.

Thus they retained their formula of the dictatorship of the proletariat. They did not understand the principle (cp. chapter 8) that all large-scale politics must be institutional, not personal ; and when clamouring for the extension of state powers (in contrast to Marx's view of the state) they never considered that the wrong persons might one day get hold of these extended powers. This is part of the reason why, as far as they proceeded to consider state-intervention, they planned to give the state practically limitless powers in the economic realm. They retained Marx's holistic and Utopian belief that only a brand-new ' social system ' can improve matters.

I have criticized this Utopian and Romantic approach to social engineering in a previous chapter (chapter 9). But I wish to add here that economic intervention, even the piecemeal methods advocated here, will tend to increase the power of the state. Interventionism is therefore extremely dangerous. This is not a decisive argument against it ; state power must always remain a dangerous though necessary evil. But it should be a warning that if we relax our watchfulness, and if we do not strengthen our democratic institutions while giving more power to the state by interventionist ' planning ', then we may lose our freedom. And if freedom is lost, everything is lost, including ' planning '. For why should plans for the welfare of the people be carried out if the people have no power to enforce them ? Only freedom can make security secure.

We thus see that there is not only a paradox of freedom but also a paradox of state planning. If we plan too much, if we give too much power to the state, then freedom will be lost, and that will be the end of planning.

Such considerations lead us back to our plea for piecemeal, and against Utopian or holistic, methods of social engineering. And they lead us back to our demand that measures should be planned to fight concrete evils rather than to establish some ideal good. State intervention should be limited to what is really necessary for the protection of freedom.

But it is not enough to say that our solution should be a minimum solution ; that we should be watchful ; and that we should not give more power to the state than is necessary for the protection of freedom. These remarks may raise problems, but they do not show a way to a solution. It is even conceivable that there is no solution ; that the acquisition of new economic powers by a state—whose powers, as compared to those of its

citizens, are always dangerously great—will make it irresistible.
So far, we have shown neither that freedom can be preserved,
nor how it can be preserved.

Under these circumstances it may be useful to remember our
considerations of chapter 7 concerning the question of the control
of political power and the paradox of freedom.

VII

The important distinction which we made there was that
between persons and institutions. We pointed out that, while
the political question of the day may demand a personal solution,
all long-term policy—and especially all democratic long-term
policy—must be conceived in terms of impersonal institutions.
And we pointed out that, more especially, the problem of con-
trolling the rulers, and of checking their powers, was in the main
an institutional problem—the problem, in short, of designing
institutions for preventing even bad rulers from doing too much
damage.

Analogous considerations will apply to the problem of the
control of the economic power of the state. What we shall have
to guard against is an increase in the power of the rulers. We
must guard against persons and against their arbitrariness. Some
types of institutions may confer arbitrary powers upon a person ;
but other types will deny them to that person.

If we look upon our labour legislation from this point of view,
then we shall find both types of institutions. Many of these laws
add very little power to the executive organs of the state. It is
conceivable, to be sure, that the laws against child labour, for
example, may be misused, by a civil servant, to intimidate, and
to dominate over, an innocent citizen. But dangers of this kind
are hardly serious if compared with those which are inherent in
a legislation that confers upon the rulers discretionary powers,
such as the power of directing labour [28]. Similarly, a law establishing that a citizen's misuse of his property should be punished
by its forfeiture will be incomparably less dangerous than one
which gives the rulers, or the servants of the state, discretionary
powers of requisitioning a citizen's property.

We thus arrive at a distinction between two entirely different
methods [29] by which the economic intervention of the state may
proceed. The first is that of designing a ' legal framework ' of
protective institutions (laws restricting the powers of the owner
of an animal, or of a landowner, are an example). The second

is that of empowering organs of the state to act—within certain limits—as they consider necessary for achieving the ends laid down by the rulers for the time being.   We may describe the first procedure as 'institutional' or 'indirect' intervention, and the second as 'personal' or 'direct' intervention.   (Of course, intermediate cases exist.)

There can be no doubt, from the point of view of democratic control, which of these methods is preferable.   The obvious policy for all democratic intervention is to make use of the first method wherever this is possible, and to restrict the use of the second method to cases for which the first method is inadequate.   (Such cases exist.   The classical example is the Budget—this expression of the Chancellor's discretion and sense of what is equitable and just.   And it is conceivable although highly undesirable that a counter-cycle measure may have to be of a similar character.)

From the point of view of piecemeal social engineering, the difference between the two methods is highly important.   Only the first, the institutional method, makes it possible to make adjustments in the light of discussion and experience.   It alone makes it possible to apply the method of trial and error to our political actions.   It is long-term ; yet the permanent legal framework can be slowly changed, in order to make allowances for unforeseen and undesired consequences, for changes in other parts of the framework, etc.   It alone allows us to find out, by experience and analysis, what we actually were doing when we intervened with a certain aim in mind.   Discretionary decisions of the rulers or civil servants are outside these rational methods.   They are short-term decisions, transitory, changing from day to day, or at best, from year to year.   As a rule (the Budget is the great exception) they cannot even be publicly discussed, both because necessary information is lacking, and because the principles on which the decision is taken are obscure. If they exist at all, they are usually not institutionalized, but part of an internal departmental tradition.

But it is not only in this sense that the first method can be described as rational and the second as irrational.   It is also in an entirely different and highly important sense.   The legal framework can be known and understood by the individual citizen ; and it should be designed to be so understandable.   Its functioning is predictable.   It introduces a factor of certainty and security into social life.   When it is altered, allowances can be made, during a transitional period, for those individuals who have laid their plans in the expectation of its constancy.

As opposed to this, the method of personal intervention must introduce an ever-growing element of unpredictability into social life, and with it will develop the feeling that social life is irrational and insecure. The use of discretionary powers is liable to grow quickly, once it has become an accepted method, since adjustments will be necessary, and adjustments to discretionary short-term decisions can hardly be carried out by institutional means. This tendency must greatly increase the irrationality of the system, creating in many the impression that there are hidden powers behind the scenes, and making them susceptible to the conspiracy theory of society with all its consequences—heresy hunts, national, social, and class hostility.

In spite of all this, the obvious policy of preferring where possible the institutional method is far from being generally accepted. The failure to accept it is, I suppose, due to different reasons. One is that it needs a certain detachment to embark on the long-term task of re-designing the ' legal framework '. But governments live from hand to mouth, and discretionary powers belong to this style of living—quite apart from the fact that rulers are inclined to love those powers for their own sake. But the most important reason is, undoubtedly, that the significance of the distinction between the two methods is not understood. The way to its understanding is blocked to the followers of Plato, Hegel, and Marx. They will never see that the old question ' Who shall be the rulers ? ' must be superseded by the more real one ' How can we tame them ? '

VIII

If we now look back at Marx's theory of the impotence of politics and of the power of historical forces, then we must admit that it is an imposing edifice. It is the direct result of his socio-logical method ; of his economic historicism, of the doctrine that the development of the economic system, or of man's metabolism, determines his social and political development. The experience of his time, his humanitarian indignation, and the need of bringing to the oppressed the consolation of a prophecy, the hope, or even the certainty, of their victory, all this is united in one grandiose philosophic system, comparable or even superior to the holistic systems of Plato and Hegel. It is only due to the accident that he was not a reactionary that the history of philosophy takes so little notice of him and assumes that he was mainly a propagandist. The reviewer of *Capital* who wrote : ' At the first glance . . we come to the conclusion that the author is one of the greatest among the idealist philosophers, in the German, that is to say, the bad sense of the word " idealist ". But in actual fact, he is enormously more realistic than any of his predecessors . .' [30], this reviewer hit the nail on the head. Marx was the last of the great holistic system builders. We should take care to leave it at that, and not to replace his by another Great System. What we need is not holism. It is piecemeal social engineering.

With this, I conclude my critical analysis of Marx's philosophy of the *method* of social science, of his economic determinism as well as of his prophetic historicism. The final test of a method, however, must be its practical results. I therefore proceed now to a more detailed examination of the main result of his method, the prophecy of the impending advent of a classless society.

CHAPTER 18 : THE COMING OF SOCIALISM

I

Economic historicism is the method applied by Marx to an analysis of the impending changes in our society. According to Marx, every particular social system must destroy itself, simply because it must create the forces which produce the next historical period. A sufficiently penetrating analysis of the feudal system, undertaken shortly before the industrial revolution, might have led to the detection of the forces which were about to destroy feudalism, and to the prediction of the most important characteristics of the coming period, capitalism. Similarly, an analysis of the development of capitalism might enable us to detect the forces which work for its destruction, and to predict the most important characteristics of the new historical period which lies ahead of us. For there is surely no reason to believe that capitalism, of all social systems, will last for ever. On the contrary, the material conditions of production, and with them, the ways of human life, have never changed so quickly as they have done under capitalism. By changing its own foundations in this way, capitalism is bound to transform itself, and to produce a new period in the history of mankind.

According to Marx's method, the principles of which have been discussed above, the fundamental or essential [1] forces which will destroy or transform capitalism must be searched for in the evolution of the material means of production. Once these fundamental forces have been discovered, it is possible to trace their influence upon the social relationships between classes as well as upon the juridical and political systems.

The analysis of the fundamental economic forces and the suicidal historical tendencies of the period which he called ' capitalism ' was undertaken by Marx in *Capital*, the great work of his life. The historical period and the economic system he dealt with was that of western Europe and especially England, from about the middle of the eighteenth century to 1867 (the year of the first publication of *Capital*). The ' ultimate aim of this work ', as Marx explained in his preface [2], was ' to lay bare the economic law of motion of modern society ', in order to prophesy its fate. A secondary aim [3] was the refutation of the apologists of capitalism, of the economists who presented the laws of the capitalist mode of production as if they were inexorable laws of nature, declaring with Burke : ' The laws of commerce are the laws of nature, and therefore the laws of God.' Marx contrasted these allegedly inexorable laws with those which he maintained to be the only inexorable laws of society, namely, its laws of development ; and he tried to show that what the economists declared to be eternal and immutable laws were in fact merely temporary regularities, doomed to be destroyed together with capitalism itself.

Marx's historical prophecy can be described as a closely knit argument. But *Capital* elaborates only what I shall call the ' first step ' of this argument, the analysis of the fundamental economic forces of capitalism and their influence upon the relations between the classes. The ' second step ', which leads to the conclusion that a social revolution is inevitable, and the ' third step ', which leads to the prediction of the emergence of a classless, i.e. socialist, society, are only sketched. In this chapter, I shall first explain more clearly what I call the three steps of the Marxist argument, and then discuss the third of these steps in detail. In the two following chapters, I shall discuss the second and the first steps. To reverse the order of the steps in this way turns out to be best for a detailed critical discussion ; the advantage lies in the fact that it is then easier to assume without prejudice the truth of the premises of each step in the argument, and to concentrate entirely upon the question whether the conclusion reached in this particular step follows from its premises. Here are the three steps.

In the *first step* of his argument, Marx analyses the method of capitalist production. He finds that there is a tendency towards an *increase in the productivity* of work, connected with technical improvements as well as with what he calls the increasing *accumulation* of the means of production. Starting from here, the argument leads him to the conclusion that in the realm of the social relations between the classes this tendency must lead to the accumulation of more and more wealth in fewer and fewer hands ; that is to say, the conclusion is reached that there will be a tendency towards an *increase of wealth and misery* ; of wealth in the ruling class, the bourgeoisie, and of misery in the ruled class, the workers. This first step will be treated in chapter 20 (' Capitalism and its Fate ').

In the *second step* of the argument, the result of the first step is taken for granted. From it, two conclusions are drawn ; first, that all classes except a small ruling bourgeoisie and a large exploited working class are bound to disappear, or to become insignificant ; secondly, that the increasing tension between these two classes must lead to a *social revolution*. This step will be analysed in chapter 19 (' The Social Revolution ').

In the *third step* of the argument, the conclusions of the second step are taken for granted in their turn ; and the final conclusion reached is that, after the victory of the workers over the bourgeoisie, there will be a society consisting of one class only, and, therefore, a classless society, a society without exploitation ; that is to say, *socialism*.

II

I now proceed to the *discussion of the third step*, of the final prophecy of the coming of socialism.

The main premises of this step, to be criticized in the next chapter but here to be taken for granted, are these : the development of capitalism has led to the elimination of all classes but two, a small bourgeoisie and a huge proletariat ; and the increase of misery has forced the latter to revolt against its exploiters. The conclusions are, first, that the workers must win the struggle, secondly that, by eliminating the bourgeoisie, they must establish a classless society, since only one class remains.

Now I am prepared to grant that the first conclusion follows from the premises (in conjunction with a few premises of minor importance which we need not question). Not only is the number of the bourgeoisie small, but their physical existence, their ' metabolism ', depends upon the proletariat. The exploiter, the drone, starves without the exploited ; in any case, if he destroys the exploited then he ends his own career as a drone. Thus he cannot win ; he can, at the best, put up a prolonged struggle. The worker, on the other hand, does not depend for his material subsistence on his exploiter ; once the worker revolts, once he has decided to challenge the existing order, the exploiter has no essential social function any longer. The worker can destroy his class enemy without endangering his own existence. Accordingly, there is only one outcome possible. The bourgeoisie will disappear.

But does the second conclusion follow ? Is it true that the workers' victory must lead to a classless society ? I do not think so. From the fact that of two classes only one remains, it does not follow that there will be a classless society. *Classes are not like individuals*, even if we admit that they behave nearly like individuals so long as there are *two* classes who are joined in battle. The unity or solidarity of a class, according to Marx's own analysis, is part of their class consciousness [4], which in turn is very largely a product of the class struggle. There is no earthly reason why the individuals who form the proletariat should retain their class unity once the pressure of the struggle against the common class enemy has ceased. Any latent conflict of interests is now likely to divide the formerly united proletariat into new classes, and to develop into a new class struggle. (The principles of dialectics would suggest that a new antithesis, a new class antagonism, must soon develop. Yet, of course, dialectics is sufficiently vague and adaptable to explain anything at all, and therefore a classless society also, as a dialectically necessary synthesis of an antithetical development [5].)

The most likely development is, of course, that those actually in power at the moment of victory—those of the revolutionary leaders who have survived the struggle for power and the various purges, together with their staff—will form a *New Class* : *the new ruling class of the new society*, a kind of new aristocracy or bureaucracy [6] ; and it is most likely that they will attempt to hide this fact. This they can do, most conveniently, by retaining as much as possible of the revolutionary ideology, taking advantage of these sentiments instead of wasting their time in efforts to destroy them (in accordance with Pareto's advice to all rulers). And it seems likely enough that they will be able to make fullest use of the revolutionary ideology if at the same time they exploit the fear of counter-revolutionary developments. In this way, the revolutionary ideology will serve them for apologetic purposes : it will serve them both as a vindication of the use they make of their power, and as a means of stabilizing it ; in short, as a new ' opium for the people '.

Something of this kind are the events which, on Marx's own premises, are likely to happen. Yet it is not my task here to make historical prophecies (or to interpret the past history of many revolutions). I merely wish to show that Marx's conclusion, the prophecy of the coming of a classless society, does not follow from the premises. The third step of Marx's argument must be pronounced to be inconclusive.

More than this I do not maintain. I do not think, more particularly, that it is possible to prophesy that socialism will not come, or to say that the premises of the argument make the introduction of socialism very unlikely. It is, for instance, possible that the prolonged struggle and the enthusiasm of victory may contribute to a feeling of solidarity strong enough to continue until laws preventing exploitation and the misuse of power are established. (The establishment of institutions for the democratic control of the rulers is the only guarantee for the elimination of exploitation.) The chances of founding such a society will depend, in my opinion, very largely upon the devotion of the workers to the ideas of socialism and freedom, as opposed to the immediate interests of their class. These are matters which cannot be easily foreseen ; all that can certainly be said is that class struggle as such does not always produce lasting solidarity among the oppressed. There are examples of such solidarity and great devotion to the common cause ; but there are also examples of groups of workers who pursue their particular group interest even where it is in open conflict with the interest of the other workers, and with the idea of the solidarity of the oppressed. Exploitation need not disappear with the bourgeoisie, since it is quite possible that groups of workers may obtain privileges which amount to an exploitation of less fortunate groups [7].

We see that a whole host of possible historical developments may follow upon a victorious proletarian revolution. There are certainly too many possibilities for the application of the method of historical prophecy. And in particular it must be emphasized that it would be most unscientific to close our eyes to some possibilities because we do not like them. Wishful thinking is apparently a thing that cannot be avoided. But it should not be mistaken for scientific thinking. And we should also recognize that the allegedly scientific prophecy provides, for a great number of people, a form of escape. It provides an escape from our present responsibilities into a future paradise ; and it provides the fitting complement of this paradise by overstressing the helplessness of the individual in face of what it describes as the overwhelming and demoniacal economic forces of the present moment.

III

If we now look a little more closely at these forces, and at our own present economic system, then we can see that our theoretical criticism is borne out by experience. But we must be on our guard against misinterpreting experience in the light of the Marxist prejudice that ' socialism ' or ' communism ' is the only alternative and the only possible successor to ' capitalism '. Neither Marx nor anybody else has ever shown that socialism, in the sense of a classless society, of ' an association in which the free development of each is the warrant for the free development of all ' [8], is the only possible alternative to the ruthless exploitation of that economic system which he first described a century ago (in 1845), and to which he gave the name ' capitalism ' [9]. And indeed, if anybody were attempting to prove that socialism is the only possible successor to Marx's unrestrained ' capitalism ', then we could simply refute him by pointing to historical facts. For *laissez-faire* has disappeared from the face of the earth, but it has not been replaced by a socialist or communist system as Marx understood it. Only in the Russian sixth of the earth do we find an economic system where, in accordance with Marx's prophecy, the means of production are owned by the state, whose political might however shows, in opposition to Marx's prophecy, no inclination to wither away. But all over the earth, organized political power has begun to perform far-reaching economic functions. *Unrestrained capitalism* has given way to a new historical period, to our own period of political *interventionism*, of the economic interference of the state. Interventionism has assumed various forms. There is the Russian variety ; there is the fascist form of totalitarianism ; and there is the democratic interventionism of England, of the United States, and of the ' Smaller Democracies ', led by Sweden [10], where the technology of democratic intervention has reached its highest level so far. The development which led to this intervention started in Marx's own day, with British factory legislation. It made its first decisive advances with the introduction of the 48-hour week, and later with the introduction of unemployment insurance and other forms of social insurance. How utterly absurd it is to identify the economic system of the modern democracies with the system Marx called ' capitalism ' can be seen at a glance, by comparing it with his 10-point programme for the communist revolution.

If we omit the rather insignificant points of this programme (for instance, ' 4. Confiscation of the property of all emigrants and rebels '), then we can say that in the democracies most of these points have been put into practice, either completely, or to a considerable degree ; and with them, many more important steps, which Marx had never thought of, have been made in the direction of social security. I mention only the following points in his programme : 2. A heavy progressive or graduated income tax. (Carried out.) 3. Abolition of all right of inheritance. (Largely realized by heavy death duties. Whether more would be desirable is at least doubtful.) 6. Central control by the state of the means of communication and transport. (For military reasons this was carried out in Central Europe before the war of 1914, without very beneficial results. It has also been achieved by most of the Smaller Democracies.) 7. Increase in the number and size of factories and instruments of production owned by the state . . (Realized in the Smaller Democracies ; whether this is always very beneficial is at least doubtful.) 10. Free education for all children in public (i.e. state) schools. Abolition of children's factory labour in its present form . . (The first demand is fulfilled in the Smaller Democracies, and to some extent practically everywhere ; the second has been exceeded.)

A number of points in Marx's programme [11] (for instance : ' 1. Abolition of all property in land ') have not been realized in the democratic countries. This is why Marxists rightly claim that these countries have not established ' socialism '. But if they infer from this that these countries are still ' capitalist ' in Marx's sense, then they only demonstrate the dogmatic character of their presupposition that there is no further alternative. This shows how it is possible to be blinded by the glare of a preconceived system. Not only is Marxism a bad guide to the future, but it also renders its followers incapable of seeing what is happening before their own eyes, in their own historical period, and sometimes even with their own co-operation.

IV

But it could be asked whether this criticism speaks in any way against the method of large-scale historical prophecy as such. Could we not, in principle, so strengthen the premises of the prophetic argument as to obtain a valid conclusion ? Of course we could do this. It is always possible to obtain any conclusion

we like if only we make our premises sufficiently strong. But
the situation is such that, for nearly every large-scale historical
prophecy, we would have to make such assumptions concerning
moral and other factors of the kind called by Marx ' ideological '
as are beyond our ability to reduce to economic factors. But
Marx would have been the first to admit that this would be a
highly unscientific proceeding. His whole method of prophecy
depends on the assumption that ideological influences need not
be treated as independent and unpredictable elements, but that
they are reducible to, and dependent on, observable economic
conditions, and therefore predictable.

It is sometimes admitted even by certain unorthodox Marxists
that the coming of socialism is not merely a matter of historical
development ; Marx's statement that ' we can shorten and lessen
the birth-pangs ' of the coming of socialism is sufficiently vague
to be interpreted as stating that a mistaken policy might delay
the advent of socialism even for centuries, as compared with the
proper policy which would shorten the time of the development
to a minimum. This interpretation makes it possible even for
Marxists to admit that it will depend largely upon ourselves
whether or not the outcome of a revolution will be a socialist
society ; that is to say, it will depend upon our aims, upon our
devotion and sincerity, and upon our intelligence, in other words,
upon moral or ' ideological ' factors. Marx's prophecy, they
may add, is a great source of moral encouragement, and it is
therefore likely to further the development of socialism. What
Marx really tries to show is that there are only two possibilities :
that a terrible world should continue forever, or that a better
world should eventually emerge ; and it is hardly worth our
while to contemplate the first alternative seriously. Therefore
Marx's prophecy is fully justified. For the more clearly men
realize that they can achieve the second alternative, the more
surely will they make a decisive leap from capitalism to socialism ;
but a more definite prophecy cannot be made.

This is an argument which admits the influence of irreducible
moral and ideological factors upon the course of history, and
with it, the inapplicability of the Marxist method. Concerning
that part of the argument which tries to defend Marxism, we
must repeat that nobody has ever shown that there are only
two possibilities, ' capitalism ' and ' socialism '. With the view
that we should not waste our time in contemplating the eternal
continuation of a very unsatisfactory world, I quite agree. But

the alternative need not be to contemplate the prophesied advent of a better world, or to assist its birth by propaganda and other irrational means, perhaps even by violence. It can be, for instance, the development of a technology for the immediate improvement of the world we live in, the development of a method for piecemeal engineering, for democratic intervention [12]. Marxists would of course contend that this kind of intervention is impossible since history cannot be made according to rational plans for improving the world. But this theory has very strange consequences. For if things cannot be improved by the use of reason, then it would be indeed an historical or political miracle if the irrational powers of history by themselves were to produce a better and more rational world [13].

Thus we are thrown back to the position that moral and other ideological factors which do not fall within the scope of scientific prophecy exert a far-reaching influence upon the course of history. One of these unpredictable factors is just the influence of social technology and of political intervention in economic matters. The social technologist and the piecemeal engineer may plan the construction of new institutions, or the transformation of old ones ; they may even plan the ways and means of bringing these changes about ; but ' history ' does not become more predictable by their doing so. For they do not plan for the whole of society, nor can they know whether their plans will be carried out ; in fact, they will hardly ever be carried out without great modification, partly because our experience grows during construction, partly because we must compromise [14]. Thus Marx was quite right when he insisted that ' history ' cannot be planned on paper. But *institutions* can be planned ; and they are being planned. Only by planning [15], step by step, for institutions to safeguard freedom, especially freedom from exploitation, can we hope to achieve a better world.

v

In order to show the practical political significance of Marx's historicist theory, I intend to illustrate each of the three chapters dealing with the three steps of his prophetic argument by a few remarks on the effects of his historical prophecy upon recent European history. For these effects have been far-reaching, because of the influence exercised, in Central and Eastern Europe, by the two great Marxist Parties, the Communists and the Social Democrats.

Both these parties were entirely unprepared for such a task
as the transformation of society.   The Russian Communists, who
found themselves first within reach of power, went ahead, entirely
unaware of the grave problems and the immensity of sacrifice as
well as of suffering which lay ahead.   The Social Democrats of
Central Europe, whose chance came a little later, shrank for
many years from the responsibilities which the Communists had
so readily taken upon themselves.   They doubted, probably
rightly, whether any people but that of Russia, which had been
most savagely oppressed by Tsarism, would have stood up to
the sufferings and sacrifices demanded from them by revolution,
civil war, and a long period of at first often unsuccessful experiments.   Moreover, during the critical years from 1918 to 1926,
the outcome of the Russian experiment appeared to them most
uncertain.   And, indeed, there was surely no basis for judging
its prospects.   One can say that the split between the Central
European Communists and Social Democrats was one between
those Marxists who had a kind of irrational faith in the final
success of the Russian experiment, and those who were, more
reasonably, sceptical of it.   When I say ' irrational ' and ' more
reasonably ', I judge them by their own standard, by Marxism ;
for according to Marxism, the proletarian revolution should have
been the final outcome of industrialization, and not *vice versa* [16] ;
and it should have come first in the highly industrialized countries,
and only much later in Russia [17].

This remark is not, however, intended as a defence of the
Social Democratic leaders [18] whose policy was fully determined
by the Marxist prophecy, by their implicit belief that socialism
must come.   But this belief was often combined, in the leaders,
with a hopeless scepticism concerning their own immediate functions and tasks, and what lay immediately ahead [19].   They
had learned from Marxism to organize the workers, and to
inspire them with a truly wonderful faith in their task, the
liberation of mankind [20].   But they were unable to prepare for
the realization of their promises.   They had learned their textbooks well, they knew all about ' scientific socialism ', and they
knew that the preparation of recipes for the future was unscientific Utopianism.   Had not Marx himself ridiculed a follower
of Comte who had criticized him in the *Revue Positiviste* for
his neglect of practical programmes ?   ' The *Revue Positiviste*
accuses me ', Marx had said [21] scornfully, ' of a metaphysical
treatment of economics, and further—you would hardly guess it

—of confining myself to a merely critical analysis of actual facts, instead of prescribing recipes (Comtist ones, perhaps ?) for the kitchen in which the future is cooked.' Thus the Marxist leaders knew better than to waste their time on such matters as technology. 'Workers of all countries, unite ! '—that exhausted their practical programme. When the workers of their countries were united, when there was an opportunity of assuming the responsibility of government and laying the foundations for a better world, when their hour had struck, they left the workers high and dry. The leaders did not know what to do. They waited for the promised suicide of capitalism. After the inevitable capitalist collapse, when things had gone thoroughly wrong, when everything was in dissolution and the risk of discredit and disgrace to themselves considerably diminished, then they hoped to become the saviours of mankind. (And, indeed, we should keep in mind the fact that the success of the Communist in Russia was undoubtedly made possible, in part, by the terrible things that had happened before their rise to power.) But when the great depression, which they first welcomed as the promised collapse, was running its course, they began to realize that the workers were growing tired of being fed and put off with interpretations of history [22] ; that it was not enough to tell them that according to the infallible scientific socialism of Marx fascism was definitely the last stand of capitalism before its impending collapse. The suffering masses needed more than that. Slowly the leaders began to realize the terrible consequences of a policy of waiting and hoping for the great political miracle. But it was too late. Their opportunity was gone.

These remarks are very sketchy. But they give some indication of the practical consequences of Marx's prophecy of the coming of socialism.

CHAPTER 19 : THE SOCIAL REVOLUTION

The second step of Marx's prophetic argument has as its most relevant premise the assumption that capitalism must lead to an increase of wealth and misery ; of wealth in the numerically declining bourgeoisie, and of misery in the numerically increasing working class. This assumption will be criticized in the next chapter but is here taken for granted. The conclusions drawn from it can be divided into two parts. The first part is a prophecy concerning the development of the *class structure* of capitalism. It affirms that all classes apart from the bourgeoisie and the proletariat, and especially the so-called middle classes, are bound to disappear, and that, in consequence of the increasing tension between the bourgeoisie and the proletariat, the latter will become increasingly class-conscious and united. The second part is the prophecy that this tension cannot possibly be removed, and that it will lead to a proletarian *social revolution*.

I believe that neither of the two conclusions follows from the premise. My criticism will be, in the main, similar to that propounded in the last chapter ; that is to say, I shall try to show that Marx's argument neglects a great number of possible developments.

I

Let us consider at once the *first conclusion*, i.e. the prophecy that all classes are bound to disappear, or to become insignificant, except the bourgeoisie and the proletariat whose class consciousness and solidarity must increase. It must be admitted that the premise, Marx's theory of increasing wealth and misery, provides indeed for the disappearance of a certain middle class, that of the weaker capitalists and the petty bourgeoisie. ' Each capitalist las many of his fellows low ', as Marx puts it [1] ; and these fellow capitalists may indeed be reduced to the position of wage-earners, which for Marx is the same as proletarians. This movement is part of the increase of wealth, the accumulation of more and more capital, and its concentration and centralization in fewer and fewer hands. An analogous fate is meted out to ' the lower strata of the middle class ', as Marx says [2]. ' The small tradespeople, shopkeepers, and retired tradesmen generally, the handicraftsmen and the peasants, all these sink gradually into the proletariat ; partly because their small capital, insufficient as it is for the scale on which modern industry is conducted, is overwhelmed in the competition with the bigger capitalists ; partly because their specialized skill is rendered worthless by new means of production. Thus the proletariat is recruited from all classes of the population.' This description is certainly fairly accurate, especially so far as handicrafts are concerned ; and it is also true that many proletarians come from peasant stock.

But admirable as Marx's observations are, the picture is defective. The movement he investigated is an industrial movement ; his ' capitalist ' is the industrial capitalist, his ' proletarian ' the industrial worker. And in spite of the fact that many industrial workers come from peasant stock, this does not mean that the farmers and peasants, for instance, are all gradually reduced to the position of industrial workers. Even the agricultural labourers are not necessarily united with the industrial workers by a common feeling of solidarity and class consciousness. ' The dispersion of the rural workers over large areas ', Marx admits [3], ' breaks down their power of resistance at the very time when the concentration of capital in a few hands increases the power of resistance of the urban workers.' This hardly suggests unification in one class-conscious whole. It shows, rather, that there is at least a possibility of division, and that the agricultural worker might sometimes be too dependent upon his master, the farmer or peasant, to make common cause with the industrial proletariat. But that farmers or peasants may easily choose to support the bourgeoisie rather than the workers was mentioned by Marx himself [4] ; and a workers' programme such as the one of the *Manifesto*[5], whose first demand is the ' abolition of all property in land ', is hardly designed to counteract this tendency.

This shows that it is at least possible that the rural middle classes may not disappear, and that the rural proletariat may not merge with the industrial proletariat. But this is not all. Marx's own analysis shows that it is vitally important for the bourgeoisie to foment division among the wage-earners ; and as Marx himself has seen, this might be achieved in at least two ways. One way is the creation of a *new* middle class, of a privileged group of wage-earners who would feel superior to the manual worker [6] and at the same time dependent upon the rulers' mercy. The other way is the utilization of that lowest stratum of society which Marx christened the ' rabble-prole-

tariat '. This is, as pointed out by Marx, the recruiting ground
for criminals who may be ready to sell themselves to the class
enemy. Increasing misery must tend, as he admits, to swell
the numbers of this class ; a development which will hardly
contribute to the solidarity of all the oppressed.

But even the solidarity of the class of industrial workers is
not a necessary consequence of increasing misery. Admittedly,
increasing misery must produce resistance, and it is even likely
to produce rebellious outbreaks. But the assumption of our
argument is that the misery cannot be alleviated until victory
has been won in the social revolution. This implies that the
resisting workers will be beaten again and again in their fruit-
less attempts to better their lot. But such a development need
not make the workers class-conscious in the Marxist sense [7], i.e.
proud of their class and assured of their mission ; it may make
them, rather, class-conscious in the sense of being conscious of
the fact that they belong to a beaten army. And it probably
will do so, if the workers do not find strength in the realization
that 'their numbers as well as their potential economic powers
continue to grow. This might be the case if, as Marx prophesied,
all classes, apart from their own and that of the capitalists, were
to show a tendency to disappear. But since, as we have seen,
this prophecy need not come true, it is possible that the solidarity
of even the industrial workers may be undermined by defeatism.

Thus, as opposed to Marx's prophecy which insists that there
must develop a neat division between two classes, we find that
on his own assumptions, the following class structure may possibly
develop : (1) bourgeoisie, (2) big landed proprietors, (3) other
landowners, (4) rural workers, (5) new middle class, (6) industrial workers, (7) rabble proletariat. (Any other combination
of these classes may, of course, develop too.) And we find,
furthermore, that such a development may possibly undermine
the unity of (6).

We can say, therefore, that the first conclusion of the second
step in Marx's argument does not follow. But as in my criticism
of the third step, here also I must say that I do not intend to
replace Marx's prophecy by another one. I do not assert that
the prophecy cannot come true, or that the alternative developments I have described will come to pass. I only assert that
they may come to pass. (And, indeed, this possibility can hardly
be denied by members of the radical Marxist wings who use the
accusation of treachery, bribery, and insufficient class solidarity

as favourite devices for explaining away developments which do not conform to the prophetic schedule.) That such things may happen should be clear to anybody who has observed the development which has led to fascism, in which all the possibilities I have mentioned played a part. But the mere possibility is sufficient to destroy the first conclusion reached in the second step of Marx's argument.

This of course affects the *second conclusion*, the prophecy of the coming social revolution. But before I can enter into a criticism of the way in which this prophecy is arrived at, it is necessary to discuss at some length the rôle played by it within the whole argument, as well as Marx's use of the term ' social revolution '.

II

What Marx meant when he spoke of the *social revolution* seems at first sight clear enough. His ' social revolution of the proletariat ' is a *historical concept*. It denotes the more or less rapid transition from the historical period of capitalism to that of socialism. In other words, it is the name of a transitional period of class struggle between the two main classes, down to the ultimate victory of the workers. When asked whether the term ' social revolution ' implied a violent civil war between the two classes, Marx answered [8] that this was not necessarily implied, adding, however, that the prospects of avoiding civil war were, unfortunately, not very bright. And he might have added further that, from the point of view of historical prophecy, the question appears to be perhaps not quite irrelevant, but at any rate of secondary importance. Social life is violent, Marxism insists, and the class war claims its victims every day [9]. What really matters is the result, socialism. To achieve this result is the essential characteristic of the ' social revolution '.

Now if we could take it as established, or as intuitively certain, that capitalism will be followed by socialism, then this explanation of the term ' social revolution ' might be quite satisfactory. But since we must make use of the doctrine of social revolution as a part of that scientific argument by which we try to establish the coming of socialism, the explanation is very unsatisfactory indeed. If in such an argument we try to characterize the social revolution as the transition to socialism, then the argument becomes as circular as that of the doctor who was asked to justify his prediction of the death of a patient, and had to confess that he knew neither the symptoms nor anything else of the malady—only that it would turn into a ' fatal malady '. (If the patient did not die, then it was not yet the ' fatal malady ' ; and if a revolution does not lead to socialism, then it is not yet the ' social revolution '.) We can also give to this criticism the simple form that in none of the three steps of the prophetic argument must we assume anything whatever that is deduced only in a later step.

These considerations show that, for a proper reconstruction of Marx's argument, we must find such a characterization of the social revolution as does not refer to socialism, and as permits the social revolution to play its part in this argument as well as possible. A characterization which fulfils these conditions appears to be this. The social revolution is an attempt of a largely united proletariat to conquer complete political power, undertaken with the firm resolution not to shrink from violence, should violence be necessary for achieving this aim, and to resist any effort of its opponents to regain political influence. This characterization is free from the difficulties just mentioned ; it fits the third step of the argument in so far as this third step is valid, giving it that degree of plausibility which the step un- doubtedly possesses ; and it is, as will be shown, in agreement with Marxism, and especially with its historicist tendency to avoid a definite [10] statement about whether or not violence will actually be used in this phase of history.

But although if regarded as an historical prophecy the pro- posed characterization is indefinite about the use of violence, it is important to realize that it is not so from a moral or legal point of view. Considered from such a point of view, the char- acterization of the social revolution here proposed undoubtedly makes of it a *violent uprising* ; for the question whether or not violence is actually used is less significant than the intention ; and we have assumed a firm resolution not to shrink from violence should it be necessary for achieving the aims of the movement. To say that the resolution not to shrink from violence is decisive for the character of the social revolution as a violent uprising is in agreement not only with the moral or legal point of view, but also with the ordinary view of the matter. For if a man is determined to use violence in order to achieve his aims, then we may say that to all intents and purposes he adopts a violent attitude, whether or not violence is actually used in a particular case. Admittedly, in trying to predict a future action of this man, we should have to be just as indefinite as Marxism, stating that we do not know whether or not he will actually resort to force. (Thus our characterization agrees in this point with the Marxist view.) But this lack of definiteness clearly disappears if we do not attempt historical prophecy, but try to characterize his attitude in the ordinary way.

Now I wish to make it quite clear that it is this prophecy of a possibly violent revolution which I consider, from the point of view of practical politics, by far the most harmful element in Marxism ; and I think it will be better if I briefly explain the reason for my opinion before I proceed with my analysis.

I am not in all cases and under all circumstances against a violent revolution. I believe with some medieval and Renaissance Christian thinkers who taught the admissibility of tyrannicide that there may indeed, under a tyranny, be no other possibility, and that a violent revolution may be justified. But I also believe that any such revolution should have as its *only* aim the establishment of a democracy ; and by a democracy I do not mean something as vague as ' the rule of the people ' or ' the rule of the majority ', but a set of institutions (among them especially general elections, i.e. the right of the people to dismiss their government) which permit public control of the rulers and their dismissal by the ruled, and which make it possible for the ruled to obtain reforms without using violence, even against the will of the rulers. In other words, the use of violence is justified only under a tyranny which makes reforms without violence impossible, and it should have only one aim, that is, to bring about a state of affairs which makes reforms without violence possible.

I do not believe that we should ever attempt to achieve more than that by violent means. For I believe that such an attempt would involve the risk of destroying all prospects of reasonable reform. The prolonged use of violence may lead in the end to the loss of freedom, since it is liable to bring about not a dispassionate rule of reason, but the rule of the strong man. A violent revolution which tries to attempt more than the destruction of tyranny is at least as likely to bring about another tyranny as it is likely to achieve its real aims.

There is only one further use of violence in political quarrels which I should consider justified. I mean the resistance, once democracy has been attained, to any attack (whether from within or without the state) against the democratic constitution and the use of democratic methods. Any such attack, especially if it comes from the government in power, or if it is tolerated by it, should be resisted by all loyal citizens, even to the use of violence. In fact, the working of democracy rests largely upon the understanding that a government which attempts to misuse its powers and to establish itself as a tyranny (or which tolerates the establishment of a tyranny by anybody else) outlaws itself, and that the citizens have not only a right but also a duty to consider the action of such a government as a crime, and its members as a dangerous gang of criminals. But I hold that such violent resistance to attempts to overthrow democracy should be unambiguously defensive. No shadow of doubt must be left that the only aim of the resistance is to save democracy. A threat of making use of the situation for the establishment of a counter-tyranny is just as criminal as the original attempt to introduce a tyranny ; the use of such a threat, even if made with the candid intention of saving democracy by deterring its enemies, would therefore be a very bad method of defending democracy ; indeed, such a threat would confuse the ranks of its defenders in an hour of peril, and would therefore be likely to help the enemy.

These remarks indicate that a successful democratic policy demands from the defenders the observance of certain rules. A few such rules will be listed later in this chapter ; here I only wish to make it clear why I consider the Marxist attitude towards violence one of the most important points to be dealt with in any analysis of Marx.

III

According to their interpretation of the social revolution, we may distinguish between two main groups of Marxists, a radical wing and a moderate wing (corresponding roughly, but not precisely [11], to the Communist and the Social Democratic parties).

Marxists often decline to discuss the question whether or not a violent revolution would be ' justified ' ; they say that they are not moralists, but scientists, and that they do not deal with speculations about what ought to be, but with the facts of what is or will be. In other words, they are historical prophets who confine themselves to the question of what will happen. But let us assume that we have succeeded in persuading them to discuss the justification of the social revolution. In this case, I believe that we should find all Marxists agreeing, in principle, with the old view that violent revolutions are justified only if they are directed against a tyranny.   From here on, the opinions of the two wings differ.

The radical wing insists that, according to Marx, all class rule is necessarily a dictatorship, i.e. a tyranny [12].   A real democracy can therefore be attained only by the establishment of a classless society, by overthrowing, if necessary violently, the capitalist dictatorship.   The moderate wing does not agree with this view, but insists that democracy can to some extent be realized even under capitalism, and that it is therefore possible to conduct the social revolution by peaceful and gradual reforms. But even this moderate wing insists that such a peaceful development is uncertain ;   it points out that it is the bourgeoisie which is likely to resort to force, if faced with the prospect of being defeated by the workers on the democratic battlefield ;   and it contends that in this case the workers would be justified in retaliating, and in establishing their rule by violent means [13]. Both wings claim to represent the true Marxism of Marx, and in a way, both are right.   For, as mentioned above, Marx's views in this matter were somewhat ambiguous, because of his historicist approach ;   over and above this, he seems to have changed his views during the course of his life, starting as a radical and later adopting a more moderate position [14].

I shall examine the *radical position* first, since it appears to me the only one which fits in with *Capital* and the whole trend of Marx's prophetic argument.   For it is the main doctrine of *Capital* that the antagonism between capitalist and worker must necessarily increase, and that there is no compromise possible, so that capitalism can only be destroyed, not improved.   It will be best to quote the fundamental passage of *Capital* in which Marx finally sums up the 'historical tendency of capitalist accumulation '.   He writes [15] : ' Along with the steady decrease in the number of capitalist magnates who usurp and monopolize all the advantages of this development, there grows the extent of misery, oppression, servitude, degradation, and exploitation ; but at the same time, there rises the rebellious indignation of the working class which is steadily growing in number, and which is being disciplined, unified, and organized by the very mechanism of the capitalist method of production.   Ultimately, the monopoly of capital becomes a fetter upon the mode of production which has flourished with it, and under it.   Both the centralization in a few hands of the means of production, and the social organization of labour, reach a point where their capitalist cloak becomes a strait-jacket. It bursts asunder. The hour of capitalist private property has struck. The expropriators are expropriated.'

In view of this fundamental passage, there can be little doubt that the core of Marx's teaching in *Capital* was the impossibility of reforming capitalism, and the prophecy of its violent overthrow ; a doctrine corresponding to that of the radical wing. And this doctrine fits into our prophetic argument as well as can be. For if we grant not only the premise of the second step but the first conclusion as well, then the prophecy of the social revolution would indeed follow, in accordance with the passage we have quoted from *Capital*. (And the victory of the workers would follow too, as pointed out in the last chapter.) Indeed, it seems hard to envisage a fully united and class-conscious working class which would not in the end, if their misery cannot be mitigated by any other means, make a determined attempt to overthrow the social order. But this does not, of course, save the second conclusion. For we have already shown that the first conclusion is invalid ; and from the premise alone, from the theory of increasing wealth and misery, the inevitability of the social revolution cannot be derived. As pointed out in our analysis of the first conclusion, all we can say is that rebellious outbreaks may be unavoidable ; but since we can be sure neither of class unity nor of a developed class consciousness among the workers, we cannot identify such outbreaks with the social revolution. (They need not be victorious either, so that the assumption that they represent the social revolution would not fit in with the third step.)

As opposed to the radical position which at least fits quite well into the prophetic argument, the *moderate position* destroys it completely. But as was said before, it too has the support of Marx's authority. Marx lived long enough to see reforms carried out which, according to his theory, should have been impossible. But it never occurred to him that these improvements in the workers' lot were at the same time refutations of his theory. His ambiguous historicist view of the social revolution permitted him to interpret these reforms as its prelude [16] or even as its beginning. As Engels tells us [17], Marx reached the conclusion that in England, at any rate, ' the inevitable social revolution might be effected entirely by peaceful and legal means. He certainly never forgot to add that he hardly expected the English ruling class to submit, without a " pro-slavery

rebellion ", to this peaceful and legal revolution '. This report
agrees with a letter [18] in which Marx wrote, only three years
before his death : ' My party . . considers an English revolution not *necessary* but—according to historic precedents—*possible.*'
It should be noted that in the first at least of these statements,
the theory of the ' moderate wing ' is clearly expressed ; the
theory, namely, that should the ruling class not submit, violence
would be unavoidable.

These moderate theories seem to me to destroy the whole
prophetic argument [19]. They imply the possibility of a compromise, of a gradual reform of capitalism, and therefore, of a
decreasing class-antagonism. But the sole basis of the prophetic
argument is the assumption of an increasing class-antagonism.
There is no logical necessity why a gradual reform, achieved by
compromise, should lead to the complete destruction of the
capitalist system; why the workers, who have learned by experience that they can improve their lot by gradual reform, should
not prefer to stick to this method, even if it does not yield ' complete victory ', i.e. the submission of the ruling class ; why they
should not compromise with the bourgeoisie and leave it in
possession of the means of production rather than risk all their
gains by making demands liable to lead to violent clashes. Only
if we assume that ' the proletarians have nothing to lose but
their fetters ' [20], only if we assume that the law of increasing
misery is valid, or that it at least makes improvements impossible, only then can we prophesy that the workers will be forced
to make an attempt to overthrow the whole system. An evolutionary interpretation of the ' social revolution ' thus destroys
the whole Marxist argument, from the first step to the last ;
all that is left of Marxism would be the historicist approach.
If an historical prophecy is still attempted, then it must be based
upon an entirely new argument.

If we try to construct such a modified argument in accordance with Marx's later views and with those of the moderate
wing, preserving as much of the original theory as possible, then
we arrive at an argument based entirely upon the claim that
the working class represents now, or will one day represent, the
majority of the people. The argument would run like this.
Capitalism will be transformed by a ' social revolution ', by
which we now mean nothing but the advance of the class
struggle between capitalists and workers. This revolution may
either proceed by gradual and democratic methods, or it may

be violent, or it may be gradual and violent in alternate stages.
All this will depend upon the resistance of the bourgeoisie.   But
in any case, and particularly if the development is a peaceful
one, it must end with the workers assuming ' the position of the
ruling class ' [21], as the *Manifesto* says ; they must ' win the
battle of democracy ' ; for ' the proletarian movement is the
self-conscious independent movement of the immense majority,
in the interest of the immense majority '.

It is important to realize that even in this moderate and
modified form, the prediction is untenable.   The reason is this.
The theory of increasing misery must be given up if the possibility of gradual reform is admitted ; but with it, even the
semblance of a justification for the assertion that the industrial
workers must one day form the ' immense majority ' disappears.
I do not wish to imply that this assertion would really follow
from the Marxist theory of increasing misery, since this theory
has never taken sufficient heed of the farmers and peasants.
But if the law of increasing misery, supposed to reduce the
middle class to the level of the proletariat, is invalid, then we
must be prepared to find that a very considerable middle class
continues to exist (or that a new middle class has arisen) and
that it may co-operate with the other non-proletarian classes
against a bid for power by the workers ; and nobody can say
for certain what the outcome of such a contest would be.
Indeed, statistics no longer show any tendency for the number
of industrial workers to increase in relation to the other classes
of the population.   There is, rather, the opposite tendency, in
spite of the fact that the accumulation of instruments of production continues.   This fact alone refutes the validity of the
modified prophetic argument.   All that remains of it is the
important observation (which is, however, not up to the pretentious standards of a historicist prophecy) that social reforms
are carried out largely [22] under the pressure of the oppressed,
or (if this term is preferred) under the pressure of class struggle ;
that is to say, that the emancipation of the oppressed will be
largely the achievement of the oppressed themselves [23].

IV

The prophetic argument is untenable, and irreparable, in all
its interpretations, whether radical or moderate.   But for a full
understanding of this situation, it is not enough to refute the
modified prophecy ; it is also necessary to examine the *ambiguous*

attitude towards the problem of violence which we can observe in both the radical and the moderate Marxist parties. This attitude has, I assert, a considerable influence upon the question whether or not the ' battle of democracy' will be won ; for wherever the moderate Marxist wing has won a general election, or come close to it, one of the reasons seems to have been that they attracted large sections of the middle class. This was due to their humanitarianism, to their stand for freedom and against oppression. But the *systematic ambiguity* of their attitude towards violence not only tends to neutralize this attraction, but it also directly furthers the interest of the anti-democrats, the anti-humanitarians, the fascists.

There are two closely connected ambiguities in the Marxist doctrine, and both are important from this point of view. The one is an ambiguous attitude towards violence, founded upon the historicist approach. The other is the ambiguous way in which Marxists speak about ' the conquest of political power by the proletariat', as the *Manifesto* puts it [24]. What does this mean ? It may mean, and it is sometimes so interpreted, that the workers' party has the harmless and obvious aim of every democratic party, that of obtaining a majority, and of forming a government. But it may mean, and it is often hinted by Marxists that it does mean, that the party, once in power, intends to entrench itself in this position ; that is to say, that it will use its majority vote in such a way as to make it very difficult for others ever to regain power by ordinary democratic means. The difference between these two interpretations is most important. If a party which is at a certain time in the minority plans to suppress the other party, whether by violence or by means of a majority vote, then it recognizes by implication the right of the present majority party to do the same. It loses any moral right to complain about oppression ; and, indeed, it plays into the hands of those groups within the present ruling party who wish to suppress the opposition by force.

I may call these two ambiguities briefly *the ambiguity of violence* and *the ambiguity of power-conquest*. Both are rooted not only in the vagueness of the historicist approach, but also in the Marxist theory of the state. If the state is, essentially, a class tyranny, then, on the one hand, violence is permissible, and on the other, all that can be done is to replace the dictatorship of the bourgeoisie by that of the proletariat. To worry much about formal democracy merely shows lack of historical sense ; after all 'democracy is . . only one of the stages in the course of the historical development', as Lenin says [25].

The two ambiguities play their rôle in the tactical doctrines of both the radical and the moderate wings. This is understandable, since the systematic use of the ambiguity enables them to extend the realm from which prospective followers may be recruited. This is a tactical advantage which may, however, easily lead to a disadvantage at the most critical moment ; it may lead to a split whenever the most radical members think that the hour has struck for taking violent action. The way in which the radical wing may make a systematic use of the ambiguity of violence may be illustrated by the following extracts taken from Parkes' recent critical dissection of Marxism [26]. 'Since the Communist Party of the United States now declares not only that it does not now advocate revolution, but also that it never did advocate revolution, it may be advisable to quote a few sentences from the program of the Communist International (drafted in 1928).' Parkes then quotes among others the following passages from this programme : 'The Conquest of power by the proletariat does not mean peacefully " capturing " the ready-made bourgeois state by means of parliamentary majority. . . The conquest of power . . is the violent overthrow of bourgeois power, the destruction of the capitalist state apparatus. . . The Party . . is confronted with the task of leading the masses to a direct attack upon the bourgeois state. This is done by . . propaganda . . and . . mass action. . . This mass action includes . . finally, the general strike conjointly with armed insurrection. . . The latter form . . which is the supreme form, must be conducted according to the rules of war . .' One sees, from these quotations, that this part of the programme is quite unambiguous ; but this does not prevent the party from making a systematic use of the ambiguity of violence, withdrawing, if the tactical situation [27] demands it, towards a non-violent interpretation of the term 'social revolution' ; and this in spite of the concluding paragraph of the *Manifesto* [28] (which is retained by the programme of 1928) : 'The Communists disdain to conceal their views and aims. They openly declare that their aims can be attained only by the forcible overthrow of all the existing social conditions. . .'

But the way in which the moderate wing has systematically used the ambiguity of violence as well as that of power-conquest is even more important. It has been developed especially by

Engels, on the basis of Marx's more moderate views quoted above, and it has become a tactical doctrine which has greatly influenced later developments. The doctrine I have in mind might be presented as follows [29] : We Marxists much prefer a peaceful and democratic development towards socialism, if we can have it. But as political realists we foresee the probability that the bourgeoisie will not quietly stand by when we are within reach of attaining the majority. They will rather attempt to destroy democracy. In this case, we must not flinch, but fight back, and conquer political power. And since this development is a probable one, we must prepare the workers for it ; otherwise we should betray our cause. Here is one of Engels' passages [30] on the matter : ' For the moment . . legality . . is working so well in our favour that we should be mad to abandon it as long as it lasts. It remains to be seen whether it will not be the bourgeoisie . . which will abandon it first in order to crush us with violence. *Take the first shot, gentlemen of the bourgeoisie !* Never doubt it, they will be the first to fire. One fine day the . . bourgeoisie will grow tired of . . watching the rapidly increasing strength of socialism, and will have recourse to illegality and violence.' What will happen then is left systematically ambiguous. And this ambiguity is used as a threat ; for in later passages, Engels addresses the ' gentlemen of the bourgeoisie ' in the following way : ' If . . you break the constitution . . then the Social Democratic Party is free to act, or to refrain from acting, against you—whatever it likes best. What it is going to do, however, it will hardly give away to you to-day ! '

It is interesting to see how widely this doctrine differs from the original conception of Marxism which predicted that the revolution would come as the result of the increasing pressure of capitalism upon the workers, and not as the result of the increasing pressure of a successful working-class movement upon capitalists. This most remarkable change of front [31] shows the influence of the actual social development which turned out to be one of decreasing misery. But Engels' new doctrine, which leaves the revolutionary, or more precisely, the counter-revolutionary, initiative to the ruling class, is tactically absurd, and doomed to failure. The original Marxist theory taught that the workers' revolution will break out at the depth of a depression, i.e. at a moment when the political system is weakened by the breakdown of the economic system, a situation which would

contribute greatly to the victory of the workers. But if the
' gentlemen of the bourgeoisie ' are invited to take the first shot,
is it conceivable that they will be stupid enough not to choose
their moment wisely ?   Will they not make proper preparations
for the war they are going to wage ?   And since, according to
the theory, they hold the power, will such a preparation not
mean the mobilization of forces against which the workers can
have no slightest chance of victory ?   Such criticism cannot be
met by amending the theory so that the workers should not wait
until the other side strikes but try to anticipate them, since, on
its own assumption, it must always be easy for those in power
to be ahead in their preparations—to prepare rifles, if the
workers prepare sticks, guns if they prepare rifles, dive bombers
if they prepare guns, etc.

V

But this criticism, practical as it is, and corroborated by
experience, is only superficial.   The main defects of the doctrine
lie deeper.   The criticism I now wish to offer attempts to show
that both the presupposition of the doctrine and its tactical
consequences are such that they are likely to *produce* exactly that
anti-democratic reaction of the bourgeoisie which the theory
predicts, yet claims (with ambiguity) to abhor : the strengthening of the anti-democratic element in the bourgeoisie, and, in
consequence, civil war.   And we know that this may lead to
defeat, and to fascism.

The criticism I have in mind is, briefly, that Engels' tactical
doctrine, and, more generally, the ambiguities of violence and of
power-conquest, make the working of democracy impossible,
once they are adopted by an important political party.   I base
this criticism on the contention that democracy can work only
if the main parties adhere to a view of its functions which may
be summarized in some rules such as these (cp. also section II of
chapter 7) :

(1) Democracy cannot be fully characterized as the rule of
the majority, although the institution of general elections is most
important.   For a majority might rule in a tyrannical way.
(The majority of those who are less than 6 ft. high may decide
that the minority of those over 6 ft. shall pay all taxes.)   In
a democracy, the powers of the rulers must be limited ; and
the criterion of a democracy is this : In a democracy, the rulers
—that is to say, the government—can be dismissed by the ruled

without bloodshed. Thus if the men in power do not safeguard those institutions which secure to the minority the possibility of working for a peaceful change, then their rule is a tyranny.

(2) We need only distinguish between two forms of government, viz. such as possess institutions of this kind, and all others ; i.e. democracies and tyrannies.

(3) A consistent democratic constitution should exclude only one type of change in the legal system, namely a change which would endanger its democratic character.

(4) In a democracy, the full protection of minorities should not extend to those who violate the law, and especially not to those who incite others to the violent overthrow of the democracy [32].

(5) A policy of framing institutions to safeguard democracy must always proceed on the assumption that there may be anti-democratic tendencies latent among the ruled as well as among the rulers.

(6) If democracy is destroyed, all rights are destroyed. Even if certain economic advantages enjoyed by the ruled should persist, they would persist only on sufferance [33].

(7) Democracy provides an invaluable battle-ground for any reasonable reform, since it permits reform without violence. But if the preservation of democracy is not made the first consideration in any particular battle fought out on this battle-ground, then the latent anti-democratic tendencies which are always present (and which appeal to those who suffer under the strain of civilization, as we called it in chapter 10) may bring about a breakdown of democracy. If an understanding of these principles is not yet developed, its development must be fought for. The opposite policy may prove fatal ; it may bring about the loss of the most important battle, the battle for democracy itself.

As opposed to such a policy, that of Marxist parties can be characterized as one of *making the workers suspicious of democracy*. ' In reality the state is nothing more ', says Engels [34], ' than a machine for the oppression of one class by another, and this holds for a democratic republic no less than for a monarchy.' But such views must produce :

(a) A policy of blaming democracy for all the evils which it does not prevent, instead of recognizing that the democrats are to be blamed, and the opposition usually no less than the majority. (Every opposition has the majority it deserves.)

(*b*) A policy of educating the ruled to consider the state not
as theirs, but as belonging to the rulers.

(*c*) A policy of telling them that there is only one way to
improve things, that of the *complete conquest of power*. But this
neglects the one really important thing about democracy, that
it checks and balances power.

Such a policy amounts to doing the work of the enemies of
the open society ; it provides them with an unwitting fifth
column. And against the *Manifesto* which says [35] ambiguously :
' The first step in the revolution of the working class is to raise the
proletariat to the position of the ruling class—to win the battle
of democracy ', I assert that if this is accepted as the first step,
then the battle of democracy will be lost.

These are the general consequences of Engels' tactical doctrines, and of the ambiguities grounded in the theory of the
social revolution. Ultimately, they are merely the last consequences of Plato's way of posing the problem of politics by
asking ' who should rule the state ? ' (cp. chapter 7). It is high
time for us to learn that the question ' *who* is to wield the power
in the state ? ' matters only little as compared with the question ' *how* is the power wielded ? ' and ' *how much* power is
wielded ? ' We must learn that in the long run, all political
problems are institutional problems, problems of the legal framework ather than of persons, and that progress towards more
equality can be safeguarded only by the institutional control of
power.

VI

As in the previous chapter, I shall now illustrate the second
step by showing something of the way in which the prophecy
has influenced recent historical developments. All political
parties have some sort of ' vested interest ' in their opponent's
unpopular moves. They live by them and are therefore liable
to dwell upon, to emphasize, and even to look forward to them.
They may even encourage the political mistakes of their opponents as long as they can do so without becoming involved in
the responsibility for them. This, together with Engels' theory,
has led some Marxist parties to look forward to the political
moves made by their opponents against democracy. Instead of
fighting such moves tooth and nail, they were pleased to tell
their followers : ' See what these people do. That is what they
call democracy. That is what they call freedom and equality !

Remember it when *the day of reckoning* comes.' (An ambiguous phrase which may refer to election day or to the day of revolution.) This policy of letting one's opponents expose themselves must, if extended to moves against democracy, lead to disaster. It is a policy of talking big and doing nothing in the face of real and increasing danger to democratic institutions. It is a policy of talking war and acting peace ; and it taught the fascists the invaluable method of talking peace and acting war.

There is no doubt about the way in which the ambiguity just mentioned played into the hands of those fascist groups who wanted to destroy democracy. For we must reckon with the possibility that there will be such groups, and that their influence within the so-called bourgeoisie will depend largely on the policy adopted by the workers' parties.

For instance, let us consider more closely the use made in the political struggle of the threat of revolution or even of *political* strikes (as opposed to wage disputes, etc.). As explained above, the decisive question here would be whether such means are used as offensive weapons or solely for the defence of democracy. Within a democracy, they would be justified as a purely defensive weapon, and when resolutely applied in connection with a defensive and unambiguous demand they have been successfully used in this way. (Remember the quick breakdown of Kapp's putsch.) But if used as an offensive weapon they must lead to a strengthening of the anti-democratic tendencies in the opponent's camp, since they clearly make democracy unworkable. Furthermore, such use must make the weapon ineffective for defence. If you use the whip even when the dog is good, then it won't work if you need it to deter him from being bad. The defence of democracy must consist in making anti-democratic experiments too costly for those who try them ; much more costly than a democratic compromise. . . The use by the workers of any kind of non-democratic pressure is likely to lead to a similar, or even to an anti-democratic, counter-pressure—to provoke a move against democracy. Such an anti-democratic move on the part of the rulers is, of course, a much more serious and dangerous thing than a similar move on the part of the ruled. It would be the task of the workers to fight this dangerous move resolutely, to stop it in its inconspicuous beginnings. But how can they now fight in the name of democracy ? Their own anti-democratic action must provide their enemies, and those of democracy, with an opportunity.

The facts of the development described can, if one wishes,
be interpreted differently ; they may lead to the conclusion that
democracy is 'no good'. This is indeed a conclusion which
many Marxists have drawn. After having been defeated in
what they believed to be the democratic struggle (which they
had lost in the moment they formulated their tactical doctrine),
they said : 'We have been too lenient, too humane—next time
we will make a really bloody revolution !' It is as if a man who
loses a boxing match should conclude : boxing is no good—I
should have used a club. . . The fact is that the Marxists taught
the theory of class war to the workers, but the practice of it to
the reactionary diehards of the bourgeoisie. Marx talked war.
His opponents listened attentively ; then they began to talk peace
and accuse the workers of belligerency ; this charge the Marxists
could not deny, since class war was their slogan. And the fascists
acted.

So far, the analysis mainly covers certain more 'radical'
Social Democratic parties who based their policy entirely upon
Engels' ambiguous tactical doctrine. The disastrous effects of
Engels' tactics were increased in their case by the lack of a
practical programme discussed in the last chapter. But the
Communists too adopted the tactics here criticized in certain
countries and at certain periods, especially where the other
workers' parties, for instance the Social Democrats or the Labour
Party, observed the democratic rules.

But the position was different with the Communists in so
far as they had a programme. It was : 'Copy Russia !' This
made them more definite in their revolutionary doctrines as
well as in their assertion that democracy merely means the
dictatorship of the bourgeoisie [36]. According to this assertion,
not much could be lost and something would be gained if that
hidden dictatorship became an open one, apparent to all ; for
this could only bring the revolution nearer [37]. They even hoped
that a totalitarian dictatorship in Central Europe would speed
up matters. After all, since the revolution was bound to come,
fascism could only be one of the means of bringing it about ;
and this was more particularly so since the revolution was
clearly long overdue. Russia had already had it in spite of its
backward economic conditions. Only the vain hopes created
by democracy [38] were holding it back in the more advanced
countries. Thus the destruction of democracy through the
fascists could only promote the revolution by achieving the

ultimate disillusionment of the workers in regard to democratic methods. With this, the radical wing of Marxism [39] felt that it had discovered the ' essence ' and the ' true historical rôle ' of fascism. Fascism was, essentially, *the last stand of the bourgeoisie*. Accordingly, the Communists did not fight when the fascists seized power. (Nobody expected the Social Democrats to fight.) For the Communists were sure that the proletarian revolution was overdue and that the fascist interlude, necessary for its speeding up [40], could not last longer than a few months. Thus no action was required from the Communists. They were harmless. There was never a ' communist danger ' to the fascist conquest of power. As Einstein once emphasized, of all organized groups of the community, it was only the Church, or rather a section of the Church, which seriously offered resistance.

Chapter 20 : CAPITALISM AND ITS FATE

According to Marxist doctrine, capitalism is labouring under inner contradictions that threaten to bring about its downfall. A minute analysis of these contradictions and of the historical movement which they force upon society constitutes the first step of Marx's prophetic argument. This step is not only the most important of his whole theory, it is also the one on which he spent most of his labour, since practically the whole of the three volumes of *Capital* (over 2,200 pages in the original edition [1]) is devoted to its elaboration. It is also the least abstract step of the argument since it is based upon a descriptive analysis, supported by statistics, of the economic system of his time—that of unrestrained capitalism [2]. As Lenin puts it : ' Marx deduces the inevitability of the transformation of capitalist society into socialism wholly and exclusively from *the economic law of the movement of contemporary society.*'

Before proceeding to explain in some detail the first step of Marx's prophetic argument, I shall try to describe its main ideas in the form of a very brief outline.

Marx believes that capitalist competition forces the capitalist's hand. It forces the capitalist to accumulate capital. By doing so, he works against his own long-term economic interests (since the accumulation of capital is liable to bring about a fall of his profits). But although working against his own personal interest, he works in the interest of the historical development ; he works, unwittingly, for economic progress, and for socialism. This is due to the fact that accumulation of capital means (*a*) increased productivity ; increase of wealth ; and concentration of wealth in a few hands ; (*b*) increase of pauperism and misery ; the workers are kept on subsistence or starvation wages, mainly by the fact that the surplus of workers, called the ' industrial reserve army ', keeps the wages on the lowest possible level. The trade cycle prevents, for any length of time, the absorption of the surplus of workers by the growing industry. This cannot be altered by the capitalists, even if they wish to do so ; for the falling rate of their profits makes their own economic position much too precarious for any effective action. In this way, capitalist accumulation turns out to be a suicidal and self-contradictory process, even though it fosters the technical, economic, and historical progress towards socialism.

I

The premises of the first step are the laws of capitalist competition, and of the accumulation of the means of production. The conclusion is the law of increasing wealth and misery. I begin my discussion with an explanation of these premises and conclusions.

Under capitalism, competition between the capitalists plays an important rôle. ' The battle of competition ', as analysed by Marx in *Capital* [3], is carried out by selling the commodities produced, if possible at a lower price than the competitor could afford to accept. ' But the cheapness of a commodity ', Marx explains, ' depends in its turn, other things being equal, upon the productivity of labour ; and this, again, depends on the scale of production.' For production on a very large scale is in general capable of employing more specialized machinery, and a greater quantity of it ; this increases the productivity of the workers, and permits the capitalist to produce, and to sell, at a lower price. ' Large capitalists, therefore, get the better of small ones. . . Competition always ends with the downfall of many lesser capitalists and with the transition of their capital into the hands of the conqueror.' (This movement is, as Marx points out, much accelerated by the credit system.)

According to Marx's analysis, the process described, *accumulation due to competition*, has two different aspects. One of them is that the capitalist is forced to accumulate or concentrate more and more capital, in order to survive ; this means in practice investing more and more capital in more and more as well as newer and newer machinery, thus continually increasing the *productivity* of his workers. The other aspect of the accumulation of capital is the *concentration* of more and more wealth in the hands of the various capitalists, and of the capitalist class ; and along with it goes the reduction in the number of capitalists, a movement called by Marx the *centralization* [4] of capital (in contradistinction to mere accumulation or concentration).

Now three of these terms, competition, accumulation, and increasing productivity, indicate the fundamental tendencies of all capitalist production, according to Marx ; they are the tendencies to which I alluded when I described the *premise* of the first step as ' the laws of capitalist competition and of

accumulation '. The fourth and the fifth terms, however, concentration and centralization, indicate a tendency which forms
one part of the *conclusion* of the first step ; for they describe a
tendency towards a continuous increase of wealth, and its centralization in fewer and fewer hands. The other part of the
conclusion, however, the law of increasing misery, is only reached
by a much more complicated argument. But before beginning
an explanation of this argument, I must first explain this second
conclusion itself.

The term ' increasing misery ' may mean, as used by Marx,
two different things. It may be used in order to describe the
extent of misery, indicating that it is spread over an increasing
number of people ; or it may be used in order to indicate an
increase in the intensity of the suffering of the people. Marx
undoubtedly believed that misery was growing both in extent
and in intensity. This, however, is more than he needed in
order to carry his point. For the purpose of the prophetic
argument, a wider interpretation of the term ' increasing misery '
would do just as well (if not better [5]) ; an interpretation, namely,
according to which the extent of misery increases, while its
intensity may or may not increase, but at any rate does not show
any marked decrease.

But there is a further and much more important comment
to be made. Increasing misery, to Marx, involves fundamentally
an *increasing exploitation of the employed workers ; not only in numbers
but also in intensity*. It must be admitted that in addition it involves an increase in the suffering as well as in the numbers of the
unemployed, called [6] by Marx the (relative) ' surplus population ' or the ' industrial reserve army '. But the function of the
unemployed, in this process, is to exert pressure upon the employed workers, thus assisting the capitalists in their efforts to
make profit out of the employed workers, to exploit them. ' The
industrial reserve army ', Marx writes [7], ' belongs to capitalism
just as if its members had been reared by the capitalists at their
own cost. For its own varying needs, capital creates an ever-
ready supply of exploitable human material. . . During periods
of depression and of semi-prosperity, the industrial reserve army
keeps up its pressure upon the ranks of the employed workers ;
and during periods of excessive production and boom, it serves
to bridle their aspirations.' Increasing misery, according to
Marx, is essentially the increasing exploitation of labour power ;
and since labour power of the unemployed is not exploited,

they can serve in this process only as unpaid assistants of the capitalists in the exploitation of the employed workers. The point is important since later Marxists have often referred to unemployment as one of the empirical facts that verify the prophecy that misery tends to increase ; but unemployment can be claimed to corroborate Marx's theory only if it occurs together with increased exploitation of the employed workers, i.e. with long hours of work and with low real wages.

This may suffice to explain the term ' increasing misery '. But it is still necessary to explain the *law* of increasing misery which Marx claimed to have discovered. By this I mean the doctrine of Marx on which the whole prophetic argument hinges ; namely, the doctrine that capitalism cannot possibly afford to decrease the misery of the workers, since the mechanism of capitalist accumulation keeps the capitalist under a strong economic pressure which he is forced to pass on to the workers if he is not to succumb. This is why the capitalists cannot compromise, why they cannot meet any important demand of the workers, even if they wished to do so ; this is why ' capitalism cannot be reformed but can only be destroyed ' [8]. It is clear that this law is the decisive conclusion of the first step. The other conclusion, the law of increasing wealth, would be a harmless matter, if only it were possible for the increase of wealth to be shared by the workers. Marx's contention that this is impossible will therefore be the main subject of our critical analysis. But before proceeding to a presentation and criticism of Marx's arguments in favour of this contention, I may briefly comment on the first part of the conclusion, the theory of increasing wealth.

The tendency towards the accumulation and concentration of wealth, which Marx observed, can hardly be questioned. His theory of increasing productivity is also, in the main, unexceptionable. Although there may be limits to the beneficial effects exerted by the growth of an enterprise upon its productivity, there are hardly any limits to the beneficial effects of the improvement and accumulation of machinery. But in regard to the tendency towards the centralization of capital in fewer and fewer hands, matters are not quite so simple. Undoubtedly, there is a tendency in that direction, and we may grant that under an unrestrained capitalist system there are few counteracting forces. Not much can be said against this part of Marx's analysis as a description of an unrestrained capitalism. But considered as a prophecy, it is less tenable. For we know that now there are many means by which legislation can intervene. Taxation and death duties can be used most effectively to counteract centralization, and they have been so used. And anti-trust legislation can also be used, although perhaps with less effect. To evaluate the force of Marx's prophetic argument we must consider the possibility of great improvements in this direction ; and as in previous chapters, I must declare that the argument on which Marx bases this prophecy of centralization or of a decrease in the number of capitalists is inconclusive.

Having explained the main premises and conclusions of the first step, and having disposed of the first conclusion, we can now concentrate our attention entirely upon Marx's derivation of the other conclusion, the prophetic law of increasing misery. Three different trends of thought may be distinguished in his attempts to establish this prophecy. They will be dealt with in the next four sections of this chapter under the headings : II : the theory of value ; III : the effect of the surplus population upon wages ; IV : the trade cycle ; V : the effects of the falling rate of profit.

II

Marx's *theory of value*, usually considered by Marxists as well as by anti-Marxists as a corner-stone of the Marxist creed, is in my opinion one of its rather unimportant parts ; indeed, the sole reason why I am going to treat of it, instead of proceeding at once to the next section, is that it is generally held to be important, and that I cannot defend my reasons for differing from this opinion without discussing the theory. But I wish to make it clear at once that in holding that the theory of value is a redundant part of Marxism, I am defending Marx rather than attacking him. For there is little doubt that the many critics who have shown that the theory of value is very weak in itself are in the main perfectly right. But even if they were wrong, it would only strengthen the position of Marxism if it could be established that its decisive historico-political doctrines can be developed entirely independently of such a controversial theory.

The idea of the so-called *labour theory of value*[9], adapted by Marx for his purposes from suggestions he found in his predecessors (he refers especially to Adam Smith and David Ricardo), is simple enough. If you need a carpenter, you must pay him by the hour. If you ask him why a certain job is more expensive than another one, he will point out that there is more work in it. In addition to the labour, you must pay of course for the timber. But if you go into this a little more closely, then you find that you are, indirectly, paying for the labour involved in foresting, felling, transporting, sawing, etc. This consideration suggests the general theory that you have to pay for the job, or for any commodity you may buy, roughly in proportion to the amount of work in it, i.e. to the number of labour hours necessary for its production.

I say ' roughly ' because the actual prices fluctuate. But there is, or so at least it appears, always something more stable behind these prices, a kind of average price about which the actual prices oscillate [10], christened the ' exchange-value ' or, briefly, the ' value ' of the thing. Using this general idea, Marx defined the *value* of a commodity as the average number of labour hours necessary for its production (or for its reproduction).

The next idea, that of the *theory of surplus value*, is nearly as simple. It too was adapted by Marx from his predecessors. (Engels asserts [11]—perhaps mistakenly, but I shall follow his presentation of the matter—that Marx's main source was Ricardo.) The theory of surplus value is an attempt, within the limits of the labour theory of value, to answer the question : ' How does the capitalist make his profit ? ' If we assume that the commodities produced in his factory are sold on the market at their true value, i.e. according to the number of labour hours necessary for their production, then the only way in which the capitalist can make a profit is by paying his workers less than the full value of their product. Thus the wages received by the worker represent a value which is not equal to the number of hours he has worked. And we can accordingly divide his working day into two parts, the hours he has spent in producing value equivalent to his wages and the hours he has spent in producing value for the capitalist [12]. And correspondingly, we can divide the whole value produced by the worker into two parts, the value equal to his wages, and the rest, which is called *surplus value*. This surplus value is appropriated by the capitalist and is the sole basis for his *profit*.

So far, the story is simple enough. But now there arises a theoretical difficulty. The whole value theory has been introduced in order to explain the actual prices at which all commodities are exchanged ; and it is still assumed that the capitalist is able to obtain on the market the full value of his product, i.e. a price that corresponds to the total number of hours spent on it.   But it looks as if the worker does not get the full price of the commodity which he sells to the capitalist on the labour market. It looks as if he is cheated, or robbed ; at any rate, as if he is not paid according to the general law assumed by the value theory, namely, that *all* actual prices paid are, at least in a first approximation, determined by the value of the commodity.   (Engels says that the problem was realized by the economists who belonged to what Marx called ' the school of Ricardo ' ; and he asserts [13] that their inability to solve it led to the breakdown of this school.) There appeared what seemed a rather obvious solution of the difficulty.   The capitalist possesses a monopoly of the means of production, and this superior economic power can be used for bullying the worker into an agreement which violates the law of value.   But this solution (which I consider quite a plausible description of the situation) utterly destroys the labour theory of value.   For it now turns out that certain prices, namely, wages, do not correspond to their values, not even in a first approximation.   And this opens up the possibility that this may be true of other prices for similar reasons.

Such was the situation when Marx entered the scene in order to save the labour theory of value from destruction.   With the help of another simple but brilliant idea he succeeded in showing that the theory of surplus value was not only compatible with the labour theory of value but that it could also be rigidly deduced from the latter.   In order to achieve this deduction, we have only to ask ourselves : what is, precisely, the commodity which the worker sells to the capitalist ?   Marx's reply is : not his labour *hours*, but his whole labour *power*.   What the capitalist buys or hires on the labour market is the labour *power* of the worker. Let us assume, tentatively, that this commodity is sold at its true value.   What is its value ?   According to the definition of value, the value of labour *power* is the average number of labour *hours* necessary for its production or reproduction.   But this is, clearly, nothing but the number of hours necessary for producing the worker's (and his family's) *means of subsistence*.

Marx thus arrived at the following result.   The true value of the worker's whole labour power is equal to the labour hours needed for producing the means of his subsistence.   Labour power is sold for this price to the capitalist.   If the worker is able to work longer than that, then his surplus labour belongs to the buyer or hirer of his power.   The greater the productivity of labour, that is to say, the more a worker can produce per hour, the fewer hours will be needed for the production of his subsistence, and the more hours remain for his exploitation. This shows that the basis of capitalist exploitation is a *high productivity of labour*. If the worker could produce in a day no more than his own daily needs, then exploitation would be impossible without violating the law of value ; it would be possible only by means of cheating, robbery, or murder. But once the productivity of labour has, by the introduction of machinery, risen so high that one man can produce much more than he needs, capitalist exploitation becomes possible. It is possible even in a capitalist society which is ' ideal ' in the sense that every commodity, including labour power, is bought and sold at its true value. In such a society, the injustice of exploitation does not lie in the fact that the worker is not paid a ' just price ' for his labour power, but rather in the fact that he is so poor that he is forced to sell his labour power, while the capitalist is rich enough to buy labour power in great quantities, and to make profit out of it.

By this derivation [14] of the theory of surplus value, Marx saved the labour theory of value from destruction for the time being ; and in spite of the fact that I regard the whole ' value problem ' (in the sense of an ' objective ' true value round which the prices oscillate) as irrelevant, I am very ready to admit that this was a theoretical success of the first order. But Marx had done more than save a theory originally advanced by ' bourgeois economists '. With one stroke, he gave a theory of exploitation and a theory explaining why the workers' wages tend to oscillate about the subsistence (or starvation) level. But the greatest success was that he could now give an explanation, one in keeping with his economic theory of the legal system, of the fact that the capitalist mode of production tended to adopt the legal cloak of liberalism. For the new theory led him to the conclusion that once the introduction of new machinery had multiplied the productivity of labour, there arose the possibility of a new form of exploitation which used a free market instead of brutal force, and which was based on the ' formal ' observance of justice, equality before the law, and freedom. The capitalist system, he asserted, was not only a system of ' free competition ', but it was also ' maintained by the exploitation of the labour of others, but of labour which, *in a formal sense*, is free ' [15].

It is impossible for me to enter here into a detailed account of the really astonishing number of further applications made by Marx of his value theory. But it is also unnecessary, since my criticism of the theory will show the way in which the value theory can be eliminated from all these investigations. I am now going to develop this criticism ; its three main points are (a) that Marx's value theory does not suffice to explain exploitation, (b) that the additional assumptions which are necessary for such an explanation turn out to be sufficient, so that the theory of value turns out to be redundant, (c) that Marx's theory of value is an essentialist or metaphysical one.

(a) The fundamental law of the theory of value is the law that the prices of practically all commodities, including wages, are determined by their values, or more precisely, that they are at least in a first approximation proportional to the labour hours necessary for their production. Now this ' law of value ', as I may call it, at once raises a problem. Why does it hold ? Obviously, neither the buyer nor the seller of the commodity can see, at a glance, how many hours are necessary for its production ; and even if they could, it would not explain the law of value. For it is clear that the buyer simply buys as cheaply as he can, and that the seller charges as much as he can get. This, it appears, must be one of the fundamental assumptions of any theory of market prices. In order to explain the law of value, it would be our task to show why the buyer is unlikely to succeed in buying below, and the seller in selling above, the ' value ' of a commodity. This problem was seen more or less clearly by those who believed in the labour theory of value, and their reply was this. For the purpose of simplification, and in order to obtain a first approximation, let us assume perfectly free competition, and for the same reason let us consider only such commodities as can be manufactured in practically unlimited quantities (if only the labour were available). Now let us assume that the price of such a commodity is above its value ; this would mean that excessive profits can be made in this particular branch of production. It would encourage various manufacturers to produce this commodity, and competition would lower the price. The opposite process would lead to an increase in the price of a commodity which is sold below its value. Thus there will be oscillations of price, and these will tend to centre about the values of commodities. In other words, it is a mechanism of *supply and demand* which, under free competition, tends to give force [16] to the law of value.

Such considerations as these can be found frequently in Marx, for instance, in the third volume of *Capital* [17], where he tries to explain why there is a tendency for all profits in the various branches of manufacture to approximate, and adjust themselves, to a certain average profit. And they are also used in the first volume, especially in order to show why wages are kept low, near subsistence level, or, what amounts to the same, just above starvation level. It is clear that with wages below this level, the workers would actually starve, and the supply of labour power on the labour market would disappear. But as long as men live, they will reproduce ; and Marx attempts to show in detail (as we shall see in section iv), why the mechanism of capitalist accumulation must create a surplus population, an industrial reserve army. Thus as long as wages are just above starvation level there will always be not only a sufficient but even an excessive supply of labour power on the labour market ; and it is this excessive supply which, according to Marx, prevents the rise of wages [18] : ' The industrial reserve army keeps up its pressure upon the ranks of the employed workers ; . . thus surplus population is the background in front of which there operates the law of supply and demand of labour. Surplus population restricts the range within which this law is permitted to operate to such limits as best suit the capitalist greed for exploitation and domination.'

(*b*) Now this passage shows that Marx himself realized the necessity of backing up the law of value by a more concrete theory ; a theory which shows, in any particular case, how the *laws of supply and demand* bring about the effect which has to be explained ; for instance, starvation wages. But if these laws are sufficient to explain these effects, then we do not need the labour theory of value at all, whether or not it may be tenable as a first approximation (which I do not think it is). Furthermore, as Marx realized, the laws of supply and demand are necessary for explaining all those cases in which there is no free competition, and in which his law of value is therefore clearly out of operation ; for instance, where a monopoly can be used to keep prices constantly above their ' values '. Marx considered such cases as exceptions, which is hardly the right view ; but however this may be, the case of monopolies shows not only that the laws of supply and demand are necessary to supplement his law of value, but also that they are more generally applicable.

On the other hand, it is clear that the laws of supply and demand are not only necessary but also sufficient to explain

all the phenomena of ' exploitation ' which Marx observed—
the phenomena, more precisely, of the misery of the workers side
by side with the wealth of the entrepreneurs—if we assume, as
Marx did, a free labour market as well as a chronically excessive
supply of labour. (Marx's theory of this excessive supply will
be discussed more fully in section IV below.) As Marx shows,
it is clear enough that the workers will be forced, under such
circumstances, to work long hours at low wages, in other words,
to permit the capitalist to ' appropriate the best part of the fruits
of their labour '. And in this trivial argument, which is part of
Marx's own, there is no need even to mention ' value '.

Thus the value theory turns out to be a completely redundant
part of Marx's theory of exploitation ; and this holds independently of the question whether or not the value theory is true.
But the part of Marx's theory of exploitation which remains
after the value theory is eliminated is undoubtedly correct,
provided we accept the doctrine of surplus population. It is
unquestionably true that (in the absence of a redistribution of
wealth through the state) the existence of a surplus population
must lead to starvation wages, and to provocative differences in
the standard of living.

(What is not so clear, and not explained by Marx either, is
why the supply of labour should continue to exceed the demand.
For if it is so profitable to ' exploit ' labour, how is it, then, that
the capitalists are not forced, by competition, to try to raise their
profits by employing more labour ? In other words, why do they
not compete against each other on the labour market, thereby
raising the wages to the point where they begin to become no
longer sufficiently profitable, so that it is no longer possible to
speak of exploitation ? Marx would have answered—see section
v, below—' Because competition forces them to invest more and
more capital in machinery, so that they cannot increase that part
of their capital which they use for wages '. But this answer is
unsatisfactory since even if they spend their capital on machinery,
they can do so only by buying labour to build machinery, or by
causing others to buy such labour, thus increasing the demand
for labour. It appears, for such reasons, that the phenomena of
' exploitation ' which Marx observed were due, not, as he
believed, to the mechanism of a perfectly competitive market, but
to other factors—especially to a mixture of low productivity and
imperfectly competitive markets. But a detailed and satisfactory
explanation [19] of the phenomena appears still to be missing.)

(c) Before leaving this discussion of the value theory and the part played by it in Marx's analysis, I wish to comment briefly upon another of its aspects. The whole idea—which was not Marx's invention—that there is something *behind* the prices, an objective or real or true value of which prices are only a ' form of appearance ' [20], shows clearly enough the influence of Platonic Idealism with its distinction between a hidden essential or true reality, and an accidental or delusive appearance. Marx, it must be said, made a great effort [21] to destroy this mystical character of objective ' value ', but he did not succeed. He tried to be realistic, to accept only something observable and important—labour hours—as the reality which appears in the form of price ; and it cannot be questioned that the number of labour hours necessary for producing a commodity, i.e. its Marxian ' value ', is an important thing. And in a way, it surely is a purely verbal problem whether or not we should call these labour hours the ' value ' of the commodity. But such a terminology may become most misleading and strangely unrealistic, especially if we assume with Marx that the productivity of labour increases. For it has been pointed out by Marx himself [22] that, with increasing productivity, the value of all commodities decreases, and that an increase is therefore possible in real wages as well as real profits, i.e. in the commodities consumed by workers and by capitalists respectively, together with a decrease in the ' value ' of wages and of profits, i.e. in the hours spent on them. Thus wherever we find real progress, such as shorter working hours and a greatly improved standard of living of the workers (quite apart from a higher income in money [23], even if calculated in gold), then the workers could at the same time bitterly complain that the Marxian ' value ', the real essence or substance of their income, is dwindling away, since the labour hours necessary for its production have been reduced. (An analogous complaint might be made by the capitalists.) All this is admitted by Marx himself ; and it shows how misleading the value terminology must be, and how little it represents the real social experience of the workers. In the labour theory of value, the Platonic ' essence ' has become entirely divorced from experience [24] . . .

III

After eliminating Marx's labour theory of value and his theory of surplus value, we can, of course, still retain his analysis (see the end of (*a*) in section ɪɪ) of the pressure exerted by the *surplus population* upon the wages of the employed workers. It cannot be denied that, if there is a free labour market *and* a surplus population, i.e. widespread and chronic unemployment (and there can be no doubt that unemployment played its rôle in Marx's time and ever since), then wages cannot rise above starvation wages ; and under the same assumption, together with the doctrine of accumulation developed above, Marx, although not justified in proclaiming a law of increasing misery, was right in asserting that, in a world of high profits and increasing wealth, starvation wages and a life of misery might be the permanent lot of the workers.

I think that, even if Marx's analysis was defective, his effort to explain the phenomenon of ' exploitation ' deserves the greatest respect. (As mentioned at the end of (*b*) in the foregoing section, no really satisfactory theory seems to exist even now.) It must be said, of course, that Marx was wrong when he prophesied that the conditions which he observed were to be permanent if not changed by a revolution, and even more when he prophesied that they would get worse. The facts have refuted these prophecies. Moreover, even if we could admit the validity of his analysis for an unrestrained, a non-interventionist system, even then would his prophetic argument be inconclusive. For the tendency towards increasing misery operates, according to Marx's own analysis, only under a system in which the labour market is free—in a perfectly unrestrained capitalism. But once we admit the possibility of trade unions, of collective bargaining, of strikes, then the assumptions of the analysis are no longer applicable, and the whole prophetic argument breaks down. According to Marx's own analysis, we should have to expect that such a development would either be suppressed, or that it would be equivalent to a social revolution. For collective bargaining can oppose capital by establishing a kind of monopoly of labour ; it can prevent the capitalist from using the industrial reserve army for the purpose of keeping wages down ; and in this way it can force the capitalists to content themselves with lower profits. We see here why the cry ' Workers, unite ! ' was, from a Marxian point of view, indeed the only possible reply to an unrestrained capitalism.

But we see, too, why this cry must open up the whole problem of state interference, and why it is likely to lead to the end of the unrestrained system, and to a new system, *interventionism* [25], which may develop in very different directions. For it is almost inevitable that the capitalists will contest the workers' right to unite, maintaining that unions must endanger the freedom of competition on the labour market. Non-interventionism thus faces the problem (it is part of the paradox of freedom [26]) : Which freedom should the state protect ? The freedom of the labour market, or the freedom of the poor to unite ? Whichever decision is taken, it leads to state intervention, to the use of organized political power, of the state as well as of unions, in the field of economic conditions. It leads, under all circumstances, to an extension of the economic responsibility of the state, whether or not this responsibility is consciously accepted. And this means that the assumptions on which Marx's analysis is based must disappear.

The derivation of the historical law of increasing misery is thus invalid. All that remains is a moving description of the misery of the workers which prevailed a hundred years ago, and a valiant attempt to explain it with the help of what we may call, with Lenin [27], Marx's ' economic law of the movement of contemporary society ' (that is, of the unrestrained capitalism of a hundred years ago). But in so far as it is meant as an historical prophecy, and in so far as it is used to deduce the ' inevitability ' of certain historical developments, the derivation is invalid.

IV

The significance of Marx's analysis rests very largely upon the fact that a surplus population actually existed at his time, and down to our own day (a fact which has hardly received a really satisfactory explanation yet, as I said before). So far, however, we have not yet discussed Marx's argument in support of his contention that it is the mechanism of capitalist production itself that always produces the surplus population which it needs for keeping down the wages of the employed workers. But this theory is not only ingenious and interesting in itself ; it contains at the same time Marx's *theory of the trade cycle* and of general depressions, a theory which clearly bears upon the prophecy of the crash of the capitalist system because of the intolerable misery which it must produce. In order to make as strong a case for Marx's theory as I can, I have altered it slightly [28] (namely, by introducing a distinction between two kinds of machinery, the one for the mere extension, and the other for the intensification, of production). But this alteration need not arouse the suspicion of Marxist readers ; for I am not going to criticize the theory at all.

The amended theory of surplus population and of the trade cycle may be outlined as follows. The accumulation of capital means that the capitalist spends part of his profits on new machinery ; this may also be expressed by saying that only a part of his real profits consists in goods for consumption, while part of it consists in machines. These machines, in turn, may be intended either for the *expansion* of industry, for new factories, etc., or they may be intended for *intensifying* production by increasing the productivity of labour in the existing industries. The former kind of machinery makes possible an increase of employment, the latter kind has the effect of making workers superfluous, of ' setting the workers at liberty ' as this process was called in Marx's day. (Nowadays it is sometimes called ' technological unemployment '.) Now the mechanism of capitalist production, as envisaged by the amended Marxist theory of the trade cycle, works roughly like this. If we assume, to start with, that for some reason or other there is a general expansion of industry, then a part of the industrial reserve army will be absorbed, the pressure upon the labour market will be relieved, and wages will show a tendency to rise. A period of prosperity begins. But the moment wages rise, certain mechanical improvements which intensify production and which were previously unprofitable because of the low wages may become profitable (even though the cost of such machinery will begin to rise). Thus more machinery will be produced of the kind that ' sets the workers at liberty '. As long as these machines are only in the process of being produced, prosperity continues, or increases. But once the new machines are themselves beginning to produce, the picture changes. (This change is, according to Marx, accentuated by a fall in the rate of profit, to be discussed under (v), below.) Workers will be ' set at liberty ', i.e. condemned to starvation. But the disappearance of many consumers must lead to a collapse of the home market. In consequence, great numbers of machines in the expanded factories become idle (the less efficient machinery first), and this leads to a further increase of unemployment and a further collapse of the market. The fact that much machinery now lies idle means that much capital has become worthless, that many capitalists cannot fulfil their obligations ; thus a financial crisis develops, leading to complete stagnation in the production of capital goods, etc. But while the depression (or, as Marx calls it, the ' crisis ') takes its course, the conditions are ripening for a recovery. These conditions mainly consist in the growth of the industrial reserve army and the consequent readiness of the workers to accept starvation wages. At very low wages, production becomes profitable even at the low prices of a depressed market ; and once production starts, the capitalist begins again to accumulate, to buy machinery. Since wages are very low, he will find that it is not yet profitable to use new machinery (perhaps invented in the meanwhile) of the type which sets the workers at liberty. At first he will rather buy machinery with the plan of extending production. This leads slowly to an extension of employment and to a recovery of the home market. Prosperity is coming once again. Thus we are back at our starting point. The cycle is closed, and the process can start once more.

This is the amended Marxist theory of unemployment and of the trade cycle. As I have promised, I am not going to criticize it. The theory of trade cycles is a very difficult affair, and we certainly do not yet know enough about it (at least I don't). It is very likely that the theory outlined is incomplete, and, especially, that such aspects as the existence of a monetary system based partly upon credit creation, and the effects of hoarding, are not sufficiently taken into account. But however this may be, the trade cycle is a fact which cannot easily be argued away, and it is one of the greatest of Marx's merits to have emphasized its significance as a social problem. But although all this must be admitted, we may criticize the prophecy which Marx attempts to base upon his theory of the trade cycle. First of all, he asserts that depressions will become increasingly worse, not only in their scope but also in the intensity of the workers' suffering. But he gives no argument to support this (apart, perhaps, from the theory of the fall in the rate of profit, which will be discussed presently). And if we look at actual developments, then we must say that terrible as are the effects and especially the psychological effects of unemployment even in those countries where the workers are now insured against it, there is no doubt that the workers' sufferings were incomparably worse in Marx's day. But this is not my main point.

In Marx's day, nobody ever thought of that technique of state intervention which is now called ' counter cycle policy ' ; and, indeed, such a thought must be utterly foreign to an

unrestrained capitalist system.   (But even before Marx's time, we
find the beginning of doubts about, and even of investigations into,
the wisdom of the credit policy of the Bank of England during
a depression [29].) Unemployment insurance, however, means
intervention, and therefore an increase in the responsibility of
the state, and it is likely to lead to experiments in counter cycle
policy. I do not maintain that these experiments must necessarily be successful (although I do believe that the problem
may in the end prove not so very difficult, and that Sweden [30],
in particular, has already shown what can be done in this field).
But I wish to assert most emphatically that the belief that it
is impossible to abolish unemployment by piecemeal measures
is on the same plane of dogmatism as the numerous physical
proofs (proffered by men who lived even later than Marx)
that the problems of aviation would always remain insoluble.
When the Marxists say, as they sometimes do, that Marx has
proved the uselessness of a counter cycle policy and of similar
piecemeal measures, then they simply do not speak the truth ;
Marx investigated an unrestrained capitalism, and he never
dreamt of interventionism.   He therefore never investigated the
possibility of a systematic interference with the trade cycle, much
less did he offer a proof of its impossibility.   It is strange to
find that the same people who complain of the irresponsibility
of the capitalists in the face of human suffering are irresponsible enough to oppose, with dogmatic assertions of this kind,
experiments from which we may learn how to relieve human
suffering (how to become masters of our social environment,
as Marx would have said), and how to control some of the unwanted social repercussions of our actions.   But the apologists
of Marxism are quite unaware of the fact that in the name of
their own vested interests they are fighting against progress ;
they do not see that it is the danger of any movement like Marxism
that it soon comes to represent all kinds of vested interests, and
that there are intellectual investments, as well as material ones.
    Another point must be stated here.   Marx, as we have seen,
believed that unemployment was fundamentally a gadget of the
capitalist mechanism with the function of keeping wages low,
and of making the exploitation of the employed workers easier ;
increasing misery always involved for him increasing misery of
the employed workers too ; and this is just the whole point of
the plot.   But even if we assume that this view was justified in
his day, as a prophecy it has been definitely refuted by later

experience. The standard of living of employed workers has risen everywhere since Marx's day ; and (as Parkes [31] has emphasized in his criticism of Marx) the real wages of *employed* workers tend even to increase during a depression (they did so, for example, during the last great depression), owing to a more rapid fall in prices than in wages. This is a glaring refutation of Marx, especially since it proves that the main burden of unemployment insurance was borne not by the workers, but by the entrepreneurs, who therefore lost directly through unemployment, instead of profiting indirectly, as in Marx's scheme.

V

None of the Marxist theories so far discussed do even seriously attempt to prove the point which is the most decisive one within the first step ; namely, that accumulation keeps the capitalist under a strong economic pressure which he is forced, on pain of his own destruction, to pass on to the workers ; so that capitalism can only be destroyed, but not reformed. An attempt to prove this point is contained in that theory of Marx's which aims at establishing the law *that the rate of profit tends to fall*.

What Marx calls the rate of profit corresponds to the rate of interest ; it is the percentage of the yearly average of capitalist profit over the whole invested capital. This rate, Marx says, tends to fall owing to the rapid growth of capital investments ; for these must accumulate more quickly than profits can rise.

The argument by which Marx attempts to prove this is again rather ingenious. Capitalist competition, as we have seen, forces the capitalists to make investments that increase the productivity of labour. Marx even admitted that by this increase in productivity they render a great service to mankind [32] : ' It is one of the civilizing aspects of capitalism that it exacts surplus value in a manner and under circumstances which are more favourable than previous forms (such as slavery, serfdom, etc.) to the development of the productive powers, as well as to the social conditions for a reconstruction of society on a higher plane. For this, it even creates the elements ; . . for the quantity of useful commodities produced in any given span of time depends upon the productivity of labour.' But this service to mankind is not only rendered without any intention by the capitalists ; the action to which they are forced by competition also runs counter to their own interests, for the following reason.

The capital of any industrialist can be divided into two

parts. One is invested in land, machinery, raw materials, etc. The other is used for wages. Marx calls the first part ' constant capital ' and the second ' variable capital ' ; but since I consider this terminology rather misleading, I shall call the two parts ' immobilized capital ' and ' wage capital '. The capitalist, according to Marx, can profit only by exploiting the workers ; in other words, by using his wage capital. Immobilized capital is a kind of a dead weight which he is forced by competition to carry on with, and even to increase continually. This increase is not, however, accompanied by a corresponding increase in his profits ; only an extension of the wage capital could have this wholesome effect. But the general tendency towards an increase in productivity means that the material part of capital increases relatively to its wage part. Therefore, the total capital increases also, and without a compensating increase in profits ; that is to say, the rate of profit must fall.

Now this argument has been often questioned ; indeed, it was attacked, by implication, long before Marx [33]. In spite of these attacks, I believe that there may be something in Marx's argument ; especially if we take it together with his theory of the trade cycle. (I shall return to this point briefly in the next chapter.) But what I wish to question here is the bearing of this argument upon the theory of increasing misery.

Marx sees this connection as follows. If the rate of profit tends to fall, then the capitalist is faced with destruction. All he can do is to attempt to ' take it out of the workers ', i.e. to increase exploitation. This he can do by extending working hours ; speeding up work ; lowering wages ; raising the workers' cost of living (inflation) ; exploiting more women and children. The inner contradictions of capitalism, based on the fact that competition and profit-making are in conflict, develop here into a climax. First, they force the capitalist to accumulate and to increase productivity, and so reduce the rate of profit. Next, they force him to increase exploitation to an intolerable degree, and with it the tension between the classes. Thus compromise is impossible. The contradictions cannot be removed. They must finally seal the fate of capitalism.

This is the main argument. But can it be conclusive ? We must remember that increased productivity is the very basis of capitalist exploitation ; only if the worker can produce much more than he needs for himself and his family can the capitalist appropriate surplus labour. Increased productivity, in Marx's terminology, means increased surplus labour ; it means both an increased number of hours available to the capitalist, and on top of this, an increased number of commodities produced per hour. It means, in other words, a greatly increased profit. This is admitted by Marx [34]. He does not hold that profits are dwindling ; he only holds that the total capital increases much more quickly than the profits, so that the *rate* of profit falls.

But if this is so, there is no reason why the capitalist should labour under an economic pressure which he is forced to pass on to the workers, whether he likes it or not. It is true, probably, that he does not like to see a fall in his rate of profit. But as long as his income does not fall, but, on the contrary, rises, there is no real danger. The situation for a successful average capitalist will be this : he sees his income rise quickly, and his capital still more quickly ; that is to say, his savings rise more quickly than the part of his income which he consumes. I do not think that this is a situation which must force him to desperate measures, or which makes a compromise with the workers impossible. On the contrary, it seems to me quite tolerable.

It is true, of course, that the situation contains an element of danger. Those capitalists who speculate on the assumption of a constant or of a rising rate of profit may get into trouble ; and things such as these may indeed contribute to the trade cycle, accentuating the depression. But this has little to do with the sweeping consequences which Marx prophesied.

This concludes my analysis of the third and last argument, propounded by Marx in order to prove the law of increasing misery.

VI

In order to show how completely wrong Marx was in his prophecies, and at the same time how justified he was in his glowing protest against the hell of an unrestrained capitalism as well as in his demand, ' Workers, unite ! ', I shall quote a few passages from the chapter of *Capital* in which he discusses the ' General Law of Capitalist Accumulation ' [35]. ' In factories . . young male workers are used up in masses before they reach the age of manhood ; after that, only a very small proportion remains useful for industry, so that they are constantly dismissed in large numbers. They then form part of the floating surplus population which grows with the growth of industry . . Labour power is so quickly used up by capital that the middle-aged worker is usually a worn-out man . . Dr. Lee, medical officer of health, declared not long ago " that the average age at death of the Manchester upper middle class was 38, while the average age at death of the labouring class was 17 ; while at Liverpool those figures were represented as 35 against 15 . ." . . The exploitation of working-class children puts a premium upon their production. . . The higher the productivity of labour . . the more precarious become the worker's conditions of existence. . . Within the capitalist system, all the methods for raising the social productivity of labour . . are transformed into means of domination and of exploitation ; they mutilate the worker into a fragment of a human being, they degrade him to a mere cog in the machine, they make work a torture, . . and drag his wife and children beneath the wheels of the capitalist Juggernaut . . *It follows that to the degree in which capital accumulates, the worker's condition must deteriorate, whatever his payment may be* . . the greater the social wealth, the amount of capital at work, the extent and energy of its growth, . . the larger is the surplus population. . . The size of the industrial reserve army grows as the power of wealth grows. But . . the larger the industrial reserve army, the larger are the masses of the workers whose misery is relieved only by an increase in the agony of toil ; and . . the larger is the number of those who are officially recognized as paupers. *This is the absolute and general law of capitalist accumulation.* . . The accumulation of wealth at the one pole of society involves at the same time an accumulation of misery, of the agony of toil, of slavery, ignorance, brutalization, and of moral degradation, at the opposite pole . .'

Marx's terrible picture of the economy of his time is only too true. But his law that misery must increase together with accumulation does not hold. Means of production have accumulated and the productivity of labour has increased since his day to an extent which even he would hardly have thought possible. But child labour, working hours, the agony of toil, and the precariousness of the worker's existence, have not increased ; they have declined. I do not say that this process must continue. There is no law of progress, and everything will depend on ourselves. But the actual situation is briefly and fairly summed up by Parkes [36] in one sentence : ' Low wages, long hours, and child labour have been characteristic of capitalism not, as Marx predicted, in its old age, but in its infancy.'

Unrestrained capitalism is gone.   Since the day of Marx, democratic interventionism has made immense advances, and the improved productivity of labour—a consequence of the accumu- lation of capital—has made it possible virtually to stamp out misery.   This shows that much has been achieved, in spite of undoubtedly grave mistakes, and it should encourage us to believe that more can be done.   For much remains to be done and to be undone.   Democratic interventionism can only make it possible. It rests with us to do it.

I have no illusions concerning the force of my arguments. Experience shows that Marx's prophecies were false.   But experience can always be explained away.   And, indeed, Marx himself, and Engels, began with the elaboration of an *auxiliary hypothesis* designed to explain why the law of increasing misery does not work as they expected it to do.   According to this hypothesis, the tendency towards a falling rate of profit, and with it, increasing misery, is counteracted by the effects of *colonial exploitation*, or, as it is usually called, by 'modern imperialism '.   Colonial exploitation, according to this theory, is a method of passing on economic pressure to the colonial proletariat, a group which, economically as well as politically, is weaker still than the industrial proletariat at home.   ' Capital invested in colonies ', Marx writes [37], ' may yield a higher rate of profit for the simple reason that the rate of profit is higher there where capitalist development is still in a backward stage, and for the added reason that slaves, coolies, etc., permit a better exploitation of labour.   I can see no reason why these higher rates of profit . . , when sent home, should not enter there as elements into the average rate of profit, and, in proportion, contribute to keeping it up.'   (It is worth mentioning that the main idea behind this theory of ' modern ' imperialism can be traced back for more than 160 years, to Adam Smith, who said of colonial trade that it ' has necessarily contributed to keep up the rate of profit '.)   Engels went one step further than Marx in his development of the theory.   Forced to admit that in Britain the prevailing tendency was not towards an increase in misery but rather towards a considerable improvement, he hints that this may be due to the fact that Britain ' is exploiting the whole world ' ;   and he scornfully assails ' the British working class ' which, instead of suffering as he expected them to do, ' is actually becoming more and more bourgeois '.   And he con- tinues [38] : ' It seems that this most bourgeois of all nations wants

to bring matters to such a pass as to have a bourgeois aristocracy
and a bourgeois proletariat *side by side* with the bourgeoisie.'
Now this change of front on Engels' part is at least as remarkable
as that other one of his which I mentioned in the last chapter [39];
and like that, it was made under the influence of a social development which turned out to be one of decreasing misery.   Marx
blamed capitalism for ' proletarianizing the middle class and the
lower bourgeoisie ', and for reducing the workers to pauperism.
Engels now blames the system—it is still blamed—for making
bourgeois out of workers.   But the nicest touch in Engels' complaint is the indignation that makes him call the British who
behave so inconsiderately as to falsify Marxist prophecies ' this
most bourgeois of all nations '.   According to Marxist doctrine,
we should expect from the ' most bourgeois of all nations ' a
development of misery and class tension to an intolerable degree ;
instead, we hear that the opposite takes place.   But the good
Marxist's hair rises when he hears of the incredible wickedness of
a capitalist system that transforms good proletarians into bad
bourgeois ;   quite forgetting that Marx showed that the wickedness of the system consisted solely in the fact that it was working
the other way round.   Thus we read in Lenin's analysis [40] of the
evil causes and dreadful effects of modern British imperialism :
' Causes :   (1) exploitation of the whole world by this country ;
(2) its monopolistic position in the world market ;   (3) its colonial
monopoly.   Effects :   (1) *bourgeoisification of a part of the British
proletariat* ;   (2) a part of the proletariat permits itself to be led by
people who are bought by the bourgeoisie, or who are at least
paid by it.'   Having given such a pretty Marxist name, ' the
bourgeoisification of the proletariat ', to a hateful tendency—
hateful mainly because it did not fit in with the way the world
should go according to Marx—Lenin apparently believes that it
has become a Marxist tendency.   Marx himself held that the
more quickly the whole world could go through the necessary
historical period of capitalist industrialization, the better, and he
was therefore inclined to support [41] imperialist developments.
But Lenin came to a very different conclusion.   Since Britain's
possession of colonies was the reason why the workers at home
followed ' leaders bought by the bourgeoisie ' instead of the Communists, he saw in the colonial empire a potential trigger or fuse.
A revolution there would make the law of increasing misery
operative at home, and a revolution at home would follow.   Thus
the colonies were the place from which the fire would spread. . .

I do not believe that the auxiliary hypothesis whose history I have sketched can save the law of increasing misery ; for this hypothesis is itself refuted by experience. There are countries, for instance the Scandinavian democracies, Czechoslovakia, Canada, Australia, New Zealand, to say nothing of the United States, in which a democratic interventionism secured to the workers a high standard of living, in spite of the fact that colonial exploitation had no influence there, or was at any rate far too unimportant to support the hypothesis. Furthermore, if we compare certain countries that 'exploit' colonies, like Holland and Belgium, with Denmark, Sweden, Norway, and Czechoslovakia which do not 'exploit' colonies, we do not find that the industrial *workers* profited from the possession of colonies, for the situation of the working classes in all those countries was strikingly similar. Furthermore, although the misery imposed upon the natives through colonization is one of the darkest chapters in the history of civilization, it cannot be asserted that their misery has tended to increase since the days of Marx. The exact opposite is the case ; things have greatly improved. And yet, increasing misery would have to be very noticeable there if the auxiliary hypothesis and the original theory were both correct.

VII

As I did with the second and third steps in the previous chapters, I shall now illustrate the first step of Marx's prophetic argument by showing something of its practical influence upon the tactics of Marxist parties.

The Social Democrats, under the pressure of obvious facts, tacitly dropped the theory that the intensity of misery increases ; but their whole tactics remained based upon the assumption that the law of the increasing extent of misery was valid, that is to say, that the numerical strength of the industrial proletariat must continue to increase. This is why they based their policy exclusively upon representing the interests of the industrial workers, at the same time firmly believing that they were representing, or would very soon represent, 'the great majority of the population' [42]. They never doubted the assertion of the *Manifesto* that 'All previous historical movements were movements of minorities. . . The proletarian movement is the self-conscious, independent movement of the immense majority, in the interest of the immense majority.' They waited confidently, therefore, for the day when the class consciousness and class

assuredness of the industrial workers would win them the majority
in the elections. ' There can be no doubt as to who will be
victorious in the end—the few exploiters, or the immense majority,
the workers.' They did not see that the industrial workers
nowhere formed a majority, much less an ' immense majority ',
and that statistics no longer showed any tendency towards an
increase in their numbers. They did not understand that the
existence of a democratic workers' party was fully justified only as
long as such a party was prepared to compromise or even to
co-operate with other parties, for instance with some party representing the peasants, or the middle classes. And they did not see
that, if they wanted to rule the state solely as the representatives
of the majority of the population, they would have to change
their whole policy and cease to represent mainly or exclusively the
industrial workers. Of course, it is no substitute for this change
of policy to assert naïvely that the proletarian policy as such
may simply bring (as Marx said [43]) ' the rural producers under
the intellectual leadership of the central towns of their districts,
there securing to them, in the industrial worker, the *natural
trustee* of their interests. . .'

The position of the Communist parties was different. They
strictly adhered to the theory of increasing misery, believing in
an increase not only of its extent but also of its intensity, once
the causes of the temporary bourgeoisification of the workers
were removed. This belief contributed considerably to what
Marx would have called ' the inner contradictions ' of their
policy.

The tactical situation seems simple enough. Thanks to
Marx's prophecy, the Communists knew for certain that misery
must soon increase. They also knew that the party could not
win the confidence of the workers without fighting for them,
and with them, for an improvement of their lot. These two
fundamental assumptions clearly determined the principles of
their general tactics. Make the workers demand their share,
back them up in every particular episode in their unceasing fight
for bread and shelter. Fight with them tenaciously for the fulfilment of their practical demands, whether economic or political.
Thus you will win their confidence. At the same time, the
workers will learn that it is impossible for them to better their
lot by these petty fights, and that nothing short of a wholesale
revolution can bring about an improvement. For all these
petty fights are bound to be unsuccessful ; we know from Marx

that the capitalists simply *cannot* continue to compromise and
that, ultimately, misery *must* increase. Accordingly, the only
result—but a valuable one—of the workers' daily fight against
their oppressors is an increase in their class consciousness ; it
is that feeling of unity which can be won only in battle, together
with a desperate knowledge that only revolution can help them
in their misery. When this stage is reached, then the hour has
struck for the final show-down.

This is the theory and the Communists acted accordingly.
At first they support the workers in their fight to improve their
lot. But, contrary to all expectations and prophecies, the fight
is successful. The demands are granted. Obviously, the reason
is that they had been too modest. Therefore one must demand
more. But the demands are granted again [44]. And as misery
decreases, the workers become less embittered, more ready to
bargain for wages than to plot for revolution.

Now the Communists find that their policy must be reversed.
Something must be done to bring the law of increasing misery
into operation. For instance, colonial unrest must be stirred
up (even where there is no chance of a successful revolution),
and with the general purpose of counteracting the bourgeoisification of the workers, a policy fomenting catastrophes of all sorts
must be adopted. But this new policy destroys the confidence
of the workers. The Communists lose their members, with the
exception of those who are inexperienced in real political fights.
They lose exactly those whom they describe as the ' vanguard
of the working class ' ; their tacitly implied principle : ' The
worse things are, the better they are, since misery must pre-
cipitate revolution ', makes the workers suspicious—the better
the application of this principle, the worse are the suspicions
entertained by the workers. For they are realists ; to obtain
their confidence, one must work to improve their lot.

Thus the policy must be reversed again : one is forced to
fight for the immediate betterment of the workers' lot and to
hope at the same time for the opposite.

With this, the ' inner contradictions ' of the theory produce
the last stage of confusion. It is the stage when it is hard to
know who is the traitor, since treachery may be faithfulness
and faithfulness treachery. It is the stage when those who
followed the party not simply because it appeared to them
(rightly, I am afraid) as the only vigorous movement with humanitarian ends, but especially because it was a movement based on

a scientific theory, must either leave it, or sacrifice their intellectual integrity ; for they must now learn to believe blindly in some authority. Ultimately, they must become mystics—hostile to reasonable argument.

It seems that it is not only capitalism which is labouring under inner contradictions that threaten to bring about its downfall. . .

Chapter 21 : AN EVALUATION OF THE PROPHECY

The arguments underlying Marx's historical prophecy are invalid. His ingenious attempt to draw prophetic conclusions from observations of contemporary economic tendencies failed. The reason for this failure does not lie in any insufficiency of the empirical basis of the argument. Marx's sociological and economic analyses of contemporary society may have been somewhat one-sided, but in spite of their bias, they were excellent in so far as they were descriptive. The reason for his failure as a prophet lies entirely in the poverty of historicism as such, in the simple fact that even if we observe to-day what appears to be a historical tendency or trend, we cannot know whether it will have the same appearance to-morrow.

We must admit that Marx saw many things in the right light. If we consider only his prophecy that the system of unrestrained capitalism, as he knew it, was not going to last much longer, and that its apologists who thought it would last forever were wrong, then we must say that he was right. He was right, too, in holding that it was largely the ' class struggle ', i.e. the association of the workers, that was going to bring about its transformation into a new economic system. But we must not go so far as to say that Marx predicted that new system, interventionism [1], under another name, socialism. The truth is that he had no inkling of what was lying ahead. What he called ' socialism ' was very dissimilar from any form of interventionism, even from the Russian form ; for he strongly believed that the impending development would diminish the influence, political as well as economic, of the state, while interventionism has increased it everywhere.

Since I am criticizing Marx and, to some extent, praising democratic piecemeal interventionism (especially of the institutional kind explained in section VII to chapter 17), I wish to make it clear that I feel much sympathy with Marx's hope for a decrease in state influence. It is undoubtedly the greatest danger of interventionism—especially of any direct intervention—that it leads to an increase in state power and in bureaucracy. Most interventionists do not mind this, or they close their eyes to it, which increases the danger. But I believe that once the danger is faced squarely, it should be possible to master it. For this is again merely a problem of social technology and of social piece-meal engineering. But it is important to tackle it early, for it constitutes a danger to democracy. We must plan for freedom, and not only for security, if for no other reason than that only freedom can make security secure.

But let us return to Marx's prophecy. One of the historical tendencies which he claimed to have discovered seems to be of a more persistent character than the others ; I mean the tendency towards the accumulation of the means of production, and especially towards increasing the productivity of labour. It seems indeed that this tendency will continue for some time, provided, of course, that we continue to keep civilization going. But Marx did not merely recognize this tendency and its ' civiliz-ing aspects ', he also saw its inherent dangers. More especially, he was one of the first (although he had some predecessors, for instance, Fourier [2]) to emphasize the connection between ' the development of the productive forces ' in which he saw [3] ' the historical mission and justification of capital ', and that most destructive phenomenon of the credit system—a system which seems to have encouraged the rapid rise of industrialism—the *trade cycle*.

Marx's own theory of the trade cycle (discussed in section IV of the last chapter) may perhaps be paraphrased as follows : even if it is true that the inherent laws of the free market produce a tendency towards full employment, it is also true that every single approach towards full employment, i.e. towards a shortage of labour, stimulates inventors and investors to create and to introduce new labour-saving machinery, thereby giving rise (first to a short boom and then) to a new wave of unemployment and depression. Whether there is any truth in this theory, and how much, I do not know. As I said in the last chapter, the theory of the trade cycle is a rather difficult subject, and one upon which I do not intend to embark. But since Marx's con-tention that the increase of productivity is one of the factors contributing to the trade cycle seems to me important, I may be permitted to develop some rather obvious considerations in its support.

The following list of possible developments is, of course, quite incomplete ; but it is constructed in such a way that when-ever the productivity of labour increases, then at least one of the following developments, and possibly many at a time, must commence and must proceed in a degree sufficient to balance the increase in productivity.

(A) Investments increase, that is to say, such capital goods are produced as strengthen the power for producing other goods. (Since this leads to a further increase of productivity, it cannot *alone* balance its effects for any length of time.)

(B) Consumption increases—the standard of living rises :

    (*a*) that of the whole population ;

    (*b*) that of certain parts of it (for instance, of a certain class).

(C) Labour time decreases.

    (*a*) the daily labour hours are reduced ;

    (*b*) the number of people who are not industrial workers increases, and especially

    (b_1) the number of scientists, physicians, artists, business men, etc., increases.

    . . . .

    (b_2) the number of unemployed workers increases.

(D) The quantity of goods produced but not consumed increases.

    (*a*) consumption goods are destroyed ;

    (*b*) capital goods are not used (factories are idle) ;

    (*c*) goods, other than consumption goods and goods of the type (A), are produced, for instance, arms ;

    (*d*) labour is used to destroy capital goods (and thereby to reduce productivity).

I have listed these developments—the list could, of course, be elaborated—in such a way that down to the dotted line, i.e. down to (C, b_1), the developments as such are generally recognized as desirable, whilst from (C, b_2) onward come those which are generally taken to be undesirable ; they indicate depression, the manufacture of armaments, and war.

Now it is clear that since (A) alone cannot restore the balance for good, although it may be a very important factor, one or several of the other developments must set in. It seems, further, reasonable to assume that if no institutions exist which guarantee that the desirable developments proceed in a degree sufficient to balance the increased productivity, some of the undesirable developments will begin. But all of these, with the possible exception of armament production, are of such a character that they are likely to lead to a sharp reduction of (A), which must severely aggravate the situation.

I do not think that such considerations as the above are able to ' explain ' armament or war in any sense of the word, although they may explain the success of totalitarian states in fighting unemployment. Nor do I think that they are able to ' explain ' the trade cycle, although they may perhaps contribute something to such an explanation, in which problems of credit and money are likely to play a very important part ; for the reduction of (A), for instance, may be equivalent to the hoarding of such savings as would otherwise probably be invested—a much-discussed and important factor [4]. And it is not quite impossible that the Marxist law of the falling rate of profit (if this law is at all tenable [5]) may also give a hint for the explanation of hoarding ; for assuming that a period of quick accumulation may lead to such a fall, this might discourage investments and encourage hoarding, and reduce (A).

But all this would not be a theory of the trade cycle. Such a theory would have a different task. Its main task would be to explain why the institution of the free market, as such a very efficient instrument for equalizing supply and demand, does not suffice to prevent depressions [6], i.e. overproduction or under-consumption. In other words, we should have to show that the buying and selling on the market produces, as one of the unwanted social repercussions [7] of our actions, the trade cycle. The Marxist theory of the trade cycle has precisely this aim in view ; and the considerations sketched here regarding the effects of a general tendency towards increasing productivity can at the best only supplement this theory.

I am not going to pronounce judgement on the merits of all these speculations upon the trade cycle. But it seems to me quite clear that they are most valuable even if in the light of modern theories they should by now be entirely superseded. The mere fact that Marx treated this problem extensively is greatly to his credit. This much at least of his prophecy has come true, for the time being ; the tendency towards an increase of productivity continues : the trade cycle also continues, and its continuation is likely to lead to interventionist counter-measures and therefore to a further restriction of the free market system ; a development which conforms to Marx's prophecy that the trade cycle would be one of the factors that must bring about the down-fall of the unrestrained system of capitalism. And to this, we must add that other piece of successful prophecy, namely, that the association of the workers would be another important factor in this process.

In view of this list of important and largely successful prophecies, is it justifiable to speak of the poverty of historicism ? If Marx's historical prophecies have been even partially successful, then we should certainly not dismiss his method lightly. But a closer view of Marx's successes shows that *it was nowhere his historicist method which led him to success, but always the methods of institutional analysis.* Thus it is not an historicist but a typical institutional analysis which leads to the conclusion that the capitalist is forced by competition to increase productivity. It is an institutional analysis on which Marx bases his theory of the trade cycle and of surplus population. And even the theory of class struggle is institutional ; it is part of the mechanism by which the distribution of wealth as well as of power is controlled, a mechanism which makes possible collective bargaining in the widest sense. Nowhere in these analyses do the typical historicist 'laws of historical development', or stages, or periods, or tendencies, play any part whatever. On the other hand, none of Marx's more ambitious historicist conclusions, none of his 'inexorable laws of development' and his 'stages of history which cannot be leaped over ', has ever turned out to be a success-ful prediction. Marx was successful *only* in so far as he was analysing institutions and their functions. And the opposite is true also : none of his more ambitious and sweeping historical prophecies falls within the scope of institutional analysis. Wherever the attempt is made to back them up by such an analysis, the derivation is invalid. Indeed, compared with Marx's own high standards, the more sweeping prophecies are on a rather low intellectual level. They contain not only a lot of wishful thinking, they are also lacking in political imagination. Roughly speaking, Marx shared the belief of the progressive industrialist, of the 'bourgeois' of his time : the belief in a law of progress. But this naïve historicist optimism, of Hegel and Comte, of Marx and Mill, is no less superstitious than a pessimistic historicism like that of Plato and Spengler. And it is a very bad outfit for a prophet, since it must bridle historical imagination. Indeed, it is necessary to recognize as one of the principles of any unprejudiced view of politics that everything is possible in human affairs ; and more particularly that no conceivable development can be excluded on the grounds that it may violate the so-called tendency of human progress, or any other of the alleged laws of 'human nature'. 'The fact of progress', writes [8] H. A. L. Fisher, ' is written plain and large on the page of history ; but progress is not a law of nature.

The ground gained by one generation may be lost by the next.'

In accordance with the principle that everything is possible it may be worth while to point out that Marx's prophecies might well have come true. A faith like the progressivist optimism of the nineteenth century can be a powerful political force ; it can help to bring about what it has predicted. Thus even a correct prediction must not be accepted too readily as a corroboration of a theory, and of its scientific character. It may rather be a consequence of its religious character and a proof of the force of the religious faith which it has been able to inspire in men. And in Marxism more particularly the religious element is unmistakable. In the hour of their deepest misery and degradation, Marx's prophecy gave the workers an inspiring belief in their mission, and in the great future which their movement was to prepare for the whole of mankind. Looking back at the course of events from 1864 to 1930, I think that but for the somewhat accidental fact that Marx discouraged research in social technology, European affairs might possibly have developed, under the influence of this prophetic religion, towards a socialism of a non-collectivist type. A thorough preparation for social engineering, for planning for freedom, on the part of the Russian Marxists as well as those in Central Europe, might possibly have led to an unmistakable success, convincing to all friends of the open society. But this would not have been a corroboration of a scientific prophecy. It would have been the result of a religious movement—the result of the faith in humanitarianism, combined with a critical use of our reason for the purpose of changing the world.

But things developed differently. The prophetic element in Marx's creed was dominant in the minds of his followers. It swept everything else aside, banishing the power of cool and critical judgement and destroying the belief that by the use of reason we may change the world. All that remained of Marx's teaching was the oracular philosophy of Hegel, which in its Marxist trappings threatens to paralyse the struggle for the open society.

CHAPTER 22 : THE MORAL THEORY OF HISTORICISM

The task which Marx set himself in *Capital* was to discover inexorable laws of social development. It was not the discovery of economic laws which would be useful to the social technologist. It was neither the analysis of the economic conditions which would permit the realization of such socialist aims as just prices, equal distribution of wealth, security, reasonable planning of production and, above all, freedom, nor was it an attempt to analyse and to clarify these aims.

But although Marx was strongly opposed to Utopian technology as well as to any attempt at a moral justification of socialist aims, his writings contained, by implication, an ethical theory. This he expressed mainly by moral evaluations of social institutions. After all, Marx's condemnation of capitalism is fundamentally a moral condemnation. The *system is condemned*, for the cruel injustice inherent in it which is combined with full ' formal ' justice and righteousness. The system is condemned, because by forcing the exploiter to enslave the exploited it robs both of their freedom. Marx did not combat wealth, nor did he praise poverty. He hated capitalism, not for its accumulation of wealth, but for its oligarchical character ; he hated it because in this system wealth means political power in the sense of power over other men. Labour power is made a commodity ; that means that men must sell themselves on the market. Marx hated the system because it resembled slavery.

By laying such stress on the moral aspect of social institutions, Marx emphasized our responsibility for the more remote social repercussions of our actions ; for instance, of such actions as may help to prolong the life of socially unjust institutions.

But although *Capital* is, in fact, largely a treatise on social ethics, these ethical ideas are never represented as such. They are expressed only by implication, but not the less forcibly on that account, since the implications are very obvious. Marx, I believe, avoided an explicit moral theory, because he hated preaching. Deeply distrustful of the moralist, who usually preaches water and drinks wine, Marx was reluctant to formulate his ethical convictions explicitly. The principles of humanity

and decency were for him matters that needed no discussion,
matters to be taken for granted. (In this field, too, he was an
optimist.) He attacked the moralists because he saw them as
the sycophantic apologists of a social order which he felt to be
immoral ; he attacked the eulogists of liberalism because of their
self-satisfaction, because of their identification of freedom with
the formal liberty then existing within a social system which
destroyed freedom. Thus, by implication, he admitted his love
for freedom ; and in spite of his bias, as a philosopher, for holism,
he was certainly not a collectivist, for he hoped that the state
would 'wither away'. Marx's faith, I believe, was fundamentally a faith in the open society.

Marx's attitude towards Christianity is closely connected
with these convictions, and with the fact that a hypocritical
defence of capitalist exploitation was in his day characteristic
of official Christianity. (His attitude was not unlike that of his
contemporary Kierkegaard, the great reformer of Christian
ethics, who exposed [1] the official Christian morality of his day as
anti-Christian and anti-humanitarian hypocrisy.) A typical
representative of this kind of Christianity was the High Church
priest J. Townsend, author of *A Dissertation on the Poor Laws,
by a Wellwisher of Mankind*, an extremely crude apologist for
exploitation whom Marx exposed. 'Hunger', Townsend begins
his eulogy [2], ' is not only a peaceable, silent, unremitted pressure
but, as the most natural motive of industry and labour, it calls
forth the most powerful exertions.' In Townsend's ' Christian '
world order, everything depends (as Marx observes) upon making
hunger permanent among the working class ; and Townsend
believes that this is indeed the divine purpose of the principle
of the growth of population ; for he goes on : ' It seems to be
a law of nature that the poor should be to a certain degree
improvident, so that there may always be some to fulfil the most
servile, the most sordid, the most ignoble offices in the community.
The stock of human happiness is thereby much increased, whilst
the more delicate . . are left at liberty without interruption to
pursue those callings which are suited to their various dispositions.'
And the ' delicate priestly sycophant ', as Marx called him for
this remark, adds that the Poor Law, by helping the hungry,
' tends to destroy the harmony and beauty, the symmetry and
order, of that system which God and nature have established
in the world.'

If this kind of ' Christianity ' has disappeared to-day from the face of the better part of our globe, it is in no small degree due to the moral reformation brought about by Marx. I do not suggest that the reform of the Church's attitude towards the poor in England did not commence long before Marx had any influence in England ; but he influenced this development especially on the Continent, and the rise of socialism had the effect of strengthening it in England also. His influence on Christianity may be perhaps compared with Luther's influence on the Roman Church. Both were a challenge, both led to a counter-reformation in the camps of their enemies, to a revision and re-valuation of their ethical standards. Christianity owes not a little to Marx's influence if it is to-day on a different path from the one it was pursuing only thirty years ago. It is even partly due to Marx's influence that the Church has listened to the voice of Kierkegaard, who, in his *Book of the Judge*, described his own activity as follows [3] : ' He whose task it is to produce a corrective idea, has only to study, precisely and deeply, the rotten parts of the existing order—and then, in the most partial way possible, to stress the opposite of it.' (' Since that is so ', he adds, ' an apparently clever man will easily raise the objection of partiality against the corrective idea—and he will make the public believe that this was the whole truth about it.') In this sense one might say that the early Marxism, with its ethical rigour, its emphasis on deeds instead of mere words, was perhaps the most important corrective idea of our time [4]. This explains its tremendous moral influence.

The demand that men should prove themselves in deeds is especially marked in some of Marx's earlier writings. This attitude, which might be described as his *activism*, is most clearly formulated in the last of his *Theses on Feuerbach* [5] : ' The philosophers have only interpreted the world in various ways ; the point however is to *change* it.' But there are many other passages which show the same ' activist ' tendency ; especially those in which Marx speaks of socialism as the ' kingdom of freedom ', a kingdom in which man would become the ' master of his own social environment '. Marx conceived of socialism as a period in which we are largely free from the irrational forces that now determine our life, and in which human reason can actively control human affairs. Judging by all this, and by Marx's general moral and emotional attitude, I cannot doubt that, if faced with the alternative ' *are we to be the makers of our fate, or shall we be content to be its prophets ?* ' he would have decided to be a maker and not merely a prophet.

But as we already know, these strong ' activist ' tendencies of Marx's are counteracted by his historicism.   Under its influence, he became mainly a prophet.   He decided that, at least under capitalism, we must submit to ' inexorable laws ' and to the fact that all we can do is ' to shorten and lessen the birth-pangs ' of the ' natural phases of its evolution ' [6].   There is a wide gulf between Marx's activism and his historicism, and this gulf is further widened by his doctrine that we must submit to the purely irrational forces of history.   For since he denounced as Utopian any attempt to make use of our reason in order to plan for the future, *reason can have no part in bringing about a more reasonable world.*   I believe that such a view cannot be defended, and must lead to mysticism.   But I must admit that there seems to be a theoretical possibility of bridging this gulf, although I do not consider the bridge to be sound.   This bridge, of which there are only rough plans to be found in the writings of Marx and Engels, I call their *historicist moral theory* [7].

Unwilling to admit that their own ethical ideas were in any sense ultimate and self-justifying, Marx and Engels preferred to look upon their humanitarian aims in the light of a theory which explains them as the product, or the reflection, of social circumstances.   Their theory can be described as follows.   If a social reformer, or a revolutionary, believes that he is inspired by a hatred of ' injustice ', and by a love for ' justice ', then he is largely a victim of illusion (like anybody else, for instance the apologists of the old order).   Or, to put it more precisely, his moral ideas of ' justice ' and ' injustice ' are by-products of the social and historical, development.   But they are by-products of an important kind, since they are part of the mechanism by which the development propels itself.   To illustrate this point, there are always at least two ideas of ' justice ' (or of ' freedom ' or of ' equality '), and these two ideas differ very widely indeed. The one is the idea of ' justice ' as the ruling class understands it, the other, the same idea as the oppressed class understands it. These ideas are, of course, products of the class situation, but at the same time they play an important part in the class struggle— they have to provide both sides with that good conscience which they need in order to carry on their fight.

This theory of morality may be characterized as historicist because it holds that all moral categories are dependent on the historical situation ; it is usually described as *historical relativism* in the field of ethics.   From this point of view, it is an incomplete question to ask : Is it right to act in this way ? The complete question would run like this : Is it right, in the sense of fifteenth-century feudal morality, to act in this way ? Or perhaps : Is is right, in the sense of nineteenth-century proletarian morality, to act in this way ? This historical relativism was formulated by Engels as follows [8] : ' What morality is preached to us to-day ? There is first Christian-feudal morality, inherited from past centuries ; and this again has two main subdivisions, Roman Catholic and Protestant moralities, each of which in turn has no lack of further subdivisions, from the Jesuit-Catholic and Orthodox-Protestant to loose " advanced " moralities. Alongside of these, we find the modern bourgeois morality, and with it, too, the proletarian morality of the future . .'

But this so-called ' historical relativism ' by no means exhausts the historicist character of the Marxist theory of morals. Let us imagine we could ask those who hold such a theory, for instance Marx himself : Why do you act in the way you do ? Why would you consider it distasteful and repulsive, for instance, to accept a bribe from the bourgeoisie for stopping your revolutionary activities ? I do not think that Marx would have liked to answer such a question ; he would probably have tried to evade it, asserting perhaps that he just acted as he pleased, or as he felt compelled to. But all this does not touch our problem. It is certain that in the practical decisions of his life Marx followed a very rigorous moral code ; it is also certain that he demanded from his collaborators a high moral standard. Whatever the terminology applied to these things may be, the problem which faces us is how to find a reply which he might have possibly made to the question : Why do you act in such a way ? Why do you try, for instance, to help the oppressed ? (Marx did not himself belong to this class, either by birth or by upbringing or by his way of living.)

If pressed in this way, Marx would, I think, have formulated his moral belief in the following terms, which form the core of what I call his historicist moral theory. As a social scientist (he might have said) I know that our moral ideas are weapons in the class struggle. As a scientist, I can consider them without adopting them. But as a scientist I find also that I cannot avoid taking sides in this struggle ; that any attitude, even aloofness, means taking sides in some way or other. My problem thus assumes the form : Which side shall I take ? When I have chosen a certain side, then I have, of course, also decided upon my morality. I shall have to adopt the moral system necessarily bound up with the interests of the class which I have decided to support. But before making this fundamental decision, I have not adopted any moral system at all, provided I can free myself from the moral tradition of my class ; but this, of course, is a necessary prerequisite for making any conscious and rational decision regarding the competing moral systems. Now since a decision is ' moral ' only in relation to some previously accepted moral code, my fundamental decision can be no ' moral ' decision at all. But it can be a *scientific* decision. For as a social scientist, I am able to see what is going to happen. I am able to see that the bourgeoisie, and with it its system of morals, is bound to disappear, and that the proletariat, and with it a new system of morals, is bound to win. I see that this development is inevitable. It would be madness to attempt to resist it, just as it would be madness to attempt to resist the law of gravity. This is why my fundamental decision is in favour of the proletariat and of its morality. And this decision is based only on scientific foresight, on scientific historical prophecy. Although itself not a moral decision, since it is not based on any system of morality, it leads to the adoption of a certain system of morality. To sum up, my fundamental decision is not (as you suspected) the sentimental decision to help the oppressed, but the scientific and rational decision not to offer vain resistance to the developmental laws of society. Only after I have made this decision am I prepared to accept, and to make full use of, those moral sentiments which are necessary weapons in the fight for what is bound to come in any case. In this way, I adopt the facts of the coming period as the standards of my morality. And in this way, I solve the apparent paradox that a more reasonable world will come without being planned by reason ; for according to my moral standards now adopted, the future world must be better, and therefore more reasonable. And I also bridge the gap between my activism and my historicism. For it is clear that even though I have discovered the natural law that determines the movement of society, I cannot shuffle the natural phases of its evolution out of the world by a stroke of the pen. But this much I can do. I can actively assist in shortening and lessening its birth-pangs.

This, I think, would have been Marx's reply, and it is this reply which to me represents the most important form of what I have called ' historicist moral theory '. It is this theory to which Engels alludes when he writes [9] : ' Certainly, that morality which contains the greatest number of elements that are going to last is the one which, within the present time, represents the overthrow of the present time ; it is the one which represents the future ; it is the proletarian morality. . . According to this conception, the ultimate causes of all social changes and political revolutions are not increasing insight into justice ; they are to be sought not in the *philosophy* but in the *economics* of the epoch concerned. The growing realization that existing social institutions are irrational and unjust is only a symptom . .' It is the theory of which a modern Marxist says : ' In founding socialist aspirations on a rational economic law of social development, *instead of justifying them on moral grounds*, Marx and Engels proclaimed socialism a historical necessity.' [10] It is a theory which is very widely held ; but it has rarely been formulated clearly and explicitly. Its criticism is therefore more important than might be realized at first sight.

First, it is clear enough that the theory depends largely on the possibility of correct historical prophecy. If this is questioned —and it certainly must be questioned—then the theory loses most of its force. But for the purpose of analysing it, I shall assume at first that historical foreknowledge is an established fact ; and I shall merely stipulate that this historical foreknowledge is limited ; I shall stipulate that we have foreknowledge for, say, the next 500 years, a stipulation which should not restrict even the boldest claims of Marxist historicism.

Now let us first examine the claim of historicist moral theory that the fundamental decision in favour of, or against, one of the moral systems in question is itself not a moral decision ; that it is not based on any moral consideration or sentiment, but on a scientific historical prediction. This claim is, I think, untenable. In order to make this quite clear, it will suffice to make explicit the imperative, or principle of conduct, implied in this fundamental decision. It is the following principle : Adopt the moral system of the future ! or : Adopt the moral system held by those whose actions are most useful for bringing about the future ! Now it seems clear to me that even on the assumption that we know exactly what the next 500 years will be like, it is not at all necessary for us to adopt such a principle. It is, to give an example, at least conceivable that some humanitarian pupil of Voltaire who foresaw in 1764 the development of

France down to, say, 1864 might have disliked the prospect ;
it is at least conceivable that he would have decided that this
development was rather distasteful and that he was not going
to adopt the moral standards of Napoleon III as his own.   I shall
be faithful to my humanitarian standards, he might have said,
I shall teach them to my pupils ; perhaps they will survive this
period, perhaps some day they will be victorious.   It is likewise
at least conceivable (I do not assert more, at present) that a
man who to-day foresees with certainty that we are heading for
a period of slavery, that we are going to return to the cage of
the arrested society, or even that we are about to return to the
beasts, may nevertheless decide not to adopt the moral standards
of this impending period but to contribute as well as he can to
the survival of his humanitarian ideals, hoping perhaps for a
resurrection of his morality in some dim future.

All that is, at least, conceivable.   It may perhaps not be the
' wisest' decision to make.   But the fact that such a decision is
excluded neither by foreknowledge nor by any sociological or
psychological law shows that the first claim of historicist moral
theory is untenable.   Whether we should accept the morality
of the future just because it is the morality of the future, this in
itself is just a moral problem.   The fundamental decision cannot
be derived from any knowledge of the future.

In previous chapters I have mentioned *moral positivism*
(especially that of Hegel), the theory that there is no moral
standard but the one which exists ; that what is, is reasonable
and good ; and therefore, that *might is right*.   The practical
aspect of this theory is this.   A moral criticism of the existing
state of affairs is impossible, since this state itself determines the
moral standard of things.   Now the historicist moral theory
we are considering is nothing but another form of moral positivism.   For it holds that *coming might is right*.   The future is
here substituted for the present—that is all.   And the practical
aspect of the theory is this.   A moral criticism of the coming
state of affairs is impossible, since this state determines the moral
standard of things.   The difference between ' the present ' and
' the future ' is here, of course, only a matter of degree.   One
can say that the future starts to-morrow, or in 500 years, or in
100.   *In their theoretical structure there is no difference between moral
conservatism, moral modernism, and moral futurism.*   Nor is there
much to choose between them in regard to moral sentiments.
If the moral futurist criticizes the cowardice of the moral

conservative who takes sides with the powers that be, then the moral conservative can return the charge ; he can say that the moral futurist is a coward since he takes sides with the powers that will be, with the rulers of to-morrow.

I feel sure that, had he considered these implications, Marx would have repudiated historicist moral theory. Numerous remarks and numerous actions prove that it was not a scientific judgement but a moral impulse, the wish to help the oppressed, the wish to free the shamelessly exploited and miserable workers, which led him to socialism. I do not doubt that it is this moral appeal that is the secret of the influence of his teaching. And the force of this appeal was tremendously strengthened by the fact that he did not preach morality in the abstract. He did not pretend to have any right to do so. Who, he seems to have asked himself, lives up to his own standard, provided it is not a very low one ? It was this feeling which led him to rely, in ethical matters, on under-statements, and which led him to the attempt to find in prophetic social science an authority in matters of morals more reliable than he felt himself to be.

Surely, in Marx's practical ethics such categories as freedom and equality played the major rôle. He was, after all, one of those who took the ideals of 1789 seriously. And he had seen how shamelessly a concept like ' freedom ' could be twisted. This is why he did not preach freedom in words—why he preached it in action. He wanted to improve society and improvement meant to him more freedom, more equality, more justice, more security, higher standards of living, and especially that shortening of the working day which at once gives the workers *some* freedom. It was his hatred of hypocrisy, his reluctance to speak about these ' high ideals ', together with his amazing optimism, his trust that all this would be realized in the near future, which led him to veil his moral beliefs behind historicist formulations.

Marx, I assert, would not seriously have defended moral positivism in the form of moral futurism if he had seen that it implies the recognition of future might as right. But there are others who do not possess his passionate love of humanity, who are moral futurists just because of these implications, i.e. opportunists wishing to be on the winning side. Moral futurism is widespread to-day. Its deeper, non-opportunist basis is probably the belief that goodness must ' ultimately ' triumph over wickedness. But moral futurists forget that we are not going to live to witness the ' ultimate ' outcome of present events. ' History

will be our judge ! ' What does this mean ? That *success* will
judge. The worship of success and of future might is the highest
standard of many who would never admit that present might is
right. (They quite forget that the present is the future of the
past.) The basis of all this is a half-hearted compromise between
a moral optimism and a moral scepticism. It seems to be hard
to believe in one's conscience. And it seems to be hard to resist
the impulse to be on the winning side.

All these critical remarks are consistent with the assumption
that we can predict the future for the next, say, 500 years. But
if we drop this entirely fictitious assumption, then historicist moral
theory loses all its plausibility. And we must drop it. For
there is no prophetic sociology to help us in selecting a moral
system. We cannot shift our responsibility for such a selection
on to anybody, not even on to ' the future '.

Marx's historicist moral theory is, of course, only the result
of his view concerning the method of social science, of his
sociological determinism, a view which has become rather fashionable
in our day. All our opinions, it is said, including our moral
standards, depend upon society and its historical state. They
are the products of society or of a certain class situation. Education is defined as a special process by which the community
attempts to ' pass on ' to its members ' its culture including the
standards by which it would have them to live ' [11], and the
' relativity of educational theory and practice to a prevailing
order ' is emphasized. Science, too, is said to depend on the
social stratum of the scientific worker, etc.

A theory of this kind which emphasizes the sociological
dependence of our opinions is sometimes called *sociologism* ; if
the historical dependence is emphasized, it is called *historism*.
(Historism must not, of course, be mixed up with historicism.)
Both sociologism and historism, in so far as they maintain the
determination of scientific knowledge by society or history, will
be discussed in the next two chapters. In so far as sociologism
bears upon moral theory, a few remarks may be added here.
But before going into any detail, I wish to make quite clear my
opinion concerning these Hegelianizing theories. I believe that
they chatter trivialities clad in the jargon of oracular philosophy.

Let us examine this moral ' sociologism '. That man, and
his aims, are *in a certain sense* a product of society is true enough.
But it is also true that society is a product of man and of his aims
and that it may become increasingly so. The main question is :

Which of these two aspects of the relations between men and society is more important ?   Which is to be stressed ?

We shall understand sociologism better if we compare it with the analogous ' naturalistic ' view that man and his aims are a product of heredity and environment. Again we must admit that this is true enough. But it is also quite certain that man's environment is to an increasing extent a product of him and his aims (to a limited extent, the same might be said even of his heredity). Again we must ask : which of the two aspects is more important, more fertile ? The answer may be easier if we give the question the following more practical form. We, the generation now living, and our minds, our opinions, are largely the product of our parents, and of the way they have brought us up. But the next generation will be, to a similar extent, a product of ourselves, of our actions and of the way in which we bring them up. Which of the two aspects is the more important one for us to-day ?

If we consider this question seriously, then we find that the decisive point is that our minds, our opinions, though largely de-pendent on our upbringing are not totally so. If they were totally dependent on our upbringing, if we were incapable of self-criticism, of learning from our own way of seeing things, from our experience, then, of course, the way we have been brought up by the last generation would determine the way in which we bring up the next. But it is quite certain that this is not so. Accordingly, we can concentrate our critical faculties on the difficult problem of bringing up the next generation in a way which we consider better than the way in which we have been brought up ourselves.

The situation stressed so much by sociologism can be dealt with in an exactly analogous way. That our minds, our views, are in a way a product of ' society ' is trivially true. The most important part of our environment is its social part ; thought, in particular, is very largely dependent on social intercourse ; language, the medium of thought, is a social phenomenon. But it simply cannot be denied that we can examine thoughts, that we can criticize them, improve them, and further that we can change and improve our physical environment according to our changed, improved thoughts. And the same is true of our social environment.

All these considerations are entirely independent of the metaphysical ' problem of free will '. Even the indeterminist admits a certain amount of dependence on heredity and on environmental, especially social, influence. On the other hand, the determinist must agree that our views and actions are not fully and solely determined by heredity, education, and social influences. He has to admit that there are other factors, for instance, the more ' accidental ' experiences accumulated during one's life, and that these also exert their influence. Determinism or indeterminism, as long as they remain within their metaphysical boundaries, do not affect our problem. But the point is that they may trespass beyond these boundaries ; that metaphysical determinism, for instance, may encourage sociological determinism or ' sociologism '. But in this form, the theory can be confronted with experience. And experience shows that it is certainly false.

Beethoven, to take an instance from the field of æsthetics, which has a certain similarity to that of ethics, is surely to some extent a *product* of musical education and tradition, and many who take an interest in him will be impressed by this aspect of his work. The more important aspect, however, is that he is also a *producer* of music, and thereby of musical tradition and education. I do not wish to quarrel with the metaphysical determinist who would insist that every bar Beethoven wrote was determined by some combination of hereditary and environmental influences. Such an assertion is empirically entirely insignificant, since no one could actually ' explain ' a single bar of his writing in this way. The important thing is that everyone admits that what he wrote can be explained neither by the musical works of his predecessors, nor by the social environment in which he lived, nor by his deafness, nor by the food which his housekeeper cooked for him ; not, in other words, by any definite set of environmental influences or circumstances open to empirical investigation, or by anything we could possibly know of his heredity.

I do not deny that there are certain interesting sociological aspects of Beethoven's work. It is well known, for instance, that the transition from a small to a large symphony orchestra is connected, in some way, with a socio-political development. Orchestras cease to be the private hobbies of princes, and are at least partly supported by a middle class whose interest in music greatly increases. I am willing to appreciate any sociological ' explanation ' of this sort, and I admit that such aspects may be worthy of scientific study. (After all, I myself have attempted similar things in this book, for instance, in my treatment of Plato.)

What then, more precisely, is the object of my attack ? It is the exaggeration and generalization of any aspect of this kind. If we 'explain' Beethoven's symphony orchestra in the way hinted above, we have explained very little. If we describe Beethoven as representing the bourgeoisie in the process of emancipating itself, we say very little, even if it is true. Such a function could most certainly be combined with the production of bad music (as we see from Wagner). We cannot attempt to explain Beethoven's genius in this way, or in any way at all.

I think that Marx's own views could likewise be used for an empirical refutation of sociological determinism. For if we consider in the light of this doctrine the two theories, activism and historicism, and their struggle for supremacy in Marx's system, then we will have to say that historicism would be a view more fitting for a conservative apologist than for a revolutionary or even a reformer. And, indeed, historicism was used by Hegel with that tendency. The fact that Marx not only took it over from Hegel, but in the end permitted it to oust his own activism, may thus show that the side a man takes in the social struggle need not always determine his intellectual decisions. These may be determined, as in Marx's case, not so much by the true interest of the class he supported as by accidental factors, such as the influence of a predecessor, or perhaps by shortsightedness. Thus in this case, sociologism may further our understanding of Hegel, but the example of Marx himself exposes it as an unjustified generalization. A similar case is Marx's underrating of the significance of his own moral ideas ; for it cannot be doubted that the secret of his religious influence was in its moral appeal, that his criticism of capitalism was effective mainly as a moral criticism. Marx showed that a social system can as such be unjust ; that if the system is bad, then all the righteousness of the individuals who profit from it is a mere sham righteousness, is mere hypocrisy. For our responsibility extends to the system, to the institutions which we allow to persist.

It is this moral radicalism of Marx which explains his influence ; and that is a hopeful fact in itself. This moral radicalism is still alive. It is our task to keep it alive, to prevent it from going the way which his political radicalism will have to go. 'Scientific' Marxism is dead. Its feeling of social responsibility and its love for freedom must survive.

> Rationality, in the sense of an appeal to a universa
> and impersonal standard of truth, is of supreme
> importance . . , not only in ages in which it easily
> prevails, but also, and even more, in those less
> fortunate times in which it is despised and rejected
> as the vain dream of men who lack the virility to
> kill where they cannot agree.
>
> BERTRAND RUSSELL.

CHAPTER 23 : THE SOCIOLOGY OF KNOWLEDGE

It can hardly be doubted that Hegel's and Marx's historicist philosophies are characteristic products of their time—a time of social change. Like the philosophies of Heraclitus and Plato, and like those of Comte and Mill, Lamarck and Darwin, they are philosophies of change, and they witness to the tremendous and undoubtedly somewhat terrifying impression made by a changing social environment on the minds of those who live in this environment. Plato reacted to this situation by attempting to arrest all change. The more modern social philosophers appear to react very differently, since they accept, and even welcome, change ; yet this love of change seems to me a little ambivalent. For even though they have given up any hope of arresting change, as historicists they try to predict it, and thus to bring it under rational control ; and this certainly looks like an attempt to tame it. Thus it seems that, to the historicist, change has not entirely lost its terrors.

In our own time of still more rapid change, we even find the desire not only to predict change, but to control it by centralized large-scale planning. These holistic views (which I have criticized in *The Poverty of Historicism*) represent a compromise, as it were, between Platonic and Marxian theories. Plato's will to arrest change, combined with Marx's doctrine of its inevitability, yield, as a kind of Hegelian ' synthesis ', the demand that since it cannot be entirely arrested, change should at least be ' planned ', and controlled by the state whose power is to be vastly extended.

An attitude like this may seem, at first sight, to be a kind of rationalism ; it is closely related to Marx's dream of the ' realm of freedom ' in which man is for the first time master of his own

fate. But as a matter of fact, it occurs in closest alliance with
a doctrine which is definitely opposed to rationalism (and especially to the doctrine of the rational unity of mankind ; see chapter 24), one which is well in keeping with the irrationalist and
mystical tendencies of our time. I have in mind the Marxist
doctrine that our opinions, including our moral and scientific
opinions, are determined by class interest, and more generally
by the social and historical situation of our time. Under the
name of ' sociology of knowledge ' or ' sociologism ', this doctrine
has been developed recently (especially by M. Scheler and
K. Mannheim [1]) as a theory of the social determination of
scientific knowledge.

The sociology of knowledge argues that scientific thought, and
especially thought on social and political matters, does not
proceed in a vacuum, but in a socially conditioned atmosphere.
It is influenced largely by unconscious or subconscious elements.
These elements remain hidden from the thinker's observing eye
because they form, as it were, the very place which he inhabits,
his *social habitat*. The social habitat of the thinker determines
a whole system of opinions and theories which appear to him as
unquestionably true or self-evident. They appear to him as if
they were logically and trivially true, such as, for example, the
sentence ' all tables are tables '. This is why he is not even aware
of having made any assumptions at all. But that he has made
assumptions can be seen if we compare him with a thinker who
lives in a very different social habitat ; for he too will proceed
from a system of apparently unquestionable assumptions, but
from a very different one ; and it may be so different that no
intellectual bridge may exist and no compromise be possible
between these two systems. Each of these different socially
determined systems of assumptions is called by the sociologists of
knowledge a *total ideology*.

The sociology of knowledge can be considered as a Hegelian
version of Kant's theory of knowledge. For it continues on the
lines of Kant's criticism of what we may term the ' passivist '
theory of knowledge. I mean by this the theory of the empiricists
down to and including Hume, a theory which may be described,
roughly, as holding that knowledge streams into us through our
senses, and that error is due to our interference with the sense-
given material, or to the associations which have developed within
it ; the best way of avoiding error is to remain entirely passive
and receptive. Against this receptacle theory of knowledge (I

usually call it the ' bucket theory of the mind '), Kant [2] argued that knowledge is not a collection of gifts received by our senses and stored in the mind as if it were a museum, but that it is very largely the result of our own mental activity ; that we must most actively engage ourselves in searching, comparing, unifying, generalizing, if we wish to attain knowledge. We may call this theory the ' activist ' theory of knowledge. In connection with it, Kant gave up the untenable ideal of a science which is free from any kind of presuppositions. (That this ideal is even self-contradictory will be shown in the next chapter.) He made it quite clear that we cannot start from nothing, and that we have to approach our task equipped with a system of presuppositions which we hold without having tested them by the empirical methods of science ; such a system may be called a ' categorial apparatus ' [3]. Kant believed that it was possible to discover the one true and unchanging categorial apparatus, which represents as it were the necessarily unchanging framework of our intellectual outfit, i.e. human ' reason '. This part of Kant's theory was given up by Hegel, who, as opposed to Kant, did not believe in the unity of mankind. He taught that man's intellectual outfit was constantly changing, and that it was part of his social heritage ; accordingly the development of man's reason must coincide with the historical development of his society, i.e. of the nation to which he belongs. This theory of Hegel's, and especially his doctrine that all knowledge and all truth is ' relative ' in the sense of being determined by history, is sometimes called ' historism ' (in contradistinction to ' historicism ', as mentioned in the last chapter). The sociology of knowledge or ' sociologism ' is obviously very closely related to or nearly identical with it, the only difference being that, under the influence of Marx, it emphasizes that the historical development does not produce one uniform ' national spirit ', as Hegel held, but rather several and sometimes opposed ' total ideologies ' within one nation, according to the class, the social stratum, or the social habitat, of those who hold them.

But the likeness to Hegel goes further. I have said above that according to the sociology of knowledge, no intellectual bridge or compromise between different total ideologies is possible. But this radical scepticism is not really meant quite as seriously as it sounds. There is a way out of it, and the way is analogous to the Hegelian method of superseding the conflicts which preceded him in the history of philosophy. Hegel, a spirit freely

poised above the whirlpool of the dissenting philosophies, reduced
them all to mere components of the highest of syntheses, of his
own system. Similarly, the sociologists of knowledge hold that
the ' freely poised intelligence ' of an intelligentsia which is only
loosely anchored in social traditions may be able to avoid the
pitfalls of the total ideologies ; that it may even be able to see
through, and to unveil, the various total ideologies and the
hidden motives and other determinants which inspire them.
Thus the sociology of knowledge believes that the highest degree
of objectivity can be reached by the freely poised intelligence
analysing the various hidden ideologies and their anchorage in the
unconscious. The way to true knowledge appears to be the
unveiling of unconscious assumptions, a kind of psycho-therapy,
as it were, or if I may say so, a *socio-therapy*. Only he who has
been socio-analysed or who has socio-analysed himself, and who
is freed from this social complex, i.e. from his social ideology,
can attain to the highest synthesis of objective knowledge.

In a previous chapter, when dealing with ' Vulgar Marxism '
I mentioned a tendency which can be observed in a group of
modern philosophies, the tendency to unveil the hidden motives
behind our actions. The sociology of knowledge belongs to this
group, together with psycho-analysis and certain philosophies
which unveil the ' meaninglessness ' of the tenets of their opponents [4]. The popularity of these views lies, I believe, in the ease
with which they can be applied, and in the satisfaction which
they confer on those who see through things, and through the
follies of the unenlightened. This pleasure would be harmless,
were it not that all these ideas are liable to destroy the intellectual basis of any discussion, by establishing what I have called [5]
a ' reinforced dogmatism '. (Indeed, this is something rather
similar to a ' total ideology '.) Hegelianism does it by declaring
the admissibility and even fertility of contradictions. But if
contradictions need not be avoided, then any criticism and any
discussion becomes impossible since criticism always consists in
pointing out contradictions either within the theory to be criticized, or between it and some facts of experience. The situation
with psycho-analysis is similar : the psycho-analyst can always
explain away any objections by showing that they are due to
the repressions of the critic. And the philosophers of meaning,
again, need only point out that what their opponents hold is
meaningless, which will always be true, since ' meaninglessness '
can be so defined that any discussion about it is by definition

without meaning [6].   Marxists, in a like manner, are accustomed
to explain the disagreement of an opponent by his class bias, and
the sociologists of knowledge by his total ideology.   Such
methods are both easy to handle and good fun for those who
handle them.   But they clearly destroy the basis of rational discussion, and they must lead, ultimately, to anti-rationalism and
mysticism.

In spite of these dangers, I do not see why I should entirely
forgo the fun of handling these methods.   For just like the
psycho-analysts, the people to whom psycho-analysis applies best, [7]
the socio-analysts invite the application of their own methods
to themselves with an almost irresistible hospitality.   For is not
their description of an intelligentsia which is only loosely anchored
in tradition a very neat description of their own social group ?
And is it not also clear that, assuming the theory of total ideologies
to be correct, it would be part of every total ideology to believe
that one's own group was free from bias, and was indeed that
body of the elect which alone was capable of objectivity ?   Is it
not, therefore, to be expected, always assuming the truth of this
theory, that those who hold it will unconsciously deceive themselves by producing an amendment to the theory in order to
establish the objectivity of their own views ?   Can we, then,
take seriously their claim that by their sociological self-analysis
they have reached a higher degree of objectivity ;   and their
claim that socio-analysis can cast out a total ideology ?   But we
could even ask whether the whole theory is not simply the
expression of the class interest of this particular group ;   of an
intelligentsia only loosely anchored in tradition, though just
firmly enough to speak Hegelian as their mother tongue.

How little the sociologists of knowledge have succeeded in
socio-therapy, that is to say, in eradicating their own total
ideology, will be particularly obvious if we consider their relation
to Hegel.   For they have no idea that they are just repeating
him ;   on the contrary, they believe not only that they have
outgrown him, but also that they have successfully seen through
him, socio-analysed him ;   and that they can now look at him,
not from any particular social habitat, but objectively, from a
superior elevation.   This palpable failure in self-analysis tells us
enough.

But, all joking apart, there are more serious objections.   The
sociology of knowledge is not only self-destructive, not only a
rather gratifying object of socio-analysis, it also shows an astound-

ing failure to understand precisely its main subject, the *social aspects of knowledge*, or rather, of scientific method. It looks upon science or knowledge as a process in the mind or ' consciousness ' of the individual scientist, or perhaps as the product of such a process. If considered in this way, what we call scientific objectivity must indeed become completely ununderstandable, or even impossible ; and not only in the social or political sciences, where class interests and similar hidden motives may play a part, but just as much in the natural sciences. Everyone who has an inkling of the history of the natural sciences is aware of the passionate tenacity which characterizes many of its quarrels. No amount of political partiality can influence political theories more strongly than the partiality shown by some natural scientists in favour of their intellectual offspring. If scientific objectivity were founded, as the sociologistic theory of knowledge naïvely assumes, upon the individual scientist's impartiality or objectivity, then we should have to say good-bye to it. Indeed, we must be in a way more radically sceptical than the sociology of knowledge ; for there is no doubt that we are all suffering under our own system of prejudices (or ' total ideologies ', if this term is preferred) ; that we all take many things as self-evident, that we accept them uncritically and even with the naïve and cocksure belief that criticism is quite unnecessary ; and scientists are no exception to this rule, even though they may have superficially purged themselves from some of their prejudices in their particular field. But they have not purged themselves by socio-analysis or any similar method ; they have not attempted to climb to a higher plane from which they can understand, socio-analyse, and expurgate their ideological follies. For by making their minds more ' objective ' they could not possibly attain to what we call ' scientific objectivity '. No, what we usually mean by this term rests on different grounds [8]. It is a matter of scientific method. And, ironically enough, objectivity is closely bound up with the *social aspect of scientific method*, with the fact that science and scientific objectivity do not (and cannot) result from the attempts of an individual scientist to be ' objective ', but from the *friendly-hostile co-operation of many scientists*. Scientific objectivity can be described as the inter-subjectivity of scientific method. But this social aspect of science is almost entirely neglected by those who call themselves sociologists of knowledge.

Two aspects of the method of the natural sciences are of importance in this connection. Together they constitute what

I may term the 'public character of scientific method'. First, there is something approaching *free criticism*. A scientist may offer his theory with the full conviction that it is unassailable. But this will not impress his fellow-scientists and competitors ; rather it challenges them : they know that the scientific attitude means criticizing everything, and they are little deterred even by authorities. Secondly, scientists try to avoid talking at cross-purposes. (I may remind the reader that I am speaking of the natural sciences, but a part of modern economics may be included.) They try very seriously to speak one and the same language, even if they use different mother tongues. In the natural sciences this is achieved by recognizing experience as the impartial arbiter of their controversies. When speaking of 'experience' I have in mind experience of a 'public' character, like observations, and experiments, as opposed to experience in the sense of more 'private' æsthetic or religious experience ; and an experience is 'public' if everybody who takes the trouble can repeat it. In order to avoid speaking at cross-purposes, scientists try to express their theories in such a form that they can be tested, i.e. refuted (or else corroborated) by such experience.

This is what constitutes scientific objectivity. Everyone who has learned the technique of understanding and testing scientific theories can repeat the experiment and judge for himself. In spite of this, there will always be some who come to judgements which are partial, or even cranky. This cannot be helped, and it does not seriously disturb the working of the various *social institutions* which have been designed to further scientific objectivity and criticism ; for instance the laboratories, the scientific periodicals, the congresses. This aspect of scientific method shows what can be achieved by institutions designed to make public control possible, and by the open expression of public opinion, even if this is limited to a circle of specialists. Only political power, when it is used to suppress free criticism, or when it fails to protect it, can impair the functioning of these institutions, on which all progress, scientific, technological, and political, ultimately depends.

In order to elucidate further still this sadly neglected aspect of scientific method, we may consider the idea that it is advisable to characterize science by its methods rather than by its results.

Let us first assume that a clairvoyant produces a book by dreaming it, or perhaps by automatic writing. Let us assume, further, that years later as a result of recent and revolutionary scientific discoveries, a great scientist (who has never seen that book) produces one precisely the same.   Or to put it differently, we assume that the clairvoyant ' saw ' a scientific book which could not then have been produced by a scientist owing to the fact that many relevant discoveries were still unknown at that date.   We now ask : is it advisable to say that the clairvoyant produced a scientific book ?   We may assume that, if submitted at the time to the judgement of competent scientists, it would have been described as partly ununderstandable, and partly fantastic ; thus we shall have to say that the clairvoyant's book was not when written a scientific work, since it was not the result of scientific method.   I shall call such a result, which, though in agreement with some scientific results, is not the product of scientific method, a piece of ' revealed science '.

In order to apply these considerations to the problem of the publicity of scientific method, let us assume that Robinson Crusoe succeeded in building on his island physical and chemical laboratories, astronomical observatories, etc., and in writing a great number of papers, based throughout on observation and experiment.   Let us even assume that he had unlimited time at his disposal, and that he succeeded in constructing and in describing scientific systems which actually coincide with the results accepted at present by our own scientists.   Considering the character of this Crusonian science, some people will be inclined, at first sight, to assert that it is real science and not ' revealed science '. And, no doubt, it is very much more like science than the scientific book which was revealed to the clairvoyant, for Robinson Crusoe applied a good deal of scientific method.   And yet, I assert that this Crusonian science is still of the ' revealed ' kind ; that there is an element of scientific method missing, and consequently, that the fact that Crusoe arrived at our results is nearly as accidental and miraculous as it was in the case of the clairvoyant.   For there is nobody but himself to check his results ; nobody but himself to correct those prejudices which are the unavoidable consequence of his peculiar mental history ; nobody to help him to get rid of that strange blindness concerning the inherent possibilities of our own results which is a consequence of the fact that most of them are reached through comparatively irrelevant approaches.   And concerning his scientific papers, it is only in attempts to explain his work to *somebody who has not done it* that he can acquire the discipline of clear and reasoned communication which too is part of scientific method.   In one point—a

comparatively unimportant one—is the ' revealed ' character of
the Crusonian science particularly obvious ; I mean Crusoe's
discovery of his ' personal equation ' (for we must assume that
he made this discovery), of the characteristic personal reaction-
time affecting his astronomical observations. Of course it is
conceivable that he discovered, say, changes in his reaction-
time, and that he was led, in this way, to make allowances for it.
But if we compare this way of finding out about reaction-time,
with the way in which it was discovered in ' public ' science—
through the contradiction between the results of various observers
—then the ' revealed ' character of Robinson Crusoe's science
becomes manifest.

To sum up these considerations, it may be said that what we
call ' scientific objectivity ' is not a product of the individual
scientist's impartiality, but a product of the social or public
character of scientific method ; and the individual scientist's
impartiality is, so far as it exists, not the source but rather the
result of this socially or institutionally organized objectivity of
science.

Both [9] Kantians and Hegelians make the same mistake of
assuming that our presuppositions (since they are, to start with,
undoubtedly indispensable instruments which we need in our
active ' making ' of experiences) can neither be changed by
decision nor refuted by experience ; that they are above and
beyond the scientific methods of testing theories, constituting as
they do the basic presuppositions of all thought. But this is an
exaggeration, based on a misunderstanding of the relations
between theory and experience in science. It was one of the
greatest achievements of our time when Einstein showed that,
in the light of experience, we may question and revise our presuppositions regarding even space and time, ideas which had been
held to be necessary presuppositions of all science, and to belong
to its ' categorial apparatus '. Thus the sceptical attack upon
science launched by the sociology of knowledge breaks down in
the light of scientific method. The empirical method has proved
to be quite capable of taking care of itself.

But it does so not by eradicating our prejudices all at once ;
it can eliminate them only one by one. The classical case in
point is again Einstein's discovery of our prejudices regarding
time. Einstein did not set out to discover prejudices ; he did
not even set out to criticize our conceptions of space and time.
His problem was a concrete problem of physics, the re-drafting

of a theory that had broken down because of various experiments which in the light of the theory seemed to contradict one another. Einstein together with most physicists realized that this meant that the theory was false. And he found that if we alter it in a point which had so far been held by everybody to be self-evident and which had therefore escaped notice, then the difficulty could be removed. In other words, he just applied the methods of scientific criticism and of the invention and elimination of theories, of trial and error. But this method does not lead to the abandonment of all our prejudices ; rather, we can discover the fact that we had a prejudice only after having got rid of it.

But it certainly has to be admitted that, at any given moment, our scientific theories will depend not only on the experiments, etc., made up to that moment, but also upon prejudices which are taken for granted, so that we have not become aware of them (although the application of certain logical methods may help us to detect them). At any rate, we can say in regard to this incrustation that science is capable of learning, of breaking down some of its crusts. The process may never be perfected, but there is no fixed barrier before which it must stop short. Any assumption can, in principle, be criticized. And that anybody may criticize constitutes scientific objectivity.

Scientific results are ' relative ' (if this term is to be used at all) only in so far as they are the results of a certain stage of scientific development and liable to be superseded in the course of scientific progress. But this does not mean that *truth* is ' relative '. If an assertion is true, it is true for ever [10]. It only means that most scientific results have the character of hypotheses, i.e. statements for which the evidence is inconclusive, and which are therefore liable to revision at any time. These considerations (with which I have dealt more fully elsewhere [11]), though not necessary for a criticism of the sociologists, may perhaps help to further the understanding of their theories. They also throw some light, to come back to my main criticism, on the important rôle which co-operation, intersubjectivity, and the publicity of method play in scientific criticism and scientific progress.

It is true that the social sciences have not yet fully attained this publicity of method. This is due partly to the intelligence-destroying influence of Aristotle and Hegel, partly perhaps also to their failure to make use of the social instruments of scientific objectivity. Thus they are really ' total ideologies ', or putting it differently, some social scientists are unable, and even unwilling, to speak a common language. But the reason is not class interest, and the cure is not a Hegelian dialectical synthesis, nor self-analysis. The only course open to the social sciences is to forget all about the verbal fireworks and to tackle the practical problems of our time with the help of the theoretical methods which are fundamentally the same in *all* sciences. I mean the methods of trial and error, of inventing hypotheses which can be practically tested, and of submitting them to practical tests. *A social technology is needed whose results can be tested by piecemeal social engineering.*

The cure here suggested for the social sciences is diametrically opposed to the one suggested by the sociology of knowledge. Sociologism believes that it is not their unpractical character, but rather the fact that practical and theoretical problems are too much intertwined in the field of social and political knowledge, that creates the methodological difficulties of these sciences. Thus we can read in a leading work on the sociology of knowledge [12] : ' The peculiarity of political knowledge, as opposed to "exact" knowledge, lies in the fact that knowledge and will, or the rational element and the range of the irrational, are inseparably and essentially intertwined.' To this we can reply that ' knowledge ' and ' will ' are, in a certain sense, always inseparable ; and that this fact need not lead to any dangerous entanglement. No scientist can know without making an effort, without taking an interest ; and in his effort there is usually even a certain amount of self-interest involved. The engineer studies things mainly from a practical point of view. So does the farmer. Practice is not the enemy of theoretical knowledge but the most valuable incentive to it. Though a certain amount of aloofness may be becoming to the scientist, there are many examples to show that it is not always important for a scientist to be thus disinterested. But it *is* important for him to remain in touch with reality, with practice, for those who overlook it have to pay by lapsing into scholasticism. Practical application of our findings is thus the means by which we may eliminate irrationalism from social science, and not any attempt to separate knowledge from ' will '.

As opposed to this, the sociology of knowledge hopes to reform the social sciences by making the social scientists aware of the social forces and ideologies which unconsciously beset them. But the main trouble about prejudices is that there is no such direct way of getting rid of them. For how shall we ever know that we have made any progress in our attempt to rid ourselves from prejudice ? Is it not a common experience that those who are most convinced of having got rid of their prejudices are most prejudiced ? The idea that a sociological or a psychological or an anthropological or any other study of prejudices may help us to rid ourselves of them is quite mistaken ; for many who pursue these studies are full of prejudice ; and not only does self-analysis not help us to overcome the unconscious determination of our views, it often leads to even more subtle self-deception. Thus we can read in the same work on the sociology of knowledge [13] the following references to its own activities : ' There is an increasing tendency towards making conscious the factors by which we have so far been unconsciously ruled. . . Those who fear that our increasing knowledge of determining factors may paralyse our decisions and threaten " freedom " should put their minds at rest. For only he is truly determined who does not know the most essential determining factors but acts immediately under the pressure of determinants unknown to him.' Now this is clearly just a repetition of a pet idea of Hegel's which Engels naïvely repeated when he said [14] : 'Freedom is the appreciation of necessity.' And it is a reactionary prejudice. For are those who act under the pressure of well-known determinants, for example, of a political tyranny, made free by their knowledge ? Only Hegel could tell us such tales. But that the sociology of knowledge preserves this particular prejudice shows clearly enough that there is no possible short-cut to rid us of our ideologies. (Once a Hegelian, always a Hegelian.) Self-analysis is no substitute for those practical actions which are necessary for establishing the democratic institutions which alone can guarantee the freedom of critical thought, and the progress of science.

Chapter 24 : ORACULAR PHILOSOPHY AND THE REVOLT AGAINST REASON

Marx was a rationalist. With Socrates, and with Kant, he believed in human reason as the basis of the unity of mankind. But his doctrine that our opinions are determined by class interest hastened the decline of this belief. Like Hegel's doctrine that our ideas are determined by national interests and traditions, Marx's doctrine tended to undermine the rationalist belief in reason. Thus threatened both from the right and from the left, a rationalist attitude to social and economic questions could hardly resist when historicist prophecy and oracular irrationalism made a frontal attack on it. This is why the conflict between rationalism and irrationalism has become the most important intellectual, and perhaps even moral, issue of our time.

I

Since the terms ' reason ' and ' rationalism ' are vague, it will be necessary to explain roughly the way in which they are used here. First, they are used in a wide sense [1] ; they are used to cover not only intellectual activity but also observation and experiment. It is necessary to keep this remark in mind, since ' reason ' and ' rationalism ' are often used in a different and more narrow sense, in opposition not to ' irrationalism ' but to ' empiricism ' ; if used in this way, rationalism extols intelligence above observation and experiment, and might therefore be better described as ' intellectualism '. But when I speak here of ' rationalism ', I use the word always in a sense which includes ' empiricism ' as well as ' intellectualism ' ; just as science makes use of experiments as well as of thought. Secondly, I use the word ' rationalism ' in order to indicate, roughly, an attitude that seeks to solve as many problems as possible by an appeal to reason, i.e. to clear thought and experience, rather than by an appeal to emotions and passions. This explanation, of course, is not very satisfactory, since all terms such as ' reason ' or ' passion ' are vague ; we do not possess ' reason ' or ' passions ' in the sense in which we possess certain physical organs, for example, brains or a heart, or in the sense in which we possess certain ' faculties ', for example, the power of speaking, or of gnashing our teeth. In order therefore to be a little more precise, it may be better to explain rationalism in terms of practical attitudes or behaviour. We could then say that rationalism is an attitude of readiness to listen to critical arguments and to learn from experience. It is fundamentally an attitude of admitting that ' *I may be wrong and you may be right, and by an effort, we may get nearer to the truth* '. It is an attitude which does not lightly give up hope that by such means as argument and careful observation, people may reach some kind of agreement on many problems of importance ; and that, even where their demands and their interests clash, it is often possible to argue about the various demands and proposals, and to reach—perhaps by arbitration—a compromise which, because of its equity, is acceptable to most, if not to all. In short, the rationalist attitude, or, as I may perhaps label it, the ' attitude of reasonableness ', is very similar to the scientific atti-tude, to the belief that in the search for truth we need co-oper-ation, and that, with the help of argument, we can in time attain something like objectivity.

It is of some interest to analyse this resemblance between this attitude of reasonableness and that of science more fully. In the last chapter, I tried to explain the social aspect of scientific method with the help of the fiction of a scientific Robinson Crusoe. An exactly analogous consideration can show the social character of reasonableness, as opposed to intellectual gifts, or cleverness. Reason, like language, can be said to be a product of social life. A Robinson Crusoe (marooned in early childhood) might be clever enough to master many difficult situations ; but he would invent neither language nor the art of argumentation. Admittedly, we often argue with ourselves ; but we are accus-tomed to do so only because we have learned to argue with others, and because we have learned in this way that the argument counts, rather than the person arguing. (This last consideration cannot, of course, tip the scales when we argue with ourselves.) Thus we can say that we owe our reason, like our language, to intercourse with other men.

The fact that the rationalist attitude considers the argument rather than the person arguing is of far-reaching importance. It leads to the view that we must recognize everybody with whom we communicate as a potential source of argument and of reason-able information ; it thus establishes what may be described as the ' rational unity of mankind '.

In a way, our analysis of ' reason ' may be said to resemble slightly that of Hegel and the Hegelians, who consider reason as a social product and indeed as a kind of department of the soul or the spirit of society (for example, of the nation, or the class) and who emphasize, under the influence of Burke, our indebtedness to our social heritage, and our nearly complete dependence on it. Admittedly, there is some similarity. But there are very considerable differences also. Hegel and the Hegelians are collectivists. They argue that, since we owe our reason to 'society'—or to a certain society such as a nation—'society' is everything and the individual nothing; or that whatever value the individual possesses is derived from the collective, the real carrier of all values. As opposed to this, the position presented here does not assume the existence of collectives; if I say, for example, that we owe our reason to 'society', then I always mean that we owe it to certain concrete individuals— though perhaps to a considerable number of anonymous individuals—and to our intellectual intercourse with them. Therefore, in speaking of a 'social' theory of reason (or of scientific method), I mean more precisely that the theory is an *inter-personal* one, and never that it is a collectivist theory. Certainly we owe a great deal to tradition, and tradition is very important, but the term 'tradition' also has to be analysed into concrete personal relations [2]. And if we do this, then we can get rid of that attitude which considers every tradition as sacrosanct, or as valuable in itself, replacing this by an attitude which considers traditions as valuable or pernicious, as the case may be, according to their influence upon individuals. We thus may realize that each of us (by way of example and criticism) may contribute to the growth or the suppression of such traditions.

The position here adopted is very different from the popular, originally Platonic, view of reason as a kind of 'faculty', which may be possessed and developed by different men in vastly different degrees. Admittedly, intellectual gifts may be different in this way, and they may contribute to reasonableness; but they need not. Clever men may be very unreasonable; they may cling to their prejudices and may not expect to hear anything worth while from others. According to our view, however, we not only owe our reason to others, but we can never excel others in our reasonableness in a way that would establish a claim to authority; authoritarianism and rationalism in our sense cannot be reconciled, since argument, which includes criticism, and the art of listening to criticism, is the basis of reasonableness. Thus rationalism in our sense is diametrically opposed to all those modern Platonic dreams of brave new worlds in which the growth of reason would be controlled or ' planned ' by some superior reason. Reason, like science, grows by way of mutual criticism ; the only possible way of ' planning ' its growth is to develop those institutions that safeguard the freedom of this criticism, that is to say, the freedom of thought. It may be remarked that Plato, even though his theory is authoritarian, and demands the strict control of the growth of human reason in his guardians (as has been shown especially in chapter 8), pays tribute, *by his manner of writing*, to our inter-personal theory of reason ; for most of his earlier dialogues describe arguments conducted in a very reasonable spirit.

My way of using the term ' rationalism ' may become a little clearer, perhaps, if we distinguish between a true rationalism and a false or a pseudo-rationalism. What I shall call the ' true rationalism ' is the rationalism of Socrates. It is the awareness of one's limitations, the intellectual modesty of those who know how often they err, and how much they depend on others even for this knowledge. It is the realization that we must not expect too much from reason ; that argument rarely settles a question, although it is the only means for learning—not to see clearly, but to see more clearly than before.

What I shall call ' pseudo-rationalism ' is the intellectual intuitionism of Plato. It is the immodest belief in one's superior intellectual gifts, the claim to be initiated, to know with certainty, and with authority. According to Plato, opinion—even ' true opinion ', as we can read in the *Timaeus* [3]—' is shared by all men ; but reason ' (or ' intellectual intuition ') ' is shared only by the gods, and by very few men '. This authoritarian intellectualism, this belief in the possession of an infallible instrument of discovery, or an infallible method, this failure to distinguish between a man's intellectual powers and his indebtedness to others for all he can possibly know or understand, this pseudo-rationalism is often called ' rationalism ', but it is diametrically opposed to what we call by this name.

My analysis of the rationalist attitude is undoubtedly very incomplete, and, I readily admit, a little vague ; but it will suffice for our purpose. In a similar way I shall now describe irrationalism, indicating at the same time how an irrationalist is likely to defend it.

The irrationalist attitude may be developed along the following lines. Though perhaps recognizing reason and scientific argument as tools that may do well enough if we wish to scratch the surface of things, or as means to serve some irrational end, the irrationalist will insist that ' human nature ' is in the main not rational. Man, he holds, is more than a rational animal, and also less. In order to see that he is less, we need only consider how small is the number of men who are capable of argument ; this is why, according to the irrationalist, the majority of men will always have to be tackled by an appeal to their emotions and passions rather than by an appeal to their reason. But man is also more than just a rational animal, since all that really matters in his life goes beyond reason. Even the few scientists who take reason and science seriously are bound to their rationalist attitude merely because they love it. Thus even in these rare cases, it is the emotional make-up of man and not his reason that determines his attitude. Moreover, it is his intuition, his mystical insight into the nature of things, rather than his reasoning which makes a great scientist. Thus rationalism cannot offer an adequate interpretation even of the apparently rational activity of the scientist. But since the scientific field is exceptionally favourable to a rationalist interpretation, we must expect that rationalism will fail even more conspicuously when it tries to deal with other fields of human activity. And this expectation, so the irrationalist will continue his argument, proves to be quite accurate. Leaving aside the lower aspects of human nature, we may look to one of its highest, to the fact that man can be creative. It is the small creative minority of men who really matter ; the men who create works of art or of thought, the founders of religions, and the great statesmen. These few exceptional individuals allow us to glimpse the real greatness of man. But although these leaders of mankind know how to make use of reason for their purposes, they are never men of reason. Their roots lie deeper—deep in their instincts and impulses, and in those of the society of which they are parts. Creativeness is an entirely irrational, a mystical faculty. . .

II

The issue between rationalism and irrationalism is of long standing. Although Greek philosophy undoubtedly started off as a rationalist undertaking, there were streaks of mysticism even in its first beginnings. It is (as hinted in chapter 10) the yearning for the lost unity and shelter of tribalism which expresses itself in these mystical elements within a fundamentally rational approach [4]. An open conflict between rationalism and irrationalism broke out for the first time in the Middle Ages, as the opposition between scholasticism and mysticism. (It is perhaps not without interest that rationalism flourished in the former Roman provinces, while men from the ' barbarian ' countries were prominent among the mystics.) In the seventeenth, eighteenth, and nineteenth centuries, when the tide of rationalism, of intellectualism, and of ' materialism ' was rising, irrationalists had to pay some attention to it, to argue against it ; and by exhibiting its limitations, and exposing the immodest claims and dangers of pseudo-rationalism (which they did not distinguish from rationalism in our sense), some of these critics, notably Burke, have earned the gratitude of all true rationalists. But the tide has now turned, and ' profoundly significant allusions . . and allegories ' (as Kant puts it) have become the fashion of the day. An oracular irrationalism has established (especially with Bergson and the majority of German philosophers and intellectuals) the habit of ignoring or at best deploring the existence of such an inferior being as a rationalist. To them the rationalists—or the ' materialists ', as they often say—and especially, the rationalist scientist, are the poor in spirit, pursuing soulless and largely mechanical activities [5], and completely unaware of the deeper problems of human destiny and of its philosophy. And the rationalists usually reciprocate by dismissing irrationalism as sheer nonsense. Never before has the break been so complete. And the break in the diplomatic relations of the philosophers proved its significance when it was followed by a break in the diplomatic relations of the states.

In this issue, I am entirely on the side of rationalism. This is so much the case that even where I feel that rationalism has gone too far I still sympathize with it, holding as I do that an excess in this direction (as long as we exclude the intellectual immodesty of Plato's pseudo-rationalism) is harmless indeed as compared with an excess in the other. In my opinion, the only way in which excessive rationalism is likely to prove harmful is that it tends to undermine its own position and thus to further an irrationalist reaction. It is only this danger which induces me to examine the claims of an excessive rationalism more closely and to advocate a modest and self-critical rationalism which recognizes certain limitations. Accordingly, I shall distinguish in what follows between two rationalist positions, which I label ' critical rationalism ' and ' uncritical rationalism ' or ' comprehensive rationalism'. (This distinction is independent of the previous one between a 'true' and a 'false' rationalism, even though a 'true' rationalism in my sense will hardly be other than critical.)

Uncritical or comprehensive rationalism can be described as the attitude of the person who says ' I am not prepared to accept anything that cannot be defended by means of argument or experience '. We can express this also in the form of the principle that any assumption which cannot be supported either by argument or by experience is to be discarded [6]. Now it is easy to see that this principle of an uncritical rationalism is inconsistent; for since it cannot, in its turn, be supported by argument or by experience, it implies that it should itself be discarded. (It is analogous to the paradox of the liar [7], i.e. to a sentence which asserts its own falsity.) Uncritical rationalism is therefore logically untenable; and since a purely logical argument can show this, uncritical rationalism can be defeated by its own chosen weapon, argument.

This criticism may be generalized. Since all argument must proceed from assumptions, it is plainly impossible to demand that all assumptions should be based on argument. The demand raised by many philosophers that we should start with no assumption whatever and never assume anything about ' sufficient reason ', and even the weaker demand that we should start with a very small set of assumptions (' categories '), are both in this form inconsistent. For they themselves rest upon the truly colossal assumption that it is possible to start without, or with only a few assumptions, and still to obtain results that are worth while. (Indeed, this principle of avoiding all presuppositions is not, as some may think, a counsel of perfection, but a form of the paradox of the liar [8].)

Now all this is a little abstract, but it may be restated in connection with the problem of rationalism in a less formal way. The rationalist attitude is characterized by the importance it attaches to argument and experience. But neither logical argument nor experience can establish the rationalist attitude; for only those who are ready to consider argument or experience, and who have therefore adopted this attitude already, will be impressed by them. That is to say, a rationalist attitude must be first adopted if any argument or experience is to be effective, and it cannot therefore be based upon argument or experience. (And this consideration is quite independent of the question whether or not there exist any convincing rational arguments which favour the adoption of the rationalist attitude.) We have to conclude from this that no rational argument will have a rational effect on a man who does not want to adopt a rational attitude. Thus a comprehensive rationalism is untenable.

But this means that whoever adopts the rationalist attitude does so because he has adopted, consciously or unconsciously, some proposal, or decision, or belief, or behaviour ; an adoption which may be called ' irrational '. Whether this adoption is tentative or leads to a settled habit, we may describe it as an irrational *faith in reason*. So rationalism is necessarily far from comprehensive or self-contained. This has frequently been over-looked by rationalists who thus exposed themselves to a beating in their own field and by their own favourite weapon whenever an irrationalist took the trouble to turn it against them. And indeed it did not escape the attention of some enemies of ration-alism that one can always refuse to accept arguments, either all arguments or those of a certain kind ; and that such an attitude can be carried through without becoming logically inconsistent. This led them to see that the uncritical rationalist who believes that rationalism is self-contained and can be established by argument must be wrong. Irrationalism is logically superior to uncritical rationalism.

Then why not adopt irrationalism ? Many who started as rationalists but were disillusioned by the discovery that a too comprehensive rationalism defeats itself have indeed practically capitulated to irrationalism. (This is what has happened to Whitehead [9], if I am not quite mistaken.) But such panic action is entirely uncalled for. Although an uncritical and com-prehensive rationalism is logically untenable, and although a comprehensive irrationalism is logically tenable, this is no reason why we should adopt the latter. For there are other tenable attitudes, notably that of critical rationalism which recognizes the fact that the fundamental rationalist attitude results from an (at least tentative) act of faith—from faith in reason. Accordingly, our choice is open. We may choose some form of irrationalism, even some radical or comprehensive form. But we are also free to choose a critical form of rationalism, one which frankly admits its origin in an irrational decision (and which, to that extent, admits a certain priority of irrationalism).

III

The choice before us is not simply an intellectual affair, or a matter of taste. It is a moral decision [10] (in the sense of chapter 5). For the question whether we adopt some more or less radical form of irrationalism, or whether we adopt that minimum concession to irrationalism which I have termed ' critical rationalism ', will deeply affect our whole attitude towards other men, and towards the problems of social life. It has already been said that rationalism is closely connected with the belief in the unity of mankind. Irrationalism, which is not bound by any rules of consistency, may be combined with any kind of belief, including a belief in the brotherhood of man ; but the fact that it may easily be combined with a very different belief, and especially the fact that it lends itself easily to the support of a romantic belief in the existence of an elect body, in the division of men into leaders and led, into natural masters and natural slaves, shows clearly that a moral decision is involved in the choice between it and a critical rationalism.

As we have seen before (in chapter 5), and now again in our analysis of the uncritical version of rationalism, arguments cannot *determine* such a fundamental moral decision. But this does not imply that our choice cannot be *helped* by any kind of argument whatever. On the contrary, whenever we are faced with a moral decision of a more abstract kind, it is most helpful to analyse carefully the consequences which are likely to result from the alternatives between which we have to choose. For only if we can visualize these consequences in a concrete and practical way, do we really know what our decision is about ; otherwise we decide blindly. In order to illustrate this point, I may quote a passage from Shaw's *Saint Joan*. The speaker is the Chaplain ; he has stubbornly demanded Joan's death ; but when he sees her at the stake, he breaks down : ' I meant no harm. I did not know what it would be like . . I did not know what I was doing . . If I had known, I would have torn her from their hands. You don't know. You haven't seen : it is so easy to talk when you don't know. You madden yourself with words . . But when it is brought home to you ; when you see the thing you have done ; when it is blinding your eyes, stifling your nostrils, tearing your heart, then—then—O God, take away this sight from me ! ' There were, of course, other figures in Shaw's play who knew exactly what they were doing, and yet

decided to do it ; and who did not regret it afterwards. Some
people dislike seeing their fellow men burning at the stake, and
others do not. This point (which was neglected by many Vic-
torian optimists) is important, for it shows that a rational analysis
of the consequences of a decision does not make the decision
rational ; the consequences do not determine our decision ; it is
always we who decide. But an analysis of the concrete consequences, and their clear realization in what we call our ' imagination ', makes the difference between a blind decision and a
decision made with open eyes ; and since we use our imagination
very little [11], we only too often decide blindly. This is especially
so if we are intoxicated by an oracular philosophy, one of the
most powerful means of maddening ourselves with words—to use
Shaw's expression.

The rational and imaginative analysis of the consequences of
a moral theory has a certain analogy in scientific method. For in
science, too, we do not accept an abstract theory because it is convincing in itself ; we rather decide to accept or reject it after we
have investigated those concrete and practical consequences which
can be more directly tested by experiment. But there is a fundamental difference. In the case of a scientific theory, our decision
depends upon the results of experiments. If these confirm the
theory, we may accept it until we find a better one. If they
contradict the theory, we reject it. But in the case of a moral
theory, we can only confront its consequences with our conscience. And while the verdict of experiments does not depend
upon ourselves, the verdict of our conscience does.

I hope I have made it clear in which sense the analysis of
consequences may influence our decision without determining it.
And in presenting the consequences of the two alternatives
between which we must decide, rationalism and irrationalism,
I warn the reader that I shall be partial. So far, in presenting
the two alternatives of the moral decision before us—it is, in
many senses, the most fundamental decision in the ethical field
—I have tried to be impartial, although I have not hidden my
sympathies. But now I am going to present those considerations
of the consequences of the two alternatives which appear to me
most telling, and by which I myself have been influenced in
rejecting irrationalism and accepting the faith in reason.

Let us examine the consequences of irrationalism first. The
irrationalist insists that emotions and passions rather than reason
are the mainsprings of human action. To the rationalist's reply

that, though this may be so, we should do what we can to remedy it, and should try to make reason play as large a part as it possibly can, the irrationalist would rejoin (if he condescends to a discussion) that this attitude is hopelessly unrealistic. For it does not consider the weakness of 'human nature', the feeble intellectual endowment of most men and their obvious dependence upon emotions and passions.

It is my firm conviction that this irrational emphasis upon emotion and passion leads ultimately to what I can only describe as crime. One reason for this opinion is that this attitude, which is at best one of resignation towards the irrational nature of human beings, at worst one of scorn for human reason, must lead to an appeal to violence and brutal force as the ultimate arbiter in any dispute. For if a dispute arises, then this means that those more constructive emotions and passions which might in principle help to get over it, reverence, love, devotion to a common cause, etc., have shown themselves incapable of solving the problem. But if that is so, then what is left to the irrationalist except the appeal to other and less constructive emotions and passions, to fear, hatred, envy, and ultimately, to violence? This tendency is very much strengthened by another and perhaps even more important attitude which also is in my opinion inherent in irrationalism, namely, the stress on the inequality of men.

It cannot, of course, be denied that human individuals are, like all other things in our world, in very many respects very unequal. Nor can it be doubted that this inequality is of great importance and even in many respects highly desirable [12]. (The fear that the development of mass production and collectivization may react upon men by destroying their inequality or individuality is one of the nightmares [13] of our times.) But all this simply has no bearing upon the question whether or not we should decide to treat men, especially in political issues, as equals, or as much like equals as is possible ; that is to say, as possessing equal rights, and equal claims to equal treatment ; and it has no bearing upon the question whether we ought to construct political institutions accordingly. ' Equality before the law ' is *not a fact but a political demand* [14] *based upon a moral decision* ; and it is quite independent of the theory—which is probably false—that ' all men are born equal '. Now I do not intend to say that the adoption of this humanitarian attitude of impartiality is a direct consequence of a decision in favour of rationalism. But a tendency towards impartiality is closely related to rationalism, and

can hardly be excluded from the rationalist creed.   Again, I do
not intend to say that an irrationalist could not consistently adopt
an equalitarian or impartial attitude ; and even if he could not
do so consistently, he is not bound to be consistent.   But I do
wish to stress the fact that the irrationalist attitude can hardly
avoid becoming entangled with the attitude that is opposed to
equalitarianism.   This fact is connected with its emphasis upon
emotions and passions ; for we cannot feel the same emotions
towards everybody.   Emotionally, we all divide men into those
who are near to us, and those who are far from us.   The division
of mankind into friend and foe is a most obvious emotional
division ; and this division is even recognized in the Christian
commandment, ' Love thy enemies ! '   Even the best Christian
who really lives up to this commandment (there are not many, as
is shown by the attitude of the average good Christian towards
' materialists ' and ' atheists '), even he cannot feel equal love for
all men.   We cannot really love ' in the abstract ' ; we can love
only those whom we know.   Thus the appeal even to our best
emotions, love and compassion, can only tend to divide mankind
into different categories.   And this will be more true if the appeal
is made to lesser emotions and passions.   Our ' natural ' reaction
will be to divide mankind into friend and foe ; into those who
belong to our tribe, to our emotional community, and those who
stand outside it ; into believers and unbelievers ; into com-
patriots and aliens ; into class comrades and class enemies ; and
into leaders and led.

I have mentioned before that the theory that our thoughts
and opinions are dependent upon our class situation, or upon our
national interests, must lead to irrationalism.   I now wish to
emphasize the fact that the opposite is also true.   The abandonment of the rationalist attitude, of the respect for reason and
argument and the other fellow's point of view, the stress upon the
' deeper ' layers of human nature, all this must lead to the view
that thought is merely a somewhat superficial manifestation of
what lies within these irrational depths.   It must nearly always,
I believe, produce an attitude which considers the person of the
thinker instead of his thought.   It must produce the belief that
' we think with our blood ', or ' with our national heritage ', or
' with our class '.   This view may be presented in a materialist
form or in a highly spiritual fashion ; the idea that we ' think
with our race ' may perhaps be replaced by the idea of elect or
inspired souls who ' think by God's grace '.   I refuse, on moral

grounds, to be impressed by these differences ; for the decisive similarity between all these intellectually immodest views is that they do not judge a thought on its own merits. By thus abandoning reason, they split mankind into friends and foes ; into the few who share in reason with the gods, and the many who don't (as Plato says) ; into the few who stand near and the many who stand far ; into those who speak the untranslatable language of our own emotions and passions and those whose tongue is not our tongue. Once we have done this, political equalitarianism becomes practically impossible.

Now the adoption of an anti-equalitarian attitude in political life, i.e. in the field of problems concerned with the power of man over man, is just what I should call criminal. For it offers a justification of the attitude that different categories of people have different rights; that the master has the right to enslave the slave ; that some men have the right to use others as their tools. Ultimately, it will be used, as in Plato [15], to justify murder.

I do not overlook the fact that there are irrationalists who love mankind, and that not all forms of irrationalism engender criminality. But I hold that he who teaches that not reason but love should rule opens the way for those who rule by hate. (Socrates, I believe, saw something of this when he suggested [16] that mistrust or hatred of argument is related to mistrust or hatred of man.) Those who do not see this connection at once, who believe in a direct rule of emotional love, should consider that love as such certainly does not promote impartiality. And it cannot do away with conflict either. That love as such may be unable to settle a conflict can be shown by considering a harmless test case, which may pass as representative of more serious ones. Tom likes the theatre and Dick likes dancing. Tom lovingly insists on going to a dance while Dick wants for Tom's sake to go to the theatre. This conflict cannot be settled by love ; rather, the greater the love, the stronger will be the conflict. There are only two solutions ; one is the use of emotion, and ultimately of violence, and the other is the use of reason, of impartiality, of reasonable compromise. All this is not intended to indicate that I do not appreciate the difference between love and hate, or that I think that life would be worth living without love. (And I am quite prepared to admit that the Christian idea of love is not meant in a purely emotional way.) But I insist that no emotion, not even love, can replace the rule of institutions controlled by reason.

This, of course, is not the only argument against the idea of a rule of love. Loving a person means wishing to make him happy. (This, by the way, was Thomas Aquinas' definition of love.) But of all political ideals, that of making the people happy is perhaps the most dangerous one. It leads invariably to the attempt to impose our scale of ' higher ' values upon others, in order to make them realize what seems to us of greatest importance for their happiness ; in order, as it were, to save their souls. It leads to Utopianism and Romanticism. We all feel certain that everybody would be happy in the beautiful, the perfect community of our dreams. And no doubt, there would be heaven on earth if we could all love one another. But, as I have said before (in chapter 9), the attempt to make heaven on earth invariably produces hell. It leads to intolerance. It leads to religious wars, and to the saving of souls through the inquisition. And it is, I believe, based on a complete misunderstanding of our moral duties. It is our duty to help those who need our help ; but it cannot be our duty to make others happy, since this does not depend on us, and since it would only too often mean intruding on the privacy of those towards whom we have such amiable intentions. The political demand for piecemeal (as opposed to Utopian) methods corresponds to the decision that the fight against suffering must be considered a duty, while the right to care for the happiness of others must be considered a privilege confined to the close circle of their friends. In their case, we may perhaps have a certain right to try to impose our scale of values—our preferences regarding music, for example. (And we may even feel it our duty to open to them a world of values which, we trust, can so much contribute to their happiness.) This right of ours exists only if, and because, they can get rid of us ; because friendships can be ended. But the use of political means for imposing our scale of values upon others is a very different matter. Pain, suffering, injustice, and their prevention, these are the eternal problems of public morals, the ' agenda ' of public policy (as Bentham would have said). The ' higher ' values should very largely be considered as ' non-agenda ', and should be left to the realm of *laissez-faire*. Thus we might say : help your enemies ; assist those in distress, even if they hate you ; but love only your friends.

This is only part of the case against irrationalism, and of the consequences which induce me to adopt the opposite attitude, that is, a critical rationalism. This latter attitude with its

emphasis upon argument and experience, with its device ' I may
be wrong and you may be right, and by an effort we may get
nearer to the truth ', is, as mentioned before, closely akin to the
scientific attitude. It is bound up with the idea that everybody
is liable to make mistakes, which may be found out by himself,
or by others, or by himself with the assistance of the criticism of
others. It therefore suggests the idea that nobody should be his
own judge, and it suggests the idea of impartiality. (This is
closely related to the idea of ' scientific objectivity ' as analysed in
the previous chapter.) Its faith in reason is not only a faith in
our own reason, but also—and even more—in that of others.
Thus a rationalist, even if he believes himself to be intellectually
superior to others, will reject all claims to authority [17] since he is
aware that, if his intelligence is superior to that of others (which
is hard for him to judge), it is so only in so far as he is capable of
learning from criticism as well as from his own and other people's
mistakes, and that one can learn in this sense only if one takes
others and their arguments seriously. Rationalism is therefore
bound up with the idea that the other fellow has a right to be
heard, and to defend his arguments. It thus implies the recognition of the claim to tolerance, at least [18] of all those who are not
intolerant themselves. One does not kill a man when one adopts
the attitude of first listening to his arguments. (Kant was right
when he based the ' Golden Rule ' on the idea of reason. To be
sure, it is impossible to prove the rightness of any ethical principle, or even to argue in its favour in just the manner in which
we argue in favour of a scientific statement. Ethics is not a
science. But although there is no ' rational scientific basis ' of
ethics, there is an ethical basis of science, and of rationalism.)
Also the idea of impartiality leads to that of responsibility ; we
have not only to listen to arguments, but we have a duty to
respond, to answer, where our actions affect others. Ultimately,
in this way, rationalism is linked up with the recognition of the
necessity of social institutions to protect freedom of criticism, freedom of thought, and thus the freedom of men. And it establishes
something like a moral obligation towards the support of these
institutions. This is why rationalism is closely linked up with the
political demand for practical social engineering—piecemeal
engineering, of course—in the humanitarian sense, with the demand for the rationalization of society [19], for planning for freedom,
and for its control by reason ; not by ' science ', not by a Platonic,
a pseudo-rational authority, but by that Socratic reason which is

aware of its limitations, and which therefore respects the other man and does not aspire to coerce him—not even into happiness. The adoption of rationalism implies, moreover, that there is a common medium of communication, a common language of reason ; it establishes something like a moral obligation towards that language, the obligation to keep up its standards of clarity [20] and to use it in such a way that it can retain its function as the vehicle of argument.   That is to say, to use it plainly ; to use it as an instrument of rational communication, of significant information, rather than as a means of ' self-expression ', as the vicious romantic jargon of most of our educationists has it.   (It is characteristic of the modern romantic hysteria that it combines a Hegelian collectivism concerning ' reason ' with an excessive individualism concerning ' emotions ' : thus the emphasis on language as a means of self-expression instead of a means of communication.   Both attitudes, of course, are parts of the revolt against reason.)   And it implies the recognition that mankind is united by the fact that our different mother tongues, in so far as they are rational, can be translated into one another.   It recognizes the unity of human reason.

A few remarks may be added concerning the relation of the rationalist attitude to the attitude of readiness to use what is usually called ' imagination '.   It is frequently assumed that imagination has a close affinity with emotion and therefore with irrationalism, and that rationalism rather tends towards an unimaginative dry scholasticism.   I do not know whether such a view may have some psychological basis, and I rather doubt it. But my interests are institutional rather than psychological, and from an institutional point of view (as well as from that of method) it appears that rationalism must encourage the use of imagination because it needs it, while irrationalism must tend to discourage it.   The very fact that rationalism is critical, whilst irrationalism must tend towards dogmatism (where there is no argument, nothing is left but full acceptance or flat denial), leads in this direction.   Criticism always demands a certain degree of imagination, whilst dogmatism suppresses it.   Similarly, scientific research and technical construction and invention are inconceivable without a very considerable use of imagination ; one must offer something new in these fields (as opposed to the field of oracular philosophy where an endless repetition of impressive words seems to do the trick).   At least as important is the part played by imagination in the practical application of equalitarianism and of impartiality. The basic attitude of the rationalist, ' I may be wrong and you may be right ', demands, when put into practice, and especially when human conflicts are involved, a real effort of our imagination. I admit that the emotions of love and compassion may sometimes lead to a similar effort. But I hold that it is humanly impossible for us to love, or to suffer with, a great number of people ; nor does it appear to me very desirable that we should, since it would ultimately destroy either our ability to help or the intensity of these very emotions. But reason, supported by imagination, enables us to understand that men who are far away, whom we shall never see, are like ourselves, and that their relations to one another are like our relations to those we love. A direct emotional attitude towards the abstract whole of mankind seems to me hardly possible. We can love mankind only in certain concrete individuals. But by the use of thought and imagination, we may become ready to help all who need our help.

All these considerations show, I believe, that the link between rationalism and humanitarianism is very close, and certainly much closer than the corresponding entanglement of irrationalism with the anti-equalitarian and anti-humanitarian attitude. I believe that as far as possible this result is corroborated by experience. A rationalist attitude seems to be usually combined with a basically equalitarian and humanitarian outlook ; irrationalism, on the other hand, exhibits in most cases at least some of the anti-equalitarian tendencies described, even though it may often be associated with humanitarianism also. My point is that the latter connection is anything but well founded.

IV

I have tried to analyse those consequences of rationalism and irrationalism which induce me to decide as I do. I wish to repeat that the decision is largely a moral decision. It is the decision to try to take argument seriously. This is the difference between the two views ; for irrationalism will use reason too, but without any feeling of obligation ; it will use it or discard it as it pleases. But I believe that the only attitude which I can consider to be morally right is one which recognizes that we owe it to other men to treat them and ourselves as rational.

Considered in this way, my counter-attack upon irrationalism is a moral attack. The intellectualist who finds our rationalism much too commonplace for his taste, and who looks out for the latest esoteric intellectual fashion, which he discovers in the admiration of medieval mysticism, is not, one fears, doing his duty by his fellow men. He may think himself and his subtle taste superior to our ' scientific age ', to an ' age of industrialization ' which carries its brainless division of labour and its ' mechanization ' and ' materialization ' even into the field of human thought [21]. But he only shows that he is incapable of appreciating the moral forces inherent in modern science. The attitude I am attacking can perhaps be illustrated by the following passage which I take from A. Keller [22] ; a passage that seems to me a typical expression of this romantic hostility towards science : ' We seem to be entering upon a new era where the human soul is regaining its mystical and religious faculties, and protesting, by inventing new myths, against the materialization and mechanization of life. The mind suffered when it had to serve humanity as technician, as chauffeur ; it is reawakening again as poet and prophet, obeying the command and leadership of dreams which seem to be quite as wise and reliable as, but more inspiring and stimulating than, intellectual wisdom and scientific programmes. The myth of revolution is a reaction against the unimaginative banality and conceited self-sufficiency of bourgeois society and of an old tired culture. It is the adventure of men who have lost all security and are embarking on dreams instead of concrete facts.' In analysing this passage I wish first, but only in passing, to draw attention to its typical historicist character and to its moral futurism [23] (' entering a new era ', ' old and tired culture ', etc.). But more important even than to realize the technique of the word-magic which the passage uses is to ask whether what it says is true. Is it true that our soul protests against the materialization and mechanization of our life, that it protests against the progress we have made in the fight against the untold suffering through hunger and pestilence which characterized the Middle Ages? Is it true that the mind suffered when it had to serve humanity as a technician, and was it happier to serve as a serf or a slave ? I do not intend to belittle the very serious problem of purely mechanical work, of a drudgery which is felt to be meaningless, and which destroys the creative power of the workers ; but the only practical hope lies, not in a return to slavery and serfdom, but in an attempt to make machinery take over this mechanical drudgery. Marx was right in insisting that increased productivity is the only reasonable hope of humanizing labour, and of further shortening the labour day. (Besides, I do not think that the mind always suffers when it has to serve humanity as a technician ; I suspect that often enough, the ' technicians ', including the great inventors and the great scientists, rather enjoyed it, and that they were just as adventurous as the mystics.) And who believes that the ' command and leadership of dreams ', as dreamt by our contemporary prophets, dreamers, and leaders, are really ' quite as wise and reliable as intellectual wisdom and scientific programmes ' ?   But we need only turn to the ' myth of revolution ', etc., in order to see more clearly what we are facing here.   It is a typical expression of the romantic hysteria and the radicalism produced by the dissolution of the tribe and by the strain of civilization (as I have described it in chapter 10).   This kind of ' Christianity ' which recommends the creation of myth as a substitute for Christian responsibility is a tribal Christianity. It is a Christianity that refuses to carry the cross of being human. Beware of these false prophets !   What they are after, without being aware of it, is the lost unity of tribalism.   And the return to the closed society which they advocate is the return to the cage, and to the beasts [24].

It may be useful to consider how the adherents of this kind of romanticism are likely to react to such criticism.   Arguments will hardly be offered ; since it is impossible to discuss such profundities with a rationalist, the most likely reaction will be a high-handed withdrawal, combined with the assertion that there is no language common to those whose souls have not yet ' regained their mystical faculties ', and those whose souls possess such faculties.   Now this reaction is analogous to that of the psychoanalyst (mentioned in the last chapter) who defeats his opponents not by replying to their arguments but by pointing out that their repressions prevent them from accepting psycho-analysis.   It is analogous also to that of the socio-analyst who points out that the total ideologies of his opponents prevent them from accepting the sociology of knowledge.   This method, as I admitted before, is good fun for those who practise it.   But we can see here more clearly that it must lead to the irrational division of men into those who are near to us and those who are far from us.   This division is present in every religion, but it is comparatively harmless in Mohammedanism, Christianity, or the rationalist faith, which all see in every man a potential convert, and the same may be said of psycho-analysis, which sees in every man a potential object of treatment (only that in the last case the fee for conversion constitutes a serious obstacle).   But the division

is getting less harmless when we proceed to the sociology of knowledge. The socio-analyst claims that only certain intellectuals
can get rid of their total ideology, can be freed from ' thinking
with their class ' ; he thus gives up the idea of a potential rational
unity of man, and delivers himself body and soul to irrationalism.
And this situation gets very much worse when we proceed to
the biological or naturalist version of this theory, to the racial
doctrine that we ' think with our blood ' or that we ' think with
our race '. But at least as dangerous, since more subtle, is the
same idea when it appears in the cloak of a religious mysticism ;
not in the mysticism of the poet or musician, but in that of the
Hegelianizing intellectualist who persuades himself and his
followers that their thoughts are endowed, because of special
grace, with ' mystical and religious faculties ' not possessed by
others, and who thus claim that they ' think by God's grace '.
This claim with its gentle allusion to those who do not possess
God's grace, this attack upon the potential spiritual unity of
mankind, is, in my opinion, as pretentious, blasphemous and anti-
Christian, as it believes itself to be humble, pious, and Christian.

As opposed to the intellectual irresponsibility of a mysticism
which escapes into dreams and of an oracular philosophy which
escapes into verbiage, modern science enforces upon our intellect
the discipline of practical tests. Scientific theories can be tested
by their practical consequences. The scientist, in his own field,
is responsible for what he says ; you can know him by his fruits,
and thus distinguish him from the false prophets [25]. One of the
few who have appreciated this aspect of science is the Christian
philosopher J. Macmurray (with whose views on historical
prophecy I widely disagree, as will be seen in the next chapter) :
' Science itself', he says [26], ' in its own specific fields of research,
employs a method of understanding which restores the broken
integrity of theory and practice.' This, I believe, is why science
is such an offence in the eyes of mysticism, which evades practice
by creating myths instead. ' Science, in its own field,' says
Macmurray in another place, ' is the product of Christianity,
and its most adequate expression so far ; . . its capacity for
co-operative progress, which knows no frontiers of race or nationality or sex, its ability to predict, and its ability to control, are the
fullest manifestations of Christianity that Europe has yet seen.'
I fully agree with this, for I too believe that our Western civilization owes its rationalism, its faith in the rational unity of man
and in the open society, and especially its scientific outlook, to

the ancient Socratic and Christian belief in the brotherhood of all men, and in intellectual honesty and responsibility. (A frequent argument against the morality of science is that many of its fruits have been used for bad purposes, for instance, in war. But this argument hardly deserves serious consideration. There is nothing under the sun which cannot be misused, and which has not been misused. Even love can be made an instrument of murder ; and pacifism can be made one of the weapons of an aggressive war. On the other hand, it is only too obvious that it is irrationalism and not rationalism that has the responsibility for all national hostility and aggression. There have been only too many aggressive religious wars, both before and after the Crusades, but I do not know of any war waged for a ' scientific ' aim, and inspired by scientists.)

It will have been observed that in the passages quoted, Macmurray emphasizes that what he appreciates is science ' in its own specific fields of research '. I think that this emphasis is particularly valuable. For nowadays one often hears, usually in connection with the mysticism of Eddington and Jeans, that modern science, as opposed to that of the nineteenth century, has become more humble, in that it now recognizes the mysteries of this world. But this opinion, I believe, is entirely on the wrong track. Darwin and Faraday, for instance, sought for truth as humbly as anybody, and I do not doubt that they were much more humble than the two great contemporary astronomers mentioned. For great as these are ' in their own specific fields of research ', they do not, I believe, prove their humility by extending their activities to the field of philosophical mysticism [27]. Speaking more generally, however, it may indeed be the case that scientists are becoming more humble, since the progress of science is largely by way of the discovery of errors, and since, in general, the more we know, the more clearly we realize what we do not know. (The spirit of science is that of Socrates [28].)

Although I am mainly concerned with the moral aspect of the conflict between rationalism and irrationalism, I feel that I should briefly touch upon a more ' philosophical ' aspect of the problem ; but I wish to make it clear that I consider this aspect as of minor importance here. What I have in mind is the fact that the critical rationalist can turn the tables upon the irrationalist in another way as well. He may contend that the irrationalist who prides himself on his respect for the more profound mysteries of the world and his understanding of them (as opposed to the scientist who just scratches its surface) in fact neither respects nor understands its mysteries, but satisfies himself with cheap rationalizations. For what is a myth if not an attempt to rationalize the irrational ? And who shows greater reverence for mystery, the scientist who devotes himself to discovering it step by step, always ready to submit to facts, and always aware that even his boldest achievement will never be more than a stepping-stone for those who come after him, or the mystic who is free to maintain anything because he need not fear any test ? But in spite of this dubious freedom, the mystics endlessly repeat the same thing. (It is always the myth of the lost tribal paradise, the hysterical refusal to carry the cross of civilization [29].) All mystics, as F. Kafka, the mystical poet, wrote [30] in despair, ' set out to say . . that the incomprehensible is incomprehensible, and that we knew before '. And the irrationalist not only tries to rationalize what cannot be rationalized, but he also gets hold of the wrong end of the stick altogether. For it is the particular, the unique and concrete individual, which cannot be approached by rational methods, and not the abstract universal. Science can describe general types of landscape, for example, or of man, but it can never exhaust one single individual landscape, or one single individual man. The universal, the typical, is not only the domain of reason, but it is also largely the product of reason, in so far as it is the product of scientific abstraction. But the unique individual and his unique actions and experiences and relations to other individuals can never be fully rationalized [31]. And it appears to be just this irrational realm of unique individuality which makes human relations important. Most people would feel, for example, that what makes their lives worth living would largely be destroyed if they themselves, and their lives, were in no sense unique but in all and every respect typical of a class of people, so that they repeated exactly all the actions and experiences of all other men who belong to this class. It is the uniqueness of our experiences which, in this sense, makes our lives worth living, the unique experience of a landscape, of a sunset, of the expression of a human face. But since the day of Plato, it has been a characteristic of all mysticism that it transfers this feeling of the irrationality of the unique individual, and of our unique relations to individuals, to a different field, namely, to the field of abstract universals, a field which properly belongs to the province of science. That it is this feeling which the mystic tries to transfer can hardly be doubted. It is well known that the terminology of mysticism, the mystical union, the mystical intuition of beauty, the mystical love, have in all times been borrowed from the realm of relations between individual men, and especially from the experience of sexual love. Nor can it be doubted that this feeling is transferred by mysticism to the abstract universals, to the essences, to the Forms or Ideas. It is again the lost unity of the tribe, the wish to return into the shelter of a patriarchal home and to make its limits the limits of our world, which stands behind this mystical attitude. ' The feeling of the world as a limited whole is the mystical feeling ', says [32] Wittgenstein. But this holistic and universalistic irrationalism is misplaced. The ' world ' and the ' whole ' and ' nature ', all these are abstractions and products of our reason. (This makes the difference between the mystical philosopher and the artist who does not rationalize, who does not use abstractions, but who creates, in his imagination, concrete individuals and unique experiences.) To sum up, mysticism attempts to rationalize the irrational, and at the same time it seeks the mystery in the wrong place ; and it does so because it dreams of the collective [33], and the union of the elect, since it dares not face the hard and practical tasks which those must face who realize that every individual is an end in himself.

The nineteenth-century conflict between science and religion appears to me to be superseded [34]. Since an ' uncritical ' rationalism is inconsistent, the problem cannot be the choice between knowledge and faith, but only between two kinds of faith. The new problem is : which is the right faith and which is the wrong faith ? What I have tried to show is that the choice with which we are confronted is between a faith in reason and in human individuals and a faith in the mystical faculties of man by which he is united to a collective ; and that this choice is at the same time a choice between an attitude that recognizes the unity of mankind and an attitude that divides men into friends and foes, into masters and slaves.

Enough has been said, for the present purpose, to explain the terms ' rationalism ' and ' irrationalism ', as well as my motives in deciding in favour of rationalism, and the reason why I see in the irrational and mystical intellectualism which is at present so fashionable the subtle intellectual disease of our time. It is a disease which need not be taken too seriously, and it is not more than skin-deep. (Scientists, with very few exceptions, are particularly free from it.)   But in spite of its superficiality, it is a dangerous disease, because of its influence in the field of social and political thought.

V

In order to illustrate the danger, I shall briefly criticize two of the most influential irrationalist authorities of our time.   The first of them is A. N. Whitehead, famous for his work in mathematics, and for his collaboration with the greatest contemporary rationalist philosopher, Bertrand Russell [35].   Whitehead considers himself a rationalist philosopher too ; but so did Hegel, to whom Whitehead owes a great deal ; indeed, he is one of the few Neo-Hegelians who know how much they owe to Hegel [36] (as well as to Aristotle).   Undoubtedly, he owes it to Hegel that he has the courage, in spite of Kant's burning protest, to build up grandiose metaphysical systems with a royal contempt for argument.

Let us consider first one of the few rational arguments offered by Whitehead in his *Process and Reality*, the argument by which he defends his speculative philosophical method (a method which he calls ' rationalism ').   ' It has been an objection to speculative philosophy ', he writes [37], ' that it is over-ambitious. Rationalism, it is admitted, is the method by which advance is made within the limits of particular sciences.   It is, however, held that this limited success must not encourage attempts to frame ambitious schemes expressive of the general nature of things. One alleged justification of this criticism is ill-success ; European thought is represented as littered with metaphysical problems, abandoned and unreconciled . .   (But) *the same criterion would fasten ill-success upon science*.   We no more retain the physics of the seventeenth century than we do the Cartesian philosophy of the century . .   The proper test is not that of finality, but of progress.'   Now this is in itself certainly a perfectly reasonable and even plausible argument ; but is it valid ?   The obvious objection against it is that while physics progresses, metaphysics does not.   In physics, there is a ' proper test of progress ', namely the test of experiment, of practice.   We can say why modern physics is better than the physics of the seventeenth century.   Modern physics stands up to a great number of practical tests which utterly defeat the older systems.   And the obvious objection against speculative metaphysical systems is that the progress they claim seems to be just as imaginary as any-

thing else about them. This objection is very old ; it dates back
to Bacon, Hume, and Kant. We read, for example, in Kant's
Prolegomena [38], the following remarks concerning the alleged progress of metaphysics : ' Undoubtedly there are many who, like
myself, have been unable to find that this science has progressed
by so much as a finger-breadth in spite of so many beautiful
things which have long been published on this subject. Admittedly, we may find an attempt to sharpen a definition, or to supply
a lame proof with new crutches, and thus to patch up the crazy
quilt of metaphysics, or to give it a new pattern ; but this is not
what the world needs. We are sick of metaphysical assertions.
We want to have definite criteria by which we may distinguish
dialectical fancies . . from truth.' Whitehead is probably aware
of this classical and obvious objection ; and it looks as if he
remembers it when in the sentence following the one quoted
last he writes : ' But the main objection dating from the six-
teenth century and receiving final expression from Francis Bacon,
is the uselessness of philosophic speculation.' Since it was the
experimental and practical uselessness of philosophy to which
Bacon objected, it looks as if Whitehead here had our point in
mind. But he does not follow it up. He does not reply to the
obvious objection that this practical uselessness destroys his
point that speculative philosophy, like science, is justified by the
progress it makes. Instead, he contents himself with switching
over to an entirely different problem, namely, the well-known
problem ' that there are no brute, self-contained matters of fact ',
and that all science must make use of thought, since it must
generalize, and interpret, the facts. On this consideration he
bases his defence of metaphysical systems : ' Thus the understanding of the immediate brute fact requires its metaphysical
interpretation . .' Now this may be so, or it may not be so.
But it is certainly an entirely different argument from the one
he began with. ' The proper test is . . progress ', in science
as well as in philosophy : this is what we originally heard from
Whitehead. But no answer to Kant's obvious objection is
forthcoming. Instead, Whitehead's argument, once on the
track of the problem of universality and generality, wanders off to
such questions as the (Platonic) collectivist theory of morality [39] :
' Morality of outlook is inseparably conjoined with generality
of outlook. The antithesis between the general good and the
individual interest can be abolished only when the individual
is such that its interest is the general good . .'

Now this was a sample of rational argument. But rational arguments are rare indeed. Whitehead has learned from Hegel how to avoid Kant's criticism that speculative philosophy only supplies new crutches for lame proofs. This Hegelian method is simple enough. We can easily avoid crutches as long as we avoid proofs and arguments altogether. Hegelian philosophy does not argue ; it decrees. It must be admitted that, as opposed to Hegel, Whitehead does not pretend to offer the final truth. He is not a dogmatic philosopher in the sense that he presents his philosophy as an indisputable dogma ; he even emphasizes its imperfections. But like all Neo-Hegelians, he adopts the dogmatic method of laying down his philosophy without argument. We can take it or leave it. But we cannot discuss it. (We are indeed faced with ' brute facts ' ; not with Baconian brute facts of experience, but with the brute facts of a man's metaphysical inspiration.) In order to illustrate this ' method of take it or leave it ', I shall quote just one passage from *Process and Reality*; but I must warn my readers that, although I have tried to select the passage fairly, they should not form an opinion without reading the book itself.

Its last part, entitled ' Final Interpretations ', consists of two chapters, ' The Ideal Opposites ' (where, for instance, ' Perman-ence and Flux ' occurs, a well-known patch from Plato's system ; we have dealt with it under the name ' Change and Rest '), and ' God and the World '. I quote from this latter chapter. The passage is introduced by the two sentences : ' The final summary can only be expressed in terms of a group of antitheses, whose apparent self-contradiction depends on neglect of the diverse categories of existence. In each antithesis there is a shift of meaning which converts the opposition into a contrast.' This is the introduction. It prepares us for an ' apparent contra-diction ', and tells us that this ' depends ' on some neglect. This seems to indicate that by avoiding that neglect we may avoid the contradiction. But how this is to be achieved, or what is, more precisely, in the author's mind, we are not told. We have just to take it or leave it. Now I quote the first two of the an-nounced ' antitheses ' or ' apparent self-contradictions ' which are also stated without a shadow of argument: 'It is as true to say that God is permanent and the World fluent as that the World is permanent and God fluent.—It is as true to say that God is one and the World many, as that the World is one and God many.'[40] Now I am not going to criticize these echoes of Greek philosophical fancies ; we may indeed take it for granted that the one is just ' as true ' as the other. But we have been promised an ' apparent self-contradiction ' ; and I should like to know where a self-contradiction appears here. For to me not even the appearance of a contradiction is apparent. A self-contradiction would be, for instance, the sentence : ' Plato is happy and Plato is not happy ', and all the sentences of the same ' logical form ' (that is to say, all sentences obtained from the foregoing by substituting a proper name for ' Plato ' and a property word for ' happy '). But the following sentence is clearly not a contradiction : ' It is as true to say that Plato is happy to-day as it is to say that he is unhappy to-day ' (for since Plato is dead, the one is indeed ' as true ' as the other) ; and no other sentence of the same or a similar form can be called self-contradictory, even if it happens to be false. This is only to indicate why I am at a loss as to this purely logical aspect of the matter, the ' apparent self-contradictions '. And I feel that way about the whole book. I just do not understand what its author wished it to convey. Very likely, this is my fault and not his. I do not belong to the number of the elect, and I fear that many others are in the same position. This is just why I claim that the method of the book is irrational. It divides mankind into two parts, a small number of the elect, and the large number of the lost. But lost as I am, I can only say that, as I see it, Neo-Hegelianism no longer looks like that old crazy quilt with a few new patches, so vividly described by Kant ; rather it looks now like a bundle of a few old patches which have been torn from it.

I leave it to the careful student of Whitehead's book to decide whether it has stood up to its own ' proper test ', whether it shows progress as compared with the metaphysical systems of whose stagnation Kant complained ; provided he can find the criteria by which to judge such progress. And I will leave it to the same student to judge the appropriateness of concluding these remarks with another of Kant's comments upon metaphysics [41] : ' Concerning metaphysics in general, and the views I have expressed on their value, I admit that my formulations may here or there have been insufficiently conditional and cautious. Yet I do not wish to hide the fact that I can only look with repugnance and even with something like hate upon the puffed-up pretentiousness of all these volumes filled with wisdom, such as are fashionable nowadays. For I am fully satisfied that the wrong way has been chosen ; that the accepted methods must endlessly increase these follies and blunders ; and that even the complete annihilation of all these fanciful achievements could not possibly be as harmful as this fictitious science with its accursed fertility.'

The second example of contemporary irrationalism with which I intend to deal here is A. J. Toynbee's *A Study of History*. I wish to make it clear that I consider this a most remarkable and interesting book, and that I have chosen it because of its superiority to all other contemporary irrationalist and historicist works I know of. I am not competent to judge Toynbee's merits as a historian. But as opposed to other contemporary historicist and irrationalist philosophers, he has much to say that is most stimulating and challenging ; I at least have found him so, and I owe to him many valuable suggestions. I do not accuse him of irrationalism in his own field of historical research. For where it is a question of comparing evidence in favour of or against a certain historical interpretation, he uses unhesitatingly a fundamentally rational method of argument. I have in mind, for instance, his comparative study of the authenticity of the Gospels as historical records, with its negative results [42] ; although I am not able to judge his evidence, the rationality of the method is beyond question, and this is the more admirable as Toynbee's general sympathies with Christian orthodoxy might have made it hard for him to defend a view which, to say the least, is unorthodox [43]. I also agree with many of the political tendencies expressed in his work, and most emphatically with his attack upon modern nationalism, and the tribalist and ' archaist ', i.e. culturally reactionary tendencies, which are connected with it.

The reason why, in spite of all this, I single out Toynbee's monumental historicist work in order to charge it with irrationality, is that only when we see the effects of this poison in a work of such merit do we fully appreciate its danger.

What I must describe as Toynbee's irrationalism expresses itself in various ways. One of them is that he yields to a widespread and dangerous fashion of our time. I mean the fashion of not taking arguments seriously, and at their face value, at least tentatively, but of seeing in them nothing but a way in which deeper irrational motives and tendencies express themselves. It is the attitude of socio-analysis, criticized in the last chapter ; the attitude of looking at once for the unconscious motives and determinants in the social habitat of the thinker, instead of first examining the validity of the argument itself.

This attitude may be justified to a certain extent, as I have tried to show in the two previous chapters ; and this is especially so in the case of an author who does not offer any arguments, or whose arguments are obviously not worth looking into. But if no attempt is made to take serious arguments seriously, then I believe that we are justified in making the charge of irrationalism ; and we are even justified in retaliating, by adopting the same attitude towards the procedure. Thus I think that we have every right to make the socio-analytical diagnosis that Toynbee's neglect to take serious arguments seriously is representative of a twentieth-century intellectualism which expresses its disillusionment, or even despair, of reason, and of a rational solution of our social problems, by an escape into a religious mysticism [44].

As an example of the refusal to take serious arguments seriously, I select Toynbee's treatment of Marx. My reasons for this selection are the following. First, it is a topic which is familiar to myself as well as to the reader of this book. Secondly, it is a topic on which I agree with Toynbee in most of its practical aspects. His main judgements on Marx's political and historical influence are very similar to results at which I have arrived by more pedestrian methods ; and it is indeed one of the topics whose treatment shows his great historical intuition. Thus I shall hardly be suspected of being an apologist for Marx if I defend Marx's rationality against Toynbee. For this is the point on which I disagree : Toynbee treats Marx (as he treats everybody) not as a rational being, a man who offers arguments for what he teaches. Indeed, the treatment of Marx, and of his theories, only exemplifies the general impression conveyed by Toynbee's work that arguments are an unimportant mode of speech, and that the history of mankind is a history of emotions, passions, religions, irrational philosophies, and perhaps of art and poetry ; but that it has nothing whatever to do with the history of human reason or of human science. (Names like Galileo and Newton, Harvey and Pasteur, do not play any part in the first six volumes [45] of Toynbee's historicist study of the life-cycle of civilizations.)

Regarding the points of similarity between Toynbee's and my general views of Marx, I may remind the reader of my allusions, in chapter 1, to the analogy between the chosen people and the chosen class ; and in various other places, I have commented critically upon Marx's doctrines of historical necessity, and especially of the inevitability of the social revolution. These ideas are linked together by Toynbee with his usual brilliance : 'The distinctively Jewish . . inspiration of Marxism ', he writes [46], ' is the apocalyptic vision of a violent revolution which is inevitable because it is the decree . . of God himself, and which is to invert the present rôles of Proletariat and Dominant Minority in . . a reversal of rôles which is to carry the Chosen People, at one bound, from the lowest to the highest place in the Kingdom of This World. Marx has taken the Goddess " Historical Necessity " in place of Yahweh for his omnipotent deity, and the internal proletariat of the modern Western World in place of Jewry ; and his Messianic Kingdom is conceived as a Dictatorship of the Proletariat. But the salient features of the traditional Jewish apocalypse protrude through this threadbare disguise, and it is actually the pre-Rabbinical Maccabæan Judaism that our philosopher-impresario is presenting in modern Western costume . .' Now there is certainly not much in this brilliantly phrased passage with which I do not agree, as long as it is intended as nothing more than an interesting analogy. But if it is intended as a serious analysis (or part of it) of Marxism, then I must protest ; Marx, after all, wrote *Capital*, studied *laissez-faire* capitalism, and made serious and most important contributions to social science, even if much of them has been superseded. And, indeed, Toynbee's passage is intended as a serious analysis ; he believes that his analogies and allegories contribute to a serious appreciation of Marx ; for in an Annex to this passage (from which I have quoted only an important part) he treats, under the title [47] ' Marxism, Socialism, and Christianity ', what he considers to be likely objections of a Marxist to this ' account of the Marxian Philosophy '. This Annex itself is also undoubtedly intended as a serious discussion of Marxism, as can be seen by the fact that its first paragraph commences with the words ' The advocates of Marxism will perhaps protest that . .' and the second with the words : ' In attempting to reply to a Marxian protest on such lines as these . .' But if we look more closely into this discussion, then we find that none of the rational arguments or claims of Marxism is even mentioned, let alone examined. Of Marx's theories and of the question whether they are true or false we do not hear a word. The one additional problem raised in the Annex is again one of historical origin ; for the Marxist opponent envisaged by Toynbee does not protest, as any Marxist in his senses would, that it is Marx's claim to have based an old idea, socialism, upon a new, namely a rational and scientific, basis ; instead, he 'protests' (I am quoting Toynbee) 'that in a rather summary account of Marxian Philosophy . . we have made a show of analysing this into a Hegelian and a Jewish and a Christian constituent element without having said a word about the most characteristic . . part of Marx's message. . . Socialism, the Marxian will tell us, is the essence of the Marxian way of life ; *it is an original element in the Marxian system which cannot be traced to a Hegelian or a Christian or a Jewish or any other pre-Marxian source*'. This is the protest put by Toynbee into the mouth of a Marxist, although any Marxist, even if he has read nothing but the *Manifesto*, must know that Marx himself as early as in 1847 distinguished about seven or eight different ' pre-Marxian sources ' of socialism, and among them also those which he labelled ' Clerical ' or ' Christian ' socialism, and that he never dreamt of having dis-covered socialism, but only claimed that he had made it rational ; or, as Engels expresses it, that he had developed socialism from a Utopian idea into a science [48]. But Toynbee neglects all that. ' In attempting ', he writes, ' to reply to a Marxian protest on such lines as these, we shall readily admit the humaneness and constructiveness of the ideal for which socialism stands, as well as the importance of the part which this ideal plays in the Marxian " ideology " ; but we shall find ourselves unable to accept *the Marxian contention that Socialism is Marx's original discovery*. We shall have to point out, on our part, that there is a Christian socialism which was practised as well as preached before the Marxian Socialism was ever heard of ; and, when our turn comes for taking the offensive, we shall . . maintain that the Marxian Socialism is derived from the Christian tradition . .' Now I would certainly never deny this derivation, and it is quite clear that every Marxist could admit it without sacrificing the tiniest bit of his creed ; for the Marxist creed is not that Marx was the inventor of a humane and constructive ideal but that he was the scientist who by purely rational means showed that socialism will come, and in what way it will come.

How, I ask, can it be explained that Toynbee discusses Marxism on lines which have nothing whatever to do with its rational claims ? The only explanation I can see is that the Marxist claim to rationality has no meaning whatever for Toynbee. He is interested only in the question of how it originated as a religion.   Now I should be the last to deny its religious character.   But the method of treating philosophies or religions entirely from the point of view of their historical origin and environment, an attitude described in the previous chapters as *historism* (and to be distinguished from historicism), is, to say the least, very one-sided ;   and how much this method is liable to produce irrationalism can be seen from Toynbee's neglect of, if not contempt for, that important realm of human life which we have here described as rational.

In an assessment of Marx's influence, Toynbee arrives at the conclusion [49] that ' the verdict of History may turn out to be that a re-awakening of the Christian social conscience has been the one great positive achievement of Karl Marx '.   Against this assessment, I have certainly not much to say ;   perhaps the reader will remember that I too have emphasized [50] Marx's moral influence upon Christianity.   I do not think that, as a final appraisal, Toynbee takes sufficiently into account the great moral idea that the exploited should emancipate themselves, instead of waiting for acts of charity on the part of the exploiters ;   but this, of course, is just a difference of opinion, and I would not dream of contesting Toynbee's right to his own opinion, which I consider very fair.   But I should like to draw attention to the phrase ' the verdict of history may turn out ', with its implied historicist moral theory, and even moral futurism [51].   For I hold that we cannot and must not evade deciding in such matters for ourselves ;   and that if we are not able to pass a verdict, neither will history.

So much about Toynbee's treatment of Marx.   Concerning the more general problem of his historism or historical relativism, it may be said that he is well aware of it, although he does not formulate it as a general principle of the historical determination of *all* thought, but only as a restricted principle applicable to *historical* thought ;   for he explains [52] that he takes ' as the starting point . . the axiom that all historical thought is inevitably relative to the particular circumstances of the thinker's own time and place.   This is a law of Human Nature from which no human genius can be exempt.'   The analogy of this historism with the sociology of knowledge is rather obvious ;   for ' the thinker's own time and place ' is clearly nothing but the description of what may be called his ' historical habitat ', by analogy with the ' social habitat ' described by the sociology of knowledge. The difference, if any, is that Toynbee confines his ' law of Human

Nature' to historical thought, which seems to me a slightly strange and perhaps even unintentional restriction ; for it is somewhat improbable that there should be a ' law of Human Nature from which no human genius can be exempt ' holding not for thought in general but only for historical thought.

With the undeniable but rather trivial kernel of truth contained in such a historism or sociologism I have dealt in the last two chapters, and I need not repeat what I have said there. But as regards criticism, it may be worth while to point out that Toynbee's sentence, if freed from its restriction to historical thought, could hardly be considered an ' axiom ' since it would be paradoxical. (It would be another [53] form of the paradox of the liar ; for if no genius is exempt from expressing the fashions of his social habitat then this contention itself may be merely an expression of the fashion of its author's social habitat, i.e. of the relativistic fashion of our own day.) This remark has not only a formal-logical significance. For it indicates that historism or historio-analysis can be applied to historism itself, and this is indeed a permissible way of dealing with an idea *after* it has been criticized by way of rational argument. Since historism has been so criticized, I may now risk a historio-analytical diagnosis, and say that historism is a typical though slightly obsolescent product of our time ; or more precisely, of the typical backwardness of the social sciences of our time. It is the typical reaction to interventionism and to a period of rationalization and industrial co-operation ; a period which, perhaps more than any other in history, demands the practical application of rational methods to social problems. A social science which cannot quite meet these demands is therefore inclined to defend itself by producing elaborate attacks upon the applicability of science to such problems. Summing up my historio-analytical diagnosis, I venture to suggest that Toynbee's historism is an apologetic anti-rationalism, born out of despair of reason, and trying to escape into the past, as well as into prophecy of the future [54]. If anything then historism must be understood as an historical product.

This diagnosis is corroborated by many features of Toynbee's work. An example is his stress upon the superiority of other-worldliness over action which will influence the course of this world. So he speaks, for instance, of Mohammed's ' tragic worldly success ', saying that the opportunity which offered itself to the prophet of taking action in this world was ' a challenge to which his spirit failed to rise. In accepting . . he was renouncing the sublime rôle of the nobly-honoured prophet and contenting himself with the commonplace rôle of the magnificently successful statesman.'   (In other words, Mohammed succumbed to a temptation which Jesus resisted.)   Ignatius Loyola, accordingly, wins Toynbee's approval for turning from a soldier into a saint [55].   One may ask, however, whether this saint did not become a successful statesman too ?   (But if it is a question of Jesuitism, then, it seems, all is different : this form of statesmanship is sufficiently other-worldly.)   In order to avoid misunderstandings, I wish to make it clear that I myself would rate many saints higher than most, or very nearly all, statesmen I know of, for I am generally not impressed by political success.   I quote this passage only as a corroboration of my historio-analytical diagnosis : that this historism of a modern historical prophet is a philosophy of escape.

Toynbee's anti-rationalism is prominent in many other places. For instance, in an attack upon the rationalistic conception of tolerance he uses categories like ' nobleness ' as opposed to ' lowness ' instead of arguments.   The passage deals with the opposition between the merely ' negative ' avoidance of violence, on rational grounds, and the true non-violence of other-worldliness, hinting that these two are instances of ' meanings . . which are . . positively antithetical to one another ' [56].   Here is the passage I have in mind : ' At its lowest the practice of Non-Violence may express nothing more noble and more constructive than a cynical disillusionment with . . violence . . previously practised *ad nauseam*. . .   A notorious example of Non-Violence of this unedifying kind is the religious tolerance in the Western World from the seventeenth century . . down to our day.'   It is difficult to resist the temptation to retaliate by asking—using Toynbee's own terminology—whether this edifying attack upon Western democratic religious tolerance expresses anything more noble or more constructive than a cynical disillusionment with reason ; whether it is not a notorious example of that anti-rationalism which has been, and unfortunately still is, fashionable in our Western World, and which has been practised *ad nauseam*, especially from the time of Hegel, down to our day ?

Of course, my historio-analysis of Toynbee is not a serious criticism.   It is only an unkind way of retaliating, of paying historism back in its own coin.   My fundamental criticism is on very different lines, and I should certainly be sorry if by dabbling in historism I were to become responsible for making this cheap method more fashionable than it is already.

I do not wish to be misunderstood. I feel no hostility towards religious mysticism (only towards a militant anti-rationalist intellectualism) and I should be the first to fight any attempt to oppress it. It is not I who advocate religious intolerance. But I claim that faith in reason, or rationalism, or humanitarianism, or humanism, has the same right as any other creed to contribute to an improvement of human affairs, and especially to the control of international crime and the establishment of peace. ' The humanist', Toynbee writes [57], ' purposely concentrates. all his attention and effort upon . . bringing human affairs under human control. Yet . . the unity of mankind can never be established in fact except within a framework of the unity of the superhuman whole of which Humanity is a part . . ; and our Modern Western school of humanists have been peculiar, as well as perverse, in planning to reach Heaven by raising a titanic Tower of Babel on terrestrial foundations . .' Toynbee's contention, if I understand him rightly, is that there is no chance for the humanist to bring international affairs under the control of human reason. Appealing to the authority of Bergson [58], he claims that only allegiance to a superhuman whole can save us, and that there is no way for human reason, no ' terrestrial road ', as he puts it, by which tribal nationalism can be superseded. Now I do not mind the characterization of the humanist's faith in reason as ' terrestrial ', since I believe that it is indeed a principle of rationalist politics that we cannot make heaven on earth [59]. But humanism is, after all, a faith which has proved itself in deeds, and which has proved itself as well, perhaps, as any other creed. And although I think, with most humanists, that Christianity, by teaching the fatherhood of God, may make a great contribution to establishing the brotherhood of man, I also think that those who undermine man's faith in reason are unlikely to contribute much to this end.

CHAPTER 25 : HAS HISTORY ANY MEANING?

I

In approaching the end of this book, I wish again to remind the reader that these chapters were not intended as anything like a full history of historicism ; they are merely scattered marginal notes to such a history, and rather personal notes to boot. That they form, besides, a kind of critical introduction to the philosophy of society and of politics, is closely connected with this character of theirs, for historicism is a social and political and moral (or, shall I say, immoral) philosophy, and it has been as such most influential since the beginning of our civilization. It is therefore hardly possible to comment on its history without discussing the fundamental problems of society, of politics, and of morals. But such a discussion, whether it admits it or not, must always contain a strong personal element. This does not mean that much in this book is purely a matter of opinion ; in the few cases where I am explaining my personal proposals or decisions in moral and political matters, I have always made the personal character of the proposal or decision clear. It rather means that the selection of the subject matter treated is a matter of personal choice to a much greater extent than it would be, say, in a scientific treatise.

In a way, however, this difference is a matter of degree. Even a science is not merely a ' body of facts '. It is, at the very least, a collection, and as such it is dependent upon the collector's interests, upon a point of view. In science, this point of view is usually determined by a scientific theory ; that is to say, we select from the infinite variety of facts, and from the infinite variety of aspects of facts, those facts and those aspects which are interesting because they are connected with some more or less preconceived scientific theory. A certain school of philosophers of scientific method [1] have concluded from considerations such as these that science always argues in a circle, and ' that we find ourselves chasing our own tails ', as Eddington puts it, since we can only get out of our factual experience what we have ourselves put into it, in the form of our theories. But this is not a

259

tenable argument. Although it is, in general, quite true that we select only facts which have a bearing upon some preconceived theory, it is not true that we select only such facts as confirm the theory and, as it were, repeat it ; the method of science is rather to look out for facts which may refute the theory. This is what we call testing a theory—to see whether we cannot find a flaw in it. But although the facts are collected with an eye upon the theory, and will confirm it as long as the theory stands up to these tests, they are more than merely a kind of empty repetition of a preconceived theory. They confirm the theory only if they are the results of unsuccessful attempts to overthrow its predictions, and therefore a telling testimony in its favour. So it is, I hold, the possibility of overthrowing it, or its falsifiability, that constitutes the possibility of testing it, and therefore the scientific character of a theory ; and the fact that all tests of a theory are attempted falsifications of predictions derived with its help, furnishes the clue to scientific method [2]. This view of scientific method is corroborated by the history of science, which shows that scientific theories are often overthrown by experiments, and that the overthrow of theories is indeed the vehicle of scientific progress. The contention that science is circular cannot be upheld.

But one element of this contention remains true ; namely, that all scientific descriptions of facts are highly selective, that they always depend upon theories. The situation can be best described by comparison with a searchlight (the ' searchlight theory of science ', as I usually call it in contradistinction to the ' bucket theory of the mind ' [3]). What the searchlight makes visible will depend upon its position, upon our way of directing it, and upon its intensity, colour, etc. ; although it will, of course, also depend very largely upon the things illuminated by it. Similarly, a scientific description will depend, largely, upon our point of view, our interests, which are as a rule connected with the theory or hypothesis we wish to test ; although it will also depend upon the facts described. Indeed, the theory or hypothesis could be described as the crystallization of a point of view. For if we attempt to formulate our point of view, then this formulation will, as a rule, be what one sometimes calls a working hypothesis ; that is to say, a provisional assumption whose function is to help us to select, and to order, the facts. But we should be clear that there cannot be any theory or hypothesis which is not, in this sense, a working hypothesis, and does not remain one. For no theory is final, and every theory helps us to select and order facts. This selective character of all description makes it in a certain sense ' relative ' ; but only in the sense that we would offer not this but another description, if our point of view were different. It may also affect our *belief* in the truth of the description ; but it does not affect the question of the truth or falsity of the description ; truth is not ' relative ' in this sense [4].

The reason why all description is selective is, roughly speaking, the infinite wealth and variety of the possible aspects of the facts of our world. In order to describe this infinite wealth, we have at our disposal only a finite number of finite series of words. Thus we may describe as long as we like : our description will always be incomplete, a mere selection, and a small one at that, of the facts which present themselves for description. This shows that it is not only impossible to avoid a selective point of view, but also wholly undesirable to attempt to do so ; for if we could do so, we should get not a more ' objective ' description, but only a mere heap of entirely unconnected statements. But, of course, a point of view is inevitable ; and the naïve attempt to avoid it can only lead to self-deception, and to the uncritical application of an unconscious point of view [5]. All this is true, most emphatically, in the case of *historical description*, with its ' infinite subject matter ', as Schopenhauer [6] calls it. Thus in history no less than in science, we cannot avoid a point of view ; and the belief that we can must lead to self-deception and to lack of critical care. This does not mean, of course, that we are permitted to falsify anything, or to take matters of truth lightly. Any particular historical description of facts will be simply true or false, however difficult it may be to decide upon its truth or falsity.

So far, the position of history is analogous to that of the natural sciences, for example, that of physics. But if we compare the part played by a ' point of view ' in history with that played by a ' point of view ' in physics, then we find a great difference. In physics, as we have seen, the ' point of view ' is usually presented by a physical theory which can be tested by searching for new facts. In history, the matter is not quite so simple.

II

Let us first consider a little more closely the rôle of the theories in a natural science such as physics. Here, theories have several connected tasks. They help to unify science, and they help to explain as well as to predict events. Regarding explanation and prediction, I may perhaps quote from one of my own publications [7] : ' To give a *causal explanation* of a certain event means to derive deductively a statement (it will be called a *prognosis*) which describes that event, using as premises of the deduction some *universal laws* together with certain singular or specific sentences which we may call *initial conditions*. For example, we can say that we have given a causal explanation of the breaking of a certain thread if we find that this thread was capable of carrying one pound only, and that a weight of two pounds was put on it. If we analyse this causal explanation, then we find that two different constituents are involved in it. (1) We assume some hypotheses of the character of universal laws of nature ; in our case, perhaps : " Whenever a certain thread undergoes a tension exceeding a certain maximum tension which is characteristic for that particular thread, then it will break." (2) We assume some specific statements (the initial conditions) pertaining to the particular event in question ; in our case, we may have the two statements : " For this thread, the characteristic maximum tension at which it is liable to break is equal to a one-pound weight " and " The weight put on this thread was a two-pound weight." Thus we have two different kinds of statements which together yield a complete causal explanation, viz. : (1) *universal statements of the character of natural laws*, and (2) *specific statements pertaining to the special case in question, the initial conditions*. Now from the universal laws (1), we can deduce with the help of the initial conditions (2) the following specific statement (3) : " This thread will break." This conclusion (3) we may also call a specific *prognosis*.—The initial conditions (or more precisely, the situation described by them) are usually spoken of as the *cause* of the event in question, and the prognosis (or rather, the event described by the prognosis) as the effect : for example, we say that the putting of a weight of two pounds on a thread capable of carrying one pound only was the cause of the breaking of the thread.'

From this analysis of causal explanation, we can see several things. One is that we can never speak of cause and effect in an absolute way, but that an event is a cause of another event, which is its effect, relative to some universal law. However, these universal laws are very often so trivial (as in our own example) that as a rule we take them for granted, instead of making conscious use of them. A second point is that the use of a theory for the purpose of *predicting* some specific event is just another aspect of its use for the purpose of *explaining* such an event. And since we test a theory by comparing the events predicted with those actually observed, our analysis also shows how theories can be *tested*. Whether we use a theory for the purpose of explanation, or prediction, or of testing, depends on our interest, and on what propositions we take as given or assumed.

Thus in the case of the so-called theoretical or *generalizing sciences* (such as physics, biology, sociology, etc.) we are predominantly interested in the universal laws or hypotheses. We wish to know whether they are true, and since we can never directly make sure of their truth, we adopt the method of eliminating the false ones. Our interest in the specific events, for example in experiments which are described by the initial conditions and prognoses, is somewhat limited ; we are interested in them mainly as means to certain ends, means by which we can test the universal laws, which latter are considered as interesting in themselves, and as unifying our knowledge.

In the case of applied sciences, our interest is different. The engineer who uses physics in order to build a bridge is predominantly interested in a prognosis : whether or not a bridge of a certain kind described (by the initial conditions) will carry a certain load. For him, the universal laws are means to an end and taken for granted.

Accordingly, pure and applied generalizing sciences are respectively interested in testing universal hypotheses, and in predicting specific events. But there is a further interest, that in explaining a specific or particular event. If we wish to explain such an event, for example, a certain road accident, then we usually tacitly assume a host of rather trivial universal laws (such as that a bone breaks under a certain strain, or that any motor-car colliding in a certain way with any human body will exert a strain sufficient to break a bone, etc.), and are interested, predominantly, in the initial conditions or in the cause which, together with these trivial universal laws, would explain the event in question. We then usually assume certain initial conditions hypothetically, and attempt to find some further evidence in order to find out whether or not these hypothetically assumed initial conditions are true ; that is to say, we test these specific hypotheses by deriving from them (with the help of some other and usually equally trivial universal laws) new predictions which can be confronted with observable facts.

Very rarely do we find ourselves in the position of having to worry about the universal laws involved in such an explanation. It happens only when we observe some new or strange kind of event, such as an unexpected chemical reaction. If such an event gives rise to the framing and testing of new hypotheses, then it is interesting mainly from the point of view of some generalizing science. But as a rule, if we are interested in specific events and their explanation, we take for granted all the many universal laws which we need.

Now the sciences which have this interest in specific events and in their explanation may, in contradistinction to the generalizing sciences, be called the *historical sciences*.

This view of history makes it clear why so many students of history and its method insist that it is the particular event that interests them, and not any so-called universal historical laws. For from our point of view, there can be no historical laws. Generalization belongs simply to a different line of interest, sharply to be distinguished from that interest in specific events and their causal explanation which is the business of history. Those who are interested in laws must turn to the generalizing sciences (for example, to sociology). Our view also makes it clear why history has so often been described as ' the events of the past as they actually did happen '. This description brings out quite well the specific interest of the student of history, as opposed to a student of a generalizing science, even though we shall have to raise certain objections against it. And our view explains why, in history, we are confronted, much more than in the generalizing sciences, with the problems of its ' infinite subject matter '. For the theories or universal laws of generalizing science introduce unity as well as a ' point of view ' ; they create, for every generalizing science, its problems, and its centres of interest as well as of research, of logical construction, and of presentation. But in history we have no such unifying theories ; or, rather, the host of trivial universal laws we use are taken for granted ; they are practically without interest, and totally unable to bring order into the subject matter. If we explain, for example, the first division of Poland in 1772 by pointing out that it could not possibly resist the combined power of Russia, Prussia, and Austria, then we are tacitly using some trivial universal law such as : ' If of two armies which are about equally well armed and led, one has a tremendous superiority in men, then the other never wins.' (Whether we say here ' never ' or

'hardly ever' does not make, for our purposes, as much difference as it does for the Captain of H.M.S. *Pinafore*.)   Such a law
might be described as a law of the sociology of military power ;
but it is too trivial ever to raise a serious problem for the students
of sociology, or to arouse their attention.   Or if we explain
Cæsar's decision to cross the Rubicon by his ambition and energy,
say, then we are using some very trivial psychological generalizations which would hardly ever arouse the attention of a psychologist.   (As a matter of fact, most historical explanation makes
tacit use, not so much of trivial sociological and psychological
laws, but of what I have called, in chapter 14, the *logic of the
situation* ;   that is to say, besides the initial conditions describing
personal interests, aims, and other situational factors, such as the
information available to the person concerned, it tacitly assumes,
as a kind of first approximation, the trivial general law that sane
persons as a rule act more or less rationally.)

III

We see, therefore, that those universal laws which historical
explanation uses provide no selective and unifying principle,
no 'point of view' for history.   In a very limited sense such a
point of view may be provided by confining history to a history
of something ;   examples are the history of power politics, or of
economic relations, or of technology, or of mathematics.   But
as a rule, we need further selective principles, points of view
which are at the same time centres of interest.   Some of these
are provided by preconceived ideas which in some way resemble
universal laws, such as the idea that what is important for history
is the character of the 'Great Men', or the 'national character',
or moral ideas, or economic conditions, etc.   Now it is important
to see that many 'historical theories' (they might perhaps be
better described as 'quasi-theories') are in their character vastly
different from scientific theories.   For in history (including the
historical natural sciences such as historical geology) the facts at
our disposal are often severely limited and cannot be repeated
or implemented at our will.   And they have been collected in
accordance with a preconceived point of view ;   the so-called
'sources' of history record only such facts as appeared sufficiently
interesting to record, so that the sources will often contain only
such facts as fit in with preconceived theory.   And if no further
facts are available, it will often not be possible to test this theory
or any other subsequent theory.   Such untestable historical

theories can then rightly be charged with being circular in the sense in which this charge has been unjustly brought against scientific theories. I shall call such historical theories, in contradistinction to scientific theories, ' *general interpretations* '.

Interpretations are important since they represent a point of view. But we have seen that a point of view is always inevitable, and that, in history, a theory which can be tested and which is therefore of scientific character can only rarely be obtained. Thus we must not think that a general interpretation can be confirmed by its agreement even with all our records ; for we must remember its circularity, as well as the fact that there will always be a number of other (and perhaps incompatible) interpretations that agree with the same records, and that we can rarely obtain new data able to serve as do crucial experiments in physics [8]. Historians often do not see any other interpretation which fits the facts as well as their own does ; but if we consider that even in the field of physics, with its larger and more reliable stock of facts, new crucial experiments are needed again and again because the old ones are all in keeping with both of two competing and incompatible theories (consider the eclipse-experiment which is needed for deciding between Newton's and Einstein's theories of gravitation), then we shall give up the naïve belief that any definite set of historical records can ever be interpreted in one way only.

But this does not mean, of course, that all interpretations are of equal merit. First, there are always interpretations which are not really in keeping with the accepted records ; secondly, there are some which need a number of more or less plausible auxiliary hypotheses if they are to escape falsification by the records ; next, there are some that are unable to connect a number of facts which another interpretation can connect, and in so far ' explain '. There may accordingly be a considerable amount of progress even within the field of historical interpretation. Furthermore, there may be all kinds of intermediate stages between more or less universal ' points of view ' and those specific or singular historical hypotheses mentioned above, which in the explanation of historical events play the rôle of hypothetical initial conditions rather than of universal laws. Often enough, these can be tested fairly well and are therefore comparable to scientific theories. But some of these specific hypotheses closely resemble those universal quasi-theories which I have called interpretations, and may accordingly be classed with these, as

' specific interpretations '. For the evidence in favour of such a specific interpretation is often enough just as circular in character as the evidence in favour of some universal ' point of view '. For example, our only authority may give us just that information regarding certain events which fits with his own specific interpretation. Most specific interpretations of these facts we may attempt will then be circular in the sense that they must fit in with that interpretation which was used in the original selection of facts. If, however, we can give to such material an interpretation which radically deviates from that adopted by our authority (and this is certainly so, for example, in our interpretation of Plato's work), then the character of our interpretation may perhaps take on some semblance to that of a scientific hypothesis. But fundamentally, it is necessary to keep in mind the fact that it is a very dubious argument in favour of a certain interpretation that it can be easily applied, and that it explains all we know ; for only if we can look out for counter examples can we test a theory. (This point is nearly always overlooked by the admirers of the various ' unveiling philosophies ', especially by the psycho-, socio-, and historio-analysts ; they are often seduced by the ease with which their theories can be applied everywhere.)

I said before that interpretations may be incompatible ; but as long as we consider them merely as crystallizations of points of view, then they are not. For example, the interpretation that man steadily progresses (towards the open society or some other aim) is incompatible with the interpretation that he steadily slips back or retrogresses. But the ' point of view ' of one who looks on human history as a history of progress is not necessarily incompatible with that of one who looks on it as a history of retrogression ; that is to say, we could write a history of human progress towards freedom (containing, for example, the story of the fight against slavery) and another history of human retrogression and oppression (containing perhaps such things as the impact of the white race upon the coloured races) ; and these two histories need not be in conflict ; rather, they may be complementary to each other, as would be two views of the same landscape seen from two different points. This consideration is of considerable importance. For since each generation has its own troubles and problems, and therefore its own interests and its own point of view, it follows that each generation has a right to look upon and re-interpret history in its own way, which is complementary to that of previous generations. After all, we study history because we are interested in it [9], and perhaps because we wish to learn something about our own problems. But history can serve neither of these two purposes if, under the influence of an inapplicable idea of objectivity, we hesitate to present historical problems from our point of view. And we should not think that our point of view, if consciously and critically applied to the problem, will be inferior to that of a writer who naïvely believes that he does not interpret, and that he has reached a level of objectivity permitting him to present ' the events of the past as they actually did happen '. (This is why I believe that even such admittedly personal comments as can be found in this book are justified, since they are in keeping with historical method.) The main thing is to be conscious of one's point of view, and critical, that is to say, to avoid, as far as this is possible, unconscious and therefore uncritical bias in the presentation of the facts. In every other respect, the interpretation must speak for itself ; and its merits will be its fertility, its ability to elucidate the facts of history, as well as its topical interest, its ability to elucidate the problems of the day.

To sum up, there can be no history of ' the past as it actually did happen ' ; there can only be historical interpretations, and none of them final ; and every generation has a right to frame its own. But not only has it a right to frame its own interpretations, it also has a kind of obligation to do so ; for there is indeed a pressing need to be answered. We want to know how our troubles are related to the past, and we want to see the line along which we may progress towards the solution of what we feel, and what we choose, to be our main tasks. It is this need which, if not answered by rational and fair means, produces historicist interpretations. Under its pressure the historicist substitutes for a rational question : ' What are we to choose as our most urgent problems, how did they arise, and along what roads may we proceed to solve them ? ' the irrational and apparently factual question : ' Which way are we going ? What, in essence, is the part that history has destined us to play ? '

But am I justified in refusing to the historicist the right to interpret history in his own way ? Have I not just proclaimed that anybody has such a right ? My answer to this question is that historicist interpretations are of a peculiar kind. Those interpretations which are needed, and justified, and one or other of which we are bound to adopt, can, I have said, be compared to a searchlight. We let it play upon our past, and we hope to illuminate the present by its reflection.   As opposed to this, the historicist interpretation may be compared to a searchlight which we direct upon ourselves.   It makes it difficult if not impossible to see anything of our surroundings, and it paralyses our actions. To translate this metaphor, the historicist does not recognize that it is we who select and order the facts of history, but he believes that ' history itself', or the ' history of mankind ', determines, by its inherent laws, ourselves, our problems, our future, and even our point of view.   Instead of recognizing that historical interpretation should answer a need arising out of the practical problems and decisions which face us, the historicist believes that in our desire for historical interpretation, there expresses itself the profound intuition that by contemplating history we may discover the secret, the essence of human destiny.   Historicism is out to find The Path on which mankind is destined to walk ; it is out to discover The Clue to History (as J. Macmurray calls it), or The Meaning of History.

IV

But is there such a clue ?   *Is there a meaning in history ?*

I do not wish to enter here into the problem of the meaning of ' meaning ' ;   I take it for granted that most people know with sufficient clarity what they mean when they speak of the ' meaning of history ' or of the ' meaning or purpose of life ' [10].   And in this sense, in the sense in which the question of the meaning of history is asked, I answer :   *History has no meaning.*

In order to give reasons for this opinion, I must first say something about that ' history ' which people have in mind when they ask whether it has meaning.   So far, I have myself spoken about ' history ' as if it did not need any explanation.   That is no longer possible ;   for I wish to make it clear that ' *history* ' *in the sense in which most people speak of it simply does not exist* ; and this is at least one reason why I say that it has no meaning.

How do most people come to use the term ' history ' ?   (I mean ' history ' in the sense in which we say of a book that it is *about* the history of Europe—not in the sense in which we say that it *is* a history of Europe.)   They learn about it in school and at the University.   They read books about it.   They see what is treated in the books under the name ' history of the world ' or ' the history of mankind ', and they get used to looking upon it as a more or less definite series of facts.   And these facts constitute, they believe, the history of mankind.

But we have already seen that the realm of facts is infinitely rich, and that there must be selection. According to our interests, we could, for instance, write about the history of art ; or of language ; or of feeding habits ; or of typhus fever (see Zinsser's *Rats, Lice, and History*). Certainly, none of these is the history of mankind (nor all of them taken together). What people have in mind when they speak of the history of mankind is, rather, the history of the Egyptian, Babylonian, Persian, Macedonian, and Roman empires, and so on, down to our own day. In other words : They speak about the *history of mankind*, but what they mean, and what they have learned about in school, is the *history of political power*.

There is no history of mankind, there is only an indefinite number of histories of all kinds of aspects of human life. And one of these is the history of political power. This is elevated into the history of the world. But this, I hold, is an offence against every decent conception of mankind. It is hardly better than to treat the history of embezzlement or of robbery or of poisoning as the history of mankind. For *the history of power politics is nothing but the history of international crime and mass murder* (including, it is true, some of the attempts to suppress them). This history is taught in schools, and some of the greatest criminals are extolled as its heroes.

But is there really no such thing as a universal history in the sense of a concrete history of mankind ? There can be none. This must be the reply of every humanitarian, I believe, and especially that of every Christian. A concrete history of mankind, if there were any, would have to be the history of all men. It would have to be the history of all human hopes, struggles, and sufferings. For there is no one man more important than any other. Clearly, this concrete history cannot be written. We must make abstractions, we must neglect, select. But with this we arrive at the many histories ; and among them, at that history of international crime and mass murder which has been advertised as the history of mankind.

But why has just the history of power been selected, and not, for example, that of religion, or of poetry ? There are several reasons. One is that power affects us all, and poetry only a few. Another is that men are inclined to worship power. But there can be no doubt that the worship of power is one of the worst kinds of human idolatries, a relic of the time of the cage, of human servitude. The worship of power is born of fear, an emotion which is rightly despised. A third reason why power politics has been made the core of ' history ' is that those in power wanted to be worshipped and could enforce their wishes. Many historians wrote under the supervision of the emperors, the generals and the dictators.

I know that these views will meet with the strongest opposition from many sides, including some apologists for Christianity ; for although there is hardly anything in the New Testament to support this doctrine, it is often considered a part of the Christian dogma that God reveals Himself in history ; that history has meaning ; and that its meaning is the purpose of God. Historicism is thus held to be a necessary element of religion. But I do not admit this. I contend that this view is pure idolatry and superstition, not only from the point of view of a rationalist or humanist but from the Christian point of view itself.

What is behind this theistic historicism ? With Hegel, it looks upon history—political history—as a stage, or rather, as a kind of lengthy Shakespearian play ; and the audience conceive either the ' great historical personalities ', or mankind in the abstract, as the heroes of the play. Then they ask, ' Who has written this play ? ' And they think that they give a pious answer when they reply, ' God '. But they are mistaken. Their answer is pure blasphemy, for the play was (and they know it) written not by God, but, under the supervision of generals and dictators, by the professors of history.

I do not deny that it is as justifiable to interpret history from a Christian point of view as it is to interpret it from any other point of view ; and it should certainly be emphasized, for example, how much of our Western aims and ends, humanitarianism, freedom, equality, we owe to the influence of Christianity. But at the same time, the only rational as well as the only Christian attitude even towards the history of freedom is that we are ourselves responsible for it, in the same sense in which we are responsible for what we make of our lives, and that only our conscience can judge us and not our worldly success. The theory that God reveals Himself and His judgement in history is indistinguishable from the theory that worldly success is the ultimate judge and justification of our actions ; it comes to the same thing as the doctrine that history will judge, that is to say, that future might is right ; it is the same as what I have called ' moral futurism ' [11]. To maintain that God reveals Himself in what is usually called ' history ', in the history of international crime and of mass murder, is indeed blasphemy ; for what really happens within the realm of human lives is hardly ever touched upon by this cruel and at the same time childish affair. The life of the forgotten, of the unknown individual man ; his sorrows and his joys, his suffering and death, this is the real content of human experience down the ages. If that could be told by history, then I should certainly not say that it is blasphemy to see the finger of God in it. But such a history does not and cannot exist ; and all the history which exists, our history of the Great and the Powerful, is at best a shallow comedy ; it is the opera buffa played by the powers behind reality (comparable to Homer's opera buffa of the Olympian powers behind the scene of human struggles). It is what one of our worst instincts, the idolatrous worship of power, of success, has led us to believe to be real. And in this not even man-made, but man-faked ' history ', some Christians dare to see the hand of God ! They dare to understand and to know what He wills when they impute to Him their petty historical interpretations ! ' On the contrary ', says K. Barth, the theologian, in his *Credo*, ' we have to begin with the admission . . that all that we think we know when we say " God " does not reach or comprehend Him . . , but always one of our self-conceived and self-made idols, whether it is " spirit " or " nature ", " fate " or " idea " . .' [12] (It is in keeping with this attitude that Barth characterizes the ' Neo-Protestant doctrine of the revelation of God in history ' as ' inadmissible ' and as an encroachment upon ' the kingly office of Christ '.) But it is, from the Christian point of view, not only arrogance that underlies such attempts ; it is, more specifically, an anti-Christian attitude. For Christianity teaches, if anything, that worldly success is not decisive. Christ ' suffered under Pontius Pilate '. I am quoting Barth again : ' How does Pontius Pilate get into the Credo ? The simple answer can at once be given : it is a matter of date.' Thus the man who was successful, who represented the historical power of that time, plays here the purely technical rôle of indicating when these events happened. And what were these events ? They had nothing to do with power-political success, with ' history '. They were not even the story of an unsuccessful non-violent nationalist revolution (*à la* Gandhi) of the Jewish people against the Roman conquerors. The events were nothing but the sufferings of a man. Barth insists that the word ' suffers ' refers to the whole of the life of Christ and not only to His death ; he says [13] : ' Jesus *suffers*. Therefore He does not conquer. He does not triumph. He has no success . . He achieved nothing except . . His crucifixion. The same could be said of His relationship to His people and to His disciples.' My intention in quoting Barth is to show that it is not only my ' rationalist ' or ' humanist ' point of view from which the worship of historical success appears as incompatible with the spirit of Christianity. What matters to Christianity is not the historical deeds of the powerful Roman conquerers but (to use a phrase of Kierkegaard's [14]) ' what a few fishermen have given the world '. And yet all theistic interpretation of history attempts to see in history as it is recorded, i.e. in the history of power, and in historical success, the manifestation of God's will.

To this attack upon the ' doctrine of the revelation of God in history ', it will probably be replied that it *is* success, His success after His death, by which Christ's unsuccessful life on earth was finally revealed to mankind as the greatest spiritual victory ; that it was the success, the fruits of His teaching which proved it and justified it, and by which the prophecy ' The last shall be first and the first last ' has been verified. In other words, that it was the historical success of the Christian Church through which the will of God manifested itself. But this is a most dangerous line of defence. Its implication that the worldly success of the Church is an argument in favour of Christianity clearly reveals lack of faith. The early Christians had no worldly encouragement of this kind. (They believed that conscience must judge power [15], and not the other way round.) Those who hold that the history of the success of Christian teaching reveals the will of God should ask themselves whether this success was really a success of the spirit of Christianity ; and whether this spirit did not triumph at the time when the Church was persecuted, rather than at the time when the Church was triumphant. Which Church incorporated this spirit more purely, that of the martyrs, or the victorious Church of the Inquisition ?

There seem to be many who would admit much of this, insisting as they do that the message of Christianity is to the meek, but who still believe that this message is one of historicism. An outstanding representative of this view is J. Macmurray, who, in *The Clue to History*, finds the essence of Christian teaching in historical prophecy, and who sees in its founder the discoverer of a dialectical law of ' human nature '. Macmurray holds [16] that, according to this law, political history must inevitably bring forth ' the socialist commonwealth of the world. The fundamental law of human nature cannot be broken . . It is the meek who will inherit the earth.' But this historicism, with its substitution of certainty for hope, must lead to a moral futurism. ' The law *cannot* be broken.' So we can be sure, on psychological grounds, that whatever we do will lead to the same result ; that even fascism must, in the end, lead to that commonwealth ; so that the final outcome does not depend upon our moral decision, and that there is no need to worry over our responsibilities. If we are told that we can be *certain*, on scientific grounds, that ' the last will be first and the first last ', what else is this but the substitution of historical prophecy for conscience ? Does not this theory come dangerously close (certainly against the intentions of its author) to the admonition : ' Be wise, and take to heart what the founder of Christianity tells you, for he was a great psychologist of human nature and a great prophet of history. Climb in time upon the band-waggon of the meek ; for according to the inexorable scientific laws of human nature, this is the surest way to come out on top ! ' Such a clue to history implies the worship of success ; it implies that the meek will be justified because they will be on the winning side. It translates Marxism, and especially what I have described as Marx's historicist moral theory, into the language of a psychology of human nature, and of religious prophecy. It is an interpretation which, by implication, sees the greatest achievement of Christianity in the fact that its founder was a forerunner of Hegel—a superior one, admittedly.

My insistence that success should not be worshipped, that it cannot be our judge, and that we should not be dazzled by it, and in particular, my attempts to show that in this attitude I concur with what I believe to be the true teaching of Christianity, should not be misunderstood. They are not intended to support the attitude of ' other-worldliness ' which I have criticized in the last chapter [17]. Whether Christianity is other-worldly, I do not know, but it certainly teaches that the only way to prove one's faith is by rendering practical (and worldly) help to those who need it. And it is certainly possible to combine an attitude of the utmost reserve and even of contempt towards worldly success in the sense of power, glory, and wealth, with the attempt to do one's best in this world, and to further the ends one has decided to adopt with the clear purpose of making them succeed ; not for the sake of success or of one's justification by history, but for their own sake.

A forceful support of some of these views, and especially of the incompatibility of historicism and Christianity, can be found in Kierkegaard's criticism of Hegel. Although Kierkegaard never freed himself entirely from the Hegelian tradition in which he was educated [18], there was hardly anybody who recognized more clearly what Hegelian historicism meant. ' There were ', Kierkegaard wrote [19], ' philosophers who tried, before Hegel, to explain . . history. And providence could only smile when it saw these attempts. But providence did not laugh outright, for there was a human, honest sincerity about them. But Hegel— ! Here I need Homer's language. How did the gods roar with laughter ! Such a horrid little professor who has simply seen through the necessity of anything and everything there is, and who now plays the whole affair on his barrel-organ : listen, ye gods of Olympus ! ' And Kierkegaard continues, referring to the attack [20] by the atheist Schopenhauer upon the Christian apologist Hegel : ' Reading Schopenhauer has given me more pleasure than I can express. What he says is perfectly true ; and then—it serves the Germans right—he is as rude as only a German can be.' But Kierkegaard's own expressions are nearly as blunt as Schopenhauer's ; for Kierkegaard goes on to say that Hegelianism, which he calls ' this brilliant spirit of putridity ', is the ' most repugnant of all forms of looseness ' ; and he speaks of its ' mildew of pomposity ', its ' intellectual voluptuousness ', and its ' infamous splendour of corruption '.

And, indeed, our intellectual as well as our ethical education is corrupt. It is perverted by the admiration of brilliance, of the way things are said, which takes the place of a critical appreciation of the things that are said (and the things that are done). It is perverted by the romantic idea of the splendour of the stage of History on which we are the actors. We are educated to act with an eye to the gallery.

The whole problem of educating man to a sane appreciation of his own importance relative to that of other individuals is thoroughly muddled by these ethics of fame and fate, by a morality which perpetuates an educational system that is still based upon the classics with their romantic view of the history of power and their romantic tribal morality which goes back to Heraclitus ; a system whose ultimate basis is the worship of power. Instead of a sober combination of individualism and altruism (to use these labels again [21])—that is to say, instead of a position like ' What really matters are human individuals, but I do not take this to mean that it is I who matter very much '

—a romantic combination of egoism and collectivism is taken for granted. That is to say, the importance of the self, of its emotional life and its ' self-expression ', is romantically exaggerated ; and with it, the tension between the ' personality ' and the group, the collective. This takes the place of the other individuals, the other men, but does not admit of reasonable personal relations. ' Dominate or submit ' is, by implication, the device of this attitude ; either be a Great Man, a Hero wrestling with fate and earning fame (' the greater the fall, the greater the fame ', says Heraclitus), or belong to ' the masses ' and submit yourself to leadership and sacrifice yourself to the higher cause of your collective. There is a neurotic, an hysterical element in this exaggerated stress on the importance of the tension between the self and the collective, and I do not doubt that this hysteria, this reaction to the strain of civilization, is the secret of the strong emotional appeal of the ethics of hero-worship, of the ethics of domination and submission [22].

At the bottom of all this there is a real difficulty. While it is fairly clear (as we have seen in chapters 9 and 24) that the politician should limit himself to fighting against evils, instead of fighting for ' positive ' or ' higher ' values, such as happiness, etc., the teacher, in principle, is in a different position. Although he should not *impose* his scale of ' higher ' values upon his pupils, he certainly should try to *stimulate* their interest in these values. He should care for the souls of his pupils. (When Socrates told his friends to care for their souls, *he* cared for them.) Thus there is certainly something like a romantic or æsthetic element in education, such as should not enter politics. But though this is true in principle, it is hardly applicable to our educational system. For it presupposes a relation of friendship between teacher and pupil, a relation which, as emphasized in chapter 24, each party must be free to end. (Socrates chose his companions, and they him.) The very number of pupils makes all this impossible in our schools. Accordingly, attempts to impose higher values not only become unsuccessful, but it must be insisted that they lead to *harm*—to something much more concrete and public than the ideals aimed at. And the principle that those who are entrusted to us must, before anything else, not be harmed, should be recognized to be just as fundamental for education as it is for medicine. ' Do no harm ' (and, therefore, ' give the young what they most urgently need, in order to become independent of us, and to be able to choose for themselves ') would be a very worthy aim for our educational system, and one whose realization is somewhat remote, even though it sounds modest. Instead, ' higher ' aims are the fashion, aims which are typically romantic and indeed nonsensical, such as ' the full development of the personality '.

It is under the influence of such romantic ideas that individualism is still identified with egoism, as it was by Plato, and altruism with collectivism (i.e. with the substitution of group egoism for the individualist egoism). But this bars the way even to a clear formulation of the main problem, the problem of how to obtain a sane appreciation of one's own importance in relation to other individuals. Since it is felt, and rightly so, that we have to aim at something beyond our own selves, something to which we can devote ourselves, and for which we may make sacrifices, it is concluded that this must be the collective, with its ' historical mission '. Thus we are told to make sacrifices, and, at the same time, assured that we shall make an excellent bargain by doing so. We shall make sacrifices, it is said, but we shall thereby obtain honour and fame. We shall become ' leading actors ', heroes on the Stage of History ; for a small risk we shall gain great rewards. This is the dubious morality of a period in which only a tiny minority counted, and in which nobody cared for the common people. It is the morality of those who, being political or intellectual aristocrats, have a chance of getting into the textbooks of history. It cannot possibly be the morality of those who favour justice and equalitarianism ; for historical fame cannot be just, and it can be attained only by a very few. The countless number of men who are just as worthy, or worthier, will always be forgotten.

It should perhaps be admitted that the Heraclitean ethics, the doctrine that the higher reward is that which only posterity can offer, may in some way perhaps be slightly superior to an ethical doctrine which teaches us to look out for reward now. But it is not what we need. We need an ethics which defies success and reward. And such an ethics need not be invented. It is not new. It has been taught by Christianity, at least in its beginnings. It is, again, taught by the industrial as well as by the scientific co-operation of our own day. The romantic historicist morality of fame, fortunately, seems to be on the decline. The Unknown Soldier shows it. We are beginning to realize that sacrifice may mean just as much, or even more, when it is made anonymously. Our ethical education must follow suit.

We must be taught to do our work ; to make our sacrifice for the sake of this work, and not for praise or the avoidance of blame. (The fact that we all need some encouragement, hope, praise, and even blame, is another matter altogether.) We must find our justification in our work, in what we are doing ourselves, and not in a fictitious ' meaning of history '.

History has no meaning, I contend. But this contention does not imply that all we can do about it is to look aghast at the history of political power, or that we must look on it as a cruel joke. For we can interpret it, with an eye to those problems of power politics whose solution we choose to attempt in our time. We can interpret the history of power politics from the point of view of our fight for the open society, for a rule of reason, for justice, freedom, equality, and for the control of international crime. Although history has no ends, we can impose these ends of ours upon it ; and *although history has no meaning, we can give it a meaning*.

It is the problem of nature and convention which we meet here again [23]. Neither nature nor history can tell us what we ought to do. Facts, whether those of nature or those of history, cannot make the decision for us, they cannot determine the ends we are going to choose. It is we who introduce purpose and meaning into nature and into history. Men are not equal ; but we can decide to fight for equal rights. Human institutions such as the state are not rational, but we can decide to fight to make them more rational. We ourselves and our ordinary language are, on the whole, emotional rather than rational ; but we can try to become a little more rational, and we can train ourselves to use our language as an instrument not of self-expression (as our romantic educationists would say) but of rational communication [24]. History itself—I mean the history of power politics, of course, not the non-existent story of the development of mankind—has no end nor meaning, but we can decide to give it both. We can make it our fight for the open society and against its enemies (who, when in a corner, always protest their humanitarian sentiments, in accordance with Pareto's advice) ; and we can interpret it accordingly. Ultimately, we may say the same about the ' meaning of life '. It is up to us to decide what shall be our purpose in life, to determine our ends [25].

This dualism of facts and decisions [26] is, I believe, fundamental. Facts as such have no meaning ; they can gain it only through our decisions. Historicism is only one of many attempts to get over this dualism ; it is born of fear, for it shrinks from realizing that we bear the ultimate responsibility even for the standards we choose. But such an attempt seems to me to represent precisely what is usually described as superstition. For it assumes that we can reap where we have not sown ; it tries to persuade us that if we merely fall into step with history everything will and must go right, and that no fundamental decision on our part is required ; it tries to shift our responsibility on to history, and thereby on to the play of demoniac powers beyond ourselves ; it tries to base our actions upon the hidden intentions of these powers, which can be revealed to us only in mystical inspirations and intuitions ; and it thus puts our actions and ourselves on the moral level of a man who, inspired by horoscopes and dreams, chooses his lucky number in a lottery [27]. Like gambling, historicism is born of our despair in the rationality and responsibility of our actions. It is a debased hope and a debased faith, an attempt to replace the hope and the faith that springs from our moral enthusiasm and the contempt for success by a certainty that springs from a pseudo-science ; a pseudo-science of the stars, or of ' human nature ', or of historical destiny.

Historicism, I assert, is not only rationally untenable, it is also in conflict with any religion that teaches the importance of conscience. For such a religion must agree with the rationalist attitude towards history in its emphasis on our supreme responsibility for our actions, and for their repercussions upon the course of history. True, we need hope ; to act, to live without hope goes beyond our strength. But we do *not* need more, and we must not be given more. We do not need certainty. Religion, in particular, should not be a substitute for dreams and wish-fulfilment ; it should resemble neither the holding of a ticket in a lottery, nor the holding of a policy in an insurance company. The historicist element in religion is an element of idolatry, of superstition.

This emphasis upon the dualism of facts and decisions determines also our attitude towards such ideas as ' progress '. If we think that history progresses, or that we are bound to progress, then we commit the same mistake as those who believe that history has a meaning that can be discovered in it and need not be given to it. For to progress is to move towards some kind of end, towards an end which exists for us as human beings.

' History ' cannot do that ; only we, the human individuals, can do it ; we can do it by defending and strengthening those democratic institutions upon which freedom, and with it progress, depends. And we shall do it much better as we become more fully aware of the fact that progress rests with us, with our watchfulness, with our efforts, with the clarity of our conception of our ends, and with the realism [28] of their choice.

Instead of posing as prophets we must become the makers of our fate. We must learn to do things as well as we can, and to look out for our mistakes. And when we have dropped the idea that the history of power will be our judge, when we have given up worrying whether or not history will justify us, then one day perhaps we may succeed in getting power under control. In this way we may even justify history, in our turn. It badly needs a justification.

NOTES

NOTES TO CHAPTER 11

[1] That Aristotle's criticism of Plato is very frequently, and in important places, unmerited, has been admitted by many students of the history of philosophy. It is one of the few points in which even the admirers of Aristotle find it difficult to defend him, since usually they are admirers of Plato as well. Zeller, to quote just one example, comments (cp. *Aristotle and the Earlier Peripatetics*, English translation by Costelloe and Muirhead, 1897, II, 261, n. 2), upon the distribution of land in Aristotle's Best State : ' There is a similar plan in Plato's *Laws*, 745c seqq. ; Aristotle, however, in *Politics* 1265b24 considers Plato's arrangement, merely on account of a trifling difference, highly objectionable.' A similar remark is made by G. Grote, *Aristotle* (Ch. XIV, end of second paragraph). In view of many criticisms of Plato which strongly suggest that envy of Plato's originality is part of his motive, Aristotle's much-admired solemn assurance (*Nicomachean Ethics*, I, 6, 1) that the sacred duty of giving preference to truth forces him to sacrifice even what is most dear to him, namely, his love for Plato, sounds to me somewhat hypocritical.

[2] Cp. Th. Gomperz, *Greek Thinkers* (I am quoting from the German Edition, III, 298, i.e. Book 7, Ch. 31, § 6). See especially Aristotle's *Politics*, 1313a. —

G. C. Field (in *Plato and His Contemporaries*, 114 f.) defends Plato and Aristotle against the ' reproach . . that, with the possibility, and, in the case of the latter, the actuality of this ' (i.e. the Macedonian conquest) ' before their eyes, they . . say nothing of these new developments '. But Field's defence (perhaps directed against Gomperz) is unsuccessful, in spite of his strong comments upon those who make such a reproach. (Field says : ' this criticism betrays . . a singular lack of understanding.') Of course, it is correct to claim, as Field does, ' that a hegemony like that exercised by Macedon . . was no new thing ' ; but Macedon was in Plato's eyes at least half-barbarian and therefore a natural enemy. Field is also right in saying that ' the destruction of independence by Macedon ' was not a complete one ; but did Plato or Aristotle foresee that it was not to become complete ? I believe that a defence like Field's cannot possibly succeed, simply because it would have to prove too much ; namely, that the significance of Macedon's threat could not have been clear, at the time, to any observer ; but this is disproved, of course, by the example of Demosthenes. The question is : why did Plato, who like Isocrates had taken some interest in pan-Hellenic nationalism (cp. notes 48–50 to chapter 8, *Rep.*, 470, and the *Eighth Letter*, 353e, which Field claims to be ' certainly genuine ') and who was apprehensive of a ' Phœnician and Oscan ' threat to Syracuse, why did he ignore Macedon's threat to Athens ? A likely reply to the corresponding question concerning Aristotle is : because he belonged to the pro-Macedonian party. A reply in Plato's case is suggested by Zeller (*op. cit.*, II, 41) in his defence of Aristotle's right to support Macedon : ' So satisfied was Plato of the intolerable character of the existing political position that he advocated sweeping changes.' (' Plato's follower ', Zeller continues, referring to Aristotle, ' could the less evade the same convictions, since he had a keener insight into men and things . .') In other words, the answer might be that Plato's hatred of Athenian democracy exceeded so much even his pan-Hellenic nationalism that he was, like Isocrates, looking forward to the Macedonian conquest.

³ This and the following three quotations are from Aristotle's *Politics*, 1254b–1255a ; 1254a ; 1255a ; 1260a.—See also : 1252a, f. (I, 2, 2–5) ; 1253b, ff. (I, 4, 386, and especially I, 5) ; 1313b (V, 11, 11). Furthermore : *Metaphysics*, 1075a, where freemen and slaves are also opposed 'by nature'. But we find also the passage : ' Some slaves have the souls of freemen, and others their bodies' (*Politics*, 1254b). Cp. with Plato's *Timaeus*, 51e, quoted in note 50 (2), to chapter 8.—For a trifling mitigation, and a typically 'balanced judgement' of Plato's *Laws*, see *Politics*, 1260b : ' Those' (this is a somewhat typical Aristotelian way of referring to Plato) ' are wrong who forbid us even to converse with slaves and say that we should only use the language of command ; for slaves must be admonished' (Plato had said, in *Laws*, 777e, that they should not be admonished) ' even more than children.' Zeller, in his long list of the personal virtues of Aristotle (*op. cit.*, I, 44), mentions his ' nobility of principles' and his ' benevolence to slaves'. I cannot help remembering the perhaps less noble but certainly more benevolent principle put forward much earlier by Alcidamas and Lycophron, namely, that there should be no slaves at all. W. D. Ross (*Aristotle*, 2nd ed., 1930, pp. 241 ff.) defends Aristotle's attitude towards slavery by saying : ' Where to us he seems reactionary, he may have seemed revolutionary to them', viz., to his contemporaries. In support of this view, Ross mentions Aristotle's doctrine that Greek should not enslave Greek. But this doctrine was hardly very revolutionary since Plato had taught it, probably half a century before Aristotle. And that Aristotle's views were indeed reactionary can be best seen from the fact that he repeatedly finds it necessary to defend them against the doctrine that no man is a slave by nature, and further from his own testimony to the anti-slavery tendencies of the Athenian democracy.

An excellent statement on Aristotle's *Politics* can be found in the beginning of Chapter XIV of G. Grote's *Aristotle*, from which I quote a few sentences : ' The scheme . . of government proposed by Aristotle, in the two last books of his *Politics*, as representing his own ideas of something like perfection, is evidently founded upon the *Republic* of Plato : from whom he differs in the important circumstance of not admitting either community of property or community of wives and children. Each of these philosophers recognizes one separate class of inhabitants, relieved from all private toil and all money-getting employments, and constituting exclusively the citizens of the commonwealth. This small class is in effect *the city—the commonwealth* : the remaining inhabitants are not a part of the commonwealth, they are only appendages to it—indispensable indeed, but still appendages, in the same manner as slaves or cattle.' Grote recognizes that Aristotle's Best State, where it deviates from the *Republic*, largely copies Plato's *Laws*. Aristotle's dependence upon Plato is prominent even where he expresses his acquiescence in the victory of democracy ; cp. especially *Politics*, III, 15 ; 11–13 ; 1286b (a parallel passage is IV, 13 ; 10 ; 1297b). The passage ends by saying of democracy : ' No other form of government appears to be possible any longer' ; but this result is reached by an argument that follows very closely Plato's story of the decline and fall of the state in Books VIII-IX of the *Republic* ; and this in spite of the fact that Aristotle criticizes Plato's story severely (for instance in V, 12 ; 1316a, f.).

⁴ Aristotle's use of the word ' banausic' in the sense of ' professional' or ' money earning' is clearly shown in *Politics*, VIII, 6, 3 ff. (1340b) and especially 15 f. (1341b). Every professional, for example a flute player, and of course every artisan or labourer, is ' banausic', that is to say, not a free man, not a citizen, even though he is not a real slave ; the status of a ' banausic' man is one of ' partial or limited slavery' (*Politics*, I, 14 ; 13 ; 1260a/b). The word ' *banausos*' derives, I gather, from a pre-Hellenic word for ' fire-worker'. Used as an attribute it means that a man's origin and caste ' disqualify him

from prowess in the field '. (Cp. Greenidge, quoted by Adam in his edition of the *Republic*, note to 495e30.) It may be translated by ' low-caste ', ' cringing ', ' degrading ', or in some contexts by ' upstart '. Plato used the word in the same sense as Aristotle. In the *Laws* (741e and 743d), the term ' *banausia* ' is used to describe the depraved state of a man who makes money by means other than the hereditary possession of land. See also the *Republic*, 495e and 590c. But if we remember the tradition that Socrates was a mason ; and Xenophon's story (*Mem.* II, 7) ; and Antisthenes' praise of hard work ; and the attitude of the Cynics ; then it seems unlikely that Socrates agreed with the aristocratic prejudice that money earning must be degrading. (The *Oxford English Dictionary* proposes to render ' banausic ' as ' merely mechanical, proper to a mechanic ', and quotes Grote, *Eth. Fragm.*, vi, 227 = *Aristotle*, 2nd ed., 1880, p. 545 ; but this rendering is much too narrow, and Grote's passage does not justify this interpretation, which may originally rest upon a misunderstanding of Plutarch. It is interesting that in Shakespeare's *Midsummer Night's Dream* the term ' mere mechanicals ' is used precisely in the sense of ' banausic ' men ; and this use might well be connected with a passage on Archimedes in North's translation of the *Life of Marcellus*.)

In *Mind*, vol. 47, there is an interesting discussion between A. E. Taylor and F. M. Cornford, in which the former (pp. 197 ff.) defends his view that Plato, when speaking of ' the god ' in a certain passage of the *Timaeus*, may have had in mind a ' peasant cultivator ' who ' serves ' by bodily labour ; a view which is, I think most convincingly, criticized by Cornford (pp. 329 ff.). Plato's attitude towards all ' banausic ' work, and especially manual labour, bears on this problem ; and when (p. 198, note) Taylor uses the argument that Plato compares his gods ' with shepherds or sheep-dogs in charge of a flock of sheep ' (*Laws*, 901e, 907a), then we could point out that the activities of *nomads* and *hunters* are quite consistently considered by Plato as noble or even divine ; but the sedentary ' peasant cultivator ' is banausic and depraved. Cp. note 32 to chapter 4, and text.

⁵ The two passages that follow are from *Politics* (1337b, 4 and 5).

⁶ The 1939 edition of the *Pocket Oxford Dictionary* still says : ' liberal . . (of education) fit for a gentleman, of a general literary rather than technical kind '. This shows most clearly the everlasting power of Aristotle's influence.

I admit that there is a serious problem of a professional education, that of *narrow-mindedness*. But I do not believe that a ' literary ' education is the remedy ; for it may create its own peculiar kind of narrow-mindedness, its peculiar snobbery. And in our day no man should be considered educated if he does not take an interest in science. The usual defence that an interest in electricity or stratigraphy need not be more enlightening than an interest in human affairs only betrays a complete lack of understanding of human affairs. For science is not merely a collection of facts about electricity, etc. ; it is one of the most important spiritual movements of our day. Anybody who does not attempt to acquire an understanding of this movement cuts himself off from the most remarkable development in the history of human affairs. Our so-called Arts Faculties, based upon the theory that by means of a literary and historical education they introduce the student into the spiritual life of man, have therefore become obsolete in their present form. There can be no history of man which excludes a history of his intellectual struggles and achievements ; and there can be no history of ideas which excludes the history of scientific ideas. But literary education has an even more serious aspect. Not only does it fail to educate the student, who is often to become a teacher, to an understanding of the greatest spiritual movement of his own day, but it also often fails to educate him to intellectual honesty. Only if the student experiences how easy it is to err, and how hard to make even a small advance in the field of knowledge, only then can he obtain a feeling for the standards of intellectual honesty, a respect for truth, and a disregard of authority and bumptiousness. But nothing is more necessary to-day than the spread of these modest intellectual virtues. ' The mental power ', T. H. Huxley wrote in *A Liberal Education*, ' which will be of most importance in your . . life will be the power of seeing things as they are without regard to authority. . . But at school and at college, you shall know of no source of truth but authority.' I admit that, unfortunately, this is true also of many courses in science, which by some teachers is still treated as if it was a ' body of knowledge ', as the ancient phrase goes. But this idea will one day, I hope, disappear ; for science can be taught as a fascinating part of human history—as a quickly developing growth of bold hypotheses, controlled by experiment, and by *criticism*. Taught in this way, as a part of the history of ' natural philosophy ', and of the history of problems and of ideas, it could become the basis of a new liberal University education ; of one whose aim, where it cannot produce experts, will be to produce at least *men who can distinguish between a charlatan and an expert*. This modest and liberal aim will be far beyond anything that our Arts faculties nowadays achieve.

⁷ *Politics*, VIII, 3, 2 (1337b) : ' I must repeat over and over again, that the first principle of all action is leisure.' Previously, in VII, 15, 1 f. (1334a), we read : ' Since the end of individuals and of states is the same . . they should both contain the virtues of leisure. . . For the proverb says truly, " There is no leisure for slaves ".' Cp. also the reference in note 9 to this section, and *Metaphysics*, 1072b23.

Concerning Aristotle's ' admiration and deference for the leisured classes ', cp. for example the following passage from the *Politics*, IV, (VII), 8, 4–5 (1293b/1294a) : ' Birth and education as a rule go together with wealth. . . The rich are already in possession of those advantages the want of which is a temptation to crime, and hence they are called noblemen and gentlemen. Now it appears to be impossible that a state should be badly governed if the best citizens rule . .' Aristotle, however, not only admires the rich, but is also, like Plato, a racialist (cp. *op. cit.*, III, 13, 2–3, 1283a) : ' The nobly born are citizens in a truer sense of the word than the low born. . . Those who come from better ancestors are likely to be better men, for nobility is excellence of race.'

⁸ Cp. Th. Gomperz, *Greek Thinkers*. (I am quoting from the German edition, vol. III, 263, i.e. book 6, ch. 27, § 7.)

⁹ Cp. *Nicomachean Ethics*, X, 7, 6. The Aristotelian phrase, ' *the good life* ', seems to have caught the imagination of many modern admirers who associate with this phrase something like a ' good life ' in the Christian sense— a life devoted to help, service, and the quest for the ' higher values '. But this interpretation is the result of a mistaken idealization of Aristotle's intentions ; Aristotle was exclusively concerned with the ' good life ' of feudal gentlemen, and this ' good life ' he did not envisage as a life of good deeds, but as a *life of refined leisure*, spent in the pleasant company of friends who are equally well situated.

¹⁰ I do not think that even the term ' vulgarization ' would be too strong, considering that to Aristotle himself ' professional ' means ' vulgar ', and considering that he certainly made a profession of Platonic philosophy. Besides, he made it dull, as even Zeller admits in the midst of his eulogy (*op. cit.*, I, 46) : ' He cannot inspire us . . at all in the same way as Plato does. His work is drier, more professional . . than Plato's has been.'

¹¹ Plato presented in the *Timaeus* (42a f., 90e f., and especially 91d f. ; see note 6 (7) to chapter 3) a general theory of the *origin of species by way of degeneration*, down from the Gods and the first man. Man first degenerates into a woman, then further to the higher and lower animals and to the plants.

It is, as Gomperz says (*Greek Thinkers*, book 5, ch. 19, § 3 ; I am quoting from the German edition, vol. II, 482), ' a theory of descent in the literal sense or a theory of devolution, as opposed to the modern theory of evolution which, since it assumes an ascending sequence, might be called a theory of ascent.' Plato's mythical and possibly semi-ironical presentation of this theory of descent by degeneration makes use of the Orphic and Pythagorean theory of the transmigration of the soul. All this (and the important fact that evolutionary theories which made the lower forms precede the higher were in vogue at least as early as Empedocles) must be remembered when we hear from Aristotle that Speusippus, together with certain Pythagoreans, believed in an evolutionary theory according to which the best and most divine, which are first in rank, come last in the chronological order of development. Aristotle speaks (*Met.*, 1072b30) of ' those who suppose, with the Pythagoreans and Speusippus, that supreme beauty and goodness are not present in the beginning '. From this passage we may conclude, perhaps, that some Pythagoreans had used the myth of transmigration (possibly under the influence of Xenophanes) as the vehicle of a ' theory of ascent '. This surmise is supported by Aristotle, who says (*Met.*, 1091a34) : ' The mythologists seem to agree with some thinkers of the present day ' (an allusion, I suppose, to Speusippus) ' . . who say that the good as well as the beautiful make their appearance in nature only after nature has made some progress.' It also seems as if Speusippus had taught that the world will in the course of its development become a Parmenidian *One*—an organized and ully harmonious whole. (Cp. *Met.*, 1092a14, where a thinker who maintains that the more perfect always comes from the imperfect, is quoted as saying that ' the One itself does not yet exist ' ; cp. also *Met.*, 1091a11.) Aristotle himself consistently expresses, at the places quoted, his opposition to these ' theories of ascent '. His argument is that it is a complete man that produces man, and that the incomplete seed is not prior to man. In view of this attitude, Zeller can hardly be right in attributing to Aristotle what is practically the Speusippian theory. (Cp. Zeller, *Aristotle*, etc., vol. II, 28 f. A similar interpretation is propounded by H. F. Osborn, *From the Greeks to Darwin*, 1908, pp. 48–56.) We may have to accept Gomperz's interpretation, according to which Aristotle taught the *eternity and invariability of the human species and at least of the higher animals.* Thus his morphological orders must be interpreted as neither chronological nor genealogical. (Cp. *Greek Thinkers*, book 6, ch. 11, § 10, and especially ch. 13, § 6 f., and the notes to these passages.) But there remains, of course, the possibility that Aristotle was inconsistent in this point, as he was in many others, and that his arguments against Speusippus are due to his wish to assert his independence. See also note 6 (7) to chapter 3, and notes 2 and 4 to chapter 4.

[12] Aristotle's First Mover, that is, God, is prior in time (though he is eternal) and has the predicate of goodness. For the evidence concerning the identification of formal and final cause mentioned in this paragraph, see note 15 to this chapter.

[13] For Plato's biological teleology see *Timaeus*, 73a–76e. Gomperz comments rightly (*Greek Thinkers*, book 5, ch. 19, § 7 ; German ed., vol. II, 495 f.) that Plato's teleology is only understandable if we remember that ' animals are degenerate men, and that their organization may therefore exhibit purposes which were originally only the ends of man '.

[14] For Plato's version of the theory of the *natural places*, see *Timaeus*, 60b–63a, and especially 63b f. Aristotle adopts the theory with only minor changes and explains like Plato the ' lightness ' and ' heaviness ' of bodies by the ' upward ' and ' downward ' direction of their natural movements towards their natural places ; cp. for instance *Physics*, 192b13 ; also *Metaphysics*, 1065b10.

¹⁵ Aristotle is not always quite definite and consistent in his statements on this problem. Thus he writes in the *Metaphysics* (1044a35) : ' What is the formal cause (of man) ? His Essence. The final cause ? His end. But *perhaps* these two are the same.' In other parts of the same work he seems to be more assured of the identity between the *Form* and the *end* of a change or movement. Thus we read (1069b/1070a) : ' Everything that changes . . is changed *by* something *into* something. That by which it is changed is the immediate mover ; . . that into which it is changed, the Form.' And later (1070a, 9/10) : ' There are three kinds of substance : first, matter . . ; secondly, the nature towards which it moves ; and thirdly, the particular substance which is composed of these two.' Now since what is here called ' nature ' is as a rule called ' Form ' by Aristotle, and since it is here described as an end of movement, we have : *Form = end*.

¹⁶ For the doctrine that movement is the realization or actualization of potentialities, see for instance *Metaphysics*, Book IX ; or 1065b17, where the term ' buildable ' is used to describe a definite potentiality of a prospective house : 'When the " buildable " . . actually exists, then it is being built ; and this is the process of building.' Cp. also Aristotle's *Physics*, 201b4 f. ; furthermore, see Gomperz, *op. cit.*, book 6, ch. 11, § 5.

¹⁷ Cp. *Metaphysics*, 1049b5. See further Book V, ch. IV, and especially 1015a12 f., Book VII, ch. IV, especially 1029b15.

¹⁸ For the definition of the soul as the First Entelechy, see the reference given by Zeller, *op. cit.*, vol. II, p. 3, n. 1. For the meaning of Entelechy as formal cause, see *op. cit.*, vol. I, 379, note 2. Aristotle's use of this term is anything but precise. (See also *Met.*, 1035b15.) Cp. also note 19 to chapter 5, and text.

¹⁹ For this and the next quotation see Zeller, *op. cit.*, I, 46.

²⁰ Cp. *Politics*, II, 8, 21 (1269a), with its references to Plato's various Myths of the Earthborn (*Rep.*, 414c ; *Pol.*, 271a ; *Tim.*, 22c ; Laws, 677a).

²¹ Cp. Hegel, *Lectures on the Philosophy of History*, transl. by J. Sibree, London 1914, Introduction, 23 ; see also Loewenberg's *Hegel—Selections* (The Modern Student's Library), 366.—The whole Introduction, especially this and the following pages, shows clearly Hegel's dependence upon Aristotle. That Hegel was aware of it is shown by the way in which he alluded to Aristotle on p. 59 (Loewenberg's edition, 412).

²² Hegel, *op. cit.*, 23 (Loewenberg's edition, 365).

²³ Cp. Caird, *Hegel* (Blackwood 1911), 26 f.

²⁴ The next quotations are from the place referred to in notes 21 and 22.

²⁵ For the following remarks, see *Hegel's Philosophical Propaedeutics*, 2nd Year, *Phenomenology of the Spirit*. Transl. by W. T. Harris (Loewenberg's edition, 68 ff.). I deviate slightly from this translation. My remarks allude to the following interesting passages : § 23 : ' The impulse of self-consciousness ' (' self-consciousness ' in German means also self-assertion ; cp. the end of chapter 16) ' consists in this : to realize its . . " true nature ". . . It is therefore . . active . . in asserting itself externally . .' § 24 : ' Self-consciousness has in its culture, or movement, three stages : . . . (2) *in so far as it is related to another self* . . : *the relation of master and slave (domination and servitude)*.' Hegel does not mention any other ' relation to another self '.— We read further : ' (3) *The Relation of Master and Slave*. . . § 32 : In order to assert itself as free being and *to obtain recognition* as such, self-consciousness must exhibit itself to another self. . . § 33 : . . With the reciprocal demand for recognition there enters . . the relation of master and slave between them . . § 34 : Since . . each must strive to assert and prove himself . . the one who prefers life to freedom enters into a condition of slavery, thereby showing that he has not the capacity ' (' nature ' would have been Aristotle's

or Plato's expression) ' . . for his independence. . . § 35 : . . The one who serves is devoid of selfhood and has another self in place of his own. . . The master, on the contrary, looks upon the servant as reduced, and upon his own individual will as preserved and elevated . . § 36 : The individual will of the servant . . is cancelled in his fear of the master . .' etc. It is difficult to overlook an element of hysteria in this theory of human relations and their reduction to mastership and servitude. I hardly doubt that Hegel's method of burying his thoughts under heaps of words, which one must remove in order to get to his meaning (as a comparison between my various quotations and the original may show) is one of the symptoms of his hysteria ; it is a kind of escape, a way of shunning the daylight. I do not doubt that this method of his would make as excellent an object for psycho-analysis as his wild dreams of domination and submission. (It must be mentioned that Hegel's dialectics—see the next chapter—carries him, at the end of § 36 here quoted, beyond the master-slave relation ' to the universal will, the transition to positive freedom '. As will be seen from chapter 12 (especially sections II and IV), these terms are just euphemisms for the totalitarian state. Thus, mastership and servitude are very appropriately ' reduced to components ' of totalitarianism.)

With Hegel's remark quoted here (cp. § 35) that the slave is the man who prefers life to freedom, compare Plato's remark (*Republic*, 387a) that free men are those who fear slavery more than death. In a sense, this is true enough ; those who are not prepared to fight for their freedom will lose it. But the theory which is implied by both Plato and Hegel, and which is very popular with later authors also, is that men who give in to superior force, or who do not die rather than give in to an armed gangster, are, by nature, ' born slaves ' who do not deserve to fare better. This theory, I assert, can be held only by the most violent enemies of civilization.

[26] For a criticism of Wittgenstein's view that, while science investigates matters of fact, the business of philosophy is the clarification of meaning, see notes 46 and especially 51 and 52 to this chapter. (Cp. further, H. Gomperz, *The Meanings of Meaning*, in *Philosophy of Science*, vol. 8, 1941, especially p. 183.)

For the whole problem to which this digression (down to note 54 to this chapter) is devoted, viz. the problem of *methodological essentialism versus methodological nominalism*, cp. notes 27–30 to chapter 3, and text ; see further especially note 38 to the present chapter.

[27] For Plato's, or rather Parmenides', distinction between knowledge and opinion (a distinction which continued to be popular with more modern writers, for example with Locke and Hobbes), see notes 22 and 26 to chapter 3, and text ; further, notes 19 to chapter 5, and 25–27 to chapter 8. For Aristotle's corresponding distinction, cp. for example *Metaphysics* 1039b31 and *Anal. Post.*, I, 33 (88b30 ff.) ; II, 19 (100b5).

For Aristotle's distinction between *demonstrative* and *intuitive* knowledge, see the last chapter of the *Anal. Post.* (II, 19, especially 100b 5–17 ; see also 72b 18–24, 75b31, 84a31, 90a6–91a11.) For the connection between demonstrative knowledge and the ' causes ' of a thing which are ' distinct from its essential nature ' and thereby require a middle term, see *op. cit.* II, 8 (especially 93a5, 93b26). For the analogous connection between intellectual intuition and the ' indivisible form ' which it grasps—the indivisible essence and individual nature which is identical with its cause—see *op. cit.*, 72b24, 77a4, 85a1, 88b35. See also *op. cit.* 90a31 : ' To know the nature of a thing is to know the reason why it is ' (i.e. its cause) ; and 93b21 : ' There are essential natures which are immediate, i.e. basic premises.'

For Aristotle's recognition that we must stop somewhere in the regression of proofs or demonstrations, and accept certain *principles* without proof, see for example *Metaphysics*, 1006a7 : ' It is impossible to prove everything, for then there would arise an infinite regression . .' See also *Anal. Post.*, II, 3 (90b, 18–27).

I may mention that my analysis of Aristotle's theory of definition agrees largely with that of Grote, but partly disagrees with that of Ross. The very great difference between the interpretations of these two writers may be just indicated by two quotations, both taken from chapters devoted to the analysis of Aristotle's *Anal. Post.*, Book II. ' In the second book, Aristotle turns to consider demonstration as the instrument whereby *definition* is reached.' (Ross, *Aristotle*, 2nd ed., p. 49.) This may be contrasted with : ' The Definition can never be demonstrated, for it declares only the essence of the subject . . ; whereas Demonstration assumes the essence to be known . .' (Grote, *Aristotle*, 2nd ed., 241 ; see also 240/241. Cp. also end of note 29 below.)

²⁸ Cp. Aristotle's *Metaphysics*, 1031b7 and 1031b20. See also 996b20 : ' We have knowledge of a thing if we know its essence.'

²⁹ ' A definition is a statement that describes the essence of a thing ' (Aristotle, *Topics*, I, 5, 101b36 ; VII, 3, 153a, 153a15, etc. See also *Met.*, 1042a17)—' The definition . . reveals the essential nature.' (*Anal. Post.*, II, 3., 91a1).—' Definition is . . a statement of the nature of the thing ' (93b28). —' Only those things have essences whose formulæ are definitions.' (*Met.*, 1030a5 f.)—' The essence, whose formula is a definition, is also called the substance of a thing.' (*Met.*, 1017b21)—' Clearly, then, the definition is the formula of the essence . .' (*Met.*, 1031a13).

Regarding the principles, i.e. the starting points or basic premises of proofs, we must distinguish between two kinds. (1) The logical principles (cp. *Met.*, 996b25 ff.) and (2) the premises from which proofs must proceed and which cannot be proven in turn if an infinite regression is to be avoided (cp. note 27 to this chapter). The latter are definitions : ' The basic premises of proofs are definitions ' (*Anal. Post.*, II, 3., 90b23 ; cp. 89a17, 90a35, 90b23). See also Ross, *Aristotle*, p. 45/46, commenting upon *Anal. Post.*, I, 4., 20–74a4 : ' The premises of science ', Ross writes (p. 46), ' will, we are told, be *per se* in either sense (*a*) or sense (*b*).' On the previous page we learn that a premise is necessary *per se* (or essentially necessary) on the senses (*a*) and (*b*) *if it rests upon a definition*.

³⁰ ' If it has a name, then there will be a formula of its meaning ', says Aristotle (*Met.*, 1030a14 ; see also 1030b24) ; and he explains that not every formula of the meaning of a name is a definition ; but if the name is one of a species of a genus, then the formula will be a definition.

It is important to note that in my use (I follow here the modern use of the word) ' definition ' always refers to the whole definition sentence, while Aristotle (and others who follow him in this, e.g. Hobbes) sometimes uses the word also as a synonym for ' definiens '.

Definitions are not of particulars, but only of universals (cp. *Met.*, 1036a28) and only of essences, i.e. of something which is the species of a genus (i.e. a *last differentia* ; cp. *Met.*, 1038a19) and an indivisible form, see also *Anal. Post.* II, 13., 97b6 f.

³¹ That Aristotle's treatment is not very lucid may be seen from the end of note 27 to this chapter, and from a further comparison of these two interpretations. The greatest obscurity is in Aristotle's treatment of the way in which, by a process of induction, we rise to definitions that are principles ; cp. especially *Anal. Post.*, II, 19, pp. 100a f.

³² For Plato's doctrine, see notes 25–27 to chapter 8, and text.

Grote writes (*Aristotle*, 2nd ed., 260) : ' Aristotle had inherited from Plato his doctrine of an infallible Nous or Intellect, enjoying complete immunity from error.' Grote continues to emphasize that, as opposed to Plato, Aristotle does not despise observational experience, but rather assigns to his Nous (i.e. intellectual intuition) 'a position as terminus and correlate to the process of Induction' (*loc. cit.*, see also *op. cit.*, p. 577). This is so ; but observational experience has apparently only the function of priming and developing our intellectual intuition for its task, the intuition of the universal essence ; and, indeed, nobody has ever explained how definitions, *which are beyond error*, can be reached by induction.

[33] Aristotle's view amounts to the same as Plato's in so far as there is for both, in the last instance, no possible appeal to argument. All that can be done is to assert *dogmatically* of a certain definition that it is a true description of its essence ; and if asked why this and no other description is true, all that remains is an appeal to the 'intuition of the essence'.

Aristotle speaks of induction in at least two senses—in a more heuristic sense of a method leading us to 'intuit the general principle' (cp. *An. Pri.*, 67a22f., 27b25-33, *An. Post.*, 71a7, 81a38-b5, 100b4 f.) and in a more empirical sense (cp. *An. Pri.*, 68b15-37, 69a16, *An. Post.*, 78a35, 81b5 ff., *Topics*, 105a13, 156a4, 157a34).

A case of an apparent contradiction, which, however, might be cleared up, is 77a4, where we read that a definition is neither universal nor particular. I suggest that the solution is not that a definition is 'not strictly a judgement at all' (as G. R. G. Mure suggests in the Oxford translation), but that it is not *simply* universal but 'commensurate', i.e. universal and *necessary*. (Cp. 73b26, 96b4, 97b25.)

For the 'argument' of *Anal. Post.* mentioned in the text, see 100b6 ff. For the mystical union of the knowing and the known in *De Anima*, see especially 425b30 f., 430a20, 431a1 ; the decisive passage for our purpose is 430b27 f. : 'The intuitive grasp of the definition . . of the essence is never in error . . just as . . the seeing of the special object of sight can never be in error.' For the theological passages of the *Metaphysics*, see especially 1072b20 ('contact') and 1075a2. See also notes 59 (2) to chapter 10, 36 to chapter 12, and notes 3, 4, 6, 29–32, and 58 to chapter 24.

For 'the whole body of fact' mentioned in the next paragraph, see the end of *Anal. Post.* (100b15 f.).

It is remarkable how similar the views of Hobbes (a nominalist but *not* a methodological nominalist) are to Aristotle's methodological essentialism. Hobbes too believes that definitions are the basic premises of all knowledge (as opposed to opinion).

[34] I have developed this view of scientific method in my *Logic of Scientific Discovery* ; see, e.g. pp. 278 ff. and pp. 315 ff., for a fuller translation from *Erkenntnis*, vol. 5 (1934) where I say : 'We shall have to get accustomed to interpreting sciences as systems of hypotheses (instead of "bodies of knowledge"), i.e. of anticipations that cannot be established, but which we use as long as they are corroborated, and of which we are not entitled to say that they are "true" or "more or less certain" or even "probable".'

[35] The quotation is from my note in *Erkenntnis*, vol. 3 (1933), now retranslated in *The Logic of Scientific Discovery*, pp. 312 ff. ; it is a variation and generalization of a statement on geometry made by Einstein in his *Geometry and Experience*.

[36] It is, of course, not possible to estimate whether theories, argument, and reasoning, or else observation and experiment, are of greater significance for science ; for science is always *theory tested by observation and experiment*. But it is certain that all those 'positivists' who try to show that science is the 'sum total of our observations', or that it is observational rather than theoretical, are quite mistaken. The rôle of theory and argument in science can hardly be overrated.—Concerning the relation between proof and logical argument in general, see note 47 to this chapter.

[37] Cp. e.g. *Met.*, 1030a, 6 and 14 (see note 30 to this chapter).

[38] I wish to emphasize that I speak here about *nominalism versus essentialism* in a purely methodological way. I do not take up any position towards the *metaphysical* problem of universals, i.e. towards the metaphysical problem of nominalism versus essentialism (a term which I suggest should be used instead of the traditional term ' realism ') ; and I certainly do not advocate a metaphysical nominalism, although I advocate a methodological nominalism. (See also notes 27 and 30 to chapter 3.)

The opposition between *nominalist and essentialist definitions* made in the text is an attempt to reconstruct the traditional distinction between ' verbal ' and ' real ' definitions. *My main emphasis, however, is on the question whether the definition is read from the right to the left or from the left to the right ; or, in other words, whether it replaces a long story by a short one, or a short story by a long one.*

[39] My contention that in science *only* nominalist definitions occur (I speak here of explicit definitions only and neither of implicit nor of recursive definitions) needs some defence. It certainly does not imply that terms are not used more or less ' intuitively ' in science ; this is clear if only we consider that all chains of definitions must start with *undefined* terms, whose meaning can be exemplified but not defined. Further, it seems clear that in science, especially in mathematics, we often first use a term, for instance ' dimension ' or ' truth ', intuitively, but proceed later to define it. But this is a rather rough description of the situation. A more precise description would be this. Some of the undefined terms used intuitively can be sometimes replaced by defined terms of which it can be shown that they fulfil the intentions with which the undefined terms have been used ; that is to say, to every sentence in which the undefined terms occurred (e.g. which was interpreted as analytic) there is a corresponding sentence in which the newly defined term occurs (which follows from the definition).

One certainly can say that K. Menger has recursively defined ' Dimension ' or that A. Tarski has defined ' Truth ' ; but this way of expressing matters may lead to misunderstandings. What has happened is that Menger gave a purely nominal definition of classes of sets of points which he labelled ' *n*-dimensional ', because it was possible to replace the intuitive mathematical concept ' *n*-dimensional ' by the new concept in all important contexts ; and the same can be said of Tarski's concept ' Truth '. Tarski gave a nominal definition (or rather a method of drafting nominal definitions) which he labelled ' Truth ', since a system of sentences could be derived from the definition corresponding to those sentences (like the law of the excluded middle) which had been used by many logicians and philosophers in connection with what they called ' Truth '.

[40] If anything, our language would gain precision if we were to avoid definitions and take the immense trouble of always using the defining terms instead of the defined terms. For there is a source of imprecision in the current methods of definition : Carnap has developed (in 1934) what appears to be the first method of avoiding inconsistencies in a language using definitions. Cp. *Logical Syntax of Language*, 1937, § 22, p. 67. (See also Hilbert-Bernays, *Grundlagen d. Math.*, 1939, II, p. 295, note 1.) Carnap has shown that in most cases a language admitting definitions will be inconsistent even if the definitions satisfy the general rules for forming definitions. The comparative practical unimportance of this inconsistency merely rests upon the fact that we can always eliminate the defined terms, replacing them by the defining terms.

[41] Several examples of this method of introducing the new term only after the need has arisen may be found in the present book. Dealing, as it does, with philosophical positions, it can hardly avoid introducing, for the sake of brevity, *names* for these positions. This is the reason why I have to make use of so many ' isms '. But in many cases these names are introduced only after the positions in question have been described.

[42] In a more systematic criticism of the essentialist method, three problems might be distinguished which essentialism can neither escape nor solve. (1) The problem of distinguishing clearly between a mere verbal convention and an essentialist definition which 'truly' describes an essence. (2) The problem of distinguishing 'true' essential definitions from 'false' ones. (3) The problem of avoiding an infinite regression of definitions.—I shall briefly deal with the second and third of these problems only. The third of these problems will be dealt with in the text; for the second, see notes 44 (1) and 54 to this chapter.

[43] The fact that a statement is true may sometimes help to explain why it appears to us as self-evident. This is the case with '2 + 2 = 4', or with the sentence 'the sun radiates light as well as heat'. But the opposite is clearly not the case. The fact that a sentence appears to some or even to all of us to be 'self-evident', that is to say, the fact that some or even all of us believe firmly in its truth and cannot conceive of its falsity, is no reason why it should be true. (The fact that we are unable to conceive of the falsity of a statement is in many cases only a reason for suspecting that our power of imagination is deficient or undeveloped.) It is one of the gravest mistakes if a philosophy ever offers self-evidence as an argument in favour of the truth of a sentence; yet this is done by practically all idealist philosophies. It shows that idealist philosophies are often systems of apologetics for some dogmatic beliefs.

The excuse that we are often in such a position that we must accept certain sentences for no better reason than that they are self-evident, is not valid. The principles of logic and of scientific method (especially the 'principle of induction' or the 'law of uniformity of nature') are usually mentioned as statements which we must accept, and which we cannot justify by anything but self-evidence. Even if this were so, it would be franker to say that we cannot justify them, and leave it at that. But, in fact, there is no need for a 'principle of induction'. (Cp. my *The Logic of Scientific Discovery*.) And as far as the 'principles of logic' are concerned, much has been done in recent years which shows that the self-evidence theory is obsolete. (Cp. especially Carnap's *Logical Syntax of Language* and his *Introduction to Semantics*.) See also note 44 (2).

[44] (1) If we apply these considerations to the intellectual intuition of essences, then we can see that essentialism is unable to solve the problem: How can we find out whether or not a proposed definition which is formally correct is true also; and especially, how can we decide between two competing definitions? It is clear that for the methodological nominalist the answer to a question of this kind is trivial. For let us assume that somebody maintains (with the *Oxford Dictionary*) that 'A puppy is a vain, empty-headed, impertinent young man', and that he insists upon upholding this definition against somebody who clings to our previous definition. In this case, the nominalist, if he is patient enough to do so, will point out that a quarrel about labels does not interest him, since their choice is arbitrary; and he may suggest, *if there is any danger of ambiguity*, that one can easily introduce two different labels, for example 'puppy$_1$' and 'puppy$_2$'. And if a third party should support that 'A puppy is a brown dog', then the nominalist will patiently suggest the introduction of the label 'puppy$_3$'. But should the contesting parties continue to quarrel, either because somebody insists that only his puppy is the legitimate one, or because he insists that his puppy must, at least, be labelled 'puppy$_1$', then even a very patient nominalist would only shrug his shoulders. (In order to avoid misunderstandings, it should be said that *methodological nominalism* does not discuss the question of the existence of universals; Hobbes, accordingly, is not a methodological nominalist, but what I should call an ontological nominalist.)

The same trivial problem, however, raises insurmountable difficulties for the essentialist method. We have already supposed that the essentialist

insists that, for instance, ' A puppy is a brown dog ' is not a correct definition
of the essence of ' puppiness '.   How can he defend this view ?   Only by an
appeal to his intellectual intuition of essences.   But this fact has the practical
consequence that the essentialist is reduced to complete helplessness, if his
definition is challenged.   For there are only two ways in which he can react.
The one is to reiterate stubbornly that his intellectual intuition is the only
true one, to which, of course, his opponent may reply in the same way, so
that we reach a deadlock instead of the absolutely final and indubitable
knowledge which we were promised by Aristotle.   The other is to admit
that his opponent's intuition may be as true as his own, but that it is of a
different essence, which he unfortunately denotes by the same name.   This
would lead to the suggestion that two different names should be used for the
two different essences, for example ' puppy₁' and ' puppy₂'.   But this step
means giving up the essentialist position altogether.   For it means that
we start with the defining formula and attach to it some label, i.e. that we
proceed ' from the right to the left ' ;   and it means that we shall have to
attach these labels arbitrarily.   This can be seen by considering that the
attempt to insist that a puppy₁ is, essentially, a young dog, while the brown dog
can only be a puppy₂, would clearly lead to the same difficulty which has driven
the essentialist into his present dilemma.   Accordingly, every definition must
be considered as equally admissible (provided it is formally correct) ;   which
means, in Aristotelian terminology, that one basic premise is just as true as
another (which is contrary to it) and that ' *it is impossible to make a false statement* '.   (This seems to have been pointed out by Antisthenes ;   see note 54 to
this chapter.)   Thus the Aristotelian claim that intellectual intuition is a
source of knowledge as opposed to opinion, unerringly and indubitably true,
and that it furnishes us with definitions which are the safe and necessary basic
premises of all scientific deduction, is baseless in every single one of its points.
And a definition turns out to be nothing but a sentence which tells us that the
defined term means the same as the defining formula, and that each can be
replaced by the other.   Its nominalist use permits us to cut a long story short
and is therefore of some practical advantage.   But its essentialist use can only
help us to replace a short story by a story which means the same but is much
longer.   This use can only encourage verbalism.

(2) For a criticism of Husserl's intuition of essences, cp. J. Kraft, *From
Husserl to Heidegger* (in German, 1932).   See also note 8 to chapter 24.   Of all
authors who hold related views, M. Weber had probably the greatest influence
upon the treatment of sociological problems.   He advocated for the social
sciences a ' method of intuitive understanding ' ;   and his ' ideal types ' largely
correspond to the essences of Aristotle and Husserl.   It is worth mentioning
that Weber saw, in spite of these tendencies, the inadmissibility of appeals to
self-evidence.   ' The fact that an interpretation possesses a high degree of
self-evidence proves in itself nothing about its empirical validity ' (*Ges. Aufsaetze*,
1922, p. 404) ;   and he says quite rightly that intuitive understanding ' *must
always be controlled by ordinary methods* '.   (*Loc. cit.*, italics mine.)   But if that
is so, then it is not a characteristic method of a science of ' human behaviour '
as he thinks ;   it also belongs to mathematics, physics, etc.   And it turns out
that those who believe that intuitive understanding is a method peculiar to
sciences of ' human behaviour ' hold such views mainly because they cannot
imagine that a mathematician or a physicist could become so well acquainted
with his object that he could ' get the feel of it ', in the way in which a sociologist ' gets the feel ' of human behaviour.

[45] ' Science assumes the definitions of all its terms . .' (Ross, *Aristotle*,
44 ;   cp. *Anal. Post.*, I, 2) ;   see also note 30 to this chapter.

[46] The following quotation is from R. H. S. Crossman, *Plato To-Day*
1937), pp. 71 f.

A very similar doctrine is expressed by M. R. Cohen and E. Nagel in their book, *An Introduction to Logic and Scientific Method* (1936), p. 232 : ' Many of the disputes about the true nature of property, of religion, of law, . . would assuredly disappear if the precisely defined equivalents were substituted for these words.' (See also notes 48 and 49 to this chapter.)

The views concerning this problem expressed by Wittgenstein in his *Tractatus Logico-Philosophicus* (1921/22) and by several of his followers are not as definite as those of Crossman, Cohen, and Nagel. Wittgenstein is an anti-metaphysician. ' The book ', he writes in the preface, ' deals with the problems of philosophy and shows, I believe, that the method of formulating these problems rests on the misunderstanding of the logic of our language.' He tries to show that metaphysics is ' simply nonsense ' and tries to draw a limit, in our language, between sense and nonsense : ' The limit can . . be drawn in languages and what lies on the other side of the limit will be simply nonsense.' According to Wittgenstein's book, propositions have sense. They are true or false. Philosophical propositions do not exist ; they only look like propositions, but are, in fact, nonsensical. The limit between sense and nonsense coincides with that between natural science and philosophy : ' The totality of true propositions is the total natural science (or the totality of the natural sciences).—Philosophy is not one of the natural sciences.' *The true task of philosophy, therefore, is not to formulate propositions ; it is, rather, to clarify propositions* : ' The result of philosophy is not a number of " philo- sophical propositions ", but to make propositions clear.' Those who do not see that, and propound philosophical propositions, talk metaphysical nonsense.

(It should be remembered, in this connection, that a sharp distinction between meaningful statements which have sense, and meaningless linguistic expressions which may look like statements but which are without sense, was first made by Russell in his attempt to solve the problems raised by the para- doxes which he had discovered. Russell's division of expressions which look like statements is three-fold, since statements which may be *true* or *false*, and *meaningless* or nonsensical pseudo-statements, may be distinguished. It is important to note that this use of the terms ' meaningless ' or ' senseless ' partly agrees with ordinary use, but is much sharper, since ordinarily one often calls real statements ' meaningless ', for example, if they are 'absurd ', i.e. self-contradictory, or obviously false. Thus a statement asserting of a certain physical body that it is at the same time in two different places is not meaningless but a false statement, or one which contradicts the use of the term ' body ' in classical physics ; and similarly, a statement asserting of a certain electron that it has a precise place and momentum is not meaningless— as some physicists have asserted, and as some philosophers have repeated— but it simply contradicts modern physics.)

What has been said so far can be summed up as follows. Wittgenstein looks for a line of demarcation between sense and nonsense, and finds that this demarcation coincides with that between science and metaphysics, i.e. between scientific sentences and philosophical pseudo-propositions. (That he wrongly identifies the sphere of the natural sciences with that of *true* sentences shall not concern us here ; see, however, note 51 to this chapter.) This interpretation of his aim is corroborated when we read : ' Philosophy limits the . . sphere of natural science.' (All sentences so far quoted are from pp. 75 and 77.)

How is the line of demarcation ultimately drawn ? How can ' science ' be distinguished from ' metaphysics ', and thereby ' sense ' from ' nonsense ' ? It is the reply given to this question which establishes the similarity between Wittgenstein's theory and that of Crossman and the rest. Wittgenstein implies that the terms or ' signs ' used by scientists have meaning, while the metaphysician ' has given no meaning to certain signs in his propositions ' ; this is what he writes (pp. 187 and 189) : ' The right method of philosophy would be this. To say nothing except what can be said, i.e. the propositions of natural science, i.e. something that has nothing to do with philosophy : and then always when someone else wished to say something metaphysical, to demonstrate to him that he had given no meaning to certain signs in his propositions.' In practice, this implies that we should proceed by asking the metaphysician : ' What do you mean by this word ? What do you mean by that word ? ' In other words, *we demand a definition from him ; and if it is not forthcoming, we assume that the word is meaningless.*

This theory, as will be shown in the text, overlooks the facts (*a*) that a witty and unscrupulous metaphysician every time he is asked, ' What do you mean by this word ? ', will quickly proffer a definition, so that the whole game develops into a trial of patience ; (*b*) that the natural scientist is in no better logical position than the metaphysician ; and even, if compared with a metaphysician who is unscrupulous, in a worse position.

It may be remarked that Schlick, in *Erkenntnis*, 1, p. 8, where he deals with Wittgenstein's doctrine, mentions the difficulty of an infinite regress ; but the solution he suggests (which seems to lie in the direction of inductive definitions or ' constitutions ', or perhaps of operationalism ; cp. note 50 to this chapter) is neither clear nor able to solve the problem of demarcation. I think that certain of the intentions of Wittgenstein and Schlick in demanding a philosophy of meaning are fulfilled by that logical theory which Tarski has called ' Semantics '. But I also believe that the correspondence between these intentions and Semantics does not go far ; for Semantics *propounds propositions* ; it does not only ' clarify ' them.—These comments upon Wittgenstein are continued in notes 51–52 to the present chapter. (See also notes 8 (2) and 32 to chapter 24 ; and 10 and 25 to chapter 25.)

[47] It is important to distinguish between a logical deduction in general, and a proof or demonstration in particular. A *proof* or *demonstration* is a deductive argument by which the truth of the conclusion is finally established ; this is how Aristotle uses the term, demanding (for example, in *Anal. Post.*, I, 4, pp. 73a, ff.) that the ' necessary ' truth of the conclusion should be established ; and this is how Carnap uses the term (see especially *Logical Syntax*, § 10, p. 29, § 47, p. 171), showing that conclusions which are ' demonstrable ' in this sense are ' analytically ' true. (Into the problems concerning the terms ' analytic ' and ' synthetic ', I shall not enter here

Since Aristotle, it has been clear that not all logical deductions are proofs (i.e. demonstrations) ; there are also logical deductions which are not proofs ; for example, we can deduce conclusions from admittedly false premises, and such deductions are not called proofs. Non-demonstrative deductions are called by Carnap ' derivations ' (*loc. cit.*). It is interesting that a name for these non-demonstrative deductions has not been introduced earlier ; it shows the preoccupation with proofs, a preoccupation which arose from the Aristotelian prejudice that ' science ' or ' scientific knowledge ' must establish all its statements, i.e. accept them either as self-evident premises, or prove them. But the position is this. *Outside of pure logic and pure mathematics nothing can be proved.* Arguments in other sciences (and even some within mathematics, as I. Lakatos has shown) are not proofs but merely *derivations*.

It may be remarked that there is a far-reaching parallelism between the problems of *derivation* on the one side and *definition* on the other, and between the problems of the *truth of sentences* and that of the *meaning of terms*.

A derivation starts with premises and leads to a conclusion ; a definition starts (if we read it from the right to the left) with the defining terms and leads to a defined term. A derivation informs us about the truth of the conclusion, *provided* we are informed about the truth of the premises ; a definition informs us about the meaning of the defined term, *provided* we are informed about the meaning of the defining terms. Thus a derivation shifts the problem of *truth* back to the premises, without ever being able to solve it ; and a definition shifts the problem of *meaning* back to the defining terms, without ever being able to solve it.

[48] The reason why the defining terms are likely to be rather less clear and precise than the defined terms is that they are as a rule more abstract and general. This is not necessarily true if certain modern methods of definition are employed (' definition by abstraction ', a method of symbolic logic) ; but it is certainly true of all those definitions which Crossman can have in mind, and especially of all Aristotelian definitions (by *genus* and *differentia*).

It has been held by some positivists, especially under the influence of Locke and Hume, that it is possible to define abstract terms like those of science or of politics (see text to next note) in terms of particular, concrete observations or even of sensations. Such an ' inductive ' method of definition has been called by Carnap ' constitution '. But we can say that it is impossible to ' constitute ' universals in terms of particulars. (With this, cp. my *The Logic of Scientific Discovery*, especially sections 14, pp. 64 ff., and 25, p. 93 ; and Carnap's *Testability and Meaning*, in *Philosophy of Science*, vol. 3, 1936, pp. 419 ff., and vol. 4, pp. 1 ff.)

[49] The examples are the same as those which Cohen and Nagel, *op. cit.*, 232 f., recommend for definition. (Cp. note 46 to this chapter.)

Some general remarks on the uselessness of essentialist definitions may be added here. (Cp. also end of note 44 (1) to this chapter.)

(1) The attempt to solve a factual problem by reference to definitions usually means the substitution of a merely verbal problem for the factual one. (There is an excellent example of this method in Aristotle's *Physics*, II, 6, towards the end.) This may be shown for the following examples. (*a*) There is a factual problem : Can we return to the cage of tribalism ? And by what means ? (*b*) There is a moral problem : Should we return to the cage ?

The philosopher of meaning, if faced by (*a*) or (*b*), will say : It all depends on what you mean by your vague terms ; tell me how you define ' return ', ' cage ', ' tribalism ', *and with the help of these definitions I may be able to decide your problem*. Against this, I maintain that if the decision can be made with the help of the definitions, if it follows from the definitions, then the problem so decided was merely a verbal problem ; for it has been solved independently of facts or of moral decisions.

(2) An *essentialist* philosopher of meaning may do even worse, especially in connection with problem (*b*) ; he may suggest, for example, that it depends upon ' the essence ' or ' the essential character ' or perhaps upon ' the destiny ' of our civilization whether or not we should try to return. (See also note 61 (2) to this chapter.)

(3) Essentialism and the theory of definition have led to an amazing development in Ethics. The development is one of increasing abstraction and loss of touch with *the basis of all ethics*—the practical moral problems, to be decided by us here and now. It leads first to the general question, ' What is good ? ' or ' What is the Good ? ' ; next to ' What does " Good " mean ? ' and next to ' Can the problem " What does ' Good ' mean ? " be answered ? ' or ' Can " good " be defined ? ' G. E. Moore, who raised this last problem in his *Principia Ethica*, was certainly right in insisting that ' good ' in the moral sense cannot be defined in ' naturalistic ' terms. For, indeed, if we could, it would mean something like ' bitter ' or ' sweet ' or ' green ' or ' red ' ; and it would be utterly irrelevant from the point of view of morality. Just as we need not attain the bitter, or the sweet, etc., there would be no reason to take any moral interest in a naturalistic ' good '. But although Moore was right

in what is perhaps justly considered his main point, it may be held that an analysis of good or of any other concept or essence can in no way contribute to an ethical theory which bears upon the only relevant basis of all ethics, the immediate moral problem that must be solved here and now. Such an analysis can lead only to the substitution of a verbal problem for a moral one. (Cp. also note 18 (1) to chapter 5, especially upon the irrelevance of moral judgements.)

⁵⁰ I have in mind the methods of ' constitution ' (see note 48 to this chapter), ' implicit definition ', ' definition by correlation ', and ' operational definition '. The arguments of the ' operationalists ' seem to be in the main true enough ; but they cannot get over the fact that in their operational definitions, or descriptions, they need universal terms which have to be taken as undefined ; and to them, the problem applies again.

A few hints or allusions may be added here concerning the way we ' use our terms '. For the sake of brevity, these hints will refer without explanation to certain technicalities ; they may therefore, in the present form, not be generally understandable.

Of the so-called *implicit definitions*, especially in mathematics, Carnap has shown (*Symposion* I, 1927, 355 ff. ; cp. also his *Abriss*) that they do not ' define ' in the ordinary sense of this word ; a system of implicit definitions cannot be considered as defining a ' model ', but it defines a whole class of ' models '. Accordingly, the system of symbols defined by a system of implicit definitions cannot be considered as a system of *constants*, but they must be considered as *variables* (with a definite range, and bound by the system in a certain way to one another). I believe that there is a limited analogy between this situation and the way we ' use our terms ' in science The analogy can be described in this way. In a branch of mathematics i.n which we operate with signs defined by implicit definition, the fact that these signs have no ' definite meaning ' does not affect our operating with them, or the precision of our theories. Why is that so ? Because we do not overburden the signs. We do not attach a ' meaning ' to them, beyond that shadow of a meaning that is warranted by our implicit definitions. (And if we attach to them an intuitive meaning, then we are careful to treat this as a private auxiliary device, which must not interfere with the theory.) In this way, we try to keep, as it were, within the ' penumbra of vagueness ' or of ambiguity, and to avoid touching the problem of the precise limits of this penumbra or range ; and it turns out that we can achieve a great deal without discussing the meaning of these signs ; for nothing *depends* on their meaning. In a similar way, I believe, we can operate with these terms whose meaning we have learned ' operationally '. We use them, as it were, so that nothing depends upon their meaning, or as little as possible. Our ' operational definitions ' have the advantage of helping us to shift the problem into a field in which nothing or little depends on words. *Clear speaking is speaking in such a way that words do not matter.*

⁵¹ Wittgenstein teaches in the *Tractatus* (cp. note 46 to this chapter where further cross-references are given) that philosophy cannot propound propositions, and that all philosophical propositions are in fact senseless pseudopropositions. Closely connected with this is his doctrine that the true task of philosophy is not to propound sentences but to clarify them : ' The object of philosophy is the logical clarification of thoughts.—Philosophy is not a theory but an activity. A philosophical work consists essentially of elucidations.' (*Op. cit.*, p. 77.)

The question arises whether this view is in keeping with Wittgenstein's fundamental aim, the destruction of metaphysics by unveiling it as meaningless nonsense. In my *The Logic of Scientific Discovery* (see especially pp. 311 ff.), I have tried to show that Wittgenstein's method leads to a merely verbal solution and that it must give rise, in spite of its apparent radicalism, not to the destruction or to the exclusion or even to the clear demarcation of metaphysics, but to their intrusion into the field of science, and to their confusion with science. The reasons for this are simple enough.

(1) Let us consider one of Wittgenstein's sentences, for example, ' Philosophy is not a theory but an activity '. Surely, this is not a sentence belonging to ' total natural science (or the totality of the natural sciences) '. Therefore, according to Wittgenstein (see note 46 to this chapter), it cannot belong to ' the totality of true propositions '. On the other hand, it is not a false proposition either (since if it were, its negation would have to be true, and to belong to natural science). *Thus we arrive at the result that it must be ' meaningless ' or ' senseless ' or ' nonsensical ' ; and the same holds for most of Wittgenstein's propositions.* This consequence of his doctrine is recognized by Wittgenstein himself, for he writes (p. 189): ' My propositions are elucidatory in this way : he who understands me finally recognizes them as senseless . .' The result is important. Wittgenstein's own philosophy is senseless, and it is admitted to be so. ' On the other hand ', as Wittgenstein says in his Preface, ' the truth of the thoughts communicated here seems to me unassailable and definite. I am, therefore, of the opinion that the problems have in essentials been finally solved.' This shows that we can communicate *unassailably and definitely true thoughts* by way of propositions which are admittedly nonsensical, and that we can solve problems ' finally ' by propounding nonsense. (Cp. also note 8 (2, b) to chapter 24.)

Consider what this means. It means that all the metaphysical nonsense against which Bacon, Hume, Kant, and Russell have fought for centuries may now comfortably settle down, and even frankly admit that it is nonsense. (Heidegger does so ; cp. note 87 to chapter 12.) For now we have a new kind of nonsense at our disposal, nonsense that communicates thoughts whose truth is unassailable and definitive ; in other words, *deeply significant nonsense*.

I do not deny that Wittgenstein's thoughts are unassailable and definitive. For how could one assail them ? Obviously, whatever one says against them must be philosophical and therefore nonsense. And it can be dismissed as such. We are thus faced with that kind of position which I have described elsewhere, in connection with Hegel (cp. note 33 to chapter 12) as a *reinforced dogmatism*. ' All you need ', I wrote in my *Logik der Forschung* (now translated as *The Logic of Scientific Discovery* : see p. 51), p. 21, ' is to determine the conception of " sense " or of " meaning " in a suitably narrow way, and you can say of all uncomfortable questions that you cannot find any " sense " or " meaning " in them. By recognizing the problems of natural science alone as " meaningful ", every debate about the concept of meaning must become nonsensical. Once enthroned, the dogma of meaning is for ever raised above the possibility of attack. It is " unassailable and definitive ".'

(2) But not only does Wittgenstein's theory invite every kind of metaphysical nonsense to pose as deeply significant ; it also blurs what I have called (*op. cit.*, p. 7) the *problem of demarcation*. This he does because of his naïve idea that there is something ' essentially ' or ' by nature ' scientific and something ' essentially ' or ' by nature ' metaphysical and that it is our task to discover the ' natural ' demarcation between these two. ' Positivism ', I may quote myself again (*op. cit.*, p. 8), ' interprets the problem of demarcation in a naturalistic way ; instead of interpreting this question as one to be decided according to practical usefulness, it asks for a difference that exists " by nature ", as it were, between natural science and metaphysics.' But it is clear that the philosophical or methodological task can only be to suggest and to devise a useful demarcation between these two. This can hardly be done by characterizing metaphysics as 'senseless' or 'meaningless'. First, because these terms are better fitted for giving vent to one's personal indignation

about metaphysicians and metaphysical systems than for a technical character-ization of a line of demarcation. Secondly, because the problem is only shifted, for we must now ask : ' What do " meaningful " and " meaningless " mean?' If ' meaningful ' is only an equivalent for ' scientific ', and ' meaning-less ' for ' non-scientific ', then we have clearly made no progress. For reasons such as these I suggested (*op. cit.*, 8 ff., 21 f., 227) that we eliminate the emotive terms ' meaning ', ' meaningful ', ' meaningless ', etc., from the methodological discussion altogether. (Recommending that we solve the problem of demarca-tion by using falsifiability or testability, or dergees of testability, as criterion of the empirical character of a scientific system, I suggested that it was of no advantage to introduce ' meaningful ' as an emotive equivalent of ' testable '.) * In spite of my explicit refusal to regard falsifiability or testability (or any-thing else) as a ' *criterion of meaning* ', I find that philosophers frequently attribute to me the proposal to adopt this as a criterion of meaning or of ' meaningfulness '. (See, for example, *Philosophic Thought in France and in the United States*, edited by M. Farber, 1950, p. 570.) *

But even if we eliminate all reference to ' meaning ' or ' sense ' from Wittgenstein's theories, his solution of the problem of demarcating science from metaphysics remains most unfortunate. For since he identifies ' the totality of true propositions ' with the totality of natural science, he excludes all those hypotheses from ' the sphere of natural science ' which are not true. And since we can never know of a hypothesis whether or not it is true, we can never know whether or not it belongs to the sphere of natural science. The same unfortunate result, namely, a demarcation that excludes all hypotheses from the sphere of natural science, and therefore includes them in the field of metaphysics, is attained by Wittgenstein's famous ' principle of verifi-cation ', as I pointed out in *Erkenntnis*, 3 (1933), p. 427. (For a hypothesis is, strictly speaking, not verifiable, and if we speak loosely, then we can say that even a metaphysical system like that of the early atomists has been verified.) Again, this conclusion has been drawn in later years by Wittgenstein himself, who, according to Schlick (cp. my *The Logic of Scientific Discovery*, note 7 to section 4), asserted in 1931 that scientific theories are ' not really propositions ', i.e. not meaningful. Theories, hypotheses, that is to say, the most important of all scientific utterances, are thus thrown out of the temple of natural science, and therefore put on a level with metaphysics.

Wittgenstein's original view in the *Tractatus* can only be explained by the assumption that he overlooked the difficulties connected with the status of a scientific hypothesis which always goes *far beyond a simple enunciation of fact* ; he overlooked the problem of universality or generality. In this, he followed in the footsteps of earlier positivists, notably of Comte, who wrote (cp. his *Early Essays on Social Philosophy*, edited by H. D. Hutton, 1911, p. 223 ; see F. A. von Hayek, *Economica*, VIII, 1941, p. 300) : ' Observation of facts is the only solid basis of human knowledge . . . a proposition which does not admit of being reduced to a simple enunciation of fact, special or general, can have no real and intelligible sense.' Comte, although he remained unaware of the gravity of the problem hidden behind the simple phrases ' general fact ', at least *mentions* this problem, by inserting the words ' special or general '. If we omit these words, then the passage becomes a very clear and concise formulation of Wittgenstein's fundamental criterion of sense or meaning, as formulated by him in the *Tractatus* (all propositions are truth-functions of, and therefore reducible to, atomic propositions, i.e. pictures of atomic facts), and as expounded by Schlick in 1931.—Comte's criterion of meaning was adopted by J. S. Mill.

To sum up. The anti-metaphysical theory of meaning in Wittgenstein's *Tractatus*, far from helping to combat metaphysical dogmatism and oracular philosophy, represents a reinforced dogmatism that opens wide the door to the enemy, deeply significant metaphysical nonsense, and throws out, by the same door, the best friend, that is to say, scientific hypothesis.

⁵² It appears that irrationalism in the sense of a doctrine or creed that does not propound connected and debatable arguments but rather propounds aphorisms and dogmatic statements which must be ' understood ' or else left alone, will generally tend to become the property of an esoteric circle of the initiated. And, indeed, this prognosis seems to be partly corroborated by some of the publications that come from Wittgenstein's school. (I do not wish to generalize ; for example, everything I have seen of F. Waismann's writing is presented as a chain of rational and exceedingly clear arguments, and entirely free from the attitude of ' *take it or leave it* '.)

Some of these esoteric publications seem to be without a serious problem ; to me, they appear to be subtle for subtlety's sake. It is significant that they come from a school which started by denouncing philosophy for the barren subtlety of its attempts to deal with pseudo-problems.

I may end this criticism by stating briefly that I do not think that there is much justification for fighting metaphysics in general, or that anything worth while will result from such a fight. It is necessary to solve the problem of the demarcation of science from metaphysics. But we should recognize that many metaphysical systems have led to important scientific results. I mention only the system of Democritus ; and that of Schopenhauer which is very similar to that of Freud. And some, for instance those of Plato or Male-branche or Schopenhauer, are beautiful structures of thought. But I believe, at the same time, that we should fight those metaphysical systems which tend to bewitch and to confuse us. But clearly, we should do the same even with un-metaphysical and anti-metaphysical systems, if they exhibit this dangerous tendency. And I think that we cannot do this at one stroke. We have rather to take the trouble to analyse the systems in some detail ; we must show that we understand what the author means, but that what he means is not worth the effort to understand it. (It is characteristic of all these dogmatic systems and especially of the esoteric systems that their admirers assert of all critics that ' they do not understand ' ; but these admirers forget that understanding must lead to agreement only in the case of sentences with a trivial content. In all other cases, one can understand *and* disagree.)

⁵³ Cp. Schopenhauer, *Grundprobleme* (4th ed., 1890, p. 147). He comments upon ' intellectually intuiting reason that makes its pronouncements from the tripod of the oracle ' (hence my term ' oracular philosophy ') ; and he continues : ' This is the origin of that philosophic method which entered the stage immediately after Kant, of this method of mystifying and imposing upon people, of deceiving them and throwing dust in their eyes—the method of windbaggery. One day this era will be recognized by the history of philosophy as the *age of dishonesty*.' (Then follows the passage quoted in the text.) Concerning the irrationalist attitude of ' *take it or leave it* ', cp. also text to notes 39–40 to chapter 24.

⁵⁴ Plato's theory of definition (cp. note 27 to chapter 3 and note 23 to chapter 5), which Aristotle later developed and systematized, met its main opposition (1) from Antisthenes, (2) from the school of Isocrates, especially Theopompus.

(1) Simplicius, one of the best of our sources on these very doubtful matters, presents Antisthenes (*ad Arist. Categ.*, pp. 66b, 67b) as an opponent of Plato's theory of Forms or Ideas, and in fact, of the doctrine of essentialism and intellectual intuition altogether. ' I can see a horse, Plato ', Antisthenes is reported to have said, ' but I cannot see its horseness.' (A very similar argument is attributed by a lesser source, *D.L.*, VI, 53, to Diogenes the Cynic, and there is no reason why the latter should not have used it too.) I think that we may rely upon Simplicius (who appears to have had access to Theophrastus),

considering that Aristotle's own testimony in the *Metaphysics* (especially
in *Met.*, 1043b24) squares well with this anti-essentialism of Antisthenes.
    The two passages in the *Metaphysics* in which Aristotle mentions Antis-
thenes' objection to the essentialist theory of definitions are both very interesting.   In the first (*Met.*, 1024b32) we hear that Antisthenes raised the point
discussed in note 44 (1) to this chapter ; that is to say, that there is no way
of distinguishing between a ' true ' and a ' false ' definition (of ' puppy ', for
example) so that two apparently contradictory definitions would only refer
to two different essences, ' puppy$_1$' and ' puppy$_2$' ; thus there would be no
contradiction, and it would hardly be possible to speak of false sentences.
' Antisthenes ', Aristotle writes about this criticism, ' showed his crudity by
claiming that nothing could be described except by its proper formula, one
formula for one thing ; from which it followed that there could be no contradiction ; and almost that it was impossible to make a false statement.'   (The
passage has usually been interpreted as containing Antithenes' positive theory,
instead of his criticism of the doctrine of definition.   But this interpretation
neglects Aristotle's context.   The whole passage deals with the possibility
of false definitions, i.e. with precisely that problem which gives rise, in view
of the inadequacy of the theory of intellectual intuition, to the difficulties
described in note 44 (1).   And it is clear from Aristotle's text that he is
troubled by these difficulties as well as by Antisthenes' attitude towards them.)
The second passage (*Met.*, 1043b24) also agrees with the criticism of essentialist
definitions developed in the present chapter.   It shows that Antisthenes
attacked essentialist definitions as useless, as *merely substituting a long story for
a short one* ; and it shows further that Antisthenes very wisely admitted that,
although it is useless to *define*, it is possible to describe or to *explain* a thing by
referring to the similarity it bears to a thing already known, or, if it is composite, by explaining what its parts are.   ' Indeed there is ', Aristotle writes,
' something in that difficulty which has been raised by the Antisthenians and
other such-like uneducated people.   They said that what a thing is ' (or the
' what is it ' of a thing) ' cannot be defined ; for the so-called definition,
they say, is nothing but a long formula.   But they admit that it is possible
to explain, for example of silver, what sort of a thing it is ; for we may say
that it is similar to tin.'   From this doctrine it would follow, Aristotle adds,
' that it is possible to give a definition and a formula of the *composite* kind of
things or substances, whether they are sensible things, or objects of intellectual
intuition ; but not of their primary parts . .'   (In the sequel, Aristotle
wanders off, trying to link this argument with his doctrine that a defining
formula is *composed* of two parts, genus and differentia, which are related, and
united, like matter and form.)
    I have dealt here with this matter since it appears that the enemies of
Antisthenes, for example Aristotle (cp. *Topics*, I, 104b21), cited what he
said in a manner which has led to the impression that it is not Antisthenes'
criticism of essentialism but rather his positive doctrine.   This impression
was made possible by mixing it up with another doctrine probably held by
Antisthenes ; I have in mind the simple doctrine that we must speak plainly,
just using each term in one meaning, and that in this way we can avoid all
those difficulties whose solution is unsuccessfully attempted by the theory of
definitions.
    All these matters are, as mentioned before, very uncertain, owing to the
scantiness of our evidence.   But I think that Grote is likely to be right when
he characterizes ' this debate between Antisthenes and Plato ' as the ' first
protest of Nominalism against the doctrine of an extreme Realism ' (or in
our terminology, of an extreme essentialism).   Grote's position may be thus
defended against Field's attack (*Plato and His Contemporaries*, 167) that it is
' quite wrong ' to describe Antisthenes as a nominalist.

In support of my interpretation of Antisthenes, I may mention that against the scholastic theory of definitions, very similar arguments were used by Descartes (cp. *The Philosophical Works*, translated by Haldane and Ross, 1911, vol. I, p. 317) and, less clearly, by Locke (Essay, Book III, ch. III, § 11, to ch. IV, § 6 ; also ch. X, §§ 4 to 11 ; see especially ch. IV, § 5). Both Descartes and Locke, however, remained essentialists. Essentialism itself was attacked by Hobbes (cp. note 33 above) and by Berkeley who might be described as one of the first to hold a *methodological nominalism*, quite apart from his ontological nominalism ; see also note 7 (2) to chapter 25.

(2) Of other critics of the Platonic-Aristotelian theory of definition, I mention only Theopompus (quoted by Epictetus, II, 17, 4–10 ; see Grote, *Plato*, I, 324). I think it likely that, as opposed to the generally accepted view, Socrates himself would not have favoured the theory of definitions ; what he seems to have combated was the merely verbal solution of ethical problems ; and his so-called attempted definitions of ethical terms, considering their negative results, may well be attempts to destroy verbalist prejudices.

(3) I wish to add here that in spite of all my criticism I am very ready to admit Aristotle's merits. He is the founder of logic, and down to *Principia Mathematica*, all logic can be said to be an elaboration and generalization of the Aristotelian beginnings. (A new epoch in logic has indeed begun, in my opinion, though not with the so-called ' non-Aristotelian ' or ' multi-valued ' systems, but rather with the clear distinction between ' object-language ' and ' meta-language '.) Furthermore, Aristotle has the great merit of having tried to tame idealism by his common-sense approach which insists that only individual things are ' real ' (and that their ' forms ' and ' matter ' are only aspects or abstractions). * Yet this very approach is responsible for the fact that Aristotle does not even attempt to solve Plato's problem of universals (see notes 19 and 20 to chapter 3, and text), i.e., the problem of explaining why certain things resemble one another and others do not. For why should there not be as many different Aristotelian essences in things as there are things ? *

[55] The influence of Platonism especially upon the Gospel of St. John is clear ; and this influence is less noticeable in the earlier Gospels, though I do not assert that it is absent. Nevertheless the Gospels exhibit a clearly anti-intellectualist and anti-philosophizing tendency. They avoid an appeal to philosophical speculation, and they are definitely against scholarship and dialectics, for instance, that of the ' scribes ' ; but scholarship means, in this period, interpreting the scriptures in a dialectical and philosophical sense, and especially in the sense of the Neo-Platonists.

[56] The problem of nationalism and the superseding of Jewish parochial tribalism by internationalism plays a most important part in the early history of Christianity ; the echoes of these struggles can be found in the *Acts* (especially 10, 15 ff. ; 11, 1–18 ; see also *St. Matthew* 3, 9, and the polemics against tribal feeding taboos in *Acts* 10, 10–15). It is interesting that this problem turns up together with the social problem of wealth and poverty, and with that of slavery ; see *Galatians* 3, 28 ; and especially *Acts* 5, 1–11, where the retention of private property is described as mortal sin.

The survival in the Ghettos of eastern Europe, down to 1914 and even longer, of arrested and petrified forms of Jewish tribalism is very interesting (Cp. the way in which the Scottish tribes attempted to cling to their tribal life.)

[57] The quotation is from Toynbee, *A Study of History*, vol. VI, p. 202 ; the passage deals with the motive for the persecution of Christianity by the Roman rulers, who were usually very tolerant in matters of religion. ' The element in Christianity ', Toynbee writes, ' that was intolerable to the Imperial Government was the Christians' refusal to accept the Government's claim that it was entitled to compel its subjects to act against their conscience. . . So

far from checking the propagation of Christianity, the martyrdoms proved the most effective agencies of conversion . .'

⁵⁸ For Julian's Neo-Platonic Anti-Church with its Platonizing hierarchy, and his fight against the ' atheists ', i.e. Christianity, cp. for example Toynbee, *op. cit.*, V, pp. 565 and 584 ; I may quote a passage from J. Geffken (quoted by Toynbee, *loc. cit.*) : ' In Jamblichus ' (a pagan philosopher and number-mystic and founder of the Syrian school of Neo-Platonists, living about A.D. 300) ' the individual religious experience . . is eliminated. Its place is taken by a mystical church with sacraments, by a scrupulous exactness in carrying out the forms of worship, by a ritual that is closely akin to magic, and by a clergy. . . Julian's ideas about the elevation of the priesthood reproduce . . exactly the standpoint of Jamblichus, whose zeal for the priests, for the details of the forms of worship, and for a systematic orthodox doctrine has prepared the ground for the construction of a pagan church.' We can recognize in these principles of the Syrian Platonist and of Julian the development of the genuine Platonic (and perhaps also late Jewish ; cp. note 56 to this chapter) tendency to resist the revolutionary religion of individual conscience and humaneness by arresting all change and by introducing a rigid doctrine kept pure by a philosophic priest caste and by rigid taboos. (Cp. text to notes 14 and 18–23 to chapter 7 ; and chapter 8, especially text to note 34.) With Justinian's prosecution of non-Christians and heretics and his suppression of philosophy in 529, the tables are turned ; it is now Christianity which adopts totalitarian methods and the control of conscience by violence. The dark ages begin.

⁵⁹ For Toynbee's warning against an interpretation of the rise of Christianity in the sense of Pareto's advice (for which cp. notes 65 to chapter 10 and 1 to chapter 13) see, for example, *A Study of History*, V, 709.

⁶⁰ For Critias' and Plato's and Aristotle's cynical doctrine that religion is opium for the people, cp. notes 5 to 18 (especially 15 and 18) to chapter 8. (See also Aristotle's *Topics*, I, 2, 101a30 ff.) For later examples (Polybius and Strabo) see, for example, Toynbee, *op. cit.*, V, 646 f., 561. Toynbee quotes from Polybius (*Historiae*, VI, 56) : ' The point in which the Roman constitution excels others most conspicuously is to be found, in my opinion, in its handling of Religion. . . The Romans have managed to forge the main bond of their social order . . out of superstition.' etc. And he quotes from Strabo : ' A rabble . . cannot be induced to answer to the call of Philosophic Reason. . . In dealing with people of that sort, you cannot do without superstition.' etc. In view of this long series of Platonizing philosophers who teach that religion is ' opium for the people ' I fail to see how the imputation of similar motives to Constantine can be described as *anachronistic*.

It may be mentioned that it is a formidable opponent of whom Toynbee says, by implication, that he lacks historical sense : Lord Acton. For he writes (cp. his *History of Freedom*, 1909, p. 30 f., italics mine) of Constantine's relation to the Christians : ' Constantine, in adopting their faith, intended neither to abandon his predecessor's scheme of policy nor to renounce the fascinations of arbitrary authority, *but to strengthen his throne with the support of a religion* which had astonished the world by its power of resistance . .'

⁶¹ I admire the mediæval cathedrals as much as anybody, and I am perfectly prepared to recognize the greatness and uniqueness of mediæval craftsmanship. But I believe that æstheticism must never be used as an argument against humanitarianism.

The eulogy of the Middle Ages seems to begin with the Romantic movement in Germany, and it has become fashionable with the renaissance of this Romantic movement which unfortunately we are witnessing at the present time. It is, of course, an anti-rationalist movement ; it will be discussed from another point of view in chapter 24.

The two attitudes towards the Middle Ages, rationalism and anti-rational-ism, correspond to two *interpretations of ' history '* (cp. chapter 25).

(1) The rationalist interpretation of history views with hope those periods in which man attempted to look upon human affairs rationally.   It sees in the Great Generation and especially in Socrates, in early Christianity (down to Constantine), in the Renaissance and the period of the Enlightenment, and in modern science, parts of an often interrupted movement, the efforts of men to free themselves, to break out of the cage of the closed society, and to form an open society.   It is aware that this movement does not represent a ' law of progress ' or anything of that sort, but that it depends solely upon ourselves, and must disappear if we do not defend it against its antagonists as well as against laziness and indolence.   This interpretation sees in the intervening periods dark ages with their Platonizing authorities, their hierarchies of priest and tribalist orders of knights.

A classical formulation of this interpretation has been made by Lord Acton (*op. cit.*, p. 1 ; italics mine).   ' Liberty,' he writes, ' next to religion, has been the motive of good deeds and the common pretext of crime, from the sowing of the seed at Athens, two thousand five hundred and sixty years ago. . .   In every age its progress has been beset by its natural enemies, by ignorance and superstition, by lust of conquest and by love of ease, by the strong man's craving for power, and the poor man's craving for food.   During long intervals it has been utterly arrested . .   No obstacle has been so con-stant, or so difficult to overcome, as uncertainty and confusion touching the nature of true liberty.   *If hostile interests have wrought much injury, false ideas have wrought still more.*'

It is strange how strong a feeling of darkness prevails in the dark ages.   Their science and their philosophy are both obsessed by the feeling that *the truth has once been known, and has been lost.*   This expresses itself in the belief in the lost secret of the ancient philosophers' stone and in the ancient wisdom of astrology no less than in the belief that an idea cannot be of any value if it is new, and that every idea needs the backing of ancient authority (Aristotle and the Bible).   But the men who felt that the secret key to wisdom was lost in the past were right.   For this key is faith in reason, and liberty.   It is the free competition of thought, which cannot exist without freedom of thought.

(2) The other interpretation agrees with Toynbee in seeing, in Greek as well as in modern rationalism (since the Renaissance), an *aberration* from the path of faith.   ' To the present writer's eye ', Toynbee says (*A Study of History*, vol. V, p. 6 f., note ; italics mine), ' the common element of rationalism which may be discernible in the Hellenic and Western Civilization is not so distinctive as to mark this pair of societies off from all other representatives of the species. . .   If we regard the Christian element of our Western Civilization as being the essence of it, then our reversion to Hellenism might be taken to be, *not a fulfilment of the potentialities of Western Christendom, but an aberration from the proper path of Western growth—in fact, a false step which it may or may not be possible now to retrieve.*'

In contrast to Toynbee, I do not doubt for a minute that it is possible to retrieve this step and to return to the cage, to the oppressions, superstition, and pestilences, of the Middle Ages.   But I believe that we had much better not do so.   And I contend that what we ought to do will have to be decided by ourselves, through free decisions, and not by historicist essentialism ; nor, as Toynbee holds (see also note 49 (2) to this chapter), by ' the question of what the essential Character of the Western Civilization may be '.

(The passages here quoted from Toynbee are parts of his reply to a letter from Dr. E. Bevan ; and Bevan's letter, i.e. the first of his two letters quoted by Toynbee, seems to me to present very clearly indeed what I call the rationalist interpretation.)

⁶² See H. Zinsser, *Rats, Lice, and History* (1937), pp. 80 and 83 ; italics mine. Concerning my remark in the text, at the end of this chapter, that Democritus' science and morals still live with us, I may mention that a direct historical connection leads from Democritus and Epicurus via Lucretius not only to Gassendi but undoubtedly to Locke also. ' Atoms and the void ' is the characteristic phrase whose presence always reveals the influence of this tradition ; and as a rule, the natural philosophy of ' atoms and the void ' goes together with the moral philosophy of an altruistic hedonism or utilitarianism. In regard to hedonism and utilitarianism, I believe that it is indeed necessary to replace their principle : *maximize pleasure !* by one which is probably more in keeping with the original views of Democritus and Epicurus, more modest, and much more urgent. I mean the rule : *minimize pain !* I believe (cp. chapters 9, 24, and 25) that it is not only impossible but very dangerous to attempt to maximize the pleasure or the happiness of the people, since such an attempt must lead to totalitarianism. But there is little doubt that most of the followers of Democritus (down to Bertrand Russell, who is still interested in atoms, geometry, and hedonism) would have little quarrel with the suggested re-formulation of their pleasure principle provided it is taken for what it is meant, and not for an ethical criterion.

NOTES TO CHAPTER 12

General Note to this Chapter. Wherever possible, I refer in these notes to *Selections*, i.e. to *Hegel : Selections*, edited by J. Loewenberg, 1929. (From *The Modern Student's Library of Philosophy*.) This excellent and easily accessible selection contains a great number of the most characteristic passages from Hegel, so that it was possible in many cases to choose the quotations from them. Quotations from the *Selections* will, however, be accompanied by references to editions of the original texts. Wherever possible I have referred to ' *WW* ', i.e. to *Hegel's Sämtliche Werke*, herausgegeben von H. Glockner, Stuttgart (from 1927 on). An important version of the *Encyclopedia*, however, which is not included in *WW*, is quoted as ' *Encycl.* 1870 ', i.e., G. W. F. Hegel, *Encyclopädie*, herausgegeben von K. Rosenkranz, Berlin 1870. Passages from the *Philosophy of Law* (or *Philosophy of Right*) are quoted by paragraph numbers, and the letter L indicates that the passage is from the lecture notes added by Gans in his edition of 1833. I have not always adopted the wording of the translators.

¹ In his Inaugural Dissertation, *De Orbitis Planetarum*, 1801. (The asteroid Ceres had been discovered on the 1st of January, 1801.)

² Democritus, fragm., 118 (D²) ; cp. text to note 29 to chapter 10.

³ Schopenhauer, *Grundprobleme* (4th ed., 1890), p. 147 ; cp. note 53 to chapter 11.

⁴ The whole *Philosophy of Nature* is full of such definitions. H. Stafford Hatfield, for instance, translates (cp. his translation of Bavink, *The Anatomy of Modern Science*, p. 30) Hegel's definition of heat : ' Heat is the self-restoration of matter in its formlessness, its liquidity the triumph of its abstract homogeneity over specific definiteness, its abstract, purely self-existing continuity, as negation of negation, is here set as activity.' Similar is, for example, Hegel's definition of electricity.

For the next quotation see Hegel's *Briefe*, I, 373, quoted by Wallace, *The Logic of Hegel* (transl., p. xiv f., italics mine).

⁵ Cp. Falkenberg, *History of Modern Philosophy* (6th German ed., 1908, 612 ; cp. the English translation by Armstrong, 1895, 632).

⁶ I have in mind the various philosophies of ' evolution ' or ' progress ' or

emergence ' such as those of H. Bergson, S. Alexander, Field-Marshal Smuts or A. N. Whitehead.

[7] The passage is quoted and analysed in note 43 (2), below.

[8] For the eight quotations in this paragraph, cp. *Selections*, pp. 389 (= *WW*, vi, 71), 447, 443, 446 (three quotations) ; 388 (two quotations) (=*WW*, xi, 70). The passages are from *The Philosophy of Law* (§§ 272L, 258L, 269L, 270L) ; the first and the last are from the *Philosophy of History*.

For Hegel's holism, and for his organic theory of the state, see for example his reference to Menenius Agrippa (*Livy*, II, 32 ; for a criticism, see note 7 to chapter 10) in the *Philosophy of Law*, § 269L ; and his classical formulation of the opposition between the power of an organized body and the powerless ' heap, or aggregate, of atomic units ', at the end of § 290L (cp. also note 70 to this chapter).

Two other very important points in which Hegel adopts Plato's political teaching are : (1) The theory of the One, the Few, and the Many ; see, for example, *op. cit.*, § 273 : The monarch is *one* person ; the *few* enter the scene with the executive ; and the *many* . . with the legislative ; also the reference is to ' the many ' in § 301, etc. (2) The theory of the opposition between knowledge and opinion (cp. the discussion of *op. cit.*, § 270, on *freedom of thought*, in the text between notes 37 and 38, below), which Hegel uses for characterizing public opinion as the ' opinion of the many ' or even as the 'caprice of the many ', cp. *op. cit.*, §§ 316 ff., and note 76, below.

For Hegel's interesting criticism of Plato, and the even more interesting twist he gives to his own criticism, cp. note 43 (2) to this chapter.

[9] For these remarks, cp. especially chapter 25.

[10] Cp. *Selections*, xii (J. Loewenberg in the Introduction to the *Selections*).

[11] I have in mind not only his immediate philosophical predecessors (Fichte, Schlegel, Schelling, and especially Schleiermacher), or his ancient sources (Heraclitus, Plato, Aristotle), but especially Rousseau, Spinoza, Montesquieu, Herder, Burke (cp. section IV to this chapter), and the poet Schiller. Hegel's indebtedness to Rousseau, Montesquieu (cp. *The Spirit of the Laws*, XIX, 4 f.), and Herder, for his *Spirit of the Nation*, is obvious. His relations to Spinoza are of a different character. He adopts, or rather adapts, two important ideas of the determinist Spinoza. The first is that there is no freedom but in the rational recognition of the necessity of all things, and in the power which reason, by this recognition, may exert over the passions. This idea is developed by Hegel into an identification of reason (or ' Spirit ') with freedom, and of his teaching that freedom is the truth of necessity (*Selections*, 213, *Encycl.* 1870, p. 154). The second idea is Spinoza's strange moral positivism, his doctrine that might is right, an idea which he contrived to use for the fight against what he called tyranny i.e. the attempt to wield power beyond the limits of one's actual power. Spinoza's main concern being the freedom of thought, he taught that it is impossible for a ruler to force men's thoughts (for thoughts are free), and that the attempt to achieve the impossible is tyrannical. On this doctrine, he based his support of the power of the secular state (which, he naïvely hoped, would not curtail the freedom of thought) as against the church. Hegel also supported the state against the church, and he paid lip-service to the demand for freedom of thought whose great political significance he realized (cp. the preface to the *Phil. of Law*) ; but at the same time he perverted this idea, claiming that the state must decide what is true and false, and may suppress what it deems to be false (see the discussion of the *Phil. of Law*, § 270, in the text between notes 37 and 38, below). From Schiller, Hegel took (incidentally without acknowledgement or even indication that he was quoting) his famous dictum ' The history of the world is the World's court of justice '. But this dictum (at the end of § 340 of the *Phil. of Law* ; cp. text to note 26) implies a good deal

of Hegel's historicist political philosophy ; not only his worship of success and thus of power, but also his peculiar moral positivism, and his theory of the reasonableness of history.

The question whether Hegel was influenced by Vico seems to be still open. (Weber's German translation of the *New Science* was published in 1822.)

[12] Schopenhauer was an ardent admirer not only of Plato but also of Heraclitus. He believed that the mob fill their bellies like the beast ; he adopted Bias' dictum ' all men are wicked ' as his device ; and he believed that a Platonic aristocracy was the best government. At the same time, he hated nationalism, and especially German nationalism. He was a cosmopolite. The rather repulsive expressions of his fear and hatred of the revolutionaries of 1848 can be partly explained by his apprehension that under ' mob rules ' he might lose his independence, and partly by his hatred of the nationalist ideology of the movement.

[13] For Schopenhauer's suggestion of this motto (taken from *Cymbeline*, Act V, Sc. 4) see his *Will in Nature* (4th ed., 1878), p. 7. The two following quotations are from his *Works* (2nd ed., 1888), vol. V, 103 f., and vol. II, p. xvii, f. (i.e. Preface to the second ed. of the *World as Will and Idea* ; the italics are mine). I believe that everybody who has studied Schopenhauer must be impressed by his sincerity and truthfulness. Cp. also the judgement of Kierkegaard, quoted in the text to notes 19/20 to chapter 25.

[14] Schwegler's first publication (1839) was an essay in memory of Hegel. The quotation is from his *History of Philosophy*, transl. by H. Stirling, 7th ed., p. 322.

[15] ' To English readers Hegel was first introduced in the powerful statement of his principles by Dr. Hutchinson Stirling ', writes E. Caird (*Hegel*, 1883, Preface, p. vi) ; which may show that Stirling was taken quite seriously. The following quotation is from Stirling's *Annotations* to Schwegler's *History*, p. 429. I may remark that the motto of the present chapter is taken from p. 441 of the same work.

[16] Stirling writes (*op. cit.*, 441) : ' The great thing at last for Hegel was a good citizen, and for him who was already that, there was to Hegel's mind no call for philosophy. Thus he tells a M. Duboc who writes to him about his difficulties with the system, that, as a good head of a house and father of a family, possessed of a faith that is firm, he has pretty well enough, and may consider anything further, in the way of philosophy, for instance, as but . . an intellectual luxury.' Thus, according to Stirling, *Hegel was not interested in clearing up a difficulty in his system, but merely in converting ' bad ' citizens into ' good ' ones.*

[17] The following quotation is from Stirling, *op. cit.*, 444 f. Stirling continues the last sentence quoted in the text : ' I have gained much from Hegel, and will always thankfully acknowledge that much, but my position in his regard has been simply that of one who, in making the unintelligible intelligible, would do a service to the public.' And he ends the paragraph by saying : ' My general aim . . I conceive to be identical with Hegel's . . that, namely, of a Christian philosopher.'

[18] Cp., for example, *A Textbook of Marxist Philosophy*.

[19] I take this passage from the most interesting study, *Nationalism and the Cultural Crisis in Prussia, 1806-1815*, by E. N. Anderson (1939), p. 270. Anderson's analysis is critical of nationalism, and he clearly recognizes the neurotic and hysterical element in it (cp., for example, p. 6 f.). And yet I cannot entirely agree with his attitude. Led, I suppose, by the historian's desire for objectivity, he seems to me to take the nationalist movement too seriously. I cannot agree, more particularly, with his condemnation of King Frederick William for his lack of understanding of the nationalist movement. ' Frederick

William lacked the capacity for appreciating greatness ', Anderson writes on p. 271, ' whether in an ideal or in an action.   The course into nationalism which the rising German literature and philosophy opened so brilliantly for others remained closed to him.'   But by far the best of German literature and philosophy was anti-nationalistic ;   Kant and Schopenhauer were both anti-national, and even Goethe kept away from nationalism ;   and it is unjustifiable to demand of anybody, and especially of a simple, candid, conservative like the king, that he should get excited about Fichte's windbaggery.   Many will fully agree with the king's judgement when he spoke (*loc. cit.*) of ' eccentric, popular scribbling '.   Although I agree that the king's conservatism was very unfortunate, I feel the greatest respect for his simplicity, and his resistance to the wave of nationalist hysteria.

²⁰ Cp. *Selections*, xi (J. Loewenberg in the Introduction to the *Selections*).

²¹ Cp. notes 19 to chapter 5 and 18 to chapter 11, and text.

²² For this quotation see *Selections*, 103 (= *WW*, iii, 116) ;   for the next one, see *Selections*, 130 (= G. W. F. Hegel, *Werke*, Berlin and Leipzig 1832–1887, vol. vi, 224).   For the last quotation in this paragraph, see *Selections*, 131 (= *Werke*, 1832–1887, vol. vi, 224–5).

²³ Cp. *Selections*, 103 (= *WW*, iii, 103).

²⁴ Cp. *Selections*, 128 (= *WW*, iii, 141).

²⁵ I am alluding to Bergson, and especially to his *Creative Evolution*.   (Engl. transl. by A. Mitchell, 1913.)   It appears that the Hegelian character of this work is not sufficiently recognized ;   and, indeed, Bergson's lucidity and reasoned presentation of his thought sometimes make it difficult to realize how much his philosophy depends on Hegel.   But if we consider, for example, that Bergson teaches that *the essence is change*, or if we read passages like the following (cp. *op. cit.*, 275 and 278), then there remains little doubt.

' Essential also is the progress to reflection ', writes Bergson.   ' If our analysis is correct, it is consciousness, or rather super-consciousness, that is at the origin of life. . .   Consciousness corresponds exactly to the living being's power of choice ;   it is co-extensive with the fringe of possible action that surrounds real action :   *consciousness is synonymous* with invention and *with freedom.*'   (Italics mine.)   The identification of consciousness (or Spirit) with freedom is the Hegelian version of Spinoza.   This goes so far that theories can be found in Hegel which I feel inclined to describe as ' unmistakably Bergsonian ' ;   for example, ' The very essence of Spirit is activity ;   it realizes its potentiality ;   it makes itself its own deed, its own work . .' (*Selections*, 435 = *WW*, xi, 113.)

²⁶ Cp. notes 21 to 24 to chapter 11, and text.   Another characteristic passage is this (cp. *Selections*, 409 = *WW*, xi, 89) :   ' The principle of *Development* involves also the existence of a latent germ of being—a capacity or potentiality striving to realize itself.'—For the quotation later in the paragraph, cp. *Selections*, 468 (i.e. *Phil. of Law*, § 340 ;   see also note 11, above).

²⁷ Considering, on the other hand, that even a second-hand Hegelianism, i.e. a third- or fourth-hand Fichteanism and Aristotelianism, has often been noisily acclaimed as an original achievement, it is perhaps a little hard on Hegel to say that he was unoriginal.   (But cp. note 11.)

²⁸ Cp. Kant's *Critique of Pure Reason*, 2nd ed., p. 514 (top) ;   see also p. 518 (end of section 5) ;   for the motto of my Introduction, see Kant's letter to Mendelssohn of April 8th, 1766.

²⁹ Cp. note 53 to chapter 11, and text.

³⁰ It is perhaps reasonable to assume that what one usually calls the ' spirit of a language ' is very largely the *traditional standard of clarity* introduced by the great writers of that particular language.   There are some further traditional standards in a language, apart from clarity, for example, standards

of simplicity, of ornamentation, of brevity, etc. ; but the standard of clarity is perhaps the most important of them ; and it is a cultural inheritance which should be carefully guarded. Language is one of the most important institutions of social life, and its clarity is a condition of its functioning as a means of rational communication. Its use for the communication of emotions is much less important, for we can communicate a great deal of emotion without saying a word.

* It may be worth saying that Hegel, who had learned from Burke something about the importance of the historical growth of traditions, did in fact do much to destroy the intellectual tradition which Kant had founded, both by his doctrine of ' the cunning of reason ' which reveals itself in passion (see notes 82, 84 and text), and by his actual method of arguing. But he did more. By his historical relativism—by his theory that truth is relative, dependent on the spirit of the age—he helped to destroy the tradition of searching for truth, and of respecting truth. See also the section IV of this chapter, and my paper, *Towards a Rational Theory of Tradition* (in *The Rationalist Annual*, 1949 ; now in my *Conjectures and Refutations*).*

[31] Attempts to refute Kant's Dialectics (his doctrine of Antinomies) seem to be very rare. Serious criticism attempting to clarify and restate Kant's arguments can be found in Schopenhauer's *World as Will and Idea* and in J. F. Fries' *New or Anthropological Critique of Reason*, second German ed., 1828, pp. xxiv ff. I have tried to interpret Kant as holding that mere speculation cannot establish anything where experience cannot help to weed out false theories. (Cp. *Mind*, 49, 1940, p. 416 ; also, *Conjectures and Refutations*, p. 326 f. In the same volume of *Mind*, pp. 204 ff., there is a careful and interesting criticism of Kant's argument by M. Fried.) For an attempt to make sense of Hegel's dialectical theory of reason as well as of his collectivist interpretation of reason (his ' objective spirit '), see the analysis of the social or interpersonal aspect of scientific method in chapter 23, and the corresponding interpretation of ' reason ' in chapter 24.

[32] I have given a detailed justification of this in *What is Dialectic ?* (*Mind*, 49, pp. 403 ff. ; see especially the last sentence on p. 410 : also, *Conjectures and Refutations*, p. 321). See also a further note under the title, *Are Contradictions Embracing ?* *This has since appeared in *Mind*, 52, 1943, pp. 47 ff. After it was written I received Carnap's *Introduction to Semantics*, 1942, where he uses the term ' comprehensive ', which seems preferable to ' embracing '. See especially § 30 of Carnap's book.*

In *What is Dialectic ?* a number of problems are treated which are only touched upon in the present book ; especially the transition from Kant to Hegel, Hegel's dialectics, and his philosophy of identity. Although a few statements from that paper have been repeated here, the two presentations of the problems are in the main complementary to one another. Cp. also the next notes, down to note 36.

[33] Cp. *Selections*, xxviii (the German quotation ; for similar quotations see *WW*, iv, 618, and *Werke* 1832–1887, vol. vi, 259). For the idea of a *reinforced dogmatism* mentioned in this paragraph, cp. *What is Dialectic?*, p. 417, and *Conjectures and Refutations*, p. 327 ; see also note 51 to chapter 11.

[34] Cp. *What is Dialectic ?* especially from p. 414, where the problem, ' How can our mind grasp the world ? ' is introduced, down to p. 420 (*Conjectures and Refutations*, pp. 325–30).

[35] ' Everything actual is an Idea ', says Hegel. Cp. *Selections*, 103 (= *WW*, iii, 116) ; and from the perfection of the Idea, moral positivism follows. See also *Selections*, 388 (= *WW*, xi, 70), i.e. the last passage quoted in the text to note 8 ; see, furthermore, § 6 of the *Encyclopædia*, and the Preface as well as § 270L of the *Philosophy of Right*.—I need hardly add that the ' Great Dictator ' in the previous paragraph is an allusion to Chaplin's film.

[36] Cp. *Selections*, 103 (= *WW*, iii, 116). See also *Selections*, 128, § 107 (= *WW*, iii, 142).

Hegel's philosophy of identity shows, of course, the influence of the mystic theory of knowledge of Aristotle—the doctrine of the unity of the knowing subject and the known object. (Cp. notes 33 to chapter 11, 59–70 to chapter 10, notes 4, 6, and 29–32, and 58, to chapter 24.)

To my remarks in the text about Hegel's philosophy of identity, it may be added that Hegel believed, with most of the philosophers of his time, that logic is the theory of thinking or of reasoning. (See *What is Dialectic?* p. 418.) This, together with the philosophy of identity, has the consequence that logic is considered as the theory of thought, or of reason, or of the Ideas or notions, or of the Real. From the further premise that thought develops dialectically, Hegel can deduce that reason, the Ideas or notions, and the Real, all develop dialectically ; and he further gets *Logic = Dialectics* and *Logic = Theory of Reality*. This latter doctrine is known as Hegel's *pan-logism*.

On the other hand, Hegel can derive from these premises that notions develop dialectically, i.e. are capable of a kind of self-creation and self-development, out of nothing. (Hegel begins this development with the Idea of Being which presupposes its opposite, i.e. Nothing, and creates the transition from Nothing to Being, i.e. Becoming.) There are two motives for this attempt to develop notions out of nothing. The one is the mistaken idea that philosophy has to start without any presuppositions. (This idea has been recently reaffirmed by Husserl ; it is discussed in chapter 24 ; cp. note 8 to that chapter, and text.) This leads Hegel to start from ' nothing '. The other motive is the hope of giving a systematic development and justification of Kant's Table of Categories. Kant had made the remark that the first two categories of each group are opposed to each other, and that the third is a kind of synthesis of the first. This remark (and the influence of Fichte) led Hegel to hope that he could derive all categories ' dialectically ', out of nothing, and thereby justify the ' necessity ' of all the categories.

[37] Cp. *Selections*, xvi (= *Werke*, 1832–1887, vi, 153–4).

[38] Cp. Anderson, *Nationalism*, etc., 294.—The king promised the constitution on May 22, 1815.—The story of the ' constitution ' and the court-physician seems to have been told of most of the princes of the period (for example, of the emperor Francis I as well as his successor Ferdinand I of Austria).—The next quotation is from *Selections*, 246 f. (= *Encycl.* 1870, pp. 437–8).

[39] Cp. *Selections*, 248 f. (= *Encycl.* 1870, pp. 437–8 ; italics partly mine).

[40] Cp. note 25 to chapter 11.

[41] For the *paradox of freedom*, cp. note 43 (1) below ; the four paragraphs in the text before note 42 to chapter 6 ; notes 4 and 6 to chapter 7, and note 7 to chapter 24 ; and the passages in the text. (See also note 20 to chapter 17.) For Rousseau's restatement of the paradox of freedom, cp. the *Social Contract*, Book I, chapter VIII, second paragraph. For Kant's solution, cp. note 4 to chapter 6. Hegel frequently alludes to this Kantian solution (cp. Kant's *Metaphysics of Morals*, Introduction to the Theory of Law, § C ; *Works*, ed. by Cassirer, VII, p. 31) ; for example in his *Philosophy of Law*, § 29 ; and § 270, where, following Aristotle and Burke (cp. note 43 to chapter 6 and text), Hegel argues against the theory (due to Lycophron and Kant) that ' the state's specific function consists in the protection of everybody's life, property, and caprice ', as he sneeringly puts it.

For the two quotations at the beginning and end of this paragraph, cp. *Selections*, 248 f., and 249 (= *Encycl.* 1870, p. 439).

[42] For the quotations, cp. *Selections*, 250 (= *Encycl.* 1870, pp. 440–41).

[43] (1) For the following quotations, cp. *Selections*, 251 (§ 540 = *Encycl.* 1870, p. 441) ; 251 f., (first sentence of § 541 = *Encycl.* 1870, p. 442) ; and 253 f.

(beginning of § 542, italics partly mine = *Encycl.* 1870, p. 443). These are the passages from the *Encyclopædia*. The 'parallel passage' from the *Philosophy of Law* is : § 273 (last paragraph) to § 281. The two quotations are from § 275, and from § 279, end of first paragraph (italics mine). For a similarly dubious use of the paradox of freedom, cp. *Selections*, 394 (= *WW*, xi, 76) : ' If the principle of regard for the individual will is recognized as the only basis of political liberty . . then we have, properly speaking, *no Constitution.*' See also *Selections*, 400 f. (= *WW*, xi, 80–81), and 449 (see the *Philosophy of Law*, § 274).

Hegel himself summarizes his twist (*Selections*, 401 = *WW*, xi, 82) : ' At an earlier stage of the discussion, we established . . *first*, the Idea of Freedom as the absolute and final aim. . . We *then* recognized the State as the moral Whole and the Reality of Freedom . .' Thus we begin with freedom and end with the totalitarian state. One can hardly present the twist more cynically.

(2) For another example of a dialectic twist, viz., that of *reason into passion and violence*, see end of (*g*) in section IV, below, of the present chapter (text to note 84). Particularly interesting in this connection is *Hegel's criticism of Plato*. (See also notes 7 and 8 above, and text.) Hegel, paying lip-service to all modern and ' Christian ' values, not only to freedom, but even to the ' subjective freedom ' of the individual, criticizes Plato's holism or collectivism (*Phil. of Law*, § 187) : ' The principle of the self-sufficient . . personality of the individual, the principle of subjective freedom, is denied its right by . . Plato. This principle dawned . . in the Christian religion and . . in the Roman World.' This criticism is excellent, and it proves that Hegel knew what Plato was about ; in fact, Hegel's reading of Plato agrees very well with my own. For the untrained reader of Hegel, this passage might even prove the injustice of branding Hegel as a collectivist. But we have only to turn to § 70L of the same work in order to see that Plato's most radical collectivist saying, ' You are created for the sake of the whole, and not the whole for the sake of you ', is fully subscribed to by Hegel, who writes : ' A single person, it hardly needs saying, is something subordinate, and as such he must dedicate himself to the ethical whole ', i.e. the state. This is Hegel's ' individualism '.

But why, then, does he criticize Plato ? Why does he emphasize the importance of ' subjective freedom ' ? §§ 316 and 317 of the *Philosophy of Law* give an answer to this question. Hegel is convinced that revolutions can be avoided only by granting the people, as a kind of safety valve, a certain small amount of freedom which should not go beyond an irrelevant opportunity to give vent to their feelings. Thus he writes (*op. cit.*, §§ 316, 317L, italics mine) : ' In our day . . the principle of subjective freedom is of great importance and significance. . . Everybody wishes to participate in discussions and deliberations. But once he has had his say, . . his subjectivity is gratified and *he will put up with a lot*. In France, freedom of speech has proved far less dangerous than silence imposed by force ; with the latter . . men have to swallow everything, while if they are permitted to argue, they have an outlet as well as some satisfaction ; *and in this way, a thing may be pushed ahead more easily.*' It must be difficult to surpass the cynicism exhibited by this discussion in which Hegel gives vent, so freely, to his feeling concerning ' subjective freedom ' or, as he often calls it so solemnly, ' *the principle of the modern world* '.

To sum up. Hegel agrees with Plato completely, except that he criticizes Plato's failure to provide the ruled with the illusion of ' subjective freedom '.

44 The astonishing thing is that these despicable services could be successful, that even serious people have been deceived by Hegel's dialectical method. As an example it may be mentioned that even such a critical and enlightened fighter for freedom and reason as C. E. Vaughan fell a victim to Hegel's hypocrisy, when he expressed his belief in Hegel's ' belief in freedom and progress which, *on Hegel's own showing*, is . . the essence of his creed '. (Cp. C. E. Vaughan, *Studies in the History of Political Philosophy*, vol. II, 296 ; italics mine.)   It must be admitted that Vaughan criticized Hegel's ' undue leaning towards the established order ' (p. 178) ; he even said of Hegel that ' no one could . . be more ready . . to assure the world that the most retrograde and oppressive institutions . . must . . be accepted as indisputably rational ' (p. 295) ; yet he trusted ' Hegel's own showing ' so much that he took features of this kind as mere ' extravagances ' (p. 295), as ' shortcomings for which it is easy to allow ' (p. 182).   Moreover, his strongest and perfectly justified comment, that Hegel ' discovers the last word of political wisdom, the coping stone . . of history, in the Prussian Constitution ' (p. 182), was not fated to be published without an antidote restoring the reader's confidence in Hegel ; for the editor of Vaughan's posthumous *Studies* destroys the force of Vaughan's comment by adding in a foot-note, with reference to a passage from Hegel which he assumes to be the one alluded to by Vaughan (he does not refer to the passage quoted here in the text to notes 47, 48, and 49), ' but perhaps the passage hardly justifies the comment . .'

⁴⁵ See note 36 to this chapter.   An indication of this dialectical theory may be found as early as in Aristotle's *Physics*, I, 5.

⁴⁶ I am greatly indebted to E. H. Gombrich, who permitted me to adopt the main ideas of this paragraph from his excellent criticism of my presentation of Hegel (communicated to me by letter).

For Hegel's view that ' the Absolute Spirit manifests itself in the history of the world ', see his *Philosophy of Law*, § 259L. For his identification of the ' Absolute Spirit ' with the ' World Spirit ', see *op. cit.*, § 339L. For the view that perfection is the aim of Providence, and for Hegel's attack on the (Kantian) view that the plan of Providence is inscrutable, see *op. cit.*, § 343.   (For M. B. Foster's interesting counter-attacks, see note 19 to chapter 25.)   For Hegel's use of (dialectical) syllogisms, see especially the *Encyclopædia*, § 181 (' the syllogism is the rational, and everything rational ') ; § 198, where the state is described as a triad of syllogisms ; and §§ 575 to 577, where Hegel's whole system is presented as such a triad of syllogisms.   According to this last passage, we might infer that ' history ' is the realm of the ' second syllogism ' (§ 576) ; cp. *Selections*, 309 f. For the first passage (from section III of the Introduction to the *Philosophy of History*), see *Selections*, 348 f.—For the next passage (from the *Encyclopædia*) see *Selections*, 262 f.

⁴⁷ Cp. *Selections*, 442 (last paragraph = *WW*, xi, 119–20). The last quotation in this paragraph is from the same place.

Concerning the three steps, cp. *Selections*, 360, 362, 398 (= *WW*, xi, 44, 46, 79–80). See also Hegel's *Philosophy of History* (transl. by J. Sibree, 1857, quoted from the edition of 1914), p. 110 : ' The East knew . . only that *One* is free ; the Greek and the Roman World, that *some* are free ; the German World knows that *All* are free.   The first political form therefore which we observe in History is *Despotism*, the second *Democracy* and *Aristocracy*, the third *Monarchy*.'

(For the further treatment of the three steps, cp. *op. cit.*, pp. 117, 260, 354.)

⁴⁸ For the next three quotations cp. Hegel's *Philosophy of History*, 429; *Selections*, 358, 359 (= *WW*, xi, 43–44).

The presentation in the text simplifies the matter somewhat ; for Hegel first divides (*Phil. of Hist.*, 356 ff.) the Germanic World into three periods which he describes (p. 358) as the ' Kingdoms of the Father, the Son and the Spirit ' ; and the kingdom of the Spirit is again subdivided into the three periods mentioned in the text.

⁴⁹ For the following three passages, cp. the *Philosophy of History*, pp. 354, 476, 476–7.

⁵⁰ See especially text to note 75 to this chapter.

⁵¹ Cp. especially notes 48–50 to chapter 8.

⁵² Cp. Hegel's *Philosophy of History*, p. 418. (The translator writes: 'Germanized Sclaves'.)

⁵³ Masaryk has been described sometimes as a 'philosopher king'. But he was certainly not a ruler of the kind Plato would have liked ; for he was a democrat. He was very interested in Plato, but he idealized Plato and interpreted him democratically. His nationalism was a reaction to national oppression, and he always fought against nationalist excesses. It may be mentioned that his first printed work in the Czech language was an article on Plato's patriotism. (Cp. K. Capek's biography of Masaryk, the chapter on his period as a University student.) Masaryk's Czechoslovakia was probably one of the best and most democratic states that ever existed ; but in spite of all that, it was built on the principle of the national state, on a principle which in this world is inapplicable. An inter-national federation in the Danube basin might have prevented much.

⁵⁴ See chapter 7. For the quotation from Rousseau, later in the paragraph, cp. the *Social Contract*, book I, ch. VII (end of second paragraph). For Hegel's view concerning the doctrine of the sovereignty of the people, see the passage from § 279 of the *Philosophy of Law* quoted in text to note 61 to this chapter.

⁵⁵ Cp. Herder, quoted by Zimmern, *Modern Political Doctrines* (1939), p. 165 f. (The passage quoted in my text is not characteristic of Herder's empty verbalism, which was criticized by Kant.)

⁵⁶ Cp. note 7 to chapter 9. For the two quotations from Kant, further on in this paragraph, cp. *Works* (ed. by E. Cassirer), vol. IV, p. 179 ; and p. 195.

⁵⁷ Cp. Fichte's *Briefwechsel* (ed. Schulz, 1925), II, p. 100. The letter is partly quoted by Anderson, *Nationalism*, etc., p. 30. (Cp. also Hegemann, *Entlarvte Geschichte*, 2nd ed., 1934, p. 118.)—The next quotation is from Anderson, *op. cit.*, p. 34 f.—For the quotations in the next paragraph, cp. *op. cit.*, 36 f. ; italics mine.

It may be remarked that an originally anti-German feeling is common to many of the founders of German nationalism ; which shows how far nationalism is based upon a feeling of inferiority. (Cp. notes 61 and 70 to this chapter.) As an example, Anderson says (*op. cit.*, 79) about E. M. Arndt, later a famous nationalist : ' When Arndt travelled through Europe in 1798–9, he called himself a Swede because, as he said, the name German "stinks in the world " ; not, he added characteristically, through the fault of the common people.' Hegemann insists rightly (*op. cit.*, 118) that the German spiritual leaders of the time turned especially against the barbarism of Prussia, and he quotes Winckelmann, who said, ' I would rather be a Turkish eunuch than a Prussian ' ; and Lessing, who said, ' Prussia is the most slavish country in Europe ' ; and he refers to Goethe, who passionately hoped that relief would come from Napoleon. And Hegemann, who is also the author of a book against Napoleon, adds : ' Napoleon was a despot ; . . whatever we have to say against him, it must be admitted that by his victory of Jena he had forced the reactionary state of Frederick to introduce a few reforms that had been long overdue.'

An interesting judgement on the Germany of 1800 can be found in Kant's *Anthropology* (1800), where he deals, not quite seriously, with *national characteristics*. Kant writes (*Works*, vol. VIII, 213, 211, 212 ; italics mine) of the German ' His bad side is the compulsion to imitate others and *his low opinion of himself* with respect to his own originality . . ; and especially a certain pedantic inclination to classify himself painstakingly in relation to other citizens, according to a system of rank and of prerogatives. In this system of rank, he is inexhaustible in the invention of titles, and thus *slavish out of pedantry*. . . Of all civilized peoples, the German submits most easily and most lastingly to the government under which he happens to live, and he is further removed than any other from a love of change and from resistance to the established order. His character is a kind of phlegmatic reason.'

⁵⁸ Cp. Kant's *Works*, vol. VIII, 516. Kant, who had been immediately ready to help when Fichte appealed to him as an unknown author in distress, hesitated for seven years after the anonymous publication of Fichte's first book to speak his mind about Fichte, although he was pressed to do so from various sides, for example by Fichte himself, who posed as the fulfiller of the Kantian promise. Ultimately, Kant published his *Public Explanation Regarding Fichte*, as a reply ' to the solemn demand made by a reviewer in the name of the public ', that he should speak his mind. He declared that, in his view, ' Fichte's system was totally untenable ' ; and he declined to have anything to do with a philosophy which consisted of ' barren subtleties '. And after praying (as quoted in the text) that God may protect us from our friends, Kant goes on to say : ' For there may be also . . fraudulent and perfidious friends who are scheming for our ruin, although they speak the language of benevolence ; one cannot be sufficiently cautious in order to avoid the traps they set for us.' If Kant, a most balanced, benevolent, and conscientious person, was moved to say things such as these, then we have every reason to consider his judgement seriously. *But I have seen so far no history of philosophy which clearly states that, in Kant's opinion, Fichte was a dishonest impostor ;* although I have seen many histories of philosophy that try to explain away Schopenhauer's indictments, for example, by hinting that he was envious.

But Kant's and Schopenhauer's accusations are by no means isolated. A. von Feuerbach (in a letter of January 30th, 1799 ; cp. Schopenhauer's *Works*, vol. V, 102) expressed himself as strongly as Schopenhauer ; Schiller arrived at a similar opinion, and so did Goethe ; and Nicolovius called Fichte a ' sycophant and a deceiver '. (Cp. also Hegemann, *op. cit.*, pp. 119 ff.)

It is astonishing to see that, thanks to a conspiracy of noise, a man like Fichte succeeded in perverting the teaching of his ' master ', *in spite of Kant's protests, and in Kant's lifetime*. This happened only a hundred years ago and can easily be checked by anybody who takes the trouble to read Kant's and Fichte's letters, and Kant's public announcements ; and it shows that my theory of Plato's perversion of the teaching of Socrates is by no means so fantastic as it may appear to Platonists. Socrates was dead then, and he had left no letters. (Were the comparison not one that does too much honour to Fichte and Hegel, one would be tempted to say : without Plato, there could have been no Aristotle ; and without Fichte, no Hegel.)

⁵⁹ Cp. Anderson, *op. cit.*, p. 13.

⁶⁰ Cp. Hegel's *Philosophy of History*, 465. See also *Philosophy of Law*, § 258. With Pareto's advice, cp. note 1 to chapter 13.

⁶¹ Cp. *Philosophy of Law*, § 279 ; for the next quotation, see *Selections*, 256 f. (= *Encycl.* 1870, p. 446). The attack upon England, further below in the paragraph, follows on p. 257 (= *Encycl.* 1870, p. 447). For Hegel's reference to the German empire, cp. *Philosophy of History*, p. 475 (see also note 77 to this chapter).—Feelings of inferiority, especially in relation to England, and clever appeals to such feelings, play a considerable part in the story of the rise of nationalism ; cp. also notes 57 and 70 to this chapter. For other passages on England, see the next note and note 70 to this chapter, and text. (The words ' arts and science ' are italicized by me.)

⁶² Hegel's disparaging reference to merely ' formal ' rights, to merely ' formal ' freedom, to a merely ' formal ' constitution, etc., is interesting, since

it is the dubious source of the modern Marxist criticism of merely ' formal '
democracies which offer merely ' formal ' freedom.   Cp. note 19 to chapter 17
and text.

A few characteristic passages in which Hegel denounces merely ' formal '
freedom, etc., may be quoted here.   They are all taken from the *Philosophy
of History*—(p. 471) : ' Liberalism sets up, in opposition to all this ' (i.e. to the
Prussian ' holistic ' restoration), ' the atomistic principle which insists upon
the sway of individual wills, maintaining that all governments should . .
have their ' (the people's) ' explicit sanction.   In thus asserting the *formal
side of Freedom*—this mere abstraction—the party in question makes it impossible firmly to establish any political organization.'—(p. 474) : ' The Constitution of England is a complex of *mere particular rights* and particular privileges,
. . Of institutions characterized by real freedom ' (as opposed to merely
formal freedom) ' there are nowhere fewer than in England.   In point of
private rights and the freedom of possessions they present an incredible
deficiency : sufficient proof of which is afforded in the rights of primogeniture
which make it necessary to provide (by purchase or otherwise) military or
ecclesiastical appointments for the younger sons of the aristocracy.'   See
further the discussion of the French declaration of the Rights of Man and Kant's
principles on pp. 462 ff. with its reference to ' nothing more than *formal* Will '
and the ' principle of Freedom ' that ' remained merely formal ' ; and contrast this, for example, with the remarks on p. 354, which show that the German
Spirit is ' true ' and ' absolute ' freedom : ' The German Spirit is the Spirit
of the new World.   Its aim is the realization of absolute Truth as the unlimited
self-determination of Freedom ; of that Freedom which has its own absolute
form itself as its purport.'   If I were to use the term ' formal freedom ' in
a disparaging sense, then I should apply it to Hegel's ' subjective freedom ', as treated by him in *Philosophy of Law*, § 317L (quoted at the end of
note 43).

⁶³ Cp. Anderson, *Nationalism*, etc., p. 279.   For Hegel's reference to England (quoted in brackets at the end of this paragraph), cp. *Selections*, 263
(= *Encycl.* 1870, p. 452) ; see also note 70 to this chapter.

⁶⁴ This quotation is from the *Philosophy of Law*, § 331.   For the following
two quotations, cp. *Selections*, 403 (= *WW*, xi, 84) and 267 f. (= *Encycl.* 1870,
pp. 455–56).   For the quotation further below (illustrating juridical positivism), cp. *Selections*, 449 (i.e. *Phil. of Law*, § 274).   With the theory of world
dominion, cp. also the theory of domination and submission, and of slavery,
outlined in note 25 to chapter 11, and text.   For the theory of national spirits
or wills or geniuses asserting themselves in history, i.e. in the history of wars
see text to notes 69 and 77.

In connection with the *historical theory of the nation*, cp. the following remarks
of Renan (quoted by A. Zimmern in *Modern Political Doctrines*, p. 190 f.) :
' To forget and—I will venture to say—to get one's history wrong, are essential
factors in the making of a nation [or, as we now know, of a totalitarian state] ;
and thus the advance of historical studies is often a danger to nationality. . .
Now it is of the essence of a nation that all individuals should have much in
common, and further that they should all have forgotten much.'   One would
hardly believe that Renan is a nationalist ; but he is, although one of the
democratic type ; and his nationalism is typically Hegelian ; for he writes
(p. 202) : ' A nation is a soul, a spiritual principle.'

⁶⁵ Haeckel can hardly be taken seriously as a philosopher or scientist.
He called himself a free thinker, but his thinking was not sufficiently independent to prevent him from demanding in 1914 ' the following fruits of
victory ' : ' (1) Emancipation from England's tyranny : (2) the invasion of
the British pirate state by the German navy and army ; the capture of London;
(3) the partitioning of Belgium ' ; and so forth for quite a time.   (In : *Das*

Monistische Jahrhundert, 1914, No. 31/32, pp. 65 f., quoted in *Thus Spake Germany*, 270.)

W. Schallmayer's prize essay has the title : *Heredity and Selection in the Life of the Nations*. (See also note 71 to chapter 10, above.)

⁶⁶ For Bergson's Hegelianism, cp. note 25 to this chapter. For Shaw's characterization of the religion of creative evolution, cp. *Back to Methuselah*, the last section of the Preface (' My Own Part in The Matter ') : ' . . as the conception of Creative Evolution developed, I saw that we were at last within reach of a faith which complied with the first condition of all the religions that have ever taken hold of humanity : namely that it must be, first and fundamentally, a science of metabiology.'

⁶⁷ Cp. A. Zimmern's excellent Introduction to his *Modern Political Doctrines*, p. xviii.—Regarding Platonic totalitarianism, cp. text to note 8 to this chapter. For the theory of master and slave, and of domination and submission, cp. note 25 to chapter 11 ; see also note 74 to the present chapter.

⁶⁸ Cp. Schopenhauer, *Grundprobleme*, p. xix.

⁶⁹ For the eight quotations in this paragraph, cp. *Selections*, 265, 402, 403, 435, 436, 399, 407, 267 f. (= *Encycl.* 1870, p. 453, *WW*, xi, 83, 84, 113–4, 81, 88, *Encycl.* pp. 455–6). Cp. also § 347 of the *Philosophy of Law*.

⁷⁰ Cp. *Selections*, 435 f. (= *WW*, xi, 114). For the problem of inferiroity, cp. also notes 57 and 61 to this chapter, and text. For the other passage on England, see notes 61–63, and text to this chapter. A very interesting passage (*Phil. of Law*, § 290L) containing a classical formulation of holism shows that Hegel not only thought in terms of holism or collectivism and power, but also that he saw the applicability of these principles towards the organization of the proletariat. ' The lower classes ', Hegel writes, ' have been left more or less unorganized. And yet, it is of the utmost importance that they should be organized, for only in this way can they become powerful. Without organization, they are nothing but a heap, an aggregate of atoms.' Hegel comes pretty close to Marx in this passage.

⁷¹ The passage is from H. Freyer, *Pallas Athene* (1935), quoted by A. Kolnai, *The War against the West* (1938), p. 417. I am greatly indebted to Kolnai's book, which has made it possible for me to quote in the remaining part|of this chapter a considerable number of authors who would otherwise have been inaccessible to me. (I have, however, not always followed the wording of Kolnai's translations.)

For the characterization of Freyer as one of the leading sociologists of contemporary Germany, cp. F. A. von Hayek, *Freedom and the Economic System* (Public Policy Pamphlet No. 29, 2nd impression, 1940), p. 30.

For the four passages in this paragraph from Hegel's *Philosophy of Law*, §§ 331, 340, 342L (cp. also 331 f.) and 340, see *Selections*, 466, 467, 465, 468. For the passages from the *Encyclopædia*, cp. *Selections*, 260 f. (= *Encycl.* 1870, pp. 449–50). (The last sentence quoted is a different version of the first sentence of § 546.)

For the passage from H. von Treitschke, cp. *Thus Spake Germany* (1941), p. 60.

⁷² Cp. *Philosophy of Law*, § 257, i.e. *Selections*, 443. For the next three quotations, see *Philosophy of Law*, §§ 334 and 339L, i.e. *Selections*, 467. For the last quotation in this paragraph, cp. Hegel's *Philosophy of Law*, §§ 330L and 333.

⁷³ Cp. *Selections*, 365 (= *WW*, xi, 49) ; italics partly mine. For the next quotation, cp. *Selections*, 468, i.e. *Philosophy of Law*, § 340.

⁷⁴ Quoted by Kolnai, *op. cit.*, 418.—For Heraclitus, cp. text to note 10 to chapter 2.—For Haiser, see Kolnai, *loc. cit.* ; cp. also Hegel's theory of slavery, mentioned in note 25 to chapter 11.—For the concluding quotation of this paragraph, cp. *Selections*, 467, i.e. *Philosophy of Law*, 334. For the ' war of defence ' that turns into a ' war of conquest ', see *op. cit.*, § 326.

⁷⁵ For all the passages from Hegel in this paragraph, cp. *Selections*, 426 f. (= *WW*, xi, 105–6). (Italics mine.) For another passage expressing the postulate that world-history must overrule morals, see the *Philosophy of Law*, § 345. For E. Meyer, cp. end of note 15 (2) to chapter 10.

⁷⁶ See *Philosophy of Law*, § 317 f. ; cp. *Selections*, 461 ; for similar passages, see § 316 : ' Public opinion as it exists is a continuous self-contradiction ' ; see also § 301, i.e. *Selections*, 456, and § 318L. (For further views of Hegel on public opinion, cp. also text to note 84 to this chapter.)—For Haiser's remark, cp. Kolnai, *op. cit.*, 234.

⁷⁷ Cp. *Selections*, 464, 465, for the passages from the *Philosophy of Law*, §§ 324 and 324L. For the next passages from the *Philosophy of History*, cp. *Selections*, 436 f. (= *WW*, xi, 114–5). (The next passage quoted continues characteristically : '. . . naturally dead in itself, as e.g. the German Imperial Cities, the German Imperial Constitution.' With this, cp. note 61 to this chapter, and text.)

⁷⁸ Cp. *Philosophy of Law*, §§ 327L and 328, i.e. *Selections*, 465 f. (Italics mine.) For the remark on gunpowder, cp. Hegel's *Philosophy of History*, p. 419.

⁷⁹ For the quotations from Kaufmann, Banse, Ludendorff, Scheler, Freyer, Lenz, and Jung, cp. Kolnai, *op. cit.*, 411, 411 f., 412, 411, 417, 411, and 420.— For the quotation from J. G. Fichte's *Addresses to the German Nation* (1808), cp. the German edition of 1871 (edited by I. H. Fichte), p. 49 f. ; see also A. Zimmern, *Modern Political Doctrines*, 170 f.—For Spengler's repetition, see his *Decline of the West*, I, p. 12 ; for Rosenberg's repetition, cp. his *Myth of the Twentieth Century* (1935), p. 143 ; see also my note 50 to chapter 8, and Rader, *No Compromise* (1939), 116.

⁸⁰ Cp. Kolnai, *op. cit.*, 412.

⁸¹ Cp. Caird, *Hegel* (1883), p. 26.

⁸² Kolnai, *op. cit.*, 438.—For the passages from Hegel, cp. *Selections*, 365 f., italics partly mine ; cp. also text to note 84 to this chapter. For E. Krieck, cp. Kolnai, *op. cit.*, 65 f., and E. Krieck, *National-Political Education* (in German, 1932, p. 1 ; quoted in *Thus Spake Germany*, p. 53).

⁸³ Cp. *Selections*, 268 (= *Encycl.* 1870, p. 456) ; for Stapel, cp. Kolnai, *op. cit.*, 292 f.

⁸⁴ For Rosenberg, cp. Kolnai, *op. cit.*, 295. For Hegel's views on public opinion, cp. also text to note 76 to this chapter ; for the passages quoted in the present paragraph, see *Philosophy of Law*, § 318L, i.e. *Selections*, pp. 461 (italics mine), 375, 377, 377, 378, 367/368, 380, 368, 364, 388, 380 (= *WW*, xi, 59, 60, 60, 60–61, 51–2, 63, 52, 48, 70–1, 63). (Italics partly mine.) For Hegel's eulogy of emotion and passion and self-interest, cp. also text to note 82 to this chapter.

⁸⁵ For Best, cp. Kolnai, *op. cit.*, 414 f.—For the quotations from Hegel, cp. *Selections*, 464 f., 464, 465, 437 (= *WW*, xi, 115, a noteworthy similarity to Bergson), 372. (The passages from *Phil. of Law* are from §§ 324, 324L, 327L.)—For the remark on Aristotle, cp. *Pol.*, VII, 15, 3 (1334a).

⁸⁶ For Stapel, cp. Kolnai, *op. cit.*, 255–257.

⁸⁷ Cp. *Selections*, p. 100 : ' If I neglect *all* the determinations of an object, then *nothing* remains.'—For Heidegger's *What is Metaphysics?* cp. Carnap, *Erkenntnis*, 2, 229. For Heidegger's relation to Husserl and Scheler, cp. J. Kraft, *From Husserl to Heidegger* (2nd German ed., 1957). Heidegger recognizes that his sentences are meaningless : ' Question and answer concerning nothingness are in themselves equally nonsensical ', Heidegger writes (cp. *Erkenntnis*, 2, 231). What could be said, from the point of view of Wittgenstein's *Tractatus*, against this kind of philosophy which admits that it talks nonsense—but deeply significant nonsense ? (Cp. note 51 (1) to chapter 11.) G. Schneeberger, *Nachlese zu Heidegger*, 1962, contains a collection of documents on Heidegger's political activity.

⁸⁸ For these quotations from Heidegger, cp. Kolnai, *op. cit.*, 221, 313.—
For Schopenhauer's advice to the guardian, cp. *Works*, vol. V, p. 25 (note).

⁸⁹ For Jaspers, cp. Kolnai, *op. cit.*, 270 f. Kolnai (p. 282) calls Jaspers
' Heidegger's lesser brother '. I cannot agree with that. For, as opposed
to Heidegger, Jaspers has undoubtedly written books which contain much
of interest, even books which contain much that is based on experience, for
instance his *General Psycho-Pathology*. But I may quote here a few passages
from an early work, his *Psychology of World-Views* (first published in 1919 ;
I quote from the third German ed., 1925), which show that Jaspers' world-
views were far advanced, at any rate, before Heidegger took to writing. ' To
visualize the life of man, one would have to see how he lives in the Moment.
The Moment is the sole reality, it is reality in itself, in the life of the soul.
The Moment that has been lived is the Last, the Warm-Blooded, the Immediate, the Living, the Bodily-Present, the Totality of the Real, the only Concrete
Thing. . . Man finds Existence and the Absolute ultimately in the Moment
alone.' (p. 112.)—(From the chapter on the *Enthusiastic Attitude*, p. 112) :
' Wherever Enthusiasm is the absolute leading motive, i.e. wherever one
lives in Reality and for Reality, and still dares and risks all, there one may
well speak of Heroism : of heroic Love, heroic Strife, heroic Work, etc. § 5.
The Enthusiastic Attitude is Love . .'—(Subsection 2, p. 128) : ' *Compassion is
not Love . .*'—(p. 127) : ' This is why Love is cruel, ruthless ; and why it
is believed in, by the genuine Lover, only if it is so.'—(pp. 256 ff.) : ' III.
Single Marginal Situations. . . (A) *Strife.* Strife is a fundamental form of
all Existence. . . The *reactions* to the Marginal Situations of Strife are the
following : . . 2. *Man's lack of understanding of the fact that Strife is Ultimate* :
He skulks . .' And so on. We always find the same picture : A hysterical
romanticism, combined with a brutal barbarism and the professorial pedantry
of sub-sections and sub-sub-sections.

⁹⁰ Cp. Kolnai, *op. cit.*, 208.
For my remark on ' philosophy of the gambler ', cp. O. Spengler
(*The Hour of Decision. Germany and World-Historical Evolution.*—German ed.,
1933, p. 230 ; quoted in *Thus Spake Germany*, 28) : ' He whose sword compels
victory here will be lord of the world. The dice are there, ready for this
stupendous game. Who dares to throw them ? '
Of the gangster philosophy, a book by the very talented author, E. von
Salomon, is perhaps even more characteristic. I quote a few passages from
this book, *The Outlaws* (1930 ; the passages quoted are from pp. 105, 73, 63,
307, 73, 367) : ' Satanic lust ! Am I not one with my gun ? . . The
first lust of man is destruction. . . They shot quite indiscriminately, just
because it was good fun. . . We are free of the burden of plan, method or
system. . . What we wanted we did not know, and what we knew we did
not want. . . My greatest lust was always for destruction.' And so on.
(Cp. also Hegemann, *op. cit.*, 171.)

⁹¹ Cp. Kolnai, *op. cit.*, 313.

⁹² For Ziegler, cp. Kolnai, *op. cit.*, 398.

⁹³ This quotation is from Schopenhauer, *Grundprobleme* (4th ed., 1890),
Introduction to the first edition (1840), p. xix.—Hegel's remark on ' the
most lofty depth ' (or ' the most elevated depth ') is from the *Jahrbuecher d.
wiss. Lit.*, 1827, No. 7 ; it is quoted by Schopenhauer, *op. cit.*—The concluding
quotation is from Schopenhauer, *op. cit.*, xviii.

NOTES TO CHAPTER 13

General Note to the Chapters on Marx. Wherever possible, I refer in these
notes to *Capital* or to *H.o.M.* or to both. I use *Capital* as abbreviation for the

Everyman Double Volume Edition of K. Marx, *Capital*, translated by E. and C. Paul.—*H.o.M.* stands for *A Handbook of Marxism*, edited by E. Burns, 1935, but references to complete editions of the texts have always been added. For quotations from Marx and Engels, I refer to the Moscow standard edition (Gesamtausgabe, abbreviated *GA*), published from 1927 onwards and edited by D. Ryazanow and others but still incomplete. For quotations from Lenin, I refer to the *Little Lenin Library*, published by Martin Lawrence, later Lawrence and Wishart, abbreviated L.L.L. The later volumes of *Capital* are quoted as *Das Kapital* (of which vol. I was first published in 1867) ; the references are to vol. II, 1885, or to vol. III, part 1, and vol. III, part 2 (quoted as III/1 and III/2), both 1894. I wish to make it quite clear that although I refer where possible to the translations mentioned above, I do not always adopt their wording.

¹ Cp. V. Pareto, *Treatise on General Sociology*, § 1843. (English transl. : *The Mind and Society*, 1935, vol. III, p. 1281 ; cp. also text to note 65 to chapter 10.) Pareto writes (p. 1281 f.) : ' The art of government lies in finding ways to take advantage of such sentiments, not wasting one's energy in futile efforts to destroy them ; very frequently the sole effect of the latter course is to strengthen them. The person capable of freeing himself from the blind domination of his own sentiments will be able to utilize the sentiments of other people for his own ends. . . This may be said in general of the relation between ruler and ruled. The statesman who is of greatest service to himself and to his party is the man without prejudice who knows how to profit by the prejudices of others.' The prejudices Pareto has in mind are of diverse character—nationalism, love of freedom, humanitarianism. And it may be just as well to remark that Pareto, though he has freed himself from many prejudices, has certainly not succeeded in freeing himself from all of them. This can be seen in nearly every page he writes, especially, of course, where he speaks of what he describes not inappropriately as ' the humanitarian religion '. His own prejudice is the anti-humanitarian religion. Had he seen that his choice was not between prejudice and freedom from prejudice, but only between the humanitarian prejudice and the anti-humanitarian prejudice, he might perhaps have felt a little less confident of his superiority. (For the problem of prejudices, cp. note 8 (1) to chapter 24, and text.)

Pareto's ideas concerning the ' art of government ' are very old ; they go back at least to Plato's uncle Critias, and have played their part in the Platonic school tradition (as pointed out in note 18 to chapter 8).

² (1) Fichte's and Hegel's ideas led to the principle of the national state and of national self-determination, a reactionary principle in which, however, a fighter for the open society such as Masaryk sincerely believed, and which the democrat Wilson adopted. (For Wilson, cp. for instance *Modern Political Doctrines*, ed. by A. Zimmern, 1939, pp. 223 ff.) This principle is obviously inapplicable on this earth, and especially in Europe, where the nations (i.e. linguistic groups) are so densely packed that it is quite impossible to disentangle them. The terrible effect of Wilson's attempt to apply this romantic principle to European politics should be clear by now to everybody. That the Versailles settlement was harsh, is a myth ; that Wilson's principles were not adhered to, is another myth. The fact is that such principles could not be more consistently applied ; and Versailles failed mainly because of the attempt to apply Wilson's inapplicable principles. (For all this, cp. note 7 to chapter 9, and text to notes 51-64 to chapter 12.)

(2) In connection with the Hegelian character of Marxism mentioned in the text in this paragraph, I give here a list of important views which Marxism takes over from Hegelianism. My treatment of Marx is not based on this list, since I do not intend to treat him just as another Hegelian, but rather as a serious investigator who can, and must, answer for himself. This is the

list, ordered approximately according to the importance of the various views for Marxism.

(a) Historicism : The method of a science of society is the study of history, and especially of the tendencies inherent in the historical development of mankind.

(b) Historical relativism : What is a law in one historical period need not be a law in another historical period. (Hegel maintained that what is true in one period need not be true in another.)

(c) There is an inherent law of progress in historical development.

(d) The development is one towards more freedom and reason, although the instrumentality of bringing this about is not our reasonable planning but rather such irrational forces as our passions and our self-interests. (Hegel calls this ' the cunning of reason '.)

(e) Moral positivism, or in Marx's case, moral ' futurism '. (This term is explained in chapter 22.)

(f) Class consciousness is one of the instruments by which the development propels itself. (Hegel operates with the consciousness of the nation, the ' national Spirit ' or ' national Genius '.)

(g) Methodological essentialism. Dialectics.

(h) The following Hegelian ideas play a part in Marx's writings but have become more important with later Marxists.

(h_1) The distinction between merely ' formal ' freedom or merely ' formal ' democracy and ' real ' or ' economic ' freedom or ' economic ' democracy, etc. ; in connection with this, there is a certain ' ambivalent ' attitude towards liberalism, i.e. a mixture of love and hate.

(h_2) Collectivism.

In the following chapters, (a) is again the main theme. In connection with (a) and (b), see also note 13 to this chapter. For (b), cp. chapters 22–24. For (c), cp. chapters 22 and 25. For (d), cp. chapter 22 (and regarding Hegel's ' cunning of reason ', cp. text to note 84 to chapter 12). For (f), cp. chapters 16 and 19. For (g), cp. notes 4 to the present chapter, 6 to chapter 17, 13 to chapter 15, 15 to chapter 19, and notes 20–24 to chapter 20, and text. For (h_1), cp. note 19 to chapter 17. (h_2) has its influence on Marx's anti-psychologism (cp. text to note 16 to chapter 14) ; it is under the influence of the Platonic-Hegelian doctrine of the superiority of the state over the individual that Marx develops his theory that even the ' consciousness ' of the individual is determined by social conditions. Yet, fundamentally, Marx was an individualist ; his main interest was to help suffering human individuals. Thus collectivism as such certainly does not play an important part in Marx's own writings. (Apart from his emphasis upon a collective class consciousness, mentioned under (f) ; cp., for example, note 4 to chapter 18.) But it plays its part in Marxist practice.

³ In *Capital* (387–9), Marx makes some interesting remarks both on Plato's theory of the division of labour (cp. note 29 to chapter 5 and text) and on the caste character of Plato's state. (Marx refers, however, only to Egypt and not to Sparta ; cp. note 27 to chapter 4.) In this connection, Marx quotes also an interesting passage from Isocrates' *Busiris*, 15 f., 224/5, where Isocrates first proffers arguments for the division of labour very similar to those of Plato (text to note 29 to chapter 5) ; Isocrates then continues : ' The Egyptians . . . were so successful that the most celebrated philosophers who discuss such topics extol the constitution of Egypt above all others, and that the Spartans . . . govern their own city in such an excellent manner because they have copied the ways of the Egyptians.' I think it most probable that Isocrates refers here to Plato ; and he may in turn be referred to by Crantor, when he spoke of those who accuse Plato of becoming a disciple of the Egyptians, as mentioned in note 27 (3) to chapter 4.

⁴ Or, 'intelligence destroying'; cp. text to note 68 to chapter 12. For *dialectics* in general, and Hegelian dialectics in particular, cp. chapter 12, especially text to notes 28–33. With Marx's dialectics, I do not intend to deal in this book, since I have dealt with it elsewhere. (Cp. *What is Dialectic ?*, *Mind*, N.S., vol. 49, 1940, pp. 403 ff. ; or, revised, in *Conjectures and Refutations*, pp. 312 ff.) I consider Marx's dialectics, like Hegel's, a rather dangerous muddle ; but its analysis can be avoided here, especially since the criticism of his historicism covers all that may be taken seriously in his dialectics.

⁵ Cp., for instance, the quotation in the text to note 11 to this chapter.

⁶ Utopianism is first attacked by Marx and Engels in the *Communist Manifesto*, III, 3. (Cp. *H.o.M.*, 55 ff. = *GA*, Series I, vol. 6, 553–5.) For Marx's attacks upon the 'bourgeois economists' who 'try to reconcile . . political economy with the claims of the proletariat', attacks directed especially against Mill and other members of the Comtist school, cp. especially *Capital*, 868 (against Mill ; see also note 14 to this chapter), and 870 (against the Comtist *Revue Positiviste* ; see also text to note 21 to chapter 18). For the whole problem of social technology versus historicism, and of piecemeal social engineering versus Utopian social engineering, cp. especially chapter 9, above. (See also the notes 9 to chapter 3 ; 18 (3) to chapter 5 ; and 1 to chapter 9 ; with references to M. Eastman's *Marxism: is it Science ?*)

⁷ (1) The two quotations from Lenin are taken from Sidney and Beatrice Webb, *Soviet Communism* (2nd ed., 1937), p. 650 f., who say, in a note, that the second of the quotations is from a speech made by Lenin in May, 1918. It is most interesting to see how quickly Lenin grasped the situation. On the eve of his party's rise to power, in August, 1917, when he published his book *State and Revolution*, he was still a pure historicist. Not only was he as yet unaware of the most difficult problems involved in the task of constructing a new society ; he even believed, with most Marxists, that the problems were non-existent, or that they would be solved by the process of history. Cp. especially the passages from *State and Revolution* in *H.o.M.*, p. 757 f. (= Lenin, *State and Revolution*, L.L.L., vol. 14, 77–9), where Lenin emphasizes the simplicity of the problems of organization and administration in the various phases of the evolving Communist society. 'All that is required', he writes, 'is that they should work equally, should regularly do their share of work, and should receive equal pay. The accounting and control necessary for this have been *simplified*' (italics in the original) ' by capitalism to the utmost.' They can thus be simply taken over by the workers, since these methods of control are ' within reach of anybody who can read and write, and knows the first four rules of arithmetic.' These astonishingly naïve statements are representative. (We find similar views expressed in Germany and in England ; cp. this note, under (2).) They must be contrasted with Lenin's speeches made a few months later. They show how free the prophetic ' scientific socialist ' was from any foreboding of the problems and disasters ahead. (I mean the disaster of the period of war-communism, that period which was the outcome of this prophetic and anti-technological Marxism.) But they show also Lenin's capability of finding, and of admitting to himself, the mistakes made. He abandoned Marxism in practice, although not in theory. Compare also Lenin's chapter V, sections 2 and 3, *H.o.M.*, pp. 742 ff. (= *State and Revolution*, 67–73), for the purely historicist, i.e. prophetic and anti-technological (' anti-Utopian ', Lenin might have said ; cp. p. 747 = *State and Revolution* 70–71), character of this ' scientific socialism ' before its rise to power.

But when Lenin confessed that he knew no book dealing with the more constructive problems of social engineering, then he only demonstrated that Marxists, faithful to Marx's commandments, did not even read the ' Utopian stuff' of the ' professorial armchair socialists ' who tried to make a beginning with these very problems ; I am thinking of some of the Fabians in England

and of A. Menger (e.g. *Neue Staatslehre*, 2nd ed. 1904, especially pp. 248 ff.) and J. Popper-Lynkeus in Austria. The latter developed apart from many other suggestions a technology of collective farming, and especially of giant farms of the kind later introduced in Russia (see his *Allgemeine Nährpflicht*, 1912 ; cp. pp. 206 ff. and 300 ff. of the 2nd ed., 1923). But he was dismissed by Marxists as a' half-socialist '. They called him a ' half-socialist ' because he envisaged a private enterprise sector in his society ; he confined the economic activity of the state to the care for the basic needs of everybody—for the ' guaranteed minimum of subsistence '. Everything beyond this was to be left to a strictly competitive system.

(2) Lenin's view in *State and Revolution* quoted above is (as J. Viner has pointed out) very similar to that of John Carruthers, *Socialism and Radicalism* (cp. note 9 to chapter 9) ; see especially pp. 14–16. He says : ' The capitalists have invented a system of finance which, although complex, is sufficiently simple to be practically worked, and which fully instructs everyone as to the best manner of managing his factory. A very similar although greatly simpler finance would in the same way instruct the elected manager of a socialist factory how he should manage it, and he would have no more need for advice from a professional organizer than a capitalist has.'

⁸ This naïve naturalistic slogan is Marx's ' principle of communism ' (taken over by Marx from Louis Blanc's article *L'organisation de travail* ', as Bryan Magee has kindly pointed out to me). Its origin is Platonic and early Christian (cp. note 29 to chapter 5 ; the *Acts*, 2, 44–45, and 4, 34–35 ; see also note 48 to chapter 24, and the cross-references given there). It is quoted by Lenin in *State and Revolution* ; see *H.o.M.*, 752 (= *State and Revolution*, 74). Marx's ' principle of socialism ', which is incorporated in the *New Constitution* of the U.S.S.R. (1936), is slightly but significantly weaker ; compare the *Article 12* : ' In the U.S.S.R.', we read there, ' the principle of socialism is realized : " From each according to his ability, to each according to his work ".' The substitution of ' work ' for the early Christian term ' needs ' transforms a romantic and economically quite indefinite naturalistic phrase into a fairly practical but commonplace principle—and into one which even ' capitalism ' may claim as its own.

⁹ I am alluding to the title of a famous book by Engels : ' The Development of Socialism From a Utopia Into a Science.' (The book has been published in English under the title : *Socialism : Utopian and Scientific*.)

¹⁰ See my *The Poverty of Historicism* (*Economica*, 1944 : now published separately).

¹¹ This is the eleventh of Marx's *Theses on Feuerbach* (1845), cp. *H.o.M.*, 231 (= F. Engels, *Ludwig Feuerbach und der Ausgang der Klassischen deutschen Philosophie*, J. W. Dietz, Nachf. Berlin 1946, 56). See also notes 14–16 to this chapter, and the sections 1, 17 and 18 of *The Poverty of Historicism*.

¹² I do not intend to discuss here the metaphysical or the methodological problem of determinism in any detail. (A few further remarks on the problem will be found in chapter 22, below.) But I wish to point out how little adequate it is if ' determinism ' and ' scientific method ' are taken as synonyms. This is still done, even by a writer of the excellence and clarity of B. Malinowski. Cp., for instance, his paper in *Human Affairs* (ed. by Cattell, Cohen, and Travers, 1937), chapter XII. I fully agree with the methodological tendencies of this paper, with its plea for the application of scientific method in social science as well as with its brilliant condemnation of romantic tendencies in anthropology (cp. especially pp. 207 ff., 221–4.) But when Malinowski argues in favour of ' determinism in the study of human culture ' (p. 212 ; cp., for instance, also p. 252), I fail to see what he means by ' determinism ' if not simply ' scientific method '. This equation is, however, not tenable, and has its grave dangers, as shown in the text ; for it may lead to historicism.

[13] For a criticism of historicism, see *The Poverty of Historicism* (*Economica*, 1944). Marx may be excused for holding the mistaken belief that there is a 'natural law of historical development'; for some of the best scientists of his time (e.g. T. H. Huxley; cp. his *Lay Sermons*, 1880, p. 214) believed in the possibility of discovering a *law of evolution*. But there can be no empirical 'law of evolution'. There is a specific evolutionary hypothesis, stating that life *on earth* has developed in certain ways. But a universal or natural law of evolution would have to state a hypothesis concerning the course of development of life on *all* planets (at least). In other words, wherever we are confined to the observation of one unique process, there we cannot hope to find, and to test, a 'law of nature'. (Of course, there are laws of evolution pertaining to the development of young organisms, etc.).

There can be *sociological laws*, and even sociological laws pertaining to the problem of progress; for example, the hypothesis that, wherever the freedom of thought, and of the communication of thought, is effectively protected by legal institutions and institutions ensuring the publicity of discussion, there will be scientific progress. (Cp. chapter 23.) But there are reasons for holding the view that we should do better not to speak of *historical laws* at all. (Cp. note 7 to chapter 25, and text.)

[14] Cp. *Capital*, 864 (Preface to the First Edition. For a similar remark of Mill's, see note 16, below.) At the same place, Marx also says : 'It is the ultimate aim of this work to lay bare the economic law of motion of modern society.' (For this, cp. *H.o.M.*, 374, and text to note 16 to the present chapter.) The clash between Marx's pragmatism and his historicism becomes fairly obvious if we compare these passages with the eleventh of his *Theses on Feuerbach* (quoted in text to note 11 to this chapter). In *The Poverty of Historicism*, section 17, I have tried to make this clash more obvious by characterizing Marx's historicism in a form which is exactly analogous to his attack on Feuerbach. For we can paraphrase Marx's passage quoted in the text by saying : The historicist can only *interpret* social development, and aid it in various ways; his point, however, is that *nobody can change it*. See also chapter 22, especially text to notes 5 ff.

[15] Cp. *Capital*, 469 ; the next three quotations are from *Capital*, 868 (Preface to the Second Edition. The translation 'shallow syncretism' is not quite in keeping with the very strong expression of the original) ; *op. cit.*, 673 ; and *op. cit.*, 830. For the 'ample circumstantial evidence' mentioned in the text, see, for instance, *op. cit.*, 105, 562, 649, 656.

[16] Cp. *Capital*, 864 = *H.o.M.*, 374 ; cp. note 14 to this chapter. The following three quotations are from J. S. Mill, *A System of Logic* (1st ed., 1843 ; quoted from the 8th ed.), Book VI, Chapter X ; § 2 (end) ; § 1 (beginning) ; § 1 (end). An interesting passage (which says nearly the same as Marx's famous remark quoted in text to note 14) can be found in the same chapter of Mill's *Logic*, § 8. Referring to the historical method, which searches for the 'laws of social order and of social progress', Mill writes : 'By its aid we may hereafter succeed not only in looking far forward into the future history of the human race, but in determining what artificial means may be used, and to what extent, *to accelerate the natural progress in so far as it is beneficial* ; to compensate for whatever may be its inherent inconveniences or disadvantages, and to guard against the dangers or accidents to which our species is exposed from the necessary incidents of its progression.' (Italics mine.) Or as Marx puts it, to 'shorten and lessen its birth-pangs'.

[17] Cp. Mill, *loc. cit.*, § 2 ; the next remarks are from the first paragraph of § 3. The 'orbit' and the 'trajectory' are from the end of the second paragraph of § 3. When speaking of 'orbits' Mill thinks, probably, of such cyclical theories of historical development as formulated in Plato's *Statesman*, or perhaps in Machiavelli's *Discourses on Livy*.

¹⁸ Cp. Mill, *loc. cit.*, the beginning of the last paragraph of § 3.—For all these passages, cp. also notes 6–9 to chapter 14, and *The Poverty of Historicism*, sections 22, 24, 27, 28.

¹⁹ Concerning *psychologism* (the term is due to E. Husserl), I may here quote a few sentences by the excellent psychologist D. Katz ; the passages are taken from his article *Psychological Needs* (Chapter III of *Human Affairs*, ed. by Cattell, Cohen, and Travers, 1937, p. 36). ' In philosophy there has been for some time a tendency to make psychology " the " fundamental basis of all other sciences . . This tendency is usually called psychologism . . But even such sciences, which, like sociology and economics, are more closely related to psychology, have a neutral nucleus which is not psychological . .' Psychologism will be discussed at length in chapter 14. Cp. also note 44 to chapter 5.

²⁰ Cp. Marx's Preface to *A Contribution to the Critique of Political Economy* (1859), quoted in *H.o.M.*, 371 (= Karl Marx, *Zur Kritik der politischen Oekonomie*, edited by K. Kautsky, J. W. Dietz, Nachf. Berlin 1930, LIV–LV, also in *Capital*, p. xv f.). The passage is quoted more fully in text to note 13 to chapter 15, and in text to note 3 to chapter 16 ; see also note 2 to chapter 14.

NOTES TO CHAPTER 14

¹ Cp. note 19 to the last chapter.

² Cp. Marx's Preface to *A Contribution to the Critique of Political Economy*, quoted also in note 20 to chapter 13 and in text to notes 13 to chapter 15 and 4 to chapter 16 ; cp. *H.o.M.*, 372 = *Capital*, p. xvi. See also Marx and Engels, *German Ideology* (*H.o.M.*, 213 = *GA*, Series I, vol. v, 16) : ' It is not consciousness that determines life, but life that determines consciousness.'

³ Cp. M. Ginsberg, *Sociology* (Home University Library, 130 ff.), who discusses this problem in a similar context, without, however, referring to Marx.

⁴ Cp., for instance, *Zoology Leaflet 10*, published by the Field Museum of Natural History, Chicago, 1929.

⁵ For institutionalism, cp. especially chapter 3 (text to notes 9 and 10) and chapter 9.

⁶ Cp. Mill, *A System of Logic*, VI ; IX, § 3. (Cp. also notes 16–18 to chapter 13.)

⁷ Cp. Mill, *op. cit.*, VI ; VI, § 2.

⁸ Cp. Mill, *op. cit.*, VI ; VII, § 1. For the opposition between ' methodological individualism ' and ' methodological collectivism ', see F. A. von Hayek's *Scientism and the Study of Society*, Part II, section VII (*Economica*, 1943, pp. 41 ff.).

⁹ For this and the following quotation see Mill, *op. cit.*, VI ; X, § 4.

¹⁰ I am using the term ' sociological laws ' to denote the natural laws of social life, as opposed to its normative laws ; cp. text to notes 8–9 to chapter 5.

¹¹ Cp. note 10 to chapter 3. (The passage is from p. 122 of part II of my *The Poverty of Historicism* (*Economica*, N.S. xi, 1944), and p. 65 of the book.

I owe the suggestion that it was Marx who first conceived social theory as the study of the *unwanted social repercussions of nearly all our actions* to K. Polanyi, who emphasized this aspect of Marxism in private discussions (1924).

* (1) It should be noted, however, that in spite of the aspect of Marxism which has been just mentioned and which constitutes an important point of agreement between Marx's views on method and mine, there is a considerable disagreement between Marx's and my views about the way in which these unwanted or unintended repercussions have to be analysed. For Marx is a *methodological collectivist*. He believes that it is the ' system of economic relations ' as such which gives rise to the unwanted consequences—a system of institutions which, in turn, may be explicable in terms of ' means of production ', but which is not analysable in terms of individuals, their relations, and their actions. As opposed to this, I hold that institutions (and traditions) must be analysed in individualistic terms—that is to say, in terms of the relations of individuals acting in certain situations, and of the unintended consequences of their actions.

(2) The reference in the text to ' canvas-cleaning ', and to chapter 9 is to notes 9 to 12, and the text, of this chapter.

(3) Concerning the remarks in the text (in the paragraph to which this note is appended, and in some of those which follow) about the unintended social repercussions of our actions, I wish to draw attention to the fact that the situation in the physical sciences (and in the field of mechanical engineering and technology) is somewhat similar. The task of technology is here also largely to inform us about unintended consequences of what we are doing (e.g. that a bridge may become too heavy if we strengthen certain of its components). But the analogy goes even further. Our mechanical inventions do rarely turn out according to our original plans. The inventors of the motor car probably did not foresee the social repercussions of their doings, but they certainly did not foresee the purely mechanical repercussions—the many ways in which their cars broke down. And while their cars were altered in order to avoid these breakdowns, they changed beyond recognition. (And with them, some people's motives and aspirations changed also.)

(4) With my criticism of the Conspiracy Theory (pp. 94–6), cp. my *Prediction and Prophecy and their Significance for Social Theory* (in *Proceedings of the Xth International Congress of Philosophy*, 1948, vol. i, pp. 82 ff., especially p. 87 f.), and *Towards a Rational Theory of Tradition* (*The Rationalist Annual*, 1949, pp. 36 ff., especially p. 40 f.). Both papers are now in my *Conjectures and Refutations.**

[12] See the passage from Mill cited in note 8 to this chapter.

[13] Cp. note 63 to chapter 10. Important contributors to the logic of power are Plato (in Books VIII and IX of the *Republic*, and in the *Laws*), Aristotle, Machiavelli, Pareto, and many others.

[14] Cp. Max Weber's *Ges. Aufsaetze zur Wissenschaftslehre* (1922), especially pp. 408 ff.

A remark may be added here concerning the often repeated assertion that the social sciences operate with a method different from that of the natural sciences, in so far as we know the ' social atoms ', i.e. ourselves, by direct acquaintance, while our knowledge of physical atoms is only hypothetical. From this, it is often concluded (e.g. by Karl Menger) that the method of social science, since it makes use of our knowledge of ourselves, is psychological, or perhaps ' subjective ', as opposed to the ' objective ' methods of the natural sciences. To this, we may answer : There is surely no reason why we should not use any ' direct ' knowledge we may have of ourselves. But such knowledge is useful in the social sciences only if we generalize, i.e. if we assume that what we know of ourselves holds good for others too. But this generalization is of a hypothetical character, and it must be tested and corrected by experience of an ' objective ' kind. (Before having met anybody who does not like chocolate, some people may easily believe that everybody likes it.) Undoubtedly, in the case of ' social atoms ' we are in certain ways more favourably situated than in the case of physical atoms, owing not only to our knowledge of ourselves, but also to the use of language. Yet from the point of view of scientific method, a social hypothesis suggested by self-intuition is in no different position from a physical hypothesis about atoms. The latter may also be suggested to the physicist by a kind of intuition about what atoms are like. And in both cases, this intuition is a private affair of the man who proposes the hypothesis. What is ' public ', and important for science, is merely the question whether the hypotheses could be tested by experience, and whether they stood up to tests.

From this point of view, social theories are no more 'subjective' than physical ones. (And it would be clearer, for example, to speak of 'the theory of subjective values' or of 'the theory of acts of choice' than of the subjective theory of value': see also note 9 to chapter 20.)

¹⁵ The present paragraph has been inserted in order to avoid the misunderstanding mentioned in the text. I am indebted to Prof. E. Gombrich for drawing my attention to the possibility of such a misunderstanding.

¹⁶ Hegel contended that his 'Idea' was something existing 'absolutely', i.e. independently of anybody's thought. One might contend, therefore, that he was not a psychologist. Yet Marx, quite reasonably, did not take seriously this 'absolute idealism' of Hegel; he rather interpreted it as a disguised *psychologism*, and combated it as such. Cp. *Capital*, 873 (italics mine) : 'For Hegel, the *thought process* (which he even presents in disguise under the name "Idea" as an independent agent or subject) is the creator of the real.' Marx confines his attack to the doctrine that the thought process (or consciousness, or mind) creates the 'real'; and he shows that it does not even create the social reality (to say nothing about the material universe).

For the Hegelian theory of the dependence of the individual upon society, see (apart from section iii of chapter 12) the discussion, in chapter 23, of the social, or more precisely, the inter-personal element in scientific method, as well as the corresponding discussion, in chapter 24, of the inter-personal element in rationality.

NOTES TO CHAPTER 15

¹ Cp. Cole's Preface to *Capital*, xvi. (But see also the next note.)

² Lenin too sometimes used the term 'Vulgar Marxists', but in a somewhat different sense.—How little Vulgar Marxism has in common with the views of Marx may be seen from Cole's analysis, *op. cit.*, xx, and from the text to notes 4 and 5 to chapter 16, and from note 17 to chapter 17.

³ According to Adler, lust for power, of course, is really nothing but the urge towards compensation for one's feelings of inferiority by proving one's superiority.

Some Vulgar Marxists even believe that the finishing touch to the philosophy of the modern man was added by Einstein, who, so they think, discovered 'relativity' or 'relativism', i.e. that 'everything is relative'.

⁴ J. F. Hecker writes (*Moscow Dialogues*, p. 76) of Marx's so-called 'historical materialism' : 'I would have preferred to call it "dialectical historicism" or . . something of that sort.'—I again draw the reader's attention to the fact that in this book I am not dealing with Marx's *dialectics*, since I have dealt with them elsewhere. (Cp. note 4 to chapter 13.)

⁵ For Heraclitus' slogan, cp. especially text to note 4 (3) to chapter 2, notes 16/17 to chapter 4, and note 25 to chapter 6.

⁶ Both the following quotations are from *Capital*, 873 (Epilogue to the second ed. of vol. I).

⁷ Cp. *Das Kapital*, vol. III/2 (1894), p. 355 ; i.e. chapter 48, section III, from where the following quotations are taken.

⁸ Cp. *Das Kapital*, vol. III/2, *loc. cit.*

⁹ For the quotations in this paragraph, cp. F. Engels, *Anti-Dühring* ; see *H.o.M.*, 298, 299 (= F. Engels, *Herrn Eugen Duehring's* Umwaelzung der Wissenschaft, *GA* special volume, 294–5).

¹⁰ I have in mind questions concerning, for example, the influence of economic conditions (such as the need for land surveying) upon Egyptian geometry, and upon the different development of early Pythagorean geometry in Greece.

¹¹ Cp. especially the quotation from *Capital* in note 13 to chapter 14 ;

also the full passages from the Preface to *A Contribution to the Critique of Political Economy*, quoted only partially in the text to the next note. For the problem of Marx's essentialism, and the distinction between ' reality ' and appearance, see note 13 to this chapter, and notes 6 and 16 to chapter 17.

¹² But I feel inclined to say that it is a little better than an idealism of the Hegelian or Platonic brand ; as I said in *What is Dialectic ?*, if I were forced to choose, which, fortunately, I am not, I would choose materialism. (Cp. p. 422 of *Mind*, vol. 49, or *Conjectures and Refutations*, p. 331, where I deal with problems very similar to those dealt with here.)

¹³ For this and the following quotations, cp. Marx's Preface to *A Contribution to the Critique of Political Economy*, H.o.M., 372 (= *Zur Kritik der politischen Oekonomie*, LV).

Some further light is thrown upon these passages (and on the text to note 3 to chapter 16) by the *Second Observation* of part II of Marx's *Poverty of Philosophy* (cp. H.o.M., 354 f. = GA, Series I, vol. vi, 179–80) ; for Marx here analyses society very clearly into *three layers*, if I may call them so. The first of these layers corresponds to ' reality ' or ' essence ', the second and the third to a primary and a secondary form of appearance. (This is very similar to Plato's distinction of Ideas, sensible things, and images of sensible things ; cp. for the problem of Plato's essentialism chapter 3 ; for Marx's corresponding ideas, see also notes 8 and 16 to chapter 17). The *first* or fundamental layer (or ' reality ') is the material layer, the machinery and other material means of production that exist in society ; this layer is called by Marx the material ' productive forces ', or ' material productivity '. The *second* layer he calls ' productive relationship ' or ' social relations ' ; they are dependent on the first layer : ' Social relations are closely bound up with productive forces. In acquiring new productive forces men change their mode of production ; and in changing their mode of production, they change their way of earning their living—they change all their social relations.' (For the first two layers, cp. text to note 3 to chapter 16.) The *third* layer is formed by the ideologies, i.e. by legal, moral, religious, scientific ideas : ' The same men who establish their social relations in conformity with material productivity, produce also principles, ideas, and categories, in conformity with their social relations.' In terms of this analysis, we may say that in Russia the first layer was transformed in conformity with the third, a striking refutation of Marx's theory. (See also the next note.)

¹⁴ It is easy to make very general prophecies ; for instance, to prophesy that, within a reasonable time, it will rain. Thus there would not be much in the prophecy that, in some decades, there will be a revolution somewhere. But, as we see, Marx said just a little more than that, and just enough to be falsified by events. Those who try to interpret this falsification away remove the last bit of empirical significance from Marx's system. It then becomes purely ' metaphysical ' (in the sense of my *The Logic of Scientific Discovery*).

How Marx conceived the general mechanism of any revolution, in accordance with his theory, is illustrated by the following description of the social revolution of the bourgeoisie (also called the ' industrial revolution '), taken from the *Communist Manifesto* (H.o.M., 28 ; italics mine= GA, Series I, vol. vi, 530–31) : 'The means of production and of exchange, on whose foundation the bourgeoisie built itself up, were generated in feudal society. At a certain stage in the development of the means of production and of exchange . . the feudal relations of property became no longer compatible with the *already developed productive forces*. They became so many fetters. They had to be burst asunder. And they were burst asunder.' (Cp. also text to note 11, and note 17 to chapter 17.)

¹⁵ Cp. H. Heine, *Religion and Philosophy in Germany*. (Engl. transl., 1882) here quoted from the appendix to P. Carus, *Kant's Prolegomena*, 1912, p. 267.;

¹⁶ A testimony to this friendship can be found in *Capital*, at the end of footnote 2 to p. 671.

Marx, I admit, was often intolerant. Nevertheless, I feel—but I may easily be mistaken—that he had sufficient critical sense to see the weakness of all dogmatism, and that he would have disliked the way in which his theories were converted into a set of dogmas. (See note 30 to chapter 17, and p. 425— p. 334 in *Conjectures and Refutations*—of *What is Dialectic ?* Cp. note 4 to chapter 13.) It seems, however, that Engels was prepared to tolerate the intolerance and orthodoxy of the Marxists. In his Preface to the first English translation of *Capital*, he writes (cp. *Capital*, 886) of the book that it ' is often called, on the Continent, '' the Bible of the working class ''.' And instead of protesting against a description which converts ' scientific ' socialism into a religion, Engels proceeds to show, in his comments, that *Capital* is worthy of this title, since ' the conclusions arrived at in this work are daily more and more becoming the fundamental principles of the great working-class movement ' all over the world. From here there was only one step to the heresy-hunting and excommunication of those who retain the critical, i.e. scientific, spirit, the spirit which had once inspired Engels as well as Marx.

NOTES TO CHAPTER 16

¹ Cp. Marx and Engels, *The Communist Manifesto* ; see *H.o.M.*, p. 22 (= *GA*, Series I, vol. vi, 525). As pointed out in chapter 4 (see text to notes 5/6 and 11/12), Plato had very similar ideas.

² Cp. text to note 15 to chapter 14.

³ Cp. Marx, *The Poverty of Philosophy*, *H.o.M.*, 355 (= *GA*, Series I, vol. vi, 179). (The quotation is from the same place as that from which the passages quoted in note 13 to chapter 15 are taken.)

⁴ Cp. the preface to *A Contribution to the Critique of Political Economy* ; cp. *Capital*, xvi, and *H.o.M.*, 371 f. (= *Zur Kritik der politischen Oekonomie*, LIV–LV. See also note 20 to chapter 13, note 1 to chapter 14, note 13 to chapter 15, and text.) The passage quoted here, and especially the terms ' material productive forces ' and ' productive relationships ' receive some light from those quoted in note 13 to chapter 15.

⁵ Cp. *Capital*, 650 f. See also the parallel passage on capitalist and miser in *Capital*, 138 f., = *H.o.M.*, 437 ; cp. also note 17 to chapter 17. In *The Poverty of Philosophy*, *H.o.M.*, 367 (= *GA*, Series I, vol. vi, 189), Marx writes : ' Although all the members of the modern bourgeoisie have the same interest in so far as they form a class against another class, they have opposite, antagonistic interests, in so far as they stand face to face with one another. This opposition of interests results from the economic conditions of their bourgeois life.'

⁶ *Capital*, 651.

⁷ This is exactly analogous to Hegel's nationalist historicism, where the true interest of the nation gains consciousness in the subjective minds of the nationals, and especially of the leader.

⁸ Cp. the text to note 14 to chapter 13.

⁹ Cp. *Capital*, 651.

¹⁰ * I originally used the term ' *laissez-faire* capitalism ' ; but in view of the fact that ' *laissez-faire* ' indicates the absence of trade barriers (such as customs)—something highly desirable, I believe—and of the fact that I consider the economic policy of non-interference of the early nineteenth century as undesirable, and even as paradoxical, I decided to change my terminology, and to use the term ' unrestrained capitalism ' instead.*

NOTES TO CHAPTER 17

[1] Cp. the Preface to *A Contribution to the Critique of Political Economy* (*H.o.M.*, 372 = *Zur Kritik der politischen Oekonomie*, LV). For the theory of the strata or layers of the ' superstructures ', see the quotations in note 13 to chapter 15.

[2] For Plato's recommendation of ' both persuasion and force', see, for instance, text to note 35 to chapter 5, and notes 5 and 10 to chapter 8.

[3] Cp. Lenin, *State and Revolution* (*H.o.M.*, 733/4 and 735 = *State and Revolution*, 15 and 16).

[4] The two quotations are from Marx-Engels, *The Communist Manifesto* (*H.o.M.*, 46 = *GA*, Series I, vol. vi, 546).

[5] Cp. Lenin, *State and Revolution* (*H.o.M.*, 725 = *State and Revolution*, 8–9).

[6] For the characteristic problems of a historicist essentialism, and especially for problems of the type ' What is the state ? ' or ' What is government ? ' cp. the text to notes 26–30 to chapter 3, 21–4 and 26 ff. to chapter 11 and 26 to chapter 12.

For the *language of political demands* (or better, of *political 'proposals'*, as L. J. Russell puts it) which in my opinion must replace this kind of essentialism, cp. especially text between notes 41 and 42 to chapter 6 and note 5(3) to chapter 5. For Marx's essentialism, see especially text to note 11, and note 13, to chapter 15 ; note 16 to the present chapter ; and notes 20–24 to chapter 20. Cp. especially the methodological remark in the third volume of *Capital* (*Das Kapital*, III/2, p. 352), quoted in note 20 to chapter 20.

[7] This quotation is from the *Communist Manifesto* (*H.o.M.*, 25 = *GA*, Series I, vol. vi, 528). The text is from Engels' Preface to the first English translation of *Capital*. I quote here the whole concluding passage of this Preface ; Engels speaks there about Marx's conclusion ' that at least in Europe, England is the only country where the inevitable social revolution might be effected entirely by peaceful and legal means. He certainly never forgot to add that he hardly expected the English ruling class to submit, without a " pro-slavery rebellion ", to this peaceful and legal revolution '. (Cp. *Capital*, 887 ; see also text to note 7 to chapter 19.) This passage shows clearly that, according to Marxism, the violence or non-violence of the revolution will depend on the resistance or non-resistance of the old ruling class. Cp. also text to notes 3 ff. to chapter 19.

[8] Cp. Engels, *Anti-Dühring* (*H.o.M.*, 296 = *GA*, Special volume, 292) ; see also the passages mentioned in note 5 to this chapter.

The resistance of the bourgeoisie has been broken for some years in Russia ; but there are no signs of the ' withering away ' of the Russian state, not even in its internal organization.

The theory of the withering away of the state is highly unrealistic, and I think that it may have been adopted by Marx and Engels mainly in order to take the wind out of their rivals' sails. The rivals I have in mind are Bakunin and the anarchists ; Marx did not like to see anyone else's radicalism outdoing his own. Like Marx, they aimed at the overthrow of the existing social order, directing their attack, however, against the politico-legal, instead of the economic system. To them, the state was the fiend who had to be destroyed. But for his anarchist competitors, Marx, from his own premises, might have easily granted the possibility that the institution of the state, under socialism, might have to fulfil new and indispensable functions ; namely those functions of safeguarding justice and freedom allotted to it by the great theorists of democracy.

[9] Cp. *Capital*, 799.

[10] In the chapter, ' Primary accumulation ', Marx is, as he says (p. 801), ' not concerned . . with the purely economic causes of the agricultural

revolution. Our present interest is the forcible ' (i.e. political) ' means that were used to bring about the change.'

[11] For the many passages, and the superstructures, cp. note 13 to chapter 15.

[12] Cp. the text to the notes referred to in the last note.

[13] One of the most noteworthy and valuable parts of *Capital*, a truly imperishable document of human suffering, is Chapter VIII of the First Volume, entitled *The Working Day*, in which Marx sketches the early history of labour legislation. From this well-documented chapter, the following quotations are taken.

It must, however, be realized that this very chapter contains the material for a complete refutation of Marxist ' Scientific Socialism ', which is based upon the *prophecy of ever-increasing exploitation* of the workers. No man can read this chapter of Marx without realizing that this prophecy has fortunately not come true. It is not impossible, however, that this is due, in part, to the activities of the Marxists in organizing labour ; but the main contribution comes from the increased productivity of labour—in its turn, according to Marx, a result of ' Capitalist accumulation '.

[14] Cp. *Capital*, 246. (See the footnote 1 to this passage.)

[15] Cp. *Capital*, 257 f. Marx's comment in his footnote 1 to this page is most interesting. He shows that such cases as these were used by the pro-slavery Tory reactionaries for *propaganda for slavery*. And he shows that among others, Thomas Carlyle, the oracle (a forerunner of facism), partici- pated in this pro-slavery movement. Carlyle, to quote Marx, reduced ' the one great event of contemporary history, the American Civil War, to this level, that the Peter of the North wants to break the head of the Paul of the South because the Peter of the North hires his workers " by the day, and the Paul of the South hires them by the lifetime ".' Marx is here quoting Carlyle's article *Ilias Americana in Nuce* (*Macmillan's Magazine*, August, 1863). And Marx concludes : ' Thus the bubble of the Tory sympathy for the urban workers (the Tories never had any sympathy for agricultural workers) has burst at last. Inside it we find—slavery ! '

One of my reasons for quoting this passage is that I wish to emphasize Marx's complete disagreement with the belief that there is not much to choose between slavery and ' wage-slavery '. Nobody could stress more strongly than Marx the fact that the abolition of slavery (and consequently the introduction of ' wage-slavery ') is a most important and necessary step in the emancipation of the oppressed. The term ' wage-slavery ' is therefore dangerous and misleading ; for it has been interpreted, by Vulgar Marxists, as an indication that Marx agreed with what is in fact Carlyle's appraisal of the situation.

[16] Marx defines the ' value ' of a commodity as the average number of labour hours necessary for its reproduction. This definition is a good illus- tration of his *essentialism* (cp. note 8 to this chapter). For he introduces *value* in order to get at the essential reality which corresponds to what appears in the form of the *price* of a commodity. Price is a delusive kind of appearance. ' A thing may have a price without having value ', writes Marx (*Capital*, 79 ; see also Cole's excellent remarks in his Introduction to *Capital*, especially pp. xxvii, ff.). A sketch of Marx's ' value theory ' will be found in chapter 20. (Cp. notes 9-27 to that chapter, and text.)

[17] For the problem of the ' wage-slaves ', cp. end of note 15 to this chapter ; also *Capital*, 155 (especially footnote 1). For Marx's analysis the results of which are briefly sketched here, see especially *Capital*, 153 ff., also the footnote 1 to p. 153 ; cp. also my chapter 20, below.

My presentation of Marx's analysis may be supported by quoting a state- ment made by Engels in his *Anti-Dühring* on the occasion of a summary of *Capital*. Engels writes (*H.o.M.*, 269 = *GA*, Special volume, 160-67) : ' In

other words, even if we exclude all possibility of robbery, violence, and fraud a
even if we assume that all private property was originally produced by the
owner's own labour ; and that throughout the whole subsequent process,
there was only exchange of equal values for equal values ; even then the
progressive development of production and exchange would necessarily
bring about the present capitalist system of production ; with its monopoliza-
tion of the instruments of production as well as of the goods of consumption
in the hands of a class weak in numbers ; with its degradation into proletarian
paupers of the other class comprising the immense majority ; with its periodic
cycle of production booms and of trade depressions ; in other words, with the
whole anarchy of our present system of production. The whole process is
explained by purely economic causes : robbery, force, and the assumption
of political interference of any kind are unnecessary at any point whatever.'

Perhaps this passage may one day convince a Vulgar Marxist that Marxism
does not explain depressions by the conspiracy of ' big business '.   Marx
himself said (*Das Kapital*, II, 406 f., italics mine) : ' Capitalist production
involves conditions which, *independently of good or bad intentions*, permit only
a temporary relative prosperity of the working class, and always only as
a forerunner of a depression.'

[18] For the doctrine ' property is theft ' or ' property is robbery ', cp. also
Marx's remark on John Watts in *Capital*, 601, footnote 1.

[19] For the Hegelian character of the distinction between merely ' formal '
and ' actual ' or ' real ' freedom, or democracy, cp. note 62 to chapter 12.
Hegel likes to attack the British constitution for its cult of merely ' formal '
freedom, as opposed to the Prussian State in which ' real ' freedom is ' actualized '.   For the quotation at the end of this paragraph, cp. the passage quoted
in the text to note 7 to chapter 15.   See also notes 14 and 15 to chapter 20,
and text.

[20] For the *paradox of freedom* and the need for the protection of freedom by
the state, cp. the four paragraphs in the text before note 42 to chapter 6, and
especially notes 4 and 6 to chapter 7, and text ; see also note 41 to chapter 12,
and text, and note 7 to chapter 24.

[21] Against this analysis, it may be said that, if we assume perfect competition between the entrepreneurs as producers, and especially as buyers of
labour on the labour markets (and if we further assume that there is no
' industrial reserve army ' of unemployed to exert pressure on this market),
then there could be no talk of exploitation of the economically weak by the
economically strong, i.e. of the workers by the entrepreneurs.   But is the
assumption of perfect competition between the buyers on the labour markets
at all realistic ?   Is it not true that, for example, on many local labour markets,
there is only one buyer of any significance ?   Besides, we cannot assume that
perfect competition would automatically eliminate the problem of unemployment, if for no other reason because labour cannot easily be moved.

[22] For the problem of economic intervention by the state, and for a characterization of our present economic system as *interventionism*, see the next three
chapters, especially note 9 to chapter 18 and text.   It may be remarked that
interventionism as used here is the economic complement of what I have called
in chapter 6, text to notes 24–44, political *protectionism*.   (It is clear why the
term ' protectionism ' cannot be used instead of ' interventionism '.)   See
especially note 9 to chapter 18, and 25/26 to chapter 20, and text.

[23] The passage is quoted more fully in the text to note 14 to chapter 13 ;
for the contradiction between practical action and historicist determinism,
see that note, and text to notes 5 ff. to chapter 22.

[24] Cp. section II of chapter 7.

[25] See Bertrand Russell, *Power* (1938) ; cp. especially pp. 123 ff. ; Walter
Lippmann, *The Good Society* (1937), cp. especially pp. 188 ff.

²⁶ Russell, *Power*, pp. 128 f.   Italics mine.

²⁷ Laws to safeguard democracy are still in a rather rudimentary state of development.   Very much could and should be done.   The freedom of the press, for instance, is demanded because of the aim that the public should be given correct information ; but viewed from this standpoint, it is a very insufficient institutional guarantee that this aim will be achieved.   What good newspapers usually do at present on their own initiative, namely, giving the public all important information available, might be established as their duty, either by carefully framed laws, or by the establishment of a moral code, sanctioned by public opinion.   Matters such as, for instance, the Zinovief letter, could be perhaps controlled by a law which makes it possible to nullify elections won by improper means, and which makes a publisher who neglects his duty to ascertain as well as possible the truth of published information liable for the damage done ; in this case, for the expenses of a fresh election.   I cannot go into details here, but it is my firm conviction that we could easily overcome the technological difficulties which may stand in the way of achieving such ends as the conduct of election campaigns largely by appeal to reason instead of passion.   I do not see why we should not, for instance, standardize the size, type, etc., of the electioneering pamphlets, and eliminate placards.   (This need not endanger freedom, just as reasonable limitations imposed upon those who plead before a court of justice protect freedom rather than endanger it.)   The present methods of propaganda are an insult to the public as well as to the candidate.   Propaganda of the kind which may be good enough for selling soap should not be used in matters of such consequence.

²⁸ * Cp. the British ' Control of Engagement Order ', 1947.   The fact that this order is hardly used (it is clearly not abused) shows that legislation of even the most dangerous character is enacted without compelling need— obviously because the fundamental difference between the two types of legislation, viz. the one that establishes general rules of conduct, and the one that gives the government discretionary powers, is not sufficiently understood.*

²⁹ * For this distinction, and for the use of the term ' legal framework ', see F. A. Hayek, *The Road to Serfdom* (I am quoting from the 1st English Edition, London, 1944).   See, for example, p. 54, where Hayek speaks of ' the distinction . . between the creation of a *permanent framework of laws* within which productive activity is guided by individual decision, and the *direction of economic activity* by a central authority.'   (Italics mine.)   Hayek emphasizes the significance of the *predictability of the legal framework* ; see, for example, p. 56.*

³⁰ The review, published in the *European Messenger* of St. Petersburg, is quoted by Marx in the Preface to the 2nd edition of *Capital.*   (See *Capital*, 871.)

In fairness to Marx, we must say that he did not always take his own system too seriously, and that he was quite prepared to deviate a little from his fundamental scheme ; he considered it as a point of view (and as such it was certainly most important) rather than as a system of dogmas.

Thus we read, on two consecutive pages of *Capital* (832 f.), a statement which emphasizes the usual Marxist theory of the secondary character of the legal system (or of its character as a cloak, an ' appearance '), and another statement which ascribes a very important rôle to the political might of the state and raises it explicitly to the rank of a full-grown *economic force.*   The first of these statements, ' The author would have done well to remember that revolutions are not made by laws ', refers to the industrial revolution, and to an author who asked for the enactments by which it was effected.   The second statement is a comment (and one most unorthodox from the Marxist point of view) upon the methods of accumulating capital ; all these methods, Marx says, ' make use of the power of the state, which is the centralized

political might of society.   Might is the midwife of every old society pregnant
with a new one.   *It is itself an economic force.*'   Up to the last sentence, which
I have put in italics, the passage is clearly orthodox.   But the last sentence
breaks through this orthodoxy.

Engels was more dogmatic.   One should compare especially one of his
statements in his *Anti-Dühring* (*H.o.M.*, 277), where he writes, ' The rôle played
in history by political might as opposed to economic developments is now
clear.'   He contends that whenever ' political might works against economic
developments, then, as a rule, with only few exceptions, it succumbs ;   these
few exceptions are isolated cases of conquest in which barbarian conquerors
. . have laid waste . . productive forces which they did not know how to
use '.   (Compare, however, notes 13/14 to chapter 15, and text.)

The dogmatism and authoritarianism of most Marxists is a really astonishing
phenomenon.   It just shows that they use Marxism irrationally, as a metaphysical system.   It is to be found among radicals and moderates alike.   E.
Burns, for example, makes (in *H.o.M.*, 374) the surprisingly naïve statement
that ' refutations . . inevitably distort Marx's theories ' ;   which seems to
imply that Marx's theories are irrefutable, i.e. unscientific ;   for every scientific
theory is refutable, and can be superseded.   L. Laurat, on the other hand,
in *Marxism and Democracy*, p. 226, says : ' In looking at the world in which
we live, we are staggered at the almost mathematical precision with which
the essential predictions of Karl Marx are being realized.'

Marx himself seems to have thought differently.   I may be wrong in this,
but I do believe in the sincerity of his statement (at the end of his Preface
to the first edition of *Capital* ; see 865) : ' I welcome scientific criticism, however
harsh.   But in the face of the prejudices of a so-called public opinion, I
shall stick to my maxim . . : Follow your course, and let them chatter ! '

NOTES TO CHAPTER 18

[1] For Marx's essentialism, and the fact that the material means of production play the part of essences in his theory, cp. especially note 13 to chapter 15.   See also note 6 to chapter 17 and notes 20-24 to chapter 20, and
text.

[2] Cp. *Capital*, 864 = *H.o.M.*, 374, and notes 14 and 16 to chapter 13.

[3] What I call the secondary aim of *Capital*, its anti-apologetic aim, includes
a somewhat academic task, namely, the *critique of political economy with regard
to its scientific status*.   It is this latter task to which Marx alluded both in the
title of the forerunner of *Capital*, namely in *A Contribution to the Critique of
Political Economy*, and in the sub-title of *Capital* itself, which reads, in literal
translation, *Critique of Political Economy*.   For both these titles allude unmistakably to Kant's *Critique of Pure Reason*.   And this title, in turn, was intended
to mean : ' Critique of pure or metaphysical philosophy in regard to its
scientific status '.   (This is more clearly indicated by the title of the paraphrase of Kant's Critique which reads in an almost literal translation : *Prolegomena To Any Metaphysics Which In Future May Justly Claim Scientific Status*.)
By alluding to Kant, Marx apparently wished to say : ' Just as Kant criticized
the claim of metaphysics, revealing that it was *no science* but largely *apologetic
theology*, so I criticize here the corresponding claims of bourgeois economics.'
That the main tendency of Kant's *Critique* was, in Marx's circles, considered to
be directed against apologetic theology can be seen from its representation
in *Religion and Philosophy in Germany* by Marx's friend, H. Heine (cp. notes 15
and 16 to chapter 15).   It is not quite without interest that, in spite of Engels'
supervision, the first English translators of *Capital* translated its sub-title as
A Critical Analysis of Capitalist Production, thus substituting an emphasis upon

what I have described in the text as Marx's first aim for an allusion to his second aim.

Burke is quoted by Marx in *Capital*, 843, note 1. The quotation is from E. Burke, *Thoughts and Details on Scarcity*, 1800, p. 31 f.

⁴ Cp. my remarks on class consciousness towards the end of section I, in chapter 16.

Concerning the continued existence of class-unity after the class struggle against the class enemy has ceased, it is, I think, hardly in keeping with Marx's assumptions, and especially with his dialectics, to assume that class consciousness is a thing that *can* be accumulated and afterwards stored, that it *can* survive the forces that produced it. But the further assumption that it *must necessarily* outlive these forces contradicts Marx's theory which looks upon consciousness as a mirror or as a product of hard social realities. And yet, this further assumption must be made by anybody who holds with Marx that the dialectic of history must lead to socialism.

The following passage from the *Communist Manifesto* (*H.o.M.*, 46 f. = *GA*, Series I, vol. vi, 46) is particularly interesting in this context ; it contains a clear statement that the class consciousness of the workers is a mere consequence of the ' force of circumstances ', i.e. the pressure of the class situation ; but it contains, at the same time, the doctrine criticized in the text, namely, the prophecy of the classless society. This is the passage : ' In spite of the fact that the proletariat is compelled, by the force of circumstances, to organize itself as a class during its struggle with the bourgeoisie ; in spite of the fact that, by means of revolution, it makes itself the ruling class, and, as such, sweeps away by force the old conditions of production ; in spite of these facts, it will sweep away, along with these conditions, also the conditions for the existence of any class antagonism and of any classes, and will thereby abolish its own supremacy as a class.—In place of the old bourgeois society, with its classes and class antagonism, we shall have an association in which the free development of each is the warrant for the free development of all.' (Cp. also text to note 8 to this chapter.) It is a beautiful belief, but it is an æsthetic and romantic belief ; it is a wishful ' Utopianism ', to use Marxist terminology, not a ' scientific socialism '.

Marx fought against what he called ' Utopianism ', and rightly so. (Cp. chapter 9.) But since he was himself a romantic, he failed to discern the most dangerous element in Utopianism, its romantic hysteria, its æstheticist irrationalism ; instead, he fought against its (admittedly most immature) attempts at rational planning, opposing to them his historicism. (Cp. note 21 to the present chapter.)

For all his acute reasoning and for all his attempts to use scientific method, Marx permitted irrational and æsthetic sentiments to usurp, in places, complete control of his thoughts. Nowadays one calls this wishful thinking. It was romantic, irrational, and even mystical wishful thinking that led Marx to assume that the collective class unity and class solidarity of the workers would last after a change in the class situation. It is thus wishful thinking, a mystical collectivism, and an irrational reaction to the strain of civilization which leads Marx to prophesy the necessary advent of socialism.

This kind of romanticism is one of the elements of Marxism which appeals most strongly to many of its followers. It is expressed, for example, most touchingly in the dedication of Hecker's *Moscow Dialogues*. Hecker speaks here of socialism as of ' a social order where the strife of class and race shall be no more, and where truth, goodness and beauty shall be the share of all '. Who would not like to have heaven on earth ! And yet, it must be one of the first principles of rational politics that *we cannot make heaven on earth*. We are not going to become Free Spirits or angels at least not for the next couple of centuries or so. We are bound to this earth by our metabolism, as Marx once wisely declared ; or as Christianity puts it, we are spirits *and* flesh. Thus we must be more modest. In politics and in medicine, he who promises too much is likely to be a quack. We must try to improve things, but we must get rid of the idea of a philosophers' stone, of a formula which will convert our corrupt human society into pure, lasting gold.

At the back of all this is the hope of casting out the devil from our world. Plato thought he could do it by banishing him to the lower classes, and ruling over him. The anarchists dreamt that once the state, the Political System, was destroyed, everything must turn out well. And Marx dreamt a similar dream of banishing the devil by destroying the economic system.

These remarks are not intended to imply that it is impossible to make even rapid advances, perhaps even through the introduction of comparatively small reforms, such as, for example, a reform of taxation, or a reduction of the rate of interest. I only wish to insist that we must expect every elimination of an evil to create, as its unwanted repercussion, a host of new though possibly very much lesser evils, which may be on an altogether different plane of urgency. Thus the second principle of sane politics would be : *all politics consists in choosing the lesser evil* (as the Viennese poet and critic K. Kraus put it). And politicians should be zealous in the search for the evils their actions must necessarily produce instead of concealing them, since a proper evaluation of competing evils must otherwise become impossible.

[5] Although I do not intend to deal with Marx's dialectics (cp. note 4 to chapter 13), I may show that it would be possible to 'strengthen' Marx's logically inconclusive argument by so-called 'dialectical reasoning'. In accordance with this reasoning, all we need is to describe the antagonistic trends within capitalism in such a manner that socialism (for instance in the form of a totalitarian state-capitalism) appears as the necessary synthesis. The two antagonistic tendencies of capitalism can then perhaps be described thus. *Thesis* : The tendency towards the accumulation of capital in a few hands ; towards industrialization and bureaucratic control of industry ; towards economic and psychological levelling of the workers through the standardization of needs and desires. *Antithesis* : The increasing misery of the great masses ; their increasing class consciousness in consequence of (a) class war, and (b) their increasing realization of their paramount significance within an economic system like that of an industrial society in which the working class is the only productive class, and accordingly the only essential class. (Cp. also note 15 to chapter 19, and text.)

It is hardly necessary to show how the desired Marxist synthesis emerges ; but it may be necessary to insist that a slightly changed emphasis in the description of the antagonistic tendency may lead to very different ' syntheses ' ; in fact, to any other synthesis one wishes to defend. For instance, one could easily present fascism as a necessary synthesis ; or perhaps ' technocracy ' ; or else, a system of democratic interventionism.

[6] * Bryan Magee writes about this passage : ' This is what *The New Class* by Djilas is all about : a fully worked out theory of the realities of the Communist revolution, written by an unrepentant Communist.'*

[7] The history of the working-class movement is full of contrasts. It shows that the workers have been ready for the greatest sacrifices in their fight for the liberation of their own class, and beyond this, of mankind. But there are also many chapters telling a sorry tale of quite ordinary selfishness and of the pursuit of sectional interest to the detriment of all.

It is certainly understandable that a trade union which obtains a great advantage for its members through solidarity and collective bargaining should try to exclude those from these benefits who are not prepared to join the union ; for instance, by incorporating in their collective contracts the condition that only members of the union are to be employed. But it is a very different matter, and indeed indefensible, if a union which in this way has obtained a monopoly closes its membership list, thus keeping out fellow workers who want to join, without even establishing a just method (such as the strict adherence to a waiting list) of admitting new members. That such things can occur shows that the fact that a man is a worker does not always prevent him from forgetting all about the solidarity of the oppressed and from making full use of the economic prerogatives he may possess, i.e. from exploiting his fellow workers.

⁸ Cp. *The Communist Manifesto* (*H.o.M.*, 47 = *GA*, Series I, vol. vi, 546) ; the passage is quoted more fully in note 4 to this chapter, where Marx's romanticism is dealt with.

⁹ The term ' capitalism ' is much too vague to be used as a name of a definite historical period. The term ' capitalism ' was originally used in a disparaging sense, and it has retained this sense (' system favouring big profits made by people who do not work ') in popular usage. But at the same time it has also been used in a neutral scientific sense, but with many different meanings. In so far as, according to Marx, all accumulations of means of production may be termed ' capital ', we may even say that ' capitalism ' is in a certain sense synonymous with ' industrialism '. We could in this sense quite correctly describe a communist society, in which the state owns all capital, as ' state-capitalism '. For these reasons, I suggest using the name ' *unrestrained capitalism* ' for that period which Marx analysed and christened ' capitalism ', and the name *interventionism* for our own period. The name ' interventionism ' could indeed cover the three main types of social engineering in our time : the collectivist interventionism of Russia ; the democratic interventionism of Sweden and the ' Smaller Democracies ' and the New Deal in America ; and even the fascist methods of regimented economy. What Marx called ' capitalism '—i.e. unrestrained capitalism—has completely ' withered away ' in the twentieth century.

¹⁰ The Swedish ' social democrats ', the party which inaugurated the Swedish experiment, had once been Marxist ; but it gave up its Marxist theories shortly after its decision to accept governmental responsibilities and to embark upon a great programme of social reform. One of the aspects in which the Swedish experiment deviates from Marxism is its emphasis upon the consumer, and the rôle played by the consumer co-operatives, as opposed to the dogmatic Marxist emphasis upon production. The technological economic theory of the S wedes is strongly influenced by what Marxists would call ' bourgeois economics ', while the orthodox Marxist theory of value plays no rôle in it whatever.

¹¹ For this programme, see *H.o.M.*, 46 (= *GA*, Series I, vol. vi, 545).— With point (1), cp. text to note 15 to chapter 19.

It may be remarked that even in one of the most radical statements ever made by Marx, the *Address to the Communist League* (1850), he considered a progressive income tax a most revolutionary measure. In the final description of revolutionary tactics towards the end of this address which culminates in the battle cry ' Revolution in permanence ! ' Marx says : ' If the democrats propose proportional taxation, the workers must demand progressive taxation. And should the democrats themselves declare for a moderate progressive tax, the workers must insist upon a steeply graduated tax ; so steeply graduated as to cause the collapse of large capital.' (Cp. *H.o.M.*, 70, and especially note 44 to chapter 20.)

¹² For my conception of piecemeal social engineering, cp. especially chapter 9. For political intervention in economic matters, and a more precise explanation of the term *interventionism*, see note 9 to this chapter and text.

¹³ I consider this criticism of Marxism very important. It is mentioned in sections 17/18 of my *The Poverty of Historicism* ; and as stated there, it can

be parried by proffering a *historicist moral theory*. But I believe that only if such a theory (cp. chapter 22, especially notes 5 ff. and text) is accepted can Marxism escape the charge that it teaches ' *the belief in political miracles* '. (This term is due to Julius Kraft.) See also notes 4 and 21 to the present chapter.

¹⁴ For the problem of *compromise*, cp. a remark at the end of the paragraph to which note 3 to chapter 9 is appended. For a justification of the remark in the text, ' For they do not plan for the whole of society ', see chapter 9, and my The *Poverty of Historicism, II* (especially the criticism of holism).

¹⁵ F. A. von Hayek (cp., for example, his *Freedom and the Economic System*, Chicago, 1939) insists that a centralized ' planned economy ' must involve the gravest dangers to individual freedom. But he also emphasizes that *planning for freedom* is necessary. (' Planning for freedom ' is also advocated by Mannheim, in his *Man and Society in an Age of Reconstruction*, 1941. But since his idea of ' planning ' is emphatically *collectivistic* and *holistic*, I am convinced that it must lead to tyranny, and not to freedom ; and, indeed, Mannheim's ' freedom ' is the offspring of Hegel's. Cp. the end of chapter 23, and my paper quoted at the end of the preceding note.)

¹⁶ This contradiction between the Marxist historical theory and the Russian historical reality is discussed in chapter 15, notes 13/14, and text.

¹⁷ This is another contradiction between Marxist theory and historical practice ; as opposed to that mentioned in the last note, this second contradiction has given rise to many discussions and attempts to explain the matter by the introduction of auxiliary hypotheses. The most important of these is the theory of imperialism and colonial exploitation. This theory asserts that the revolutionary development is frustrated in countries in which the proletarian in common with the capitalist reaps where not he but the oppressed natives of the colonies have sown. This hypothesis which is undoubtedly refuted by developments like those in the non-imperialistic Smaller Democracies will be discussed more fully in chapter 20 (text to notes 37–40).

Many social democrats interpreted the Russian revolution, in accordance with Marx's scheme, as a belated ' bourgeois revolution ', insisting that this revolution was bound up with an economic development parallel to the ' industrial revolution ' in the more advanced countries. But this interpretation assumes, of course, that history must conform with the Marxist scheme. In fact, such an essentialist problem as whether the Russian revolution is a belated industrial revolution or a premature ' social revolution ' is of a purely verbal character ; and if it leads to difficulties within Marxism, then this shows only that Marxism has verbal difficulties in describing events which have not been foreseen by its founders.

¹⁸ The leaders were able to inspire in their followers an enthusiastic faith in their mission—to liberate mankind. But the leaders also were responsible for the ultimate failure of their politics, and the breakdown of the movement. This failure was due, very largely, to intellectual irresponsibility. The leaders had assured the workers that Marxism was a science, and that the intellectual side of the movement was in the best hands. But they never adopted a scientific, i.e. a critical, attitude towards Marxism. As long as they could apply it (and what is easier than this ?), as long as they could interpret history in articles and speeches, they were intellectually satisfied. (Cp. also notes 19 and 22 to this chapter.)

¹⁹ For a number of years prior to the rise of fascism in Central Europe a very marked defeatism within the ranks of the social democratic leaders was noticeable. They began to believe that fascism was an unavoidable stage in social development. That is to say, they began to make some amendments to Marx's scheme, but they never doubted the soundness of the historicist

approach ; they never saw that such a question as ' Is fascism an unavoidable stage in the development of civilization ? ' may be totally misleading.

²⁰ The Marxist movement in Central Europe had few precedents in history. It was a movement which, in spite of the fact that it professed atheism, can truly be called a great religious movement. (Perhaps this may impress some of those intellectuals who do not take Marxism seriously.) Of course, it was a collectivist and even a tribalist movement, in many ways. But it was a movement of the workers to educate themselves for their great task ; to emancipate themselves, to raise the standard of their interests and of their pastimes ; to substitute mountaineering for alcohol, classical music for swing, serious books for thrillers. ' The emancipation of the working class can only be achieved by the workers themselves ' was their belief. (For the deep impression made by this movement on some observers, see, for example, G. E. R. Gedye's *Fallen Bastions*, 1939.)

²¹ The quotation is from Marx's Preface to the second edition of *Capital*, (cp. *Capital*, 870 ; cp. also note 6 to chapter 13.) It shows how fortunate Marx was in his reviewers (cp. also note 30 to chapter 17, and text).

Another most interesting passage in which Marx expresses his anti-Utopianism and historicism can be found in *The Civil War in France* (*H.o.M.*, 150, K. Marx, *Der Buergerkrieg in Frankreich*, A. Willaschek, Hamburg 1920, 65–66), where Marx says approvingly of the Paris *Commune* of 1871 : ' The working class did not expect miracles from the Commune. They have no ready-made Utopias, to be introduced by the decree of the people. They know that in order to achieve their own emancipation, and with it, those higher forms to which our present society is irresistibly tending, . . they will have to pass through long struggles, through a series of historic processes, transforming circumstances and men. They have no ideals to realize, but to set free the elements of the new society with which the old collapsing bourgeois society itself is pregnant.' There are few passages in Marx which exhibit the historicist lack of plan more strikingly. ' They have to pass through long struggles . .', Marx says. But if they have no plan to realize, ' no ideals to realize ', as Marx says, what are they struggling for ? They ' did not expect miracles ', Marx says ; but he himself expected miracles in believing that the historical struggle irresistibly tends to ' higher forms ' of social life. (Cp. notes 4 and 13 to the present chapter.) Marx was to a certain extent justified in his refusal to embark upon social engineering. To organize the workers was undoubtedly the most important practical task of his day. If such a suspect excuse as ' the time was not ripe for it ' can ever be justly applied, it must be applied to Marx's refusal to dabble in the problems of rational institutional social engineering. (This point is illustrated by the childish character of the Utopian proposals down to and including, say, Bellamy). But it was unfortunate that he supported this sound political intuition by a theoretical attack upon social technology. This became an excuse for his dogmatic followers to continue in the same attitude at a time when things had changed, and technology had become politically more important even than organizing the workers.

²² The Marxist leaders interpreted the events as the dialectical ups and downs of history. They thus functioned as cicerones, as guides through the hills (and valleys) of history rather than as political leaders of action. This dubious art of interpreting the terrible events of history instead of fighting them was forcefully denounced by the poet K. Kraus (mentioned in note 4 to this chapter).

NOTES TO CHAPTER 19

[1] Cp. *Capital*, 846 = *H.o.M.*, 403.

[2] The passage is from Marx-Engels, *The Communist Manifesto*. (Cp. *H.o.M.*, 31 = *GA*, Series I, vol. vi, 533.)

[3] Cp. *Capital*, 547 = *H.o.M.*, 560 (where it is quoted by Lenin).

A remark may be made concerning the term ' concentration of capital ' (which I have translated in the text ' concentration of capital in a few hands ').

In the third edition of *Capital* (cp. *Capital*, 689 ff.) Marx introduced the following distinctions : (*a*) by *accumulation* of capital he means merely the growth in the total amount of capital goods, for example, within a certain region ; (*b*) by *concentration* of capital he means (cp. 689/690) the normal growth of the capital in the hands of the various individual capitalists, a growth which arises from the general tendency towards accumulation and which gives them command over an increasing number of workers. (*c*) by *centralization* he means (cp. 691) that kind of growth of capital which is due to the expropriation of some capitalists by other capitalists (' one capitalist lays many of his fellows low ').

In the second edition, Marx had not yet distinguished between concentration and centralization ; he used the term ' concentration ' in both senses (*b*) and (*c*). To show the difference, we read in the third edition (*Capital*, 691) : ' Here we have genuine centralization, in contradistinction to accumulation and concentration.' In the second edition, we read at this place : ' Here we have genuine concentration, in contradistinction to accumulation.' The alteration, however, was not made throughout the book, but only in a few passages (especially pp. 690–3, and 846). In the passage here quoted in the text, the wording remained the same as in the second edition. In the passage (p. 846) quoted in the text to note 15 to this chapter, Marx replaced ' concentration ' by ' centralization '.

[4] Cp. Marx's *Eighteenth Brumaire* (*H.o.M.*, 123 ; italics mine = Karl Marx, *Der Achtzehnte Brumaire des Louis Bonaparte*, Verlag fuer Literatur und Politik. Wien-Berlin 1927, 28–29) : ' The bourgeois republic triumphed. On its side stood the aristocracy of finance, the industrial bourgeoisie, *the middle class*, the petty bourgeoisie, the army, *the rabble proletariat*, organized as the Mobile Guard, *the intellectual lights*, the clergy, *and the rural population*. On the side of the Paris proletariat stood none but the proletariat itself.'

For an incredibly naïve statement made by Marx concerning the ' rural producers ', cp. also note 43 to chapter 20.

[5] Cp. text to note 11 to chapter 18.

[6] Cp. the quotation in note 4 to the present chapter, especially the reference to the middle class and to the ' intellectual lights '.

For the ' rabble proletariat ', cp. the same place and *Capital*, 711 f. (The term is there translated as ' tatterdemalion proletariat '.)

[7] For the meaning of ' class consciousness ' in Marx's sense, see end of section I in chapter 16.

Apart from the possible development of a defeatist spirit, as mentioned in the text, there are other things which may undermine the class consciousness of the workers, and which may lead to disunion among the working class. Lenin, for example, mentions that imperialism may split the workers by offering them a share in its spoils ; he writes (*H.o.M.*, 707 = V. I. Lenin, L.L.L., *Imperialism, the Highest State of Capitalism*, vol. xv, 96 ; cp. also note 40 to chapter 20) : ' . . in Great Britain, the tendency of imperialism to split the workers, to strengthen the opportunists among them, and to cause temporary decay in the working-class movement, revealed itself much earlier than at the end of the nineteenth and the beginning of the twentieth centuries.'

H. B. Parkes rightly mentions in his excellent analysis, *Marxism—A Post Mortem* (1940 ; also published under the title *Marxism—An Autopsy*), that it is quite possible that entrepreneurs and workers may together exploit the consumer ; in a protected or monopolist industry, they may share in the spoil. This possibility shows that Marx exaggerates the antagonism between the interests of the workers and entrepreneurs.

And lastly it may be mentioned that the tendency of most governments to proceed along the line of least resistance is liable to lead to the following result. Since workers and entrepreneurs are the best organized and politically most powerful groups in the community, a modern government may easily tend to satisfy both at the expense of the consumer. And it may do so without a guilty conscience ; for it will persuade itself that it has done well by establishing peace between the most antagonistic parties in the community.

[8] Cp. text to notes 17 and 18 to this chapter.

[9] Some Marxists even dare to assert that there would be far less suffering involved in a violent social revolution than in the chronic evils inherent in what they call ' capitalism '. (Cp. L. Laurat, *Marxism and Democracy*, translated by E. Fitzgerald, 1940 ; p. 38, note 2 ; Laurat criticizes Sidney Hook, *Towards an Understanding of Marx*, for holding such views.) These Marxists do not, however, disclose the scientific basis of this estimate ; or to speak more bluntly, of this utterly irresponsible piece of oracular pretence.

[10] ' It should be plain without any further comment ', Engels says about Marx, remembering his Hegel, ' that if things and their mutual relations are taken to be variable instead of fixed, then their mental images, their notions, will be subject to variation and transformation also ; that one does not attempt to force them into the pigeonholes of rigid definitions ; but that one treats them, as the case may be, according to the historical or logical character of the process by which they have been formed.' (Cp. Engels' Preface to *Das Kapital*, III/1, p. xvi.)

[11] It does not correspond precisely because the Communists sometimes profess the more moderate theory, especially in those countries where this theory is not represented by the Social Democrats. Cp., for example, text to note 26 to this chapter.

[12] Cp. notes 4 and 5 to chapter 17, and text ; as well as note 14 to the present chapter ; and contrast with notes 17 and 18 to the present chapter, and text.

[13] There are, of course, positions between these two ; and there are also more moderate Marxist positions : especially A. Bernstein's so-called ' revisionism '. This latter position, in fact, gives up Marxism altogether ; it is nothing but the advocacy of a strictly democratic and non-violent workers' movement.

[14] This development of Marx's is, of course, an interpretation, and not a very convincing one ; the fact is that Marx was not very consistent, and that he used the terms ' revolution ', ' force ', ' violence ', etc., with a systematic ambiguity. This position was partly forced upon him by the fact that history during his lifetime did not proceed according to his plan. It conformed to the Marxist theory in so far as it exhibited most clearly a tendency away from what Marx called ' capitalism ', i.e. away from non-intervention. Marx frequently referred with satisfaction to this tendency, for example, in his Preface to the first edition of *Capital*. (Cp. the quotation in note 16 to the present chapter ; see also the text.) On the other hand, this same tendency (towards interventionism) led to an improvement of the lot of the workers in opposition to Marx's theory ; and it thereby reduced the likelihood of a revolution. Marx's wavering and ambiguous interpretations of his own teaching are probably the result of this situation.

In order to illustrate the point, two passages may be quoted, one from an early and one from a late work of Marx. The early passage is from the

Address to the Communist League (1850 ; cp. *H.o.M.*, pp. 60 ff. = *Labour Monthly*, September 1922, 136 ff.). The passage is interesting because it is practical. Marx assumes that the workers together with the bourgeois democrats have won the battle against feudalism and have set up a democratic regime. Marx insists that after having achieved this, the battle-cry of the workers must be ' Revolution in permanence ! ' What this means is explained in detail (p. 66) : ' They must act in such a manner that the revolutionary excitement does not collapse immediately after the victory. On the contrary, they must maintain it as long as possible. Far from opposing so-called excesses, such as the sacrificing to popular revenge of hated individuals or public buildings to which hateful memories are attached, such deeds must not only be tolerated, but their direction must be taken in hand, for example's sake.' (Cp. also note 35 (1) to this chapter, and note 44 to chapter 20.)

A moderate passage which contrasts with the previous one may be chosen from Marx's *Address to the First International* (Amsterdam, 1872 ; cp. L. Laurat, *op. cit.*, p. 36) : ' We do not deny that there are countries, such as the United States and Great Britain—if I knew your institutions better, I should perhaps add Holland—where the workers will be able to achieve their aims by peaceful means. But this is not the case in all countries.' For these more moderate views, cp. also text to notes 16–18 to the present chapter.l

But the whole confusion can be found in a nutshell as eary as in the final summary of the *Manifesto* where we find the following two contradictory statements, separated by one sentence only : (1) ' In short, the Communists support everywhere every revolutionary movement against the existing social and political order of things.' (This must include England, for example.) (2) Finally, they labour everywhere for the union and agreement of the democratic parties of all countries.' To make the confusion complete, the next sentences run : ' The communists disdain to conceal their views and aims. They openly declare that their ends can be attained only by the forcible overthrow of all existing social conditions.' (Democratic conditions are not excluded.)

¹⁵ Cp. *Capital*, 846 = *H.o.M.*, 403 f. (Concerning the term ' centralization ', substituted in the third edition for the term ' concentration ' of the second edition, cp. note 3 to the present chapter. Concerning the translation ' their capitalist cloak becomes a straight jacket ', it may be remarked that a more literal translation would be : ' they become incompatible with their capitalist wrapper ' or ' cloak ' ; or slightly more freely : ' their capitalist cloak becomes intolerable '.)

This passage is strongly influenced by Hegelian *dialectics*, as is shown by its continuation. (Hegel called the *antithesis* of a *thesis* sometimes its negation, and the *synthesis* the ' negation of the negation '.) ' The capitalist method of appropriation ', Marx writes, ' . . is the first negation of individual private property based upon individual labour. But with the inexorability of a law of nature, capitalist production begets its own negation. It is the negation of the negation. This second negation . . establishes . . the common ownership of the land and of the means of production.' (For a more detailed dialectical derivation of socialism, cp. note 5 to chapter 18.)

¹⁶ This was the attitude taken up by Marx in his Preface to the first edition of *Capital* (*Capital*, 865), where he says : ' Still, progress is undeniable. . . The foreign representatives of the British crown . . tell us . . that in the more advanced countries of the European continent, a change in the relations between capital and labour is just as obvious and as inevitable as in England. . . Mr. Wade, the vice-president of the United States of North America . . declares at public meetings that, after the abolition of slavery, a radical change in the conditions of capital and landed property comes next on the agenda ! ' (Cp. also note 14 to this chapter.)

¹⁷ Cp. Engels' Preface to the first English edition of *Capital*. (*Capital*, 887.)   The passage is quoted more fully in note 9 to chapter 17.

¹⁸ Cp. Marx's letter to Hyndman, dated December 8th, 1880 ; see H. H. Hyndman, *The Record of an Adventurous Life* (1911), p. 283.   Cp. also L. Laurat, *op. cit.*, 239.   The passage may be quoted here more fully : ' If you say that you do not share the views of my party for England I can only reply that that party considers an English revolution not *necessary*, but—according to historic precedents—*possible*.   If the unavoidable evolution turns into a revolution, it would not only be the fault of the ruling classes, but also of the working class.'   (Note the ambiguity of the position.)

¹⁹ H. B. Parkes, *Marxism—A Post Mortem*, p. 101 (cp. also pp. 106 ff.), expresses a similar view ; he insists that the Marxist ' belief that capitalism cannot be reformed but can only be destroyed ' is one of the characteristic tenets of the Marxist theory of accumulation.   ' Adopt some other theory ', he says, ' . . and it remains possible for capitalism to be transformed by gradual methods.'

²⁰ Cp. the end of the *Manifesto* (*H.o.M.*, 59 = *GA*, Series I, vol. vi, 557) : ' The proletarians have nothing to lose but their fetters.   They have a world to win.'

²¹ Cp. the *Manifesto* (*H.o.M.*, 45 = *GA*, Series I, vol. vi, 545) ; the passage is quoted more fully in text to note 35 to this chapter.—The last quotation in this paragraph is from the *Manifesto*, *H.o.M.*, 35 (= *GA*, Series I, vol. vi, 536).   Cp. also note 35 to this chapter.

²² But social reforms have rarely been carried out under the pressure of those who suffer ; religious movements—I include the Utilitarians—and individuals (like Dickens) may influence public opinion greatly.   And Henry Ford discovered, to the astonishment of all Marxists and many ' capitalists ' that a rise in wages may benefit the employer.

²³ Cp. notes 18 and 21 to chapter 18.

²⁴ Cp. *H.o.M.*, 37 (= *GA*, Series I, vol. vi, 538).

²⁵ Cp. *The State and Revolution*, *H.o.M.*, 756 (= *State and Revolution*, 77). Here is the passage in full : ' Democracy is of great importance for the working class in its struggle for freedom against the capitalists.   But democracy is by no means a limit one may not overstep ; it is only one of the stages in the course of the development from feudalism to capitalism, and from capitalism, to Communism.'

Lenin insists that democracy means only ' *formal* equality '.   Cp. also *H.o.M.*, 834 (= V. I. Lenin, *The Proletarian Revolution and the Renegade Kautsky*. L.L.L., vol. xviii, 34), where Lenin uses this Hegelian argument of merely ' formal ' equality against Kautsky : ' . . he accepts the formal equality, which under capitalism is merely a fraud and a piece of hypocrisy at its face value as a de facto equality . .'

²⁶ Cp. Parkes, *Marxism—A Post Mortem*, p. 219.

²⁷ Such a tactical move is in keeping with the *Manifesto* which announces that the Communists ' labour everywhere for the union and agreement of the democratic parties of all countries ', but which announces at the same time ' that their ends can be attained only by the forcible overthrow of existing social conditions ', which include democratic conditions.

But such a tactical move is also in keeping with the party programme of 1928 ; for this says (*H.o.M.*, 1036 ; italics mine = *The Programme of the Communist International*, Modern Books Ltd., London 1932, 61) : ' In determining its line of tactics each Communist Party must take into account the concrete internal and external situation. . .   The party determines slogans . . with a view to organizing . . the masses *on the broadest possible scale*.'   But this cannot be achieved without making full use of the systematic ambiguity of the term revolution.

²⁸ Cp. *H.o.M.*, 59 and 1042 (= *GA*, Series I, vol. vi, 557, and *Programme of the Communist International*, 65) ; and end of note 14 to this chapter. (See also note 37.)

²⁹ This is not a quotation but a paraphrase. Cp., for example, the passage from Engels' Preface to the first English edition of *Capital* quoted in note 9 to chapter 17. See also L. Laurat, *op. cit.*, p. 240.

³⁰ The first of the two passages is quoted by L. Laurat, *loc. cit.* ; for the second, cp. *H.o.M.*, 93 (= Karl Marx, *The Class Struggle in France 1848–1850*. Introduction by F. Engels. Co-operative Publishing Society of Foreign Workers in the U.S.S.R., Moscow 1934, 29). Italics mine.

³¹ Engels was partly conscious that he had been forced to a change of front since ' History has proved us wrong, and all who thought like us ', as he said (*H.o.M.*, 79 = Karl Marx, *Die Klassenkampfe in Frankreich*, Vorwaerts, Berlin 1890, 8). But he was conscious mainly of one mistake : that he and Marx had overrated the speed of the development. That the development was, in fact, in a different direction, he never admitted, although he complained of it ; cp. text to notes 38–9 to chapter 20, where I quote Engels' paradoxical complaint that the ' working class is actually becoming more and more bourgeois '.

³² Cp. notes 4 and 6 to chapter 7.

³³ They may continue for other reasons also ; for example, because the tyrant's power depends on the support of a certain section of the ruled. *But this does not mean that the tyranny must in fact be a class rule*, as the Marxists would say. For even if the tyrant is forced to bribe a certain section of the population, to grant them economic or other advantages, this does not mean that he is forced *by this section*, or that this section has the power to claim and to enforce these advantages as their right. If there are no *institutions* in existence enabling that section to enforce its influence, the tyrant may withdraw the benefits enjoyed by this section and seek support from another one.

³⁴ Cp. *H.o.M.*, 171 (= Karl Marx, *Civil War in France*, Introduction by F. Engels. Martin Lawrence, London 1933, 19). (See also *H.o.M.*, 833 = *The Proletarian Revolution*, 33–34.)

³⁵ Cp. *H.o.M.*, 45 (= *GA*, Series I, vol. vi, 545). See also note 21 to this chapter. Cp. further the following passage from the *Manifesto* (*H.o.M.*, 37 = *GA*, Series I, vol. vi, 538) : ' The immediate aim of the Communists is the . . conquest of political power by the proletariat.'

(1) Tactical advice that must lead to the loss of the battle of democracy is given in detail by Marx in his *Address to the Communist League.* (*H.o.M.*, 67 = *Labour Monthly*, September 1922, 143 ; cp. also note 14 to this chapter and note 44 to chapter 20.) Marx explains there the attitude to be taken up, after democracy has been attained, towards the democratic party with whom, according to the *Manifesto* (cp. note 14 to this chapter), the communists have had to establish ' union and agreement '. Marx says : ' In short, from the first moment of victory, we must no longer direct our distrust against the beaten reactionary enemy, but against our former allies' (i.e. the democrats).

Marx demands that ' the arming of the whole proletariat with rifles, guns, and ammunition should be carried out at once ' and that ' the workers must try to organize themselves into an independent guard, with their own chiefs and general staff '. The aim is ' that the bourgeois democratic Government not only immediately loses all backing among the workers, but from the commencement finds itself under the supervision and threats of authorities behind whom stands the entire mass of the working class '.

It is clear that this policy is bound to wreck democracy. It is bound to make the Government turn against those workers who are not prepared to abide by the law, but try to rule by threats. Marx tries to excuse his politics by prophecy (*H.o.M.*, 68 and 67 = *Labour Monthly*, Sept. 1922, 143) :

' As soon as the new Government is established they will commence to fight the workers ', and he says : ' In order that this party ' (i.e. the democrats) ' whose betrayal of the workers will begin with the first hour of victory, should be frustrated in its nefarious work, it is necessary to organize and to arm the proletariat.' I think that his tactics would produce precisely the nefarious effect he prophesies. They would make his historical prophecy come true. Indeed, if the workers were to proceed in this way, every democrat in his senses would be forced (even if, and particularly if, he wished to promote the cause of the oppressed) to join in what Marx describes as the betrayal of the workers, and to fight against those who were out to wreck the democratic institutions for the protection of the individual from the benevolence of tyrants and Great Dictators.

I may add that the passages quoted are comparatively early utterance, of Marx and that his more mature opinions were probably somewhat differents and at any rate more ambiguous. But this does not detract from the fact that these early passages had a lasting influence, and that they have often been acted upon, to the detriment of all concerned.

(2) In connection with point (*b*) in the text above, a passage from Lenin may be quoted (*H.o.M.*, 828 = *The Proletarian Revolution*, 30) : '. . the working class realizes perfectly well that the bourgeois parliaments are institutions *foreign* to them, that they are *instruments of the oppression* of the proletariat by the bourgeoisie, that they are institutions of the hostile class, of the exploiting minority.' It is clear that these stories did not encourage the workers to defend parliamentary democracy against the assault of the fascists.

[36] Cp. Lenin, *State and Revolution* (*H.o.M.*, 744 = *State and Revolution*, 68) : ' Democracy . . for the rich, that is the democracy of capitalist society. . . Marx brilliantly grasped the *essence* of capitalist democracy when . . he said that the oppressed were allowed, once every few years, to decide which particular representatives of the oppressing class should . . oppress them ! ' See also notes 1 and 2 to chapter 17.

[37] Lenin writes in *Left-Wing Communism* (*H.o.M.*, 884 f. ; italics mine = V. I. Lenin, *Left-Wing Communism, An Infantile Disorder*. L.L.L. vol. xvi, 72–73) : '. . all attention must be concentrated on the *next* step . . on seeking out the forms of *transition or approach* to the proletarian revolution. The proletarian vanguard has been ideologically won over. . . But from this first step it is still a long way to victory. . . In order that the entire class . . may take up such a position, propaganda and agitation alone are not enough. *The masses must have their own political experience.* Such is the fundamental law of all great revolutions . . : *it has been necessary . . to realize through their own painful experience . . the absolute inevitability of a dictatorship of the extreme reactionaries . .* as the only alternative to a dictatorship of the proletariat, *in order to turn them resolutely towards communism.*'

[38] As is to be expected, each of the two Marxist parties tries to put the blame for their failure on the other ; the one blames the other for its policy of catastrophe, and in its turn is blamed by the latter for keeping up the worker's faith in the possibility of winning the battle of democracy. It is somewhat ironical to find that Marx himself has given an excellent description which fits every detail of this method of blaming the circumstances, and especially the competing party, for one's failure. (The description was, of course, aimed by Marx against a competing leftist group of his time.) Marx writes (*H.o.M.*, 130 ; last group of italics mine = V. I. Lenin, *The Teachings of Karl Marx*, L.L.L. vol. i, 55) : ' They do not need to consider their own resources too critically. They have merely to give the signal, and the people, with all its inexhaustible resources, will fall upon the *oppressors*. If, in the actual event, their . . powers prove to be sheer impotence, then the fault lies either with the pernicious sophists ' (the other party, presumably) ' who

split the *united people* into different hostile camps, or . . the whole thing has been wrecked by a detail in its execution, or else an unforeseen accident has, for the time being, spoilt the game.   In any case the democrat ' (or the anti-democrat) ' comes out of the most disgraceful defeat immaculate, just as he went into it innocent, *with the newly won conviction that he is destined to conquer ; that neither he himself nor his party have to give up their old standpoint, but, on the contrary, conditions have to ripen, to move in his direction . .*'

[39] I say ' the radical wing ', for this historicist interpretation of fascism as being an inevitable stage in the inexorable development was believed in, and defended, by groups far beyond the ranks of the Communists.   Even some of the leaders of the Viennese workers who offered a heroic but belated and badly organized resistance to fascism believed faithfully that fascism was a necessary step in the historical development towards socialism.   Much as they hated it, they felt compelled to regard even fascism as a step forward, bringing the suffering people nearer to the ultimate goal.

[40] Cp. the passage quoted in note 37 to this chapter.

NOTES TO CHAPTER 20

[1] The only complete English translation of the three volumes of *Capital* has nearly 2,500 pages.   To these have to be added the three volumes which were published in German under the title *Theories of Surplus Value* ;   they contain material, largely historical, which Marx intended to use in *Capital*.

[2] Cp. the opposition between an unrestrained capitalism and interventionism introduced in chapters 16 and 17.   (See notes 10 to chapter 16, 22 to chapter 17 and 9 to chapter 18, and text.)
For Lenin's statement, cp. *H.o.M.*, 561 (= *The Teachings of Karl Marx*, 29, italics mine).   It is interesting that neither Lenin nor most of the Marxists appear to realize that society has changed since Marx.   Lenin speaks in 1914 of ' contemporary society '. as if it were Marx's as well as his contemporary society.   But the *Manifesto* was published in 1848.

[3] For all quotations in this paragraph, cp. *Capital*, 691.

[4] Cp. the remarks on these terms made in note 3 to chapter 19.

[5] It would do better because the defeatist spirit, which might endanger class consciousness (as mentioned in the text to note 7 to chapter 19), would be less likely to develop.

[6] Cp. *Capital*, 697 ff.

[7] The two quotations are from *Capital*, 698 and 706.   The term translated by ' semi-prosperity ' would be, in a more literal translation, ' medium prosperity '.   I translate ' excessive production ' instead of ' over-production ' because Marx does *not* mean ' over-production ' in the sense that more is produced than can be sold *now*, but in the sense that so much is produced that a difficulty of selling it will soon develop.

[8] As Parkes puts it ;   cp. note 19 to chapter 19.

[9] The labour theory of value is, of course, very old.   My discussion of the value theory, it must be remembered, is confined to the so-called ' objective value theory ' ;   I do not intend to criticize the ' subjective value theory ' (which should perhaps better be described as the theory of subjective evaluation, or of acts of choice ;   cp. note 14 to chapter 14).   J. Viner kindly pointed out to me that almost the only connection between Marx's value theory and Ricardo's arises out of Marx's misunderstanding of Ricardo, and that Ricardo never held that, unit for unit, labour had any more creating power than capital.

[10] It appears to me certain that Marx never doubted that his ' values ' *in some way* correspond to market prices.   The value of a commodity, he taught, is equal to that of another one if the average number of labour hours

needed for their production is the same. If one of the two commodities is *old*, then its weight can be considered as the *price* of the other commodity, expressed in gold ; and since money is based (by law) upon gold, we thus arrive at the money price of a commodity.

The actual exchange ratios on the market, Marx teaches (see especially the important footnote 1 to p. 153 of *Capital*), will oscillate about the value ratios ; and accordingly, the market price in money will also oscillate about the corresponding value ratio to gold of the commodity in question. ' If the magnitude of value is transformed into price ', Marx says, a bit clumsily (*Capital*, 79 ; italics mine), ' then this . . relation assumes the form of an . . exchange ratio to *that commodity which functions as money* ' (i.e. gold). ' In this ratio expresses itself, however, not only the magnitude of the value of the commodity, but also the ups and downs, the more or less, for which special circumstances are responsible ' ; in other words, prices may fluctuate. ' The possibility . . of a derivation of price from . . value is therefore inherent in the price form. This is not a defect ; on the contrary, it shows that the price form is quite adequate to a method of production in which *regularities can manifest themselves only as averages of irregularities.*' It seems to me clear that the ' regularities ' of which Marx speaks here are the values, and that he believes that values ' manifest themselves ' (or ' assert themselves ') only as averages of the actual market prices, which are therefore oscillating about the value.

The reason why I emphasize this is that it has sometimes been denied. G. D. H. Cole, for example, writes in his ' Introduction ' (*Capital*, xxv ; italics mine) : ' Marx . . speaks usually as if commodities had actually a tendency, *subsequent* to temporary market fluctuations, to exchange at their " values ". But he says explicitly (on page 79) that he does not mean this ; and in the third volume of *Capital* he . . makes the inevitable divergence of prices and " values " abundantly clear.' But although it is true that Marx does not consider the fluctuations as merely ' temporary ', he does hold that commodities have a tendency, *subject* to market fluctuations, to exchange at their ' values ' ; for as we have seen in the passage quoted here, and referred to by Cole, Marx does not speak of any *divergence* between value and price, but describes fluctuations and averages. The position is somewhat different in the third volume of *Capital*, where (in Chapter IX) the place of the ' value ' of a commodity is taken by a new category, the ' production-price ', which is the sum of its production cost plus the average rate of surplus value. But even here it remains characteristic of Marx's thinking that this new category, the production-price, is related to the actual market price as a kind of regulator of averages only. It does not determine the market price directly, but it expresses itself (just as does ' value ' in the first volume) as an average about which the actual prices oscillate or fluctuate. This may be shown with the help of the following passage (*Das Kapital*, III/2, p. 396 f.) : ' The market prices rise above or fall below these regulating production-prices, but these oscillations compensate one another. . . The same principle of regulative averages rules here that has been established by Quételet for social phenomena in general.' Similarly, Marx speaks there (p. 399) of the ' regulative price . . , i.e. the price about which market prices oscillate ' ; and on the next page, where he speaks of the influence of competition, he says that he is interested in the ' *natural* price . . , i.e. the price . . that is not regulated by competition, but regulates it.' (Italics mine.) Apart from the fact that the ' natural ' price clearly indicates that Marx hopes to find the essence of which the oscillating market prices are the ' forms of appearance ' (cp. also note 23 to this chapter), we see that Marx consistently clings to the view that this essence, whether value or production-price, manifests itself as the *average* of the market prices. See also *Das Kapital*, III/1, 171 f.

¹¹ Cole, *op. cit.*, xxix, says in his otherwise excellently clear statement of Marx's theory of Surplus Value that it was ' his distinctive contribution to economic doctrine '. But Engels, in his Preface to the second volume of *Capital*, has shown that this theory was not Marx's, that Marx not only never claimed that it was, but also had dealt with its history (in his *Theories of Surplus Value* ; cp. note 1 to this chapter). Engels quotes from Marx's manuscript in order to show that Marx deals with Adam Smith's and Ricardo's contribution to that theory and quotes at length from the pamphlet, *The Source and Remedy of the National Difficulties*, mentioned in *Capital*, 646, in order to show that the main ideas of the doctrine, apart from the Marxian distinction between labour and labour power, can be found there. (Cp. *Das Kapital*, II, xii-xv.)

¹² The first part is called by Marx (cp. *Capital*, 213 f.) *necessary labour time*, the second part *surplus labour time*.

¹³ Cp. Engels' Preface to the second volume of *Capital*. (*Das Kapital*, II, xxi, f.)

¹⁴ Marx's derivation of the doctrine of surplus value is of course closely connected with his criticism of ' formal ' freedom, ' formal ' justice, etc. Cp. especially notes 17 and 19 to chapter 17, and text. See also the text to the next note.

¹⁵ Cp. *Capital*, 845. See also the passages referred to in the foregoing note.

¹⁶ Cp. the text to note 18 (and note 10) to this chapter.

¹⁷ See especially chapter X of the third volume of *Capital*.

¹⁸ For this quotation, cp. *Capital*, 706. From the words ' thus surplus population ', the passage follows immediately after the one quoted in the text to note 7 to this chapter. (I have omitted the word ' relative ' before ' surplus population ', since it is irrelevant in the present context, and perhaps confusing. There seems to be a misprint in the Everyman edition : ' overproduction ' instead of ' surplus population '.) The quotation is of interest in connection with the problem of supply and demand, and with Marx's teaching that these must have a ' background ' (or ' essence ') ; cp. notes 10 and 20 to this chapter.

¹⁹ It may be mentioned in this connection that the phenomena in question —misery in a period of rapidly expanding industrialization (or of ' early capitalism ' ; cp. note 36 below, and text) has recently been explained by a hypothesis which, if it can be upheld, would show that there was a great deal in Marx's theory of exploitation. I have in mind a theory based on Walter Euken's doctrine of the two pure monetary systems (the gold and the credit system), and his method of analysing the various historically given economic systems as ' mixtures ' of pure systems. Applying this method, Leonhard Miksch has recently pointed out (in a paper *Die Geldordnung der Zukunft*, Zeitschrift für das Gesamte Kreditwesen, 1949) that the credit system leads to *forced investments*, i.e. the consumer is forced to save, to abstain ;' ' but the capital saved by way of these forced investments ', Miksch writes, ' does not belong to those who were forced to abstain from consumption, but to the entrepreneurs '.

If this theory proves acceptable, then Marx's analysis (but neither his ' laws ' nor his prophecies) would be vindicated to a considerable extent. For there is only a small difference between Marx's ' surplus value ' which, by rights, belongs to the worker but is ' appropriated ' or ' expropriated ' by the ' capitalist ', and Miksch's ' forced savings ' which become the property, not of the consumer who was forced to save, but of the ' entrepreneur '. Miksch himself hints that these results explain much of the economic development of the nineteenth century (and of the rise of socialism).

It should be noted that Miksch's analysis explains the relevant facts in terms of *imperfections* in the competitive system (he speaks of an ' economic monopoly of money creation which is possessed of stupendous power ') while Marx attempted to explain corresponding facts with the help of the assumption of a free market, i.e. of competition. (Furthermore, 'consumers' and 'industrial workers' cannot, of course, be completely identified.) But whatever the explanation, the facts—described by Miksch as 'intolerably anti-social'—remain ; and it is to Marx's credit, both that he did not accept these facts, and that he tried hard to explain them.

²⁰ Cp. note 10 to this chapter, especially the passage on the ' natural ' price (also note 18 and text) ; it is interesting that in the third volume of *Capital*, not far from the passages quoted in note 10 to this chapter (see *Das Kapital*, III/2, 352 ; italics mine), and in a similar context, Marx makes the following methodological remark : ' *All science would be superfluous if the forms of appearance of things coincided with their essences.*' This is, of course, pure essentialism. That this essentialism borders on metaphysics is shown in note 24 to this chapter.

It is clear that when Marx speaks repeatedly, especially in the first volume, of the price-form, he has a ' form of appearance ' in mind ; the essence is ' value '. (Cp. also note 6 to chapter 17 and text.)

²¹ In *Capital*, pp. 43 ff. : ' The Mystery of the Fetishistic Character of Commodities.'

²² Cp. *Capital*, 567 (see also 328), with Marx's summary : ' If the productivity of labour is doubled then, if the ratio of necessary labour to surplus labour remains unaltered, . . the only result will be that each of them will represent twice as many use-values ' (i.e. commodities) ' as before. These use-values are now twice as cheap as before. . . Thus it is possible, when the productivity of labour is increasing, that the price of labour power should keep on falling, and yet that *this fall should be accompanied by a constant growth in the quantity of the worker's means of subsistence.*'

²³ If productivity increases more or less generally, then the productivity of the gold companies may also increase ; and this would mean that gold, like every other commodity, becomes cheaper if appraised in labour hours. Accordingly, the same would hold for gold as for other commodities ; and when Marx says (cp. the foregoing note) that the quantity of the worker's real income increases, this would, in theory, also be true of his income in gold, i.e. in money. (Marx's analysis in *Capital*, p. 567, of which I have quoted only a summary in the foregoing note, is therefore not correct wherever he speaks of ' prices ' ; for ' prices ' are ' values ' expressed in gold, and these may remain *constant* if productivity increases equally in all lines of production, including the production of gold.)

²⁴ The strange thing about Marx's value theory (as distinct from the English classical school, according to J. Viner) is that it considers human labour as fundamentally different from all other processes in nature, for example, from the labour of animals. This shows clearly that the theory is based ultimately upon a *moral* theory, the doctrine that human suffering and a human lifetime spent is a thing fundamentally different from all natural processes. We can call this the doctrine of the *holiness of human labour*. Now I do not deny that this theory is right in the moral sense ; that is to say, that we should act according to it. But I also think that an economic analysis should not be based upon a moral or metaphysical or religious doctrine of which the holder is unconscious. Marx who, as we shall see in chapter 22, did not consciously believe in a humanitarian morality, or who repressed such beliefs, was building upon a moralistic basis where he did not suspect it—in his abstract theory of value. This is, of course, connected with his essentialism : the essence of all social and economic relations is human labour.

²⁵ For interventionism, cp. notes 22 to chapter 17 and 9 to chapter 18. (See also note 2 to the present chapter.)

²⁶ For the *paradox of freedom* in its application to economic freedom, cp. note 20 to chapter 17, where further references are given.

The problem of the *free market*, mentioned in the text only in its application to the labour market, is of very considerable importance. Generalizing from what has been said in the text, it is clear that the idea of a free market is paradoxical. If the state does not interfere, then other semi-political organizations such as monopolies, trusts, unions, etc., may interfere, reducing the freedom of the market to a fiction. On the other hand, it is most important to realize that without a carefully protected free market, the whole economic system must cease to serve its only rational purpose, that is, *to satisfy the demands of the consumer*. If the consumer cannot choose ; if he must take what the producer offers ; if the producer, whether a private producer or the state or a marketing department, is master of the market, instead of the consumer ; then the situation must arise that the consumer serves, ultimately, as a kind of money-supply and rubbish-remover for the producer, instead of the producer serving the needs and desires of the consumer.

Here we are clearly faced with an important problem of social engineering : the market must be controlled, but in such a way that the control does not impede the free choice of the consumer and that it does not remove the need for the producers to compete for the favour of the consumer. Economic ' planning ' that does not plan for economic freedom in this sense will lead dangerously close to totalitarianism. (Cp. F. A. von Hayek's *Freedom and the Economic System*, Public Policy Pamphlets, 1939/40.)

[27] Cp. note 2 to this chapter, and text.

[28] This distinction between machinery serving mainly for the *extension* and machinery serving mainly for the *intensification* of production is introduced in the text largely with the aim of making the presentation of the argument more lucid. Apart from that, it is also, I hope, an improvement of the argument.

I may give here a list of the more important passages of Marx, bearing on the trade cycle (*t-c*), and on its connection with unemployment (*u*) : *Manifesto*, 29 f. (*t-c*).—*Capital*, 120 (monetary crisis = general depression), 624 (*t-c* and currency), 694 (*u*), 698 (*t-c*), 699 (*t-c* depending on *u* ; automatism of the cycle), 703–705 (*t-c* and *u* in interdependence), 706 f. (*u*). See also the third volume of *Capital*, especially chapter XV, section on *Surplus of Capital and Surplus of Population*, H.o.M., 516–528 (*t-c* and *u*) and chapters XXV–XXXII (*t-c* and currency ; cp. especially *Das Kapital*, III/2, 22 ff.) See also the passage from the second volume of *Capital* from which a sentence is quoted in note 17 to chapter 17.

[29] Cp. the *Minutes of Evidence, taken before the Secret Committee of the House of Lords appointed to inquire into the causes of Distress*, etc., 1875, quoted in *Das Kapital*, III/1, pp. 398 ff.

[30] Cp. for example the two articles on *Budgetary Reform* by C. G. F. Simkin in the Australian *Economic Record*, 1941 and 1942 (see also note 3 to chapter 9). These articles deal with counter cycle policy, and report briefly on the Swedish measures.

[31] Cp. Parkes, *Marxism—A Post Mortem*, especially p. 220, note 6.

[32] The quotations are from *Das Kapital*, III/2, 354 f. (I translate ' useful commodities ' although ' use-value ' would be more literal.)

[33] The theory I have in mind (held, or very nearly held, by J. Mill as J. Viner informs me) is frequently alluded to by Marx, who struggled against it without, however, succeeding in making his point quite clear. It can be expressed briefly as the doctrine that all capital reduces ultimately to wages, since the ' immobilized ' (or as Marx says, ' constant ') capital has been produced, and paid for, in wages. Or in Marx's terminology : There is no constant but only variable capital.

This doctrine has been very clearly and simply presented by Parkes (*op. cit.*, 97) : ' All capital is variable capital. This will be plain if we consider a hypothetical industry which controls the whole of its processes of production from the farm or the mine to the finished product, without buying any machinery or raw material from outside.   The entire cost of production in such an industry will consist of its wage bill.'   And since an economic system as a whole can be considered as such a hypothetical industry, within which machinery (constant capital) is always paid for in terms of wages (variable capital), the sum total of constant capital must form part of the sum total of variable capital.

I do not think that this argument, in which I once believed myself, can invalidate the Marxian position.   (This is perhaps the only major point in which I cannot agree with Parkes's excellent criticism.)   The reason is this. If the hypothetical industry decides to *increase* its machinery—not only to replace it, or to make necessary improvements—then we can look upon this process as a typical Marxian process of accumulation of capital *by the investment of profits*.   In order to measure the success of this investment, we should have to consider whether the profits in succeeding years had increased in proportion to it.   Some of these new profits may be invested again.   Now during the year in which they were invested (or profits were accumulated by conversion into constant capital), they were paid for in the form of variable capital.   But once they have been invested, they are, in the following periods, considered as part of the constant capital, since they are expected to contribute proportionally to new profits.   If they do not, the rate of profit must fall, and we say that it was a mal-investment.   The rate of profit is thus a measure of the success of an investment, of the productivity of the newly added constant capital, which, though originally always paid for in the form of variable capital, none the less becomes constant capital in the Marxian sense, and exerts its influence upon the rate of profit.

³⁴ Cp. chapter XIII of the third volume of *Capital*, for example, H.o.M., 499 : ' We see then, that in spite of the progressive fall in the rate of profit, there may be . . an absolute increase in the mass of the produced profit. And this increase may be progressive.   And it *may* not only be so.   On the basis of capitalist production, it *must* be so, aside from temporary fluctuations.'

³⁵ The quotations in this paragraph are from *Capital*, 708 ff.

³⁶ For Parkes's summary, cp. *Marxism—A Post Mortem*, p. 102.

It may be mentioned here that the Marxian theory that revolutions depend on misery has been to some extent confirmed in the last century by the outbreak of revolutions in countries in which misery actually increased. But contrary to Marx's prediction, these countries were not those of developed capitalism.   They were either peasant countries or countries where capitalism was at a primitive stage of development.   Parkes has given a list to substantiate this statement.   (Cp. *op. cit.*, 48.)   It appears that revolutionary tendencies decrease with the advance of industrialization.   Accordingly, the Russian revolution should not be interpreted as premature (nor the advanced countries as over-ripe for revolution), but rather as a product of the typical misery of capitalist infancy and of peasant misery, enhanced by the misery of war and the opportunities of defeat.   See also note 19, above.

³⁷ Cp. H.o.M., 507.

In a footnote to this passage (i.e. *Das Kapital*, III/1, 219), Marx contends that Adam Smith is right, against Ricardo.

The passage from Smith to which Marx probably alludes is quoted further below in the paragraph : it is from the *Wealth of Nations* (vol. II, p. 95 of the Everyman edition).

Marx quotes a passage from Ricardo (*Works*, ed. MacCulloch, p. 73 = Ricardo, Everyman edition, p. 78).   But there is an even more characteristic passage in which Ricardo holds that the mechanism described by Smith ' cannot . . affect the rate of profit ' (*Principles*, 232).

³⁸ For Engels, cp. H.o.M., 708 (= Quoted in *Imperialism*, 96).

[39] For this change of front, cp. note 31 to chapter 19, and text.

[40] Cp. Lenin, *Imperialism : The Highest Stage of Capitalism* (1917) ; *H.o.M.*, 708 (= *Imperialism*, 97).

[41] This may be an excuse, though only a very unsatisfactory excuse, for certain most depressing remarks of Marx, quoted by Parkes, *Marxism—A Post Mortem* (213 f., note 3).—They are most depressing since they raise the question whether Marx and Engels were the genuine lovers of freedom one would like them to be ; whether they were not more influenced by Hegel's irresponsibility and by his nationalism than one should, from their general teaching, expect.

[42] Cp. *H.o.M.*, 295 (= *GA*, Special Volume, 290–1) : ' By more and more transforming the great majority of the population into proletarians, the capitalist mode of production creates the force which . . is compelled to carry out this revolution.' For the passage from the *Manifesto*, cp. *H.o.M.*, 35 (= *GA*, Series I, vol. vi, 536).—For the following passage, cp. *H.o.M.*, 156 f. (= *Der Buergerkrieg in Frankreich*, 84).

[43] For this amazingly naïve passage, cp. *H.o.M.*, 147 f. (= *Der Buergerkrieg in Frankreich*, 75 f.).

[44] For this policy, cp. Marx's *Address to the Communist League*, quoted in notes 14 and 35–37 to chapter 19. (Cp. also, for example, notes 26 f. to that chapter.) See further the following passage from the *Address* (*H.o.M.*, 70 f. ; italics mine = *Labour Monthly*, Sept. 1922, 145–6) : ' Thus, for instance, if the petty bourgeoisie purpose to purchase the railways and factories, the workers must demand that such railways and factories shall simply be confiscated by the State without compensation ; for they are the property of the reactionaries. If the democrats propose proportional taxation, the workers must demand progressive taxation. If the democrats themselves declare for a moderate progressive tax, the workers must insist on a steeply graduated tax ; so steeply graduated as to cause the collapse of large capital. If the democrats propose the regulation of the National Debt, the workers must demand State bankruptcy. *The demands of the workers will depend on the proposals and measures of the democrats.*' These are the tactics of the Communists, of whom Marx says : ' Their battle-cry must be : " Revolution in permanence ! " ' '

NOTES TO CHAPTER 21

[1] Cp. notes 22 to chapter 17 and 9 to chapter 18, and text.

[2] Engels says in the *Anti-Dühring* that Fourier long ago discovered the ' vicious circle ' of the capitalist mode of production ; cp. *H.o.M.*, 287.

[3] Cp. *H.o.M.*, 527 (= *Das Kapital*, III/1, 242).

[4] Cp., for example, Parkes, *Marxism—A Post Mortem*, pp. 102 ff.

[5] This is a question which I wish to leave open.

[6] This point has been emphasized by my colleague, Prof. C. G. F. Simkin, in discussions.

[7] Cp. text to note 11 to chapter 14, and end of note 17 to chapter 17.

[8] Cp. H. A. L. Fisher, *History of Europe* (1935), Preface, vol. I, p. vii. The passage is quoted more fully in note 27 to chapter 25.

NOTES TO CHAPTER 22

[1] For Kierkegaard's fight against ' official Christianity ', cp. especially his *Book of the Judge*. (German ed., by H. Gottsched, 1905.)

[2] Cp. J. Townsend, *A Dissertation on the Poor Laws, by a Wellwisher of Mankind* (1817) ; quoted in *Capital*, 715.

On p. 711 (note 1) Marx quotes ' the spirited and witty Abbé Galiani ' as holding similar views : ' Thus it comes to pass ', Galiani says, ' that the men who practise occupations of primary utility breed abundantly.' See Galiani, *Della Moneta*, 1803, p. 78.

The fact that even in Western countries, Christianity is not yet entirely free from the spirit of defending the return to the closed society of reaction and oppression can be seen from the excellent polemic of H. G. Wells against Dean Inge's biased and pro-fascist attitude towards the Spanish civil war. Cp. H. G. Wells, *The Common Sense of War and Peace* (1940), pp. 38-40. (In referring to Wells's book, I do not wish to associate myself with anything he says on federation, whether critical or constructive ; and especially not with the idea propounded on pp. 56 ff., regarding fully empowered world commissions. The fascist dangers involved in this idea seem to me enormous.) On the other hand, there is the opposite danger, that of a pro-communist Church ; cp. note 12 to chapter 9.

³ Cp. Kierkegaard, *op. cit.*, 172.

⁴ But Kierkegaard said something of Luther that may be true of Marx also : ' Luther's corrective idea . . produces . . the most sophisticated form of . . paganism.' (*Op. cit.*, 147.)

⁵ Cp. *H.o.M.*, 231 (= Ludwig Feuerbach, 56) ; cp. notes 11 and 14 to chapter 13.

⁶ Cp. note 14 to chapter 13, and text.

⁷ Cp. my *The Poverty of Historicism*, section 19.

⁸ Cp. *H.o.M.*, 247 f. (= *GA*, Special Volume, 97).

⁹ For these quotations, cp. *H.o.M.*, 248, and 279 (the latter passage is shortened = *GA*, Special Volume, 97 and 277).

¹⁰ Cp. L. Laurat, *Marxism and Democracy*, p. 16. (Italics mine.)

¹¹ For these two quotations, cp. *The Churches Survey Their Task* (1937), p. 130, and A. Loewe, *The Universities in Transformation* (1940), p. 1. With the concluding remark of this chapter, cp. also the views expressed by Parkes in the last sentences of his criticism of Marxism (*Marxism—A Post Mortem*, 1940, p. 208).

NOTES TO CHAPTER 23

¹ Concerning Mannheim, see especially *Ideology and Utopia* (quoted here from the German ed., 1929). The terms ' social habitat ' and ' total ideology ' are both due to Mannheim ; the terms ' sociologism ' and ' historism ' have been mentioned in the last chapter. The idea of a ' social habitat ' is Platonic.

For a criticism of Mannheim's *Man and Society in an Age of Reconstruction* (1941), which combines historicist tendencies with a romantic and even mystical holism, see my *The Poverty of Historicism*, II (*Economica*, 1944).

² Cp. my interpretation in *What is Dialectic?* (*Mind*, 49, especially p. 414 ; also *Conjectures and Refutations*, especially p. 325.)

³ This is Mannheim's term (cp. *Ideology and Utopia*, 1929, p. 35). For the ' freely poised intelligence ', see *op. cit.*, p. 123, where this term is attributed to Alfred Weber. For the theory of an intelligentsia loosely anchored in tradition, see *op. cit.*, pp. 121-34, and especially p. 122.

⁴ For the latter theory, or, rather, practice, cp. notes 51 and 52 to chapter 11.

⁵ Cp. *What is Dialectic?* (p. 417 ; *Conjectures and Refutations*, p. 327). Cp. note 33 to chapter 12.

⁶ The analogy between the psycho-analytic method and that of Wittgenstein is mentioned by Wisdom, *Other Minds* (*Mind*, vol. 49, p. 370, note) : ' A doubt such as " I can never really know what another person is feeling " may arise from more than one of these sources. This over-determination of sceptical symptoms complicates their cure. The treatment is like psychot analytic treatment (to enlarge Wittgenstein's analogy) in that the treatmen- is the diagnosis and the diagnosis is the description, the very full description, of the symptoms.' And so on. (I may remark that, using the word ' know '

in the ordinary sense, we can, of course, never know what another person is feeling. We can only make hypotheses about it. This solves the so-called problem. It is a mistake to speak here of doubt, and a still worse mistake to attempt to remove the doubt by a semiotico-analytic treatment.)

[7] The psycho-analysts seem to hold the same of the individual psychologists, and they are probably right. Cp. Freud's *History of the Psycho-Analytic Movement* (1916), p. 42, where Freud records that Adler made the following remark (which fits well within Adler's individual-psychological scheme, according to which feelings of inferiority are predominantly important) : ' Do you believe that it is such a pleasure for me to stand in your shadow my whole life ? ' This suggests that Adler had not successfully applied his theories to himself, at that time at least. But the same seems to be true of Freud : None of the founders of psycho-analysis were psycho-analysed. To this objection, they usually replied that they had psycho-analysed themselves. But they would never have accepted such an excuse from anybody else ; and, indeed, rightly so.

[8] For the following analysis of scientific objectivity, cp. my *The Logic of Scientific Discovery*, section 8 (pp. 44 ff.).

[9] I wish to apologize to the Kantians for mentioning them in the same breath as the Hegelians.

[10] Cp. notes 23 to chapter 8 and 39 (second paragraph) to chapter 11.

[11] Cp. notes 34 ff., to chapter 11.

[12] Cp. K. Mannheim, *Ideology and Utopia* (German ed., p. 167).

[13] For the first of these two quotations, cp. *op. cit.*, 167. (For simplicity's sake, I translate ' conscious ' for ' reflexive '.) For the second, cp. *op. cit.*, 166.

[14] Cp. *Handbook of Marxism*, 255 (= *GA*, Special Volume, 117–18) : ' Hegel was the first to state correctly the relation between freedom and necessity. To him, freedom is the appreciation of necessity.' For Hegel's own formulation of his pet idea, cp. *Hegel Selections*, 213 (= *Werke*, 1832–1887, vi, 310) : ' The truth of necessity, therefore, is freedom.' 361 (= *WW*, xi, 46) : ' . . the *Christian* principle of self-consciousness—Freedom.' 362 (= *WW*, xi, 47) : ' The essential nature of freedom, which involves in it absolute necessity, is to be displayed as the attainment of a consciousness of itself (for it is in its very nature, self-consciousness) and it thereby realizes its existence.' And so on.

NOTES TO CHAPTER 24

[1] I am here using the term ' rationalism ' in opposition to ' irrationalism ' and not to ' empiricism '. Carnap writes in his *Der Logische Aufbau der Welt* (1928), p. 260 : ' The word " rationalism " is now often meant . . in a modern sense : *in contradistinction to irrationalism*.'

In using the term ' rationalism ' in this way, I do not wish to suggest that the other way of using this term, namely, in opposition to empiricism, is perhaps less important. On the contrary, I believe that this opposition characterizes one of the most interesting problems of philosophy. But I do not intend to deal with it here ; and I feel that, in opposition to empiricism, we might do better to use another term—perhaps ' intellectualism ' or ' intellectual intuitionism '—in place of ' rationalism ' in the Cartesian sense. I may mention in this context that I do not *define* the terms ' reason ' or ' rationalism ' ; I am using them as labels, taking care that nothing depends on the words used. Cp. chapter 11, especially note 50. (For the reference to Kant, see note 56 to chapter 12, and text.)

[2]* This is what I tried to do in *Towards a Rational Theory of Tradition* (*The Rationalist Annual*, 1949, pp. 36 ff., and now in *Conjectures and Refutations*, pp. 120 ff.).

³ Cp. Plato's *Timaeus* 51e. (See also the cross-references in note 33 to chapter 11.)

⁴ Cp. chapter 10, especially notes 38–41, and text.

In Pythagoras, Heraclitus, Parmenides, Plato, mystical and rationalist elements are mixed. Plato especially, in spite of all his emphasis on ' reason ', incorporated into his philosophy such a weighty admixture of irrationalism that it nearly ousted the rationalism he inherited from Socrates. This enabled the Neo-Platonists to base their mysticism on Plato ; and most subsequent mysticism goes back to these sources.

It may perhaps be accidental, but it is in any case remarkable that there is still a cultural frontier between Western Europe and the regions of Central Europe which coincide very nearly with those regions that did not come under the administration of Augustus' Roman Empire, and that did not enjoy the blessings of the Roman peace, i.e. of the Roman civilization. The same ' barbarian ' regions are particularly prone to be affected by mysticism, even though they did not invent mysticism. Bernard of Clairvaux had his greatest successes in Germany, where later Eckhart and his school flourished, and also Boehme.

Much later Spinoza, who attempted to combine Cartesian intellectualism with mystical tendencies, rediscovered the theory of a mystical intellectual intuition, which, in spite of Kant's strong opposition, led to the post-Kantian rise of ' Idealism ', to Fichte, Schelling, and Hegel. Practically all modern irrationalism goes back to the latter, as is briefly indicated in chapter 12. (Cp. also notes 6, 29–32 and 58, below, and notes 32–33 to chapter 11, and the cross-references on mysticism there given.)

⁵ With the ' mechanical activities ', cp. notes 21 and 22 to this chapter.

⁶ I say ' discarded ' in order to cover the views (1) that such an assumption would be false, (2) that it would be unscientific (or impermissible), though it might perhaps be accidentally true, (3) that it would be ' senseless ' or ' meaningless ', for example in the sense of Wittgenstein's *Tractatus* ; cp. note 51 to chapter 12, and note 8 (2) to the present chapter.

In connection with the distinction between ' critical ' and ' uncritical ' rationalism, it may be mentioned that the teaching of Duns Scotus as well as of Kant could be interpreted as approaching ' critical ' rationalism. (I have in mind their doctrines of the ' primacy of will ', which may be interpreted as the primacy of an irrational decision.)

⁷ In this and the following note a few remarks on paradoxes will be made, especially on the *paradox of the liar*. In introducing these remarks, it may be said that the so-called ' logical ' and ' semantical ' paradoxes are no longer merely playthings for the logicians. Not only have they proved to be important for the development of mathematics, but they are also becoming important in other fields of thought. There is a definite connection between these paradoxes and such problems as the *paradox of freedom* which, as we have seen (cp. note 20 to chapter 17 and notes 4 and 6 to chapter 7), is of considerable significance in political philosophy. In point (4) of this note, it will be briefly shown that the various *paradoxes of sovereignty* (cp. note 6 to chapter 7, and text) are very similar to the paradox of the liar. On the modern methods of solving these paradoxes (or perhaps better : of constructing languages in which they do not occur), I shall not make any comments here, since it would take us beyond the scope of this book.

(1) *The paradox of the liar* can be formulated in many ways. One of them is this. Let us assume that somebody says one day : ' All that I say to-day is a lie ' ; or more precisely : ' All statements I make to-day are false ' ; and that he says nothing else the whole day. Now if we ask ourselves whether he spoke the truth, this is what we find. If we start with the assumption that what he said was true, then we arrive, considering *what* he said, at the result

that it must have been false. And if we start with the assumption that what he said was false, then we must conclude, considering *what* he said, that it was true.

(2) Paradoxes are sometimes called ' contradictions '. But this is perhaps slightly misleading. An ordinary contradiction (or a self-contradiction) is simply a logically false statement, such as ' Plato was happy yesterday and he was not happy yesterday '. If we assume that such a sentence is false, no further difficulty arises. But of a paradox, we can neither assume that it is true *nor that it is false*, without getting involved in difficulties.

(3) There are, however, statements which are closely related to paradoxes, but which are, more strictly speaking, only self-contradictions. Take for example the statement : ' All statements are false.' If we assume that this statement is true, then we arrive, considering *what* it says, at the result that it is false. But if we assume that it is false, then we are out of the difficulty ; for this assumption leads only to the result that not all statements are false, or in other words, that there are some statements—at least one—that are true. And this result is harmless ; for it does not imply that our original statement is one of the true ones. (This does not imply that we can, in fact, construct a language *free of paradoxes* in which ' All statements are false ' or ' All statements are true ' can be formulated.)

In spite of the fact that this statement ' All propositions are false ' is not really a paradox, it may be called, by courtesy, ' a form of the paradox of the liar ', because of its obvious resemblance to the latter ; and indeed, the old Greek formulation of this paradox (Epimenides the Cretan says : ' All Cretans always lie ') is, in this terminology, rather ' a form of the paradox of the liar ' i.e. a contradiction rather than a paradox. (Cp. also next note, and note 54 to this chapter, and text.)

(4) I shall now show briefly the similarity between the paradox of the liar and the various *paradoxes of sovereignty*, for example, of the principle that the best or the wisest or the majority should rule. (Cp. note 6 to chapter 7 and text.)

C. H. Langford has described various ways of putting the paradox of the liar, among them the following. We consider two statements, made by two people, A and B.

A says : ' What B says is true.'
B says : ' What A says is false.'

By applying the method described above, we easily convince ourselves that each of these sentences is paradoxical. Now we consider the following two sentences, of which the first is the principle that the wisest should rule :

(A) The principle says : What the wisest says under (B) should be law.
(B) The wisest says : What the principle states under (A) should not be law.

⁸ (1) That the principle of avoiding all presuppositions is ' a form of the paradox of the liar ' in the sense of note 7 (3) to this chapter, and therefore self-contradictory, will be easily seen if we describe it like this. A philosopher starts his investigation by assuming without argument the principle : ' All principles assumed without argument are impermissible.' It is clear that if we assume that tnis principle is true, we must conclude, considering what it says, that it is impermissible. (The opposite assumption does not lead to any difficulty.) The remark ' a counsel of perfection ' alludes to the usual criticism of this principle which was laid down, for example, by Husserl. J. Laird (*Recent Philosophy*, 1936, p. 121) writes about this principle that it ' is a cardinal feature of Husserl's philosophy. Its success may be more doubtful, for presuppositions have a way of creeping in.' So far, I fully agree ; but not quite with the next remark : ' . . the avoidance of all presuppositions may well be a counsel of perfection, impracticable in an inadvertent world.' (See also note 5 to chapter 25.)

(2) We may consider at this place a few further ' principles ' which are, in the sense of note 7 (3) to this chapter, ' forms of the paradox of the liar ', and therefore self-contradictory.

(a) From the point of view of social philosophy, the following ' principle of sociologism ' (and the analogous ' principle of historism ') are of interest. They can be formulated in this way. ' No statement is absolutely true, and all statements are inevitably relative to the social (or historical) habitat of their originators.' It is clear that the considerations of note 7 (3) apply practically without alteration. For if we assume that such a principle is true, then it follows that it is not true but only ' relative to the social or historical habitat of its originator '. See also note 53 to this chapter, and text.

(b) Some examples of this kind can be found in Wittgenstein's *Tractatus*. The one is Wittgenstein's proposition (quoted more fully in note 46 to chapter 11) : ' The totality of true propositions is . . the totality of natural science.' Since this proposition does not belong to natural science (but, rather, to a meta-science, i.e. a theory that speaks about science) it follows that it asserts its own untruth, and is therefore contradictory.

Furthermore, it is clear that this proposition violates Wittgenstein's own principle (*Tractatus*, p. 57), ' No proposition can say anything about itself. . .'

* But even this last quoted principle which I shall call ' W ' turns out to be a form of the paradox of the liar, and to assert its own untruth. (It therefore can hardly be—as Wittgenstein believes it to be—equivalent to, or a summary of, or a substitute for, ' the whole theory of types ', i.e. Russell's theory, designed to avoid the paradoxes which he discovered by dividing expressions which look like propositions into three classes—true propositions, false propositions, and meaningless expressions or pseudo-propositions.) For Wittgenstein's principle W may be re-formulated as follows :

(W^+) Every expression (and especially one that looks like a proposition) which contains a reference to itself—either by containing its own name or an individual variable ranging over a class to which it itself belongs—is not a proposition (but a meaningless pseudo-proposition).

Now let us assume that W^+ is true. Then, considering the fact that it is an expression, and that it refers to every expression, it cannot be a proposition, and is therefore *a fortiori* not true.

The assumption that it is true is therefore untenable ; W^+ cannot be true. But this does not show that it must be false ; for both, the assumption that it is false and the other that it is a meaningless (or senseless) expression, do not involve us in immediate difficulties.

Wittgenstein might perhaps say that he saw this himself when he wrote (p. 189 ; cp. note 51 (1) to chapter 11) : ' My propositions are elucidatory in this way : he who understands me finally recognizes them as senseless . .' ; in any case, we may conjecture that he would incline to describing W^+ as meaningless rather than false. I believe, however, that it is not meaningless but simply false. Or more precisely, I believe that in every formalized language (e.g. in one in which Goedel's undecidable statements can be expressed) which contains means for speaking about its own expressions, and in which we have names of classes of expressions such as ' propositions ' and ' non-propositions ', *the formalization of a statement which, like W^+, asserts its own meaninglessness, will be self-contradictory and neither meaningless nor genuinely paradoxical ;* it will be a meaningful proposition merely because it asserts of every expression of a certain kind that it is not a proposition (i.e. not a well-formed formula) ; and such an assertion will be true or false, but not meaningless, simply because to be (or not to be) a well-formed proposition is a property of expressions. For example, ' All expressions are meaningless ' will be self-contradictory, but not genuinely paradoxical, and so will be the expression

' The expression x is meaningless ', if we substitute for ' x ' a name of this expression. Modifying an idea of J. N. Findlay's, we can write :

The expression obtained by substituting for the variable in the following expression, ' *The expression obtained by substituting for the variable in the following expression* x *the quotation name of this expression, is not a statement* ', *the quotation name of this expression, is not a statement.*

And what we have just written turns out to be a self-contradictory statement. (If we write twice ' is a false statement ' instead of ' is not a statement ', we obtain a paradox of the liar ; if we write ' is a non-demonstrable statement ', we obtain a Goedelian statement in J. N. Findlay's writing.)

To sum up. Contrary to first impressions, we find that a theory which implies its own meaninglessness is not meaningless but false, since the predicate ' meaningless ', as opposed to ' false ', does not give rise to paradoxes. And Wittgenstein's theory is therefore not meaningless, as he believes, but simply false (or, more specifically, self-contradictory).

(3) It has been claimed by some positivists that a tripartition of the expressions of a language into (i) true statements, (ii) false statements, and (iii) meaningless expressions (or, better, expressions other than well-formed statements), is more or less ' natural ' and that it provides, because of their meaninglessness, for the elimination of the paradoxes and, at the same time, of metaphysical systems. The following may show that this tripartition is not enough.

The General's Chief Counter-Espionage Officer is provided with three boxes, labelled (i) ' General's Box ', (ii) ' Enemy's Box ' (to be made accessible to the enemy's spies), and (iii) ' Waste Paper ', and is instructed to distribute all information arriving before 12 o'clock among these three boxes, according to whether this information is (i) true, (ii) false, or (iii) meaningless.

For a time, he receives information which he can easily distribute (among it true statements of the theory of natural numbers, etc., and perhaps statements of logic such as L : ' From a set of true statements, no false statement can be validly derived '). The last message M, arriving with the last incoming mail just before 12 o'clock, disturbs him a little, for M reads : ' From the set of all statements placed, or to be placed, within the box labelled " General's Box ", the statement " $0 = 1$ " cannot validly be derived.' At first, the Chief Counter-Espionage Officer hesitates whether he should not put M into box (ii). But since he realizes that, if put into (ii), M would supply the enemy with valuable true information, he ultimately decides to put M into (i).

But this turns out to be a big mistake. For the symbolic logicians (experts in logistic ?) on the General's staff, after formalizing (and ' arithmetizing ') the contents of the General's box, discover that they obtain a set of statements which contains an assertion of its own consistency ; and this, according to Goedel's second theorem on decidability, leads to a contradiction, so that ' $0 = 1$ ' can actually be deduced from the presumably true information supplied to the General.

The solution of this difficulty consists in the recognition of the fact that the tripartition-claim is unwarranted, at least for ordinary languages ; and we can see from Tarski's theory of truth that no definite number of boxes will suffice. At the same time we find that ' meaninglessness ' in the sense of ' not belonging to the well-formed formulæ ' is by no means an indication of ' nonsensical talk ' in the sense of ' words which just don't mean anything, although they may pretend to be deeply significant ' ; but to have revealed that metaphysics was just of this character was the chief claim of the positivists.*

[9] It appears that it was the difficulty connected with the so-called ' problem of induction ' which led Whitehead to the disregard of argument displayed in *Process and Reality*. (Cp. also notes 35-7 to this chapter.)

¹⁰ It is a moral decision and not merely ' a matter of taste ' since it is not a private affair but affects other men and their lives. (For the opposition between æsthetic matters of taste and moral problems, cp. text to note 6 to chapter 5, and chapter 9 especially text to notes 10–11.) The decision with which we are faced is most important from the point of view that the ' learned ', who are faced with it, act as intellectual trustees for those who are not faced with it.

¹¹ It is, I believe, perhaps the greatest strength of Christianity that it appeals fundamentally not to abstract speculation but to the imagination, by describing in a very concrete manner the suffering of man.

¹² Kant, the great equalitarian in regard to moral decisions, has emphasized the blessings involved in the fact of human inequality. He saw in the variety and individuality of human characters and opinions one of the main conditions of moral as well as material progress.

¹³ The allusion is to A. Huxley's *Brave New World*.

¹⁴ For the distinction between facts, and decisions or demands, cp. text to notes 5 ff. to chapter 4. For the ' language of political demands ' (or ' proposals ' in the sense of L. J. Russell) cp. text to notes 41–43, chapter 6 and note 5(3) to chapter 5.

I should be inclined to say that the theory of the innate intellectual equality of all men is false ; but since such men as Niels Bohr contend that the influence of environment is alone responsible for individual differences, and since there are no sufficient experimental data for deciding this question, ' probably false ' is perhaps all that should be said.

¹⁵ See, for example, the passage from Plato's *Statesman*, quoted in the text to note 12 to chapter 9. Another such passage is *Republic*, 409e–410a. After having spoken (409b & c) of the ' *good judge . . who is good because of the goodness of his soul* ', Plato continues (409e, f.), ' And are you not going to establish physicians and judges . . who are to look after those citizens whose physical and mental constitution is healthy and good ? Those whose physical health is bad, they will leave to die. And those whose soul is bad-natured and incurable, they will actually kill.'—' Yes,' he said, ' since you have proved that this is the best thing, both for those to whom it happens, and for the state.'

¹⁶ Cp. notes 58 to chapter 8 and 28 to chapter 10.

¹⁷ An example is H. G. Wells, who gave to the first chapter of his book, *The Common Sense of War and Peace*, the excellent title : *Grown Men Do Not Need Leaders*. (Cp. also note 2 to chapter 22.)

¹⁸ For the problem and the paradox of tolerance, cp. note 4 to chapter 7.

¹⁹ The ' world ' is not rational, but it is the task of science to rationalize it. ' Society ' is not rational, but it is the task of the social engineer to rationalize it. (This does not mean, of course, that he should ' direct ' it, or that centralized or collectivist ' planning ' is desirable.) Ordinary language is not rational, but it is our task to rationalize it, or at least to keep up its standards of clarity. The attitude here characterized could be described as ' *pragmatic rationalism* '. This pragmatic rationalism is related to an uncritical rationalism and to irrationalism in a similar way as critical rationalism is related to these two. For an uncritical rationalism may argue that the world is rational and that the task of science is to discover this rationality, while an irrationalist may insist that the world, being fundamentally irrational, should be experienced and exhausted by our emotions and passions (or by our intellectual intuition) rather than by scientific methods. As opposed to this, pragmatic rationalism may recognize that the world is not rational, but demand *that we submit or subject it to reason*, as far as possible. Using Carnap's words (*Der Logische Aufbau*, etc., 1928, p. vi) one could describe what I call ' pragmatic rationalism ' as ' the attitude which strives for clarity everywhere but recognizes the never fully understandable or never fully rational entanglement of the events of life '.

[20] For the problem of the standards of clarity of our language, cp. the last note and note 30 to chapter 12.

[21] Industrialization and the Division of Labour are attacked, for example, by Toynbee, *A Study of History*, vol. I, pp. 2 ff. Toynbee complains (p. 4) that ' the prestige of the Industrial System imposed itself upon the " intellectual workers " of the Western World . . ; and when they have attempted to " work " these materials " up " into " manufactured " or " semi-manufactured " articles, they have had recourse, once again, to the Division of Labour . .' In another place (p. 2) Toynbee says of physical scientific periodicals : ' Those periodicals were the Industrial System " in book form ", with its Division of Labour and its sustained maximum output of articles manufactured from raw materials *mechanically*.' (Italics mine.) Toynbee emphasizes (p. 3, note 2) with the Hegelian Dilthey that the spiritual sciences at least should keep apart from these methods. (He quotes Dilthey, who said : ' The real categories . . are nowhere the same in the sciences of the Spirit as they are in the sciences of Nature.')

Toynbee's interpretation of the division of labour in the field of science seems to me just as mistaken as Dilthey's attempt to open up a gulf between the methods of the natural and the social sciences. What Toynbee calls ' division of labour ' could better be described as co-operation and mutual criticism. Cp. text to notes 8 f. to chapter 23, and Macmurray's comments upon scientific co-operation quoted in the present chapter, text to note 26. (For Toynbee's anti-rationalism, cp. also note 61 to chapter 11.)

[22] Cp. Adolf Keller, *Church and State on the European Continent* (Beckly Social Service Lecture, 1936). I owe it to Mr. L. Webb that my attention has been drawn to this interesting passage.

[23] For moral futurism as a kind of moral positivism, cp. chapter 22 (especially text to notes 9 ff.).

I may draw attention to the fact that in contradistinction to the present fashion (cp. notes 51 f. to chapter 11), I attempt to take Keller's remarks seriously and question their truth, instead of dismissing them, as the positivist fashion would demand, as meaningless.

[24] Cp. note 70 to chapter 10 and text, and note 61 to chapter 11.

[25] Cp. Matthew 7, 15 f. : ' Beware of false prophets, which come to you in sheep's clothing, but inwardly they are ravening wolves. Ye shall know them by their fruits.'

[26] The two passages are from J. Macmurray, *The Clue to History* (1938), pp. 86 and 192. (For my disagreement with Macmurray cp. text to note 16 to chapter 25.)

[27] Cp. L. S. Stebbing's book, *Philosophy and the Physicists*, and my own brief remark on the Hegelianism of Jeans in *What is Dialectic?* (*Mind*, 1940, 49, p. 420 ; now in *Conjectures and Refutations*, p. 330).

[28] Cp., for example, notes 8-12 to chapter 7, and text.

[29] Cp. chapter 10, especially the end of that chapter, i.e. notes 59-70, and text (see especially the reference to McTaggart in note 59) ; the note to the *Introduction* ; notes 33 to chapter 11 and 36 to chapter 12 ; notes 4, 6, and 58 to the present chapter. See also Wittgenstein's insistence (quoted in note 32 to the present chapter) that the contemplation of, or the feeling for, the world as a *limited whole* is the mystical feeling.

A much-discussed recent work on mysticism and its proper rôle in politics is Aldous Huxley's *Grey Eminence*. It is interesting mainly because the author does not seem to realize that his own story of the mystic and politician, Father Joseph, flatly refutes the main thesis of his book. This thesis is that training in mystical practice is the only educational discipline known that is capable of securing to men that absolutely firm moral and religious ground which is so dearly needed by people who influence public policy. But his own story shows that Father Joseph, in spite of his training, fell into temptation—the usual temptation of those who wield power—and that he was unable to resist ; absolute power corrupted him absolutely. That is to say, the only historical evidence discussed at any length by the author disproves his thesis completely ; which, however, does not seem to worry him.

³⁰ Cp. F. Kafka, *The Great Wall of China* (English transl. by E. Muir, 1933), p. 236.

³¹ Cp. also note 19 to this chapter.

³² Cp. Wittgenstein's *Tractatus*, p. 187 : ' Not *how* the world is, is the mystical, but *that* it is.—The contemplation of the world *sub specie aeterni* is its contemplation as a limited whole.—The feeling of the world as a limited whole is the mystical feeling.' One sees that Wittgenstein's mysticism is typically holistic.—For other passages of Wittgenstein (*loc. cit.*) like : ' There is indeed the inexpressible. This *shows* itself ; it is the mystical ', cp. Carnap's criticism in his *Logical Syntax of Language* (1937), p. 314 f. Cp. also note 25 to chapter 25, and text. See also note 29 to the present chapter and the cross-references given there.

³³ Cp. chapter 10, for example notes 40, 41. The tribal and esoteric tendency of this kind of philosophy may be exemplified by a quotation from H. Blueher (cp. Kolnai, *The War against the West*, p. 74, italics mine) : ' Christianity is emphatically an aristocratic creed, free of morals, unteachable. The Christians know one another by their exterior type ; they form a set in human society who never fail in mutual understanding, and *who are understood by none but themselves*. They constitute a secret league. Furthermore, the kind of love that operates in Christianity is that which illuminates the pagan temples ; it bears no relation to the Jewish invention of so-called love of mankind or love of one's neighbours.' Another example may be taken from E. von Salomon's book, *The Outlaws* (quoted also in note 90 to chapter 12 ; the present quotation is from`p. 240 ; italics mine) : ' *We recognized one another in an instant*, though we came from all parts of the Reich, having got wind of skirmishes and of danger.'

³⁴ This remark is not meant in a historicist sense. I do not mean to prophesy that the conflict will play no part in future developments. I only mean that by now we could have learned that the problem does not exist, or that it is, at any rate, insignificant as compared with the problem of the *evil religions*, such as totalitarianism and racialism, with which we are faced.

³⁵ I am alluding to *Principia Mathematica*, by A. N. Whitehead and B. Russell. (Whitehead says, in *Process and Reality*, p. 10, note 1, that the ' introductory discussions are practically due to Russell, and in the second edition wholly so '.)

³⁶ Cp. the reference to Hegel (and many others, among them Plato and Aristotle) in A. N. Whitehead, *Process and Reality*, p. 14.

³⁷ Cp. Whitehead, *op. cit.*, pp. 18 f.

³⁸ Cp. Kant's Appendix to his *Prolegomena*. (*Works*, ed. by Cassirer, vol. IV, 132 f. For the translation ' crazy quilt ', cp. Carus' English edition of Kant's *Prolegomena*, 1902 and 1912, p. iv.)

³⁹ Cp. Whitehead, *Process and Reality*, p. 20 f. Concerning the attitude of *take it or leave it*, described in the next paragraph, cp. note 53 to chapter 11.

⁴⁰ Cp. Whitehead, *op. cit.*, 492. Two of the other antitheses are : ' It is as true to say that the World is immanent in God, as that God is immanent in the World. . . It is as true to say that God creates the World, as that the World creates God.' This is very reminiscent of the German mystic Scheffler (Angelus Silesius), who wrote : ' I am as great as God, God is as small as me, I cannot without him, nor he without me, be.'

Concerning my remark, later in the paragraph, that I just do not understand what the author wishes to convey, I may say that it was only with great reluctance that I wrote this. The ' I do not understand ' criticism is a rather cheap and dangerous kind of sport. I simply wrote these words because, in spite of my efforts, they remained true.

⁴¹ Cp. Kant's letter to Mendelssohn of April 8th, 1766. (*Works*, ed. by Cassirer, vol. IX, 56 f.)

⁴² Cp. Toynbee, *A Study of History*, vol. VI, 536 f.

⁴³ Toynbee says (*op. cit.*, 537) of the ' traditionally orthodox minds ' that they ' will see our investigation as an attack upon the historicity of the story of Jesus Christ as it is presented in the Gospels '. And he holds (p. 538) that God reveals himself through poetry as well as through truth ; according to his theory, God has ' revealed himself in folk-lore '.

⁴⁴ Following up this attempt to apply Toynbee's methods to himself, one could ask whether his *Study of History* which he has planned to consist of thirteen volumes is not just as much what he terms a *tour de force* as the ' histories like the several series of volumes now in course of publication by the Cambridge University Press '—undertakings which he brilliantly compares (vol. I, p. 4) to ' stupendous tunnels and bridges and dams and liners and battleships and skyscrapers '. And one could ask whether Toynbee's *tour de force* is not, more particularly, the manufacturing of what he calls a ' time machine ', i.e. an escape into the past. (Cp. especially Toynbee's medievalism, briefly discussed in note 61 to chapter 11. Cp. further note 54 to the present chapter.)

⁴⁵ I have not so far seen more than the first six volumes. Einstein is one of the few scientists mentioned.

⁴⁶ Toynbee, *op. cit.*, vol. II, 178.

⁴⁷ Toynbee, *op. cit.*, vol. V, 581 ff. (Italics mine.)

In connection with Toynbee's neglect, mentioned in the text, of the Marxian doctrines and especially of the *Communist Manifesto*, it may be said that on p. 179 (note 5) of this volume, Toynbee writes : ' The Bolshevik or Majoritarian wing of the Russian Social-Democratic Party renamed itself " the Russian Communist Party " (in homage to the Paris Commune of A.D. 1871) in March, 1918 . .' A similar remark can be found in the same volume, p. 582, note 1.

But this is not correct. The change of name (which was submitted by Lenin to the party conference of April, 1917 ; cp. *Handbook of Marxism*, 783 ; cp. also p. 787) referred, obviously enough, to the fact that ' Marx and Engels called themselves Communists ', as Lenin puts it, and to the *Communist Manifesto*.

⁴⁸ Cp. Engels, *Socialism : Utopian and Scientific* (see note 9 to chapter 13). For two historical roots of Marx's communism (Plato's and, perhaps, Pythagoras'—archaism, and the *Acts*, which seem to be influenced by it) see especially note 29 to chapter 5 ; see also notes 30 to chapter 4, 34–36 to chapter 6, and notes 3 and 8 to chapter 13 (and text).

⁴⁹ Cp. Toynbee, *op. cit.*, vol. V, 587.

⁵⁰ Cp. chapter 22, especially text to notes 1–4, and the end of that chapter.

⁵¹ The passage is not isolated ; Toynbee very often expresses his respect for the ' verdict of history ' ; a fact that is in keeping with his doctrine that it is ' the claim of Christianity . . that God has revealed Himself in history '. This ' Neo-protestant doctrine ' (as K. Barth calls it) will be discussed in the next chapter. (Cp. especially note 12 to that chapter.)

In connection with Toynbee's treatment of Marx, it may be mentioned that his whole approach is strongly influenced by Marxism. He says (*op. cit.*, vol. I, p. 41, note 3) : ' More than one of these Marxian coinages have become current even among people who reject the Marxian dogmas.' This

statement refers especially to the use of the word ' proletariat '. But it covers
more than the mere use of words.

⁵² Cp. Toynbee, *op. cit.*, vol. III, 476. The passage refers back to vol. I,
part I, A, *The Relativity of Historical Thought.* (The problem of the ' relativity '
of historical thought will be discussed in the next chapter.) For an excellent
early criticism of historical relativism (and historicism), see H. Sidgwick's
Philosophy—Its Scope and Relations (1902), Lecture IX, especially p. 180 f.

⁵³ For if *all* thought is in such a sense ' inevitably relative ' to its historical
habitat that it is not ' absolutely true ' (i.e. not true), then this must hold
for this contention as well. Thus it cannot be true, and therefore not an
inevitable ' Law of Human Nature '. Cp. also note 8 (2, *a*) to this chapter.

⁵⁴ For the contention that Toynbee escapes into the past, cp. note 44 to
this chapter and note 61 to chapter 11 (on Toynbee's medievalism). Toynbee
himself gives an excellent criticism of archaism, and I fully agree with his
attack (vol. VI, 65 f.) upon nationalist attempts to revive ancient languages,
especially in Palestine. But Toynbee's own attack upon industrialism (cp.
note 21 to the present chapter) seems to be no less archaistic.—For an escape
into the future, I have no other evidence than Toynbee's announced prophetic
title of part ʾXII of his work : *The Prospects of the Western Civilization.*

⁵⁵ The ' tragic worldly success of the founder of Islam ' is mentioned by
Toynbee in *op. cit.*, III, p. 472. For Ignatius Loyola, cp. vol. III, 270 ; 466 f.

⁵⁶ Cp. *op. cit.*, vol. V, 590.—The passage quoted next is from the same
volume, p. 588.

⁵⁷ Toynbee, *op. cit.*, vol. VI, 13.

⁵⁸ Cp. Toynbee, vol. VI, 12 f. (The reference is to Bergson's *Two Sources
of Morality and Religion.*)

The following historicist quotation from Toynbee (vol. V, 585 ; italics
mine) is interesting in this context : ' Christians believe—and *a study of History
assuredly proves them right*—that the brotherhood of Man is *impossible for Man to
achieve in any other way* than by enrolling himself as a citizen of a *Civitas Dei*
which transcends the human world and has God himself for its king.' How
can a study of history prove such a claim ? Is it not a highly responsible
matter to assert that it can be proved ?

Concerning Bergson's *Two Sources*, I fully agree that there is an irrational
or intuitive element in every creative thought ; but this element can be
found in rational scientific thought also. Rational thought is not non-
intuitive ; it is, rather, intuition *submitted to tests and checks* (as opposed to
intuition run wild). Applying this to the problem of the creation of the
open society, I admit that men like Socrates were inspired by intuition ; but
while I grant this fact, I believe that it is their *rationality* by which the founders
of the open society are distinguished from those who tried to arrest its development, and who were also, like Plato, inspired by intuition—only by an intuition
unchecked by reasonableness (in the sense in which this term has been used
in the present chapter). See also the note to the *Introduction.*

⁵⁹ Cp. note 4 to chapter 18.

NOTES TO CHAPTER 25

¹ The so-called conventionalists (H. Poincaré, P. Duhem, and more
recently, A. Eddington) ; cp. note 17 to chapter 5.

² Cp. my *The Logic of Scientific Discovery.*

³ The ' bucket theory of the mind ' has been mentioned in chapter 23.
(*For the ' searchlight theory of science ', see also my *Towards a Rationa
Theory of Tradition*, now in my *Conjectures and Refutations*, especially pp. 127 f.*)
The ' searchlight theory ' contains, perhaps, just those elements of Kantian-
ism that are tenable. We might say that Kant's mistake was to think the

searchlight itself incapable of improvement; and that he did not see that some searchlights (theories) may fail to illuminate facts which others bring out clearly. But this is how we give up using certain searchlights, and make progress.

⁴ Cp. note 23 to chapter 8.

⁵ For the attempt to avoid all presuppositions, cp. the criticism (of Husserl) in note 8 (1) to chapter 24, and text. The naïve idea that it is possible to avoid presupposition (or a point of view) has also been attacked on different lines by H. Gomperz. (Cp. *Weltanschauungslehre*, I, 1905, pp. 33 and 35 ; my translation is perhaps a little free.) Gomperz's attack is directed against radical empiricists. (Not against Husserl.) 'A philosophic or scientific attitude towards facts', Gomperz writes, 'is always an attitude of thought, and not merely an attitude of enjoying the facts in the manner of a cow, or of contemplating facts in the manner of a painter, or of being overwhelmed by the facts in the manner of a visionary. We must therefore assume that the philosopher is not satisfied with the facts as they are, but thinks about them. . . Thus it seems clear that behind that philosophical radicalism which pretends . . to go back to immediate facts or data, there is always hidden an uncritical reception of traditional doctrines. For some thoughts about the facts must occur even to these radicals ; . but since they are unconscious of them to such a degree as to hold that they merely admit the facts, we have no choice but to assume that their thoughts are . . uncritical.' (Cp. also the same author's remarks on *Interpretation* in *Erkenntnis*, vol. 7, pp. 225¶ff.)

⁶ Cp. Schopenhauer's comments on history (*Parerga*, etc., vol. II, ch. XIX, § 238 ; *Works*, second German edition, vol. VI, p. 480).

⁷ (1) To my knowledge, the theory of causality sketched here in the text was first presented in my book, *Logik der Forschung* (1935)—now translated as *The Logic of Scientific Discovery* (1959). See pp. 59 f. of the translation. As here translated, the original brackets have been eliminated, and numbers in brackets as well as four brief passages in brackets have been added, partly in order to make a somewhat compressed passage more intelligible, and partly (in the case of the two last brackets) to make allowance for a point of view I had not clearly seen in 1935, the point of view of what A. Tarski has called 'semantics'. (See, e.g., his *Grundlegung der wissenschaftlichen Semantik*, in *Actes du Congrès International Philosophique*, vol. III, Paris, 1937, pp. 1 ff., and R. Carnap, *Introduction to Semantics*, 1942). Owing to Tarski's development of the foundations of semantics, I no longer hesitate (as I did when writing the book referred to) to make full use of the terms 'cause' and 'effect'. For these can be defined, using Tarski's concept of truth, by a semantic definition such as the following : Event A is the cause of event B, and event B the effect of event A, if and only if there exists a language in which we can formulate three propositions, u, a, and b, such that u is a true universal law, a describes A, and b describes B, and b is a logical consequence of u and a. (Here the term 'event' or 'fact' may be defined by a semantic version of my definition of 'event' in my *The Logic of Scientific Discovery*, pp. 88 ff., say, by the following definition : An event E is the common designatum of a class of mutually translatable singular statements.)

(2) A few historical remarks concerning the *problem of cause and effect* may be added here. The Aristotelian concept of cause (viz., his formal and material cause, and his efficient cause ; the final cause does not interest us here, even though my remark holds good for it too) is typically essentialistic ; the problem is to explain change or motion, and it is explained by reference to the hidden structure of things. This essentialism is still to be found in Bacon's, Descartes', Locke's, and even Newton's views on this matter ; but Descartes' theory opens the way to a new view. He saw the essence of all physical bodies in their spatial extension or geometrical shape, and concluded

from this that the only way in which bodies can act upon one another is by pushing ; one moving body *necessarily* pushes another from its place because both are extended, and therefore cannot fill the same space. Thus *the effect follows the cause by necessity, and all truly causal explanation (of physical events) must be in terms of push*. This view was still assumed by Newton, who accordingly said about his own theory of gravitation—which, of course, employs the idea of pull rather than push—that nobody who knows anything of philosophy could possibly consider it a satisfactory explanation ; and it still remains influential in physics in the form of a dislike of any kind of ' action at a distance '.—Berkeley was the first to criticize the explanation by hidden essences, whether these are introduced to ' explain ' Newton's attraction, or whether they lead to a Cartesian theory of push ; he demanded that science should *describe*, rather than *explain* by essential or necessary connections. This doctrine, which became one of the main characteristics of positivism, lose its point if our theory of causal explanation is adopted ; for explanation becomes then a kind of description ; it is a description which makes use of universal hypotheses, initial conditions, and logical deduction. To Hume (who was partly anticipated by Sextus Empiricus, Al-Gazzâli, and others) is due what may be called the most important contribution to the theory of causation ; he pointed out (as against the Cartesian view) that we cannot know anything about a necessary connection between an event *A* and another event *B*. All we can possibly know is that events of the kind *A* (or events similar to *A*) have so far been followed by events of the kind *B* (or events similar to *B*). We can know that, in point of fact, such events were connected ; but since we do not know that this connection is a necessary one, we can say only that it has held good in the past. Our theory fully recognizes this Humean criticism. But it differs from Hume (1) in that it explicitly formulates the *universal hypothesis* that events of the kind *A* are always and everywhere followed by events of the kind *B* ; (2) that it asserts the truth of the statement that *A* is the cause of *B*, provided that the universal hypothesis is true.—Hume, in other words, only looked at the events *A* and *B* themselves ; and he could nlot find any trace of a causal link or a necessary connection between these two. But we add a third thing, a universal law ; and with respect to this aw, we may speak of a causal link, or even of a necessary connection. We could, for example, define : Event *B* is *causally linked* (or *necessarily connected*) with event *A* if and only if *A* is the cause of *B* (in the sense of our semantic definition given above).—Concerning the question of the truth of a universal law, we may say that there are countless universal laws whose truth we never question in daily life ; and accordingly, there are also countless cases of causation where in daily life we never question the ' necessary causal link '. From the point of scientific method, the position is different. For we can never rationally establish the truth of scientific laws ; all we can do is to test them severely, and to eliminate the false ones (this is perhaps the crux of my *The Logic of Scientific Discovery*). Accordingly, all scientific laws retain for ever a hypothetical character ; they are assumptions. And consequently, all statements about specific causal connections retain the same hypothetical character. We can never be certain (in a scientific sense) that *A* is the cause of *B*, precisely because we can never be certain whether the universal hypothesis in question is true, however well it may be tested. Yet, we shall be inclined to find the specific hypothesis that *A* is the cause of *B* the more acceptable the better we have tested and confirmed the corresponding universal hypothesis. (For my theory of *confirmation*, see chapter X and also appendix *ix of *The Logic of Scientific Discovery*, especially p. 275, where the temporal coefficients or indices of confirmation sentences are discussed.)

(3) Concerning my theory of historical explanation, developed here in the text (further below), I wish to add some critical comments to an article

by Morton G. White, entitled *Historical Explanation* and published in *Mind* (vol. 52, 1943, pp. 212 ff.). The author accepts my analysis of causal explanation, as originally developed in my *Logik der Forschung* (now translated as *The Logic of Scientific Discovery*). (He mistakenly attributes this theory to an article by C. G. Hempel, published in the *Journal of Philosophy*, 1942 ; see, however, Hempel's review of my book in *Deutsche Literaturzeitung*, 1937, (8), pp. 310 to 314.) Having found what in general we call an explanation, White proceeds to ask what is *historical* explanation. In order to answer this question, he points out that the characteristic of a biological explanation (as opposed, say, to a physical one) is the occurrence of *specifically biological terms* in the explanatory universal laws ; and he concludes that an historical explanation would be one in which *specifically historical terms* would so occur. He further finds that all laws in which anything like specific historical terms occur are better characterized as sociological, since the terms in question are of a sociological character rather than of an historical one ; and he is thus ultimately forced to identify ' historical explanation ' with ' sociological explanation '.

It seems to me obvious that this view neglects what has been described here in the text as the *distinction between historical and generalizing sciences*, and their specific problems and methods ; and I may say that discussions on the problem of the method of history have long ago brought out the fact that history is interested in specific events rather than in general laws. I have in mind, for example, Lord Acton's essays against Buckle, written in 1858 (to be found in his *Historical Essays and Studies*, 1908), and the debate between Max Weber and E. Meyer (see Weber's *Gesammelte Aufsaetze zur Wissenschaftslehre*, 1922, pp. 215 ff.). Like Meyer, Weber always rightly emphasized that history is interested in *singular events*, not in universal laws, and that, *at the same time*, it is interested in *causal explanation*. Unfortunately, however, these correct views led him to turn repeatedly (e.g. *op. cit.*, p. 8) against the view that causality is bound up with universal laws. It appears to me that our theory of historical explanation, as developed in the text, removes the difficulty and at the same time explains how it could arise.

[8] The doctrine that crucial experiments may be made in physics has been attacked by the conventionalists, especially by Duhem (cp. note 1 to this chapter). But Duhem wrote before Einstein, and before Eddington's crucial eclipse observation ; he even wrote before the experiments of Lummer and Pringsheim which, by falsifying the formulæ of Rayleigh and Jeans, led to the Quantum theory.

[9] The dependence of history upon our interest has been admitted both by E. Meyer and by his critic M. Weber. Meyer writes (*Zur Theorie und Methodik der Geschichte*, 1902, p. 37) : ' The selection of facts depends upon the historical interest taken by those living at the present time. . .' Weber writes (*Ges. Aufsaetze*, 1922, p. 259) : ' Our . . interest . . will determine the range of cultural values which determines . . history.' Weber, following Rickert, repeatedly insists that our interest, in turn, depends upon ideas of value ; in this he is certainly not wrong, but he does not add anything to the methodological analysis. None of these authors, however, draw the revolutionary consequence that, since all history depends upon our interest, *there can be only histories, and never a ' history '*, a story of the development of mankind ' as it happened '.—

For two interpretations of history which are opposed to one another, cp. note 61 to chapter 11.

[10] For this refusal to discuss the problem of the ' meaning of meaning ' (Ogden and Richards) or rather of the ' meanings of meaning ' (H. Gomperz), cp. chapter 11, especially notes 26, 47, 50, and 51. See also note 25 to the present chapter.

[11] For moral futurism, cp. chapter 22.

¹² Cp. K. Barth, *Credo* (1936), p. 12. For Barth's remark against 'the Neo-Protestant doctrine of the revelation of God in history', cp. *op. cit.*, 142. See also the Hegelian source of this doctrine, quoted in text to note 49, chapter 12. Cp. also note 51 to chapter 24. For the next quotation cp. Barth, *op. cit.*, 79.

* Concerning my remark that the story of Christ was *not* 'the story of an unsuccessful . . nationalist revolution', I am now inclined to believe that it may have been precisely this ; see R. Eisler's book *Jesus Basileus*. But in any case, it is not a story of wordly success.*

¹³ Cp. Barth, *op. cit.*, 76.

¹⁴ Cp. Kierkegaard's Journal of 1854 ; see the German edition (1905) of his *Book of the Judge*, p. 135.

¹⁵ Cp. note 57 to chapter 11, and text.

¹⁶ Cp. the concluding sentences of Macmurray's *The Clue to History* (1938 ; p. 237).

¹⁷ Cp. especially note 55 to chapter 24, and text.

¹⁸ Kierkegaard was educated at the University of Copenhagen in a period of intense and even somewhat aggressive Hegelianism. The theologian Martensen was especially influential. (For this aggressive attitude, cp. the judgement of the Copenhagen Academy against Schopenhauer's prize essay on the *Foundations of Morals*, of 1840. It is very likely that this affair was instrumental in making Kierkegaard acquainted with Schopenhauer, at a time when the latter was still unknown in Germany.)

¹⁹ Cp. Kierkegaard's *Journal* of 1853 ; see the German edition of his *Book of the Judge*, p. 129, from which the passage in the text is freely translated.

Kierkegaard is not the only Christian thinker protesting against Hegel's historicism ; we have seen (cp. note 12 to this chapter) that Barth also protests against it. A remarkably interesting criticism of Hegel's teleological interpretation of history was given by the Christian philosopher, M. B. Foster, a great admirer (if not a follower) of Hegel, at the end of his book *The Political Philosophies of Plato and Hegel*. The main point of his criticism, if I understand him rightly, is this. By interpreting history teleologically, Hegel does not see, in its various stages, ends in themselves, but merely means for bringing about the final end. But Hegel is wrong in assuming that historical phenomena or periods are means to an end which can be conceived and stated as something distinguishable from the phenomena themselves, in a way in which a purpose can be distinguished from the action which seeks to realize it, or a moral from a play (if we wrongly assume that the sole purpose of the play was to convey this moral). For this assumption, Foster contends, shows a failure to recognize the difference between the work of a *creator* and that of an instrument maker, a technician or '*Demiurge*'. '. . a series of works of creation may be understood as a development', Foster writes (*op. cit.*, pp. 201–3),'. . without a distinct conception of the end to which they progress . . the painting, say, of one era may be understood to have developed out of the era preceding it, without being understood as a nearer approximation to a perfection or end. . . Political history, similarly, . . may be understood as development, without being interpreted as a teleological process.—But Hegel, here and elsewhere, lacks insight in the significance of creation.' And later, Foster writes (*op. cit.*, p. 204 ; italics partly mine) : ' Hegel regards it as a sign of inadequacy of the religious imagery that those who hold it, while they assert that there is a plan of Providence, deny that the plan is knowable. . . To say that the plan of Providence is inscrutable is, no doubt, an inadequate expression, but the truth which it expresses inadequately is not that God's plan is knowable, but that, as Creator and not as a Demiurge, *God does not work according to plan at all.*'

I think that this criticism is excellent, even though the creation of a work of art may, in a very different sense, proceed according to a '*plan*' (although not an end or purpose) ; for it may be an attempt to realize something like the Platonic idea of that work—that perfect model before his mental eyes or ears which the painter or musician strives to copy. (Cp. note 9 to chapter 9 and notes 25–26 to chapter 8.)

²⁰ For Schopenhauer's attacks upon Hegel, to which Kierkegaard refers, cp. chapter 12, for example, text to note 13, and the concluding sentences. The partly quoted continuation of Kierkegaard's passage is *op. cit.*, 130. (In a note, Kierkegaard later inserted ' pantheist ' before ' putridity '.)

²¹ Cp. chapter 6, especially text to note 26.

²² For the Hegelian ethics of domination and submission, cp. note 25 to chapter 11.   For the ethics of hero-worship, cp. chapter 12, especially text to notes 75 ff.

²³ Cp. chapter 5 (especially text to note 5).

²⁴ We can ' express ourselves ' in many ways without communicating anything.   For our task of using language for the purpose of rational communication, and for the need of keeping up the standards of clarity of the language, cp. notes 19 and 20 to chapter 24 and note 30 to chapter 12.

²⁵ This view of the problem of the ' meaning of life ' may be contrasted with Wittgenstein's view of the problems of the ' sense of life ' in the *Tractatus* (p. 187) : ' The solution of the problem of life is seen in the vanishing of this problem.—(Is not this the reason why men to whom after long doubting the sense of life became clear, could not then say wherein this sense consisted ?)' For Wittgenstein's mysticism, see also note 32 to chapter 24.   For the interpretation of history here suggested, cp. notes 61 (1) to chapter 11, and 27 to the present chapter.

²⁶ Cp., for example, note 5 to chapter 5 and note 19 to chapter 24.

It may be remarked that the world of facts is in itself complete (since every decision can be interpreted as a fact).   It is therefore for ever impossible to *refute* a monism which insists that there are only facts.   But irrefutability is not a virtue.   Idealism, for example, cannot be refuted either.

²⁷ It appears that one of the motives of historicism is that the historicist does not see that there is a third alternative, besides the two which he allows : either that the world is ruled by superior *powers*, by an ' essential destiny ' or Hegelian ' Reason ', or that it is a mere wheel of chance, irrational, on the level of a gamble.   *But there is a third possibility* : that *we* may introduce reason into it (cp. note 19 to chapter 24) ; that although the world does not progress, *we* may progress, individually as well as in co-operation.

This third possibility is clearly expressed by H. A. L. Fisher in his *History of Europe* (vol. I, p. vii, italics mine ; partly quoted in text to note 8 to chapter 21) : ' One intellectual excitement has . . been denied me.   Men wiser and more learned than I have discerned in history a plot, a rhythm, a predetermined pattern.   These harmonies are concealed from me.   I can see only one emergency following upon another as wave follows wave, only one great fact with respect to which, *since it is unique, there can be no generalizations*, only one safe rule for the historian : that he should recognize . . the play of the contingent and the unforeseen.'   And immediately after this excellent attack upon historicism (with the passage in italics, cp. note 13 to chapter 13), Fisher continues : ' This is not a doctrine of cynicism and despair.   *The fact of progress is written plain and large on the page of history ; but progress is not a law of nature.   The ground gained by one generation may be lost by the next.*'

These last three sentences represent very clearly what I have called the ' third possibility ', the belief in our responsibility, the belief that everything rests with us.   And it is interesting to see that Fisher's statement is interpreted by Toynbee (*A Study of History*, vol. V, 414) as representing ' the modern Western belief in the omnipotence of Chance '.   Nothing could show more clearly the attitude of the historicist, his inability to see the third possibility.

And it explains perhaps why he tries to escape from this alleged ' omnipotence of chance ' into a belief in the omnipotence of the *power* behind the historical scene—that is, into historicism. (Cp. also note 61 to chapter 11.)

I may perhaps quote more fully Toynbee's comments on Fisher's passage (which Toynbee quotes down to the words ' the unforeseen ') : ' This brilliantly phrased passage ', Toynbee writes, ' cannot be dismissed as a scholar's conceit ; for the writer is a Liberal who is formulating a creed which Liberalism has translated from theory into action. . . This modern Western belief in the omnipotence of Chance gave birth in the nineteenth century of the Christian Era, when things still seemed to be going well with Western Man, to the policy of *laissez faire* . .' (Why the belief in a progress for which we ourselves are responsible should imply a belief in the omnipotence of Chance, or why it should produce the policy of *laissez faire*, Toynbee leaves unexplained.)

[28] By the ' realism ' of the choice of our ends I mean that we should choose ends which can be realized within a reasonable span of time, and that we should avoid distant and vague Utopian ideals, unless they determine more immediate aims which are worthy in themselves. Cp. especially the principles of piecemeal social engineering, discussed in chapter 9.

The final manuscript of volume I of the first edition of this book was completed in October, 1942, and that of volume II in February, 1943.

FACTS, STANDARDS, AND TRUTH:
A FURTHER CRITICISM OF RELATIVISM (1961)

The main philosophical malady of our time is an intellectual and moral relativism, the latter being at least in part based upon the former. By relativism—or, if you like, scepticism—I mean here, briefly, the theory that the choice between competing theories is arbitrary; since either, there is no such thing as objective truth ; or, if there is, no such thing as a theory which is true or at any rate (though perhaps not true) nearer to the truth than another theory ; or, if there are two or more theories, no ways or means of deciding whether one of them is better than another.

In this *addendum* [1] I shall first suggest that a dose of Tarski's theory of truth (see also the references to A. Tarski in the Index of this book), stiffened perhaps by my own theory of getting nearer to the truth, may go a long way towards curing this malady, though I admit that some other remedies might also be required, such as the non-authoritarian theory of knowledge which I have developed elsewhere.[2] I shall also try to show (in sections 12 ff. below) that the situation in the realm of standards— especially in the moral and political field—is somewhat analogous to that obtaining in the realm of facts.

1. *Truth*

Certain arguments in support of relativism arise from the question, asked in the tone of the assured sceptic who knows for certain that there is no answer : ' *What is truth ?* ' But Pilate's question can be answered in a simple and reasonable way— though hardly in a way that would have satisfied him—as follows : an assertion, proposition, statement, or belief, is true if, and only if, it corresponds to the facts.

Yet what do we mean by saying that a statement corresponds to the

---

[1] I am deeply indebted to Dr. William W. Bartley's incisive criticism which not only helped me to improve chapter 24 of this book (especially page 231) but also induced me to make important changes in the present *addendum*.

[2] See for example ' On the Sources of Knowledge and of Ignorance ', now the Introduction to my *Conjectures and Refutations* and, more especially, Chapter 10 of that book ; also, of course, my *The Logic of Scientific Discovery*.

facts ? Though to our sceptic or relativist this second question may seem just as unanswerable as the first, it actually can be equally readily answered. The answer is not difficult—as one might expect if one reflects upon the fact that every judge assumes that the witness knows what truth (in the sense of correspondence with the facts) means. Indeed, the answer turns out to be almost trivial.

In a way it *is* trivial—that is, once we have learnt from Tarski that the problem is one in which we *refer to or speak about* statements and facts and some relationship of correspondence holding between statement and facts ; and that, therefore, the solution must also be one that *refers to or speaks about* statements and facts, and some relation between them. Consider the following :

The statement ' Smith entered the pawnshop shortly after 10.15 ' corresponds to the facts if, and only if, Smith entered the pawnshop shortly after 10.15.

When we read this italicized paragraph, what is likely to strike us first is its triviality. But never mind its triviality : if we look at it again, and more carefully, we see (1) that it refers to a statement, and (2) to some facts ; and (3) that it can therefore state the very obvious conditions which we should expect to hold whenever we wish to say that the statement referred to corresponds to the facts referred to.

Those who think that this italicized paragraph is too trivial or too simple to contain anything interesting should be reminded of the fact, already referred to, that since everybody knows what truth, or correspondence with the facts, means (as long as he does not allow himself to speculate about it) this must be, in a sense, a trivial matter.

That the idea formulated in the italicized paragraph is correct, may be brought out by the following second italicized paragraph.

The assertion made by the witness, ' Smith entered the pawnshop shortly after 10.15 ' is true if and only if Smith entered the pawnshop shortly after 10.15.

It is clear that this second italicized paragraph is again very trivial. Nevertheless, it states in full the conditions for applying the predicate ' is true ' to any statement made by a witness.

Some people might think that a better way to formulate the paragraph would be the following :

The assertion made by the witness ' I saw that Smith entered the pawnshop shortly after 10.15 ' is true if and only if the witness saw that Smith entered the pawnshop shortly after 10.15.

Comparing this third italicized paragraph with the second we see that while the second gives the conditions for the truth of a statement about Smith and what he did, the third gives the conditions for the truth of a statement about the witness and what he did (or saw). But this is the only difference between the two paragraphs : both state the full conditions for the truth of the two different statements which are quoted in them.

It is a rule of *giving evidence* that eye-witnesses should confine themselves to stating what they *actually saw*. Compliance with this rule may sometimes make it easier for the judge to *distinguish* between true evidence and false evidence. Thus the third italicized paragraph may perhaps be said to have some advantages over the second, if regarded from the point of view of truth-*seeking* and truth-*finding*.

But it is essential for our present purpose not to mix up questions of actual truth-seeking or truth-finding (i.e. epistemological or methodological questions) with the question of what we mean, or what we intend to say, when we speak of truth, or of correspondence with the facts (the logical or ontological question of truth). Now from the latter point of view, the third italicized paragraph has no advantage whatever over the second. Each of them states to the full the conditions for the truth of the statement to which it refers.

Each, therefore, answers the question—' What is truth ? ' in precisely the same way ; though each does it only indirectly, by giving *the conditions for the truth for a certain statement*—and each for a different statement.

2. *Criteria*

It is decisive to realize that knowing what truth means, or under what conditions a statement is called true, is not the same as, and must be clearly distinguished from, possessing a means of deciding—a *criterion* for deciding—whether a given statement is true or false.

The distinction I am referring to is a very general one, and it is of considerable importance for an assessment of relativism, as we shall see.

We may know, for example, what we mean by ' good meat ' and by ' meat gone bad ' ; but we may not know how to tell the one from the other, at least in some cases : it is this we have in mind when we say that we have no *criterion* of the ' goodness ' of good meat. Similarly, every doctor knows, more or less, what he means by 'tuberculosis'; but he may not always recognize it. And even though there may be (by now) batteries of tests which amount almost to a decision method,—that is to say, to a *criterion*—sixty years ago there certainly were no such batteries of tests at the disposal of doctors, and no criterion. But doctors knew then very well what they meant—a lung infection due to a certain kind of microbe.

Admittedly, a criterion—a definite method of decision—if we could obtain one, might make everything clearer and more definite and more precise. It is therefore understandable that some people, hankering after precision, demand criteria. And if we can get them, the demand may be reasonable.

But it would be a mistake to believe that, before we have a criterion for deciding whether or not a man is suffering from tuberculosis, the phrase 'X is suffering from tuberculosis' is meaningless; or that, before we have a criterion of the goodness or badness of meat, there is no point in considering whether or not a piece of meat has gone bad; or that, before we have a reliable lie-detector, we do not know what we mean when we say that X is deliberately lying, and should therefore not even consider this 'possibility', since it is no possibility at all, but meaningless; or that, before we have a criterion of truth, we do not know what we mean when we say of a statement that it is true.

Thus those who insist that, without a criterion—a reliable test —for tuberculosis, or lying, or truth, we cannot mean anything by the words 'tuberculosis' or 'lying' or 'true', are certainly mistaken. In fact, construction of a battery of tests for tuberculosis, or for lying, comes *after* we have established—perhaps only roughly—what we mean by 'tuberculosis' or by 'lying'.

It is clear that in the course of developing tests for tuberculosis, we may learn a lot more about this illness; so much, perhaps, that we may say that the very meaning of the term 'tuberculosis' has changed under the influence of our new knowledge, and that after the establishment of the criterion the meaning of the term is no longer the same as before. Some, perhaps, may even say that 'tuberculosis' can now be defined in terms of the criterion. But this does not alter the fact that we meant something before— though we may, of course, have known less about the thing. Nor does it alter the fact that there are few diseases (if any) for which we have either a criterion or a clear definition, and that few criteria (if any) are reliable. (But if they are not reliable, we had better not call them 'criteria'.)

There may be no criterion which helps us to establish whether a pound note is, or is not, genuine. But should we find two pound notes with the same serial number, we should have good reasons to assert, even in the absence of a criterion, that one of them at least is a forgery ; and this assertion would clearly not be made meaningless by the absence of a criterion of genuineness.

To sum up, the theory that in order to determine what a word means we must establish a criterion for its correct use, or for its correct application, is mistaken : we practically never have such a criterion.

3. *Criterion Philosophies*

The view just rejected—the view that we must have criteria in order to know what we are talking about, whether it is tuberculosis, lying, or existence, or meaning, or truth—is the overt or implicit basis of many philosophies. A philosophy of this kind may be called a ' *criterion philosophy* '.

Since the basic demand of a criterion philosophy cannot as a rule be met, it is clear that the adoption of a criterion-philosophy will, in many cases, lead to disappointment, and to relativism or scepticism.

I believe that it is the demand for a *criterion of truth* which has made so many people feel that the question ' What is truth ? ' is unanswerable. *But the absence of a criterion of truth does not render the notion of truth non-significant any more than the absence of a criterion of health renders the notion of health non-significant. A sick man may seek health even though he has no criterion for it. An erring man may seek truth even though he has no criterion for it.*

And both may simply seek health, or truth, without much bothering about the meanings of these terms which they (and others) understand well enough for their purposes.

One immediate result of Tarski's work on truth is the following theorem of logic : *there can be no general criterion of truth* (except with respect to certain artificial language systems of a somewhat impoverished kind).

This result can be exactly established ; and its establishment makes use of the notion of truth as correspondence with the facts.

We have here an interesting and philosophically very important result (important especially in connection with the problem of an authoritarian theory of knowledge [1]). But this result

---

[1] For a description and criticism of authoritarian (or non-fallibilist) theories of knowledge see especially sections v, vi, and x. ff.. of the Introduction to my *Conjectures and Refutations*.

has been established with the help of a notion—in this case the notion of truth—for which we have no criterion. The unreasonable demand of the criterion-philosophies that we should not take a notion seriously before a criterion has been established would therefore, if adhered to in this case, have for ever prevented us from attaining a logical result of great philosophical interest.

Incidentally, the result that there can be no general criterion of truth is a direct consequence of the still more important result (which Tarski obtained by combining Gödel's undecidability theorem with his own theory of truth) that there can be no general criterion of truth even for the comparatively narrow field of number theory, or for any science which makes full use of arithmetic. It applies *a fortiori* to truth in any extra-mathematical field in which unrestricted use is made of arithmetic.

4. *Fallibilism*

All this shows not only that some still fashionable forms of scepticism and relativism are mistaken, but also that they are obsolete ; that they are based on a logical confusion—between the meaning of a term and the criterion of its proper application —although the means for clearing up this confusion have been readily available for some thirty years.

It must be admitted, however, that there is a kernel of truth in both scepticism and relativism. The kernel of truth is just that there exists no general criterion of truth. But this does not warrant the conclusion that the choice between competing theories is arbitrary. It merely means, quite simply, that we can always err in our choice—that we can always miss the truth, or fall short of the truth ; that certainty is not for us (nor even knowledge that is highly probable, as I have shown in various places, for example in chapter 10 of *Conjectures and Refutations*) ; that we are fallible.

This, for all we know, is no more than the plain truth. There are few fields of human endeavour, if any, which seem to be exempt from human fallibility. What we once thought to be well-established, or even certain, may later turn out to be not quite correct (but this means false), and in need of correction.

A particularly impressive example of this is the discovery of heavy water, and of heavy hydrogen (*deuterium*, first separated by Harold C. Urey in 1931). Prior to this discovery, nothing more certain and more settled could be imagined in the field of chemistry than our knowledge of water (H_2O) and of the chemical elements of which it is composed. Water was even used for the

' operational ' definition of the gramme, the unit standard of mass of the ' absolute ' metric system ; it thus formed one of the basic units of experimental physical measurements. This illustrates the fact that our knowledge of water was believed to be so well established that it could be used as the firm basis of all other physical measurements. But after the discovery of heavy water, it was realized that what had been believed to be a chemically pure compound was actually a mixture of chemically indistinguishable but physically very different compounds, with very different densities, boiling points, and freezing points—though for the definitions of all these points, ' water ' had been used as a standard base.

This historical incident is typical ; and we may learn from it that we cannot foresee which parts of our scientific knowledge may come to grief one day. Thus the belief in scientific certainty and in the authority of science is just wishful thinking : *science is fallible, because science is human.*

But the fallibility of our knowledge—or the thesis that all knowledge is guesswork, though some consists of guesses which have been most severely tested—must not be cited in support of scepticism or relativism. From the fact that we can err, and that a criterion of truth which might save us from error does not exist, it does not follow that the choice between theories is arbitrary, or non-rational : that we cannot learn, or get nearer to the truth : that our knowledge cannot grow.

5. *Fallibilism and the Growth of Knowledge*

By ' fallibilism ' I mean here the view, or the acceptance of the fact, that we may err, and that the quest for certainty (or even the quest for high probability) is a mistaken quest. But this does not imply that the quest for truth is mistaken. On the contrary, the idea of error implies that of truth as the standard of which we may fall short. It implies that, though we may seek for truth, and though we may even find truth (as I believe we do in very many cases), we can never be quite certain that we have found it. There is always a possibility of error ; though in the case of some logical and mathematical proofs, this possibility may be considered slight.

But fallibilism need in no way give rise to any sceptical or relativist conclusions. This will become clear if we consider that all the *known* historical examples of human fallibility—including all the *known* examples of miscarriage of justice—are *examples of the advance of our knowledge.* Every discovery of a mistake constitutes a real advance in our knowledge. As Roger Martin du Gard says in *Jean Barois*, ' it is something if we know where truth is not to be found '.

For example, although the discovery of heavy water showed that we were badly mistaken, this was not only an advance in our knowledge, but it was in its turn connected with other advances, and it produced many further advances. *Thus we can learn from our mistakes.*

This fundamental insight is, indeed, the basis of all epistemology and methodology ; for it gives us a hint how to learn more systematically, how to advance more quickly (not necessarily in the interests of technology : for each individual seeker after truth, the problem of how to hasten one's advance is most urgent). This hint, very simply, is that *we must search for our mistakes*—or in other words, that *we must try to criticize our theories.*

Criticism, it seems, is the only way we have of detecting our mistakes, and of learning from them in a systematic way.

6. *Getting Nearer to the Truth*

In all this, the idea of the growth of knowledge—of getting nearer to the truth—is decisive. Intuitively, this idea is as clear as the idea of truth itself. A statement is true if it corresponds to the facts. It is nearer to the truth than another statement if it corresponds to the facts more closely than the other statement.

But though this idea is intuitively clear enough, and its legitimacy is hardly questioned by ordinary people or by scientists, it has, like the idea of truth, been attacked as illegitimate by some philosophers (for example quite recently by W. V. Quine [1]). It may therefore be mentioned here that, combining two analyses of Tarski, I have recently been able to give a ' definition ' of the idea of approaching to truth in the purely logical terms of Tarski's theory. (I simply combined the ideas of truth and of content, obtaining the idea of the truth-content of a statement a, i.e. the class of all true statements following from a, and its falsity content, which can be defined, roughly, as its content minus its truth content. We can then say that a statement a gets nearer to the truth than a statement b if and only if its truth content has increased without an increase in its falsity content ; see chapter 10 of my *Conjectures and Refutations*.) There is therefore no reason whatever to be sceptical about the notion of getting nearer to

[1] See W. V. Quine, *Word and Object*, 1959, p. 23.

the truth, or of the advancement of knowledge. And though we may always err, we have in many cases (especially in cases of crucial tests deciding between two theories) a fair idea of whether or not we have in fact got nearer to the truth.

It should be very clearly understood that the idea of one statement *a* getting nearer to the truth than another statement *b* in no way interferes with the idea that every statement is either true or false, and that there is no third possibility. It only takes account of the fact that there may be a lot of truth in a false statement. If I say ' It is half past three—too late to catch the 3.35 ' then my statement might be false because it was not too late for the 3.35 (since the 3.35 happened to be four minutes late). But there was still a lot of truth—of true information— in my statement ; and though I might have added ' unless indeed the 3.35 is late (which it rarely is) ', and thereby added to its truth-content, this additional remark might well have been taken as understood. (My statement might also have been false because it was only 3.28 not 3.30, when I made it. But even then there was a lot of truth in it.)

A theory like Kepler's which describes the track of the planets with remarkable accuracy may be said to contain a lot of true information, even though it is a false theory because deviations from Kepler's ellipses do occur. And Newton's theory (even though we may assume here that it is false) contains, for all we know, a staggering amount of true information—much more than Kepler's theory. Thus Newton's theory is a better approximation than Kepler's—it gets nearer to the truth. But this does not make it true : it can be nearer to the truth and it can, at the same time, be a false theory.

7. *Absolutism*

The idea of a philosophical absolutism is rightly repugnant to many people since it is, as a rule, combined with a dogmatic and authoritarian claim to possess the truth, or a criterion of truth.

But there is another form of absolutism—a fallibilistic absolutism—which indeed rejects all this : it merely asserts that our mistakes, at least, are absolute mistakes, in the sense that if a theory deviates from the truth, it is simply false, even if the mistake made was less glaring than that in another theory. Thus the notions of truth, and of falling short of the truth, can represent absolute standards for the fallibilist. This kind of absolutism is completely free from any taint of authoritarianism. And it is a great help in serious critical discussions. Of course, it can be criticized in its turn, in accordance with the principle that *nothing is exempt from criticism*. But at least at the moment it seems to me unlikely that criticism of the (logical) theory of truth and the theory of getting nearer to the truth will succeed.

8. *Sources of Knowledge*

The principle that *everything is open to criticism* (from which this principle itself is not exempt) leads to a simple solution of the problem of the sources of knowledge, as I have tried to show elsewhere (see the Introduction to my *Conjectures and Refutations*), It is this : every ' source '—tradition, reason, imagination. observation, or what not—is admissible and may be used, *but none has any authority*.

This denial of authority to the sources of knowledge attributes to them a role very different from that which they were supposed to play in past and present epistemologies. But it is part of our critical and fallibilist approach : every source is welcome, but no statement is immune from criticism, whatever its ' source ' may be. Tradition, more especially, which both the intellectu-alists (Descartes) and the empiricists (Bacon) tended to reject, can be admitted by us as one of the most important ' sources ', since almost all that we learn (from our elders, in school, from books) stems from it. I therefore hold that anti-traditionalism must be rejected as futile. Yet traditionalism—which stresses the authority of traditions—must be rejected too ; not as futile, but as mistaken—just as mistaken as any other epistemology which accepts some source of knowledge (intellectual intuition, say, or sense intuition) as an authority, or a guarantee, or a criterion, of truth.

9. *Is a Critical Method Possible ?*

But if we really reject any claim to authority, of any particular source of knowledge, how can we then criticize any theory ? Does not all criticism proceed from some assumptions ? *Does not the validity of any criticism, therefore, depend upon the truth of these assumptions ?* And what is the good of criticizing a theory if the criticism should turn out to be invalid ? Yet in order to show that it is valid, must we not establish, or justify, its assumptions ? And is not the establishment or the justification of any assumption just the thing which everybody attempts (though often in vain) and which I here declare to be impossible ? But if it is impossible, is not then (valid) criticism impossible too ?

I believe that it is this series of questions or objections which has largely barred the way to a (tentative) acceptance of the point of view here advocated : as these questions show, one may easily be led to believe that the critical method is, logically considered, in the same boat with all other methods : since it cannot work without making assumptions, it would have to establish or justify those assumptions ; yet the whole point of our argument was that we cannot establish or justify anything as certain, or even as probable, but have to content ourselves with theories which withstand criticism.

Obviously, these objections are very serious. They bring out the importance of our principle that nothing is exempt from criticism, or should be held to be exempt from criticism—not even this principle of the critical method itself.

Thus these objections constitute an interesting and important criticism of my position. But this criticism can in its turn be criticized ; and it can be refuted.

First of all, even if we were to admit that all criticism starts from certain assumptions, this would not necessarily mean that, for it to be valid criticism, these assumptions must be established and justified. For the assumptions may, for example, be part of the theory against which the criticism is directed. (In this case we speak of ' immanent criticism '.) Or they may be assumptions which would be generally found acceptable, even though they do not form part of the theory criticized. In this case the criticism would amount to pointing out that the theory criticized contradicts (unknown to its defenders) some generally accepted views. This kind of criticism may be very valuable even when it is unsuccessful ; for it may lead the defenders of the criticized theory to question those generally accepted views, and this may lead to important discoveries. (An interesting example is the history of Dirac's theory of anti-particles.)

Or they may be assumptions which are of the nature of a competing theory (in which case the criticism may be called ' transcendent criticism ', in contradistinction to ' immanent criticism ') : the assumptions may be, for example, hypotheses, or guesses, which can be independently criticized and tested. In this case the criticism offered would amount to a challenge to carry out certain crucial tests in order to decide between two competing theories.

These examples show that the important objections raised here against my theory of criticism are based upon the untenable dogma that criticism, in order to be ' valid ', must proceed from assumptions which are established or justified.

Moreover, criticism may be important, enlightening, and even fruitful, without being valid : the arguments used in order to reject some invalid criticism may throw a lot of new light upon a theory, and can be used as a (tentative) argument in its favour ; and of a theory which can thus defend itself against criticism we may well say that it is supported by critical arguments.

Quite generally, we may say that valid criticism of a theory consists in pointing out that a theory does not succeed in solving the *problems* which it was supposed to solve ; and if we look at criticism in this light then it certainly need not be dependent on any particular set of assumptions (that is, it can be ' immanent '), even though it may well be that some assumptions which were foreign to the theory under discussion (that is, some ' transcendent ' assumptions) inspired it to start with.

10. *Decisions*

From the point of view here developed, theories are not, in general, capable of being established or justified ; and although they may be supported by critical arguments, this support is never conclusive. Accordingly, we shall frequently have to make up our minds whether or not these critical arguments are strong enough to justify the *tentative* acceptance of the theory—or in other words, whether the theory seems preferable, in the light of the critical discussion, to the competing theories.

In this sense, *decisions* enter into the critical method. But it is always a tentative decision, and a decision subject to criticism.

As such it should be contrasted with what has been called ' decision ' or ' leap in the dark ' by some irrationalist or anti-rationalist or existentialist philosophers. These philosophers, probably under the impact of the argument (rejected in the preceding section) of the impossibility of criticism without presuppositions, developed the theory that all our tenets must be based on some fundamental decision—on some leap in the dark. It must be a decision, a leap, which we take with closed eyes, as it were ; for as we cannot ' know ' without assumptions, without already having taken up a fundamental position, this fundamental position cannot be taken up on the basis of knowledge. It is, rather, a choice—but a kind of fateful and almost irrevocable choice, one which we take blindly, or by instinct, or by chance, or by the grace of God.

Our rejection of the objections presented in the preceding section shows that the irrationalist view of decisions is an exaggeration as well as an over-dramatization. Admittedly, we must decide. But unless we decide against listening to argument and reason, against learning from our mistakes, and against listening to others who may have objections to our views, our decisions need not be final ; not even the decision to consider criticism. (It is only in its decision *not* to take an irrevocable leap into the darkness of irrationality that rationalism may be said not to be self-contained, in the sense of chapter 24.)

I believe that the critical theory of knowledge here sketched throws some light upon the great problems of all theories of knowledge : how it is that we know so much and so little ; and how it is that we can lift ourselves slowly out of the swamp of ignorance —by our own bootstraps, as it were. We do so by working with guesses, and by improving upon our guesses, through criticism.

11. *Social and Political Problems*

The theory of knowledge sketched in the preceding sections of this *addendum* seems to me to have important consequences for the evaluation of the social situation of our time, a situation influenced to a large extent by the decline of authoritarian religion. This decline has led to a widespread relativism and nihilism : to the decline of all beliefs, even the belief in human reason, and thus in ourselves.

But the argument here developed shows that there are no grounds whatever for drawing such desperate conclusions. The relativistic and the nihilistic (and even the ' existentialistic ') arguments are all based on faulty reasoning. In this they show, incidentally, that these philosophies actually do accept reason, but are unable to use it properly ; in their own terminology we might say that they fail to understand ' the human situation ', and especially man's ability to grow, intellectually and morally.

As a striking illustration of this misunderstanding—of desperate consequences drawn from an insufficient understanding of the epistemological situation—I will quote a passage from one of Nietzsche's *Tracts Against the Times* (from section 3 of his essay on Schopenhauer).

' This was the first danger in whose shadow Schopenhauer grew up : isolation. The second was : despair of finding the truth. This

latter danger is the constant companion of every thinker who sets out
from Kant's philosophy ; that is if he is a real man, a living human
being, able to suffer and yearn, and not a mere rattling automaton,
a mere thinking and calculating machine . . . Though I am reading
everywhere that [owing to Kant] . . . a revolution has started in all
fields of thought, I cannot believe that this is so as yet . . . But should
Kant one day begin to exert a more general influence, then we shall
find that this will take the form of a creeping and destructive scepticism
and relativism ; and only the most active and the most noble of minds
. . . will instead experience that deep emotional shock, and that despair
of truth, which was felt for example by Heinrich von Kleist . . .
" Recently ", he wrote, in his moving way, " I have become acquainted
with the philosophy of Kant ; and I must tell you of a thought of which
I need not be afraid that it will shake you as deeply and as painfully as it
shook me :—It is impossible for us to decide whether that to which we
appeal as truth is in truth the truth, or whether it merely seems to us
so. If it is the latter, then all that truth to which we may attain here
will be as nothing after our death, and all our efforts to produce and
acquire something that might survive us must be in vain.—If the sharp
point of this thought does not pierce your heart, do not smile at
one who feels wounded by it in the holiest depth of his soul. My
highest, my only aim has fallen to the ground, and I have none left." '

I agree with Nietzsche that Kleist's words are moving ; and
I agree that Kleist's reading of Kant's doctrine that it is impossible
to attain any knowledge of things in themselves is straightforward
enough, even though it conflicts with Kant's own intentions ;
for Kant believed in the possibility of science, and of finding the
truth. (It was only the need to explain the paradox of the
existence of an *a priori* science of nature which led him to adopt
that subjectivism which Kleist rightly found shocking.) Moreover, Kleist's despair is at least partly the result of disappointment
—of seeing the downfall of an over-optimistic belief in a simple
criterion of truth (such as self-evidence). Yet whatever may be
the history of this philosophic despair, it is not called for. Though
truth is not self-revealing (as Cartesians and Baconians thought),
though certainty may be unattainable, the human situation with
respect to knowledge is far from desperate. On the contrary,
it is exhilarating : here we are, with the immensely difficult task
before us of getting to know the beautiful world we live in, and
ourselves ; and fallible though we are we nevertheless find that
our powers of understanding, surprisingly, are almost adequate
for the task—more so than we ever dreamt in our wildest dreams.
We really do learn from our mistakes, by trial and error. And
at the same time we learn how little we know—as when, in climb-
ing a mountain, every step upwards opens some new vista into the

unknown, and new worlds unfold themselves of whose existence we knew nothing when we began our climb.

Thus we can *learn*, we can *grow* in knowledge, even if we can never *know*—that is, know for certain. Since we can learn, there is no reason for despair of reason ; and since we can never know, there are no grounds here for smugness, or for conceit over the growth of our knowledge.

It may be said that this new way of knowing is too abstract and too sophisticated to replace the loss of authoritarian religion. This may be true. But we must not underrate the power of the intellect and the intellectuals. It was the intellectuals—the ' second-hand dealers in ideas ', as F. A. Hayek calls them—who spread relativism, nihilism, and intellectual despair. There is no reason why some intellectuals—some more enlightened intellectuals—should not eventually succeed in spreading the good news that the nihilist ado was indeed about nothing.

12. *Dualism of Facts and Standards*

In the body of this book I spoke about the *dualism of facts and decisions*, and I pointed out, following L. J. Russell (see note 5 (3) to chapter 5, vol. i, p. 234), that this dualism may be described as one of propositions and proposals. The latter terminology has the advantage of reminding us that both propositions, which state facts, and proposals, which propose policies, including principles or standards of policy, are open to rational discussion. Moreover, a decision—one, say, concerning the adoption of a principle of conduct—reached after the discussion of a proposal, may well be tentative, and it may be in many respects very similar to a decision to adopt (also tentatively), as the best available hypothesis, a proposition which states a fact.

There is, however, an important difference here. For the proposal to adopt a policy or a standard, its discussion, and the decision to adopt it, may be said to *create* this policy or this standard. On the other hand, the proposal of a hypothesis, its discussion, and the decision to adopt it—or to accept a proposition —does not, in the same sense, create a fact. This, I suppose, was the reason why I thought that the term ' decision ' would be able to express the contrast between the acceptance of policies or standards, and the acceptance of facts. Yet there is no doubt that it would have been clearer had I spoken of a *dualism of facts and policies*, or of a *dualism of facts and standards*, rather than of a dualism of facts and decisions.

Terminology apart, the important thing is the irreducible dualism itself : whatever the facts may be, and whatever the standards may be (for example, the principles of our policies), the first thing is to distinguish the two, and to see clearly why standards cannot be reduced to facts.

13. *Proposals and Propositions*

There is, then, a decisive asymmetry between standards and facts : through the decision to accept a proposal (at least tentatively) we create the corresponding standard (at least tentatively) ; yet through the decision to accept a proposition we do *not* create the corresponding fact.

Another asymmetry is that standards always *pertain to* facts, and that facts are *evaluated by* standards ; these are relations which cannot be simply turned round.

Whenever we are faced with a fact—and more especially, with a fact which we may be able to change—we can ask whether or not it complies with certain standards. It is important to realize that this is very far from being the same as asking whether we like it ; for although we may often adopt standards which correspond to our likes or dislikes, and although our likes and dislikes may play an important role in inducing us to adopt or reject some proposed standard, there will as a rule be many other possible standards which we have not adopted ; and it will be possible to judge, or evaluate, the facts by any of them. This shows that the relationship of evaluation (of some questionable fact by some adopted or rejected standard) is, logically considered, totally different from a person's psychological relation (which is not a standard but a fact), of like or dislike, to the fact in question, or to the standard in question. Moreover, our likes and dislikes are facts which can be evaluated like any other facts.

Similarly, the fact that a certain standard has been adopted or rejected by some person or by some society must, as a fact, be distinguished from *any* standard, including the adopted or rejected standard. And since it is a fact (and an alterable fact) it may be judged or evaluated by some (other) standards.

These are a few reasons why standards and facts, and therefore proposals and propositions, should be clearly and decisively distinguished. Yet once they have been distinguished, we may look not only at the dissimilarities of facts and standards but also at their similarities.

First, both proposals and propositions are alike in that we

can discuss them, criticize them, and come to some decision about them. Secondly, there is some kind of regulative idea about both. In the realm of facts it is the idea of correspondence between a statement or a proposition and a fact ; that is to say, the idea of truth. In the realm of standards, or of proposals, the regulative idea may be described in many ways, and called by many terms, for example, by the terms ' right ' or ' good '. We may say of a proposal that it is right (or wrong) or perhaps good (or bad) ; and by this we may mean, perhaps, that it corresponds (or does not correspond) to certain standards which we have decided to adopt. But we may also say of a standard that it is right or wrong, or good or bad, or valid or invalid, or high or low ; and by this we may mean, perhaps, that the corresponding proposal should or should not be accepted. It must therefore be admitted that the logical situation of the regulative ideas, of ' right ', say, or ' good ', is far less clear than that of the idea of correspondence to the facts.

As pointed out in the book, this difficulty is a logical one and cannot be got over by the introduction of a religious system of standards. The fact that God, or any other authority, commands me to do a certain thing is no guarantee that the command is right. It is I who must decide whether to accept the standards of any authority as (morally) good or bad. God is good only if His commandments are good ; it would be a grave mistake— in fact an immoral adoption of authoritarianism—to say that His commandments are good simply because they are His, unless we have first decided (at our own risk) that He can only demand good or right things of us.

This is Kant's idea of autonomy, as opposed to heteronomy.

Thus no appeal to authority, not even to religious authority, can get us out of the difficulty that the regulative idea of absolute ' rightness ' or ' goodness ' differs in its logical status from that of absolute truth ; and we have to admit the difference. This difference is responsible for the fact, alluded to above, that in a sense we *create* our standards by proposing, discussing, and adopting them.

All this must be admitted ; nevertheless we may take the idea of absolute truth—of correspondence to the facts—as a kind of model for the realm of standards, in order to make it clear to ourselves that, just as we may *seek* for absolutely true propositions in the realm of facts or at least for propositions which come nearer to the truth, so we may *seek* for absolutely right or valid proposals in the realm of standards—or at least for better, or more valid, proposals.

However, it would be a mistake, in my opinion, to extend this attitude beyond the *seeking* to the *finding*. For though we should seek for absolutely right or valid proposals, we should never persuade ourselves that we have definitely found them ; for clearly, there cannot be a *criterion of absolute rightness*—even less than a criterion of absolute truth. The maximization of happiness *may* have been intended as a criterion. On the other hand I certainly never recommended that we adopt the minimization of misery as a criterion, though I think that it is an improvement on some of the ideas of utilitarianism. I also suggested that the reduction of avoidable misery belongs to the agenda of public policy (which does not mean that any question of public policy is to be decided by a calculus of minimizing misery) while the maximization of one's happiness should be left to one's private endeavour. (I quite agree with those critics of mine who have shown that if used as a *criterion*, the minimum misery principle would have absurd consequences ; and I expect that the same may be said about any other moral criterion.)

But although we have no criterion of absolute rightness, we certainly can make progress in this realm. As in the realm of facts, we can make discoveries. That cruelty is always ' bad ' ; that it should always be avoided where possible ; that the golden rule is a good standard which can perhaps even be improved by doing unto others, wherever possible, as *they* want to be done by : these are elementary and extremely important examples of discoveries in the realm of standards.

These discoveries create standards, we might say, out of nothing : as in the field of factual discovery, we have to lift ourselves by our own bootstraps. This is the incredible fact : that we can learn ; by our mistakes, and by criticism ; and that we can learn in the realm of standards just as well as in the realm of facts.

14. *Two Wrongs do Not Make Two Rights*

Once we have accepted the absolute theory of truth it is possible to answer an old and serious yet deceptive argument in favour of relativism, of both the intellectual and the evaluative kind, by making use of the analogy between true facts and valid standards. The deceptive argument I have in mind appeals to the discovery that other people have ideas and beliefs which differ

widely from ours. Who are we to insist that ours are the right
ones? Already Xenophanes sang, 2500 years ago (Diels-Kranz,
B, 16, 15) :

The Ethiops say that their gods are flat-nosed and black,
While the Thracians say that theirs have blue eyes and red hair.
Yet if cattle or horses or lions had hands and could draw,
And could sculpture like men, then the horses would draw their gods
Like horses, and cattle like cattle ; and each they would shape
Bodies of gods in the likeness, each kind, of their own.

So each of us sees his gods, and his world, from his own point
of view, according to his tradition and his upbringing ; and none
of us is exempt from this subjective bias.

This argument has been developed in various ways ; and it
has been argued that our race, or our nationality, or our historical
background, or our historical period, or our class interest, or our
social habitat, or our language, or our personal background knowledge, is an insurmountable, or an almost insurmountable, barrier
to objectivity.

The facts on which this argument is based must be admitted ;
and indeed, we can never rid ourselves of bias. There is, however, no need to accept the argument itself, or its relativistic
conclusions. For first of all, we can, in stages, get rid of some
of this bias, by means of critical thinking and especially of listening
to criticism. For example, Xenophanes doubtless was helped, by
his own discovery, to see things in a less biassed way. Secondly,
it is a fact that people with the most divergent cultural backgrounds
can enter into fruitful discussion, provided they are interested in
getting nearer to the truth, and are ready to listen to each other,
and to learn from each other. This shows that, though there
are cultural and linguistic barriers, they are not insurmountable.

Thus it is of the utmost importance to profit from Xenophanes'
discovery in every field ; to give up cocksureness, and become
open to criticism. Yet it is also of the greatest importance not
to mistake this discovery, this step towards criticism, for a step
towards relativism. If two parties disagree, this may mean that
one is wrong, or the other, or both : this is the view of the criticist.
It does not mean, as the relativist will have it, that both may be
equally right. They may be equally wrong, no doubt, though
they need not be. But anybody who says that to be equally
wrong means to be equally right is merely playing with words,
or with metaphors.

It is a great step forward to learn to be self-critical ; to learn to think that the other fellow may be right—more right than we ourselves. But there is a great danger involved in this : we may think that both, the other fellow and we ourselves, may be right. But this attitude, modest and self-critical as it may appear to us, is neither as modest nor as self-critical as we may be inclined to think ; for it is more likely that both, we ourselves and the other fellow, are wrong. Thus self-criticism should not be an excuse for laziness and for the adoption of relativism. And as two wrongs do not make a right, two wrong parties to a dispute do not make two right parties.

15. ' Experience ' and ' Intuition ' as Sources of Knowledge

The fact that we can learn from our mistakes, and through criticism, in the realm of standards as well as in the realm of facts, is of fundamental importance. But is the appeal to criticism sufficient ? Do we not have to appeal to the authority of experience or (especially in the realm of standards) of intuition ?

In the realm of facts, we do not merely criticize our theories, we criticize them by an appeal to experimental and observational *experience*. It is a serious mistake, however, to believe that we can appeal to anything like an *authority* of experience, though philosophers, particularly empiricist philosophers, have depicted sense perception, and especially sight, as a source of knowledge which furnishes us with definite ' data ' out of which our experience is composed. I believe that this picture is totally mistaken. For even our experimental and observational experience does not consist of ' data '. Rather, it consists of a web of guesses—of conjectures, expectations, hypotheses, with which there are interwoven accepted, traditional, scientific, and unscientific, lore and prejudice. There simply is no such thing as *pure* experimental and observational experience—experience untainted by expectation and theory. There are no pure ' data ', no empirically given ' sources of knowledge ' to which we can appeal, in our criticism. ' Experience ', whether ordinary or scientific experience, is much more like what Oscar Wilde had in mind in *Lady Windermere's Fan*, Act iii :

> *Dumby :* Experience is the name everyone gives to their mistakes.
> *Cecil Graham :* One shouldn't commit any.
> *Dumby :* Life would be very dull without them.

Learning from our mistakes—without which life would indeed be dull—is also the meaning of ' experience ' which is implied in

Dr. Johnson's famous joke about 'the triumph of hope over experience'; or in C. C. King's remark (in his *Story of the British Army*, 1897, p. 112): 'But the British leaders were to learn . . . in the "only school fools learn in, that of experience".'

It seems, then, that at least some of the ordinary uses of 'experience' agree much more closely with what I believe to be the character of both 'scientific experience' and 'ordinary empirical knowledge' than with the traditional analyses of the philosophers of the empiricist schools. And all this seems to agree also with the original meaning of '*empeiria*' (from '*peiraō*' —to try, to test, to examine) and thus of '*experientia*' and '*experimentum*'. Yet it must not be held to constitute an argument; neither one from ordinary usage nor one from origin. It is intended only to illustrate my logical analysis of the structure of experience. According to this analysis, experience, and more especially scientific experience, is the result of usually mistaken guesses, of testing them, and of learning from our mistakes. Experience (in this sense) is not a 'source of knowledge'; nor does it carry any authority.

Thus criticism which appeals to experience is not of an authoritative character. It does not consist in contrasting dubious results with established ones, or with 'the evidence of our senses' (or with 'the given'). It consists, rather, in comparing some dubious results with others, often equally dubious, which may, however, be taken as unproblematic for the moment, although they may at any time be challenged as new doubts arise, or else because of some inkling or conjecture; an inkling or a conjecture, for example, that a certain experiment may lead to a new discovery.

Now the situation in acquiring knowledge about standards seems to me altogether analogous.

Here, too, philosophers have looked for the authoritative *sources* of this knowledge, and they found, in the main, two: feelings of pleasure and pain, or a moral sense or a moral intuition for what is right or wrong (analogous to perception in the epistemology of factual knowledge), or, alternatively, a source called 'practical reason' (analogous to 'pure reason', or to a faculty of 'intellectual intuition', in the epistemology of factual knowledge). And quarrels continually raged over the question whether all, or only some, of these authoritative sources of moral knowledge existed.

I think that this problem is a pseudo-problem. The main

point is not the question of the ' existence ' of any of these faculties
—a very vague and dubious psychological question—but whether
these may be authoritative ' sources of knowledge ' providing us
with ' data ' or other definite starting-points for our constructions
or, at least, with a definite frame of reference for our criticism.
I deny that we have any authoritative sources of this kind, either
in the epistemology of factual knowledge or in the epistemology
of the knowledge of standards. And I deny that we need any
such definite frame of reference for our criticism.

How do we learn about standards ? How, in this realm, do
we learn from our mistakes ? First we learn to imitate others
(incidentally, we do so by trial and error), and so learn to look
upon standards of behaviour as if they consisted of fixed, ' given '
rules. Later we find (also by trial and error) that we are making
mistakes—for example, that we may hurt people. We may thus
learn the golden rule ; but soon we find that we may misjudge
a man's attitude, his background knowledge, his aims, his
standards ; and we may learn from our mistakes to take care
even beyond the golden rule.

Admittedly, such things as sympathy and imagination may
play an important rôle in this development ; but they are not
authoritative sources of knowledge—no more than any of our
sources in the realm of the knowledge of facts. And though
something like an intuition of what is right and what is wrong
may also play an important rôle in this development, it is, again,
not an authoritative source of knowledge. For we may see today
very clearly that we are right, and yet learn tomorrow that we
made a mistake.

' Intuitionism ' is the name of a philosophical school which
teaches that we have some faculty or capacity of intellectual
intuition allowing us to ' see ' the truth ; so that what we have
seen to be true must indeed be true. It is thus a theory of some
authoritative source of knowledge. Anti-intuitionists have usually
denied the existence of this source of knowledge while asserting,
as a rule, the existence of some other source such as sense-percep-
tion. My view is that both parties are mistaken, for two reasons.
First, I assert that there exists something like an intellectual
intuition which makes us feel, most convincingly, that we see
the truth (a point denied by the opponents of intuitionism).
Secondly, I assert that this intellectual intuition, though in a
way indispensable, often leads us astray in the most dangerous
manner. Thus we do not, in general, see the truth when we are

most convinced that we see it ; and we have to learn, through
mistakes, to distrust these intuitions.

What, then, are we to trust ?   What are we to accept ?   The
answer is : whatever we accept we should trust only tentatively,
always remembering that we are in possession, at best, of partial
truth (or rightness), and that we are bound to make at least
some mistake or misjudgment somewhere—not only with respect
to facts but also with respect to the adopted standards ; secondly,
we should trust (even tentatively) our intuition only if it has been
arrived at as the result of many attempts to use our imagination ;
of many mistakes, of many tests, of many doubts, and of searching
criticism.

It will be seen that this form of anti-intuitionism (or some may
say, perhaps, of intuitionism) is radically different from the
older forms of anti-intuitionism.   And it will be seen that there
is one essential ingredient in this theory : the idea that we may
fall short—perhaps always—of some standard of absolute truth, or
of absolute rightness, in our opinions as well as in our actions.

It may be objected to all this that, whether or not my views
on the nature of ethical knowledge and ethical experience are
acceptable, they are still ' relativist ' or ' subjectivist '.   For they
do not *establish* any absolute moral standards : at best they show
that the idea of an absolute standard is a regulative idea, of use
to those who are already converted—who are already eager to
learn about, and search for, true or valid or good moral standards.
My reply is that even the ' establishment '—say, by means of
pure logic—of an absolute standard, or a system of ethical norms,
would make no difference in this respect.   For assuming we have
succeeded in logically proving the validity of an absolute standard,
or a system of ethical norms, so that we could logically prove to
somebody how he ought to act : even then he might take no
notice ; or else he might reply : ' I am not in the least interested
in your " ought ", or in your moral rules—no more so than in
your logical proofs, or, say, in your higher mathematics.'   Thus
even a logical proof cannot alter the fundamental situation that
only he who is prepared to take these things seriously and to
learn about them will be impressed by ethical (or any other)
arguments.   You cannot force anybody by arguments to take
arguments seriously, or to respect his own reason.

16. *The Dualism of Facts and Standards and the Idea of Liberalism*

The dualism of facts and standards is, I contend, one of the bases of the liberal tradition. For an essential part of this tradition is the recognition of the injustice that does exist in this world, and the resolve to try to help those who are its victims. This means that there is, or that there may be, a conflict, or at least a gap, between facts and standards : facts may fall short of right (or valid or true) standards—especially those social or political facts which consist in the actual acceptance and enforcement of some code of justice.

To put it in another way, liberalism is based upon the dualism of facts and standards in the sense that it believes in searching for ever better standards, especially in the field of politics and of legislation.

But this dualism of facts and standards has been rejected by some relativists who have opposed it with arguments like the following :

(1) The acceptance of a proposal—and thus of a standard— is a social or political or historical fact.

(2) If an accepted standard is judged by another, not yet accepted standard, and found wanting, then this judgment (whoever may have made it) is also a social or political or historical fact.

(3) If a judgment of this kind becomes the basis of a social or political movement, then this is also a historical fact.

(4) If this movement is successful, and if in consequence the old standards are reformed or replaced by new standards, then this is also a historical fact.

(5) Thus—so argues the relativist or moral positivist—we never have to transcend the realm of facts, if only we include in it social or political or historical facts : there is no dualism of facts and standards.

I consider this conclusion (5) to be mistaken. It does not follow from the premises (1) to (4) whose truth I admit. The reason for rejecting (5) is very simple : we can always ask whether a development as here described—a social movement based upon the acceptance of a programme for the reform of certain standards —was ' good ' or ' bad '. In raising this question, we re-open the gulf between standards and facts which the monistic argument (1) to (5) attempts to close.

From what I have just said, it may be rightly inferred that the monistic position—*the philosophy of the identity of facts and standards*—is dangerous ; for even where it does not identify standards with existing facts—even where it does not identify present might and right—it leads necessarily to the identification of future might and right.   Since the question whether a certain movement for reform is right or wrong (or good or bad) cannot be raised, according to the monist, except in terms of another movement with opposite tendencies, nothing can be asked except the question which of these opposite movements succeeded, in the end, in establishing its standards as a matter of social or political or historical fact.

In other words, the philosophy here described—the attempt to ' transcend ' the dualism of facts and standards and to erect a monistic system, a world of facts only—leads to *the identification of standards either with established might or with future might :* it leads to a moral positivism, or to a moral historicism, as described and discussed in chapter 22 of this book.

17. *Hegel Again*

My chapter on Hegel has been much criticized.   Most of the criticism I cannot accept, because it fails to answer my main objections against Hegel—that his philosophy exemplifies, if compared with that of Kant (I still find it almost sacrilegious to put these two names side by side), a terrible decline in intellectual sincerity and intellectual honesty ; that his philosophical arguments are not to be taken seriously ; and that his philosophy was a major factor in bringing about the ' age of intellectual dishonesty ', as Konrad Heiden called it, and in preparing for that contemporary *trahison des clercs* (I am alluding to Julien Benda's great book) which has helped to produce two world wars so far.

It should not be forgotten that I looked upon my book as my war effort : believing as I did in the responsibility of Hegel and the Hegelians for much of what happened in Germany, I felt that it was my task, as a philosopher, to show that this philosophy was a pseudo-philosophy.

The time at which the book was written may perhaps also explain my optimistic assumption (which I could attribute to Schopenhauer) that the stark realities of the war would show up the playthings of the intellectuals, such as relativism, as what they were, and that this verbal spook would disappear.

I certainly was too optimistic.   Indeed, it seems that most of my critics took some form of relativism so much for granted that they were quite unable to believe that I was really in earnest in rejecting it.

I admit that I made some factual mistakes : Mr. H. N. Rodman, of Harvard University, has told me that I was mistaken in writing ' two years ' in the third line from the bottom of p. 28, and that I ought to have written ' four years '. He also told me that there are, in his opinion, a number of more serious—if less clear-cut—historical errors in the chapter, and that some of my attributions of ulterior motives to Hegel are, in his opinion, historically unjustified.

Such things are very much to be regretted, although they have happened to better historians than I. But the question of real importance is this : do these mistakes affect my assessment of Hegel's philosophy, and of its disastrous influence ?

My own answer to the question is : ' No.' It is his philosophy which has led me to look upon Hegel as I do, not his biography. In fact, I am still surprised that serious philosophers were offended by my admittedly partly playful attack upon a philosophy which I am still unable to take seriously. I tried to express this by the scherzo-style of my Hegel chapter, hoping to expose the ridiculous in this philosophy which I can only regard with a mixture of contempt and horror.

All this was clearly indicated in my book ; also the fact that I neither could [1] nor wished to spend unlimited time upon deep researches into the history of a philosopher whose work I abhor. As it was, I wrote about Hegel in a manner which assumed that few would take him seriously. And although this manner was lost upon my Hegelian critics, who were decidedly not amused, I still hope that some of my readers got the joke.

But all this is comparatively unimportant. What may be important is the question whether my attitude towards Hegel's philosophy was justified. It is a contribution towards an answer to this question which I wish to make here.

I think most Hegelians will admit that one of the fundamental motives and intentions of Hegel's philosophy is precisely to replace and ' transcend ' the dualistic view of facts and standards which had been presented by Kant, and which was the philosophical basis of the idea of liberalism and of social reform.

To transcend this dualism of facts and standards is the decisive

---

[1] See my Introduction, my Preface to the Second Edition, and the second paragraph of vol. i, p. 202.

aim of Hegel's *philosophy of identity*—the identity of the ideal and the real, of right and might. All standards are historical : they are *historical facts*, stages in the development of reason, which is the same as the development of the ideal and of the real. There is nothing but fact ; and some of the social or historical facts are, at the same time, standards.

Now Hegel's argument was, fundamentally, the one I stated (and criticized) here in the preceding section—although Hegel presented it in a surpassingly vague, unclear, and specious form. Moreover, I contend that this identity philosophy (despite some ' progressivist ' suggestions, and some mild expressions of sympathy with various ' progressive ' movements which it contained) played a major role in the downfall of the liberal movement in Germany ; a movement which, under the influence of Kant's philosophy, had produced such important liberal thinkers as Schiller and Wilhelm von Humboldt, and such important works as Humboldt's *Essay towards the Determination of the Limits of the Powers of the State.*

This is my first and fundamental accusation. My second accusation, closely connected with the first, is that Hegel's identity philosophy, by contributing to historicism and to an identification of might and right, encouraged totalitarian modes of thought.

My third accusation is that Hegel's argument (which admittedly required of him a certain degree of subtlety, though not more than a great philosopher might be expected to possess) was full of logical mistakes and of tricks, presented with pretentious impressiveness. This undermined and eventually lowered the traditional standards of intellectual responsibility and honesty. It also contributed to the rise of totalitarian philosophizing and, even more serious, to the lack of any determined intellectual resistance to it.

These are my principal objections to Hegel stated, I believe, fairly clearly in chapter 12. But I certainly did not analyse the fundamental issue—the philosophy of identity of facts and standards—quite as clearly as I ought to have done. So I hope I have made amends in this addendum—not to Hegel, but to those who may have been harmed by him.

18. *Conclusion*

In ending my book once again, I am as conscious as ever of its imperfections. In part, these imperfections are a consequence of its scope, which transcends what I should consider as my more professional interests. In part they are simply a consequence of my personal fallibility : it is not for nothing that I am a fallibilist.

But though I am very conscious of my personal fallibility, even as it affects what I am going to say now, I do believe that a fallibilist approach has much to offer to the social philosopher. By recognizing the essentially critical and therefore revolutionary character of all human thought—of the fact that we learn from our mistakes, rather than by the accumulation of data—and by recognizing on the other hand that almost all the problems as well as the (non-authoritative) sources of our thought are rooted in traditions, and that it is almost always traditions which we criticize, a critical (and progressive) fallibilism may provide us with a much-needed perspective for the evaluation of both, tradition and revolutionary thought. Even more important, it can show us that the role of thought is to carry out revolutions by means of critical debates rather than by means of violence and of warfare ; that it is the great tradition of Western rationalism to fight our battles with words rather than with swords. This is why our Western civilization is an essentially pluralistic one, and why monolithic social ends would mean the death of freedom : of the freedom of thought, of the free search for truth, and with it, of the rationality and the dignity of man.

II

NOTE ON SCHWARZSCHILD'S BOOK ON MARX (1965)

Some years after I wrote this book, Leopold Schwarzschild's book on Marx, *The Red Prussian* (translated by Margaret Wing : London 1948) became known to me. There is no doubt in my mind that Schwarzschild looks at Marx with unsympathetic and even hostile eyes, and that he often paints him in the darkest possible colours. But even though the book may be not always fair, it contains documentary evidence, especially from the Marx-Engels correspondence, which shows that Marx was less of a humanitarian, and less of a lover of freedom, than he is made to appear in my book. Schwarzschild describes him as a man who saw in ' the proletariat ' mainly an instrument for his own personal ambition. Though this may put the matter more harshly than the evidence warrants, it must be admitted that the evidence itself is shattering.

INDEX OF NAMES

INDEX OF SUBJECTS

Italicized page-numbers indicate that the reference is of special importance. The letter t, which stands for ' term ', placed after a page number, indicates that the meaning of the term in question is discussed. There is an Index of Platonic Passages at the end of the first volume.

essentialism, ii, 9–21 (see also methodological essentialism).

ethics, morals, morality, equalitarian, humanitarian and Christian, i, *65*, 66, 73, *235*, ch. 5, n. 6, 257, 263, ii, 151, 200 ; totalitarian collectivist and tribalist, i, 101–3, 107–8, 112–113, 139, 256, 258, 325, 331, 339 f. ; ii, 44, 52, 65–76, 310, 314 ; historicist, ii, 202t, *205–6*, 255 (see also historicism, and ethics) ; and æsthetics, i, *65*, *165*, 292, ii, 210, 357 ; and politics, i, 113, 139, 260 ; and religion, see religion ; and science, ii, 233, 238, 243–4 ; 'scientific', i, 237, ch. 5, n. 18 ; see also dualism of facts and decisions ; naturalism ; positivism ; relativism ; futurism ; utilitarianism ; ends and means ; pain and pleasure.

evolutionism, i, 40, ii, 322 (cp. i, 314 ; see also progressivism) ; fascist, ii, 61–2 ; of Hegel, i, 314, ii, 36–7 ; of Speusippus and Aristotle, ii, 5, 285, ch. 11, n. 11.

existentialism, ii, 76–7, 380–1.

exogamy, rules of, ii, 89t.

experiment, ii, 218, 220, 233, 238 ; crucial, ii, 12, 266, 364 ; social, i, *162*, 163, 167 ; planning ; social engineering (see also social science).

explanation, ii, 210 f., 362–4, ch. 25, n. 7 ; causal, i, 210 f., ii, 262–3, 362–4 ; historical, ii, 263t, 266, 364.

exploitation, ii, 122–4, 168, 173, 178, 184, 329 ; colonial, Marxist hypothesis of, ii, 187–9, ch. 20(VI), 336, 338.

faith in reason, i, 185, ii, 231t, 233, 243, 246, 258.

fallibilism, ii, 374, 375, 377.

falsifiability, see refutability.

fame and fate, Heraclitean and Hegelian philosophy of, i, 17t, ii, 8t, 71–2, 276–7.

fascism, ii, 30–1, 60–78 (see also nationalism ; racialism) ; attitude of Marxist parties towards, 162–4, ch. 19(VI), 336–7, 343–4.

feudalism (used in the metaphorical sense of landed proprietorship), ii, 3, 30, 113, 135, 345.

Fichte, the father of German nationalism, ii, 53–4, 71 ; and Kant, ii, 54, 313, ch. 12, n. 58.

fire, Heraclitus' theory of, i, *14*, 15, 73, 206–7, ch. 2, n. 7, 212.

flux, Heraclitus' theory of, i, 12, *189*, *204–7*, ch. 2, n. 2, 208, 211, 214, 217, 300, 301, 314, ii, 36, 249.

forms, see ideas.

freedom, ii, 126–9, ch. 17(V) ; limitations of, i, 110–11, 247, 131, ii, 44, 331 (see also paradox of freedom) ; Hegel on, ii, 56, 72 ; Marx on, ii, 101, 103, 105, 207 (see also freedom, merely formal) ; Spinoza on, ii, 305 ; merely formal, ii, 57, 124t, 127, 173, 199, 314, ch. 12, n. 62, 330, 341, 346 (cp. ii, 207) ; of criticism, ii, 238 (cp. ii, 220, 222) ; of thought and speech, Plato against, i, 267, 268, 270, 275 (see also state, state censorship ; education) ; Hegel on, ii, 42–3, 305, 310.

French Revolution, the, i, 17, 203, 208, 294, 334 ; ii, *30*, 52, 53, 55, 87, 207 ; Heine on, ii, 109.

funeral oration of Pericles, i, 186, 255, ch. 6, n. 16.

futurism, moral ; ii, 206t–208, 271, 274 ; æsthetic, i, 230.

general will, ii, 52, 81.

geometrical theory of the world, i, 248–53, 320, 343.

geometry, Plato's, i, 248–53, ch. 6, n. 9, 267, 319–20 ; *vs.* arithmetic, i, 248.

German idealism, ii, 28, 32, 134, 353 ; inferiority feelings, ii, 64, 312, 313, ch, 12, n. 57 ; nationalism, ii, 49–58, ch. 12(III), 311, 314 (see also imperialism) ; nihilism, ii, 78 ; romanticism, ii, 21, 60, 302, 317.

Germany, the other, ii, 78, 307.

'Glauconic edict', the, i, 150t, 151.

God (see monotheism) ; Antisthenes on, i, 276, 278 ; Aristotle on, ii, 285 ; Plato on, i, 213, *276*, ii, 283 ; will of, and historicism, i, 8, 24.

Golden Age, i, 11, 19, 21, 25, 43, 204, 209, 210, 218.

'golden rule', Kant's, i, 102, 256 ; justification of, ii, 238, 386.

good, the, i, 237–8, ii, 296 ; Aristotle on, ii, 5, 285 ; Moore on, ii, 295–6 ;